THE PROCESS
OF LEGAL RESEARCH

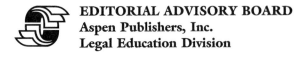

THE PROCESS OF LEGAL RESEARCH

Fifth Edition

Christina L. Kunz
Professor of Law

Deborah A. Schmedemann
Professor of Law

Matthew P. Downs
Professor of Law

Ann L. Bateston
Director of the Law Library
Associate Dean
Professor of Law

all of William Mitchell College of Law

ASPEN LAW & BUSINESS
A Division of Aspen Publishers, Inc.
Gaithersburg   New York

Permissions
Aspen Law & Business
1185 Avenue of the Americas
New York, NY 10036

Printed in the United States of America

ISBN: 0-7355-1223-X

1 2 3 4 5 6 7 8 9 0

Library of Congress Cataloging-in-Publication Data

The process of legal research / Christina L/ Kunz ... [et al.].—5th ed.
        p. cm,
    Includes index.
    ISBN 0-7355-1223-X (softcover)
      1. Legal research—United States.   2. Information storage and retrieval systems—Law—United States. I. Kunz, Christina L.

KF240.P76   2000
340′.07′2073—dc21   00-033133

This book is dedicated to the thousands of students of William Mitchell College of Law who have worked with and helped us improve these material during the past fifteen years

and

to the faculty, administrators, and staff of William Mitchell College of Law, whose unwavering support for skills instruction has made this book possible.

Summary of Contents

CONTENTS

UNIT V ADMINISTRATIVE MATERIALS   257

EXHIBITS AND ILLUSTRATIONS

UNIT III   CASE LAW

CHAPTER 11   CASE CITATORS

UNIT IV   ENACTED LAW

CHAPTER 12   CODES AND SESSION LAWS

CHAPTER 15   **AGENCY DECISIONS**

CHAPTER 16   **MINI-LIBRARIES**

UNIT VI   RULES OF PROCEDURE AND LEGAL ETHICS

CHAPTER 17   RULES OF PROCEDURE

CHAPTER 18   RULES OF LEGAL ETHICS

PREFACE

The first edition of this book was published in 1986, nearly fifteen years ago. Since then, legal research has changed little and greatly.

What has changed little is legal authority. Now, as then, the purpose of legal research is to locate pertinent cases, statutes, and rules—the law—governing the client's situation. Now, as then, commentators' discussion of the law is used to lead one to the law and to help one fully understand the law. Now, as then, it is critical for new researchers to learn how the law is made, how different lawmaking bodies interact, how to discern which law is applicable when, how to read the law carefully, and how to integrate the insights of commentators. As with all earlier editions, this book emphasizes these matters. Today, as always, you must master these fundamentals to research competently.

What has changed greatly is the technology of legal research. Legal materials have long been published, of course, in books and microforms (such as microfilm and microfiche). With the development of computers and related technology, legal research has become a multimedia endeavor. The researcher now has a (sometimes bewilderingly) wide range of options for locating a governing statute, for example: books, online subscription services offered by private publishers, CD-ROMs, Internet web sites maintained by the government, and so forth. Indeed, some sources and tools are available only in computer-based media.

Technological change has brought other changes as well. The rate of product development has increased rapidly. Sources published in books tend to change infrequently; computer-based sources are reprogrammed far more easily and, hence, far more often. Furthermore, the corporate structure of legal publishing is in flux, with large, well established companies merging and small, new companies arising.

So, it is an interesting time to be teaching and learning legal research. For us, it has been a challenge to write about a moving target. And we suspect you will find it challenging to adjust your research techniques on a nearly continual basis as publishers change their products.

In writing this book, we chose to take the following approach: As noted above, we have set forth at some length what you need to know about legal authority. Then we have described what we deem the "best practices" currently employed by lawyers as they research a particular type of legal authority. Some practices have been in use for many years and likely will continue to be best practices. Others are newer and may well evolve as technology and research sources evolve. We have sought to cover the basics as to the various practices; we hope that you will learn and appreciate the analytical processes lawyers employ in legal research. We have not discussed the mechanics and details of the best practices at length; these matters change, and you will be able to learn them easily enough once you master the basics.

A final observation: Excellent researchers are curious, persistent, flexible people. We hope you approach this book with curiosity, persistence, and flexibility. If you do, we believe you will learn a great deal about an important and interesting process.

A Note to Professors: If you have used previous editions of this book, you will notice a number of changes in this edition. Regarding the text, we would flag the following:

- expanded and somewhat reconceived discussions of the core analytical steps of legal research—generating research terms and issues, looking up concepts, and searching for words;
- substantial discussion of the Internet and CD-ROM research, along with discussion of subscription online services (primarily, but not exclusively, LEXIS and Westlaw);
- coverage of new products, such as KeyCite, Congressional Universe, and THOMAS:
- presentation of what we deem to be the handful of best research practices currently available for each type of authority, each separately presented so as to permit you to choose which to teach when;
- strengthened discussion of the authoritativeness of various legal authorities in our complex federal system;
- reconfiguration of the text into smaller chapters, grouped into units of related materials; and
- a cleaner layout, with simpler presentation of exhibits and illustrations alongside text.

Regarding the problem sets, we would flag the following:

- all new research situations for the problem sets;
- a problem set for rules of legal ethics;
- problem set design that reflects increasing levels of autonomy and source-neutrality as one moves from beginning chapters (commentary) to more advanced chapters (such as administrative materials);
- self-verifying answers to some questions (in which students attach copies or printouts); and
- more questions requiring students to link their research results to legal analysis of the facts of the situation.

We hope these changes work well for you and your students.

Deborah Schmedemann
Matthew Downs
Ann Bateson
Christina Kunz

St. Paul, Minnesota
May 2000

ACKNOWLEDGMENTS

First and foremost, we would like to recognize the work of our research assistants: Stephen Brunn, Ann Diachuk, Myrna Erickson, Chris Heffelbower, Jennifer Henderson, Nicole Hill, Elizabeth Holland, Vickie Loher, Beau McGraw, Hien Nguyen, Richard Soderberg, and Tony Wachewicz. They worked hard, long, and diligently on the new research situations for this edition. We would also like to salute the work of our many research assistants on the previous editions. The perspectives and contributions of our research assistants have been invaluable in making this book more useful to our readers.

More so than other publications by law school faculty, this book draws on the talents and hard work of the College's professional librarians: Anne Anderson, Mary Ann Archer, Anna Cherry, Pat Dolan, Elvira Embser, Paul Healey, Mary Rumsey, and Paddy Satzer. They tracked down the sources, answered our questions, and offered top-notch suggestions. Paddy Satzer prepared the Index as well.

Our colleagues Eric Janus, Neil Hamilton, and Russ Pannier graciously provided their substantive expertise. Professor Peter Erlinder and Professor Clifford Greene, now in practice in Minneapolis, were our co-authors on portions of earlier editions. Former Professor Kevin Millard, now in practice in Colorado, wrote the final draft of a chapter for the first edition of this book.

We are grateful for the expertise of Cal Bonde, Linda Thorstad, and Sara McDowell, who made sense of contorted and detailed revisions and constructed sophisticated exhibits from our mere sketches. Darlene Finch has provided valuable administrative support on this edition.

The College's faculty and administration have shown considerable interest and support for the project. In particular, we want to thank current Dean Harry Haynsworth for his generous support.

This book has been blessed with talented professionals on the publisher's end of the phone. Larry Wexler, our editor on this edition, presided over the complex process of assembling this complicated book with great patience and a sharp eye for detail. We want to recognize the work of Karen Quigley in the redesign of the book and Kathy Porzio in coordinating its manufacture and production. We are grateful for the efforts of the following people who nurtured this book and its predecessors for the past (nearly) twenty years: Nick Niemeyer and Richard Heuser (formerly at Little, Brown and Company), Carol McGeehan, Elizabeth Kenny, and Melody Davies.

On a larger scale, we would like to thank the community of legal writing and research teachers who have encouraged us and enriched us over the years with their ideas about the pedagogy of legal skills education. The same measure of gratitude and recognition goes to our students, who remain our best source of insights about the process of learning legal research.

We especially thank our spouses, companions, families, and friends for their support and their interest in this project. Every three or four years, they, like us, have been called upon to endure long hours and high stress. We thank them from the bottom of our hearts.

We would also like to acknowledge those publishers who permitted us to reprint copyrighted material in this book:

CHAPTER 2: LEGAL AUTHORITY AND RESEARCH MEDIA

Illustration 2-1: *Lukoski* Case, from *Michie's Law on Disc* for New Mexico. Lukoski v. Sandia Indian Management Co., LEXIS Law Publishing Law on Disc—New Mexico, Aug. 1999. Copyright (c) 1999 by LEXIS Law Publishing, a division of Reed Elsevier, Inc. Reprinted with permission of LEXIS Law Publishing. All rights reserved.

Illustration 2-2: Employee Privacy Statute, from *New Mexico Statutes Annotated*. Chapter 50 Labor Law, Article 11, pp. 57-58, 1993 replacement pamphlet. The statutes reprinted in the following pages are taken from the New Mexico Statutes Annotated, copyright 1993, by the State of New Mexico and are reprinted with permission of the State of New Mexico (New Mexico Compilation Commission) and The Michie Company, a division of Matthew Bender, Inc. All rights reserved.

Illustration 2-3: Encyclopedia Text, from *American Jurisprudence 2d*. Vol. 82, Wrongful Discharge, p. 774, 1992. Reprinted with permission of West Group.

Illustration 2-4: Periodical Article Text, from *Georgetown Law Journal* through Westlaw. Michele L. Tyler, Blowing Smoke: Do Smokers Have a Right? Limiting the Privacy Rights of Cigarette Smokers. Georgetown Law Journal, vol. 86, issue 3, p. 780, 1998. Reprinted with permission of the publisher, Georgetown University and Georgetown Law Journal © 1998. Reprinted with permission of West Group.

CHAPTER 3: LEGAL LANGUAGE AND RESEARCH TERMS

Illustration 3-2: Overall Table of Contents (Table of Abbreviations), from *American Jurisprudence 2d*. General Index S-Z vol., p. xviii, 2000 edition. Reprinted with permission of West Group.

Illustration 3-3: Detailed Table of Contents, from *American Jurisprudence 2d*. Vol. 82, Wrongful Discharge, p. 663, 1992. Reprinted with permission of West Group.

Illustration 3-4: Index, from *American Jurisprudence 2d*. General Index S-Z vol., p. 1154, 2000 edition. Reprinted with permission of West Group.

Illustration 3-5: Table of Authorities (Statutes), from *American Jurisprudence 2d*. General Index S-Z vol., popular names table, p. 1210, 2000 edition. Reprinted with permission of West Group.

Illustration 3-6: Citation List (Partial) Resulting from Boolean Search, Run in LEXIS Combined Law Reviews Database. Oct. 18, 1999. Copyright by LEXIS Publishing; all rights reserved. Reprinted with permission of LEXIS Publishing.

CHAPTER 4: ENCYCLOPEDIAS

Illustration 4-1: Encyclopedia Text, from *American Jurisprudence 2d*. Vol. 82, Wrongful Discharge, p. 774, 1992. Reprinted with permission of West Group.

Illustration 4-2: Encyclopedia Text, from *Corpus Juris Secundum*. Vol. 30, Employer-Employee Relationship, p. 48, 1992. Reprinted with permission of West Group.

Illustration 4-3: Encyclopedia Introductory Material, from *American Jurisprudence 2d*. Vol. 82, Wrongful Discharge, p. 657, 1992. Reprinted with permission of West Group.

Illustration 4-4: Encyclopedia Pocket Part, from *Corpus Juris Secundum*. Vol. 30, Employer-Employee Relationship, p. 68, 1999 pocket part. Reprinted with permission of West Group.

CHAPTER 5: TREATISES

Illustration 5-1: Treatise Text, from *Employment Discrimination*. Lex K. Larson. Vol. 9, p. 155-28, 2d ed., June 1999. Copyright © 2000 by Matthew Bender & Co., Inc. Reprinted with permission from Lex. K. Larson, Employment Discrimination, 2d ed. All rights reserved.

CHAPTER 6: LEGAL PERIODICALS

Illustration 6-1: Law Review Article, from *Georgetown Law Journal*. Michele L. Tyler, Blowing Smoke: Do Smokers Have a Right? Limiting the Privacy Rights of Cigarette Smokers. Georgetown Law Journal, vol. 86, issue 3, pp. 789-790, 1998. Reprinted with permission of the publisher, Georgetown University and Georgetown Law Journal © 1998.

Illustration 6-2: *Shepard's Law Review Citations*. Vol. 32, no. 5, p. 279, Sept. 1999. Reproduced by permission of Shepard's. Further reproduction of any kind is strictly prohibited.

CHAPTER 7: A.L.R. ANNOTATIONS

Illustration 7-1: A.L.R. Annotation Case Descriptions. Theresa L. Kruk, Right to Discharge Allegedly "At-Will" Employee as Affected by Employer's Promulgation of Employment Policies as to Discharge. American Law Reports Annotations 4th, vol. 33, p. 135, 1984. Reprinted with permission of West Group.

Illustration 7-2: A.L.R. Annotation Editorial Aids and Opening Sections. Theresa L. Kruk, Right to Discharge Allegedly "At-Will" Employee as Affected by Employer's Promulgation of Employment Policies as to Discharge. American Law Reports Annotations 4th, vol. 33, pp. 120-123, 1984. Reprinted with permission of West Group.

Illustration 7-3: A.L.R. Annotation Pocket Part. Theresa L. Kruk, Right to Discharge Allegedly "At-Will" Employee as Affected by Employer's Promulgation of Employment Policies as to Discharge. American Law Reports Annotations 4th, vol. 33, p. 31, 1999 pocket part. Reprinted with permission of West Group.

CHAPTER 8: RESTATEMENTS

Illustration 8-1: Restatement Rule, Comments, Illustrations, and Reporter's Note, from Restatement (Second) of Contracts. Main vol., pp. 8-10, 12, 1981. © 1981 by the American Law Institute. Reproduced with permission.

Illustration 8-2: Restatement Case Summaries, from Restatement (Second) of Contracts Appendix. Vol. 8 (July 1984 through June 1989), p. 37, 1990. © 1990 by The American Law Institute. Reproduced with permission.

Illustration 8-3: Recent Case Citations, from *Interim Case Citations to the Restatement of the Law*. July 1998 through August 1999 vol., p. 720, 1999. © 1999 by The American Law Institute. Reproduced with permission.

CHAPTER 10: REPORTERS, DIGESTS, AND THEIR ALTERNATIVES

Exhibit 10.1: Federal Circuit Map, *1999 Winter Judicial Staff Directory*. Dorothy C. Countryman. P. 587, 13th ed. Reprinted with permission of CQ Press, a division of Congressional Quarterly, Inc.

Illustration 10-1: *Lukoski* Case, from *Pacific Reporter 2d*. Vol. 48, pp. 507-510, 1988. Reprinted with permission of West Group.

Illustration 10-2: Digest Paragraphs, from *New Mexico Digest*. Vol. 4B, p. 45, 1999. Reprinted with permission of West Group.

Illustration 10-3: Topic List, from *New Mexico Digest*. Vol. 4B, p. xiv, 1999. Reprinted with permission of West Group.

Illustration 10-4: Descriptive Word Index, from *New Mexico Digest*. Descriptive Word Index, p. 443, 1948. Reprinted with permission of West Group.

Illustration 10-5: Outline of Digest Topic, from *New Mexico Digest*. Vol. 4B, p. 16, 1999. Reprinted with permission of West Group.

Illustration 10-6: Westlaw Partial Citation Lists, Run in NM-CS Database. Sept. 23, 1999. Reprinted with permission of West Group.

Illustration 10-7: *Michie's Law on Disc* Partial Citation List, Run in New Mexico Judicial Decisions. Aug. 1999 disc. Copyright by LEXIS Publishing; all rights reserved. Reprinted with permission of LEXIS Publishing.

CHAPTER 11: CASE CITATORS

Illustration 11-1: Shepard's Online Display, from LEXIS. Dec. 31, 1999. Reproduced by permission of Shepard's. Further reproduction of any kind is prohibited.

Illustration 11-2: KeyCite Display, from Westlaw. Dec. 30, 1999. Reprinted with permission of West Group.

Illustration 11-3: Shepard's Citations in Paper, from *Shepard's Pacific Reporter Citations*. Vol. 2, part 7, p. 649, 1994. Reproduced by permission of Shepard's. Further reproduction of any kind is strictly prohibited.

Illustration 11-4: Shepard's Citations Abbreviations, from *Shepard's Pacific Reporter Citations*. Vol. 2, part 7, pp. xi-xii, 1994. Reproduced by permission of Shepard's. Further reproduction of any kind is strictly prohibited.

CHAPTER 12: CODES AND SESSION LAWS

Illustration 12-1: New Mexico Constitution, from *New Mexico Statutes Annotated*. Article II, § 4, p. 3, 1992 replacement pamphlet. The constitution reprinted in

Chapter 13: Legislative Process Materials

sional and Administrative News. Vol. 4, p. 601, 1990. Reprinted with permission of West Group.

Illustration 13-6: Legislative History References in Statutory Code, from *United States Code Annotated.* Title 42, § 12102. Public Health and Welfare §§ 10401-12700 vol., p. 630, 1995. Reprinted with permission of West Group.

Illustration 13-7: Bibliography of Compiled Legislative Histories, from *Sources of Compiled Legislative Histories.* Compiled by Nancy P. Johnson. Sources of Compiled Legislative Histories: A Bibliography of Government Documents, Periodical Articles, and Books 1st Congress-104nd Congress, p. B210, rev. 1993. Reprinted with permission of American Association of Law Libraries.

Illustration 13-8: Special Legislative History, from *CIS/Legislative Histories.* Report for Public Law 101-336. CIS/Annual Legislative Histories of U.S. Public Laws, pp. 68, 70, 77, Jan.-Dec. 1990. Reprinted with permission of CIS/NEXIS.

Illustration 13-9: Legislative History, from *CIS Congressional Universe.* Report for Public Law 101-336, run, Jan. 20, 2000. Reprinted with permission of CIS/NEXIS.

Illustration 13-14: Status of Senate Bills, from *Congressional Index.* Vol. 1, p. 21,002, Dec. 23, 1999. Reproduced with permission from CONGRESSIONAL INDEX published and copyrighted by CCH INCORPORATED, 2700 Lake Cook Road, Riverwoods, Illinois 60015.

Illustration 13-15: Bill Tracking Report, from *CIS Congressional Universe.* Report for 106th Congress, 1st Session, S. 121, run Jan. 19, 2000. Reprinted with permission of CIS/NEXIS.

Illustration 13-17: STATE NET's US-BILLTRK, from Westlaw. Report for 1999 US S.B. 121, run Jan. 21, 2000. Copyright © 2000 State Net. All rights reserved. Reprinted with permission of State Net and West Group.

CHAPTER 14: REGULATIONS

Illustration 14-2: Statute re National Labor Relations Board Jurisdiction and Annotation, from *United States Code Service.* Title 29 Labor §§161-205 vol., pp. 30, 31, 68, 1993. The code sections reprinted in the following pages are taken from the United States Code Service, Copyright 1993, by LEXIS® Law Publishing, a division of Reed Elsevier Inc. and Reed Elsevier Properties, Inc. and are reprinted with permission of LEXIS® Law Publishing. All rights reserved.

Illustration 14-9: LEXIS Citations List, Run in CFR-Labor Titles Database. Nov. 22, 1999. Copyright by LEXIS Publishing; all rights reserved. Reprinted with permission of LEXIS Publishing.

Illustration 14-10: KeyCite Display, from Westlaw. Nov. 20, 1999. Reprinted with permission of West Group.

CHAPTER 15: AGENCY DECISIONS

Illustration 15-2: Case Descriptions in Annotated Code, from *United States Code Service.* Title 29 Labor §§1-157 vol., p. 580, 1994. The code section reprinted in the following pages is taken fromUnited States Code Service, Copyright 1994, by LEXIS® Law Publishing, a division of Reed Elsevier Inc. and Reed Elsevier Properties, Inc. and are reprinted with permission of LEXIS® Law Publishing. All rights reserved.

Illustration 15-5: Westlaw Partial Citations List, Run in FLB-NLRB Database. Nov. 24, 1999. Reprinted with permission of West Group.

Illustration 15-7: Shepard's Online Display (Partial), from LEXIS. Nov. 24, 1999. Reproduced by permission of Shepard's. Further reproduction of any kind is strictly prohibited.

CHAPTER 16: MINI-LIBRARIES

Illustration 16-1: Looseleaf Service General Index, from *BNA's Labor Relations Reporter.* Reproduced with permission from Labor Relations Reporter, Master Index, p. A 955. Copyright 1999 by The Bureau of National Affairs, Inc. (800-372-1033) <http://www. bna.com>

Illustration 16-2: Looseleaf Service Commentary, from *BNA's Labor Relations Reporter.* Reprinted with permission from *BNA's Labor & Employment Law Library,* LRX 510:207-208. Copyright 1988 by The Bureau of National Affairs, Inc. (800-372-1033, www.bna.com).

Illustration 16-3: Looseleaf Service State Statute Reprint, from *BNA's Labor Relations Reporter.* Reprinted with permission from *Labor Relations Reporter-Labor Relations Reporter,* SLL 41:221. Copyright 1999 by The Bureau of National Affairs, Inc. (800-372-1033, www.bna.com).

Illustration 16-4: Looseleaf Service Outline of Case Digest, from *BNA's Labor Relations Reporter.* Reprinted with permission from *BNA's Labor & Employment Law Library,* Outline of Classifications, p. C-I 112. Copyright 1995 by The Bureau of National Affairs, Inc. (800-372-1033, www.bna.com).

Illustration 16-5: Looseleaf Service Case Digest, from *BNA's Labor Relations Reporter.* Reprinted with permission from *BNA's Labor & Employment Law Library,* Cumulative Digest and Index, 1991-1995 volume, p. 1169. Copyright 1996 by The Bureau of National Affairs, Inc. (800-372-1033, www.bna.com).

Illustration 16-6: BNA's Labor and Employment Law Library Citations List, Run in LRRM-Decisions of Court and LRRM-Decisions of NLRB Directories. Source: decisions search list run on Nov. 21, 1999 from *BNA's Labor & Employment Law Library,* by The Bureau of National Affairs, Inc. (800-372-1033, www.bna.com).

Illustration 16-7: *Morton International* Case Headnotes, from BNA's Online Labor and Employment Law Library. Reprinted with permission from Labor Relations Reporter Reference Manual, 147 LRRM 1280. Copyright 1994 by The Bureau of National Affairs, Inc. (800-372-1033) <http://www. bna.com>

Illustration 16-8: Outline of Digest Topics, from BNA's Online Labor and Employment Law Library. Reproduced with permissions from BNA's Labor & Employment Law Library, Outline of Classifications, Sec. 52.2536 et seq. Copyright 2000 by The Bureau of National Affairs, Inc.(800-372-1033) <http://www. bna.com>

CHAPTER 17: RULES OF PROCEDURE

Illustration 17-1: Federal Rule of Civil Procedure 11 and Advisory Committee Notes, from *Federal Civil Judicial Procedure and Rules.* Pp. 85-86, 88, 1999 edition. Reprinted with permission of West Group.

Illustration 17-2: New Mexico Rule of Civil Procedure 1-011 and Annotation, from *New Mexico Rules Annotated.* Vol. 1, pp. 44-45, 1999 edition. The rules reprinted in the following pages are taken from the New Mexico Rules Annotated, copyright 1999, by the State of New Mexico and are reprinted with permission of the State of New Mexico (New Mexico Compilation Commission) and The Michie Company, a division of Matthew Bender, Inc. All rights reserved.

Illustration 17-3: Deskbook's Table of Contents, from *Federal Civil Judicial Procedure and Rules.* P. VII, 1999 edition. Reprinted with permission of West Group.

Illustration 17-4: Sample Form, from *Federal Civil Judicial Procedure and Rules.* Form 2, p. 270, 1999 edition. Reprinted with permission of West Group.

Illustration 17-5: Findex, from *Federal Rules Service.* Finding Aids vol., Rule 11—Page 3, April 1996. Reprinted with permission of West Group.

Illustration 17-6: Case Descriptions, from *Federal Rules Digest, Federal Rules Service.* Rules 10-11 vol., p. 35, 1997. Reprinted with permission of West Group.

Illustration 17-7: Local Civil Rule 10 of the United States District Court for the District of New Mexico, from *Federal Local Court Rules,* Vol. 3 Missouri to Oklahoma, p. 12, 2d ed. 1997. Reprinted with permission of West Group.

CHAPTER 18: RULES OF LEGAL ETHICS

Illustration 18-1: ABA Model Rules of Professional Conduct 17.1 and Comment, from *ABA Compendium of Professional Responsibility Rules and Standards.* Pp. 31-33, 1999. © 1999 by the American Bar Association. All rights reserved. Reprinted with permission of the American Bar Association. Copies of this publication are available from Service Center, American Bar Association, 750 North Lake Shore Drive, Chicago, IL 60611.

Illustration 18-2: New Mexico Rule of Professional Conduct 16.107 and Annotation, from *New Mexico Rules Annotated.* Vol. 2, pp. 476-478, 1999 edition. The rules reprinted in the following pages are taken from the New Mexico Rules Annotated, copyright 1999, by the State of New Mexico and are reprinted with permission of the State of New Mexico (New Mexico Compilation Commission) and The Michie Company, a division of Matthew Bender, Inc. All rights reserved.

Illustration 18-3: Synopses of New Mexico Ethics Opinions, from *ABA/BNA Lawyers' Manual on Professional Conduct.* Reprinted with permission of the American Bar Association and Bureau of National Affairs from *ABA/BNA's Lawyers' Manual on Professional Conduct,* Ethics Opinions, p. 1001:6001. Copyright 1996 by the American Bar Association and Bureau of National Affairs, Inc. (800-372-1033, www.bna.com).

Illustration 18-4: Commentary, from *Annotated Model Rules of Professional Conduct.* P. 98, 4th ed. 1999. © 1999 by the American Bar Association. All rights reserved. Reprinted with permission of the American Bar Association. Copies of this publication are available from Service Center, American Bar Association, 750 North Lake Shore Drive, Chicago, IL 60611.

Illustration 18-5: Illustrative Case and Commentary, from *The Law of Lawyering.* Geoffrey C. Hazard, Jr. and W. William Hodes. The Law of Lawyering: A Handbook on the Model Rules of Professional Conduct. Vol. 1, p. 232.10, 1998 supp. Reprinted with permission of Aspen Law & Business.

Illustration 18-6: ABA Formal Ethics Opinion, from Westlaw. Opinion 92-367, 1992. © 1992 by the American Bar Association. Reprinted by permission of the American Bar Association. Copies of ABA Ethics Opinions are available from Service Center, American Bar Association, 750 North Lake Shore Drive, Chicago, IL 60611. 800-286-2211.

PROBLEM SET MATERIALS:

Utah Legislative Survey—1983, 1984 Utah L. Rev. 209-12. Reprinted with permission from the Utah Law Review.

Kugler v. Koscot Interplanetary, Inc., 293 A.2d 682-684. Reprinted with permission of West Group.

Shepard's Atlantic Reporter Citations, Part 5, p. 1583, 1994. Reproduced by permission of Shepard's. Further reproduction of any kind is strictly prohibited.

The following illustrations are from federal government sources:

CHAPTER 12: CODES AND SESSION LAWS

Illustration 12-3: Outline of Federal Statute re Disability Discrimination, from *United States Code.* Vol. 23, pp. 643-644 (1994).

Illustration 12-7: Portion of Public Law 101-336, from *Statutes at Large.* Vol. 104, p. 369, 1990.

Illustration 12-9: Facsimile Citation List, from U.S. House of Representatives Code Web Site. Nov. 4, 1999.

CHAPTER 13: LEGISLATIVE PROCESS MATERIALS

Illustration 13-1: Senate Bill, from U.S. Government Printing Office. 101st Congress S. 933.

Illustration 13-4: Floor Debate, from *Congressional Record.* Vol. 136, p. 13,063, 1990.

Illustration 13-10: Bill Summary & Status Report for Enacted Bill, from THOMAS. Report for S. 933. Jan. 21, 2000.

Illustration 13-11: History of Bills and Resolutions, from *Congressional Record.* Vol. 136, p. 2523, 1990.

Illustration 13-12: Title Keyword Index, from *Monthly Catalog of U.S. Government Publications.* P. I-3452, July 1991.

Illustration 13-13: Document Description, from *Monthly Catalog of U.S. Government Publications.* P. 195, July 1991.

Illustration 13-16: Bill Summary & Status Report for Pending Bill, from THOMAS. Report for S. 121. Jan. 21, 2000.

CHAPTER 14: REGULATIONS

Illustration 14-1: National Labor Relations Board Regulation, from *Code of Federal Regulations.* Title 29, § 103.2, p. 111, 1999.

Illustration 14-3: List of CFR Titles, Chapters, Subchapters, and Parts, from *CFR Index.* P. 903, 1999.

Illustration 14-4: CFR Parallel Table of Authorities and Rules, from *CFR Index.* P. 759, 1999.

Illustration 14-5: Final Rule, from *Federal Register.* Vol. 38, no. 44, pp. 6176-6177, Mar. 7, 1973.

CHAPTER 15: AGENCY DECISIONS

THE PROCESS
OF LEGAL RESEARCH

# OVERVIEW	**UNIT** **I**

INTRODUCTION

A. THE CANOGA CASE

Imagine yourself a lawyer or legal assistant* in a small firm in Taos, New Mexico. Consider the following fictional client problem:

> Your client, Emilia Canoga, began her career as a flutist for a small symphony orchestra in Taos, New Mexico, when she graduated from the Juilliard School five years ago. She has enjoyed her job and performed well. However, she has disagreed from time to time with the orchestra's general manager, especially over personnel issues. One such disagreement led to her termination on January 7, 1999.
>
> Throughout the preceding year, the general manager had been pressuring all smoking members of the orchestra to quit smoking. He argued that smoking is a health risk and increased the orchestra's health care costs substantially. More particularly, he argued that smoking impairs the wind capacity, and hence performance, of brass and woodwind players. In September 1998, he banned smoking at work. In early December, he issued a memo asking brass and woodwind players to sign either a statement indicating that they did not smoke, whether on-

---

*This text has several primary audiences: students in law schools, lawyers, students in legal assistant programs, and legal assistants. For ease of discussion, we generally refer to lawyers or law students; we trust that readers who plan to be or are legal assistants will read "legal assistant" where appropriate.

duty or off-duty, or a pledge to embark on a no-smoking program. This memo was met with varying reactions and provoked significant discussion among the orchestra's members.

In particular, Ms. Canoga, a smoker who had tried to quit several times, was perturbed by the manager's early efforts and incensed by the December memo. She returned it with a signed note indicating that she intended to sign neither the statement nor the pledge.

The general manager called Ms. Canoga to his office shortly after receiving the note. A heated discussion ensued. Ms. Canoga accused the general manager of overstepping his bounds as an employer and intruding into her personal life. He told her she was fired for insubordination. Ms. Canoga angrily left his office.

Two days later, Ms. Canoga received her paycheck with a note stating that her employment was no longer needed by the orchestra. Ms. Canoga sought advice from a senior colleague about how to get her job back. He suggested that she exercise her right to plead her case before the board of directors, as stated in the orchestra's employee handbook. The handbook reads:

> It is the Orchestra's intent to resolve all employment disagreements amicably. If at any time, during your employment or thereafter, you are unable to resolve a disagreement by discussing the issue with management, you may bring the matter to the board. The board will make every effort to listen to both sides and facilitate a just solution.

Ms. Canoga wrote a letter to the board president requesting board consideration of her termination according to the handbook. About a week later, she received a letter stating that the board was aware of her situation, believed management had handled it appropriately, did not intend to revisit the topic, appreciated her contributions to the orchestra, and wished her well in her future endeavors. Hoping to get her job back or at least some type of compensation and a good reference, Ms. Canoga has sought your assistance.

In asking a lawyer for assistance, Ms. Canoga is seeking not just sympathy, but a resolution of her problem according to the law and within the legal system. The lawyer's role in bringing about that resolution is described well in the first rule of a widely adopted ethics code for lawyers: "A lawyer shall provide competent representation to a client. Competent representation requires the legal knowledge, skill, thoroughness and preparation reasonably necessary for the representation." Model Rules of Professional Conduct Rule 1.1 (1999).

In Ms. Canoga's case, as in any client representation, the lawyer employs various skills to solve the problem: listening to Ms. Canoga to determine the facts of her situation and her interests; investigating the facts through other sources; researching the law; analyzing the facts in light of applicable legal rules; identifying and assessing means of obtaining a resolution, such as negotiating with the orchestra's lawyer, mediating the case, working through a government agency, or pursuing civil litigation; advocating for Ms. Canoga in those processes, in writing and orally; and, at all steps along the way, helping Ms. Canoga to determine which actions should be taken on her behalf.

B. THE ROLE OF LEGAL RESEARCH

This text teaches you how lawyers acquire the legal knowledge necessary for competent client representation—through legal research. As Ms. Canoga's advocate, you could not assess the strengths and weaknesses of her case against the orchestra if you did not know the pertinent law; nor could you negotiate effectively with the orchestra's lawyer or argue her case convincingly before a tribunal without a firm understanding of the law. Similarly, had the orchestra sought your advice before adopting its no-smoking policy, you could be of service only if you knew the legal constraints on employers in such situations. If you served as an advocate for an employer association before a legislature or administrative agency contemplating new laws on smoking by employees, you would need to be well informed about the current state of the law.

Furthermore, legal research is central to the ethical obligation that accompanies client representation: service to the legal system. *See* Preamble, Model Rules of Professional Conduct (1999). As Ms. Canoga's advocate, your efforts would help to ensure the proper functioning of the legal system as a peaceful mode of resolving disputes and contribute to the rational development and application of the law, should the dispute enter the court system and yield a judicial decision. As the lawyer advising the orchestra, you would seek to secure the orchestra's compliance with the law. In either setting, you could not fulfill these roles without a firm understanding of the pertinent law.

Thus it is fitting and not surprising that incompetent legal research can have serious personal consequences for the lawyer. Failure to know the law may lead to disciplinary action. *See, e.g., People v. Yoakum,* 552 P.2d 291 (Colo. 1976); *State ex. rel. Nebraska State Bar Ass'n v. Holscher,* 230 N.W.2d 75 (Neb. 1975). Inadequate research also may result in liability to the client for legal malpractice. For example, in *Smith v. Lewis,* 530 P.2d 589 (Cal. 1975), *overruled on other grounds, In re Marriage of Brown,* 544 P.2d 561 (Cal. 1976), the court approved an award of $100,000 against a lawyer who had failed to apply principles of law commonly known to well-informed attorneys and to discover principles readily accessible through standard research techniques. Furthermore, no attorney can afford to tarnish his or her professional reputation, by becoming known for poor research.

C. THE PROCESS OF LEGAL RESEARCH

As you will soon see, legal research materials are voluminous and complex. To research competently, you must research strategically. Webster's defines "strategy" as "the art of devising or employing plans or stratagems toward a goal." *Merriam-Webster's Collegiate Dictionary* 1162 (10th ed. 1993). Your goal is research that is:

> *correct:* law that governs situations like your client's and that applies to the time when your client's situation occurred;
> *comprehensive:* a full range of pertinent authorities;
> *credible:* authority that carries weight because of its nature and quality; and
> *cost-effective:* results that justify the efforts devoted to research, in light of the client's interests and available research options.

These criteria are further developed throughout this text.

Furthermore, to research strategically, you must have a plan. For most research projects, your plan will proceed through the following stages:

- a careful consideration of the range of legal authorities and sources available to you;
- a careful analysis of the client's facts, so as to generate terms to use as you work with those materials;
- preliminary research in secondary sources—sources that are not themselves the law but comment upon it and lead you to it; and
- research in sources of primary authority—the law itself.

Your specific research plan will vary somewhat from project to project, of course, reflecting the difficulty of the topic, your initial knowledge of the pertinent law, the time available, cost considerations, and other factors. You will make choices at many points, e.g., which of various similar secondary sources to consult, which media to employ for an authority appearing in more than one medium. As you will see, legal research is not a mechanical process, but rather an art requiring creativity as well as skill.

Furthermore, although the list above suggests that research is a tidy linear process, legal research is actually rather untidy. The general course of most research projects tracks the steps set forth above—but with frequent backward loops along the way. For example, if the first set of research terms you develop yields no useful authority, you will need to return to that step to generate more. As another example, you may encounter a reference to a promising article or treatise (secondary source) within a case (primary authority) and decide to return briefly to secondary-source research.

D.   THE ORGANIZATION OF THIS BOOK

Not surprisingly, the organization of this text mirrors the sequence of research steps suggested in part C, as follows:

Overview*	**Unit I**
▶ Consider the range of legal authorities and media.	**Chapter 2**
▶ Analyze the client's facts to generate research terms.	**Chapter 3**
Research in secondary sources.	**Unit II**
▶ Encyclopedias	**Chapter 4**
▶ Treatises	**Chapter 5**
▶ Legal Periodicals	**Chapter 6**
▶ A.L.R. Annotations	**Chapter 7**
▶ Restatements	**Chapter 8**
▶ Additional Secondary Sources	**Chapter 9**
Research in primary authority: case law.	**Unit III**
▶ Reporters, Digests, and Their Alternatives	**Chapter 10**
▶ Citators	**Chapter 11**
Research in primary authority: enacted law.	**Unit IV**
▶ Codes and Session Laws	**Chapter 12**
▶ Legislative Process Materials	**Chapter 13**
Research in primary authority: administrative materials.	**Unit V**
▶ Regulations	**Chapter 14**
▶ Agency Decisions	**Chapter 15**
▶ Mini-Libraries	**Chapter 16**
Research in primary authority: rules of procedure and legal ethics.	**Unit VI**
▶ Rules of Procedure	**Chapter 17**
▶ Rules of Legal Ethics	**Chapter 18**
Conclusion*	**Unit VII**

*NOTE: The Table shows only those chapters in the book that cover the steps of the research process. Hence Chapter 1 in Unit I, this Introduction, and concluding Chapter 19, Developing an Integrated Research Strategy in Unit VII, which do not specifically cover these research steps, are not listed.

Chapters 2 and 3 of Unit I develop two analytical processes that inform all research: consideration of research materials and analysis of the client's facts. Unit II contains six short chapters, each of the first five covering a

major secondary source, with the sixth wrapping up secondary-source research. Units III through VI each cover one of the major forms of primary
authority; all have multiple chapters, because the materials for researching
the law itself are numerous and complex. Unit VII, a single chapter, presents
research journals written by upper-level law students as they researched a
typical client situation; these journals demonstrate various ways in which the
processes described in this book fit together.

Most chapters cover a set of closely related research materials and follow
a standard format. They address the following questions:

- What is the source?
- Why would you research in it?
- How do you research in it?
- What else should you know?
- How do you cite it?

Two of these subtopics merit a paragraph of explanation here.

First, as to the "how do you research in it" discussion: Many types of
legal authority can be researched multiple ways, in multiple sources. For
example, you can research case law through a set of books, through online
commercial computer services, via a CD-ROM disk, or in web sites available
through the Internet. If we were to describe all ways of conducting legal
research, this book would be enormous, and your capacity to fully learn any
particular technique would be limited. Thus we have chosen to describe in
each chapter no more than a handful or two of research practices. We think
of these practices as "best practices": likely to lead to correct, comprehensive,
credible, and cost-effective research in most situations. As you become more
expert, and the technology used in legal research evolves, you may develop
new best practices, but they probably will build on the practices discussed
here. We have synopsized the practices in shaded boxes, each of which presents
either steps (signified by arrow bullets) or options (signified by round bullets).

Second, as to the "how do you cite it" discussion: Citation is the practice
of providing the reader with a precise reference to a source. As you will see,
legal citation is complicated and technical—but also manageable if you work
through it in a systematic way. This text provides you with starting information
on citation and refers you to the predominant manual on legal citation, *The
Bluebook: A Uniform System of Citation*. At the time this book was written,
The Bluebook was in its sixteenth edition; the seventeenth was in progress.
There are alternatives to the *The Bluebook*, including manuals prepared by
the American Association of Law Libraries and the Association of Legal
Writing Directors. Furthermore, some courts have developed their own citation protocols. Should your work be governed by one of these alternatives,
you should adjust the forms presented here accordingly.

Most of the chapters present their topics in three forms: a general description, a specific example, and illustrative pages from the sources pertinent to
the Canoga case. (Please note: This book does not present all legal materials
pertinent to the Canoga case, but rather a range of major authorities on
point.) In addition, the problem sets at the end of this book present you

with fairly straightforward client situations to research, using the materials and practices covered in the chapters. Working the problem sets will not make you an accomplished researcher; no single practice opportunity could do that. The problem sets do give you an occasion to put what you have learned into practice and to acquaint yourself with the many and varied processes of legal research.

LEGAL AUTHORITY AND RESEARCH MEDIA

A. Introduction
B. Categories of Legal Research Materials
C. Media
D. Choosing Among Sources

A. INTRODUCTION

In researching Ms. Canoga's case, you would encounter a wide range of legal materials. Materials used in legal research are not all created equal; rather, the law is a strongly hierarchical field. This chapter describes the hierarchy of legal materials; it lists and explains types of primary authority, secondary sources, and finding tools. Furthermore, this chapter provides an overview of the media in which these materials are published: paper, microforms, CD-ROMs, and online services, including the Internet. This chapter concludes by presenting factors to consider in choosing among sources.

B. CATEGORIES OF LEGAL RESEARCH MATERIALS

Legal research materials are divided into three categories: primary authority, secondary sources, and finding tools. This hierarchy is depicted in Exhibit 2.1 on page 11. Note: This text uses the term "authority" to refer to the content of research materials, while "source" refers to the publications in which they are located. For instance, the legislature enacts a statute as law ("primary authority"), and that statute may appear in several publications ("primary sources").

EXHIBIT 2.1	Categories of Legal Research Materials

Primary Authority
  Judicial case law
  Enacted legislation
  Administrative regulations and decisions
  Rules of procedure and ethics

Secondary Sources (major forms)
  Encyclopedias
  Treatises
  Periodicals
  A.L.R. Annotations
  Restatements

Finding Tools (examples)
  External/broad
  Library catalogs
  Internet search engines and directories
  External/narrow
  Periodical indexes
  Case digests
  Internal
  Indexes
  Tables of contents
  Tables of cases or statutes
  Computer-based searches

1. Primary Authority

"Primary authority" constitutes the law. It is issued by a branch of the government acting in its lawmaking capacity. In basic terms, United States law emanates from three types of government bodies: the judiciary, the legislature, and administrative agencies.

First, the federal and state judiciaries decide cases based on specific disputes that have arisen between two litigants (whether individuals or entities). In doing so, a court not only resolves the dispute for the litigants, but also creates precedent. The result, rules, and reasoning in a decided case generally are to be followed in the resolution of future similar disputes. See Illustration 2-1 on pages 13–16, a case with significant implications for Ms. Canoga's case.

Second, legislative bodies at the federal, state, and local levels create constitutions, statutes, charters, and ordinances. Constitutions and charters create the government and define the rights of citizens vis-à-vis the government. Statutes and ordinances regulate a wide range of behavior by individuals, private entities, and the government. Legislation typically is written in broad, general terms. It is interpreted according to the legislature's intent, thereby rendering the materials created during the legislative process of some importance. See Illustration 2-2 on pages 17–18, a statute pertaining to Ms. Canoga's case.

Third, administrative agencies at the federal, state, and local levels generate law through two chief mechanisms. Agencies issue decisions, which resemble judicial cases in that they simultaneously resolve specific disputes and stand as precedent for future disputes. Agencies also promulgate regulations, which resemble statutes in that they address a range of behavior and are stated in general terms.

Any particular subject may be governed by some combination of legislative, judicial, and administrative agency law. For example, the legislature may pass a statute that the courts interpret in specific disputes. In a more complicated example, the legislature may create an agency by statute, that agency may promulgate a regulation and then apply it in a series of agency decisions, and the courts may then review the agency's actions in a series of judicial opinions.

In addition, all three branches create rules governing the functioning of the legal system. Rules governing the operation of the court system are created by the legislature, courts, or jointly. The procedural rules promulgated by an agency govern litigation before the agency.

For any particular client's situation, some primary authority is weightier than other primary authority. The weightier primary authority is called "mandatory" or "binding" authority, and it emanates from the legislature, courts, or agency with jurisdiction over, or the power to regulate, the client's situation. The less-weighty primary authority is called "persuasive" authority, and it emanates from a lawmaker without jurisdiction.

For example, as you will see, the Canoga case is governed by the following forms of primary authority: statutes, judicial cases, regulations, and agency decisions at the federal level; New Mexico cases and a New Mexico statute; and rules governing litigation within the federal or New Mexico state courts (depending on where a suit might be brought). All of these authorities are mandatory because they emanate from the federal or New Mexico governments, which have jurisdiction over the Canoga case.

2.   Secondary Sources

Secondary authority is defined by what it is not: it is not primary authority. Rather, it is created by individuals, nongovernmental bodies, or government bodies not acting in a lawmaking capacity. Because most secondary authority comments on the law, it also is called "commentary." All secondary authority describes what the law says, much also explains how the law came to be, and some analyzes and critiques the law. Some secondary authority represents the author's attempt to state what the law should be, and some of this secondary authority has proven influential with lawmakers.

You will find that some sources containing secondary authority resemble sources you have seen before in other fields, such as encyclopedias, treatises, and periodical articles. Some secondary sources have formats unique to the law, such as A.L.R. (*American Law Reports*) Annotations and the Restatements. As you will see, every secondary source has a particular place in legal research.

Illustration 2-3 on page 19 is an excerpt from *American Jurisprudence, Second Edition*, a legal encyclopedia; Illustration 2-4 on page 20 is from a legal periodical article. Both pertain to the Canoga case.

ILLUSTRATION 2-1   *Lukoski Case,* from *Michie's Law on Disc* for New Mexico

1

---

106 N.M. 664, 748 P.2d 507 LUKOSKI V. SANDIA INDIAN MGT. CO. (S. Ct. 1988) 1988 N.M. Lexis 17

Scott J. L. Lukoski, Plaintiff-Appellee,

vs.

Sandia Indian Management Company, Defendant-Appellant.

No. 16462
SUPREME COURT OF NEW MEXICO
106 N.M. 664, 748 P.2d 507, 1988 N.M. LEXIS 17
January 07, 1988, Filed

Appeal from the District Court of Bernalillo County, William W. Deaton, District Judge.

COUNSEL

Grammer & Grammer, David A. Grammer III, for Appellant.
Turpen & Wolfe, Donald C. Turpen, for Appellee.
 AUTHOR: RANSOM

OPINION

{*665} RANSOM, Justice.

Scott J. L. Lukoski brought a wrongful discharge action against his employer, Sandia Indian Management Co. (SIMCO). Lukoski had been employed as general manager of the Sandia Pueblo bingo operation. In a bench trial, the court decided that SIMCO violated the termination procedures prescribed for "less serious" offenses by an employee handbook. For salary due on the remaining term of his one-year oral contract, Lukoski was awarded $18,629.05. We affirm.

The court found that, in October 1983, Lukoski and SIMCO entered into a one-year oral employment agreement under which Lukoski would provide services as the general manager of a bingo hall operation for a specified annual salary plus commission. There was no written agreement between the parties. In February 1984, SIMCO distributed to all employees an employee handbook and requested each to sign the last page as verification of receipt, acknowledgment of acceptance, and agreement to conform with the stated policies and procedures. After Lukoski signed the back page as requested, it was placed in his personnel file. The court concluded that:

The parties amended the oral employment contract * * * when [SIMCO] proffered, and [Lukoski] signed, [the] Employee's Handbook containing new duties and obligations on the part of employee and employer over and above said oral contract, including Rules to be obeyed by [Lukoski] and a termination procedure to be followed by [SIMCO].

Although we determine the above-quoted language is a finding of ultimate fact, rather than a conclusion of law, that is of no consequence. **See Hoskins v. Albuquerque Bus Co.**, 72 N.M. 217, 382 P.2d 700 (1963); **Wiggs v. City of Albuquerque**, 57 N.M. 770, 263 P.2d 963 (1952).

ILLUSTRATION 2-1   *(continued)*

2

SIMCO challenges this finding and for the first time on appeal raises two other issues. First, it claims that Lukoski, as general manager, was not the type of employee intended to be covered by the handbook. Distribution to all employees with request for signatures constituted evidence to the contrary, and resolution of any ambiguity regarding management personnel would have been a specific question of fact. **See Shaeffer v. Kelton**, 95 N.M. 182, 619 P.2d 1226 (1980). Second, SIMCO claims that any breach was not material because it neither went to the substance of the contract nor defeated the object of the parties. Materiality is likewise a specific question of fact. **See Bisio v. Madenwald (In re Estate of Bisio)**, 33 Or. App. 325, 576 P.2d 801 (1978). As the contract stood after amendment, it was not materiality, as argued by SIMCO, but rather severity of offense that was at issue under the termination procedures. In any event, by failing to tender requested findings, SIMCO waived specific *{*666}* findings on these fact issues. SCRA 1986, 1-052(B)(1)(f).

There is substantial evidence supporting the court's findings of ultimate fact that the termination procedures became an amendment to Lukoski's contract, and that personality -- not the severe offenses of insubordination or disobedience -- was the cause for termination. He was terminated without warning or suspension for a cause not so severe as to constitute cause for immediate termination. His personality and interpersonal dealings were found by the court to create an atmosphere of fear and anxiety and bad morale among employees and managers.

Relying only on **Ellis v. El Paso Natural Gas Co.**, 754 F.2d 884 (10th Cir.1985), the thrust of SIMCO's appeal is that the language of the employee handbook is "too indefinite to constitute a contract" and lacks "contractual terms which might evidence the intent to form a contact." It maintains that the parties did not conduct themselves as if the employee handbook was to govern Lukoski or as if they expected it to form the basis of a contractual relationship. In support of its position, SIMCO refers to the disciplinary action, suspension, and warning provisions,[1] and argues that the language of the termination policy is ambiguous and contains no required policy for termination.

SIMCO's argument, however, overlooks the handbook's characterization of the disciplinary policy regarding warnings, suspensions and terminations as "an **established procedure** regarding suspension of problem employees and termination for those who cannot conform to Company Policy." (Emphasis added.) Moreover, the language of the handbook does nothing to alert an employee against placing reliance on any statement contained therein or against viewing such discipline and termination policy as only a unilateral expression of SIMCO's intention that is subject to revocation or change at any time, in any manner, at the pleasure of SIMCO. To the contrary, from the language of the handbook and the conduct of SIMCO in adopting the policy, it could properly be found that the policy was part of the employment agreement.

Whether an employee handbook has modified the employment relationship is a question of fact "to be discerned from the totality of the parties' statements and actions regarding the employment relationship." **Wagenseller v. Scottsdale Memorial Hosp.**, 147 Ariz. 370, 383, 710 P.2d 1025, 1038 (1985) (en banc).

Evidence relevant to this factual decision includes the language used in the personnel manual

ILLUSTRATION 2-1   *(continued)*

3

as well as the employer's course of conduct and oral representations regarding it. We do not mean to imply that all personnel manual will become part of employment contracts. Employers are certainly free to issue no personnel manual at all or to issue a personnel manual that clearly and conspicuously tells their employees that the manual is not part of the employment contract and that their jobs are terminable *{*667}* at the will of the employer with or without reason. Such actions * * * instill no reasonable expectations of job security and do not give employees any reason to rely on representations in the manual. However, if an employer does choose the issue a policy statement, in a manual or otherwise, and, by its language or by the employer's actions, encourages reliance thereon, the employer cannot be free to only selectively abide by it. Having announced a policy, the employer may not treat it as illusory.

Leikvold v. Valley View Community Hosp., 141 Ariz. 544, 548, 688 P.2d 170, 174 (1984). Here, substantial evidence supports the finding of the trial court that the employee handbook modified the employment relationship and created warning and suspension procedures which were not followed in this case.

Accordingly, based upon the foregoing, the judgment of the trial court is affirmed.

IT IS SO ORDERED.

SCARBOROUGH, C.J., SOSA, Senior Justice, and WALTERS, J., concur.

DISSENT

STOWERS, J., dissents.

STOWERS, Justice, dissenting.

I respectfully dissent from the majority's holding that SIMCO did not abide with the termination procedures.

Substantial evidence does support the findings of the trial court that the employee handbook modified the employment relationship and that Lukoski was terminated for just cause. The trial court erred, however, in concluding that SIMCO did not follow the proper termination procedures. To the contrary, SIMCO did not breach any of the provisions in the employee handbook when it discharged Lukoski without a warning and suspension. The handbook explicitly states that, "there are violations which are so severe that **immediate termination may be necessary**." (Emphasis added).

Overwhelming evidence was presented at trial to show that Lukoski's violations of company policies were of the type to fall within the category of "so severe" that a warning and any suspension procedures were not required. **See State ex rel. Goodmans Office Furnishings, Inc. v. Page & Wirtz Constr. Co.**, 102 N.M. 22, 24, 690 P.2d 1016, 1018 (1984). Generally, this evidence indicated that Lukoski had an overall attitude problem towards his employees, other managers and representatives of the Sandia Pueblo to the extent that SIMCO was in jeopardy of losing its bingo contract with the Pueblo; moreover, he was abusive towards the accountants, argued or fought publicly with customers, the assistant bingo manager, the construction

ILLUSTRATION 2-1   *(continued)*

4

supervisor and an admittance clerk; Lukoski also failed to install proper security measures and verification methods, and hired unqualified personnel. Further, testimony indicated that on several occasions, Walker, Lukoski's supervisor, spoke to Lukoski about this attitude problem, and, in fact, interceded on Lukoski's behalf when the Sandia Pueblo desired to discharge Lukoski.

As enumerated in the handbook, Lukoski's violations included, "fighting on company property, refusal to obey reasonable orders of a supervisor, discourtesy to customers, and disobeying or ignoring established written or oral work rules or policies." These are, and I again quote from the handbook, "violations which are so severe that **immediate termination** may be necessary." (Emphasis added.) Therefore, the trial court was in error when it decided that SIMCO violated the termination procedures prescribed for "less serious" offenses in the handbook. Lukoski was not entitled to those termination procedures since his offenses were not of the "less serious" type. Under the circumstances in this case, the only process due Lukoski for the seriousness of his violations was immediate termination. Thus, there was no breach by SIMCO when it discharged him for just cause.

The judgment of the district court should be reversed and this case remanded for dismissal.

OPINION FOOTNOTES

1 1. The referenced handbook provisions state:

OTHER DISCIPLINARY ACTION:

In order to protect the good employees [sic] jobs and Sandia Indian Bingo, there is an established procedure regarding suspension of problem employees and termination for those who can not conform to Company Policy. Suspensions without pay may be given to employees who violate company policies. There are violations which are so severe [including insubordination and disobedience] that immediate termination may be necessary....

SUSPENSIONS:

Suspension without pay may be given when the incident is not sufficiently serious to warrant discharge and/or the particular employee's overall value to the Company [is considered], if [in] the opinion of the Department Manager [the employee] warrants another chance. Minimum suspensions are (3) three days, maximum suspensions are (5) five days. No employee may be suspended more than once in a year; thereafter, if the incident would normally warrant suspension he/she must be discharged.

DISCIPLINARY WARNING:

Disciplinary warning slips will be issued where the offense is less serious and where corrective action may salvage an employee. More than one (1) disciplinary warning, whether for the same offense or not, may subject an employee to suspension or termination. Warning slips become a permanent part of an employee's personnel record.

ILLUSTRATION 2-2   Employee Privacy Statute, from *New Mexico Statutes Annotated*

50-10-4   EMPLOYEE PRIVACY   50-11-2

50-10-4. [Safety measures and devices; duty of employer to supply.]

Nothing herein shall be construed to relieve any person, firm or corporation requiring, authorizing or knowingly permitting a person in the employ or subject to the control of such person, firm or corporation, to enter into or remain in a sewer in this state from any duty of taking or supplying proper and reasonable safety measures, practices and devices during the time or times that its said employee or other controlled person shall be in such sewer, to the end that no dangerous concentration of flammable gas or gases, or noxious gas or gases, shall occur; and the requirements of this act [50-10-1 to 50-10-6 NMSA 1978] shall be cumulative of such other duty or duties.

History: 1953 Comp., § 12-10-4, enacted by
Laws 1959, ch. 175, § 4.

50-10-5. [Definitions.]

The term "sewer" as used herein shall mean any underground conduit composed of metal, concrete, clay, vitreous or other materials designed for the flowage of water or any waste product or products (including, without being limited to, storm sewers and sanitary sewers), and shall include any and all junction boxes, manholes and gutters and other appurtenances constituting any part of the sewer or of a sewer system.

The term "apparatus to detect the presence of any flammable gas or vapor", as used herein, shall mean any of the standard devices commercially available designed to detect, by the principle of the wheatstone bridge or other recognized technique, the presence in the atmosphere of flammable gas or vapor.

History: 1953 Comp., § 12-10-5, enacted by
Laws 1959, ch. 175, § 5.

50-10-6. [Penalties for violation.]

Any person, firm or corporation violating this act [50-10-1 to 50-10-6 NMSA 1978] shall be deemed guilty of a misdemeanor, and upon conviction thereof shall be punished by a fine not less than one hundred dollars ($100) nor more than one thousand dollars ($1,000), or by imprisonment from one day to ten days, or by both such fine and imprisonment, and each day of violation shall constitute a separate offense.

History: 1953 Comp., § 12-10-6, enacted by
Laws 1959, ch. 175, § 6.

ARTICLE 11

Employee Privacy

50-11-1. Short title.

This act [50-11-1 to 50-11-6 NMSA 1978] may be cited as the "Employee Privacy Act".

History: Laws 1991, ch. 244, § 1.

50-11-2. Definitions.

As used in the Employee Privacy Act [50-11-1 to 50-11-6 NMSA 1978]:

57

ILLUSTRATION 2-2   *(continued)*

A. "employee" means a person that performs a service for wages or other remuneration under a contract of hire, written or oral, express or implied, and includes a person employed by the state or a political subdivision of the state;

B. "employer" means a person that has one or more employees and includes an agent of an employer and the state or a political subdivision of the state; and

C. "person" means an individual, sole proprietorship, partnership, corporation, association or any other legal entity.

History: Laws 1991, ch. 244, § 2.

50-11-3. Employers; unlawful practices.

A. It is unlawful for an employer to:

(1) refuse to hire or to discharge any individual, or otherwise disadvantage any individual, with respect to compensation, terms, conditions or privileges of employment because the individual is a smoker or nonsmoker, provided that the individual complies with applicable laws or policies regulating smoking on the premises of the employer during working hours; or

(2) require as a condition of employment that any employee or applicant for employment abstain from smoking or using tobacco products during nonworking hours, provided the individual complies with applicable laws or policies regulating smoking on the premises of the employer during working hours.

B. The provisions of Subsection A of this section shall not be deemed to protect any activity that:

(1) materially threatens an employer's legitimate conflict of interest policy reasonably designed to protect the employer's trade secrets, proprietary information or other proprietary interests; or

(2) relates to a bona fide occupational requirement and is reasonably and rationally related to the employment activities and responsibilities of a particular employee or a particular group of employees, rather than to all employees of the employer.

History: Laws 1991, ch. 244, § 3.

50-11-4. Remedies.

Any employee claiming to be aggrieved by any unlawful action of an employer pursuant to Section 3 of the Employee Privacy Act [50-11-1 to 50-11-6 NMSA 1978] may bring a civil suit for damages in any district court of competent jurisdiction. The employee may be awarded all wages and benefits due up to and including the date of the judgment.

History: Laws 1991, ch. 244, § 4.

50-11-5. Court fees and costs.

In any civil suit arising from the Employee Privacy Act [50-11-1 to 50-11-6 NMSA 1978], the court shall award the prevailing party court costs and reasonable attorneys' fees.

History: Laws 1991, ch. 244, § 5.

50-11-6. Mitigation of damages.

Nothing in the Employee Privacy Act [50-11-1 to 50-11-6 NMSA 1978] shall be construed to relieve a person from the obligation to mitigate damages.

History: Laws 1991, ch. 244, § 6.

58   5390

ILLUSTRATION 2-3   Encyclopedia Text, from *American Jurisprudence 2d*

---

§ 96   WRONGFUL DISCHARGE   82 Am Jur 2d

rules in the manual, and the courts increasingly recognize that employers have a like duty to abide by the promises they make.[40]

IIII *Practice guide:* In one state it is provided by statute that a discharge is wrongful if the employer violates express provisions of its own personnel policy.[41]

Employee handbooks are viewed as one component or term of the employment agreement.[42] Unless an employee handbook or manual specifically negates any intention on the part of the employer to have it become a part of the employment contract,[43] a court may conclude from a review of the employee handbook that a question of fact is created regarding whether the handbook was intended[44] by the parties to impliedly express a term of the employment agreement.[45] Accordingly, where unilateral contracts are recognized, employment handbooks which contain provisions specifying progressive discharge procedures,[46] or specifying the grounds on which employees could be discharged,[47] or providing that discharge may be for cause only,[48] have been found binding on the employer, constituting a promise not to terminate the employee in violation of such provisions.[49]

---

40. Toussaint v. Blue Cross & Blue Shield, 408 Mich 579, 292 NW2d 880, 895 ("having announced the policy, presumably with a view to obtaining the benefit of improved employee attitudes and behavior and improved quality of the workforce, the employer may not treat its promise as illusory"); Lukoski v Sandia Indian Management Co., 106 NM 664, 748 P2d 507, 2 BNA IER Cas 1650; Thompson v St. Regis Paper Co., 102 Wash 2d 219, 685 P2d 1081, 1 BNA IER Cas 392, 116 BNA LRRM 3142, 105 CCH LC ¶55616 ("promises of specific treatment in specific situations found in an employee manual or handbook issued by the employer . . . may, in appropriate situations, obligate the employer to act in accord with those promises").

41. See Meech v Hillhaven West, Inc., 238 Mont 21, 776 P2d 488, 4 BNA IER Cas 737, 112 CCH LC ¶ 56073, upholding the constitutionality of the Montana Wrongful Discharge from Employment Act.

42. Lincoln v Sterling Drug, Inc. (DC Conn) 622 F Supp 66; Loffa Intel Corp. (App) 153 Ariz 539, 738 P2d 1146; Finley v Aetna Life & Casualty Co., 202 Conn 190, 520 A2d 208, 2 BNA IER Cas 942; Watson v Idaho Falls Consol. Hospitals, Inc., 111 Idaho 44, 720 P2d 632; Duldulao v St. Mary of Nazareth Hospital Center, 115 Ill 2d 482, 106 Ill Dec 8, 505 NE2d 314, 1 BNA IER Cas 1428; Small v Springs Industries, Inc., 292 SC 481, 357 SE2d 452, 2 BNA IER Cas 266, 106 CCH LC

774

¶55766, appeal after remand 300 SC 481, 388 SE2d 808, 5 BNA IER Cas 145, 115 CCH LC ¶56241.

The employment agreement is composed of written and verbal statements, custom, policy, past practice, industry practice, and any other fact which may define the terms of the contract. Shah v American Synthetic Rubber Corp. (Ky) 655 SW2d 489, 114 BNA LRRM 3343, 99CCH LC ¶55423.

43. As to manuals not constituting part of the employment contract, see § 97.

44. Generally, as to intent needed to form a contract, see § 88.

45. Metcalf v Intermountain Gas Co., 116 Idaho 622, 778 P2d 744, 4 BNA IER Cas 961, 113 CCH LC ¶56136.

See Lukoski v Sandia Indian Management Co., 106 NM 664, 748 P2d 507, 2 BNA IER Cas 1650, noting that the handbook did nothing to alert employees that it was subject to revocation or that employees should not rely on it.

46. § 117.

47. § 119.

48. § 120.

49. Towns v Emery Air Freight, Inc. (SD Ohio) 3 BNA IER Cas 911 (applying Ohio law);

ILLUSTRATION 2-4   Periodical Article Text, from *Georgetown Law Journal* through Westlaw

86 GEOLJ 783
(Cite as: 86 Geo. L.J. 783)

Page 1

Georgetown Law Journal
January, 1998

Note

*783 BLOWING SMOKE: DO SMOKERS HAVE A RIGHT? LIMITING THE PRIVACY RIGHTS OF CIGARETTE SMOKERS

Michele L. Tyler [FNa1]

INTRODUCTION

Despite the recent settlement negotiations between the tobacco industry and a group of state attorneys general, the day-to-day debate between smokers and nonsmokers is anything but civil. For example, at a Denny's restaurant in California in 1993, nonsmoker Rachelle Rashan Houston asked Daphnye Luster, a smoker, to extinguish her cigarette. Ms. Luster, who was seated in the nonsmoking section, complied and shortly thereafter left the restaurant. Later, Ms. Luster returned with a 12-gauge shotgun and killed Ms. Houston as Ms. Houston was driving away from the restaurant. [FN1] This violent example illustrates the growing tension between smokers and nonsmokers over whether an individual has a "right" to smoke.

Change in the social acceptance of smoking has occurred rapidly, with nonsmokers' passive tolerance of smoking turning within a single lifetime to vocal demands for protection from exposure to tobacco smoke. Not so long ago, smoking was considered an acceptable adult choice; its health effects limited to smoker's cough and yellowed teeth. Smoking was portrayed on television and film as part of a glamorous and sophisticated lifestyle. Lucy and Ricky Ricardo smoked cigarettes they kept in a silver case; [FN2] Humphrey Bogart, who died of lung cancer, and his co-stars smoked in nearly every scene of Casablanca. [FN3] Yet the tide of public opinion began to turn after the 1964 Surgeon General's Report, [FN4] which concluded that smoking increases a person's risk of lung cancer, chronic bronchitis, and emphysema. [FN5] Until the recent settlement negotiations, [FN6] ***784** the tobacco industry steadfastly denied the negative effects of smoking, [FN7] even in the face of numerous studies and reports by the Surgeon General and the Environmental Protection Agency that demonstrated otherwise. [FN8] Nevertheless, as social attitudes about smoking have changed, nonsmokers have had greater success in passing legislation aimed at controlling smoking. [FN9] As of 1993, forty- four states had passed restrictions on smoking in public places. [FN10] Additionally, some states and many localities have enacted even more restrictive smoking laws and ordinances to prohibit smoking in workplaces, restaurants, and stadiums. [FN11] Moreover, the private sector, which includes businesses, universities, hospitals, and nonprofit organizations, has responded to the growing health concerns of nonsmokers. By the early 1990s, eighty-five percent of private businesses had put some type of smoking policy in place, although the terms of these policies vary greatly. [FN12]

Yet there are signs of a smoker backlash. As of 1995, twenty-nine states had passed some type of legislation prohibiting employers from requiring employees to abstain from smoking outside the course of employment. [FN13] Additionally, many of the cities and private businesses attempting to enact restrictive smoking legislation have faced political opposition and negative public relations campaigns funded by the tobacco industry. [FN14]

*785 Recently, however, the tobacco company Liggett-Myers acknowledged that tobacco is addictive, causes cancer, and that tobacco companies have consciously marketed cigarettes to young teenagers. [FN15] In light of such acknowledgment, the tobacco industry and smokers can no longer plausibly deny the addictive effects of cigarette smoking. The industry's denials of the harmful effects of "second-hand" tobacco smoke [FN16] will likely become suspect even to long-time smokers. Nevertheless, many people will continue to smoke, often asserting a privacy right to do so. [FN17] This note will address that assertion, analyzing controversial anti-smoking legislation and court decisions with regard to three different meanings of the right to privacy: informational privacy, physical privacy, and

3.   Finding Tools

As you would no doubt guess, you will need assistance in locating pertinent primary authority and secondary sources. Finding tools help you to do so. They do not constitute authority of any sort, however, because they do not themselves assert legal propositions.

Some finding tools cover a wide range of sources. For example, a library catalog covers the paper, microform, and, with increasing frequency, computer-based sources owned by or accessible in a particular library. Internet search engines and directories index the content of World Wide Web sites.

Other finding tools are narrower, covering only a particular type of authority. For example, periodical indexes are used to locate periodical articles. Digests are used to locate cases.

Once you identify an appropriate source, you may use its internal finding tools to locate pertinent material within the source. You are no doubt already familiar with indexes and tables of contents; these are common in legal sources. Legal sources also have distinctive internal finding tools, such as a treatise's table of cases or statutes discussed therein. The searches one can run in a computer-based source operate as an internal finding tool. (Illustrations of internal finding tools appear in Chapter 3.)

Finally, most authorities operate as finding tools for other authorities. For example, a court may refer in its opinion to a statute, or a treatise author may list cases from which he or she has drawn the legal rule under discussion. Similarly, people, including colleagues, professors, and reference librarians, can sometimes be helpful "finding tools."

C.   MEDIA

The three categories of materials described above—primary authority, secondary sources, and finding tools—appear in various media. Each medium is either paper-based or computer-based.

Books (whether hardbound or softcover), periodicals, and newspapers are the clearest examples of paper-based media. Microforms, which are tiny photographs of paper sources, also qualify as paper-based media. Microfilm is available in both rolls and cartridges. A microfiche is a flat sheet of film that resembles a note card.

Computer-based media consist of CD-ROMs and online products. Both contain computer-readable collections of text and graphics (and sometimes even audio and video).

CD-ROM stands for "compact disk, read only memory." A CD-ROM is a plastic disk that contains information stored in pits molded into the surface of the disk; a typical CD-ROM disk holds the equivalent of about 200,000 pages of text. You use a computer program to call up the information you want, a laser beam reads the information, and the information is displayed on your computer monitor.

"Online" means that the information in a database is stored in a computer at a remote location. Again, you use a computer program to call up the information you want, it is sent over a telecommunication line to you, and the information is displayed on your computer monitor.

The Internet is a vast, unregulated international network that connects thousands of other computer networks, including government, university, and business networks. It is not well organized; it has no comprehensive directory, standardized search methods, uniform editorial practices, or quality control; its documentation is weak; and there is no system-wide customer service to help you.

You will most likely search the Internet using the World Wide Web (WWW), which you navigate using a web browser, a program that is installed on your computer. The most common web browsers are Netscape Navigator and Microsoft Internet Explorer. Once on a browser, you may use one of three ways to locate sources. First, you may go directly to a known site by keying its address. A typical web address, also called a Uniform Resource Locator (URL), looks something like this: http://www.law.cornell.edu. Second, you may search an Internet subject directory and site constructed by other people to help you find relevant sources. Yahoo, which is found at www.yahoo.com, is the best known of these directories and sites. Third, you may use a search engine to locate relevant sites. Search engines use computer programs, known as "robots," to search the web and retrieve web pages for indexing. (Robots work by following the hypertext links within one or more starting documents to other documents, then following the links in those documents to still other documents, and so on.) When you search the web using a search engine, you search the index created by the search engine, not the web itself. Exhibit 2.2 on page 23 lists addresses of some commonly used search engines. Once at a site, you use the site's search techniques to locate pertinent material therein.

At present, two online subscription services are of particular importance to the legal researcher: LEXIS and Westlaw. LEXIS and Westlaw provide, for a significant price, a wide variety of primary and secondary legal authority. Both also provide access to nonlegal material, LEXIS through its NEXIS component and Westlaw through the Dialog Information Service. (The corporate name of the LEXIS company is LEXIS-NEXIS.) LEXIS and Westlaw are both highly organized commercial databases with good directories, well developed search methods, strong quality controls, good documentation, and training support. Both have long track records, dating to the 1970s. The web provides a link to Westlaw and LEXIS; you (or your law school or employer) must still pay a fee for using them, because they are subscription services.

In addition, various government and educational institutions have created public web sites on which major legal authorities are made available for free (beyond the basic cost of your Internet provider). While these public web sites are not yet as sophisticated or extensive as Westlaw and LEXIS, they are expanding rapidly. Exhibit 2.2 on page 23 lists URLs for several such legal sites.

Furthermore, the web affords a mechanism for rapid and inexpensive publication of legal materials. Some smaller commercial companies are taking

| **EXHIBIT 2.2** | Selected Internet Search Engines and Sites |

Selected Search Engines

Alta Vista	www.altavista.com
Excite	www.excite.com
HotBot	www.hotbot.com
Infoseek	www.infoseek.go.com
Lycos	www.lycos.com

Public Web Sites for Legal Information

Findlaw	www.findlaw.com
Hieros Gamos	www.hg.org
Legal Information Institute (Cornell Law School)	www.law.cornell.edu
WashLaw Web (Washburn University School of Law)	www.washlaw.edu
WWW Virtual Law Library	www.law.indiana.edu/law/v-lib/ lawindex.html

Subscription Web Sites

LEXIS	www.lexis.com
Westlaw	www.westlaw.com
Loislaw	www.loislaw.com
VersusLaw	www.versuslaw.com

advantage of this opportunity and creating subscription services that are (at least at present) both less expansive and less expensive than Westlaw and LEXIS. For example, Loislaw.com, a relative newcomer, now provides a wide range of primary sources at the federal and state levels. Again, see Exhibit 2.2 above.

As the technological side of legal research evolves, you should strive to stay current on your media options. You may determine the media in which a particular authority is available by checking a library catalog, using the directory of a particular computer-based service, or doing an Internet search. You also may consult reference titles, such as:

Directory of Law-Related CD-ROMs
Gale Guide to Internet Databases
The Legal List: Research on the Internet.

Some researchers develop overly strong preferences for one medium or another. To research competently, you must become adept in all media, for several reasons. Some legal research materials are available in only one medium. Sometimes the medium you prefer will be unavailable or cost-prohibitive. And different media work better for different purposes and different research situations.

The illustrations in this chapter come from the following media: books—Illustration 2-2 on pages 17–18 (the statute) and Illustration 2-3 on page 19 (the encyclopedia); CD-ROM—Illustration 2-1 on pages 13–16 (the case); Westlaw—Illustration 2-4 on page 20 (the periodical article).

D.   CHOOSING AMONG SOURCES

Sometimes you will have a choice of sources for researching a particular type of authority. For example, the decisions of the New Mexico Supreme Court appear (among other places) in an official publication of the New Mexico government, in book form; a commercial publication, called the *Pacific Reporter*, which also appears in book form; various databases within Westlaw and LEXIS; a CD-ROM product; and a public web site. In choosing among sources, you should consider various factors:

Content: Be sure the source has as full a range of the particular authority you are seeking as you need. For example, if you are researching case law for the Canoga case, does your source include only New Mexico Supreme Court cases? Or does it also include lower court cases? Might you seek cases not typically published in paper?

Time period: Be sure the source is both sufficiently retrospective and up to date. For example, how old is the oldest case in the source? Are the newest cases included? How quickly?

Accuracy: Most legal research materials are highly accurate, but you may find some errors from time to time. If so, you should use an alternative source.

Reputation of publisher: As to any particular authority for which there is more than one source, you should be sure you are consulting a credible source. For example, regarding case law for the Canoga case, is the source the official publisher of New Mexico cases, or a commercial publisher with a strong track record, or a web site with indicia of credibility such as sponsorship of the courts or an educational institution?

Furthermore, as you will see, a fairly small number of companies publish most of the major legal resources. It is useful to know which sources are published by the same publisher or by affiliated publishers, in particular how paper sources relate to online and CD-ROM sources. Sources published by the same publisher are likely to draw on each other and to provide cross-references to each other (but not to other publishers' sources).

Ease of access: Be sure your source affords readily usable and reliable means of locating pertinent information. Paper-based sources usually offer indexes, tables of contents, and tables of authorities. Computer-based media may offer indexes and tables; they also typically offer additional research methods, such as Boolean searches, natural-language searches, segment searches, and find searches. (These research methods are explained in Chapter 3.) For example, can you easily locate cases with legal issues and facts parallel to the Canoga case?

Ease of reading: Be sure the source presents the pertinent information in a way that facilitates careful and efficient reading. Paper-based media and computer-based media differ in this respect. In paper-based media, you generally will find references to pages or sections of text, which you then will peruse. It is easy to browse from your starting point to related nearby material, by flipping pages. Unless you own the source, you will need to photocopy pertinent pages if you wish to have a copy for your file.

In computer-based media, you typically will run a search and retrieve a list of citations; you will then select the documents you wish to view and how to view those documents. You may choose to peruse them in full text, or you may be able to focus in on selected excerpts of the text that contain your search terms. It is not always easy to browse a nearby document not retrieved by your search, but you may be able to move to a document referred to in the document you initially retrieved through hypertext links. Most computer-based sources permit you to make your own file copy by downloading onto a disk or printing.

Ease of updating: Similarly, be sure the source presents the newest information in a way that facilitates careful and efficient reading. When you research in paper-based sources, you often will need to consult multiple volumes to obtain both the basic and the newest information. When you research in computer-based sources, you often will find the newest information fully integrated with older information. For example, in researching case law for the Canoga case, must you consult several volumes of a digest (a sophisticated finding tool for cases), or can you rely on a single list of retrieved cases?

Cost: Be sure that the source, as you use it, is not unduly costly. Total costs for a source include initial product cost, update costs, space costs, equipment costs, maintenance costs, training costs, and the cost of your time. Some costs (such as the purchase price of a book or the monthly rate of some online services) are more or less fixed and become a factor in the overhead of the office (which is indirectly reflected in billing rates). Others (such as online time for a service imposing per-use fees) are incurred as the source is used. For example, should you locate pertinent cases by working through a digest the office owns, which can be a fairly time-consuming process, or should you run an online search, which takes little time but may incur a fee?

As a beginning researcher, you will not be able to easily evaluate all of these factors for the sources you encounter. However, you will become more adept at evaluating them as you become an experienced researcher.

<table>
<tr><td>

LEGAL LANGUAGE AND RESEARCH TERMS

</td><td>

CHAPTER

3

</td></tr>
</table>

A. INTRODUCTION

The law (primary authority) consists of words chosen to express concepts. So too do secondary sources, which comment on the law. Most finding tools operate primarily through words. As you think about your client's situation, you also will use words, however imperfect, to describe the events and the people, their motivations, actions, and reactions.

This chapter first explains how language is used in legal research materials—something you must understand before you can research in those materials. This chapter then teaches you three critical steps of legal research: (1) generating research terms and issues, (2) using legal dictionaries and thesauri, and (3) employing your research terms and issues to look up concepts and search for words.

B. LEGAL LANGUAGE

1. The Language of Legal Rules

The core of a primary authority is the rule (or rules) of law it expresses. A rule of law links factual conditions with legal consequences. For example, consider this excerpt from the New Mexico statute illustrated in Chapter 2:

It is unlawful for an employer to . . . require as a condition of employment that any employee . . . abstain from smoking or using tobacco
products during nonworking hours. . . . Any employee claiming to be
aggrieved by [such an] unlawful action . . . may bring a civil suit for
damages. . . . The employee may be awarded all wages and benefits due
up to and including the date of the judgment.

This rule refers to the following factual condition: an employer prohibits an
employee from smoking during nonworking hours. That factual condition
leads to the following legal consequence: the employee may sue the employer
for wages and benefits.

Most of the words in this rule are familiar words. Indeed, some words
are used just as you would use them in everyday speech, for example, "smoking" and "tobacco products." Other words carry a legal connotation, for
example, "aggrieved," "civil suit," and "judgment." Still other words have
a mixed meaning. For example, an everyday understanding of "employment"
is the work one does for another person for pay; various laws govern the
employment relationship.

In some legal rules, one or more words are defined for purposes of the
particular rule; the definition may or may not accord with its common meaning. For example, the New Mexico legislature defined "employer" to include
various legal entities, including the state and its political subdivisions, that
have one or more employees. See Illustration 2-2 on page 18. In another
statute, "employer" might include only private employers or entities with a
minimum number of employees.

Most words in a legal rule are quite general, because rules describe classes
of situations, not specific situations. For example, the New Mexico statute
excerpt does not describe a specific employer or employee, certain tobacco
products, or a particular means of prohibiting smoking.

Many concepts are expressed not in one word, but in a phrase. Sometimes, the words appear in a fixed order; sometimes, the words may be
inverted with no loss of meaning. As examples, consider the fixed-order
phrase used in the New Mexico statute, "during nonworking hours," and
the invertible phrase "employment contract," which appears in the *Lukoski*
case, Illustration 2-1 on pages 13–16.

Some concepts can be stated in one of several words or phrases with
virtually the same meaning, i.e., synonyms. The encyclopedia excerpt in Illustration 2-3 on page 19 refers to "employment contract" and "employment
agreement" interchangeably. Similarly, some words and phrases used in legal
rules are antonyms. The New Mexico statute excerpted above also has another
rule pertinent to "during working hours," an antonym of "during nonworking hours."

Some concepts can be expressed in broad or narrow terms. For example,
the New Mexico statute employs a very broad term—"unlawful"—to convey
that certain employer action is prohibited. The statute also conveys the same
idea through a narrower term—"civil suit for damages."

Finally, some legal concepts are subsets of other legal concepts. The
following are subsets of the statute's overall concept of unlawful employer

practice: employer, employee, requirement of abstention from smoking, during nonworking hours.

2. Non-Rule Language of Legal Authorities

Many legal authorities, especially secondary authorities (which comment on the law), do more than state legal rules. They also elaborate upon the rule, explain its development, discuss the reasons for it, describe specific situations and predict the outcomes of those situations, critique the rule, and propose alternatives to it. Some of this language is very similar to the language used to express a legal rule.

Yet there also are important differences between rule language and non-rule language. For example, in describing the facts of a case, a court uses specific factual terms, such as the name of a specific person or company. You can see this in the *Lukoski* case in Illustration 2-1 on pages 13–16, which refers to Mr. Lukoski, his employer SIMCO, and specific provisions of the SIMCO employee handbook. As another example, in critiquing or explaining a rule, a commentary writer may refer to abstract legal and nonlegal concepts. For example, a discussion of legal rules prohibiting smoking may refer to such broad legal concepts as fairness and autonomy, or to public health concepts such as second-hand smoke or environmental tobacco smoke. See Illustration 2-4 on page 20.

C. GENERATING RESEARCH TERMS AND ISSUES

To research effectively in legal sources, you must excel in generating research terms and issues. A "research term" is an expression of a concept you wish to research; a "research issue" is a combination of terms in question form. Take the time to accomplish each of the following steps properly; you will not obtain good results unless you know what you are seeking.

Generate research terms and issues:

- ▶ analyze your research problem to identify its factual and legal concepts
- ▶ develop a full set of research terms by working with related terms, roots, and phrases
- ▶ formulate potential research issues using those terms

Analyze your research problem. As you begin your research, you should carefully analyze what you know of your client's situation and concern, that is, your research problem. You may not yet know everything there is or will be to know, typically because you know your client's view but not those of other people, or because you are advising a client before all events have occurred. Nonetheless, you should think about the following factual dimensions of what you do know:

(1)   *Who* is involved? The answer may be people or entities, such as a corporation or government body. Focus not on the exact identities of those involved, but on their roles.

(2)   *What* is involved? The answer may be physical items, activities, or intangibles.

(3)   *When* did (or will) the important events occur? Think not only about the precise date and time, but also about the sequence of events.

(4)   *Where* did (or will) the important events occur? Think not only about the precise location, but also about the significance of the location.

(5)   *Why* did (or will) the participants act in this way? Analyze their motives or states of mind.

Many of the concepts you identify will appear in some form in the factual conditions of the legal rule or rules governing your problem. Furthermore, your answer to the "where" question will help you identify the jurisdiction whose law you should research. Your answer to the "when" question will help you identify law that is current as of your client's situation. Of course, not every factual concept will prove to be a useful research term. To avoid overlooking something critical, you should include, rather than exclude, too much.

You also should think about your problem's legal dimensions. Even before you research the problem, you may have some sense of what it might entail. Many legal rules are based on common notions of what is just and fair, and many legal rules are within common parlance. Hence you should think about the following legal dimensions:

(6)   What is the *legal theory* applicable to this situation? What is the legal basis for penalizing the wrongdoer, benefiting the wronged party, or excusing the wrong?

(7)   What *relief* does the wronged party seek through the legal system?

(8)   What is the *procedural posture* of the case? At what stage of the litigation process is the case at this point?

Many of the concepts you identify will appear as the legal consequences of the rule. Although these questions, especially the third, assume that there is litigation, your problem may not actually involve litigation, now or ever. Nonetheless, as lawyers research, they imagine what the courts would do with a case involving the client's situation; hence you should look at your problem in this light.

As these eight questions—five factual questions, three legal questions—are phrased here, they probably seem fairly distinct. In practice, you will find them to be less than distinct. Fortunately, it is not important that you properly categorize a particular concept; it is important that you use these questions to think through your problem thoroughly.

As an example, if you were researching the Canoga problem, you might identify the factual and legal concepts stated below:

Factual Concepts
(1)   who: musician, flutist, smoker (tried to quit; failed), employee; employer, orchestra, general manager, board of directors
(2)   what: employment, termination, smoking, insubordination, denial of board review, employee manual, no-smoking policy, protest against smoking rules
(3)   when: January 7, 1999; five years after hire; smoking during nonworking hours
(4)   where: Taos, New Mexico; smoking away from the orchestra's premises
(5)   why: protest against policy for privacy reasons, termination for insubordination or refusal to cease smoking

Legal Concepts
(1)   legal theory: breach of contract, discrimination against smokers, violation of privacy rights
(2)   relief sought: money (damages), return to work (reinstatement), cleared work record
(3)   procedure: nothing yet

Develop research terms. Your next step is to develop a full set of research terms, a process that entails several substeps: spinning off additional words, analyzing the roots of your words, and examining your phrases.

For each important concept, you should think of words that are synonyms, antonyms, broader or narrower terms, subconcepts or main concepts for your initial words. Two useful devices for doing so are a hub-and-spokes diagram and a ladder diagram. In the former, the original word appears at the center, with additional words circling it. In the latter, a broad term appears at the top rung and consecutively narrower terms appear below it. Examples appear below:

a wheel of terms related to contract:

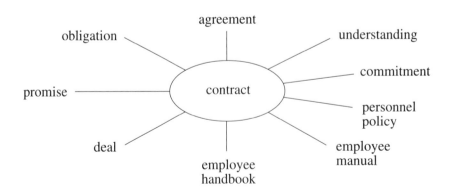

a ladder of terms relating to the right to smoke:

privacy
right to engage in legal activities
right to smoke
right to smoke off-duty, away from employer premises

Then consider each word from a linguistic perspective. Consider whether a word has a root that is shared with other potentially pertinent words. For example, the root "employ" appears in several words: employment, employee, employer. You would want to use all of these words. Consider also whether a word's root is shared by nonuseful words, or indeed whether a word has a nonpertinent meaning. For example, the word "employ" is used in many settings unrelated to working for another for pay, as in employing one's energies for a good purpose. You would want to avoid these nonpertinent usages to the extent possible.

Finally, carefully examine any phrases you have generated. Be sure you know whether the words always appear in a specific order or whether the order may be inverted.

At the end of this process, you should have a well-developed set of research terms: lists of related words, roots, and phrases covering your various factual and legal concepts. Two sets of research terms for two key concepts in the Canoga case appear below:

Employee	*Discharge*
employ . . .	discharg(e) . . . of / from employment
employer	dismiss . . . "
employee	separat(e) . . . "
employment	terminat(e) . . . "
worker	fir(e) . . . "
labor	
job	involuntary
master / servant	
orchestra / musician / flutist	

Formulate research issues. As you analyze your problem and develop research terms, you probably will note that some concepts seem closely connected. More specifically, certain factual concepts will seem to connect to certain legal concepts. From these connections, you may be able to formulate tentative research issues, that is, questions for which you are seeking legal answers.

For example, in the Canoga case, breach of contract (a legal theory) probably connects to the employee manual and denial of board review. Several possible issues for the Canoga case appear below:

> Is there a *breach of contract* when the board denied review to a terminated employee though review was promised in the employee handbook?
>
> Is there a *violation of privacy rights* when an orchestra's policy prohibits smoking off-duty, a flutist resists and is discharged?
>
> Is there unlawful *discrimination against a smoker* when a flutist-smoker who could not quit smoking was fired by an orchestra for refusing to agree not to smoke off-duty off-premises?
>
> [Legal theories are italicized.]

D. USING DICTIONARIES AND THESAURI

1. What Are Legal Dictionaries and Thesauri?

Legal dictionaries and thesauri provide information about words used in the law. You will find quite an array of legal dictionaries and thesauri, each with strengths and weaknesses. Exhibit 3.1 on page 33 presents an overview of dictionaries and thesauri that provide general coverage of legal vocabulary.

The more comprehensive dictionaries, such as *Black's Law Dictionary*, cover a very wide range of terms and phrases, including legal maxims and foreign-language phrases; comprehensive dictionaries typically include pronunciations, word derivations, and illustrative references to legal authorities. The more compact dictionaries, such as those by Gifis, Oran, and Rothenberg and Gilbert, contain only the definitions of essential or basic legal terms. Thesauri primarily provide synonyms, antonyms, and associated concepts; some include basic definitions.

2. Why Are Legal Dictionaries and Thesauri Useful?

Dictionaries and thesauri have two primary uses. First, many words have legal connotations that differ somewhat from their nonlegal connotations. Hence, you should look up your most important research terms in a legal dictionary, to be sure that your understanding comports with legal usage. (Of course, if your research involves a term defined outside of the law, you should use an appropriate nonlegal dictionary.) Second, these tools can help you identify additional research terms.

Dictionaries that contain references to primary authority or secondary sources also function, to a limited extent, as a finding tool. However the references are illustrative, not exhaustive; the cited authorities may not accord with current law in your jurisdiction. Thus, the finding-tool function is only incidental.

EXHIBIT 3.1	General-Coverage Law Dictionaries and Thesauri

Dictionary or Thesauruus	Size	Primary Orientation
Ballentine's Law Dictionary (3d ed. 1969).	full-size	legal audience
Black's Law Dictionary (Bryan A. Garner ed., 7th ed. 1999).	full-size (also abridged edition)	legal audience
Gerry W. Beyer & Kenneth R. Redden, *Modern Dictionary for the Legal Profession* (Margaret M. Beyer ed., 2d ed. 1996 & Supp. 1999).	intermediate	both
Amy B. Brann, *The Law Dictionary* (7th ed. 1997).	pocket-size	legal audience
William C. Burton, *Burton's Legal Thesaurus* (3d ed. 1998).	intermediate	both
Steven H. Gifis, *Dictionary of Legal Terms* (3d ed. 1998).	pocket-size	legal novice
Steven H. Gifis, *Law Dictionary* (4th ed. 1996).	pocket-size	legal novice
Jonathan S. Lynton, *Ballentine's Legal Dictionary and Thesaurus* (1995).	intermediate	both
Daniel Oran, *Oran's Dictionary of the Law* (2d ed. 1991).	pocket-size	both
The Plain-Language Law Dictionary (Robert E. Rothenberg & Stephen A. Gilbert eds., 2d ed. 1996).	pocket-size	legal novice
William P. Statsky, *West's Legal Thesaurus/Dictionary* (1985).	intermediate	both

3.   How Do You Use Legal Dictionaries and Thesauri?

Your first task is to select a suitable dictionary or thesaurus. For example, if you are simply seeking to generate a wider range of related terms, consult a thesaurus. If you are seeking a working definition of a common legal term, consult one of the compact dictionaries. If you are seeking a more complete definition of a less common term or a legal maxim, consult one of the full-size dictionaries.

You are most likely to use these sources in book form. As you do so, keep in mind that legal words and phrases can be alphabetized letter-by-letter or word-by-word. For instance, the phrase "contract remedy" would appear before "contractor" in word-by-word indexing, but the order would be reversed in letter-by-letter indexing.

You might use a computer-based dictionary if it is expedient to do so. Both Westlaw and LEXIS have searchable legal dictionaries and thesauri. Only a few searchable legal dictionaries were available via the Internet when this book was written; they were not very comprehensive.

Regardless of how you explore these sources, as you discover new potential terms within the definitions, be sure to look them up too. And keep track of where you locate key definitions, in case you need to cite them.

Researching the Canoga case, we looked up various words. Illustration 3-1 on pages 35–36 presents pertinent excerpts from various sources. Note that the "contract" definitions confirm the concept of contract as involving an obligation derived from a promise; the thesaurus entry provides numerous synonyms meriting consideration (agreement, covenant, pledge, etc.). Note that the law formerly used "master" to refer to employers. A potentially important term is "employment at will," which means employment that may be terminated at any time, with or without cause. Yet there also are legal concepts for "retaliatory" and "wrongful discharge," discharges that violate the law or public policy.

4. What Else?

Legal Usage Texts: Two texts that resemble dictionaries not only provide definitions but also address stylistic choices in legal writing. Bryan Garner's *A Dictionary of Modern Legal Usage* (2d ed. 1995) contains definitions of common legal terms, notes on frequently misused or confused terms, and short essays on points of grammar and style. Similarly, David Mellinkoff's *Mellinkoff's Dictionary of American Legal Usage* (1992) supplements definitions with the author's opinions about preferred usage and clear writing.

Specialized Dictionaries: If you experience difficulty finding your term in the dictionaries described above or need additional detail, you may wish to consult a specialized legal dictionary. They exist in many subjects, such as constitutional, international, and business law. There also are special-purpose dictionaries, such as *Bieber's Dictionary of Legal Abbreviations* (Prince's 4th ed. 1993).

5. How Do You Cite Dictionaries?

Citation to a legal dictionary is relatively rare; it is better to cite a primary authority providing a definition than a dictionary. You may, however, cite a dictionary for a definition of a term that is undefined in the primary authority in your jurisdiction. Depending on the source, you will need to provide the title, author or editor, page number, edition, and date. For example, here are correct citations to several of the definitions presented in this chapter (according to Rule 15 of *The Bluebook*):

Ballentine's Law Dictionary 399 (3d ed. 1969)
Black's Law Dictionary 545, 475-76 (7th ed. 1999)
Daniel Oran, *Oran's Dictionary of the Law* 100 (2d ed. 1991)
The Plain-Language Law Dictionary 110 (Robert E. Rothenberg &
Stephen A. Gilbert eds., 2d ed. 1996).

ILLUSTRATION 3-1   Excerpts from Dictionaries and Thesauri

The Plain-Language Law Dictionary 110 (Robert E. Rothenberg & Stephen A. Gilbert eds., 2d ed. 1996).
Contract. An AGREEMENT between two or more people, one PARTY (or parties) agreeing to perform certain acts, the other party (or parties) agreeing to pay for or give other consideration for said performance. A contract places an OBLIGATION on one party to do something and an obligation upon the other party to reward the doer.

Daniel Oran, *Oran's Dictionary of the Law* 100 (2d ed. 1991).
Contract An agreement that affects or creates legal relationships between two or more persons. To be a *contract,* an agreement must involve: at least one promise, **consideration** (something of value promised or given), persons legally capable of making binding agreements, and a reasonable certainty about the meaning of the terms. A contract is called **bilateral** if both sides make promises (such as the promise to deliver a book on one side and a promise to pay for it on the other) or **unilateral** if the promises are on one side only. According to the **Uniform Commercial Code,** a contract is the "total legal obligation which results from the parties' agreement," and according to the Restatement of the Law of Contracts, it is "a promise or set of promises for the breach of which the law in some way recognizes a duty." For different types of contracts, such as **output**, **requirements**, etc., see those words.

William C. Burton, *Legal Thesaurus* 122 (3d ed. 1999).
CONTRACT, *noun* accord, accordance, agreement, arrangement, articles of agreement, assurance, avouchment, avowal, bargain, binding agreement, bond, charter, collective agreement, commitment, compact, compromise, concordat, *condicio, conductio,* confirmation, *conventio,* covenant, deal, embodied terms, engagement, *entente,* guarantee, instrument evidencing an agreement, ironclad agreement, legal document, mutual agreement, mutual pledge, mutual promise, mutual undertaking, negotiated agreement, obligation, pact, paction, *pactum,* pledge, pledged word, private understanding, promise, ratified agreement, set terms, settlement, stated terms, stipulation, terms for agreement, understanding, undertaking, warranty, written terms

Ballentine's Law Dictionary 399 (3d ed. 1969).
employer. One, formerly known as "master," who is in such relation to another person that he may control the work of that other person and direct the manner in which it is to be done. 35 Am Jlst M & S § 2. The person by and for whom an independent contractor is engaged. 27 Am Jlst Ind Contr § 27.

William P. Statsky, *West's Legal Thesaurus/Dictionary: A Resource for the Writer and the Computer Researcher* 273 (1985).
Employee, n. A person in the service of another under an express or implied, oral or written

ILLUSTRATION 3-1   *(continued)*

contract of hire, in which the employer has the power and the right to control and direct the employee in the material details of how the work is to be performed (the employee acted within the scope of her employment). Servant, salaried worker, agent, wage earner, laborer, jobholder, staff member, hand, apprentice, journeyman, retainer, hireling, lackey, messenger, attendant, subordinate, workman, artisan, mechanic, craftsman, workaholic, breadwinner, helper, aide, henchman, valet, underling, domestic, retainer, white-collar worker, proletarian, hustler, flunky, man Friday, personnel. See also assistant. <u>Ant</u>. Employer.

Black's Law Dictionary 545, 475-76 (7th ed. 1999).
employment. 1. The act of employing; the state of being employed. **2.** Work for which one has been hired and is being paid by an employer.

> . . .

> **employment at will.** Employment that is usu. undertaken without a contract and that may be terminated at any time, by either the employer or the employee, without cause.—Also termed *at-will employment; hiring at will.*

> . . .

> "The doctrine of employment at will prescribed that an employee without a contract for a fixed term could be hired or fired for any reason or no reason at all. . . . [The] rule provided that employees categorized as 'at will' had no legal interest in continuing job security. Whereas early American masters had some responsibility to the public as well as to their servants when they turned dependent servants out on the world, under [this] formulation, masters could simply fire employees who had no contracts." Mark A. Rothstein et al., *Employment Law* § 1.4, at 9-10 (1994).

discharge (**dis**-charhrj), *n.* . . . . 7. The firing of an employee.

> . . .

> **retaliatory discharge.** A discharge that is made in retaliation for the employee's conduct (such as reporting unlawful activity by the employer to the government) and that clearly violates public policy. • Most states have statutes allowing an employee who is dismissed by retaliatory discharge to recover damages.

> . . .

> **wrongful discharge.** A discharge for reasons that are illegal or that violate public policy.

E.   EMPLOYING YOUR RESEARCH TERMS AND ISSUES

Legal research sources permit you to use words in various ways. Some legal research sources permit you to look up concepts, others permit you to search for specific words of your choosing, and yet others permit both types of research.

Looking up concepts is a conceptual process; searching for words is a literal process. When you look up a concept, you are looking for material discussing that concept, in whatever words that concept might be expressed. When you search for specific words, you are searching for a particular configuration of letters within the material in which you are researching. Those characters may appear in a document that is pertinent to your research problem—or in a document that is not pertinent to your research problem.

This part provides an overview of the major methods of looking up concepts and searching for words. You will learn more about methods to use with particular research materials in later chapters.

1. Looking Up Concepts

As an example of looking up concepts, consider the following: You are researching in a legal encyclopedia, in a book, seeking basic information about employment contracts promising employees protection against unfair termination. You would use a table of contents or index to the encyclopedia to locate pertinent topics and subtopics discussed within the encyclopedia, which you then would read.

This process has advantages and disadvantages. The chief advantage is that your research benefits from the editorial process that created the encyclopedia. The editors of the encyclopedia developed a set of fairly standard terms to describe the various concepts covered in the encyclopedia and internal finding tools (such as the index and the table of contents) to help you learn their terms. Hence, once you discern the editors' terms, you can work with a concept and overcome linguistic variations that may exist for the concept.

On the other hand, your research will succeed only if you can tap into the source's vocabulary. The vocabulary can be idiosyncratic to the source, or it can become stale if it does not evolve as concepts and usage evolve. For example, the terms "master" and "servant" have been used for "employer" and "employee"; if a resource continues to use this terminology and you do not think of it, you may not locate pertinent material.

Main options for looking up concepts:

- table of contents
- index
- table of authorities

When you look up a concept, you generally will employ a table of contents, an index, or a table of cited authorities. The first two processes are the most common.

Many legal research sources have overall tables of contents, which list the main topics in the order they appear in the resource. The overall design may be alphabetical or topical. You should skim the list of topics, looking for entries that correspond to or are similar to the research terms you have generated for your research problem.

Many resources also have detailed tables of contents, which list the sections within a topic. The sections typically are arrayed according to the logical structure of the topic. You should skim the detailed table of contents for two purposes: to get a sense of the topic's logical structure and to identify the most probable pertinent sections for your research problem.

For example, when we researched the Canoga problem, we found the following in the alphabetical list of topics (the table of abbreviations) in the encyclopedia *American Jurisprudence 2d* (Am. Jur. 2d): Contracts, Employment Relationship, Job Discrimination, Wrongful Discharge. See Illustration 3-2 on page 39. Skimming the detailed table of contents for the Wrongful Discharge topic, we located a discussion of employee handbooks in sections 96 through 100 and discharge and discipline in sections 116 through 122. See Illustration 3-3 on page 40.

The second common means of looking up a concept is by use of the index. An index presents an alphabetical list of covered subjects with references to where each subject is discussed. Legal indexes typically are long and complex, with multiple minor subjects listed below major subjects and with cross-references to other subjects. Your task is to look for various major and minor subjects that correspond to or are similar to your research terms. Once you have located such subjects, you would consult the listed locations within the source (chapters, pages, sections, etc.).

For example, in the Am. Jur. 2d index, the "employment relationship" listing runs over twenty pages and includes a cross-reference for "wrongful discharge." Illustration 3-4 on page 41 is a portion of the Am. Jur. 2d index listing for "wrongful discharge"; various entries point to sections 96 through 98 of the Wrong(ful) Disch(arge) topic.

The third means of looking up a concept is useful only when you already have some idea of a pertinent primary authority, such as a key case or statute. Some sources have tables of authorities for specific types of authorities, discussed therein, such as cases or statutes. You can consult such a table, using the name of the known authority as your research term; if the authority appears in or is discussed in your source, you will be directed to the pertinent location in the source.

For example, if we were researching the Canoga problem and a colleague had alerted us to a federal statute titled the Americans with Disabilities Act, we could look up that statute in an Am. Jur. 2d statutes table. See Illustration 3-5 on page 42.

ILLUSTRATION 3-2	Overall Table of Contents (Table of Abbreviations), from *American Jurisprudence 2d*

TABLE OF ABBREVIATIONS   xvii

Subscrip	Subscriptions
Sum Judg	Summary Judgment
Sun & H	Sundays and Holidays
Support Per	Support of Persons
Surety	Suretyship
Taxp Act	Taxpayers' Actions
Telecom	Telecommunications
Tender	Tender
Time	Time
Torts	Torts
Trademark	Trademarks and Tradenames
Treat	Treaties
Tresp	Trespass
Trial	Trial
Trusts	Trusts
Unempl C	Unemployment Compensation
U S	United States
Vag	Vagrancy
V & P	Vendor and Purchaser
Ven	Venue
Vet	Veterans and Veterans Laws
Veterinar	Veterinarians
War	War
Wareh	Warehouses
Waste	Waste
Waters	Waters
Watwks	Waterworks and Water Companies
Weap	Weapons and Firearms
Wts & M	Weights and Measures
Welf L	Welfare Laws
Whar	Wharves
Wills	Wills
Witn	Witnesses
Work C	Workers' Compensation
Wrong Disch	Wrongful Discharge
Zoning	Zoning and Planning

| ILLUSTRATION 3-3 | Detailed Table of Contents, from *American Jurisprudence 2d* |

ILLUSTRATION 3-4   Index, from *American Jurisprudence 2d*

AMERICAN JURISPRUDENCE 2d

WRONGFUL DISCHARGE—Cont'd
Husband of discharged employee as plaintiff, **Wrong Disch § 229**
Illegal act, refusal to commit
 intentional infliction of emotional distress, outrageousness of conduct, **Wrong Disch § 147**
 public policy exception to at-will doctrine, below
Illness. Health and safety, above
Ill will. Malice, below
Implied-in-fact contract claims
 generally, **Wrong Disch § 83-128**
 additional consideration doctrine, **Wrong Disch § 86, 93**
 agents of employer, authority to enter contracts, **Wrong Disch § 90**
 bilateral contract theory, generally, **Wrong Disch § 85**
 bonus provisions, employer representations as to, **Wrong Disch § 106**
 cause, employer representations as to discharge only for, **Wrong Disch § 120-122**
 consideration, **Wrong Disch § 84, 86, 87**
 continuing benefits, employer representations as to, **Wrong Disch § 111 et seq.**
 contract of employment, manuals as not part of, **Wrong Disch § 97**
 detrimental reliance by employee
  generally, **Wrong Disch § 123-128**
  forgoing other employment opportunities, **Wrong Disch § 125**
  former job, giving up, **Wrong Disch § 124**
  inference of contractual rights from change in employee's position, **Wrong Disch § 123**
  length of service and level of performance, **Wrong Disch § 126**
  moving to new location, **Wrong Disch § 127**
  promissory estoppel, **Wrong Disch § 91**
  union protection, giving up, **Wrong Disch § 128**
 discharge and discipline, employer representations as to
  generally, **Wrong Disch § 116-122**
  cause, discharge only for, **Wrong Disch § 120-122**
  grievance and appeals procedures, **Wrong Disch § 118**
  progressive discipline, **Wrong Disch § 117**
  specification of grounds for discharge or discipline, **Wrong Disch § 119**
 disclaimers, effect of, **Wrong Disch § 99, 100**
 evidence of consideration, **Wrong Disch § 87**
 fair treatment of employees, employer representations as to, **Wrong Disch § 104**
 forgoing other employment opportunities, detrimental reliance by employee, **Wrong Disch § 125**
 former job, giving up as detrimental reli-

WRONGFUL DISCHARGE—Cont'd
Implied-in-fact contract claims—Cont'd
 ance by employee, **Wrong Disch § 124**
 grievance and appeals procedures, employer representations as to, **Wrong Disch § 118**
 handbooks and policy manuals
  generally, **Wrong Disch § 84, 96-98**
  agent of employer, authority to enter contract, **Wrong Disch § 90**
  discharge and discipline, employer representations as to, above in this group
  intent, **Wrong Disch § 88**
 industry provisions as employer representations, **Wrong Disch § 115**
 intent, **Wrong Disch § 88**
 layoff policies, employer representations as to, **Wrong Disch § 114**
 length of service and level of performance, detrimental reliance by employee, **Wrong Disch § 126**
 modification of implied contracts, **Wrong Disch § 93, 94**
 moving to new location, detrimental reliance by employee, **Wrong Disch § 127**
 mutuality of obligation, **Wrong Disch § 84, 85**
 oral modifications of written representations establishing employment at will, effect of, **Wrong Disch § 94**
 pension and retirement plans, employer representations as to, **Wrong Disch § 112**
 performance reviews, employer representations, **Wrong Disch § 108, 109**
 periodic compensation terms, employer representations as to, **Wrong Disch § 105**
 permanent or steady employment, **Wrong Disch § 84, 102, 103, 177**
 policy manuals. Handbooks and policy manuals, above in this group
 preemption by state statutory remedies, **Wrong Disch § 217**
 probationary period, effect on employer representations, **Wrong Disch § 107**
 progressive discipline, employer representations as to, **Wrong Disch § 117**
 promissory estoppel, **Wrong Disch § 91, 92**
 promotion policies, employer representations as to, **Wrong Disch § 110**
 public policy exception to at-will doctrine, action as sounding in contract, **Wrong Disch § 17**
 punitive damages, **Wrong Disch § 262**
 raise provisions in performance reviews, employer representations, **Wrong Disch § 109**
 reliance. Detrimental reliance by employee, above in this group
 representations by employer, generally, **Wrong Disch § 95-122**
 seniority provisions, employer representations as to, **Wrong Disch § 114**
 specification of grounds for discharge or

WRONGFUL DISCHARGE—Cont'd
Implied-in-fact contract claims—Cont'd
 discipline, employer representations as to, **Wrong Disch § 119**
 stock option plans, employer representations as to, **Wrong Disch § 113**
 time and date
  formation of implied contracts, **Wrong Disch § 89**
  oral modifications of written representations establishing employment at will, **Wrong Disch § 94**
 undistributed manuals, **Wrong Disch § 98**
 unilateral contract theory, generally, **Wrong Disch § 84**
 union protection, giving up as detrimental reliance by employee, **Wrong Disch § 128**
 verbal promises, effect of, **Wrong Disch § 101**
Incompetence or inadequate performance
 defenses, **Wrong Disch § 190**
 public policy exception to at-will doctrine, **Wrong Disch § 82**
Independent contractors, **Wrong Disch § 229**
Industry practices as employer representations, implied-in-fact contract claims, **Wrong Disch § 115**
In-house counsel, application of at-will doctrine to employee who is, **Wrong Disch § 9**
Injunctions, **Wrong Disch § 250**
Insomnia as severe distress, intentional infliction of emotional distress, **Wrong Disch § 153**
Insubordination
 defenses, **Wrong Disch § 191**
 public policy exception to at-will doctrine, **Wrong Disch § 74**
Insurance
 action for wrongful discharge of agent, **Ins § 116**
 damages, **Wrong Disch § 253**
 defendants, insurers of employers as, **Wrong Disch § 232**
 disability insurance and benefits, above
 employer's representations, **Wrong Disch § 111**
 life insurance, below
 medical insurance and benefits, below
 public policy exception to at-will doctrine for refusal to falsify records, **Wrong Disch § 46**
Intent
 emotional distress, infliction of, above
 fraud, **Wrong Disch § 175**
 implied-in-fact contract claims, **Wrong Disch § 88**
 interference with contractual relations, **Wrong Disch § 161**
 malice, below
 malicious discharge, prima facie tort, **Wrong Disch § 180, 181**
 punitive damages, **Wrong Disch § 263**
Interest, recovery of, **Wrong Disch § 251**
Interference with contractual relations
 generally, **Wrong Disch § 161-166**
 agents of employers as third parties,

ILLUSTRATION 3-5   Table of Authorities (Statutes), from *American Jurisprudence 2d*

AMERICAN JURISPRUDENCE 2d

ALL WRITS ACT—Cont'd
§ 263; Exec § 29; Ne Ex § 14; Pat § 762; Prohib § 9

AMERICANS WITH DISABILITIES ACT
Main Treatment, Amer with Disab Act § 1 et seq. (New Topic Serv); Job Discrim § 18, 19, 30, 37, 38

ANATOMICAL GIFT ACT
Main Treatment, Dead B § 20

ANCILLARY ADMINISTRATION OF ESTATES ACT
Main Treatment, Ex & Ad § 1169

ANIMAL WELFARE ACT
Main Treatment, Ani § 36-40

ANTI-GAMBLING ACT
Main Treatment, Gambl § 32, 36, 121 et seq.

ANTI-INJUNCTION ACT
Main Treatment, Civ R § 275; Decl J § 52

ANTI-TERRORISM AND EFFECTIVE DEATH PENALTY ACT
Main Treatment, Hab Corp § 138-144

ANTITRUST CIVIL PROCESS ACT
Main Treatment, Depos & D § 38, 40, 80, 435; Monop § 554 et seq.; Monop § 554-571

APARTMENT OWNERSHIP ACT
Main Treatment, Condomin § 10

ARBITRATION ACT
Main Treatment, Admir § 13-16, 187, 279, 281; Alt Disp Res § 115 et seq.

ARCHEOLOGICAL RESOURCES PROTECTION ACT
Main Treatment, Reward § 11

ARMED CAREER CRIMINAL ACT
Main Treatment, Appel Rev § 256; Habit Crim § 18

ARMED SERVICES FORMER SPOUSES' PROTECTION ACT
Main Treatment, Community Prop § 10

ASSIMILATIVE CRIMES ACT
Main Treatment, Incest § 2; Indians § 192

ATOMIC ENERGY ACT
Main Treatment, Atomic E § 2-39

ATOMIC ENERGY ACT OF 1954
Main Treatment, Energy § 72 et seq.

ATOMIC ENERGY COMMISSION
Main Treatment, Atomic E § 3-10

ATOMIC ENERGY COMMUNITY ACT
Main Treatment, Atomic E § 42, 43

ATTRACTIVE NUISANCE DOCTRINE
Main Treatment, Prem Liab § 270 et seq.

AVIATION ACT
Main Treatment, Job Discrim § 2126; Monop § 285, 1147 et seq.

BABY BROKER ACTS
Main Treatment, Adopt § 47-51

BAIL REFORM ACTS
Main Treatment, Bail & R § 12

BANK ROBBERY ACT
Main Treatment, Larc § 86; Rec St P § 37-39; Rob § 92-130

BANKRUPTCY ACT OF 1898
Main Treatment, Bankr § 14, 928, 1088, 2605

BANKRUPTCY AMENDMENTS AND FEDERAL JUDGESHIP ACT OF 1984
Main Treatment, Bankr § 144, 401, 542-546

BANKRUPTCY REFORM ACT OF 1978
Main Treatment, Bankr § 12, 13

BANK SECRECY ACT
Main Treatment, Banks § 89-91; Const L § 605

BEST EVIDENCE RULE
Main Treatment, Evid § 1049-1052

BETTERMENT ACTS
Main Treatment, Improv § 6, 7, 33, 34

BILLS OF LADING ACTS
Main Treatment, Attach § 90; Carriers § 264, 289, 290; Comm Code § 4, 38, 43

BIOMASS ENERGY AND ALCOHOL FUELS ACT OF 1980
Main Treatment, Energy § 63

BLUE LAWS
Main Treatment, Sun & H § 2

BLUE SKY LAWS
Main Treatment, Secur Reg St § 1 et seq.

BOTTLE BILL
Main Treatment, Sales § 83

BRADY RULE
Main Treatment, Depos & D § 450

BULK SALES LAW
Main Treatment, Assign for Crs § 63; Fraud Conv § 238 et seq.

BUSINESS CORPORATION ACT
Main Treatment, Corp § 6, 1341 et seq., 2104 et seq.

BUSINESS RECORDS ACTS
Main Treatment, Evid § 1296 et seq.

CABLE COMMUNICATIONS POLICY ACT
Main Treatment, Telecom § 185.5

CAPEHEART HOUSING ACT
Main Treatment, Cont Bond § 235

CAPPER-VOLSTEAD ACT
Main Treatment, Mark & M § 42

CARMACK AMENDMENT
Main Treatment, Carriers § 375, 387, 518, 547, 680, 720

CARRIAGE OF GOODS BY SEA ACT
Main Treatment, Admir § 77, 126; Ship § 37, 690-693

CHANDLER ACT
Main Treatment, Assign for Crs § 6

CHILD ABUSE PREVENTION AND TREATMENT AND ADOPTION REFORM ACT
Main Treatment, Adopt § 40-42

CHILD NUTRITION ACT
Main Treatment, Sch § 308, 322; Welf L § 31

CIGARETTE LABELING AND ADVERTISING ACT
Main Treatment, Monop § 1311 et seq.; Monop § 1311, 1312; 2017,2028

CIVIL DAMAGE ACTS
Main Treatment, Indem § 41; Negl § 1492, 1511, 1737

CIVIL LIABILITY FOR SUPPORT ACT
Main Treatment, Desert & N § 116

1210   For assistance using this Index, call 1-800-328-4880

2.   Searching for Words

As an example of a search for words, consider the following: You are researching in a computer database that contains many legal periodical articles, and you ask the computer to find articles with the words "smoking" and "workplace." The computer will scan the articles in its database and retrieve articles in which those words appear. You then skim the retrieved articles, select the most pertinent, and read those.

This process has advantages and disadvantages. It permits you to customize a search for your problem, using words tailored to your research problem. If those words are distinctive enough, you should obtain excellent results. Because computers run searches quickly, such research can be time-efficient.

On the other hand, you may retrieve documents that are not pertinent to your research problem, even though they use the words you have identified. For example, an article about health insurance coverage of tobacco addiction could meet the requirements stated above. Conversely, you may fail to retrieve articles that are pertinent, because they do not use the words you have identified. For example, an article pertinent to your research problem may refer to "worksite" instead of "workplace."

The better your search, the more likely it is to succeed. Success is measured by two criteria: (1) recall, that is, retrieval of all pertinent documents, and (2) precision, that is, nonretrieval of nonpertinent documents. Exhibit 3.2 on page 44 depicts these concepts. P stands for pertinent documents; X stands for nonpertinent documents; the box represents the boundaries of the search. The depicted search has both recall problems (the Ps outside the box) and precision problems (the Xs inside the box).

You can achieve success through skillful use of various search-drafting options. The options are fairly standard across most computer-based sources, although the expression varies from source to source. For simplicity, the examples in this section reflect the protocols of Westlaw and LEXIS, which have dominated computer-based legal research for the past two decades.

Main tools for searching for words:

- Boolean search
  - single-word term (with or without root expander or universal character)
  - several-word phrase
  - multiple terms for the same concept
  - exclusion of nonpertinent usage
  - multiple-concept search employing connectors
- natural-language search
- restricted searches: date restrictor and segment searches
- find search for a document

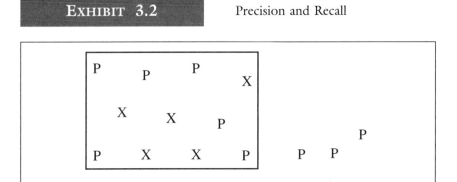

EXHIBIT 3.2   Precision and Recall

Boolean searching. For many situations, you probably will use a Boolean search (named after a nineteenth-century mathematician). Boolean searches can be simple or rather intricate.

One simple option is to enter one single-word term, such as "smoking"; you thereby ask the computer to look for any document containing that term. The word you select may itself be or contain a root word. For example, "smoking" contains the root "smok," used not only in "smoking," but also in "smoke," "smoker," "smokes," etc. Some services automatically truncate a search word to its root and search for various words with the root. Others automatically retrieve standard variations of search words, such as plurals and possessives, but require you to designate other variations. In the latter situation, you may use symbols, called root expanders, to indicate a specific number or any number of additional letters beyond the root. For example, on both Westlaw and LEXIS, [smok!] will retrieve any word starting with "smok"; [smok***] will retrieve any word starting with "smok" and continuing for up to three letters. If a letter in the middle of a word might vary, you can use * as a universal character. For example, [mari*uana] will retrieve "marijuana" and "marihuana."

Some concepts are stated not with single words, but with several-word phrases. Although phrases can be entered as such, you should be careful in doing so. You should be reasonably sure that the phrase will appear exactly as you frame it. Some phrases can be inverted or phrased in slightly different terms. Furthermore, some phrases might be written with or without hyphens, and you will want to search for all versions. Finally you should be sure you are entering the phrase as a phrase, rather than as a set of distinct search words. For example on Westlaw, ["non-working hours"] will retrieve "non-working hours" or "non working hours" or "nonworking hours." LEXIS requires two forms—non-working and nonworking—and does not require the quotation marks for the phrase.

Oftentimes, you will not have a single word or phrase in mind for a concept; recall the discussion above of synonyms, antonyms, broader terms, and narrower terms. When this occurs, you will want to search for various or multiple terms for the same concept. You do so by entering the terms, joined by the symbol for the connector "or." For example, [cigarette tobacco] on Westlaw or [cigarette or tobacco] in LEXIS would retrieve documents containing "cigarette" or "tobacco" or both. See Exhibit 3.3 below, in which the shaded area represents the retrieved documents.

On occasion, you will be aware that one of your search words has a distinct nonpertinent usage. Sometimes you can exclude documents in which the nonpertinent usage appears by asking the computer to reject documents with some other specific word associated with the nonpertinent usage. You should use such a search cautiously, only when you are reasonably certain that documents with the excluded term really are not pertinent. For example, [smok! % marijuana] on Westlaw or [smoke! and not marijuana] on LEXIS retrieves documents that both do contain variants of "smoke" and do not contain "marijuana." Again, see Exhibit 3.3.

Often you will believe that several concepts are likely to appear together in the same pertinent document. If so, you should consider a multiple-concept search. Such a search is more focused than a single-concept search and hence more efficient. However, you should take care not to combine so many concepts that you narrow your search too much and inadvertently exclude pertinent documents. Once you decide which concepts to include, you must decide how to connect them. Most legal research services offer several types of connectors.

The broadest is the connector signifying "and," which requires that the two terms appear in the same document. Often you will prefer a tighter connector, linking concepts in the same sentence, paragraph, or fixed number

EXHIBIT 3.3	Diagrams of Connectors

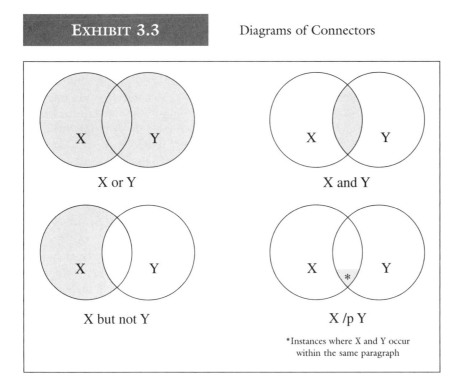

of words. In the rare instances when you are sure that one concept will precede another, you can use a sequencing connector. As examples, consider the following:

[smok! & "non-working hours"]	Both must appear anywhere in the document.
[smok! /p "non-working hours"]	Both must appear in the same paragraph.
[smok! /s "non-working hours"]	Both must appear in the same sentence.
[smok! /20 "non-working hours"]	Both must appear within twenty words of each other.
[smok! +20 "non-working hours]	Both must appear within twenty words of each other, smok! first.

Again, see Exhibit 3.3 on page 45. As you draft a search with connectors, be sure you understand exactly how they work. For example, you should know whether the service counts insignificant words (such as articles or prepositions) when given a numerical search.

You should know the service's order of operations, the order in which the computer will process multiple connectors. Westlaw and LEXIS prioritize the commonly used connectors similarly: starting with phrases and "or"; moving through numerical, sentence, paragraph, and "and" connectors; and concluding with the "not" connector. Because it can be difficult to work with multiple connectors properly, some services permit you to create your own order of operations. Placing search words and a connector within parentheses typically places a priority on that operation. For example, [discharg! (terminat! /3 employ!)] tells the computer to search first for variants of "terminate" within three words of variants of "employ," then seek documents with variants of "discharge." Without the parentheses, the computer would search for variants of "discharge" or "terminate" within three words of a variant of "employ."

Here is an example of a search involving multiple concepts and connectors that we ran, while researching the Canoga case, in a LEXIS database of periodical articles: [(priv! w/3 right) w/5 (workplace or employ!) w/10 smok!]. The citation list that resulted from that search is excerpted in Illustration 3-6 on page 48.

Natural-language searching. As an alternative to Boolean searching, some services also permit you to enter a question that resembles ordinary English. This type of searching is called natural-language searching. Services offering this method may provide a thesaurus to help you identify alternative words for the key concepts in your question. You may also be able to add your own alternative search terms, designate a phrase (the program may recognize common phrases for you), require a specific search word, or exclude a specific search word. To the extent you use these options, your search will come to resemble a Boolean search. For example, a natural-language search for the Canoga case (at least the starting point) might be [Can an employer prohibit an employee from smoking during nonworking hours?].

Boolean and natural-language searches, even when written so as to closely resemble each other, may well differ in how they are processed. In response to a Boolean search, the computer typically retrieves all documents meeting the requirements of the search. In response to a natural-language search, the computer typically retrieves a prespecified number of the most pertinent documents, identified through application of a semantic-statistical algorithm that, among other steps, ranks your search words for distinctiveness and assesses the prevalence of your search words in the many documents in the database you selected.

Restricted searches. Some services permit you to restrict your search in various ways for greater efficiency. To start, you should select a database containing only the type of document you want, for example, cases from New Mexico, periodical articles. Restricted searches permit you to narrow your search by specifying which documents within the database or which parts of the documents will be searched. For example, you may limit the search to documents dating to a specified time period by adding a date restrictor. In a segment search, you confine your search to a particular segment of a document; this is useful when a document has standard segments, and you are fairly certain that your words would appear in a specific segment. For example, if a colleague had referred you to a periodical article written during the 1990s with the words "blowing smoke" in the title, you could enter the following search: [ti("blowing smoke") & da(aft 1989)] on Westlaw or [title(blowing smoke) and date > 1989] on LEXIS.

Find search for a document. In an even more focused search, if you already knew the location of a pertinent authority and wished simply to obtain it through a computer-based source, you would use a find search. For example, if you wished to retrieve the article in Illustration 2-4 on page 20, and you knew it appeared in volume 86 of the *Georgetown Law Journal*, at page 783, you would enter [fi 86 geolj 783] on Westlaw or [lexsee 86 geo l j 783] in LEXIS (or click on the appropriate button along with keying in the citation).

| ILLUSTRATION 3-6 | Citation List (Partial) Resulting from Boolean Search, Run in LEXIS Combined Law Reviews Database |

---

lexis.com℠   (Change Client | Options | Feedback | Sign Off | Help)

Search▶ Search Advisor▶ Get a Document▶ Check a Citation▶   ECLIPSE™ History

View: **Cite** | KWIC | Full ◀━━━ **1 - 10** of 19 ▬NEXT▬ Text Only | Print | Download | Fax | Email
FOCUS™ - Narrow Results | Save As ECLIPSE | Hide Hits

Source: All Sources : / . . . / : **Law Reviews, Combined**
Terms: **(priv! w/3 right) w/5 (workplace or employ!) w/10 smok!** (Edit Search)

1. Copyright (c) 1995 Boston College Law School Boston College Law Review, September, 1995,
   36 B.C. L. Rev 1089, 21708 words, NOTE: A SPARK IN THE BATTLE BETWEEN
   SMOKERS AND NONSMOKERS: JOHANNESEN V. NEW YORK CITY DEPARTMENT OF
   HOUSING PRESERVATION & DEVELOPMENT, Kathleen Sablone
   ... F. Calder, The Emergence of **Employees' Privacy Rights: Smoking and the Workplace**, 8
   LAB. LAW. ...

2. Copyright (c) 1995 Florida Law Review Florida Law Review, April, 1995, 47 Fla. L. Rev. 287,
   6741 words, CASE COMMENTS: CONSTITUTIONAL LAW: IS THE EXPECTATION OF
   PRIVACY UNDER THE FLORIDA CONSTITUTION BROADER IN SCOPE THAN IT IS
   UNDER THE FEDERAL CONSTITUTION?, Joseph Beatty*
   ... a regulation that restricts **smoking** outside the work place and ...
   ... work hours implicates an **employee's right of privacy.** n90 - - - - - - - - - - - - - - - - -
   -Footnotes- - - - - - - - - - - - - - - - - -n86 ...

3. Copyright (c) 1998 Georgetown Law Journal Georgetown Law Journal, January, 1998, 86 Geo.
   L.J. 783, 19482 words, NOTE: Blowing Smoke: Do Smokers Have a Right? Limiting the
   Privacy Rights of Cigarette Smokers, MICHELE L. TYLER*
   ... Footnotes- - - - - - - - - - - - - - - - -First, in the **workplace,** informational **privacy rights** have
   been implicated when some government **employers** refused to hire **smokers,** insisting that new
   employees refrain from **smoking,** even while off ...
   ... a legal activity to their **employer.** Second, physical **privacy rights** associated with the home
   are implicated in two anti-**smoking** developments: (1) child ...
   ... End Footnotes- - - - - - - - - - - - - - - A. THE **WORKPLACE:** INFORMATIONAL
   PRIVACY RIGHTS Although neither a constitutional right to **smoke,** nor a constitutional right to
   ...
   ... H. Zgrodnik, Comment, **Smoking** Discrimination: Invading an Individual's **Right to Privacy** in
   the Home and Outside the **Workplace?,** 21 OHIO N.U. ...
   ... federal and state constitutional **privacy right to smoke** outside the course of **employment** and
   seeking to enjoin enforcement of the ...
   ... decisional privacy right to **smoke.** Although these concerns are persuasive in overriding
   smokers' privacy rights to smoke in the **workplace** n179 or at home, n180 ...
   ... question then is whether, assuming there is no **privacy right** that protects **smoking** in either the
   workplace, n193 the home, n194 or ...
   ... n195 the government should ban **smoking** altogether. The next Part ...

4. Copyright (c) 1993 Houston Law Review Houston Law Review, Fall, 1993, 30 Hous. L. Rev.
   1263, 52709 words, INVASION OF PRIVACY IN THE PRIVATE EMPLOYMENT SECTOR:
   TORTIOUS AND ETHICAL ASPECTS, Frank J. Cavico *
   ... F. Calder, The Emergence of **Employees' Privacy Rights: Smoking and the Workplace**, 8
   Lab. Law. ...

5. Copyright (c) 1995 Law and Psychology Review Law and Psychology Review, SPRING, 1995,
   19 Law & Psychol. Rev. 217, 9116 words, STUDENT ARTICLE: Smoking in the Workplace:
   A Conflict Between Personal Rights and Economic Realities, G. Robert Mitchell
   ... sufficient to override the prospective **employee's right to privacy.** n74 Whereas such decisions
   may somewhat ease **smokers'** anxiety over the possibility that ...

SECONDARY SOURCES

PRELIMINARY POINTS

As you learned in Chapter 1, your ultimate goal is to discern the rule of law governing your client's situation. That rule derives from primary authority, whether cases, statutes, administrative materials, or court rules. Yet this text suggests that your start your research in secondary sources.

There are several reasons for this seemingly circuitous approach. First, secondary sources "comment on" primary authority; they describe, explain, analyze, and, in some cases, critique and suggest changes in rules derived from primary authority. You often will find it easier to grasp the law when you begin with commentary than when you begin with the law itself. Second, secondary sources include references to primary authority, and you can use these references to locate leading primary authorities. Third, compared to primary authority, secondary sources are fairly accessible. As you will soon see, it is easier to locate a pertinent portion of a treatise, for example, than it is to locate a pertinent case, if you are starting with little background knowledge.

Each secondary source has its strengths and weaknesses. As you research in secondary sources, evaluate your research by the four criteria for competent research introduced in Chapter 1: correct, comprehensive, credible, and cost-effective. For most research projects, you will want to combine secondary sources to best achieve these goals.

As you read secondary sources, you should focus on information pertinent to your client's situation. Of course, you should take notes on what the source says the law is, as well as the policies underlying the law. You should note examples or illustrations that parallel your client's situation. You should note any critique of the current law and suggestions for reform, to the extent these points pertain to your client's case.

Finally, you should note pertinent references to primary and other secondary authorities. A good set of notes includes five components:

(1) research terms and modes of access (for example, an index) you used;
(2) useful pertinent information (such as legal rules and examples) along with where you located it (which volume, which page or section);
(3) a list of references to primary authority and other secondary sources;
(4) the means you used to update your research within the source (for example, a supplement pamphlet); and
(5) the information needed to cite the source correctly.

Of course, you may want to photocopy or print out long passages of pertinent material.

Time spent taking meticulous notes is time well spent. If you take meticulous notes, you are less likely to need to backtrack to obtain a missing bit of information for a citation, to check whether you looked up a particular research term, or to verify that you updated the research. Needless to say, backtracking undermines the cost-effectiveness of your research.

Chapters 4 through 8 of this unit each cover one of the major types of secondary sources. The sequence starts with sources that are analogous to nonlegal sources (such as encyclopedias and treatises) and then moves into sources that are unique to the law (such as Restatements of the Law). Chapter 9 covers, in briefer form, several minor secondary sources and then discusses strategies for secondary-source research that is correct, comprehensive, credible, and cost-effective.

ENCYCLOPEDIAS

A. WHAT IS AN ENCYCLOPEDIA?

Like nonlegal encyclopedias, legal encyclopedias cover a wide range of topics, present fairly general information, and order the topics alphabetically. Some topics are quite narrow, others very broad. Within each topic, the discussion is organized by subtopics into sections, as dictated by the legal rules and principles involved. Generally, the opening sections cover the substantive legal rules, while the closing sections cover procedure and remedies. Each section consists of text as well as fairly extensive footnotes referring to supporting authorities. Encyclopedias are written by authors on the publisher's editorial staff, who generally are not well known experts.

Two encyclopedias seek to provide broad coverage of American law, including state and federal law. They are *American Jurisprudence, Second Edition* (Am. Jur. 2d) and *Corpus Juris Secundum* (C.J.S.). Both are successors to older encyclopedias, *American Jurisprudence* and *Corpus Juris*.

Other encyclopedias have narrower scopes. In many states, a state encyclopedia covers all or many legal topics under that state's law. A hint: Some state encyclopedias do not have "encyclopedia" in their titles; they go by such names as "digests" or "jurisprudence." In some areas of law, such as criminal and international law, specialized encyclopedias exist.

As examples pertinent to the Canoga case, examine Illustration 4-1 on page 52, from Am. Jur. 2d's discussion of Wrongful Discharge, and Illustration 4-2 on page 53, from C.J.S.'s discussion of the Employer-Employee Relationship.

ILLUSTRATION 4-1   Encyclopedia Text, from *American Jurisprudence 2d*

§ 96   WRONGFUL DISCHARGE   82 Am Jur 2d

rules in the manual, and the courts increasingly recognize that employers have a like duty to abide by the promises they make.[40]

▌▌▌▌ *Practice guide:* In one state it is provided by statute that a discharge is wrongful if the employer violates express provisions of its own personnel policy.[41]

Employee handbooks are viewed as one component or term of the employment agreement.[42] Unless an employee handbook or manual specifically negates any intention on the part of the employer to have it become a part of the employment contract,[43] a court may conclude from a review of the employee handbook that a question of fact is created regarding whether the handbook was intended[44] by the parties to impliedly express a term of the employment agreement.[45] Accordingly, where unilateral contracts are recognized, employment handbooks which contain provisions specifying progressive discharge procedures,[46] or specifying the grounds on which employees could be discharged,[47] or providing that discharge may be for cause only,[48] have been found binding on the employer, constituting a promise not to terminate the employee in violation of such provisions.[49]

40. Toussaint v. Blue Cross & Blue Shield, 408 Mich 579, 292 NW2d 880, 895 ("having announced the policy, presumably with a view to obtaining the benefit of improved employee attitudes and behavior and improved quality of the workforce, the employer may not treat its promise as illusory"); Lukoski v Sandia Indian Management Co., 106 NM 664, 748 P2d 507, 2 BNA IER Cas 1650; Thompson v St. Regis Paper Co., 102 Wash 2d 219, 685 P2d 1081, 1 BNA IER Cas 392, 116 BNA LRRM 3142, 105 CCH LC ¶55616 ("promises of specific treatment in specific situations found in an employee manual or handbook issued by the employer . . . may, in appropriate situations, obligate the employer to act in accord with those promises").

41. See Meech v Hillhaven West, Inc., 238 Mont 21, 776 P2d 488, 4 BNA IER Cas 737, 112 CCH LC ¶ 56073, upholding the constitutionality of the Montana Wrongful Discharge from Employment Act.

42. Lincoln v Sterling Drug, Inc. (DC Conn) 622 F Supp 66; Loffa Intel Corp. (App) 153 Ariz 539, 738 P2d 1146; Finley v Aetna Life & Casualty Co., 202 Conn 190, 520 A2d 208, 2 BNA IER Cas 942; Watson v Idaho Falls Consol. Hospitals, Inc., 111 Idaho 44, 720 P2d 632; Duldulao v St. Mary of Nazareth Hospital Center, 115 Ill 2d 482, 106 Ill Dec 8, 505 NE2d 314, 1 BNA IER Cas 1428; Small v Springs Industries, Inc., 292 SC 481, 357 SE2d 452, 2 BNA IER Cas 266, 106 CCH LC

¶55766, appeal after remand 300 SC 481, 388 SE2d 808, 5 BNA IER Cas 145, 115 CCH LC ¶56241.

The employment agreement is composed of written and verbal statements, custom, policy, past practice, industry practice, and any other fact which may define the terms of the contract. Shah v American Synthetic Rubber Corp. (Ky) 655 SW2d 489, 114 BNA LRRM 3343, 99CCH LC ¶55423.

43. As to manuals not constituting part of the employment contract, see § 97.

44. Generally, as to intent needed to form a contract, see § 88.

45. Metcalf v Intermountain Gas Co., 116 Idaho 622, 778 P2d 744, 4 BNA IER Cas 961, 113 CCH LC ¶ 56136.

See Lukoski v Sandia Indian Management Co., 106 NM 664, 748 P2d 507, 2 BNA IER Cas 1650, noting that the handbook did nothing to alert employees that it was subject to revocation or that employees should not rely on it.

46. § 117.

47. § 119.

48. § 120.

49. Towns v Emery Air Freight, Inc. (SD Ohio) 3 BNA IER Cas 911 (applying Ohio law);

774

ILLUSTRATION 4-2   Encyclopedia Text, from *Corpus Juris Secundum*

---

§ 25 EMPLOYER-EMPLOYEE   30 C.J.S.

expressly included in them.[99] However, under other authority, provisions of an employer's personnel handbook or manual may become part of an employment contract,[1] and whether an employment manual or handbook creates an employment contract is a question which must be determined on a case by case basis.[2]

The creation of contractual rights by such handbook or manual depends upon whether the elements of a unilateral contract are present;[3] the language of a handbook must constitute an offer definite in form which is communicated to the employee, the offer must be accepted, and consideration must be furnished before a handbook becomes part of an employment contract.[4] An employee's continued service,[5] or the benefit of an orderly, cooperative and loyal work force,[6] may constitute consideration.

An employer is bound by provisions in a handbook or manual where both the employer and employee have obligations thereunder,[7] regardless of whether the manual was actually bargained for,[8] and regardless of whether it modifies an existing employment relationship.[9] A handbook which contains general,[10] or indefinite,[11] language is ordinarily not deemed part of an employment contract.

It has been held that provisions in an employer's handbook or manual may create a term of an employment agreement without any showing of particular reliance by the employee,[12] without any specific words incorporating the manual into the agreement,[13] and notwithstanding that in other respects the employment relationship would be

---

98. U.S.—Spearman v. Delco Remy Div. of General Motors Corp., 717 F.Supp. 1351—Bowser v. McDonald's Corp., S.D.Tex., 714 F.Supp. 839.

Mo.—Johnson v. McDonnell Douglas Corp., 745 S.W.2d 661.

N.C.—Walker v. Westinghouse Elec. Corp., 335 S.E.2d 79, 77 N.C.App. 253, review denied 341 S.E.2d 39, 315 N.C. 597.

Manual alone

An employment manual cannot alone be the basis of an implied contract between employee and employer, where manual is merely a unilateral expression of company policy, it is not bargained for between employer and employee, and is not a reflection of mutual assent between the parties; nonetheless, an employment manual may be one of the relevant circumstances from which an implied contract can be inferred.

U.S.—Rouse v. Peoples Natural Gas Co., D.C.Kan., 605 F.Supp. 230.

99. N.C.—Buffaloe v. United Carolina Bank, 366 S.E.2d 918, 89 N.C.App. 693.

1. U.S.—Thompson v. Kings Entertainment Co., E.D.Va., 674 F.Supp. 1194.

Ariz.—Leikvold v. Valley View Community Hosp., 688 P.2d 170, 141 Ariz. 544.

Minn.—Hoemberg v. Watco Publishers, Inc., App., 343 N.W.2d 676.

Ohio—Brown v. Otto C. Epp Memorial Hosp., 482 N.E.2d 988, 19 Ohio App.3d 25, 19 O.B.R. 90, appeal after remand 535 N.E.2d 325, 41 Ohio App.3d 198.

Tenn.—Hamby v. Genesco, Inc., App., 627 S.W.2d 373.

Wyo.—Leithead v. American Colloid Co., 721 P.2d 1059.

Implied-in-fact contract

U.S.—Marsh v. Digital Equipment Corp., D.Ariz., 675 F.Supp. 1186.

Incorporation

Under Illinois law, personnel policies contained in an employee handbook will be deemed incorporated into employment contract where another document exists which can be construed as an express employment contract and the contract can be construed as subject to "policies" of employer.

U.S.—Enis v. Continental Illinois Nat. Bank and Trust Co. of Chicago, D.C.Ill., 582 F.Supp. 876, affirmed 795 F.2d 39.

2. Ark.—Proctor v. East Cent. Arkansas EOC, 724 S.W.2d 163, 291 Ark. 265.

3. Minn.—Lewis v. Equitable Life Assur. Soc. of the U.S., 389 N.W.2d 876.

4. Ala.—Hoffman–La Roche, Inc. v. Campbell, 512 So.2d 725.

Hawaii—Kinoshita v. Canadian Pacific Airlines, Ltd., 724 P.2d 110, 68 Haw. 594.

Iowa—Fogel v. Trustees of Iowa College, 446 N.W.2d 451.

Minn.—Fitzgerald v. Norwest Corp., App., 382 N.W.2d 290, review denied.

Neb.—Stratton v. Chevrolet Motor Div., General Motors Corp., 428 N.W.2d 910, 229 Neb. 771.

5. U.S.—Vinyard v. King, C.A.Okl., 728 F.2d 428.

Ala.—Hoffman–La Roche, Inc. v. Campbell, 512 So.2d 725.

Colo.—Cronk v. Intermountain Rural Elec. Ass'n, App., 765 P.2d 619, certiorari denied.

Ill.—DeFosse v. Cherry Elec. Products Corp., 510 N.E.2d 141, 109 Ill.Dec. 520, 156 Ill.App.3d 1030.

Iowa—Fogel v. Trustees of Iowa College, 446 N.W.2d 451.

Mass.—Jackson v. Action for Boston Community Development, Inc., 525 N.E.2d 411, 403 Mass. 8.

W.Va.—Cook v. Heck's Inc., 342 S.E.2d 453, 176 W.Va. 368.

6. Wyo.—Leithead v. American Colloid Co., 721 P.2d 1059.

7. U.S.—Pudil v. Smart Buy, Inc., D.C.Ill., 607 F.Supp. 440.

8. U.S.—Pelizza v. Reader's Digest Sales and Services Inc., N.D.Ill., 624 F.Supp. 806.

9. U.S.—Pelizza v. Reader's Digest Sales and Services Inc., N.D.Ill., 624 F.Supp. 806.

10. S.D.—Bauer v. American Freight System, Inc., 422 N.W.2d 435.

General code of conduct

U.S.—Gaiardo v. Ethyl Corp., M.D.Pa., 697 F.Supp. 1377.

11. U.S.—Ellis v. El Paso Natural Gas Co., C.A.N.M., 754 F.2d 884.

Minn.—Hunt v. IBM Mid America Employees Federal Credit Union, 384 N.W.2d 853.

N.M.—Sanchez v. The New Mexican, 738 P.2d 1321, 106 N.M. 76.

12. Ariz.—Loffa v. Intel Corp., App., 738 P.2d 1146, 153 Ariz. 539.

B.   WHY ARE ENCYCLOPEDIAS USEFUL?

As secondary sources, encyclopedias describe the law and operate as finding tools for primary authority. They do not, however, critique the law or suggest legal reforms.

For the typical research project, encyclopedias are most useful at the very beginning of the research process. You very likely will find some pertinent material, which will provide a broad overview of your topic and which can be skimmed fairly easily. Furthermore, you can easily browse within an encyclopedia; that is, you can move from subtopic to subtopic or from one topic to related topics. Most encyclopedias are updated annually, with the references typically more current than the text. For these reasons, encyclopedias are useful in providing a broad overview.

If you use Am. Jur. 2d or C.J.S., the text is likely to present general principles, but not precisely state the law of your jurisdiction. Similarly, although you may well find a reference to a leading primary authority from your jurisdiction in Am. Jur. 2d or C.J.S., you should not expect to find exhaustive references. Because these encyclopedias are not written by well recognized experts, they are not as credible as some of the other sources covered in this chapter. They are cited most frequently for broad, well established points.

A state or specialized encyclopedia can be more useful than Am. Jur. 2d or C.J.S. Such encyclopedias generally may have more credibility, the text generally is more detailed, and there are more pertinent references.

C.   HOW DO YOU RESEARCH IN ENCYCLOPEDIAS?

You are most likely to use an encyclopedia when your knowledge of your subject is sketchy and you are seeking big-picture information. Hence, you should take advantage of the encyclopedia's editorial aids and be sure to browse. For these reasons, although you can research encyclopedias in computer-based sources, paper is a more common choice. This text focuses on looking up concepts in Am. Jur. 2d and C.J.S. in book form.

Encyclopedias in paper:

► use the index or topic list (or the table of primary authorities)
► read the introductory material
► consult the topic outline
► read the pertinent sections
► check the pocket part

There are two primary means of locating pertinent material in an encyclopedia: the index and the topic list. The index is located in multiple separate volumes, typically shelved at the end of the set. Am. Jur. 2d and C.J.S. both update their indexes annually; be sure to use the index for the current year. Encyclopedia indexes are complex and detailed, so you should spend some time looking up alternative terms, pursuing cross-references, and reading through the entries and subentries. You may find more than one potentially pertinent topic listed in the index, and you also may find references to multiple specific sections within those pertinent topics.

The second primary means of locating pertinent material is through the topic list. Am. Jur. 2d lists its topics in alphabetical order in the Table of Abbreviations at the front of each index volume. In C.J.S., this list appears as the List of Titles in the beginning of each non-index volume as well as the Abbreviations of Titles in the index volumes. Although this process tends to be quicker than the use of an index, it also yields less specific information because you will not obtain information about specific sections within a topic.

If you begin your research in Am. Jur. 2d or C.J.S. with a citation to a pertinent federal statute, regulation, court rule, or a pertinent uniform act, you can consult either encyclopedia's table of primary authorities, that is, its Table of Statutes, Rules, and Regulations Cited. These tables appear in their own volumes and list the topics and sections citing these authorities. Am. Jur. 2d also has a table listing statutes by their names, the Popular Names table, located in the final index volume.

Once you have located a potentially useful topic (and perhaps one or more sections within the topic), you are ready to read the discussion of your subject. Early on you should read the introductory material, which may contain helpful cross-references to other topics as well as references to other sources published by the same publisher. See Illustration 4-3 on page 57. The topic outline at the beginning of each topic shows you the coverage and organization of the topic and permits you to pinpoint the most pertinent sections. If there are general and detailed topic outlines, you should work from the general to the specific.

Once you have located the most pertinent sections within your topic, read those sections carefully with two distinct but related purposes in mind: (1) to learn pertinent legal rules, principles, and definitions, and (2) to obtain references to other potentially pertinent authorities. Be sure that you take time to browse through adjacent sections and glance at cross-reference topics, to assure that your research is comprehensive.

Because your research must be current, you must seek the most current information in the encyclopedia. For most topics, you will read the material in the main volume and then update that material by checking the pocket part. A pocket part is a set of pages inserted into a pocket in the back of a bound volume; it is used to bring the bound volume up to date (or typically within no more than one year of the present). The pocket part may provide additional text with supporting authorities or simply additional references. See Illustration 4-4 on page 58. In addition to pocket parts, Am. Jur. 2d provides the New Topic Service, a looseleaf binder containing topics too new to be located in the appropriate bound volume. It merits a brief check as you complete your research in Am. Jur. 2d. (Occasionally, when a volume becomes very updated, a new volume is issued.)

Researching the Canoga case, we looked up "employer and employee" in the C.J.S. index; we were directed to the main entry "employer-employee relationship," which has "contracts of employment" as a subentry and "personal [sic] handbooks or manuals in general" as a subsubentry; there we found a reference to "Emp-Emp § 25." When we skimmed the C.J.S. topic list, we discovered the following potentially useful topics: Contracts, Employer-Employee Relationship, Labor Relations, and Right of Privacy and Publicity.

We also located the Wrongful Discharge topic in Am. Jur. 2d. The introductory material to the Wrongful Discharge topic, Illustration 4-3 on page 57, establishes that the topic covers pertinent legal theories (such as at-will employment and implied contract), suggests related topics elsewhere in Am. Jur. 2d, and points toward several treatises. We learned from the text of section 96, found in Illustration 4-1 on page 52, as well as the C.J.S. excerpt in Illustration 4-2 on page 53, that an employer and employee may contract, through an employee handbook, for discharge procedures or limitations on the grounds for discharge. Furthermore, both refer to New Mexico cases.

The pocket parts of both Am. Jur. 2d and C.J.S. contain additional information. Illustration 4-4 on page 58, the C.J.S. pocket part, provides additional text and new references. The Am. Jur. 2d New Topic Service includes a topic on the Americans with Disabilities Act, which could be of interest.

D.   WHAT ELSE?

Conversion Tables: If you know about a pertinent section from an older version of an encyclopedia and wish to locate the corresponding material in a newer version, you should consult a conversion table. Am. Jur. 2d has tables of parallel references at the beginning of the appropriate topic volume; analogous information for *Corpus Juris* appears at the beginning of some topics in C.J.S.

Am. Jur. 2d Desk Book: This single volume includes a wide range of miscellaneous information, such as the structure and membership of federal government bodies, statistics on various aspects of life in the United States, selected international legal documents, and financial tables.

E.   HOW DO YOU CITE ENCYCLOPEDIAS?

To properly cite to an encyclopedia, you will need to know its title, the volume number, topic name, section number, and year. Here are two examples (following Rule 15.7(a) of *The Bluebook*):

82 Am. Jur. 2d *Wrongful Discharge* § 96 (1992)
30 C.J.S. *Employer-Employee Relationship* § 25 (1992 & Supp. 1999).

ILLUSTRATION 4-3	Encyclopedia Introductory Material, from *American Jurisprudence 2d*

WRONGFUL DISCHARGE
by

Irwin J. Schiffres, J.D.

Scope of topic: This article discusses modern developments which have modified the long-standing "at-will" doctrine under which the discharge of employees was permitted for any cause or no cause at all. It considers the development of theories on which discharged private sector employees—not protected by union contracts or civil service regulations—may base an action against their former employers. Actions for wrongful discharge have been permitted under a "public policy exception" which protects employees who are discharged for exercising legal rights, for refusing to commit illegal acts and for disclosing employer misconduct ("whistleblowing"). Such actions have also been permitted under an implied contract theory (based frequently on representations in employee manuals and handbooks), on the basis of a covenant of good faith and fair dealing, and under various traditional tort remedies, including interference with contractual relations, infliction of emotional distress, invasion of privacy, and fraud. Also discussed are defenses to such actions and the remedies available, including the recoverability of compensatory and punitive damages.

Federal aspects: This articles discusses the premptive effect of various federal statutes on a state common-law claim for wrongful termination. Among the statutes included are the National Labor Relations Act, the Labor-Management Relations Act, the Labor-Management Reporting Disclosure Act, the Railway Labor Act, ERISA, federal safety and environmental laws, and federal banking and lending laws. The rights of discharged employees generally under federal statutes are discussed in other articles, as indicated under "Treated elsewhere," infra. (See "Federal Legislation," infra, for USCS citations).

Treated elsewhere:

Rights of discharged employees who:

are covered by collective bargaining agreements, see 48 Am Jur 2d, Labor Relations §§ 920 et seq.

were employed by governmental agencies, see 15A Am Jur 2d, Civil Service §§ 52 et seq.

were discharged because of age, race, color, religion, sex, or national origin, see 45A, 45B Am Jur 2d, Job Discrimination §§ 873 et seq.

Discharge of employee in violation of ERISA, see 60A Am Jur 2d, Pensions and Retirement Funds

Discharge of employee hired for a definite term, see 53 Am Jur 2d, Master and Servant §§ 43-70

Discharge of employee by reason of the fact that his earnings have been subjected to garnishment, see 6 Am Jur 2d, Attachment and Garnishment § 176 (Supp)

Effect of discharge for cause on right to unemployment compensation, see 76 Am Jur 2d, Unemployment Compensation §§ 77 et seq.

Research References

Text References:

Modjeska, Employment Discrimination Law (LCP, 2d edition)

Pepe and Dunham, Avoiding and Defending Wrongful Discharge Claims (CBC)

Tobias, Litigating Wrongful Discharge Claims (CBC)

RIA Employment Discrimination Coordinator ¶¶ 101 et seq.

657

| ILLUSTRATION 4-4 | Encyclopedia Pocket Part, from *Corpus Juris Secundum* |

---

30 CJS 3

EMPLOYER—EMPLOYEE § 37
Page 68

25. Tenn.—Williams v. Maremont Corp., App., 776 S.W.2d 78, app. den.

page 43

§ 23. —— **Contracts for Permanent or Life Employment**

39. Ill.—Martin v. Federal Life Ins. Co., 440 N.E.2d 998, 65 Ill.Dec. 143, 109 Ill.App.3d 596, app. after remand 518 N.E.2d 306, 115 Ill.Dec. 781, 164 Ill.App.3d 820, app. den. 526 N.E.2d 832, 122 Ill.Dec. 439, 121 Ill.2d 572, app. after remand 644 N.E.2d 42, 205 Ill.Dec. 826, 268 Ill.App.3d 698, app. den. 649 N.E.2d 417, 208 Ill.Dec. 361, 161 Ill.2d 528.

§ 24. Construction and Operation in General

page 45

71. More than one meaning

Mo.—Enyeart v. Shelter Mut. Ins. Co., App., 693 S.W.2d 120, op. after remand 1989 WL 380448, affd. 784 S.W.2d 205.

page 47

86. Tenn.—Williams v. Maremont Corp., App., 776 S.W.2d 78, app. den.

88. U.S.—Breen v. Norwest Bank Minnesota, N.A., D.Minn., 865 F.Supp. 574.

§ 25. Personnel Handbooks or Manuals in General

98. Wis.—Bantz v. Montgomery Estates, Inc., App., 473 N.W.2d 506, 163 Wis.2d 973.

page 48

1. Ark.—Crain Industries, Inc. v. Cass, 810 S.W.2d 910, 305 Ark. 566.

Minn.—Hoemberg v. Watco Publishers, Inc., App., 343 N.W.2d 676, review den.

Implied contract

U.S.—Jackson v. Integra Inc., C.A.10(Okl.), 952 F.2d 1260, app. after remand 30 F.3d 141.

The traditional contract requirement that knowledge of an offer is a prerequisite to acceptance will not be followed in the limited context of employee handbook cases.[4.5]

4.5 Standardized agreement

Where contract is based upon employee handbook distributed to all employees, the contract is not an individually negotiated agreement, but rather is standardized agreement between employer and a class of employees and thus, it is unnecessary that particular employee seeking to enforce promise made in handbook have knowledge of the promise and this holding produces the salutary result that all employees, those who read handbook and those who did not, are treated alike.

Iowa—Anderson v. Douglas & Lomason Co., 540 N.W.2d 277.

5. Colo.—Cronk v. Intermountain Rural Elec. Ass'n, App., 765 P.2d 619, cert. den., app. after remand 1992 WL 161811, cert. den.

10. Absence of specific disciplinary procedures

Ill.—Tolbert v. St. Francis Extended Care Center, 1 Dist., 545 N.E.2d 384, 136 Ill.Dec. 860, 189 Ill. App.3d 503, app. den. 550 N.E.2d 566, 140 Ill.Dec. 681, 129 Ill.2d 572.

11. Ill.—Lee v. Canuteson, 3 Dist., 573 N.E.2d 318, 157 Ill.Dec. 900, 214 Ill.App.3d 137, app. den. 580 N.E.2d 117, 162 Ill.Dec. 491, 141 Ill.2d 543.

page 49

15. Colo.—Cronk v. Intermountain Rural Elec. Ass'n, App., 765 P.2d 619, cert. den., app. after remand 1992 WL 161811, cert. den.

Provisions not generally known

Employee could not rely on statements in employer's policy manual that was distributed to supervisors only and not to employees to support claim that employer breached employment contract when it terminated him, where there was no evidence that provisions of manual were generally known.

Wash.—Hatfield v. Columbia Federal Sav. Bank, 790 P.2d 1258, 57 Wash.App. 876, app. after remand 846 P.2d 1380, 68 Wash.App. 817, review den. 856 P.2d 382, 121 Wash.2d 1030.

20. Contextual examination necessary

Language in employee handbook stating that handbook was for information only and was not employment contract did not automatically prevent handbook from becoming party of employment contract, but rather such language had to be examined in context with handbook as whole, where such language was located on last page of 52-page handbook, and there was nothing to distinguish that language from rest of text or highlight such language as being particularly important.

U.S.—Davis v. Connecticut General Life Ins. Co., M.D.Tenn., 743 F.Supp. 1273.

However, handbook representations are enforceable under certain circumstances despite the presence of a disclaimer.[20.5]

20.5 Ill.—Perman v. ArcVentures, Inc., 1 Dist., 554 N.E.2d 982, 143 Ill.Dec. 910, 196 Ill.App.3d 758.

Promissory estoppel shown

Employee is entitled to enforce representation in employee handbook, despite disclaimer of contract in handbook, if he can demonstrate that employer should have reasonably expected employee to consider representation as commitment from employer, employee reasonably relied upon representation to his detriment, and injustice can be avoided only by enforcement of representation.

Wyo.—McDonald v. Mobil Coal Producing, Inc., 789 P.2d 866, on reh. 820 P.2d 986.

§ 27. Commencement and Duration of Employment

page 52

54. U.S.—Sneed v. American Bank Stationary Co., Div. of ABS Corp., W.D.Va., 764 F.Supp. 65.

Prior representation of employer notwithstanding

Ga.—Richard A. Naso & Associates, Inc. v. Diffusion, 390 S.E.2d 106, 194 Ga.App. 201.

61. Verbal promise of future promotion

Worker who is verbally promised future promotion to specific position in exchange for his labor is not an at-will employee and may be discharged only for cause.

S.D.—Larson v. Kreiser's, Inc., 472 N.W.2d 761.

page 53

It has been held that a Federal Communication Commission regulation prohibiting employment discrimination by licensees does not transform the employment relationship between a radio station and its employee from an at-will into a permanent relationship.[66.5]

66.5 Ala.—Howard v. Wolff Broadcasting Corp., 611 So.2d 307, cert. den. 113 S.Ct. 1849, 507 U.S. 1031, 123 L.Ed.2d 473.

In fact, regardless of the way in which the salary is quoted in an offer letter, in

the absence of a contrary agreement, the employee is hired at will.[69.5]

69.5 N.J.—Bernard v. IMI Systems, Inc., 618 A.2d 338, 131 N.J. 91, overruling Willis v. Wyllys Corp., 119 A. 24, 98 N.J.L. 180.

§ 28. Modification or Rescission

page 57

10. Idaho—Parker v. Boise Telco Federal Credit Union, App., 923 P.2d 493, 129 Idaho 248, reh. den., review den.

Miss.—Holland v. Kennedy, 548 So.2d 982, app. after remand 678 So.2d 659, reh. den.

At-will relationship not modified

U.S.—Kreimeyer v. Hercules, Inc., D.Utah, 892 F.Supp. 1374.

page 60

§ 30. Performance or Breach by Employer; Actions

69. U.S.—Smith v. Douglas Cable Communications, D.Kan., 881 F.Supp. 1510, reconsideration den. 1995 WL 337094.

page 61

70. U.S.—Conyers v. Safelite Glass Corp., D.Kan., 825 F.Supp. 974.

86. Layoff procedure

Employer contracted to conduct layoff in accordance with seniority as stated in employee handbook and breached contract when it failed to do so where handbook provision stating that it was necessary to reduce number of employees in work force, employees would be laid off on seniority basis by department was express.

Ark.—Crain Industries, Inc. v. Cass, 810 S.W.2d 910, 305 Ark. 566.

87. Severance pay

Mont.—Kittelson v. Archie Cochrane Motors, Inc., 813 P.2d 424, 248 Mont. 512.

page 64

33. Tenn.—Williams v. Maremont Corp., App., 776 S.W.2d 78, app. den.

§ 31. Evidence of Employment

page 65

41. Md.—Brady v. Ralph Parsons Co., 520 A.2d 717, 308 Md. 486, app. after remand 572 A.2d 1115, 82 Md.App. 519, affd. 609 A.2d 297, 327 Md. 275.

There is no conclusive presumption that all newscarrier delivery persons are independent contractors, as opposed to employees.[48.5]

48.5 Fla.—Keith v. News & Sun Sentinel Co., 667 So.2d 167.

page 68

§ 37. Federal Preemption in General

99. Tex.—Hatridge v. Day & Zimmermann, Inc., App.-Texarkana. 789 S.W.2d 654, app. after remand 831 S.W.2d 65, reh. den., err. den., reh. over.

Whistleblower claim

N.J.—Maher v. New Jersey Transit Rail Operations, Inc., 593 A.2d 750, 125 N.J. 455.

1. Mont.—Foster v. Albertsons. Inc., 835 P.2d 720, 254 Mont. 117, overruling Brinkman v. State, 729 P.2d 1301, 224 Mont. 228.

| TREATISES | CHAPTER |
| | 5 |

A. WHAT IS A TREATISE?

Put simply, a treatise is a book that covers one subject at length. The subject may be quite broad (such as contracts or employment law), or it may be a narrow subject (such as a single statute protecting disabled workers). Treatises typically are written by private authors, such as law professors and lawyers, although some are written by the staff of a publishing company.

Treatises are published initially and still primarily in book form. A treatise may consist of a single volume or multiple volumes, depending on the scope of the subject matter covered and the comprehensiveness of the discussion. Treatises are published in hardbound, softbound, or looseleaf forms. A looseleaf treatise consists of separate pages held together by some type of binder.

A treatise typically contains at least three parts: (1) scholarly text, with footnotes or endnotes containing supporting citations and tangential remarks; (2) internal finding tools, such as one or more tables of contents, an index, and other tables; and (3) miscellaneous features, such as a preface and appendices containing important documents such as statutes. The text in legal treatises resembles an expository essay. All treatises explain the law, setting out rules, policies, and examples. Some also critique the law and propose legal reforms. Typically a treatise's text is organized by chapters and then by sections or paragraphs.

For example, a treatise that is pertinent to the Canoga case is Lex K. Larson's *Employment Discrimination*, a looseleaf treatise that is organized by section number. A page appears as Illustration 5-1 on page 60.

ILLUSTRATION 5-1   Treatise Text, from *Employment Discrimination*

---

§ 155.06   **EMPLOYMENT DISCRIMINATION**   155–28

denial of any and all access to coverage to the plaintiff. The insurance defense was ruled inapplicable to this situation, given this complete denial of access.[9]

§ 155.06   Restrictions on Smoking

The ADA provides that nothing in the Act prevents a covered entity from prohibiting or imposing restrictions on smoking in places of employment.[1] This clause curiously appears under the heading "Relationship to Other Laws." The legislative history does not provide any clues about how this came to be or what it means: does it imply that only government-imposed restrictions such as anti-smoking ordinances are referred to? The breadth of the language and the purposes of the ADA militate against any such narrow construction, so that purely employer-imposed workplace smoking rules are no doubt legitimized as well.

---

[9] The court did hold that the employer could attempt to defend its conduct on the basis that providing such alternative coverage would constitute an undue hardship. This and the issue of damages were the only remaining questions of fact, so the court ordered trial on these issues.

[1] 42 U.S.C. § 12201(b).

B. WHY ARE TREATISES USEFUL?

Most legal treatises provide a fairly comprehensive and scholarly overview of the subject addressed. Because the coverage is typically analytical as well as descriptive, a treatise is often an ideal place to start your research if you are unfamiliar with the subject of your research problem. Furthermore, although treatises are not primary authority, a treatise may be persuasive secondary authority, depending on the credibility of the author and the quality of the work. In addition, a good treatise provides abundant references to important primary authorities and other secondary sources.

Treatises can have drawbacks. Some treatises are updated, but many are not. Some treatises are more credible, better researched, more clearly organized, and more comprehensive than others. Finally, although treatises abound, there still may be a few topics on which no one has yet written a good treatise.

C. HOW DO YOU RESEARCH IN TREATISES?

Because you are likely to use a treatise when your knowledge is fairly minimal, you should take advantage of the editorial aids and format of a book. Furthermore, only a fraction of legal treatises are available in computer-based media. Hence, this discussion focuses on researching in books.

Treatises in paper:

► locate treatises via a catalog, shelf-browsing or the reserve desk, a recommendation, or a textbook reference

► select the best treatise for your needs

► consult the index or tables of contents or table of primary authorities

► read the pertinent sections

► check for updates

Locate a treatise. To find an appropriate treatise, think first about which area of law encompasses the problem you are researching. You then may use any of these techniques:

• Look in a catalog to find out what your library owns or can obtain from other libraries.

- Find out the call-number range of the subject matter, and browse the relevant shelves. In addition, ask at the library reserve desk to see reserve treatises within that call number range. Exhibit 5.1 on page 63 lists Library of Congress call numbers for legal topics.
- Ask a professor, librarian, legal practitioner, or colleague who is knowledgeable about the subject for a recommendation.
- Look in a textbook for a reference in footnotes, endnotes, or the bibliography.

The first two methods need some elaboration.

As to the first method, your library catalog may consist of paper cards, microfiche, or a computer database. In any medium, you most likely will be able to search for treatises by author, title, and subject. An online catalog may offer additional search options, including key-word searching.

A subject search is the broadest search, so it usually will retrieve the most titles. Of course, you must work within the subject headings used by the cataloger, which usually are based on the Library of Congress system. Be sure to try various research terms. Also take advantage of the cross-references in the catalog, which direct you to the precise subjects used in the catalog. If the terms you choose for a subject search are not fruitful, you might locate a source you already know of in the catalog by means of its author or title, and then use the subject headings listed for that source to find other sources. Or you might consult the multivolume set entitled *Library of Congress Subject Headings*; these subject headings are the starting point for the creation of many library catalogs.

Another alternative, if the catalog is computer-based, is to employ a key-word search. A key-word search does not depend on a cataloger's use of subject headings. Rather it permits you to locate catalog entries containing your desired words. Especially if your topic has distinctive terms, key-word searching may be a useful place to start, with a subject search as follow-up if you want more choices.

If, as is probable, you search a computer-based catalog, pay close attention to the example screens and help screens. Be careful to spell correctly the title, the author's name, or the subject heading because a misspelled word may cause your search to be unsuccessful. Be careful, too, about your use of singulars and plurals because the two forms may not yield the same result.

As a novice legal researcher, you may find it difficult to determine what is and what is not a treatise. Do not expect the word "treatise" to appear in the title or the subject heading for the book. Sources with the following types of titles probably are not treatises: cases and materials; problems, text, and cases; casebook; institute or seminar or legal education; Restatements.

Select the best treatise. You may find more than one treatise on your subject. Treatises vary in quality and in usefulness for a particular project. To select the best for your needs, consider the following:

Coverage: Pick a treatise with the scope and level of detail you need. In an unfamiliar area of law, first you might examine a single-volume treatise to gain familiarity with the basics of the subject; then you might read a more

| EXHIBIT 5.1 | Library of Congress Call Numbers |

Administrative Law KF 5401-5425

Antitrust KF 1631-1657

Banking KF 966-1032

Bankruptcy KF 1501-1548

Business Associations, generally KF 1355-1480

Children and Law KF 479, 540-550

Civil and Political Rights KF 4741-4788

Civil Procedure KF 8810-9075

Commercial Transactions KF 871-962

Conflict of Laws KF 410-418

Constitutional Law KF 4501-5130

Contracts, quasi-contracts KF 801-1244

Copyright KF 2986-3080

Corporations KF 1384-1480

Criminal Law KF 9201-9763

Criminal Procedure KF 9601-9797

Education Policy and Law KF 4101-4257

Employment Discrimination KF 3464-3470

Environmental Law KF 277.E5

Equity KF 398-400

Evidence
    In civil cases KF 8931-8969
    In criminal cases KF 9660-9678

Federal Courts KF 8700-8807

Immigration Law KF 4801-4848

Insurance Law KF 1146-1238

International Law JX or JZ or KZ

Jurisprudence KF 379-382

Juvenile Criminal Law and Procedure KF 9771-9827

Labor Law KF 3300-3580

Land-Use Planning KF 5691-5710

Legal History KF 350-374

The Legal Profession KF 297-334

Legal Research and Writing KF 240-251

Legislative Process KF 4945-4952

Local Government/Municipal Law KF 5300-5332

Marital Relations and Dissolution KF 501-553

Medical Legislation KF 3821-3838

Mental Health Law KF 3828-3829

Oil and Gas KF 1841-1870

Patents and Trademarks KF 3091-3193

Public Safety KF 3941-3977

Real Property KF 560-698

Regulation of Industry, Trade, and Commerce KF 1600-2940

Secured Transactions KF 1046-1062

Securities Regulations KF 1066-1083, KF 1428-1457

Social Legislation KF 3300-3771

Taxation KF 6271-6645

Torts KF 1246-1327

Trial Practice (Civil) KF 8911-8925

Uniform State Laws KF 165

Water Resources KF 5551-5590

Wills and Trusts KF 726-780

detailed discussion in a multivolume treatise. Decide whether you are seeking a critical analysis or a more descriptive discussion, and choose accordingly.

Organization: Treatises are organized in a variety of ways, including chronologically and topically, such as by statute or type of transaction. They also vary in the number and quality of the tables of contents and indexes they provide.

Currency: In general you will want to select a treatise that has been published or updated recently. As applicable, check the copyright dates of the main volume, the pocket parts or pamphlet supplements, and replacement or supplement pages. Because there always is a delay between the completion of the text and its publication, look too for any statements about the dates of coverage of the text, generally located in the preface of a bound volume or the cover of a softcover volume. In general, looseleaf treatises are updated more frequently than others.

Accuracy: If your research is to be credible, the sources you use must be accurate. If you become aware that a source contains errors (from incorrect footnotes or citations, poor reviews, or otherwise), consider using another treatise.

Reputation (book): Some treatises are known as the classics in their fields; the analysis in these treatises is considered particularly credible. To determine which titles are considered especially reputable, (1) look for a treatise that has been cited in a textbook or course syllabus, (2) pick a treatise that is kept on reserve, (3) pick a treatise cited by a court, (4) find a treatise that has been published in multiple editions, or (5) use a book review (published in a periodical) to help you judge the quality of a treatise.

Reputation (author): Where possible, you should use a treatise by a true expert in the field. Check the author's credentials as noted in the treatise or in a reference book, such as *Who's Who in American Law* or *The AALS Directory of Law Teachers.* Check periodical indexes or library catalogs to see if the author has written extensively on the topic. Or use a treatise written by the author of a textbook on the subject.

Reputation (publisher): Publishers differ in the quality of their editorial work, the design of their publications, and the subject matters of their collections. As you gain experience, you will develop your own opinions about these matters. For now, you may want to ask reference librarians and other experienced legal researchers for their opinions.

Consult the index or tables. Once you have located a potentially useful treatise, you may use either the treatise's index or a table of contents to locate pertinent information within the treatise. If you use the index approach, be sure to consult all indexes; a treatise may have both a main index and one or more updates.

You may prefer to use the tables of contents because you can skim them relatively quickly. Many treatises include both a summary table of contents and a detailed table of contents. A classic technique is to start with the summary table of contents, then move to the detailed table of contents.

As another option, if you know the name of a pertinent case or the name or citation of a statute on point, and the case or statute is cited in the treatise, you could consult a table of primary authorities. An authority table helps you locate the text and footnotes within a treatise that discuss a particular authority. The two most common tables are tables of cases and tables of statutes.

Read pertinent sections. As you read the pertinent sections of the treatise, look for several types of useful information: an explanation of the law, a critique of the law (if presented), and references to other potentially pertinent authorities, whether primary or secondary. Take time to browse through adjacent sections and glance at sections referred to in the main sections you have chosen.

Check for updates. As a final step, you should check for updates to your treatise. Most multivolume treatises have update services, as do some single-volume treatises. Update services are organized by page, paragraph, or section so as to parallel the original volume. Updates come in several forms:

Pocket parts: These updates are pamphlets that slip into a pocket on an inside cover of a volume. Pocket parts usually are replaced annually. If a pocket part becomes too large, it may be replaced by a softbound supplement.

Supplemental volumes: Some sources have separate volumes or softbound pamphlets updating the original volumes. These supplements usually are shelved next to the volumes they update.

Looseleaf supplements: Sources bound in looseleaf binders may be updated with looseleaf supplements that are inserted periodically into the looseleaf volumes. These supplements generally are printed on colored paper to distinguish them from the original material.

Looseleaf page replacements: Sources bound in looseleaf binders may be updated with replacement pages that arrive and are inserted at regular intervals or on an as-needed basis.

Update services usually contain supplementary indexes and tables, which you should be sure to consult.

Legal treatises are sometimes updated through the publication of new editions. If the treatise you are using seems dated, you should check the library catalog, consult a source such as *Books in Print* or *Bowker's Law Books & Serials in Print*, or ask a librarian for help.

Researching the Canoga case. In the Canoga case, Illustration 5-2 on page 67 is an online catalog entry for the Larson treatise. We came to this entry by a subject search in the main topic "Discrimination in employment" and subtopic "Discrimination in employment—Law and legislation—United States." "Location" tells you where that source is located (for instance, the reserve collection). "Call #" tells you where the source is placed in the KF classification scheme. Note also that the entry informs you about the author(s), date(s) of publication, edition(s), and publication format for the source.

Employment Discrimination, excerpted in Illustration 5-1 on page 60, is a well known, multivolume, looseleaf treatise now in its second edition. The set is organized in part by major statutes, making it easy to find material on the specific issue of disability discrimination. The main volumes have been published recently, beginning in 1994, and they are updated regularly. The author of the first edition was Arthur Larson, a Duke University professor who was a former Secretary of Labor. The author of the second edition is Lex K. Larson, the president of Employment Law, Inc., who also lectures at that law school. The treatise is published by a reputable legal publisher.

The summary table of contents, covering all volumes of the *Employment Discrimination* treatise, directed us to volume 9, which discusses the Americans with Disabilities Act of 1990 (ADA). The detailed table of contents in volume 9 directed us to Chapter 155 Permitted Practices; Defenses under the ADA. Section 155.06 addresses restrictions on smoking.

The excerpt in Illustration 5-1 on page 60 describes and cites a potentially important provision of the federal statute on discrimination against disabled employees, which apparently permits some restrictions on smoking in the workplace. That page is an update to the original publication. The page dates to June 1999 and replaces the 1994 page.

D.   What Else?

Hornbooks: "Hornbook" generally refers to a single-volume treatise that explains the basic principles of law in a particular field, is written by a top scholar in a field, and is designed for law students. A hornbook can be an excellent place to begin your research on an unfamiliar topic.

Additional Techniques for Finding Treatises: The *Index to Legal Periodicals and Books* (covered in more detail in Chapter 6) indexes some treatises. On occasion, periodicals publish bibliographies on certain subjects.

E.   How Do You Cite Treatises?

To cite a treatise, you need to know the full name(s) of the author(s); the volume number (if the treatise has more than one volume); the main title of the book as it appears on the title page (not the cover); the page, section, or paragraph number (if only part of the volume is cited); the edition (if other than the first); and the year of publication of the main volume or supplement you are using. Here is an example (following Rule 15 of *The Bluebook*):

> 9 Lex K. Larson, *Employment Discrimination* § 155.06 (2d ed. Supp. 1999).

ILLUSTRATION 5-2   Online Catalog Entry, from Innovative Interfaces System

Author	Larson, Lex K
Title	**Employment discrimination / by Lex K. Larson ; practice forms by Lex K. Larson and Jonathan R. Harkavy**
Imprint	New York : M. Bender, 1994-
Call #	KF3464 .L374
Location	Reserve

Location Reserve	
LIB. HAS	1994-
Latest Received:	June 1999 52

LOCATION	CALL NO.	STATUS
Reserve	KF3464 .L374 v. 1	AVAILABLE
Reserve	KF3464 .L374 v. 2	AVAILABLE
Reserve	KF3464 .L374 v. 3	AVAILABLE
Reserve	KF3464 .L374 v. 4	AVAILABLE
Reserve	KF3464 .L374 v. 5	AVAILABLE
Reserve	KF3464 .L374 v. 6	AVAILABLE
Reserve	KF3464 .L374 v. 7	AVAILABLE
Reserve	KF3464 .L374 v. 8	AVAILABLE
Reserve	KF3464 .L374 v. 9	AVAILABLE
Reserve	KF3464 .L374 tables of cases index	AVAILABLE

Edition	2nd ed
Descript	v. (loose-leaf) : forms ; 26 cm
Note	Earlier ed. by: Arthur Larson
	Includes index
Subject	Sex discrimination in employment -- Law and legislation -- United States
	Discrimination in employment -- Law and legislation -- United States
Alt author	Harkavy, Jonathan R., 1943-
	Larson, Arthur

LEGAL PERIODICALS

A. What Is A Legal Periodical?

B. Why Are Legal Periodicals Useful?

C. How Do You Research Legal Periodical Articles?

D. What Else?

E. How Do You Cite Legal Periodicals?

A.   WHAT IS A LEGAL PERIODICAL?

A legal periodical is a secondary source that provides commentary on a range of legal topics over a period of time. Articles in legal periodicals are written by professors, lawyers, lawmakers, and law students. They not only describe the current state of the law but also generally explore underlying policies, critique current legal rules, and advocate law reform.

The term "legal periodical" includes several different types of publications. The most prominent type is the law review or law journal. Most law reviews cover a wide range of legal topics. They typically carry the names of a particular law school, for example, *Pepperdine Law Review* or *The Yale Law Journal.* The students of the school serve as the editors and editorial staff; they select articles, verify the authority given for the ideas propounded, assure the accuracy of the citations, and edit the author's writing. Generally, a law review staff publishes a new volume annually in two to six separate issues.

Law reviews typically publish several types of articles. Long pieces with extensive citations written by lawyers, professors, or judges are called "articles." Shorter pieces written by these authors, with fewer footnotes, are called "essays." An article by a prominent author may be followed by short discussions, usually labeled "commentaries." Student pieces are called "comments" or "notes" if they are broad in scope, "case notes" or "case comments" if they focus on a narrow topic or on a recent court or agency decision. The labels "recent developments" and "survey" are used for a survey of an area of law written by a group of students or faculty. A "symposium issue" is an issue dedicated to one topic. Some issues contain "book reviews" of recently published treatises or texts. An issue's table of contents generally classifies its contents by these categories.

A second type of legal periodical is the special-interest legal periodical, which focuses on a specific area of law. For example, the *Employee Relations Law Journal* focuses on labor and employment law. Some special-interest periodicals, such as *Social Responsibility: Business, Journalism, Law, Medicine*, are interdisciplinary. Some are published by law schools, so they resemble general-scope law reviews. Others are published by associations of lawyers or by commercial publishers; these generally are called "journals" and are more practical than theoretical.

The third type of legal periodical is the bar association journal, such as the *ABA Journal* published by the American Bar Association. Many national, state, and local bar associations and other lawyer organizations publish such journals. These tend to be more practical than theoretical. Bar journals also report legal developments, such as changes in court rules.

A fourth type of periodical is the commercial legal newspaper. Legal newspapers typically report (in full text or summary form) on new court decisions and other important changes in the law. They also carry legal notices mandated by law (such as notices of business dissolutions) as well as feature stories about people or significant events in the legal profession. Some legal newspapers are national in coverage, such as the *National Law Journal;* others cover one city or state, such as the *Los Angeles Daily Journal.*

A fifth category consists of newsletters on specific legal topics, published by commercial publishers and public-interest organizations. These newsletters generally are short; are issued monthly, weekly, or even daily; and cover very recent developments. They provide information on new cases, statutes, and regulations, and they report on other legal and nonlegal developments.

In recent years, the Internet has become a source of "articles" on legal topics. They tend to be "published" by groups of persons with a shared interest in a specific topic. These articles may or may not be edited, reviewed, or verified before they are made available online; they may be available only through the Internet. As of yet, they are less indexed than traditional journals, and few have the credibility of more traditional periodicals.

In the Canoga case, Illustration 6-1 on pages 70–71 is a portion of a note written by Michele L. Tyler on smoking in the workplace from the *Georgetown Law Journal*, which is a general-scope law review.

B.   WHY ARE LEGAL PERIODICALS USEFUL?

A good periodical article provides at least a description and analysis of the law. Most articles cover their subjects in depth; indeed, you may find a lengthy article on a narrow topic. Many articles also provide valuable background

ILLUSTRATION 6-1   Law Review Article, from *Georgetown Law Journal*

1998]   BLOWING SMOKE   789

A. THE WORKPLACE: INFORMATIONAL PRIVACY RIGHTS

Although neither a constitutional right to smoke, nor a constitutional right to breathe clean air has been recognized,[43] *Shimp v. New Jersey Bell Telephone Co.*[44] is widely cited as recognizing an employer's common law duty to provide a safe work environment. Arguing that employers have such a duty, and taking judicial notice of the dangers of environmental tobacco smoke, the *Shimp* court held that employers must prohibit smoking in work areas.[45] Once employers realized that they could be liable to their nonsmoking employees for violating this common law duty, they began to institute restrictive smoking policies.[46] At the same time, employers were becoming knowledgeable about the health consequences of smoking and the increased costs associated with employing smokers,[47] resulting in an even greater incentive to limit smoking in the workplace. Thus, most of the enacted smoking policies serve the dual purpose of protecting the health of nonsmoking employees and customers and of reducing costs to the employer. States began to take interest as well; as of 1995, eleven states had regulated smoking in private places of employment, others were considering restrictive legislation, and still others had regulated smoking in public employment.[48] Additionally, localities have passed ordinances regulating smoking, though like the state statutes, they vary in the scope of their provisions.[49]

Yet smokers, with the help of the tobacco industry, continue to lobby Congress and state and local legislatures to protect the rights of smokers.[50] By 1995,

---

43. *See* Gasper v. Louisiana Stadium & Exposition Dist., 418 F. Supp. 716 (E.D. La. 1976) (holding that the U.S. Constitution does not guarantee a right to breathe air free of smoke). The class action suit was brought on behalf of all nonsmoking attendees of events in the Louisiana Superdome, a public facility.

44. 368 A.2d 408 (N.J. Super. Ct. Ch. Div. 1976).

45. *See id.* at 416; *see also* Smith v. Western Elec. Co., 643 S.W.2d 10 (Mo. Ct. App. 1982) (holding an employer has a duty to use due care to eliminate harmful conditions, including tobacco smoke); McCarthy v. Department of Soc. & Health Serv., 759 P.2d 351 (Wash. 1988) (holding employer has duty to take "reasonable precautions" to protect employees from environmental tobacco smoke).

46. *See* Sablone, *supra* note 5, at 1090.

47. *See infra* notes 71-77 and accompanying text. The increased cost of employing smokers is not without debate. At least one critic of strict nonsmoking policies argues that smokers' productivity is sacrificed when management denies a smoker the opportunity to smoke at work. *See* Mitchell, *supra* note 1, at 231. Smokers may not want to rely on this argument, however, because it serves as yet another reason why employers should be permitted to refuse to hire smokers altogether. Additionally, employers recognize that by not limiting smoking in the workplace, they are likely to face claims by nonsmoking employees who, years later, develop health problems. *See id.* at 232.

48. *See* Ann H. Zgrodnik, Comment, *Smoking Discrimination: Invading an Individual's Right to Privacy in the Home and Outside the Workplace?*, 21 OHIO N.U. L. REV. 1227, 1238-39 & nn.114-15 (1995). In 1995, the following states had laws regulating smoking in private places of employment: Arizona, Connecticut, Florida, Maine, Minnesota, Montana, Nebraska, New Hampshire, New Jersey, Rhode Island, and Utah. *Id.* at 1239 n.114.

49. *See id.* at 1239. Although the laws vary, most prohibit smoking in certain areas, require signs to be posted indicating whether smoking is permitted, and require that certain areas be set aside as nonsmoking areas. *See* Mark A. Rothstein, *Refusing to Employ Smokers: Good Public Health or Bad Public Policy?*, 62 NOTRE DAME L. REV. 940, 946-47 (1987).

50. *See* Zgrodnik, *supra* note 48, at 1244-45.

ILLUSTRATION 6-1   (*continued*)

twenty-nine states had passed some type of smoker-protection legislation prohibiting employers from discriminating against employees or potential employees
who smoke while off duty.[51]

Despite smoker activism, some cities and private employers continue to enact
restrictive smoking policies. By 1994, an estimated six percent of all companies
refused to hire smokers, even individual smokers who do not smoke during
work hours.[52] Companies often cite *Grusendorf v. City of Oklahoma City*[53] as
support for the constitutionality of this practice. In *Grusendorf*, the Oklahoma
City Fire Department required firefighter trainees to abstain from on-duty and
off-duty smoking for one year after they were hired.[54] Grusendorf was spotted
smoking on a lunch break and was subsequently fired.[55] Although the court
agreed that the smoking policy infringed upon Grusendorf's privacy, it held that
smoking is not a fundamental privacy right and thus the policy was valid as
long as the city could offer a rational basis for it.[56] Because firefighters must be
in top physical condition to combat their on-the-job smoke exposure, the court
held that the city had passed the rational basis test.[57] Although a firefighter's
informational privacy interests are compromised by a requirement that he report
legal behavior that he would otherwise keep from his employer, it is not
surprising that in the interests of public safety, the city could validly override
this individual interest.

More controversial, however, is *City of North Miami v. Kurtz*,[58] in which the
Florida Supreme Court upheld the city's anti-smoking regulation that required
all prospective city employees to sign an affidavit stating that they had refrained
from using tobacco products for the prior year.[59] Because Kurtz admitted that
she could not truthfully sign the affidavit, she was told that she would no longer
be a candidate for city employment.[60] She then sued, claiming a violation of her
federal and state constitutional privacy right to smoke outside the course of

---

51. *See id.*; *see also* Gerhart, *supra* note 13, at 188 & n.50 (quoting BUREAU OF NAT'L AFFAIRS, INDIVIDUAL EMPLOYMENT RIGHTS MANUAL 509:501 (1995)). Although the scope and focus of smoker protection statutes vary, some prohibit employers from refusing to hire smokers or from discriminating against present employees because of their off-duty smoking. *See* Lisa A. Frye, Comment, *"You've Come a Long Way, Smokers": North Carolina Preserves the Employee's Right to Smoke Off the Job in General Statutes Section 95-28.2*, 71 N.C. L. REV. 1963, 1964 (1993).

52. *See* Lewis L. Maltby & Bernard J. Dushman, *Whose Life Is it Anyway—Employer Control of Off-Duty Behavior*, 13 ST. LOUIS U. PUB. L. REV. 645, 645 (1994).

53. 816 F.2d 539 (10th Cir. 1987). *See, e.g.*, Operation Badlaw, Inc. v. Licking County Gen. Health Dist. Bd. of Health, 866 F. Supp. 1059, 1064 (S.D. Ohio 1992) (citing *Grusendorf* for principle that the right to smoke is not a fundamental right); Town of Plymouth v. Civil Serv. Comm'n, 686 N.E.2d 188, 190 n.4 (Mass. 1997) (citing *Grusendorf* and upholding police offficer's termination for smoking while off-duty).

54. *See Grusendorf*, 816 F.2d at 540.

55. *See id.*

56. *See id.* at 541-42.

57. *See id.* at 543.

58. 653 So. 2d 1025 (Fla. 1995).

59. *Id.* at 1026.

60. Kurtz v. City of North Miami, 625 So. 2d 899, 900 (Fla. Dist. Ct. App. 1993).

information such as historical information or statistical data. You are likely to find a wealth of references to primary authority, such as cases and statutes; other secondary sources, such as treatises and other periodical articles; and nonlegal sources.

Because the special function of some legal periodicals is to present serious, creative legal thought, you may also find critiques of present law and proposals for law reform. Indeed, you may find a series of articles on the same subject, each presenting a different viewpoint and responding directly to others. Although periodicals are merely commentary sources, a few have prompted changes in the law.

Another particular advantage of legal periodicals is that articles can be written and published in less time than other materials can be published. Hence, periodicals are a good source for a discussion of new legal topics.

Periodicals have disadvantages as well. They lose currency quickly because the information is current only to the date the article was completed, which may be some time ago, and articles are not updated as some other secondary sources are. In addition, some analysis in periodical articles is idiosyncratic; you need to consider whether it is too unusual to be accepted before you rely on it heavily. Finally, even though periodical articles abound, it is possible there will be no article on your topic.

C.   HOW DO YOU RESEARCH LEGAL PERIODICAL ARTICLES?

The traditional means of researching periodicals is, in simple terms, to use an index (which may be a paper, CD-ROM, or online product) to identify pertinent articles and then to read the articles, typically in paper. This approach entails a wide range of periodicals. A newer, narrower research approach is a key-word search in an online periodical database. A follow-up step for a narrow, but important, purpose is citing a periodical article; in law citing is often called "Shepardizing."

Traditional periodicals research:

▶   select a periodical index

▶   if a paper index, search in the subject or other division

▶   if a computer-based index, search by subject or use a key-word search

▶   read and assess the article(s)

Most often, to locate a legal periodical article you will use a system no different from that used for finding a periodical article in fields outside of law—an index. There are two major indexes for legal periodicals; both are published in paper, in CD-ROM, and online (with some variations across media). Some index features change from time to time as the publishers modify their products, so be sure to read the instructions for the index you use.

The older of the two major indexes is the *Index to Legal Periodicals & Books* (I.L.P.B.), formerly *Index to Legal Periodicals*, which dates to 1908 and covers nearly 800 journals of various sorts (as well as about 2,000 law books). In paper form, I.L.P.B. is published monthly in softbound pamphlets cumulated quarterly, and then cumulated into annual hardbound volumes. Its current format has four divisions: subject and author, table of cases, table of statutes, and book reviews. I.L.P.B. is available in CD-ROM form as *Wilsondisk* and online through Westlaw, LEXIS, and WilsonWeb (through the Internet); these forms cover articles published since 1981.

The newer of the two major indexes is *Current Law Index (C.L.I.*), which began publication in 1980. Its advantages compared to I.L.P.B. are the wider scope of journals covered (nearly 900) and more specific subject headings. In paper form, it comes out monthly with quarterly cumulations and then annual hardbound volumes. Its current format has four divisions: subject, author/title, table of cases, and table of statutes. C.L.I. is the basis of *Legal-Trac,* an even more expansive index, which includes coverage of law-related articles in general-interest periodicals and is published in CD-ROM form and on the Internet. C.L.I. is available online through Westlaw and LEXIS as *Legal Resources Index.*

note Legal-Trac to access CLI

As you select from among these indexes, consider these features: scope of coverage, access methods, vocabulary used in the subject headings, display options, frequency of updating and cumulation, and information provided about the articles. For example, while you generally will want to find a recent article, you should consult I.L.P.B. if you are seeking an older article for some reason. On the other hand, some researchers generally prefer C.L.I. in one form or another because the subject headings are easier to work with. Nearly all researchers prefer one of the computer-based sources to paper sources because they afford key-word searching as well as searching by category (such as subject or author), are totally cumulative, and (in the case of online sources) are very up-to-date. Some of the computer-based sources provide not only citations to pertinent articles, but also abstracts and links to the full text of some articles.

Furthermore, try various strategies as you work with periodical indexes. For example, in a paper index, you are most likely to consult the subject division, but consider looking as well in the author division for articles by an author you know to be an expert in the field. In a computer-based index, consider performing both a subject search and a key-word search for the best results. A subject search, even if it involves a subject with subdivisions, can be very broad, yielding a long list of articles. On the other hand, because some articles have unusual titles, a pertinent article's title may not contain your research terms, so you would not want to rely solely on a key-word search. Another option is to perform a key-word search within the set of articles listed under a particular subject heading. Be sure you know exactly what material the computer is searching for your terms, for example, titles, citations, abstracts, texts, subject headings, or some combination.

Once you locate a pertinent article, you should read it carefully. Take care to differentiate the author's descriptions of existing law, critique of the law, and proposed reforms. Cull useful references to primary authority and other secondary sources from the footnotes. Be sure to note the publication date, so you appreciate the limited currency of both the text and the footnotes.

Periodical articles vary widely in quality; hence you should carefully assess an article before relying heavily upon it. Here are some factors to consider:

> *coverage:* How completely does the article cover your topic? Is the article general enough or specific enough for your needs?
>
> *accuracy:* Are the propositions in the article adequately supported by cited authorities?
>
> *persuasiveness:* If the article critiques the law or argues for a change in the law, how well does the author convince you? Are the arguments logically ordered and well constructed?
>
> *reputation (author):* How credible is the author of the article? Check the initial footnote for the author's credentials, or check a periodical index or a library catalog for additional publications by the author.
>
> *reputation (periodical):* How well regarded is the periodical? Look at the credentials of other authors in the same periodical, or ask an experienced researcher about the periodical's reputation.

Researching the Canoga case, we looked for articles through *LegalTrac*. A subject search using the subject heading "smoking" yielded over 300 articles. When we entered a key-word search [smok* and priva*], which calls for variants of "smoke" and "privacy," we identified thirty articles, including the Tyler note excerpted as Illustration 6-1 on pages 70–71. As another example, we consulted the 1997–1998 bound volume of I.L.P.B. The Tyler note is listed under "right of privacy."

The Tyler note provides an overview of legal regulation of smoking by employees, including a reference to state legislation prohibiting employers from discriminating against employees due to off-duty smoking. The note is recent. It appears in the eighty-sixth volume of a general-scope student-run law review of a well regarded law school. The note seems well supported and reads well. Overall, it seems to be worth examining closely, but would not likely carry great persuasive authority with a court because it is a note.

Periodicals via full-text key-word searching:

▶ select a LEXIS or Westlaw database

▶ run a key-word search

▶ read and assess the article(s)

Both LEXIS and Westlaw permit you to perform a key-word search of the full texts of periodical articles in law review databases. Unfortunately, both databases are limited, although expanding. They cover fewer journals than the indexes described above; coverage for some starts in the 1980s, some in the 1990s; only selected articles of some periodicals are available. As an alternative to a broad periodicals database, you could search a subject-specific database, if you are quite sure that your topic falls within the database. Ordinarily you would use a key-word search, searching the full texts of the articles. Once you located a pertinent article, you would read and assess it as described above.

Researching the Canoga case, we searched the combined law review database on LEXIS. The search [(priva! w/3 right) w/5 (workplace or employ!) w/10 smok!] yielded nineteen articles, including a bibliography published in the *Law Library Journal* and the note written by Michele L. Tyler.

Shepardizing periodical articles:

▸ identify the cited article
▸ assemble the paper volumes, or key in the citation
▸ peruse the list of citing sources

On occasion, you might find an article that sets forth an important new idea, and you may want to know whether the idea has been received favorably by courts or other legal scholars. *Shepard's Law Review Citations* lists references to periodical articles found in recent court decisions or in other periodical articles. See Illustration 6-2 on page 76.

The first step in Shepardizing is to identify the cited article—the source you have read and would like to follow up on. If you are Shepardizing in paper, the next step is to assemble all pertinent volumes of Shepard's encompassing the cited source, which is a function not only of the Shepard's title (Shepard's covers many types of authority) but also of the dates of the various hardbound volumes and updating softcover volumes. Then you must find the entries for your cited source in the various volumes. Finding the entry for your cited source online is easier; you need only key in the citation, and a single entry, completely cumulated, appears. The final step is to peruse the list of citing sources. Each listed source cites the cited source on the listed page.

For example, the Tyler note in Illustration 6-1 on page 70 cites an article by Mark Rothstein in footnote 49, at page 789. The Rothstein article starts at page 940 in volume 62 of the *Notre Dame Law Review*. While researching the Canoga case, had we first read the Rothstein article and wished to follow up on it, we would have consulted Shepard's, with the Rothstein article our cited source. Illustration 6-2 on page 76 is a recent Shepard's page covering various volumes of the *Notre Dame Law Review*. The entry for page 940 of volume 62 includes 86Geo789—a reference to volume 86 of the *Georgetown Law Journal*, page 789, that is, the Tyler note.

ILLUSTRATION 6-2   *Shephard's Law Review Citations*

NOTRE DAME LAW REVIEW

—624—
70ILJ821
—643—
28Pcf336
—879—
Md
344Md666
689A2d1240
72NDR377
[134
{ —940—
86Geo789
60TnL905
—1024—
80F3d351
36BCR217
81ILR21
46LLJ276
36NHJ(4)33
29WFL805
31WFL1045

Vol. 63
—1—
68SCL93
68TLQ17
73WsL850
—35—
85CaL1568
42CLA1573
31SFR373
—123—
57OhLJ1609
—161—
108HLR
[1843
1997IILR507
28Suf1206
—247—
45CLA1075
63FR675
46HLJ483
89NwL1398
—358—
23ONU171
—399—
25SwR267
—609—
46HLJ716
—628—
84VaL982
—645—
45DuLJ945
49MeL368
32UCD306
32UCD125
—671—
47AkL306
39AzL490
45DuLJ984
64GW534

—693—
45DuLJ946
45FLR556
46FLR29
46FLR78
46FLR125
64GW533
81ILR1218
46KLR773
57LCP(3)
[134
46StnL1472
29TU151
82VaL1250
—720—
Miss
669So2d95
N C
117NCA42
450SE33
Vt
161Vt7
73NCL2194
57PitJ929
47SCR108
—733—
45DuLJ994
46StnL1598
29TU70
—770—
877FS420
35Duq639
79MnL25
24PLR496
84VaL990
52W&L1570
36W&M
[1668
—818—
73TxL1636

Vol. 64
—1—
76BUR606
30LWR371
73NCL339
73NYL1107
49SCR92
—73—
124F3d916
—106—
37W&M573
—157—
36SAC88
97WVL222
—200—
38AzL255
76MnL1862
59MoL65
57PitL866
32WFL418
—298—
Ark
326Ark359

931SW121
Wash
128Wsh2d
[718
130Wsh2d
[841
911P2d394
928P2d1083
45CLA1752
66CUR25
32Goz274
33IDR15
105YLJ129
—321—
81Cor433
48HLJ1305
60LCP(3)
[121
47MiL636
1996WLR17
—464—
N J
143NJ439
672A2d1143
73NbL817
—497—
24EnL1506
—571—
80VaL849
—646—
Ore
141OrA491
919P2d1187
—784—
75DJ207
32LoyL677
—805—
47EmJ179
—817—
74NCL129
27Pcf13
48StnL333
—838—
47EmJ166
—886—
16ALJ186
46AU825
85CaL184
61ChL920
43CLA1086
82Geo2435
83Geo463
84Geo458
84Geo1572
1995IILR382
95McL876
54MdL195
76NCL1862
32SDL171
46SMU465
63UCR100
1995UtLR
[1073
50VLR983
1994WLR
[843

1994WLR
[1348
32WML549
—932—
81Cor1093
21FSU1187
1994IILR342
34SDL1594
29UCD755
—945—
51FLR2

Vol. 65
—1—
N D
530NW300
70NDL1094
—32—
50HLJ98
—165—
67CUR535
1994IILR583
—206—
27Cum413
25RLJ274
36SoTR71
60TnL288
1995WLR
[551
1995WLR
[603
1995WLR
[679
—397—
70ILJ109
75OLR247
47SCR784
48StnL1341
49VLR643
—425—
Ill
174Il2d73
220IID164
672NE1176
N D
546NW358
555NW587
556NW295
47DuLJ643
46EmJ184
76NCL853
49OkLR6
144PaL1000
30SFR381
—490—
27FS2d1129
—617—
27SeH21
—671—
132F3d560
47VLR304
—803—
45EmJ37
38StLJ345

—873—
46HLJ1103
—885—
22ONU10
—896—
503US282
Pa
33DC4d248
33DC4d268
40AzL1199
110HLR
[1104
23WmM570
—983—
56OhLJ1386
—1009—
22ONU17
23PLR491
—1035—
46CLA802
56OhLJ1364
50SMU36
—1050—
56OhLJ1364
—1073—
56OhLJ1364
—1075—
38AzL312

Vol. 66
—1—
Calif
9C4th285
36CaR2d543
885P2d956
33Duq266
30McGL40
—37—
53BL462
44Cth1039
—57—
954FS233
Haw
77Haw302
884P2d365
Nebr
248Neb665
538NW741
48BLR800
36W&M
[1036
—117—
Ga
270Ga796
83Cor271
—359—
45EmJ563
51StnL96
—443—
80Cor1509
45FLR572
93McL709
—603—
68TLQ66

—661—
75BUR568
—687—
28Akr470
—721—
1997IILR196
64TnL1007
—759—
44DR732
—813—
76NbL592
20VtL141
—825—
76BUR661
33NRJ1041
33NRJ1042
51StnL1142
—863—
1996IILR738
—1025—
71NDL196
—1053—
49LLJ919
—1135—
79ILR858
—1219—
56OhLJ910
56OhLJ917
—1355—
26Cum432
—1461—
38F3d437
Conn
243Ct131
701A2d23
106YLJ541
—1539—
47EmJ228

Vol. 67
—1—
53F3d409
74F3d12
99F3d36
99F3d1248
112F3d585
123F3d46
898FS94
81MnL302
1996WLR
[718
—51—
76BUR259
—97—
30WFL23

—183—
75BUR988
98CR41
44DuLJ1055
47HLJ1279
—231—
84Geo2101
82MnL385
72TxL1284
1997WLR
[446
—253—
81MaL65
83VaL1636
—363—
30RIC973
—403—
33HUL740
29McGL318
94McL2710
95McL1075
82MnL727
90NwL498
55OhLJ858
69SCL1239
33TU305
83VaL967
23WmM543
70WsL351
—553—
87CaL577
29LoyL548
—587—
73NCL1570
—615—
26AzSJ546
82CaL776
28CnL599
47EmJ171
83Geo2279
85Geo2087
79ILR593
95McL842
82MnL107
144PaL1421
—799—
N D
564NW635
—851—
Pa
538Pa203
647A2d886
—971—
68NYL1192
63UCR659
—1037—
83Geo2273
31Goz590
78MqL325
78MqL443
—1079—
31SFR586
1996WLR
[1021

—1121—
33HUL121
—1215—
39SDR532
—1317—
50SMU499
—1365—
29RIC1295
—1385—
40AzL846
28GaL876
47HLJ593
—1455—
59LCP(4)84

Vol. 68
—11—
45AU81
142PaL2024
25RLJ672
46RLR1732
—33—
867FS153
92McL2093
—81—
888FS1145
64GW525
—271—
47VLR1804
—333—
182FRD535
—427—
18ALJ575
48BLR352
45CLA617
45DuLJ6
1996IILR744
60LCP(2)
[135
730LR539
770LR159
28SeH447
27SwR550
27SwR643
61TnL1062
61TnL1245
73TxL1660
75TxL1614
75TxL1666
48VLR646
38VR1365
39VR285
39VR511
51W&L1321
31WFL1135
—507—
109HLR
57OhLJ1321
76TxL839
—581—
30AzSJ1099
Continued

D.   WHAT ELSE?

Current Awareness Services: Although the indexes described in this chapter are fairly current, if you are seeking a very recent article, you may consult a current awareness service, such as *Current Index to Legal Periodicals* (available in paper and online).

Specialty Paper Indexes: A number of other paper indexes cover legal periodicals. Some, such as the *Index to Federal Tax Articles,* cover particular subject areas within law. The *Index to Periodical Articles Related to Law* (I.P.A.R.L.) indexes periodicals not covered in other major legal periodical indexes; it covers social science, business, and technical journals as well as popular magazines, to the extent that their articles pertain to law.

Indexes to Foreign Journals: If your research pertains to the law of a particular foreign jurisdiction, you may wish to consult an index covering journals from that country, such as the *Index to Canadian Legal Periodical Literature*, *Legal Journals Index* (for British law), and *Index to Foreign Legal Periodicals* (I.F.L.P.).

Law Review-Specific Indexes: Many law reviews periodically publish indexes to their own volumes. These indexes, which generally are bound along with the law review's issues, usually are organized by subject, title, and author.

Nonlegal Periodicals: Nonlegal periodicals often are of great interest to lawyers because many legal problems touch on fields such as medicine, business, psychology, management, and economics. The *Social Science Index*, similar indexes from other disciplines, and even the massive *Readers' Guide to Periodical Literature* may lead you to useful articles.

E.   HOW DO YOU CITE LEGAL PERIODICALS?

To cite a periodical article, you need to know the author's name, the article title, the volume number and abbreviation of the law review, the page number of the article, and its date of publication. Citations to signed pieces written by students include the label, such as "Note" or "Comment." Here is an example (following Rule 16 of *The Bluebook*):

> Michele L. Tyler, Note, *Blowing Smoke: Do Smokers Have a Right? Limiting the Privacy Rights of Cigarette Smokers,* 86 Geo. L.J. 783 (1998).

CHAPTER

7

A.L.R. ANNOTATIONS

A. What Are American Law Reports (A.L.R.) Annotations?

B. Why Is A.L.R. Useful?

C. How Do You Research in A.L.R.?

D. What Else?

E. How Do You Cite A.L.R.?

A. WHAT ARE AMERICAN LAW REPORTS (A.L.R.) ANNOTATIONS?

American Law Reports (A.L.R.) contains two kinds of material: annotations and cases. An annotation is an article that discusses, in great detail, the various cases on a fairly narrow legal topic. Most annotations focus on issues of current controversy, in which courts in different jurisdictions follow different rules, or on issues that are factually sensitive so that differing facts result in different holdings. A typical A.L.R. annotation discusses the law in many jurisdictions within the United States, citing to relevant authority in each of those jurisdictions.

Accompanying the annotation is a case, a court's opinion selected by the publisher as a leading case on the topic discussed in the annotation. Because other sources of case law are more complete, your primary focus in A.L.R. research will be on the annotations.

A.L.R. is published by a commercial publisher, West Group (formerly by Lawyers Cooperative). The annotations are written by its staff attorneys or attorneys hired to write particular annotations.

A.L.R. is a large multivolume set, first published in 1919. A.L.R. has been published in multiple series, as listed below:

Series	Dates	Topics
A.L.R.1st	1919-1948	State and federal
A.L.R.2d	1948-1965	State and federal

Series	Dates	Topics
A.L.R.3d	1965-1969	State and federal
A.L.R.3d	1969-1980	State
A.L.R.4th	1980-1991	State
A.L.R.5th	1992 to date	State
A.L.R. Fed.	1969 to date	Federal

Early on, state and federal topics appeared together. Since 1969, A.L.R. Fed. has covered federal topics, while A.L.R.3d, A.L.R.4th, and A.L.R.5th have covered state topics.

Some recent annotations cover topics covered in earlier annotations, while other recent annotations cover new topics. Because many of the annotations in the first and second series have been superseded or become outdated, you are likely to use the later sets more frequently. Thus, this text focuses on the third, fourth, fifth, and federal series.

Six to nine A.L.R. volumes are issued each year for each current series, and each volume contains approximately ten annotations. The annotations contained in each A.L.R. volume typically cover a wide range of subjects, such as contracts, torts, criminal law, and employment law. Although A.L.R. covers subjects from many areas of law, it is not comprehensive; there are some subjects on which there is no annotation.

As an example pertinent to the Canoga case, Illustration 7-1 on page 80 is an excerpt from an annotation on the impact of an employment policy on the employer's right to discharge a stated at-will employee.

B. WHY IS A.L.R. USEFUL?

A.L.R. is a helpful research tool because it describes in general terms and then analyzes in detail the case law on covered topics. An annotation thus provides a good overview of a topic. Because the case descriptions are organized by rule or outcome, it also permits you to see the different approaches taken by various courts and the importance of key facts.

Besides providing commentary, an A.L.R. annotation also refers to other sources. As already noted, cases are not only cited but also described. In addition, an annotation provides references to certain other secondary sources.

Furthermore, A.L.R. is a timely source. An annotation on a new legal topic may appear before other secondary sources. And A.L.R. is kept up to date in various ways, so the information is current.

However, A.L.R. has its limitations. There may be no annotation on your subject. Moreover, although the discussion in each A.L.R. annotation is quite comprehensive, it tends to be more descriptive than analytical or critical. Furthermore, because an annotation generally is written by a staff lawyer, the research and writing may be accurate, but the writer is not a recognized scholar or expert in the area. Thus, the annotation is not as credible a source to cite as some other secondary sources.

ILLUSTRATION 7-1   A.L.R. Annotation Case Descriptions

33 ALR4th   EMPLOYMENT AT WILL—RESTRAINTS ON DISCHARGE   § 4[b]
33 ALR4th 120

its discretion in granting the defendant's motion for a new trial.

♦

In Simpson v Western Graphics Corp. (1982) 293 **Or** 96, 643 P2d 1276, where the parties agreed that the provisions of the employee handbook were contractual terms of the plaintiffs' employment and that therefore the defendant could discharge employees only upon a determination of just cause, the court held that, absent an express provision transferring authority to for making the factual just-cause determination to an outside arbiter, the employer retained the right to make that determination. The court stated that although an employer's statement of employment policy has a degree of contractual effect, its terms are not necessarily to be construed in the same way as those of a negotiated labor contract. The court pointed out that the handbook was a unilateral statement by the employer of self-imposed limitations upon its prerogatives and was furnished to the plaintiff after they were hired and afforded no inference that the plaintiffs accepted or continued in employment in reliance upon its terms. In such a situation, the court said, the meaning intended by the employer is controlling and there was no reason to infer that the employer intended to surrender its power to determine whether facts constituting cause for just termination existed.

[b] Right of discharge held not restricted

Under the particular circumstances in the following cases, it was held that the promulgation of employment policies regarding the procedures and grounds for termination of at-will employees did not operate to restrict an employer's right to freely discharge at-will employees.

Rejecting the contention of the plaintiff, a campus security guard, that the terms of the defendant's personnel manual, in particular, the provisions relating to discharge of employees, adopted by the defendant and issued to its employees upon their appointment became an employment contract binding upon both parties and that thus the defendant's discharge of the plaintiff without first providing written allegations or an opportunity to be heard, as provided for in the personnel manual, was in breach of the contract, the court in Sargent v Illinois Institute of Technology (1979) 78 **Ill** App 3d 117, 33 Ill Dec 937, 397 NE2d 443, affirmed the dismissal of the plaintiff's action, stating that the personnel manual was not an enforceable contract. Unlike the situation presented in Carter v Kaskaskia Community Action Agency (1974) 24 **Ill** App3d 1056, 322 NE2d 574, supra § 4[a], where, the court noted, it was found that both the employees and the employer affirmatively adopted the personnel manual and thus accordingly held that the manual became part of the at-will employment contract, in the instant case, the campus police guidelines set forth in the manual were not bargained for, the plaintiff provided no additional consideration to support a predischarge hearing requirement, and the manual was given to the plaintiff at the start of his employment and thus could not be viewed as a contractual modification. Viewed as a whole, the court stated the manual defined the duties and responsibilities of a campus policeman and served as a code for appropriate conduct and that by agreeing to be bound by the guidelines, the plaintiff had merely agreed to properly perform his duties and nothing more.

135

C.   HOW DO YOU RESEARCH IN A.L.R.?

There is no dominant research approach for A.L.R. The following text describes two standard approaches: a primarily paper-based approach that relies on various editorial aids and a computer-based approach that relies on searching for key words.

A.L.R. in paper:

- ▶ consult the *ALR Index* (or tables of primary authorities)
- ▶ skim the prefatory statement and opening sections
- ▶ consult the article outline, index, and jurisdictional table
- ▶ read the text of the annotation
- ▶ skim the accompanying case
- ▶ consult the references section
- ▶ examine the pocket parts
- ▶ check for superseding annotations
- ▶ call the Latest Case Service

An efficient means of locating a pertinent A.L.R. annotation in paper is to use the *ALR Index,* a multivolume set encompassing the second, third, fourth, fifth, and federal series of A.L.R. The *ALR Index* is updated, so you should check the pocket part as well as the main volume.

As an alternative, if you already knew of a key primary authority, you could locate an annotation discussing that authority by consulting the following: the tables covering federal statutes, federal regulations, federal court rules, and state statutes in the last volume of the *ALR Index;* or tables covering federal cases, statutes, regulations, and rules in the *ALR Federal Tables* volumes.

Once you have located a potentially pertinent annotation, skim the prefatory statement (if there is one) and opening sections, to learn the scope of the annotation, to discern whether other annotations might be more helpful, and to obtain an overview of the topic. See Illustration 7-2 on pages 85–86. To locate pertinent portions of a lengthy annotation, consult the editorial aids at the outset of the annotation. Newer annotations have the following: article outline, index, and a jurisdiction-by-jurisdiction table of cited cases and/or statutes. Older annotations have the following: outline, index, and table of jurisdictions represented. Again, see Illustration 7-2 on pages 84–85.

As you read the text of the annotation, focus on cases in your jurisdiction, seek to discern patterns in the case law from other jurisdictions, and look for cases with factual parallels to your client's situation. In addition, you may wish to read the accompanying case; this leading or early case on the topic may be mandatory authority but more likely will be persuasive authority. In older series, the case appears before the corresponding annotation; in newer series, the cases appear at the end of the volume.

Next, consult the references section in the opening pages for cross-references to other secondary sources. See Illustration 7-2 on page 83.

The annotations in the third, fourth, fifth, and federal series are updated several ways. First, annual pocket parts contain additional text and case descriptions. See Illustration 7-3 on page 87. Second, check for a more recent annotation. The pocket part may indicate that the annotation has been superseded, or the Annotation History Table, in the tables volume of the *ALR Index*, may so indicate. Third, you may bring your research up-to-the-minute by calling the Latest Case Service "hot line" for cases decided since the last supplement. The telephone number is listed on the front covers of recent pocket parts.

Researching the Canoga case, we found in the *ALR Index* the entry "discharge from employment or office," which listed a number of annotations under the subentry "at-will employee"; one annotation addresses the "promulgation of policy, right to discharge allegedly at-will employee as affected by employer's promulgation of employment policies as to discharge." This annotation, found in volume 33 of A.L.R.4th beginning on page 120, is excerpted in this chapter's illustrations.

The Introduction (§ 1) indicates that the annotation covers a highly pertinent topic. The outline suggests that courts have used two theories—contract and estoppel—and that outcomes vary. The index points to various potentially pertinent sections, but the table of jurisdictions indicates that no New Mexico cases are covered. See Illustration 7-2 on pages 84–85. The annotation breaks cases out by divergent outcomes, specifying facts that did or did not prompt courts to find employer policies to restrict the employer's power to discharge employees. See Illustration 7-1 on page 80. The accompanying case, *Weiner v. McGraw-Hill, Inc.*, 443 N.E.2d 441 (N.Y. 1982), decided by the New York Court of Appeals in 1982, is a leading case that would nonetheless be only persuasive authority for the Canoga case.

We did find additional case descriptions in the pocket part. As shown in Illustration 7-3 on page 87, there are two cases from New Mexico, *Lukoski v. Sandia Indian Management Co.* and *Garcia v. Middle Rio Grande Conservancy District*. There was no indication that the annotation had been superseded.

ILLUSTRATION 7-2   A.L.R. Annotation Editorial Aids and Opening Sections

ANNOTATION

RIGHT TO DISCHARGE ALLEGEDLY "AT-WILL" EMPLOYEE AS AFFECTED BY EMPLOYER'S PROMULGATION OF EMPLOYMENT POLICIES AS TO DISCHARGE

by

Theresa Ludwig Kruk, J.D.

TOTAL CLIENT-SERVICE LIBRARY® REFERENCES

53 Am Jur 2d, Master and Servant §§ 34, 43–70

Annotations: See the related matters listed in the annotation, infra.

7 Am Jur Legal Forms 2d, Employment Contracts §§ 99:111, 99:121, 99:146–99:147

7 Am Jur Proof of Facts 2d 1, Retaliatory Termination of Private Employment; 11 Am Jur Proof of Facts 2d 679, Reduction or Mitigation of Damages—Employment Contract; 29 Am Jur Proof of Facts 2d 335, Wrongful Discharge of At-Will Employee

US L Ed Digest, Master and Servant § 21

ALR Digests, Master and Servant § 51

L Ed Index to Annos, Contracts; Labor and Employment; Waiver or Estoppel

ALR Quick Index, Contracts; Discharge from Employment; Estoppel and Waiver; Manuals; Master and Servant; Restitution and Implied Contracts

Federal Quick Index, Contracts; Discharge from Employment; Labor and Employment; Manuals and Handbooks; Restitution and Implied Contracts; Waiver and Estoppel

Auto-Cite®: Any case citation herein can be checked for form, parallel references, later history, and annotation references through the Auto-Cite computer research system.

Consult POCKET PART in this volume for later cases

120

ILLUSTRATION 7-2   *(continued)*

33 ALR4th   EMPLOYMENT AT WILL—RESTRAINTS ON DISCHARGE
33 ALR4th 120

**Right to discharge allegedly "at-will" employee as affected by
employer's promulgation of employment policies as to discharge**

§ 1. Introduction:
    [a] Scope
    [b] Related matters

§ 2. Background, summary, and comment:
    [a] Generally
    [b] Practice pointers

§ 3. View that right to discharge at-will employee not affected by employer's
    promulgation of policies as to discharge

§ 4. Particular theories restricting right of discharge—contract:
    [a] Right of discharge held restricted
    [b] Right of discharge held not restricted

§ 5. —Equitable estoppel

INDEX

121

ILLUSTRATION 7-2   *(continued)*

---

§ 1[a]   EMPLOYMENT AT WILL—RESTRAINTS ON DISCHARGE   33 ALR4th
                                  33 ALR4th 120

Union activities, § 5   Withdrawal of handbook by employer, § 3
Vacation pay loss, § 4[a]   Work force reduction, § 4[a]
Warning slip, § 3   "Writing up" of employee, § 4[b]

TABLE OF JURISDICTIONS REPRESENTED
Consult POCKET PART in this volume for later cases

US: §§ 3, 4[a]	**Mich:** § 4[a]
Ala: § 3	**Minn:** § 4[a]
Cal: § 5	**Mont:** § 4[b]
Del: § 3	**Neb:** § 3
DC: §§ 3, 4[a]	**NY:** §§ 4[a], 5
Fla: § 3	**NC:** § 3
Ill: §§ 4[a], 4[b]	**Or:** §§ 4[a], 4[b]
Ind: §§ 3, 4[a]	**Pa:** § 4[a]
Kan: §§ 3, 4[a]	**SD:** § 4[a]
Ky: § 4[a]	**Tex:** § 3
La: § 3	**Va:** § 3
Me: § 3	**Wis:** § 4[b]

---

§ 1. Introduction

[a] Scope

This annotation[1] collects the state and federal cases that consider whether an employer's promulgation of employment policies regarding the procedures and reasons for termination or discharge of employees[2] affects an employer's right to discharge an at-will employee at any time and for any or no reason.

This annotation includes only those cases in which an at-will employee relies upon the policy statements of his or her employer regarding termination or discharge and contends that his or her discharge was effectuated in a manner or for reasons contrary to the express general policy of the employer,[3] as opposed to personal assurances or representations by the employer, regardless of whether such policy was written or unwritten, and the employer defends against such a charge by asserting the at-will status of the employee.

[b] Related matters

Recovery for discharge from employment in retaliation for filing workers' compensation claim. 32 ALR4th 1221.

Modern status of rule that employer may discharge at-will employee for any reason. 12 ALR4th 544.

---

1. This annotation supersedes § 7 of 12 ALR4th 544.

2. For treatment of cases dealing with an at-will employee's right to severance pay as provided by an employer's general policy on severance, see 53 Am Jur 2d, Master and Servant § 81.

3. For a discussion of cases involving at-will employees who claim to have been hired as "permanent" employees or "for life," see generally 53 Am Jur 2d, Master and Servant §§ 20, 32–34. See also the annotation in 24 ALR3d 1412 entitled "Employer's misrepresentation as to prospect, or duration of, employment as actionable fraud."

122

ILLUSTRATION 7-2   *(continued)*

33 ALR4th   EMPLOYMENT AT WILL—RESTRAINTS ON DISCHARGE   § 2[a]
33 ALR4th 120

Liability for discharging at-will employee for refusing to participate in, or for disclosing, unlawful or unethical acts of employer or coemployees. 9 ALR4th 329.

Right of corporation to discharge employee who asserts right as stockholder. 84 ALR3d 1107.

Reduction in rank or authority or change of duties as breach of employment contract. 63 ALR3d 539.

Employee's arbitrary dismissal as breach of employment contract terminable at will. 62 ALR3d 271.

Employer's termination of professional athlete's services as constituting breach of employment contract. 57 ALR3d 257.

Nature of alternative employment which employee must accept to minimize damages for wrongful discharge. 44 ALR3d 629.

Employer's misrepresentation as to prospect, or duration of, employment as actionable fraud. 24 ALR3d 1412.

Elements and measure of damages in action by schoolteacher for wrongful discharge. 22 ALR3d 1047.

Liability of federal government officer or employee for causing discharge or separation of subordinate. 5 ALR Fed 961.

§ 2.   Background,   summary,   and comment

[a] Generally

The common-law rule regarding the termination of an at-will employment contract is that if the employment is not for a definite term, and if there is no contractual or statutory restriction on the right of discharge, an employer may lawfully discharge an employee whenever and for whatever cause, without incurring liability for wrongful discharge.[4] Few legal principles have been better settled than the at-will concept, whose roots date back to the 19th century laissez-faire policy of protecting freedom to contract. In recent years, however, there has been a growing trend toward a restricted application of this rule in order to comport with express and implied public policy, as well as statutory concerns. Some jurisdictions have been willing to depart from the traditional contract rule of terminability at will and to impose an implied contractual duty not to discharge an employee for reasons regarded as violative of public policy or to recognize the tortious nature of a discharge violative of public policy, whether such policy is expressly codified or implied.[5]

In keeping with this modern trend of judicial re-evaluation and legislative modification, a number of jurisdictions have held or recognized that under particular circumstances, the right of an employer to freely discharge at-will employees may be contractually restricted as a result of the promulgation of corporate employment policies specifying the proce-

---

4. Although the at-will rule is generally regarded as vesting in the employer absolute discretion to terminate employment, this "right" is actually a rule of contract construction rather than a right grounded in substantive law. Absent an express contractual provision specifying the term of employment, the duration depends upon the intention of the parties as determined from the circumstances of each case. It is still the general rule that an indefinite hiring, under circumstances that do not permit the implication of any fixed period of duration, is presumed to be terminable at the will of either party, with the burden on the party asserting a fixed period. 53 Am Jur 2d, Master and Servant §§ 27, 43.

5. See generally, the annotation in 12 ALR4th 544, for a discussion of the modern status of the at-will rule.

ILLUSTRATION 7-3   A.L.R. Annotation Pocket Part

SUPPLEMENT   33 ALR4th 120-138

that employee handbook modified employment relationship and created warning and suspension procedures which were not followed; termination procedures became amendment to employee's contract and personality, not severe offenses of insubordination or disobedience, caused employee's termination. Handbook characterized disciplinary policy regarding warnings, suspensions, and terminations as established procedure and language of handbook did nothing to alert employee that it was subject to revocation at any time or that employee should not rely on it. Lukoski v Sandia Indiana Management Co. (1988, **NM**) 748 P2d 507, 2 BNA IER Cas 1650. LC ¶ 55496, mod on other gnds 101 NJ 10, 1985 NJ 10, 499 A2d 515.

Personnel manual gives rise to implied contract, for purposes of implied contract exception to employment at will doctrine, if it controls employer-employee relationship and employee can reasonably expect employer to conform to procedures it outlines. Garcia v Middle Rio Grande Conservancy Dist. (1996, **NM**) 918 P2d 7, 11 BNA IER Cas 1328.

Employer may be bound by express statements in its policy manual limiting its otherwise unfettered right to discharge its employees. Disciplined or terminated employee may seek Article 78 review to determine whether employer contravened any of its own rules or regulations in taking that disciplinary action. Hanchard v Facilities Dev. Corp. (1995) 85 **NY2d** 638, 628 NYS2d 4, 651 NE2d 872, 10 BNA IER Cas 1004, 130 CCH LC ¶ 57921.

Employee can rebut presumption of employment at will by establishing that employee was made aware of written policy of limitation on employer's right to discharge at time employment commenced, and in accepting employment, employee relied on termination only for cause limitation. For manual or other written policy to limit employer's right to terminate, it must contain express limitation. Preston v Champion Home Builders, Inc. (1992, 3d Dept) 187 App Div 2d 795, 589 **NYS2d** 940.

To sustain cause of action for breach of employment contract, employee must demonstrate that employment manual contained clear and express limitation that employee would not be terminated or disciplined except for cause, and that employee specifically relied on this language. Charyn v National Westminster Bank, U.S.A. (1994, 2d Dept) 204 App Div 2d 676, 612 **NYS2d** 432.

At-will auditor for brokerage house who alleged he was discharged for reporting illegal money-laundering scheme possessed cause of action for breach of contract, where employ-

ment manual contained requirement that employees report misconduct and also contained reciprocal promise to protect reporters from retaliation. Mulder v Donaldson, Lufkin & Jenrette (1995, 1st Dept) 208 App Div 2d 301, 623 **NYS2d** 560, 10 BNA IER Cas 631.

Discharged employee may recover damages by establishing that employer made employee aware of its express written policy limiting its right of discharge and that employee detrimentally relied on that policy in accepting employment. Mika v. New York State Ass'n for Retarded Children, Inc., 230 A.D.2d 744, 646 **N.Y.S.2d** 168 (2d Dep't 1996).

Where employee manual in substance states that employment will continue so long as work performance is satisfactory, and employee relies on that statement by resigning from his prior employment or passing up other offers of employment, employee who is later discharged without cause may have viable claim for wrongful discharge. Mulder v Donaldson, Lufkin & Jenrette (1994, Sup) 161 Misc 2d 698, 611 **NYS2d** 1019.

Under New York law, at-will employee can have cause of action of breach of implied contract against employer where he or she is discharged in absence of circumstances or procedures specified in employer's handbook. Thus, terminated at-will executive of registered securities broker-dealer satisfied all elements of state cause of action for wrongful discharge alleging that employer's manual created implied contract of employment because it assured continued employment as long as employee did not transgress manual's provisions; that employer breached implied contract where it did not fire him for any stated ground contained in manual, but rather for no apparent or stated reason or cause, evidence indicated that no misconduct occurred before firing. Reeves v Continental Equities Corp. (1991, **SD NY**) 767 F Supp 469 (applying NY law).

Presumption that, absent agreement establishing fixed duration, employment relationship is at will does not apply when employer had promulgated policies in personnel manual specifying procedures or grounds for termination; these procedures become part of employment contract and must be followed. Thus, job security policy stated in handbook contractually bound employer and did not amount to nonbinding general statements of policy and supervisory guidelines, where policy set forth very specific and detailed procedure for work force reduction in mandatory and unqualified terms. Further, severance pay provision was explicitly invoked and followed in case of discharged employee asserting cause of action

31

> **A.L.R. in LEXIS and Westlaw:**
>
> ▶ select a Westlaw or LEXIS database
> ▶ run a key-word search (with segment restriction)
> ▶ read the annotation (updated automatically)
> ▶ pull in cases via links

Most A.L.R. volumes are available online as well: Westlaw and LEXIS offer all but the first series. The approach stated above works with some modifications online. For example, on Westlaw, a [ci(index)] command permits you to browse the index to locate a pertinent annotation. Because A.L.R. is a large source with many case descriptions and no overall topical organization (the annotations appear as issues arise), computer-based searching for key words is a sensible approach.

In both LEXIS and Westlaw, you can use Boolean or natural-language searches. Unless you can craft a very specific search, you may want to use segment restrictions. The entire A.L.R. database is very large, and several segments provide good synopses of the content of an annotation. For example, A.L.R. titles generally are complete and precise; hence a title search may succeed well. So might a search for a particular state in the jurisdiction table, or a date-restricted search.

Once you locate a pertinent annotation, you should read the annotation much as you would read an annotation in a book, because A.L.R. online closely resembles the book version. For example, once you identify a pertinent section in the article outline or index, you can move to that section by use of the embedded links. There are some differences, however. The accompanying cases from the book version are not part of the online version. New material that appears in pocket parts is merged into the original material, making the updating process more automatic. Furthermore, you will receive a notice if your annotation has been superseded and you can proceed to the new annotation via an embedded link. You can make the transition to case law research in just a moment by linking to the name of a pertinent case described in the annotation; you will then retrieve the case.

Researching the Canoga case, we ran the following search in Westlaw: [ti (employ! personnel & handbook policy manual)]. It yielded thirty annotations; the annotation excerpted in this chapter was eighth on the list.

D.   WHAT ELSE?

A.L.R. Digests: The A.L.R. digests contain synopses of cases covered in A.L.R., organized under broad alphabetical headings and topical subheadings. The digests also contain references to annotations and some other secondary sources. The topic headings in the A.L.R. digests do not correspond with the *ALR Index* headings, and most people find the *ALR Index* easier to use. A unified digest covers the third, fourth, fifth, and federal series.

Some Features of the Older Series: A.L.R.1st has its own index and digest; the same is true of A.L.R.2d. The annotations in the first series are supplemented by the *A.L.R. Blue Book of Supplemental Decisions*; A.L.R.2d annotations are updated by *A.L.R.2d Later Case Service.*

Shepard's Citations for Annotations: You would use Shepard's to determine whether a particularly useful annotation has been cited in later cases or newer A.L.R. annotations. Shepard's provides listings (but not descriptions) of such citations.

Lawyers' Edition Annotations: Annotations discussing United States Supreme Court cases on certain major topics appear in a publication called *United States Supreme Court Reports Lawyers' Edition.*

E. HOW DO YOU CITE A.L.R.?

To cite an annotation, you need to know the author's full name (if available), the title of the annotation, volume, series, beginning page number, and date. Here is an example (following Rule 16.5.5 of *The Bluebook*):

> Theresa L. Kruk, Annotation, *Right to Discharge Allegedly "At-Will" Employee as Affected by Employer's Promulgation of Employment Policies as to Discharge,* 33 A.L.R.4th 120 (1984 & Supp. 1999).

RESTATEMENTS

A. WHAT ARE RESTATEMENTS?

The Restatements are an authority unique to law. They differ from the other types of commentary in this unit in several respects. First, the Restatements have a unique purpose: to unify the common (case) law on a national basis. Second, they are written in the form of rules with explanations. Third, they are written and revised through a deliberative process by more than one expert. Fourth, although they are not themselves primary authority, some portions are adopted by courts; the adopted language then becomes primary authority in the adopting jurisdiction. Finally, Restatements cover a narrower range of subjects than other secondary sources.

The Restatements are products of the theoretical conflicts that shaped twentieth-century American jurisprudence. The immense geographical and industrial growth of the United States in the mid-nineteenth century led to an increase in litigation and case law. Legal scholars known as "the rationalists" were concerned about apparent inconsistencies in the flood of decisions, which left courts, attorneys, and citizens without a secure understanding of the law. The rationalists believed that the law consisted of immutable principles that could be expressed in an organized manner. They sought to impose this vision of consistency and order on the common law. Legal "realists," on the other hand, believed that laws were not derived from immutable laws of nature; rather the common law reflected the needs of particular litigants, the biases of judges, and the prevailing social ethic. In 1923, the rationalists mobilized, and they helped to organize the American Law Institute (ALI).

The objective of the ALI was (and continues to be) to reduce the complexity and uncertainty of American common law by promulgating one authoritative, rule-like source. The Restatements of the Law are the results of this effort. The authors of the first series of Restatements set a lofty goal: to "restate" precisely the principles of the existing common law, producing a secondary source with authority nearly that of case law. To some extent, the Restatement approach has evolved over time. In the first Restatement series, the drafters did not take into account what the law ought to be, so the Restatement's adoption of a majority rule had the potential of retarding the growth of a minority rule and inhibiting the evolution of new rules of law. However, in 1966 the ALI changed its policies to allow choice of a wise minority position.

When the ALI decides to prepare a Restatement on an area of the law, it appoints a reporter, who is an eminent scholar in the field. With the help of assistants, the reporter prepares a draft of the Restatement. A committee of advisers who are experts in the field review and revise the draft. The revised draft then is reviewed by the ALI's Council—a group of fifty or so judges, attorneys, and professors—who may refer the draft back to the reporter or approve a draft and submit it to the annual meeting of the ALI members. After ALI members have discussed and approved a draft, with or without changes, the draft is released to the public and to the legal profession for further debate. Eventually a proposed final draft is submitted to the ALI Council and membership. If the Council and then the ALI membership approve that draft, it is published in final form.

The ALI has published Restatements in three series: the first series was adopted in 1932–42, the second series in 1957–81, and the third series in 1986 to present. Note that the series designation reflects the year of adoption, not the number of times that a Restatement on a particular subject has been promulgated. Many subjects have been addressed in more than one series. For example, the Restatement of Contracts has appeared in the first and second series. Some Restatement subjects are covered for the first time in a second or third series. Here is a list of Restatement topics, series, and dates:

Subject	*Series and Date(s) of Adoption*
Agency	1st (1933)
	2d (1957)
Conflict of Laws	1st (1934)
	2d (1969, 1988)
Contracts	1st (1932)
	2d (1979)
Foreign Relations	2d (1962, 1964, 1965)
	3d (1986)
Judgments	1st (1942)
	2d (1980)
Property	1st (1936, 1940, 1944)
Landlord & Tenant	2d (1976)
Donative Transfers	2d (1981, 1984, 1987, 1990)
Mortgages	3d (1996)

Subject	Series and Date(s) of Adoption
Restitution	1st (1936)
Security	1st (1941)
Suretyship & Guaranty	3d (1995)
Torts	1st (1934, 1938, 1939) 2d (1963, 1964, 1976, 1977)
Products Liability	3d (1997)
Trusts	1st (1935) 2d (1957)
Prudent Investor Rule	3d (1990)
Unfair Competition	3d (1993)

Each Restatement is organized by chapters. The chapters are divided into topics, which in turn are divided into numbered sections. Each section begins with a Restatement rule, which is printed in boldface. A rule typically is followed by two explanatory aids: comments and illustrations. The comments clarify the scope and meaning of the Restatement rule; they also may offer insights into the rationale for it. The illustrations are examples of the application of the rule and the comments; many illustrations are based on real cases.

For some second and third series Restatements, the illustrations are followed by the reporter's notes, which typically explain the history of the rule, refer to cases that discuss the topic, identify the primary authorities on which the text and illustrations are based, and provide other useful references to primary authority and secondary sources. For some subjects, the reporter's notes are in a separate appendix volume.

As noted above, courts regularly cite and sometimes adopt Restatement sections. The appendices contain summaries of and citations to these cases.

In the Canoga case, Illustration 8-1 on pages 93–96 shows section 2 of the Restatement (Second) of Contracts. This section might help you determine if the employer's issuance of an employee handbook was a promise that could be the basis of a contract.

B.   WHY ARE RESTATEMENTS USEFUL?

The Restatements provide a well-organized discussion of the law in the form of rules, explanations, and examples. Additionally, they identify cases that have given rise to the rules or interpret the rules. Furthermore, when no primary authority supports an argument, or when existing primary authority is adverse, you may use a Restatement section to suggest what the law should be. Due to the prestige of the reporters and advisers, the Restatements are unusually credible compared to other secondary sources. As of March 15, 1999, the Restatements had been cited by the courts almost 145,000 times. 1999 A.L.I. Ann. Rep. 19. Hence, the Restatements are particularly useful as persuasive authority.

ILLUSTRATION 8-1	Restatement Rule, Comments, Illustrations, and Reporter's Note, from Restatement (Second) of Contracts

---

§ 1   **CONTRACTS, SECOND**   **Ch. 1**

Wis. L. Rev. 303; Macauley, Contract Law and Contract Research, 20 J. Legal Ed. 452 (1968); Farnsworth, The Past of Promise: An Historical Introduction to Contract, 69 Colum. L. Rev. 576 (1969); Macneil, The Many Futures of Contract, 47 So. Cal. L. Rev. 691 (1974); Macneil, Restatement, Second, of Contracts and Presentation, 60 Va. L. Rev. 589 (1974); Atiyah, Contracts, Promises and the Law of Obligations, 94 L. Q. Rev. 193 (1978); see also Leff, Contract as Thing, 19 Amer. U. L. Rev. 131 (1970).

Comments a and b. For a concise discussion of what constitutes a contract, how it can be created and its relation to tort actions for fraud, see Steinberg v. Chicago Medical School, 69 Ill.2d 320, 371 N.E.2d 634 (1977).

Comment e. Illustration 1 is new.

Comment f. Section 12 of the original Restatement defined unilateral and bilateral contracts. It has not been carried forward because of doubt as to the utility of the distinction, often treated as fundamental, between the two types. As defined in the original Restatement, "unilateral contract" included three quite different types of transaction: (1) the promise which does not contemplate a bargain, such as the promise under seal to make a gift, (2) certain option contracts, such as the option under seal (see §§ 25, 45), and (3) the bargain completed on one side, such as the loan which is to be repaid. This grouping of unlike transactions was productive of confusion.

Moreover, as to bargains, the distinction tends to suggest, erroneously, that the obligation to repay a loan is somehow different if the actual delivery of the money was preceded by an advance commitment from the obligation resulting from a simultaneous loan and commitment. It also causes confusion in cases where performance is complete on one side except for an incidental or collateral promise, as where an offer to buy goods is accepted by shipment and a warranty is implied. Finally, the effect of the distinction has been to exaggerate the importance of the type of bargain in which one party begins performance without making any commitment, as in the classic classroom case of the promise to pay a reward for climbing a flagpole.

The principal value of the distinction has been the emphasis it has given to the fact that a promise is often binding on the promisor even though the promisee is not bound by any promise. This value is retained in § 25 on option contracts. But the terms unilateral and bilateral are generally avoided in this Restatement.

§ 2.   Promise; Promisor; Promisee; Beneficiary

(1) A promise is a manifestation of intention to act or refrain from acting in a specified way, so made as to justify a promisee in understanding that a commitment has been made.

(2) The person manifesting the intention is the promisor.

ILLUSTRATION 8-1   *(continued)*

Ch. 1   MEANING OF TERMS   § 2

(3) The person to whom the manifestation is addressed is the promisee.

(4) Where performance will benefit a person other than the promisee, that person is a beneficiary.

Comment:

 a. Acts and resulting relations. "Promise" as used in the Restatement of this Subject denotes the act of the promisor. If by virtue of other operative facts there is a legal duty to perform, the promise is a contract; but the word "promise" is not limited to acts having legal effect. Like "contract," however, the word "promise" is commonly and quite properly also used to refer to the complex of human relations which results from the promisor's words or acts of assurance, including the justified expectations of the promisee and any moral or legal duty which arises to make good the assurance by performance. The performance may be specified either in terms describing the action of the promisor or in terms of the result which that action or inaction is to bring about.

 b. Manifestation of intention. Many contract disputes arise because different people attach different meanings to the same words and conduct. The phrase "manifestation of intention" adopts an external or objective standard for interpreting conduct; it means the external expression of intention as distinguished from undisclosed intention. A promisor manifests an intention if he believes or has reason to believe that the promisee will infer that intention from his words or conduct. Rules governing cases where the promisee could reasonably draw more than one inference as to the promisor's intention are stated in connection with the acceptance of offers (see §§ 19 and 20), and the scope of contractual obligations (see §§ 201, 219).

 c. Promise of action by third person; guaranty. Words are often used which in terms promise action or inaction by a third person, or which promise a result obtainable only by such action. Such words are commonly understood as a promise of conduct by the promisor which will be sufficient to bring about the action or inaction or result, or to answer for harm caused by failure. An example is a guaranty that a third person will perform his promise. Such words constitute a promise as here defined only if they justify a promisee in an expectation of some action or inaction on the part of the promisor.

 d. Promise of event beyond human control; warranty. Words which in terms promise that an event not within human control will occur may be interpreted to include a promise to answer for harm caused by the failure of the event to occur. An example is a warranty

---

See Appendix for Court Citations and Cross References

ILLUSTRATION 8-1   *(continued)*

§ 2   CONTRACTS, SECOND   Ch. 1

of an existing or past fact, such as a warranty that a horse is sound, or that a ship arrived in a foreign port some days previously. Such promises are often made when the parties are ignorant of the actual facts regarding which they bargain, and may be dealt with as if the warrantor could cause the fact to be as he asserted. It is then immaterial that the actual condition of affairs may be irrevocably fixed before the promise is made.

Words of warranty, like other conduct, must be interpreted in the light of the circumstances and the reasonable expectations of the parties. In an insurance contract, a "warranty" by the insured is usually not a promise at all; it may be merely a representation of fact, or, more commonly, the fact warranted is a condition of the insurer's duty to pay (see § 225(3)). In the sale of goods, on the other hand, a similar warranty normally also includes a promise to answer for damages (see Uniform Commercial Code § 2–715).

Illustrations:

1. A, the builder of a house, or the inventor of the material used in part of its construction, says to B, the owner of the house, "I warrant that this house will never burn down." This includes a promise to pay for harm if the house should burn down.

2. A, by a charter-party, undertakes that the "good ship Dove," having sailed from Marseilles a week ago for New York, shall take on a cargo for B on her arrival in New York. The statement of the quality of the ship and the statement of her time of sailing from Marseilles include promises to pay for harm if the statement is untrue.

e. Illusory promises; mere statements of intention. Words of promise which by their terms make performance entirely optional with the "promisor" whatever may happen, or whatever course of conduct in other respects he may pursue, do not constitute a promise. Although such words are often referred to as forming an illusory promise, they do not fall within the present definition of promise. They may not even manifest any intention on the part of the promisor. Even if a present intention is manifested, the reservation of an option to change that intention means that there can be no promisee who is justified in an expectation of performance.

On the other hand, a promise may be made even though no duty of performance can arise unless some event occurs (see §§ 224, 225(1)). Such a conditional promise is no less a promise because there is small likelihood that any duty of performance will arise, as in the case of a promise to insure against fire a thoroughly fireproof building. There

See Appendix for Court Citations and Cross References
10

ILLUSTRATION 8-1   *(continued; page omitted)*

§ 2   CONTRACTS, SECOND   Ch. 1

ise is made; as promise is defined here, the promisee might be the person to whom the manifestation of the promisor's intention is communicated. In many situations, however, a promise is complete and binding before the communication is received (see, for example, §§ 63 and 104(1)). To cover such cases, the promisee is defined here as the addressee. As to agents or purported agents of the addressee, see § 52 Comment *c*.

In the usual situation the promisee also bears other relations to the promisor, and the word promisee is sometimes used to refer to one or more of those relations. Thus, in the simple case of a loan of money, the lender is not only the addressee of the promise but also the person to whom performance is to be rendered, the person who will receive economic benefit, the person who furnished the consideration, and the person to whom the legal duty of the promisor runs. As the word promisee is here defined, none of these relations is essential.

Contractual rights of persons not parties to the contract are the subject of Chapter 14. The promisor and promisee are the "parties" to a promise; a third person who will benefit from performance is a "beneficiary." A beneficiary may or may not have a legal right to performance; like "promisee", the term is neutral with respect to rights and duties. A person who is entitled under the terms of a letter of credit to draw or demand payment is commonly called a beneficiary, but such a person is ordinarily a promisee under the present definition. See Uniform Commercial Code § 5–103.

REPORTER'S NOTE

This Section substitutes the concept of a "manifestation of intention to act . . . " for the phrase used in former § 2(1): "an undertaking . . . that something shall happen. . . . " The older definition did not identify the essential characteristics of an undertaking. See Gardner, An Inquiry Into the Principles of Contracts, 46 Harv. L. Rev. 1, 5 (1932). The present definition of promise is based on 1 Corbin, Contracts § 13 (1963 & Supp. 1980). See also 1 id. § 15; 1 Williston, Contracts § 1A (3d ed. 1957). The definitions of "promisor," "promise" and "beneficiary" are new. Compare Gardner, Massachusetts Annota-tions, Restatement of Contracts, Chapter 6, at 64 (1935).

Comment a. See Coffman Industries, Inc. v. Gorman-Taber Co., 521 S.W.2d 763 (Mo. Ct. App. 1975); Farnsworth, The Past of Promise: An Historical Introduction to Contract, 69 Colum. L. Rev. 576 (1969).

Comment d. This Comment is based on former § 2(2). Illustrations 1 and 2 are based on Illustrations 2 and 3 to former § 2.

Comment e. See Pappas v. Bever, 219 N.W.2d 720 (Iowa 1974). Illustration 3 is based on Illustration 4 to former § 2.

See Appendix for Court Citations and Cross References

On the other hand, Restatements are available only for a limited number of subjects. In addition, some commentators believe that the Restatements do not always dispassionately and accurately record existing common law, but rather state what the authors would like the rule to be or are more like a compromise between the divergent views of the participants in the drafting and approval process. Furthermore, Restatement rules do not fully reflect the varied approaches among jurisdictions. Finally, the law may evolve away from a position adopted by the Restatements more rapidly than the Restatements can reflect that development.

C.   HOW DO YOU RESEARCH IN RESTATEMENTS?

The traditional means of researching Restatements is in paper; it remains a common approach. Computer-based research can also work well; you are more likely to use an online service than a CD-ROM product for Restatements.

Restatements in paper:

▶   select an applicable Restatement subject and series

▶   use the table of contents or index

▶   examine the rules, comments, illustrations, reporter's notes

▶   read the summaries of citing cases in the appendix volumes and supplements

▶   check *Interim Case Citations*

▶   examine the citing cases

▶   consider whether to examine another series

To locate a relevant Restatement section, you must first determine which Restatement subject, if any, encompasses your research issue. Next you must determine which series on that subject will be useful in your research. The various Restatement series and their dates of adoption are listed in the list on pages 91–92. As a general rule, begin in the most recent series. As explained below in more detail, you may consider examining an earlier series if you have questions about the derivation or status of the rule in the current series.

Once you know the subject and series to use, you can locate an applicable Restatement section using either a table of contents or an index. A table of contents is located in the front of most Restatement volumes. It usually encompasses the entire subject in that series. However, for a few subjects, the table of contents covers only topics found in that particular volume, and you will have to examine the tables in multiple volumes. A one-volume comprehensive index covers all of the first series Restatements. However, the second and third series have no comprehensive index, so you must search the index for the particular Restatement. This index may be in the last subject (non-appendix) volume, or, for Restatements that span multiple volumes, there may be an index in the back of each volume covering only that volume.

Once you have located a section number, locate that section in a main subject volume (not an appendix volume or a supplement). Read the boldface Restatement rule carefully. Keep in mind that the language is the product of painstaking deliberation. It is instructive also to examine the comments, illustrations, and the reporter's notes (where available). In particular, look for illustrations paralleling your client's situation. The reporter's notes may tell you if the rule represents a choice between conflicting positions and, if so, whether the rule reflects the majority or minority position; the notes also cite to the parallel section in the previous Restatement series and provide references to primary and secondary authorities supporting the rule and illustrations.

As you read the Restatements, remember that the Restatements purport to set forth a unitary common law, not the common law of any particular jurisdiction. Your jurisdiction may not follow the Restatement rule. So, you should attempt to discern the status of the rule in your jurisdiction and its general acceptance.

You can locate cases that cite particular Restatement sections by consulting the case summaries. These summaries include the holding and citation of the citing case, as well as short commentary telling which portion of the Restatement was involved and how it was treated by the court. See Illustration 8-2 on page 100. The summaries usually appear in the appendix volume(s) of the most recent series for a subject, which typically cover all series of a particular Restatement subject. The appendix volumes typically are updated by pocket parts or supplement pamphlets. For some Restatements, the summaries appear in the pocket part of the main Restatement volume. Summaries of very recent cases and a list of the most recent cases appear in the softbound pamphlet, *Interim Case Citations to the Restatements of the Law,* which updates all of the Restatements. See Illustration 8-3 page 101.

As you examine cases citing the Restatement, keep in mind that a court may cite a rule so as to adopt it—or the court may cite the rule merely for purposes of discussion or to disagree with the Restatement rule. A court may adopt only portions of a rule, one comment but not another, a comment but not the illustration, etc. You must fully understand how the court discussed the rule.

If the Restatement you are using is a newer series and the subject was covered in an older series, you should consider whether to research the older series as well. If your jurisdiction's court has adopted the newer series rule, you probably would not research the older series. On the other hand, you probably would research the older series if you are unclear about the status of the newer series rule in your jurisdiction, especially if the newer rule varies from the older rule or the newer rule appears to be a minority rule little supported in other states. Keep in mind that the promulgation of a new

Restatement by the ALI does not by itself disturb a court's adoption of an older series rule. To locate an older series rule on the same topic as a newer series, consult the reporter's notes or a cross-reference table in the newer series.

Researching the Canoga case, we worked with the Restatement of Contracts, Second Series. We found in the table of contents multiple sections worth checking: § 1, Contract Defined; § 2, Promise; Promisor; Promisee; Beneficiary; and § 4, How a Promise May Be Made. Similarly, we found the same leads in the index; for example, it has an entry for "promise, defined."

Section 2 defines "promise." Comment b notes that different people may understand the same language differently and indicates that the proper focus is the "manifestation of intention" by the promisor. The reporter's note explains that "manifestation of intention" is new language, indicates that the corresponding section in the first series was section 2, and lists a handful of influential cases and secondary authorities.

The Restatement appendix volumes, their updates, and *Interim Case Citations* provided a wealth of case citations. Illustration 8-2 on page 100 shows the summaries of several cases with facts somewhat parallel to the Canoga case, although none are from New Mexico. In Illustration 8-3 on page 101, a page from the *Interim Case Citations*, the table for section 2 shows one case citation, not from New Mexico.

If the point made in section 2 appeared to be of sufficient importance, it would be wise to consult the first Restatement on the topic. The current Restatement rule appears to be well grounded and widely accepted, but there are no New Mexico decisions citing it, and it does represent a change from the first Restatement (as explained in the reporter's notes).

Restatements in Westlaw and LEXIS:

▶ select a Westlaw or LEXIS database, probably for a specific Restatement and series

▶ skim the table of contents, or perform a key-word or natural-language search

▶ examine the rule, comments, illustrations, reporter's notes

▶ review the case summaries

▶ use embedded links to pull up cases

An alternative to the paper-based approach is online research. Some older-series Restatements and current-series Restatements are available in LEXIS and Westlaw. The LEXIS and Westlaw databases contain the complete text of the rules, comments, illustrations, reporter's notes, and summaries of cases that have interpreted Restatement sections. You can search a database that covers all Restatement subjects, or you can select a database for a specific Restatement and series. Searching all Restatement subjects may be valuable

ILLUSTRATION 8-2   Restatement Case Summaries, from Restatement (Second) of Contracts Appendix

Ch. 1   CITATIONS TO RESTATEMENT, SECOND   § 2

injustice can be avoided only by enforcement. Continental Air Lines, Inc. v. Keenan, 731 P.2d 708, 712.

Hawaii, 1986. Cit. in case cit. in sup. A federal court of appeals certified a question to this court as to whether an airline's employment manual constituted a contract enforceable by the employees. This court answered affirmatively that an employer is held to the policies set forth in an employment manual because it constitutes a promise. The court reasoned that announcing employment policies in a manual manifested an intent to abide by them, and that because employees could not selectively choose by which policies to abide, the employer should be similarly bound. Kinoshita v. Canadian Pacific Airlines, Ltd., 68 Hawaii 594, 724 P.2d 110, 117.

Mass.1986. Quot. in sup., cit. in sup. A driver injured in an automobile accident sued the other driver's insurance agent, alleging that the agent was negligent in failing to fulfill his preaccident promise to the insured to obtain optional liability coverage on his motor vehicle. The superior court granted the agent's motion for dismissal. The plaintiff's application for direct appellate review was granted, and this court reversed and remanded. The court held that, unlike an incidental beneficiary who was owed no duty and had no right to bring an action for breach of contract, the injured driver was an intended beneficiary of the alleged agreement for optional liability coverage between the insured and his agent, and was thus owed a duty by the insured's agent and entitled to bring an action for the agent's breach of contract. The court reasoned that the injured driver was an intended beneficiary because he was to receive the amount of his judgment against the insured, up to the limit of the optional insurance, as a result of the contract between the insured and the insurance agent. Flattery v. Gregory, 397 Mass. 143, 489 N.E.2d 1257, 1261.

Mass.App.1985. Quot. in sup. Prospective tenants brought an action against the building owner for disavowance of a lease. This court affirmed a judgment awarding the tenants compensatory and punitive damages. The court held that the owner's misrepresentations of the true situation were calculated to make the tenants conclude that only a bureaucratic formality remained to complete the lease and that such misrepresentations worked an estoppel in favor of the tenants. Greenstein v. Flatley, 19 Mass.App. 351, 474 N.E.2d 1130, 1134.

N.D.1986. Cit. in case quot. in sup. A discharged at-will employee sued her employer for wrongful termination on the ground that the employer did not follow the progressive discipline policy provisions of its employee handbook. The trial court granted summary judgment to the defendant. Affirming, this court held that the employer had clearly and conspicuously stated that the handbook was not to be construed as a contract. The court reasoned that the employer had not acted or refrained from acting in a specified way so as to justify an understanding that a commitment had been made. Bailey v. Perkins Restaurants, Inc., 398 N.W.2d 120, 122.

N.D.1987. Cit. in case quot. in disc. A charge nurse assigned to the position of in-service director of individual resident care plans sued her employer and immediate supervisor for breach of employment contract, after being relieved of her in-service director duties. This court affirmed the trial court's grant of summary judgment to the defendants, holding that the personnel policy handbook did not constitute an employment contract and that the disclaimer in the handbook's closing statement preserved the presumption that the plaintiff was an at-will employee. The court said that, although an employer may be bound when the employer makes a unilateral objective manifestation of intent, creating in the employee an expectation and in the employer an obligation of treatment, here the employer's disclaimer negated any such manifestation or creation. Eldridge v. Evan. Luth. Good Sam. Soc., 417 N.W.2d 797, 799.

Ohio App.1984. Cit. in case quot. in disc. Employees sued their former employer to recover severance benefits. On appeal of the lower court's grant of summary judgment in favor of the employer, this court held that the sale of the company by the former employer triggered the employees' rights to severance pay pursuant to their employee manual, and that the agree-

Abbreviations: cit.—cited; com.—comment; fol.—followed; quot.—quoted;
sec.—section; subsec.—subsection; sup.—support.

37

ILLUSTRATION 8-3	Recent Case Citations, from *Interim Case Citations to the Restatements of the Law*

RECENT CASE CITATIONS

CONTRACTS 2D

Section 2

Kay–Cee Enterprises, Inc. v. Amoco Oil, Co., 45 F.Supp.2d 840, 847

Section 3

Braddock v. Madison County, 34 F.Supp.2d 1098, 1104

Pacific Preferred Properties, Inc. v. Moss, 84 Cal.Rptr.2d 500, 504

Section 4

Canter v. West Pub. Co., Inc., 31 F.Supp.2d 1193, 1201

Section 6

Grigerik v. Sharpe, 247 Conn. 293, 315, 721 A.2d 526, 537

Section 7

LeGault v. Erickson, 70 Cal.App.4th 369, 82 Cal.Rptr.2d 692, 695

Yang Ming Transport Corp. v. Oceanbridge Shipping Intern., Inc., 48 F.Supp.2d 1032, 1043

Section 9

Pacific Preferred Properties, Inc. v. Moss, 84 Cal.Rptr.2d 500, 503

Section 17

Braddock v. Madison County, 34 F.Supp.2d 1098, 1104

Johnson Enterprises of Jacksonville, Inc. v. FPL Group, 162 F.3d 1290, 1311

Weston Securities Corp. v. Aykanian, 46 Mass.App.Ct. 72, 78, 703 N.E.2d 1185, 1190

Section 19

Buesing v. United States, 42 Fed.Cl. 679, 696

Section 24

Arenberg v. Central United Life Ins. Co., 18 F.Supp.2d 1167, 1174

Retrofit Partners I, L.P. v. Lucas Industries, Inc., 47 F.Supp.2d 256, 262

Section 26

Retrofit Partners I, L.P. v. Lucas Industries, Inc., 47 F.Supp.2d 256, 262

Section 27

Johnson Intern., Inc. v. City of Phoenix, 967 P.2d 607, 611

Naimie v. Cytozyme Laboratories, Inc., 174 F.3d 1104, 1112

Section 30

Quality Truck and Auto Sales, Inc. v. Yassine, 730 So.2d 1164, 1169

Section 31

Arenberg v. Central United Life Ins. Co., 18 F.Supp.2d 1167, 1175

Section 32

Arenberg v. Central United Life Ins. Co., 18 F.Supp.2d 1167, 1175

Section 36

Shelton v. Sloan, 977 P.2d 1012, 1016

Section 38

Guzman v. Visalia Community Bank, 84 Cal.Rptr.2d 581, 584

Section 45

Phillips v. Cigna Investments, Inc., 27 F.Supp.2d 345

Section 57

HLO Land Ownership Associates Ltd. Partnership v. City of Hartford, 727 A.2d 1260, 1264

Section 59

Guzman v. Visalia Community Bank, 84 Cal.Rptr.2d 581, 584

Guzman v. Visalia Community Bank, 83 Cal.Rptr.2d 665, 669

Rule v. Tobin, 719 A.2d 869, 873

Section 71

DeMauro v. Szukis, 594 N.W.2d 419

Fleming & Hall, Ltd. v. Cope, 30 F.Supp.2d 459, 464

GenCorp, Inc. v. American Intern. Underwriters, 167 F.3d 249, 256

GenCorp, Inc. v. American Intern. Underwriters, 178 F.3d 804, 812

Section 73

Singleton, United States v., 165 F.3d 1297, 1314

Section 79

Johnson Enterprises of Jacksonville, Inc. v. FPL Group, 162 F.3d 1290, 1312

Lex Associates, State v., 730 A.2d 38, 43

Section 90

Bouwens v. Centrilift, 974 P.2d 941, 947

720

if you are uncertain which subject is appropriate, but this approach often is unwieldy. Generally, you should search a specific Restatement and series.

To locate a pertinent section, although the indexes are not available online, you can review the tables of contents. You also can search for key words online or conduct a natural-language search, in the entire Restatement or in portions, such as the rules themselves or the case summaries. Once you have located a pertinent section, you can read the rule and any accompanying comments, illustrations, or reporter's notes, much as you did in paper. To determine the courts' response to a Restatement section, you may read the case summaries online, and you then can use the embedded links to move directly to the full text of the citing case.

Researching the Canoga case, we selected LEXIS' Restatement (Second) of Contracts case citations database and used this natural-language search: [Does an employment handbook give rise to a promise that forms a contract?]. We retrieved a long list of cases, most pertaining to one of several sections, including section 2. To retrieve that section (the rule and its explanatory material), we searched for section 2 in the rules database. To retrieve pertinent cases citing section 2, we could use the links from the initial search's case citation list.

D.   WHAT ELSE?

Special Features of the Restatements: Some Restatements have the following features which permit you to link Restatement sections to other research materials: (1) tables of cases and statutes cited, from which you may be able to find a pertinent Restatement section by looking up a leading case or a statute; (2) citations to A.L.R. annotations that pertain to the topic of a particular Restatement section; and (3) references to West key numbers, an important tool in case law research (see Chapter 10).

Work in Progress: You can learn about work in progress on Restatements in the ALI's current *Annual Report,* the ALI's annual *Proceedings,* or *The ALI Reporter,* the Institute's quarterly newsletter. In addition, the American Law Institute Microfiche Publications set contains, among other documents, the drafts of many Restatements.

Shepard's Restatement of the Law Citations: This tool lists cases, A.L.R. annotations, and selected legal periodical articles and treatises that cite each Restatement section, comment, and illustration. It usually is within a month of being current. Generally, the only information provided about the citing source is the citation, which imparts much less information than the Restatement summaries provide. However, Shepard's is more current than the summaries and covers a wider range of secondary sources.

E.   HOW DO YOU CITE RESTATEMENTS?

To cite a Restatement, you need to know the subject, series, and date the Restatement was adopted or amended. Sometimes you may seek to cite a specific comment, illustration, or reporter's note, or to a tentative draft. Here are some examples (following Rule 12.8.5 of *The Bluebook*):

Restatement (Second) of Contracts § 2 (1979)
Restatement (Second) of Contracts § 2 cmt. a (1979)
Restatement (Second) of Contracts § 2 cmt. d, illus. 1 (1979)
Restatement (Second) of Contracts § 2 (Tentative Draft No. 1, 1964)

ADDITIONAL SECONDARY SOURCES AND STRATEGY

A. Additional Secondary Sources
B. Research Strategy for Secondary Sources

A.   ADDITIONAL SECONDARY SOURCES

In addition to the major secondary sources described in the other chapters in this unit, four other categories of secondary sources merit mention.

Casebooks.   Casebooks are course texts containing cases and supplementary materials, such as statutes, regulations, excerpts from articles and treatises, notes by the author, and problems. While a casebook may provide useful starting references, it is not designed as a reference tool.

Practice Materials.   After researching and analyzing a client's problem, a lawyer often moves on to various activities designed to solve that problem, such as drafting documents or litigating a case. Some secondary sources provide practical advice and model forms for such activities. These sources may also provide an overview of the law behind the advice or form. Examples of such sources with broad coverage are *American Jurisprudence Trials, American Jurisprudence Proof of Facts, Causes of Action, American Jurisprudence Legal Forms 2d, American Jurisprudence Pleading and Practice Forms Annotated,* and *West's Legal Forms 2d.* There are numerous subject-specific sources of this type, such as form books focused on corporate or tax law. Practice materials are rarely used as authority for the legal propositions they state, but they can provide a helpful bridge between legal analysis and actions to be taken on the client's behalf.

Pattern Jury Instructions.   At the end of a jury trial, the jury is instructed on the law applicable to the case. Often the instructions are drawn from a set of pattern jury instructions or a jury instruction guide (JIG). JIGs typically are written by private authors (professors or lawyers), a group of judges, a bar association committee, or a combination of these. An instruction states the rule in a form paralleling a Restatement section and typically is supplemented by notes stating the source of the instruction and discussing the pertinent cases and statutes. Thus JIGs can be useful not only when you are seeking sample instructions in a trial setting, but also in nonlitigation settings.

CLE Materials.   Many states require lawyers to take courses to continuously improve their skills. Presenters at continuing legal education (CLE) programs prepare written materials containing outlines, checklists, sample documents, and important cases and statutes. CLE materials can be useful because they address practical aspects of a topic, typically provide significant detail about a specific jurisdiction's law, and may provide the first discussion of new developments. They are rarely cited.

B.   RESEARCH STRATEGY FOR SECONDARY SOURCES

1.   Choosing Among Types of Secondary Sources

All of the secondary sources covered in this unit serve dual functions as both commentary sources and finding tools for primary authority and other secondary sources. You do not need to use every source on every research project. But how do you know when to use which source, so as to produce comprehensive, correct, and credible research and yet avoid costly excessive effort?

Exhibit 9.1 on pages 106–107 is designed to help you see more clearly the differences among these sources. Although the characteristics are grouped under the four research goals (cost-effectiveness, comprehensiveness, etc.), many of the characteristics relate to more than one research goal. For instance, accuracy and lack of bias relate to both correctness and credibility of research. As you fill in the chart, you may notice some patterns.

A wider scope of coverage usually comes at the expense of detailed coverage. As examples, encyclopedias try to cover the full range of legal topics in general terms, while A.L.R. annotations and legal periodical articles seek to give detailed coverage of certain significant issues. The generality of an encyclopedia can be helpful at the outset of a research project when you need big-picture information. A narrow yet pertinent A.L.R. annotation or legal periodical article may be more helpful when you have come to focus on a well-defined question.

Some sources excel at providing a coherent and comprehensive overview of a subject that is fairly static; others excel at providing a shorter analysis of targeted hot topics. For example, periodicals and A.L.R. annotations are published periodically rather than as a set, so they are better able to respond

EXHIBIT 9.1	Secondary Source Factors

	Correctness			Comprehensiveness			
	Accuracy, Lack of Bias	*Attention to Current Topics*	*Updating Means & Frequency*	*Breadth of Topics Covered*	*Depth of Coverage of Each Topic*	*Attention to Rules, Facts, & Principles*	*Description Only, or Critique Too*
Encyclopedias							
Periodicals							
A.L.R. Annotations							
Treatises							
Restatements							

quickly to the changing profile of the law than are encyclopedias and Restatements.

Sources written by staff members of publishers tend to differ in nature from those produced other ways. The former tend to be descriptive, the latter analytical and critical. Not coincidentally, the citability of sources varies accordingly. Treatises and periodicals, especially those written by recognized experts, are quite citable, and Restatements, promulgated by a group of experts in a deliberative process, are highly citable.

2.   Choosing Among Sources or Sections

When you use an index, table of contents, or key-word search in a secondary source to find pertinent material, you may generate a long list of potentially pertinent sources or sections. If you plow through a list of possible sources in no particular order, you may find yourself reading more material than you need to; this is not cost-effective research. Instead, you first should rank your sources by how much promise they show. Give high priority to the leads with your research terms in their titles and subject descriptions. Pursue sources that appear narrowly focused on your research topic before you pursue ones with a broader focus. If you come across more than one reference to a source, pursue that source first.

| EXHIBIT 9.1 | (continued) |

	Credibility				Cost-Effectiveness		
	Reputation of Publisher(s) or Book	*Reputation of Author(s)*	*Clarity, persua-siveness*	*Other Strengths & Weaknesses*	*Type of Organization (alphabetical, topical, serial)*	*Access Methods (index, table of contents, etc.)*	*Connections to Other Research Tools*
Encyclopedias							
Periodicals							
A.L.R. Annotations							
Treatises							
Restatements							

3.   Deciding When to Cite Secondary Sources

As you research, keep in mind which sources you eventually will be able to cite in the final written product embodying your research. You should cite primary authority—cases, statutes, administrative materials, rules of proce-dure—whenever possible. Moreover, you should never rely on secondary sources without investigating and reading the related primary authority. Only by reading the full text of primary authority will you get the full flavor of the law and detect ambiguities, misinterpretations, and perhaps even mistakes made by the commentary writer.

Secondary sources are cited for several purposes. A secondary source may be cited if primary authority does not support a proposition. Secondary sources can be cited for some general propositions that do not require primary authority citation, such as a statement about the number of jurisdictions adopting a certain rule of law. A secondary source also could be cited for its criticism or policy analysis of an established rule of law.

Never cite finding tools, such as library catalogs and periodical indexes.

CASE LAW

In the United States legal system, there are many sources of law: cases decided by courts; constitutions and statutes passed by legislatures; regulations and decisions issued by agencies; rules of procedure and practice created by courts and legislatures. Furthermore, law is made at the federal, state, and local levels. This unit is the first of four discussing research into the law itself, or primary authority; it focuses on the cases decided by courts.

This unit has two chapters. Chapter 10 explains what cases are and why they are so important in legal research; it then covers various ways of identifying and obtaining pertinent cases. Chapter 11 covers a critical next step in case law research: citing a case to determine the case's status and to expand your research.

This unit continues to illustrate the research of the Canoga case stated on pages 3–4. One of the issues in that case (suggested by the research in secondary sources presented in Unit II) is whether the orchestra breached its contract with Ms. Canoga when it terminated her employment without following the procedures stated in the handbook. This unit focuses on that issue.

A note about terminology: The term "case" has several meanings for lawyers: a matter handled on behalf of a client, a dispute that is litigated in the courts, and the decision of a court. This book uses the term in all three senses.

REPORTERS, DIGESTS, AND THEIR ALTERNATIVES

A. WHAT IS A CASE?

Courts decide cases for two essential purposes. First, the decision provides a peaceful and principled resolution to a dispute the parties were unable to resolve otherwise. Second, the decision serves as a guideline for participants in future similar situations as they conduct their affairs or resolve their own disputes. Both purposes are served by the court's written explanation of the case's facts, the outcome, and the reasoning behind the outcome.

1. How Does a Case Come to Be Decided?

Courts are reactive institutions. They resolve disputes brought to them by litigants; they do not render legal opinions on issues unconnected to actual disputes. The lawyers for the litigants bring the facts to the court's attention, frame the issues, and develop the arguments on both sides.

A dispute enters litigation when one party, the plaintiff, sues the other, the defendant. (Complex cases may involve more than two parties.) The case is handled initially by a trial court, typically called a "district court." This court provides the forum for presentation of the facts to a jury or judge, determination of the facts in dispute, and application of the law to the facts to yield an initial resolution of the dispute. Many cases are, of course, resolved by the parties themselves. Others are decided by the court. This decision may come through trial, at which witnesses testify orally and documents and items are reviewed. Or it may take place through motion practice, in which the judge decides the case before trial. For example, the judge may dismiss the case early in the proceedings, with little development of the facts, if the plaintiff has sued on a theory without adequate legal support.

A party that loses in whole or in part in the trial court may appeal. The party bringing the appeal is the appellant or petitioner, while the party defending against the appeal is the appellee or respondent. Appellate proceedings differ from trial court proceedings. The appellate court relies on the record of the trial court proceedings along with the written and oral arguments of the lawyers. Cases are decided by panels of three or more judges. The panel may be drawn from the court's membership, or the case may be heard by the entire court en banc.

There may be one or two tiers of appellate courts. In the typical two-tier appellate structure, the judges of the intermediate court, typically called the "court of appeals," review the trial court's handling of the case for reversible errors. The justices of the highest court, typically titled the "supreme court," conduct a secondary review for errors, but focus primarily on the development of legal doctrine. Typically, appeal to the intermediate court is as of right, while the supreme court affords discretionary review. In a simpler one-tier structure, the sole appeals court handles both appellate functions and reviews all appeals.

2.   How Are Court Systems Structured?

The federal court system is a complex court system with three tiers. The federal trial courts are called "United States District Courts"; each state has one to four district courts, each covering part or all of the state. The intermediate appellate courts are called "United States Courts of Appeals"; there are eleven numbered circuits, each covering several states, and the District of Columbia Circuit. See Exhibit 10.1 on page 113. The United States Supreme Court hears cases on discretionary review from the courts of appeals. Furthermore, specialized trial and appeals courts exist in such areas as bankruptcy and international trade.

The New Mexico state court system (which would handle the Canoga case, if it were a real case) is somewhat simpler. The trial courts are called "district courts." The New Mexico Court of Appeals handles appeals from all district courts. The highest court is the New Mexico Supreme Court. New Mexico's system is typical for state courts.

Table 1.1 of *The Bluebook: A Uniform System of Citation* lists the courts for United States jurisdictions.

| EXHIBIT 10.1 | Federal Circuit Map (*1999 Winter Judicial Staff Directory*) |

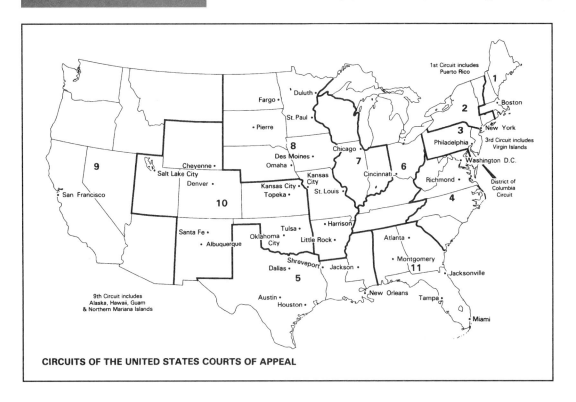

CIRCUITS OF THE UNITED STATES COURTS OF APPEAL

3.   What Does a Published Case Look Like?

Most published cases follow a fairly standard framework, labeled in the margins of Illustration 10-1 on pages 115–118, which shows the case of *Lukoski v. Sandia Indian Management Co.* The opening block includes the names of the parties and their positions in the litigation (item 2), the court deciding the case (item 4), the case's docket number (item 3), and the date of decision (item 5). The opening block also may contain a parallel citation (item 1); parallel citations are discussed in Parts C and E of this chapter.

Following the opening block are several brief paragraphs describing the main points in the case. There may be a summary, typically called a "syllabus," written by the court itself or by the court's staff as well as material written by the publisher's editorial staff. The publisher's editorial matter may include a "synopsis," a one-paragraph overview of the facts and outcome (item 6), and "headnote" paragraphs, each describing a discrete legal point made in the case (item 7). You should not view any of this material as legal authority; the opinion itself is the legal authority. The lawyers handling the case appear next (item 8).

Of course, the largest portion of the published case is comprised of the court's opinion. Each opinion begins with the name of the judge or justice who wrote the opinion (item 9). ("Judge" refers to a jurist of a trial court or intermediate appellate court; high court jurists are "justices.") The text of the opinion (item 10) typically includes a summary of the facts of the case and the course of the litigation, the court's holding, and its reasoning. The holding is the legal outcome of the case; it may be understood in procedural terms (for example, the lower court's ruling is affirmed) and in substantive terms (for example, the defendant is liable for breach of contract and must pay damages). The reasoning typically encompasses references to and discussion of pertinent legal authorities, analysis of how the law applies to the facts of the case, and perhaps discussion of public policies. The court also may opine about a situation not squarely before the court; this material is called "obiter dicta" (or "dictum" in the singular) and is not as authoritative as the rest of the opinion.

If the court consists of more than one judge, there is, of course, the potential for disagreement and multiple opinions. The opinion garnering more than half of the votes is the majority opinion; it resolves the case. A dissent (item 12) expresses the view of judges who would have reached a different result in the case. A concurrence expresses the view of judges who favor the majority's result, but for different reasons. If no opinion garners over half of the votes, the opinion garnering the largest number of votes, the plurality opinion, generally is the most influential and resolves the dispute between the parties.

Lukoski is a case you probably would read if you were researching the Canoga case. In Illustration 10-1 on pages 115–118, note that *Lukoski* was decided by the New Mexico Supreme Court on January 7, 1988, and bore the docket number 16462. Scott Lukoski, the plaintiff-appellee, sued the Sandia Indian Management Company, the defendant-appellant. Mr. Lukoski, a manager, was terminated for poor interpersonal dealings, yet the employer did not follow the suspension procedures for less serious misconduct that were outlined in its handbook. The case was tried to the judge, who ruled in favor of the employee and awarded him money damages. The case then proceeded to the New Mexico Supreme Court because contract cases did not go to the court of appeals at that time. The supreme court affirmed. Relying on various state and federal decisions, the court reasoned that the handbook language about suspensions was enforceable as a contract and Mr. Lukoski's difficulty in interpersonal dealings should have been handled through the suspension process. Justice Stowers dissented; he would have ruled that the interpersonal problems were so severe as to permit immediate termination under the disciplinary procedures provision of the handbook.

ILLUSTRATION 10-1   *Lukoski* Case, from *Pacific Reporter 2d*

LUKOSKI v. SANDIA INDIAN MANAGEMENT CO.   N. M. **507**
Cite as 748 P.2d 507 (N.M. 1988)

court's finding of damages, it is our opinion that an "as is" clause provides absolute protection to a seller such as Horizon only when the buyer and seller possess equal knowledge of the property. Here, while Lambert's knowledge of the property was equal to that of Horizon's insofar as most essentials of the contract were concerned, Lambert relied on Horizon for its knowledge of the total acreage in the property, and for such information as would have informed him about the realignment of Golf Course Road. Hence the trial court did not err in finding damages as to the realignment of Golf Course Road despite the "as is" clause. *See Archuleta v. Kopp,* 90 N.M. 273, 562 P.2d 834 (Ct.App.), *cert. dismissed,* 90 N.M. 636, 567 P.2d 485 (1977).

THE ISSUE OF THE ARROYO

[5] If as to the issue of the realignment of Golf Course Road and the total number of acres conveyed the parties were not in possession of equal knowledge, when the issue of the arroyo is raised, it is clear that Lambert did have knowledge of the property equal to that of Horizon. Indeed, it appears from the testimony of past officers of Horizon that Lambert's knowledge as to the arroyo may in some respects have been superior to that of Horizon. Lambert's principal argument against the terms of paragraph 6 of the contract insofar as it applies to the arroyo is that he talked to Horizon's legal counsel before signing the contract and was told that "natural drainageway" did not refer to the arroyo, but referred to a swale running north and south across the property.

Yet, the court found in its findings of fact that Lambert (1) "read and agreed to all the terms and conditions of the Contract," (2) "had personal knowledge of, and had inspected and investigated" the property before entering into the contract, (3) that George Lambert "is a knowledgeable and sophisticated real estate broker with 20 years of experience" and that he had available to him certain engineering drainage studies dealing with the problems of the arroyo, and (4) "[a]n Arroyo is a natural drainageway." We have no reason to dis-

pute any of these findings since they are all supported by substantial evidence. "[T]he circumstances surrounding the Agreement, the import of that Agreement as a whole, and the undisputed parol evidence of the parties show that [Lambert's] right to acquire [Horizon's] interests was not conditioned upon . . ." [an interpretation of "natural drainageway" as a "swale".] *Schaefer v. Hinkle,* 93 N.M. 129, 131, 597 P.2d 314, 316 (1979); *see also Smith v. Price's Creameries,* 98 N.M. 541, 544, 650 P.2d 825, 828 (1982), which likewise involved the issue of a conflict between contractual language and alleged oral assurances modifying the contractual language.

The judgment of the trial court is affirmed.

IT IS SO ORDERED.

WALTERS and RANSOM, JJ., concur.

106 N.M. 664

Scott J.L. LUKOSKI, Plaintiff–Appellee,

v.

SANDIA INDIAN MANAGEMENT COMPANY, Defendant–Appellant.

No. 16462.

Supreme Court of New Mexico.

Jan. 7, 1988.

Former general manager brought action against former employer for wrongful discharge. The District Court, Bernalillo County, William W. Deaton, D.J., entered judgment in favor of manager. Employer appealed. The Supreme Court, Ransom, J., held that evidence established that employee handbook amended employment contract and that employer breached contract by failing to comply with warning and suspension procedures.

Notes: 1. Parallel citation   4. Court
2. Parties   5. Date of decision
3. Docket number   6. Publisher's synopsis

ILLUSTRATION 10-1   *(continued)*

---

508 N.M.   748 PACIFIC REPORTER, 2d SERIES

Affirmed.

Stowers, J., dissented and filed opinion.

1. Trial ⟺392(1)

Defendant waived specific findings of fact on issues on which it failed to tender requested findings. SCRA 1986, Rule 1–052, subd. B(1)(f).

2. Master and Servant ⟺40(3)

Evidence supported trial court's conclusions that termination procedures in employee handbook amended general manager's employment contract, that handbook created warning and suspension procedures which were not followed, and that personality, rather than insubordination, caused employment termination; handbook characterized disciplinary policy regarding warnings, suspensions, and terminations as established procedure; and handbook did not indicate that it was subject to revocation at any time or that employees should not rely on it.

Grammer & Grammer, David A. Grammer, III, Albuquerque, for defendant-appellant.

Turpen & Wolfe, Donald C. Turpen, Albuquerque, for plaintiff-appellee.

OPINION

RANSOM, Justice.

Scott J.L. Lukoski brought a wrongful discharge action against his employer, Sandia Indian Management Co. (SIMCO). Lukoski had been employed as general manager of the Sandia Pueblo bingo operation. In a bench trial, the court decided that SIMCO violated the termination procedures prescribed for "less serious" offenses by an employee handbook. For salary due on the remaining term of his one-year oral contract, Lukoski was awarded $18,629.05. We affirm.

The court found that, in October 1983, Lukoski and SIMCO entered into a one-year oral employment agreement under which Lukoski would provide services as the general manager of a bingo hall opera-

tion for a specified annual salary plus commission. There was no written agreement between the parties. In February 1984, SIMCO distributed to all employees an employee handbook and requested each to sign the last page as verification of receipt, acknowledgement of acceptance, and agreement to conform with the stated policies and procedures. After Lukoski signed the back page as requested, it was placed in his personnel file. The court concluded that:

> The parties amended the oral employment contract * * * when [SIMCO] proffered, and [Lukoski] signed, [the] Employee's Handbook containing new duties and obligations on the part of employee and employer over and above said oral contract, including Rules to be obeyed by [Lukoski] and a termination procedure to be followed by [SIMCO].

[1] Although we determine the above-quoted language is a finding of ultimate fact, rather than a conclusion of law, that is of no consequence. *See Hoskins v. Albuquerque Bus Co.*, 72 N.M. 217, 382 P.2d 700 (1963); *Wiggs v. City of Albuquerque*, 57 N.M. 770, 263 P.2d 963 (1953). SIMCO challenges this finding and for the first time on appeal raises two other issues. First, it claims that Lukoski, as general manager, was not the type of employee intended to be covered by the handbook. Distribution to all employees with request for signatures constituted evidence to the contrary, and resolution of any ambiguity regarding management personnel would have been a specific question of fact. *See Shaeffer v. Kelton*, 95 N.M. 182, 619 P.2d 1226 (1980). Second, SIMCO claims that any breach was not material because it neither went to the substance of the contract nor defeated the object of the parties. Materiality is likewise a specific question of fact. *See Bisio v. Madenwald (In re Estate of Bisio)*, 33 Or.App. 325, 576 P.2d 801 (1978). As the contract stood after amendment, it was not materiality, as argued by SIMCO, but rather severity of offense that was at issue under the termination procedures. In any event, by failing to tender requested findings, SIMCO waived specific

---

Notes: 7. Headnotes   11. Bracketed headnote
  7a. Topic and key number   reference
    8. Counsels' names
    9. Justice who wrote majority opinion
   10. Majority opinion

ILLUSTRATION 10-1   *(continued)*

LUKOSKI v. SANDIA INDIAN MANAGEMENT CO.   N.M. **509**
Cite as 748 P.2d 507 (N.M. 1988)

findings on these fact issues. SCRA 1986, 1–052(B)(1)(f).

[2] There is substantial evidence supporting the court's findings of ultimate fact that the termination procedures became an amendment to Lukoski's contract, and that personality—not the severe offenses of insubordination or disobedience—was the cause for termination. He was terminated without warning or suspension for a cause not so severe as to constitute cause for immediate termination. His personality and interpersonal dealings were found by the court to create an atmosphere of fear and anxiety and bad morale among employees and managers.

Relying only on *Ellis v. El Paso Natural Gas Co.,* 754 F.2d 884 (10th Cir.1985), the thrust of SIMCO's appeal is that the language of the employee handbook is "too indefinite to constitute a contract" and lacks "contractual terms which might evidence the intent to form a contract." It maintains that the parties did not conduct themselves as if the employee handbook was to govern Lukoski or as if they expected it to form the basis of a contractual relationship. In support of its position, SIMCO refers to the disciplinary action, suspension, and warning provisions,[1] and argues that the language of the termination policy is ambiguous and contains no required policy for termination.

SIMCO's argument, however, overlooks the handbook's characterization of the disciplinary policy regarding warnings, suspensions and terminations as "an *estab-*

lished procedure regarding suspension of problem employees and termination for those who cannot conform to Company Policy." (Emphasis added.) Moreover, the language of the handbook does nothing to alert an employee against placing reliance on any statement contained therein or against viewing such discipline and termination policy as only a unilateral expression of SIMCO's intention that is subject to revocation or change at any time, in any manner, at the pleasure of SIMCO. To the contrary, from the language of the handbook and the conduct of SIMCO in adopting the policy, it could properly be found that the policy was part of the employment agreement.

Whether an employee handbook has modified the employment relationship is a question of fact "to be discerned from the totality of the parties' statements and actions regarding the employment relationship." *Wagenseller v. Scottsdale Memorial Hosp.,* 147 Ariz. 370, 383, 710 P.2d 1025, 1038 (1985) (en banc).

Evidence relevant to this factual decision includes the language used in the personnel manual as well as the employer's course of conduct and oral representations regarding it. We do not mean to imply that all personnel manual will become part of employment contracts. Employers are certainly free to issue no personnel manual at all or to issue a personnel manual that clearly and conspicuously tells their employees that the manual is not part of the employment contract and that their jobs are termina-

---

1. The referenced handbook provisions state:
OTHER DISCIPLINARY ACTION:
In order to protect the good employees [sic] jobs and Sandia Indian Bingo, there is an established procedure regarding suspension of problem employees and termination for those who can not conform to Company Policy. Suspensions without pay may be given to employees who violate company policies. There are violations which are so severe [including insubordination and disobedience] that immediate termination may be necessary....
SUSPENSIONS:
Suspension without pay may be given when the incident is not sufficiently serious to warrant discharge and/or the particular employee's overall value to the Company [is con-

sidered], if [in] the opinion of the Department Manager [the employee] warrants another chance. Minimum suspensions are (3) three days, maximum suspensions are (5) five days. No employee may be suspended more than once in a year; thereafter, if the incident would normally warrant suspension he/she must be discharged.
DISCIPLINARY WARNING:
Disciplinary warning slips will be issued where the offense is less serious and where corrective action may salvage an employee. More than one (1) disciplinary warning, whether for the same offense or not, may subject an employee to suspension or termination. Warning slips become a permanent part of an employee's personnel record.

ILLUSTRATION 10-1   *(continued)*

ble at the will of the employer with or without reason. Such actions * * * instill no reasonable expectations of job security and do not give employees any reason to rely on representations in the manual. However, if an employer does choose to issue a policy statement, in a manual or otherwise, and, by its language or by the employer's actions, encourages reliance thereon, the employer cannot be free to only selectively abide by it. Having announced a policy, the employer may not treat it as illusory. *Leikvold v. Valley View Community Hosp.*, 141 Ariz. 544, 548, 688 P.2d 170, 174 (1984). Here, substantial evidence supports the finding of the trial court that the employee handbook modified the employment relationship and created warning and suspension procedures which were not followed in this case.

Accordingly, based upon the foregoing, the judgment of the trial court is affirmed.

IT IS SO ORDERED.

SCARBOROUGH, C.J., SOSA, Senior Justice, and WALTERS, J., concur.

STOWERS, J., dissents.

STOWERS, Justice, dissenting.

I respectfully dissent from the majority's holding that SIMCO did not abide with the termination procedures.

Substantial evidence does support the findings of the trial court that the employee handbook modified the employment relationship and that Lukoski was terminated for just cause. The trial court erred, however, in concluding that SIMCO did not follow the proper termination procedures. To the contrary, SIMCO did not breach any of the provisions in the employee handbook when it discharged Lukoski without a warning and suspension. The handbook explicitly states that, "there are violations which are so severe that *immediate termination may be necessary.*" (Emphasis added).

Overwhelming evidence was presented at trial to show that Lukoski's violations of company policies were of the type to fall within the category of "so severe" that a

warning and any suspension procedures were not required. *See State ex rel. Goodmans Office Furnishings, Inc. v. Page & Wirtz Constr. Co.*, 102 N.M. 22, 24, 690 P.2d 1016, 1018 (1984). Generally, this evidence indicated that Lukoski had an overall attitude problem towards his employees, other managers and representatives of the Sandia Pueblo to the extent that SIMCO was in jeopardy of losing its bingo contract with the Pueblo; moreover, he was abusive towards the accountants, argued or fought publicly with customers, the assistant bingo manager, the construction supervisor and an admittance clerk; Lukoski also failed to install proper security measures and verification methods, and hired unqualified personnel. Further, testimony indicated that on several occasions, Walker, Lukoski's supervisor, spoke to Lukoski about this attitude problem, and, in fact, interceded on Lukoski's behalf when the Sandia Pueblo desired to discharge Lukoski.

As enumerated in the handbook, Lukoski's violations included, "fighting on company property, refusal to obey reasonable orders of a supervisor, discourtesy to customers, and disobeying or ignoring established written or oral work rules or policies." These are, and I again quote from the handbook, "violations which are so severe that *immediate termination* may be necessary." (Emphasis added.) Therefore, the trial court was in error when it decided that SIMCO violated the termination procedures prescribed for "less serious" offenses in the handbook. Lukoski was not entitled to those termination procedures since his offenses were not of the "less serious" type. Under the circumstances in this case, the only process due Lukoski for the seriousness of his violations was immediate termination. Thus, there was no breach by SIMCO when it discharged him for just cause.

The judgment of the district court should be reversed and this case remanded for dismissal.

B. WHY WOULD YOU RESEARCH WHICH CASES?

In a common law system, as in the United States, case law forms part of the law of the land. In the context of a particular research problem, not all cases are equal in importance. Your goal is to locate cases that are good law and either mandatory or highly persuasive precedent.

1. The Common Law, Stare Decisis, and Precedent

The operative principle in a common law system is "stare decisis et non quieta movere," which means "to adhere to precedent and not to unsettle things which are settled." According to stare decisis, a court should follow previously decided cases, or precedents, on the same legal topic. Hence, as you research the law applicable to a client's situation, even if you hope and reasonably anticipate that the situation will never come before a court, you should try to deduce how the court would handle the situation.

Stare decisis has several chief advantages. Situations involving similar facts are treated consistently. Outcomes are based on legal principles, rather than the unconstrained biases of judges and juries. Because it generally is possible to predict the outcome of a case by looking to precedents, many cases can be settled. Furthermore, people can conform their conduct to the law by looking to precedents.

Yet overly strict adherence to precedent would produce a static legal rule. Although some areas of law benefit from stability, others do not. When social values change, or information improves, or new situations develop, the law must evolve accordingly.

Fortunately the United States legal system provides for change. A court may distinguish an earlier case by finding factual differences between it and the pending case; then the court may apply a rule from some other authority. Or a court may modify the common law by refining or modifying existing precedents. Or a court may overrule precedent in response to a significant need for change. Furthermore, as you will see in Chapter 12 on statutes, legislatures may enact statutes modifying the common law to a greater or lesser degree.

2. History and Treatment of the Case

Before you rely on a case, you first must determine that it is good law. A case's status is a function primarily of its subsequent history and secondarily of its treatment. Subsequent history consists of later rulings in the same litigation. Treatment consists of decisions rendered in other, later cases that discuss the case at hand. For example:

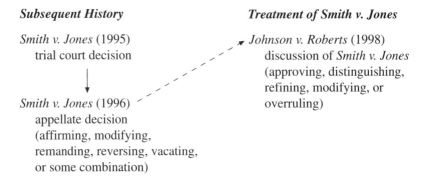

Subsequent History	*Treatment of Smith v. Jones*

Smith v. Jones (1995)
    trial court decision
	Johnson v. Roberts (1998)
	    discussion of Smith v. Jones
	    (approving, distinguishing,
	    refining, modifying, or
	    overruling)

Smith v. Jones (1996)
    appellate decision
    (affirming, modifying,
    remanding, reversing, vacating,
    or some combination)	

a.   Subsequent History

Before you rely on a decision, you must know whether it has been reviewed by a higher court and, if so, what the outcome was. The higher court may affirm the lower court's decision, reverse the lower court's decision, or take intermediate action, such as modifying or reversing and remanding to the lower court. These later decisions in the same litigation involving the same parties constitute the original decision's subsequent history.

Obviously, your research is not complete until you have identified the subsequent history of any decision you intend to rely on. Then you must carefully read any subsequent decisions. If they adversely affect the outcome and reasoning you are planning to rely on, it is incorrect to rely on the original decision. On the other hand, if your case has been affirmed in a later decision by a higher court, the original decision has greater credibility. Ordinarily you will rely on the higher court's decision. You may rely on the lower court decision when the higher court does not expressly rule on a point that is stated by the lower court, is important to your case, and is consistent with the higher court's ruling.

Furthermore, if you intend to rely on a decision that is very recent and not from the highest court, you should check whether an appeal is pending before a higher court and be prepared to adjust your analysis when the higher court rules.

For example, consider the *Lukoski* case. As already noted, the New Mexico Court of Appeals did not review *Lukoski*. But assume that you had located a court of appeals decision in *Lukoski* that reversed the trial court award in favor of Mr. Lukoski; then the supreme court ruled in favor of Mr. Lukoski. You would rely not on the court of appeals decision, but rather on the supreme court decision.

b.   Treatment

Judges often refer to decisions rendered in earlier similar cases. The court may follow an earlier decision, distinguish it, criticize it, modify it, or even overrule it. For any decided case, there may be several, a dozen, or more references in later cases.

Your research is not complete until you have discerned how later cases have treated each case you intend to rely on. You should focus on courts in the same court system because those courts have the greatest power to enhance or undermine the case's credibility. You should be especially concerned with indications that the case has been overruled; it then is no longer good law. You also should be wary of relying on a case that has been modified or criticized significantly or distinguished frequently.

For example as you will see in Chapter 11, the *Lukoski* case has been cited nine times by the New Mexico state courts; it also has been cited a few times by other courts (the federal Tenth Circuit, the federal district court for New Mexico, California and Washington state courts). It has not been overruled by later New Mexico cases or criticized by any court. Hence *Lukoski* remains good law.

3. Mandatory versus Persuasive Precedent: Federalism, Jurisdiction, and Level of Court

As to a particular situation, some cases constitute binding or mandatory precedent, while others are merely persuasive. The distinction between mandatory and persuasive precedents is critical. Stare decisis operates as to mandatory precedents only. Persuasive precedents may influence a court, but they do not bind it. The distinction between mandatory and persuasive precedent is based on two main factors: jurisdiction and level of court.

a. Federalism and Jurisdiction

The United States legal system is a federal system, that is, a collection of legal systems. A particular legal issue may be governed by federal law, or it may be governed by state law. Or it may be governed by both. A few issues are governed by local (municipal, county) law.

If the legal issue is governed by federal law, then mandatory precedents emanate from the federal courts. If the legal issue is governed by state law, then mandatory precedents emanate from the courts of the pertinent state. Other decisions are only persuasive precedent.

The term "jurisdiction" has several common meanings in the law. It often is used to refer to a legal system of a particular geographic region. In a more technical sense, "jurisdiction" is the power of a specific court to render and enforce a decision in a particular case. Generally, jurisdiction in this sense aligns with jurisdiction in the geographic sense. That is, the courts of a particular state have the power to render and enforce decisions in cases arising under the law of that state, and federal courts have the power to render and enforce decisions in cases arising under federal law and within their geographic regions.

However, this alignment is not always present. For example, in diversity jurisdiction, a federal court has the power to decide a case arising under state law if the case involves citizens of different states and the amount in controversy is high enough. Similarly, under supplemental jurisdiction, a federal court has the power to decide a case arising in part under state law if the case also involves a federal claim. Moreover, Congress has given state and federal courts concurrent jurisdiction over certain claims stated in federal law. Finally, the courts of one state may apply the law of a different state if a multistate contract identifies the second state's law as governing.

In these situations, the mandatory precedents are those decisions from the courts whose law governs. For example, when operating in diversity or supplemental jurisdiction, a federal court will follow the law of the state that governs the claim and will seek to emulate the approach of that state's supreme court; the decisions of other federal courts are not as weighty.

Unfortunately, there are few broadly applicable principles to explain the distribution of legal topics among the three levels of government, and jurisdiction can be complex. As you begin to research, you should assume that federal, state, and local law are all potentially applicable, and you should be alert to jurisdictional possibilities. Your research in secondary sources will provide preliminary guidance, which you should verify in primary authority.

In the Canoga case, the contract issue is a state law question (as is generally true of contract law). New Mexico would be the jurisdiction of the client's situation, and New Mexico state court decisions, such as *Lukoski*, would be mandatory precedent for a court in New Mexico deciding the Canoga case. The *Lukoski* court was itself bound by and cited earlier New Mexico cases—mandatory precedent—in its decision. Note that the *Lukoski* court also cited Oregon, Arizona, and federal cases—persuasive precedent. The federal case, *Ellis v. El Paso Natural Gas Co.*, involved an employee's challenge to his termination under state law; it was heard in federal court under diversity jurisdiction. The federal court in *Ellis* relied on New Mexico Supreme Court cases for guidance on the state law issue.

b. Level of Court

An additional determinant of mandatory versus persuasive precedent is the level of the court issuing the decision. Stare decisis operates hierarchically. Any particular court is bound by decisions of higher courts within the same court system and must take its own decisions into account, but is not bound by decisions issued by other courts at the same level or by lower courts. Hence, you would rely on a supreme court decision over that of an intermediate appeals court; similarly you would rely on an intermediate appeals court decision over that of a trial court.

For example, the decision in *Lukoski* binds the New Mexico Court of Appeals and the New Mexico trial courts; it also must be taken into account by the New Mexico Supreme Court in future cases. But a New Mexico Court of Appeals decision binds only the trial courts, not the supreme court. Similarly, a federal Tenth Circuit Court of Appeals decision binds the federal district courts within the Tenth Circuit (including the federal district court in New Mexico), but it does not bind the United States Supreme Court. A Tenth Circuit decision does not bind other federal circuit courts of appeals or district courts within other circuits.

4. Additional Factors

Your research may well yield multiple cases that are good law and mandatory precedent. Then you should consider the following factors as you select cases to emphasize:

> *Similarity:* The higher the degree of similarity between the facts and legal issues of your client's situation and those of the case you have located, the better. Your goal is to obtain both factual and legal parallelism, to the extent possible.
>
> *Clarity:* The clearer and more convincing the reasoning of the case you have located, the better. A clear, well reasoned case is inherently more credible than one with flawed reasoning.
>
> *Recency:* The more recent the case you have located, the better, all else being equal. Age by itself does not render a case bad law, but it may make it less credible than a more recent case, because a recent case may more closely reflect current values and perspectives.

For the Canoga case, the *Lukoski* case would be a strong case to rely on. It is less than fifteen years old, and the reasoning is fairly straightforward. Furthermore, the facts of *Lukoski* and the Canoga situation are similar, and the issues are nearly identical. Although Mr. Lukoski alleged that his employer should have suspended him, whereas Ms. Canoga would argue that the employer must provide board review, this difference is not substantial.

On some occasions, you may need to rely on persuasive precedent: when there is a dearth of mandatory precedent, the mandatory precedent is outdated, or the mandatory precedent is adverse to your client's interest and you wish to seek a change in the law. In selecting from possible persuasive precedents, you should consider the following factors, in addition to those stated above: which courts your jurisdiction's courts typically look to, which courts or cases are viewed as leaders in the subject matter, how geographically close the sister jurisdiction is to yours, how much the law of the sister jurisdiction tracks the law of your jurisdiction, and how closely the policies underlying the precedent mesh with your jurisdiction's policies. Your research in secondary sources will help you to assess some of these factors.

In the *Lukoski* case, as already noted, the court relied heavily on a persuasive precedent from Arizona, *Wagenseller v. Scottsdale Memorial Hospital. Wagenseller* then was a recent case from a nearby state. It involved fairly similar facts and the same legal issues as *Lukoski*. Based on its reasoning, it became a leading case in the developing area of employees' contract rights.

C.   HOW DO YOU RESEARCH CASES?

Cases are available in multiple media and from multiple publishers. When a case is issued by a court, it is called a "slip opinion." In some jurisdictions, the government or an authorized publisher issues books containing the jurisdiction's cases; these books are called "official reporters." Private publishers also publish case law in books called "unofficial reporters"; unofficial reporters contain significant editorial enhancements aimed at facilitating case law research. Although new cases appear fairly promptly in unofficial case reporters, some legal newspapers also print new cases even more quickly.

With the development of computers and related information technology, researchers now have additional options. For over two decades, cases have been available online from Westlaw and LEXIS, the two major online services for legal research. More recently, various publishers have published cases in CD-ROM products, which are searched much as online databases are searched. Even more recently, private publishers (such as Loislaw.com), government organizations, and educational institutions have made case law available through the Internet.

Quite often, you will find references to pertinent cases through your research in secondary sources. However, your research in secondary sources is unlikely to lead you to all of the case law you should locate because the author of the periodical or treatise, for example, did not have your specific situation in mind and probably chose only illustrative cases to discuss. Thus you will need to research cases directly.

This text discusses four case law research practices. The first involves West digests and reporters, a set of paper sources that together constitute one of the building blocks of United States case law. The second involves Westlaw, an online service that builds on the West digests and reporters. The third involves a CD-ROM product from a private publisher, Michie, which is supplemented by LEXIS. The fourth involves Internet sources generated by the government and law schools. These are not the only ways to research case law, but taken together they illustrate the major possibilities. As you will see, each has strengths and weaknesses; each fits some research situations better than others.

Furthermore, there is considerable competition in the area of case law research, especially as to computer-based sources. Established companies, such as West Group and LEXIS-NEXIS, regularly alter their products to afford additional variations on standard search options. And newer providers are trying to establish themselves in particular markets. You should follow such developments, so that your research is as effective and efficient as current sources permit.

This chapter covers the first steps of a case law research sequence: identifying, locating, obtaining, and reading pertinent cases. The critical step of discerning the subsequent history and treatment of a case is covered in Chapter 11 on citators.

Cases through West digests and reporters:

▶ select an appropriate digest

▶ identify a topic and key numbers via the topic list or Descriptive
   Word Index

▶ assemble the digest volumes and supplements you need

▶ skim the outline of the topic in the digest

▶ peruse the digest paragraphs under pertinent key numbers

▶ use the references in the digest to locate cases in reporters

▶ read each case for its rule, outcome, facts, reasoning, and
   references

▶ employ citators (see Chapter 11)

Paper-based research in case law involves two interlocking sources: digests and reporters, used in that order. A digest is a finding tool that leads you to case law published in a reporter. Because it is difficult to understand digests without an understanding of reporters, the following text provides an overview of reporters before setting out the process of using digests.

Understanding reporters and digests. A case reporter is a book containing the decisions issued during a particular time period by a single court or a set of courts. As already noted, reporters are official or unofficial. Official reporters do not contain the editorial enhancements of unofficial reporters and are not as useful for the researcher.

The most prominent reporters comprise the National Reporter System published by West Group. As synopsized in Exhibit 10.2 on pages 126–127, West currently publishes reporters containing decisions of the federal courts as follows: *Supreme Court Reporter* for decisions of the United States Supreme Court, *Federal Reporter* for decisions of the various courts of appeals, and *Federal Supplement* for decisions of the various district courts. Although all decisions of the Supreme Court are published, only some decisions of the lower federal courts appear in the West reporters; these decisions are selected by the courts because they contain significant analysis that contributes to the development of the law. (There is an official reporter for the Supreme Court, *United States Reports*, but not for the lower federal courts.)

As for case law from state courts, West has divided the country into seven regions (drawn from the perspective of a Minnesota publisher in the nineteenth century). Each region contains four to fifteen states, and each is served by one of the regional reporters. Again, see Exhibit 10.2 on pages 126–127. The regional reporters contain the decisions designated for publication by the various state appellate courts; some appellate decisions in routine cases are not published in reporters. Decisions of lower courts typically are not published. West's regions are not synonymous with jurisdiction; a case from a sister state within the same West region as your state is no more

EXHIBIT 10.2	West Reporters and Digest Paragraphs

Cases from these courts	appear in these West reporters	and are currently digested in these West digests
Federal Courts		
Supreme Court	*Supreme Court Reporter*	*United States Supreme Court Digest; Federal Practice Digest* (currently in fourth series); older cases covered by *Modern Federal Practice Digest* and *Federal Digest*
courts of appeals for various circuits	*Federal Reporter* (currently in third series)	*Federal Practice Digest;* older cases covered by *Modern Federal Practice Digest* and *Federal Digest* (also separate digests for Fifth and Eleventh Circuits)
district courts	*Federal Supplement* since 1932 (currently in second series); older cases in *Federal Reporter*	*Federal Practice Digest;* older cases covered by *Modern Federal Practice Digest* and *Federal Digest*
State Courts Connecticut Delaware District of Columbia Maine Maryland New Hampshire New Jersey Pennsylvania Rhode Island Vermont	*Atlantic Reporter* (currently in second series)	*Atlantic Digest;* state digests (except Delaware) (including federal cases from state)
Illinois Indiana Massachusetts New York Ohio	*North Eastern Reporter* (currently in second series); also *New York Supplement* (currently in second series)	state digests (including federal cases from state)
Georgia North Carolina South Carolina Virginia West Virginia	*South Eastern Reporter* (currently in second series)	*South Eastern Digest;* state digests (Virginia and West Virginia are merged) (including federal cases from state)
Alabama Florida Louisiana Mississippi	*Southern Reporter* (currently in second series)	state digests (including federal cases from state)

EXHIBIT 10.2	*(continued)*

Cases from these courts	appear in these West reporters	and are currently digested in these West digests
Arkansas Kentucky Missouri Tennessee Texas	*South Western Reporter* (currently in third series)	state digests (including federal cases from state)
Iowa Michigan Minnesota Nebraska North Dakota South Dakota Wisconsin	*North Western Reporter* (currently in second series)	*North Western Digest;* state digests (North and South Dakota are merged) (including federal cases from state)
Alaska Arizona California Colorado Hawaii Idaho Kansas Montana Nevada New Mexico Oklahoma Oregon Utah Washington Wyoming	*Pacific Reporter* (currently in second series); also *California Reporter* (currently in second series)	*Pacific Digest;* state digests (except Nevada and Utah) (including federal cases from state)

All jurisdictions also are covered in the *Century Digests, Decennial Digests,* and *General Digests.*

binding than a case from a sister state outside your state's West region. West also publishes two single-state reporters, for California and New York; these contain some cases not published in the regional reporters. (Some states publish official reporters; others in effect rely on the West reporters.)

For many reporters, West has published more than one series, for example, F., F.2d, F.3d for the *Federal Reporter.* The first series of a reporter contains the oldest cases, while the second or even third series contains the newest. The volume numbers start again with a new series.

Most volumes of a reporter are hardbound books. However, the most recent decisions appear in softcover pamphlets called "advance sheets," which can be published quickly. Once the hardbound book is prepared, it supersedes the advance sheets.

As an example of the West reporter system, consider first the *Lukoski* case, Illustration 10-1 on pages 115–118, decided by the New Mexico Supreme Court in 1988. *Lukoski* appears in volume 748 of the second series of the *Pacific Reporter* starting at page 507. As a second example, consider the *Ellis* case referred to in *Lukoski*. As a 1985 decision of the federal Tenth Circuit, *Ellis* appears in volume 754 of the second series of the *Federal Reporter* starting at page 884.

Cases are published in case reporters as they arrive at the publisher and clear the editorial process. Case reporters are organized chronologically, not topically. To locate cases on a particular topic, you need a digest. A digest is a tool for locating pertinent cases within the various volumes of a reporter for your jurisdiction. A digest presents brief statements of the legal points made in the covered cases, written by the publisher's editorial staff and then fit into a framework of major legal topics and subtopics. See Illustration 10-2 on page 131. West's digests are the most highly developed and widely used legal digests.

Select an appropriate digest. Your first step in case law research is to select an appropriate digest. There is a rough correlation between West's reporters and its digests, as indicated in Exhibit 10.2 on pages 126–127. For example, the main federal digest is the *Federal Practice Digest*, which covers the *Supreme Court Reporter*, the *Federal Reporter*, and the *Federal Supplement*. West publishes digests for the Atlantic, North Western, Pacific, and South Eastern regional reporters. It also publishes digests for most states; these digests cover state court decisions published in the regional reporters as well as federal cases arising in or appealed from the state.

West has combined the information in its various federal, regional, and state digests into master—and hence voluminous—digests: *Century Digests*, *Decennial Digests*, and *General Digests*, covering multiple decades, multiyear periods, and years, respectively. You generally will use these master digests only when you already have explored a narrower digest for your jurisdiction and have decided to seek precedent from outside your jurisdiction.

Identify a topic and key numbers. Your next step is to identify a pertinent topic and key numbers. West has divided the law into about 450 main topics. Each topic is divided into subtopics and indeed into subsubtopics. The subtopics and subsubtopics are assigned numbers, called "key numbers." This configuration of topics and key numbers is the same across the West system.

One way to find a pertinent topic is by scanning the topic list near the front of the digest volumes. See Illustration 10-3 on page 132. To find not only a pertinent topic but also pertinent key numbers, you would consult the Descriptive Word Index, which appears in its own volumes and typically is updated by pocket parts or pamphlets. See Illustration 10-4 on page 133. To obtain a thorough list of potentially pertinent topics and key numbers, look up various research terms, read the entries carefully, and check out cross-references.

Assemble a full set. The next step is to assemble the necessary digest volumes and supplements covering your topic and key numbers for the time period you are researching. Many digests consist of more than one bound series. Later series typically contain more recent information than earlier series; some later series incorporate the information from the previous series.

Typically, the most recent bound digest is updated by a pocket part inserted into the back of the bound volume; some pocket parts become so big that they are reissued as pamphlets or bound volumes. Even more recent information appears in pamphlets that generally are shelved at the end of a digest set. The most recent information appears in digest pages found within the most recent reporter hardbound volumes and advance sheets. Good researchers follow this sequence:

- bound volume for current series
- its pocket part or pamphlet
- supplementary pamphlet for the digest
- digest material in recent reporter hardbound volumes and advance sheets
- older series bound volume

Read the topic outline and headnotes. As you turn to the digest material covering your topic, skim the general and detailed outlines at the outset of your topic. See Illustration 10-5 on page 134. There may be additional pertinent key numbers you have not yet identified; rarely is there only one pertinent key number for a legal issue. Furthermore, you may find the organization of the topic to be informative.

Then peruse the entries under the pertinent key numbers. The entries are called "digest paragraphs," and they are identical to the headnote paragraphs appearing with the case in the West reporter. Compare Illustrations 10-1 on page 116 and 10-2 on page 131. The digest paragraphs appear in the digest in hierarchical order: federal cases before state cases, highest court cases before lower court cases; newer cases before older cases. At the end of each digest paragraph is a reference to the case from which it is drawn.

On occasion, you may know the name of one or both parties in a pertinent case, but not the citation of the case. Hence you need assistance locating the case in the reporter. Digests contain tables permitting you to look up the plaintiff or defendant by name, and providing the case's citation.

Locate and read the cases in reporters. When you finish with the digest, you will have a list of pertinent cases along with their locations in the case reporters and a basic idea of what each case stands for. It is essential, of course, to take the next step—to read the case in full. Relying only on the headnote is unwise because it will not tell you everything you need to know about the case, it may not reflect an important nuance of the case, and (rarely) it may be erroneous. You can use the headnotes to help you pinpoint the most pertinent portions of the case; the number preceding each headnote in the case reporter is keyed to a small bracketed number West editors insert within the opinion itself. See item 11 in Illustration 10-1 on page 116. Nonetheless, you should at least skim the apparently less pertinent portions, to be sure you fully understand the legal and factual context of the pertinent portions. As you read the case, attend to the rule the court uses to decide the case and the sources cited by the court, identify the key facts and outcome, note any factual similarities to or differences from your client's case, and trace the court's reasoning. Also watch for numbers inserted throughout the case;

these identify the page breaks in the official reporter, where there is one available before the West reporter is printed.

Finally, take advantage of the case as a finding tool for additional authorities. A case may cite authorities you have not yet located. Furthermore, there may be a pertinent headnote assigned to a topic and key number you have not yet uncovered; pursue that topic and key number in the digest, as described above.

The process described above is not complete. You still must employ a citator to verify that your case is good law, that is, to ascertain its subsequent history and treatment. Citators are discussed in Chapter 11.

Researching the Canoga case. Because we sought case law in New Mexico on a state law question of contract law, we used the *New Mexico Digest*. Another good option would be the *Pacific Digest*. We looked up "employee" and "employer" in the Descriptive Word Index. Both pointed to the "master and servant" index heading. There we found, under the subheading "discharge," a cross-reference to another index heading, "discharge of servants." Under "discharge of servant," we found references to various potentially pertinent key numbers in the Mast & S (Master and Servant) topic. See Illustration 10-4 on page 133. We also identified the Master and Servant topic by skimming the topic list. See Illustration 10-3 on page 132.

When we researched the Canoga case in fall 1999, we were fortunate to find a single bound volume, issued in summer 1999, covering New Mexico cases from 1852 forward. So the only updating to be done was in the digest pages in more recent hardbound or advance sheet reporters.

The Master and Servant topic begins with nearly 50 subtopics pertaining to the employment relationship, many pertaining to termination, discharge, and discipline. Key number 40(3.1) addresses the weight and sufficiency of evidence in such a case. One of the *Lukoski* headnote paragraphs is reprinted along with *Lukoski*'s citation under key number 40(3.1) in the main volume. See Illustration 10-2 on page 131.

The *Lukoski* case is described above in part A. The *Lukoski* case does lead to additional authority; *Lukoski* cites cases from New Mexico, other states, and the federal Tenth Circuit. On the other hand, *Lukoski* has only two headnotes: the first regarding a procedural point not pertinent to the Canoga case, the second already revealed by the digest research.

ILLUSTRATION 10-2   Digest Entries, from *New Mexico Digest*

4B N M D—45   **MASTER & SERVANT** ☞40(4)

For references to other topics, see Descriptive-Word Index

manual implied that employment would not be terminated except for a good reason and manual strictly controlled employer's and employee's conduct.

> Newberry v. Allied Stores, Inc., 773 P.2d 1231, 108 N.M. 424.

Determination that employee was discharged without a good reason and in violation of implied contract between employer and employee that allowed termination only for cause was not supported by the evidence; evidence showed that employee was discharged for removing merchandise from store in which he worked without filling out the appropriate charge ticket, as was required under company policy.

> Newberry v. Allied Stores, Inc., 773 P.2d 1231, 108 N.M. 424.

Former employee failed to establish that his employer acted in bad faith in the manner and method used to terminate him, as was required for employee to collect punitive damages from employer in his breach of contract action.

> Newberry v. Allied Stores, Inc., 773 P.2d 1231, 108 N.M. 424.

N.M. 1988. Substantial evidence supported finding that employer did not act upon reasonable grounds in terminating employee, where employer's vice-president, before he fired the employee, only reviewed a summary of an investigation into allegations of sexual harassment, illegal conduct, and mismanagement by employee, which failed to differentiate between firsthand knowledge and rumor, which made no attempt to evaluate the credibility of persons interviewed, and which was not intended to stand alone.

> Kestenbaum v. Pennzoil Co., 766 P.2d 280, 108 N.M. 20, certiorari denied 109 S.Ct. 3163, 490 U.S. 1109, 104 L.Ed.2d 1026.

N.M. 1988. Evidence supported trial court's conclusions that termination procedures in employee handbook amended general manager's employment contract, that handbook created warning and suspension procedures which were not followed, and that personality, rather than insubordination, caused employment termination; handbook characterized disciplinary policy regarding warnings, suspensions, and terminations as established procedure; and handbook did not indicate that it was subject to revocation at any time or that employees should not rely on it.

> Lukoski v. Sandia Indian Management Co., 748 P.2d 507, 106 N.M. 664.

N.M. 1984. Evidence supported trial court's finding that former employee did not violate terms of his employment agreement and that he was a good employee thereby warranting conclusion that former employee's employment was terminated by former employer with-

out good cause; therefore, former employee was not bound, as provided in the agreement, by the covenant not to compete contained in the employment agreement and was entitled to 30 days' termination pay.

> Danzer v. Professional Insurors, Inc., 679 P.2d 1276, 101 N.M. 178.

N.M.App. 1995. Presumption that an employee is at-will is rebuttable by an implied contract term that restricts employer's power to discharge.

> Kiedrowski v. Citizens Bank, 893 P.2d 468, 119 N.M. 572, certiorari denied, certiorari denied 890 P.2d 1321, 119 N.M. 389.

N.M.App. 1983. In most instances, claim under judicially created tort action based on employee's discharge which contravenes some clear mandate of public policy will assert serious misconduct; thus, proof should be made by clear and convincing evidence.

> Vigil v. Arzola, 699 P.2d 613, 102 N.M. 682, reversed in part 687 P.2d 1038, 101 N.M. 687.

N.M.App. 1972. In action alleging wrongful discharge from employment in connection with dispute as to duties employee was to perform under contract, finding that employee was employed as a manager, rather than as advisor and supervisor, was supported by substantial evidence.

> Clem v. Bowman Lumber Co., 495 P.2d 1106, 83 N.M. 659.

☞40(4). ——— **Retaliatory discharge.**

C.A.10 (N.M.) 1994. Employee did not establish that employer retaliated against her for filing written complaint claiming that she had been wrongfully denied promised promotion, based solely on her subjective belief that she did not receive promotions because of filing of complaint; moreover, adverse employment actions which occurred in 1981 and 1984 were not sufficiently close in time to 1978 complaint to support inference of retaliatory motive.

> Candelaria v. EG & G Energy Measurements, Inc., 33 F.3d 1259, rehearing denied.

C.A.10 (N.M.) 1987. Three-part analysis requiring plaintiff to establish prima facie case, requiring employer to show nondiscriminatory reason, and requiring plaintiff to prove discriminatory intent applies in retaliation cases. Age Discrimination in Employment Act of 1967, §§ 2 et seq., 15, 15(a), as amended, 29 U.S.C.A. §§ 621 et seq., 633a, 633a(a); Civil Rights Act of 1964, § 701 et seq., 42 U.S.C.A. § 2000e et seq.

> Lujan v. Walters, 813 F.2d 1051.

District court's conclusion following full trial that employee failed to prove retaliation for filing age discrimination charge was adequate

ILLUSTRATION 10-3   Topic List, from *New Mexico Digest*

DIGEST TOPICS

116	Dead Bodies	166	Extradition and	216	Inspection
117	Death		Detainers	217	Insurance
117G	Debt, Action of	167	Factors	218	Insurrection and
117T	Debtor and Creditor	168	False Imprisonmer		Sedition
118A	Declaratory	169	False Personation	219	Interest
	Judgment	170	False Pretenses	220	Internal Revenue
119	Dedication	170A	Federal Civil	221	International Law
120	Deeds		Procedure	222	Interpleader
122A	Deposits and	170B	Federal Courts	223	Intoxicating Liquors
	Escrows	171	Fences	224	Joint Adventures
123	Deposits in Court	172	Ferries	225	Joint-Stock
124	Descent and	174	Fines		Companies and
	Distribution	175	Fires		Business Trusts
125	Detectives	176	Fish	226	Joint Tenancy
126	Detinue	177	Fixtures	227	Judges
129	Disorderly Conduct	178	Food	228	Judgment
130	Disorderly House	179	Forcible Entry and	229	Judicial Sales
131	District and		Detainer	230	Jury
	Prosecuting	180	Forfeitures	231	Justices of the Peace
	Attorneys	181	Forgery	232	Kidnapping
132	District of Columbia	183	Franchises	232A	Labor Relations
133	Disturbance of	184	Fraud	233	Landlord and
	Public	185	Frauds, Statute of		Tenant
	Assemblage	186	Fraudulent	234	Larceny
134	Divorce		Conveyances	235	Levees and Flood
135	Domicile	187	Game		Control
135H	Double Jeopardy	188	Gaming	236	Lewdness
136	Dower and Curtesy	189	Garnishment	237	Libel and Slander
137	Drains	190	Gas	238	Licenses
138	Drugs and Narcotics	191	Gifts	239	Liens
141	Easements	192	Good Will	240	Life Estates
142	Ejectment	193	Grand Jury	241	Limitation of Actions
143	Election of	195	Guaranty	242	Lis Pendens
	Remedies	196	Guardian and Ward	245	Logs and Logging
144	Elections	197	Habeas Corpus	246	Lost Instruments
145	Electricity	198	Hawkers and	247	Lotteries
146	Embezzlement		Peddlers	248	Malicious Mischief
148	Eminent Domain	199	Health and	249	Malicious
148A	Employers' Liability		Environment		Prosecution
149	Entry, Writ of	200	Highways	250	Mandamus
150	Equity	201	Holidays	251	Manufactures
151	Escape	202	Homestead	252	Maritime Liens
152	Escheat	203	Homicide	253	Marriage
154	Estates in Property	204	Hospitals	255	Master and Servant
156	Estoppel	205	Husband and Wife	256	Mayhem
157	Evidence	205H	Implied and	257	Mechanics' Liens
158	Exceptions, Bill of		Constructive	257A	Mental Health
159	Exchange of		Contracts	258A	Military Justice
	Property	206	Improvements	259	Militia
160	Exchanges	207	Incest	260	Mines and Minerals
161	Execution	208	Indemnity	265	Monopolies
162	Executors and	209	Indians	266	Mortgages
	Administrators	210	Indictment and	267	Motions
163	Exemptions		Information	268	Municipal
164	Explosives	211	Infants		Corporations
165	Extortion and	212	Injunction	269	Names
	Threats	213	Innkeepers	270	Navigable Waters

XIV

ILLUSTRATION 10-4   Descriptive Word Index, from *New Mexico Digest*

1 N Mex D—443   DESCRIPTIVE-WORD INDEX   **Disclosure**
                    References are to Digest Topics and Key Numbers

DISCHARGE FROM INDEBTEDNESS, OB-
LIGATION OR LIABILITY (Cont'd)
SURETIES (Cont'd)
    Payment (Cont'd)
        Estoppel or waiver as to unauthorized
            payment to principal. **Princ & S 129**
            (5)
        Extension of time for. **Princ & S 103–**
            108
        Unauthorized payment to principal.
            Princ & S 117
    Penalty, alteration as to. **Princ & S 101**
        (4)
    Performance—
        Alteration as to time and place. **Princ**
            & S 101(5)
        Extension of time for. **Princ & S 103–**
            108
    Promise by surety after release from lia-
        bility. **Princ & S 130**
    Receiver's bonds. **Receivers 213**
    Release of—
        Cosurety. **Princ & S 116**
        Other securities. **Princ & S 115**
    Rescission of contract of principal. **Princ**
        & S 119
    Reservation by creditor of rights against
        surety in transaction with principal.
        Princ & S 127
    Satisfaction—
        By—
            Principal. **Princ & S 111–113**
            Surety. **Princ & S 131**
        Discharge of principal without satisfac-
            tion. **Princ & S 118**
    Securities, release of discharging surety.
        Princ & S 115
    Service of notice by surety to proceed
        against principal. **Princ & S 126(4)**
    Specifications for building, change in. **Princ**
        & S 100(3)
    Subsequent release or agreements. **Princ**
        & S 89
    Taking additional or new obligation as ex-
        tension of time. **Princ & S 105(3)**
    Taking additional or substituted surety.
        Princ & S 109
    Time of—
        Notice by surety to proceed against
            principal. **Princ & S 126(2)**
        Performance, alteration of instrument.
            Princ & S 101(5)
    Trustees' bonds. **Trusts 382**
    Unauthorized payment to principal. **Princ**
        & S 117
    Waiver. **Princ & S 129**
TENDER as discharging liability, see this index
    Tender
TRUSTEE administering corporation being re-
    organized in bankruptcy. **Bankr 668**
WAR risk insurance, discharge of liability.
    Army & N 76
WILLS, CONDITIONS. **Wills 664**

DISCHARGE FROM MILITARY OR NA-
VAL SERVICE
ENLISTED MEN. **Army & N 22**
OFFICERS. **Army & N 11**
PREFERENTIAL APPOINTMENT, see this index
    Officers

DISCHARGE OF SERVANT
ACTS constituting discharge. **Mast & S 31**
BREACH of contract as ground. **Mast & S 30**
    (2)
COMMENCEMENT of suit for wrongful dis-
    charge before expiration of term. **Mast &**
    S 41(3)
COMPENSATION as affected by. **Mast & S 73**
    (5, 7)
CONDITIONS precedent to action for. **Mast &**
    S 36
CONDONATION of grounds for. **Mast & S 30(7)**
DAMAGES. **Mast & S 41, 42**

DISCHARGE OF SERVANT (Cont'd)
EVIDENCE in action for wrongful discharge.
    Mast & S 40, 41(6)
EXEMPLARY DAMAGES. **Mast & S 41(5)**
FEAR of discharge inducing compliance with
    commands or threats involving risks. **Mast**
    & S 245(6)
GROUNDS—
    For discharge. **Mast & S 30**
    Of action for discharge. **Mast & S 36**
INCOMPETENCY as ground of discharge. **Mast**
    & S 30(3)
INJUNCTION, United States courts. **Courts**
    262.7(14)
INJURIES to servant by malicious procure-
    ment of discharge. **Mast & S 341**
INSUBORDINATION as ground for discharge.
    Mast & S 30(5)
INTEMPERANCE as ground for discharge. **Mast**
    & S 30(6)
LIMITATIONS of actions. **Mast & S 38**
MALICIOUS procurement of discharge. **Mast &.**
    S 341
MISCONDUCT as ground for discharge. **Mast &**
    S 30(4)
NEGLECT of duty as ground of discharge.
    Mast & S 30(3)
NOMINAL or substantial damages for wrongful
    discharge. **Mast & S 41(4)**
OPERATION and effect of discharge of servant.
    Mast & S 33½
PLEADING in action for wrongful discharge.
    Mast & S 39
REDUCTION of damages for wrongful discharge,
    effect of other employment. **Mast & S 42**
RE-EMPLOYMENT, see this index **Re-employment**
REFUSAL to serve as ground for discharge of
    servant. **Mast & S 30(2)**
STATEMENT of cause for discharge. **Mast &**
    S 32
SUPERINTENDENT of asylum. **Asylums 7**
UNEMPLOYMENT COMPENSATION, ground for.
    Mast & S 78.3(36)
UNION ACTIVITIES. **Mast & S 15(14)**
    Evidence. **Mast & S 15(47–49, 58)**
WAIVER of right to discharge servant. **Mast**
    & S 30(7)

DISCIPLINE
JUDGES. **Judges 11**
MILITIA. **Militia 14**
PUPILS—
    Private schools and academies. **Schools 8**
    Public schools. **Schools 169**
SEAMEN. **Seamen 30**

DISCLAIMER
CONTEMPT, disclaimer of intention to commit.
    Contempt 58(4)
COSTS as affected by. **Costs 47**
EJECTMENT. **Eject 71**
EQUITY. **Equity 192**
ESTOPPEL on ground of. **Estop 71**
EXEMPTIONS. **Exemp 103**
GARNISHMENT PROCEEDINGS. **Garn 208**
PARTY, effect on competency as witness. **Witn**
    139(6)
PATENTS, see this index **Patents**
PLEADING, setting aside fraudulent transfers.
    Fraud Conv 266(3)
QUIETING TITLE. **Quiet T 38**
TENANCY. **Land & Ten 16**
TITLE to property—
    Exemp 103
    Quiet T 38
TRESPASS TO TRY TITLE. **Tresp to T T 34,**
    47(2)
TRUSTS—
    Limitations as affected by. **Lim of Act 103**
WRIT of entry. **Entry Writ of 17**

DISCLOSURE
AGENCY, signature of memorandum within
    statute of frauds. **Frds St of 116(9)**

ILLUSTRATION 10-5   Outline of Digest Topic, from *New Mexico Digest*

MASTER & SERVANT   4B N M D—16

I. THE RELATION.—Continued.
  (C) TERMINATION, DISCHARGE, AND DISCIPLINE.—Continued.
    2. DISCHARGE OR DISCIPLINE.—Continued.
      ☞30. Grounds and liabilities.
            (1).   In general.
            (1.5). Cause or reason, and necessity therefor.
            (1.10). Public policy considerations.
            (1.15). Good faith and fair dealing requirement; bad faith and motive.
            (1.20). Particular reasons or grounds.
            (2).   Breach of contract or refusal to serve.
            (3).   Incompetence, disability, or neglect of duty; unsatisfactory performance.
            (4).   Misconduct.
            (5).   Disobedience and insubordination.
            (6).   Intoxication or intemperance.
            (6.5). Retaliatory discharge or discipline.
            (6.10). —— In general.
            (6.15). —— Health and safety regulations, exercise of rights under.
            (6.20). —— Workers' compensation laws, exercise of rights under.
            (6.25). Garnishment; bankruptcy.
            (6.30). Refusal to perform wrongful act.
            (6.35). Exercise of Constitutional or political rights; criticism and "whistle blowing.".
            (7).   Waiver, condonation, and effect of reparation.
      31. Acts constituting discharge.
            (1). In general.
            (2). Constructive discharge.
            (3). Procedural requirements.
      33.5. Operation and effect of discharge.
      34. Actions for wrongful discharge.
      34.1. —— In general.
      35.   —— Nature and form.
      36.   —— Conditions precedent; primary jurisdiction and exhaustion of remedies.
      37.   —— Defenses.
      38.   —— Time to sue and limitations.
      39.   —— Pleading.
            (1). In general.
            (2). Issues, proof, and variance.
      40.   —— Evidence.
            (.5). In general.
            (1). Presumptions and burden of proof.
            (2). Admissibility.
            (3). Weight and sufficiency.
            (3.1). —— In general.
            (4). —— Retaliatory discharge.
      41.   —— Damages in general.
            (.5). In general.
            (1). Measure in general.
            (2). Elements of damage.
            (3). Commencement of suit before expiration of term.

Case law in Westlaw and LEXIS:

▶ select an appropriate database

▶ draft and run a Boolean, natural-language, or key-number search, with or without a date or segment restrictor

▶ sift the results to identify pertinent cases

▶ read the cases

▶ employ citators (see Chapter 11)

Westlaw and LEXIS, the two major online subscription services for legal research, both provide access to a wide range of cases and various options for gaining access to those cases. Online research in cases has several advantages over paper research: Some cases, namely very recent cases and ones not designated for publication by the court, may be available online but not in paper. You may use research terms, such as factual concepts, beyond those used by a publisher's editorial staff to create a digest or similar tool. Information is very current and totally cumulated online, so you need not use multiple books, such as several volumes and supplements of a paper digest.

However, online research does not always work well. For some legal issues, it is difficult to draft a search that works well, chiefly when the research terms are very common legal or factual concepts. Furthermore, online legal research can be costly.

The following text focuses on Westlaw. Most of the approaches discussed here can be replicated on LEXIS. The exception is the key-number search, which is unique to Westlaw because it employs the West key-number system.

Select an appropriate database. The first step in online research is selection of an appropriate database. Case law is offered in various databases, many drawn along jurisdictional lines, others along subject-matter lines. As a general principle, you should first search in the narrowest database containing the mandatory precedent for your situation, then expand to a broader database if your initial database does not yield pertinent cases or you wish to develop some aspect of the case law further. As you begin your research, you should check the scope of your chosen database, so you know what you are and are not searching. In general, West's case law databases contain cases published in the various West reporters as well as cases too new to be in the advance sheets and some cases not designated for paper publication. Incidentally, many courts prohibit or restrict the use of unpublished cases; you should be sure you conform to any such judicial protocols.

Draft and run a search. The second step is to draft and run your search, revising it as needed to obtain better results. There are different types of searches that work well in case law; you may want to combine two or three for the most comprehensive results. (Review Chapter 3 at pages 43–48 for more detail on search drafting.)

One option is Boolean searching, in which you specify the terms you are looking for and their connection to each other. Recall from Chapter 3 that you can use general connectors, such as "and" and "or"; numerical connectors; or grammatical connectors, such as /p (same paragraph) and /s (same sentence). Such a search will obtain all cases meeting your requirements.

An alternative to Boolean searching is natural-language searching. Recall from Chapter 3 that when you draft a natural-language search, you begin with a sentence stating your research issue, and you may use an online thesaurus to expand the expression of your main concepts. Natural-language searches yield a specified number of documents (the Westlaw default number is twenty) identified as most pertinent to your topic by application of a semantic-statistical algorithm.

A third option is a key-number search (available only in Westlaw). You can discern a pertinent key number various ways: through a reference in various secondary sources (such as encyclopedias or selected treatises), by use of digests (described above), or through a pertinent case you already have located. You may also browse the key-number service on Westlaw. A key-number search works like a Boolean search, with the key number operating as the search term.

The three main search options—Boolean, natural language, and key number—will only rarely yield identical results. The three searches seek different patterns of words and symbols. Boolean and natural-language searches search more cases than the key-number search, because very recent and never-to-be-published cases lack key numbers. Boolean and key-number searches yield as many documents as fit the requirements of the search, while natural-language searching yields the top twenty cases (or whatever number you designate). Compare the partial citation lists in Illustration 10-6 on page 138.

In some circumstances, you may wish to limit the material you are searching, so as to search only portions of your selected database. For example, if you wish to confine your search to a particular time period, you could add a date restrictor to the searches described above. This is most often done when you are using an online service to update research you have performed another way, such as through digests and reporters. As another example, you might search only the publisher's synopsis of the case or the headnotes by conducting a segment search. This is most often done when your research terms are standard legal concepts and you need to reduce the material searched to a manageable volume.

Sometimes, you will use an online service not as a means of identifying pertinent cases, but only as a source of a known pertinent case. If you know the citation of a case but cannot obtain a paper copy, you can enter a find search by keying in the citation and thereby retrieve the case. If you know the name of a pertinent case, but not its citation, you can enter an appropriate database, search for one or both of the parties' names in a case-name segment, and thereby locate the case.

Sift your results, and read the cases. However you search for and identify potentially pertinent cases online, your next step is to sift through your search results to identify cases that actually are pertinent. To get a glimpse into cases retrieved online, you may skim the opening editorial material (the synopsis and headnotes), or you may read the portion of the case in which your search terms appear (typically with your search terms highlighted).

As you read a pertinent case, you should look for the information detailed above in the discussion of paper-based research in case law. As with paper-based research in cases, you must employ a citator to verify that your case is good law, that is, to ascertain its subsequent history and treatment. Citators are discussed in Chapter 11.

Researching the Canoga case. When we researched the Canoga case in the fall of 1999 on Westlaw, we first chose the NM-CS database, which contains New Mexico Supreme Court cases and New Mexico Court of Appeals cases and reaches back to 1852. A somewhat broader database is NM-CS-ALL, which includes the same cases along with federal court cases that are authoritative in New Mexico, such as Tenth Circuit cases. We entered the following search in the NM-CS database: [employ! /p (discharg! dismiss! terminat!) /p (handbook manual) /p contract]. This search yielded twenty-eight cases, including the *Lukoski* case. The first case listed, *Cockrell*, was then so new it was not yet available in paper form. See Illustration 10-6 on page 138 for a partial citation list. A search for more precise factual concepts, such as musician and smoking, yielded no documents.

To locate factually similar cases in other jurisdictions, we chose the MLB-CS database, a database containing cases from the fifty states and District of Columbia that discuss labor and employment law issues. We entered the following search in the MLB-CS database: [(discharg! dismiss! terminat!) & (smok! /p off-duty)]. This search yielded thirty-one cases, a good number involving marijuana rather than tobacco. Adding [% mari*uana], signifying "but not marijuana or marihuana," reduced the yield to fifteen. The most pertinent case, *Wood v. South Dakota Cement Plant*, 588 N.W.2d 227 (S.D. 1999), decided by the South Dakota Supreme Court, involves an assistant kiln operator fired for off-duty off-premises use of tobacco.

We also ran a natural-language search in NM-CS: [Can an employer discharge an employee without following the procedure in the employee handbook?] The thesaurus suggested the following additional terms: dismiss, fire, terminate, dismissal, firing; company manual, employee manual, employment handbook, personnel manual, and handbook. The *Lukoski* case was the first case listed. See Illustration 10-6 on page 138 for a partial citation list.

Finally, we entered the following search, drawing on the pertinent key number provided by the *Lukoski* case: [255k40]. The Master and Servant topic is the 255th topic on West's list of topics; 40 is the pertinent key number. This search yielded sixteen cases, including *Lukoski*. See Illustration 10-6 on page 138 for a partial citation list.

| ILLUSTRATION 10-6 | Westlaw Partial Citation Lists, Run in NM-CS Database |

BOOLEAN SEARCH—28 CASES

1. Cockrell v. Board of Regents of New Mexico State University, _____ P.2d _____, 1999 WL 381103, 1999-NMCA-073 (N.M.App., May 07, 1999) (NO. 19,417)
2. New Mexico Regulation & Licensing Dept. v. Lujan, 979 P.2d 744, 1999-NMCA-059 (N.M.App., Mar 17, 1999) (NO. 19,318)
3. Cates v. Regents of New Mexico Institute of Min. & Technology, 124 N.M. 633, 954 P.2d 65, 1998-NMSC-002 (N.M., Jan 07, 1998) (NO. 23,900)
4. Lopez v. Kline, 124 N.M. 539, 953 P.2d 304, 13 IER Cases 1174, 1998-NMCA-016 (N.M.App., Nov 26, 1997) (NO. 17,668)
5. Garcia v. Middle Rio Grande Conservancy Dist., 121 N.M. 728, 918 P.2d 7, 11 IER Cases 1328 (N.M., May 21, 1996) (NO. 22,790)

. . .

18. Lukoski v. Sandia Indian Management Co., 106 N.M. 664, 748 P.2d 507, 2 IER Cases 1650 (N.M., Jan 07, 1988) (NO. 16,462)

NATURAL-LANGUAGE SEARCH—20 CASES

1. Lukoski v. Sandia Indian Management Co., 106 N.M. 664, 748 P.2d 507, 2 IER Cases 1650 (N.M., Jan 07, 1988) (NO. 16,462)
2. Sanchez v. The New Mexican, 106 N.M. 76, 738 P.2d 1321, 109 Lab.Cas. P 55,918, 2 IER Cases 1427 (N.M., Jul 15, 1987) (NO. 16,362)
3. Kiedrowski v. Citizens Bank, 119 N.M. 572, 893 P.2d 468, 130 Lab.Cas. P 57,930, 134 Lab.Cas. P 58,285, 10 IER Cases 840 (N.M.App., Feb 02, 1995) (NO. 15,644)
4. Hartbarger v. Frank Paxton Co., 115 N.M. 665, 857 P.2d 776, 127 Lab.Cas. P 57,664, 8 IER Cases 1114 (N.M., Jun 14, 1993) (NO. 19,913)
5. Cates v. Regents of New Mexico Institute of Min. & Technology, 124 N.M. 633, 954 P.2d 65, 1998-NMSC-002 (N.M., Jan 07, 1998) (NO. 23,900)

KEY-NUMBER SEARCH—16 CASES

1. Weidler v. Big J Enterprises, Inc., 124 N.M. 591, 953 P.2d 1089, 66 USLW 31,559, 1998-NMCA-021 (N.M.App., Dec 15, 1997) (NO. 16,712)
2. Lihosit v. I & W, Inc., 121 N.M. 455, 913 P.2d 262, 11 IER Cases 1487 (N.M.App., Jan 17, 1996) (NO. 16,285)
3. Kiedrowski v. Citizens Bank, 119 N.M. 572, 893 P.2d 468, 130 Lab.Cas. P 57,930, 134 Lab.Cas. P 58,285, 10 IER Cases 840 (N.M.App., Feb 02, 1995) (NO. 15,644)
4. Hartbarger v. Frank Paxton Co., 115 N.M. 665, 857 P.2d 776, 127 Lab.Cas. P 57,664, 8 IER Cases 1114 (N.M., Jun 14, 1993) (NO. 19,913)
5. Shull v. New Mexico Potash Corp., 111 N.M. 132, 802 P.2d 641, 6 IER Cases 184 (N.M., Dec 04, 1990) (NO. 19,142)

. . .

10. Lukoski v. Sandia Indian Management Co., 106 N.M. 664, 748 P.2d 507, 2 IER Cases 1650 (N.M., Jan 07, 1988) (NO. 16,462)

> **Case law in CD-ROM:**
>
> ▶ select the case law portion of the CD-ROM
> ▶ draft and run a search
> ▶ sift the results to identify pertinent cases
> ▶ update your research online
> ▶ read the cases
> ▶ employ citators (see Chapter 11)

CD-ROM research mixes some of the features of paper research with some of the features of online research. Like a book, a CD-ROM contains a fixed set of legal materials. As with online research, you use a computer to gain access to the contents of the CD-ROM.

The first step in CD-ROM research is to select an appropriate portion of the CD-ROM. You may be using a state law CD-ROM, which contains not only cases but also other primary authorities and perhaps some secondary sources as well. The most direct way of researching case law is to use the case law portion. Be sure that you know exactly which courts and years the case law portion encompasses. In particular, you should know how current the CD-ROM is, because it is not updated once it leaves the publisher.

The second step is to draft and run your search. Search methods vary from CD-ROM to CD-ROM and may only loosely resemble those described above for Westlaw and LEXIS. As with online research, you may need to revise your search to improve its recall and precision.

The next step is to sift the cases you retrieved to identify cases that actually are pertinent. Again, the methods for doing so vary from CD-ROM to CD-ROM. Your options may include skimming a citation list, reviewing the text surrounding your search words, or reading cases in full.

Because CD-ROM research entails a computer, it may appear that the results should be as current as online research. This is not likely to be so; a CD-ROM disk is current only to the date of publication. Hence you should update your CD-ROM research, most probably via a supplemental online search. This process is facilitated if the CD-ROM is published by an online service provider.

As with every other approach to case law research, you must carefully read all of the pertinent cases you have found and employ a citator to verify that your case is good law.

Researching the Canoga case, we used *Michie's Law on Disc* for New Mexico, a product of LEXIS Law Publishing. The judicial decisions portion encompassed New Mexico Supreme Court decisions beginning in 1852 and New Mexico Court of Appeals decisions beginning in 1966. The coverage of the August 1999 disk that we used in the fall of 1999 stopped in mid-July 1999.

The Michie CD-ROM permitted Boolean searching with several connectors, including "or" and "and," as well as * as a root expander. We ran the following search: [employ* or personnel and handbook or manual]. As each term was entered, the computer indicated the number of hits, that is, the number of times our requirements were met, not the number of cases meeting our requirements, as follows:

employ*	→	25,013 hits
or personnel	→	25,729 hits
and handbook	→	85 hits
or manual	→	230 hits

We could review our hits (passages containing the search terms), the full text of the cases containing hits, and a citation list with the number of hits within the case noted. Illustration 10-7 below lists the first few cases on the case list as well as the *Lukoski* entry, which was the forty-seventh of 103 cases containing 230 hits; the cases are listed from newest to oldest. The numbers at the left indicate how many hits each case contained. The Michie CD-ROM printout of the *Lukoski* case appears as Illustration 2-1 on pages 13–16.

The Michie CD-ROM we used to research the Canoga case is, as noted above, a LEXIS product. To find cases newer than July 1999, we could switch into LEXIS, which would automatically run the same search, looking for recent cases in a corresponding case law database.

ILLUSTRATION 10-7	*Michie's Law on Disc* Partial Citation List, Run in New Mexico Judicial Decisions

18   -1999-NMCA-073, 38 N.M. St. B. Bull. 24 COCKRELL V. BOARD OF
      REGENTS OF NEW MEXICO STATE U (Ct. App. 1999) 1999 N.M. App.
      Lexis 14
  18   OPINION
 3   -1999-NMCA-059, 38 N.M. St. B. Bull. 20 NEW MEXICO
      REGULATION & LICENSING DEP'T V. LUJAN (Ct. App. 1999) 1999
      N.M. App. Lexis 26
   3   OPINION
 1   -1999-NMCA-032, 976 P.2d 1019 CHAVARRIA V. BASIN MOVING &
      STORAGE (Ct. App. 1999) 1999 N.M. App. Lexis 3
   1   OPINION
 1   -1998-NMCA-106, 125 N.M. 495, 964 P.2d 56 BOARD OF COUNTY
      COMM'RS OF SIERRA COUNTY V. HARRIS (Ct. App. 1998) 1998 N.M.
      App. Lexis 90
   1   OPINION

        . . .

10   -106 N.M. 664, 748 P.2d 507 LUKOSKI V. SANDIA INDIAN MGT. CO.
      (S. Ct. 1988) 1988 N.M. Lexis 17
   9   OPINION
   1   DISSENT

> **Case law via public Internet web sites:**
>
> ▶ identify an appropriate web site
>
> ▶ ascertain how to search for pertinent cases, and do so, if possible
>
> ▶ or select cases you are seeking from a case list
>
> ▶ read the cases
>
> ▶ employ citators (see Chapter 11)

Case law research in government or other public Internet web sites is highly variable. For some courts, you will find many recent cases available online and a range of search options for identifying pertinent cases. For other courts, both the collection of cases and the search options are far more limited. Hence the utility of Internet sources varies widely. As of the time this text was written, Internet research in government and public web sites was advisable primarily for the purpose of locating a known recent case, not for the purpose of identifying pertinent cases on a particular topic.

The basic process of Internet case law research is similar in outline to Westlaw or LEXIS research: First identify an appropriate web site by consulting a print directory (such as *Government on the Net* or *Guide to Finding Legal and Regulatory Information on the Internet*) or by visiting a legal-information web site (as listed in Exhibit 2.2 on page 23). Be sure to ascertain the scope of the web site you have chosen. Then figure out whether you can accomplish a search via key words, most likely through a basic Boolean technique. If not, you would use the web site as a means of obtaining known pertinent cases from a case list. Once you have located a pertinent case, read it carefully. As with cases you locate through other means, you must employ citators to verify that any case you will rely upon is good law, that is, to ascertain its subsequent history and treatment.

Researching the Canoga case on the Internet, looking for New Mexico state cases, in the fall of 1999, we found a source provided by New Mexico Technet, a private non-profit organization created by universities and government agencies in New Mexico. That source provided New Mexico Supreme Court cases from 1998 available for downloading but not on-screen reading. One could scroll down a list of cases, but not yet search for particular research terms.

Somewhat by contrast, when we shifted to the federal courts, more specifically the United States Court of Appeals for the Tenth Circuit (which includes New Mexico), we found a source initially created by Emory's law school in 1995 and continued at Washburn's law school as of 1997. At web site www.kscourts.org/ca10, we found Tenth Circuit cases. The site afforded basic Boolean search capabilities. When we entered ["New Mexico" AND employee AND contract], we obtained one case (*Trujillo v. City of Albuquerque*), which included only a line or two on our issue.

D. WHAT ELSE?

State Versions of Regional Reporters.   You may have available to you a state-specific version of a regional reporter, that is, a volume containing only the cases from one of the states covered by a regional reporter, reprinted as they appear in the regional reporter. The advantage of such a reporter is its smaller size and cost.

Updating of Key Numbers.   As the law or legal vocabulary evolves, West occasionally changes topics and key numbers. Generally, you will find a translation table at the end of the outline of the revised topic.

Specialized Reporters and Looseleaf Services.   Specialized reporters contain cases on a single area of law. For example, West publishes *Federal Rules Decisions,* a reporter with cases pertaining only to federal civil or criminal procedure. Furthermore, looseleaf services, discussed in Chapter 16, include cases and digests along with statutes, regulations, and secondary materials.

Lawyers' Edition.   Another unofficial case reporter is *United States Supreme Court Reports, Lawyers' Edition*, which encompasses United States Supreme Court cases. The set includes a digest, summaries of the lawyers' briefs, and references to secondary sources.

Paper Sources of Very New Cases.   At both the national and state levels, legal newspapers and newsletters provide copies of very recent cases, typically within a week of issuance by the court. For example, *The United States Law Week* publishes decisions of the United States Supreme Court (as well as information on cases pending before the Court) on a weekly basis. Your state may have a similar source.

LEXIS Search Advisor.   Search Advisor is a new LEXIS classification system that (like the West key-number system) provides a framework of major legal topics and numerous subtopics. You type in a research term or work through the lists of topics and subtopics, select your topic and subtopic, enter a jurisdiction, and then run a Boolean or natural-language search within the cases filed for your jurisdiction under that topic and subtopic. You may confine your search by segment or dates.

Online Searches for Particular People.   From time to time, you may want to locate cases written by a particular judge or litigated by a particular attorney. Westlaw and LEXIS permit segment searches for judges and attorneys.

National Reporter Blue Book **and State Blue Books.**   These sources contain tables of parallel citations, permitting you to look up a case by its official citation and locate the unofficial citation, and vice versa.

Words and Phrases.   West's headnotes form the basis of this multivolume set, which is organized like a dictionary and lists cases from state and federal jurisdictions defining legal terms.

E.   HOW DO YOU CITE CASES?

More than any other source, case law citation is in a state of flux. Traditionally citation format focused on paper resources. As computer-based sources become more prevalent, it seems that citation should evolve accordingly. Furthermore, some courts have promulgated their own citation rules, in part in response to technological change, in part as a reflection of the preferences of the judges.

The major open issue is how to provide information about how to locate a case. For a particular case, one could provide citations to an official reporter, an unofficial reporter, various Westlaw and LEXIS databases, one or more CD-ROMs, and possibly one or more Internet sites. Some argue that a better solution is media-neutral information; knowing a case name, decision number, court, and date should permit a reader to locate a case in various media. The current *Bluebook* does provide for use of an official public domain citation where available. However, the current *Bluebook* looks primarily to paper reporters and secondarily to Westlaw and LEXIS. For example, a state case is cited to a West regional reporter, if therein; also to an official reporter if therein (a parallel citation) if the document is written for the state court; or to an online database if the case does not appear in reporters.

Under any citation form you may be bound by, you will provide the name of the case, a means of locating it, the court and date of decision, and the case's subsequent history and adverse treatment, if any. As to each of these items, you are likely to find rather particular rules, for example, how to abbreviate party names, how many locations to provide, how to abbreviate court names, how specifically to state the date of decision, how to order this information.

Here are citations to the cases featured in this chapter (following Rule 10 and related rules of *The Bluebook*):

> *Lukoski v. Sandia Indian Management Co.,* 748 P.2d 507 (N.M. 1988)—
> for reader other than New Mexico state court
> *Lukoski v. Sandia Indian Management Co.,* 106 N.M. 664, 748 P.2d
> 507 (1988)—in document written to New Mexico state court
> *Ellis v. El Paso Natural Gas Co.,* 754 F.2d 884 (10th Cir. 1985)
> *Ellis v. El Paso Natural Gas Co.,* 754 F.2d 884 (10th Cir. 1985), *aff'd,*
> 123 U.S. 456 (1986)—if the United States Supreme Court had affirmed the Tenth Circuit
> *Cockrell v. Board of Regents,* No. 19,417, 1999 WL 381103 (N.M. Ct.
> App. May 7, 1999) Westlaw citation

F.   CONCLUDING POINTS

Because cases are primary authority, your research will not be correct, comprehensive, or credible unless you research the case law on your topic competently. As you research in case law, focus on cases from your jurisdiction (mandatory cases) that are good law. Turn to persuasive precedents only as needed to augment your mandatory authority. To research case law in a cost-effective manner, you must be proficient in both paper-based and computer-based research.

Paper research in case law entails use of an interlocking system of digests and reporters. Digests provide paragraphs setting out key points from cases, organized by topics and then by numbered subtopics. The digest paragraphs include references to cases, permitting you to locate cases within reporters.

An alternative to paper research is online research in subscription services such as Westlaw or LEXIS. To research cases effectively online, you must select a pertinent database and write a search (natural-language, Boolean, or key-number) to identify pertinent cases within your database.

A third alternative is CD-ROM research, in which you use computer-based search methods to locate pertinent cases within a fixed set of cases contained on a CD-ROM disk. CD-ROM research is a hybrid of paper-based and online research.

Yet another alternative is to research cases through Internet web sites, which may be maintained by courts or nonprofit groups. As of this writing, this alternative was most useful as a means of obtaining known pertinent cases, not as a means of researching a jurisdiction's body of case law so as to identify pertinent cases.

In many situations, you may choose to research case law through a combination of these approaches. For example, you might locate mandatory precedents expressing general rules through paper-based research in digests and reporters, then use Westlaw or LEXIS to bring your research up-to-the-minute or search for cases involving distinctive facts. However your case law research begins, once you have located a pertinent case and read it, you must employ citators as discussed in Chapter 11, to determine the subsequent history and treatment of the case.

CASE CITATORS

A.   WHAT IS A CITATOR?

A citator is a research tool that lists later sources that have cited earlier sources. The source you have located and plan to rely on is the "cited source," and it, in turn, is cited in a variety of subsequent "citing sources." Each citator covers its own tailored assortment of citing sources. The following citing sources are among those listed in a case citator: other cases, administrative materials, encyclopedias, treatises, legal periodicals, and A.L.R. Annotations. This chapter focuses exclusively on case citators—that is, citators that cover cases as the cited source. Citators are most critical in case law research. Citators for other sources are covered in other chapters; for example, Chapter 6 on periodicals discusses a periodicals citator.

The two major online legal citators are KeyCite (on Westlaw) and Shepard's (on LEXIS). Shepard's is also available on CD-ROM and in paper. Illustration 11-1 on pages 146–148 shows a sample display from Shepard's on LEXIS. Illustration 11-2 on pages 149–150 shows a sample display from KeyCite on Westlaw. Illustration 11-3 on page 151 shows a sample page from the paper *Shepard's Pacific Reporter Citations.*

ILLUSTRATION 11-1   Shepard's Online Display, from LEXIS

Copyright 1999 Shepard's - 19 Citing references

Lukoski v. Sandia Indian Management Co., 106 N.M. 664, 748 P.2d 507, 1988 N.M. LEXIS 17, 2 I.E.R. Cas. (BNA) 1650 (N.M. 1988)

SHEPARD'S(R) Signal: Caution: Possible negative treatment
Restrictions: *Unrestricted*
FOCUS Terms: *No FOCUS terms*
Print Format: *FULL*

PRIOR HISTORY (0 citing references)
(CITATION YOU ENTERED):
Lukoski v. Sandia Indian Management Co., 106 N.M. 664, 748 P.2d 507, 1988 N.M. LEXIS 17, 2 I.E.R. Cas. (BNA) 1650 (N.M. 1988)

CITING REFERENCES (14 citing references)

New Mexico Supreme Court
Cited by:
Garcia v. Middle Rio Grande Conservancy Dist., 1996 NMSC 29, 121 N.M. 728, 918 P.2d 7, 1996 N.M. LEXIS 202, 11 I.E.R. Cas. (BNA) 1328 (N.M. 1996)
Followed by:
Garcia v. Middle Rio Grande Conservancy Dist., 1996 NMSC 029, 121 N.M. 728, 918 P.2d 7, 1996 N.M. LEXIS 261, 11 I.E.R. Cas. (BNA) 1328 (N.M. 1996)
> **Followed by:**
> 1996 NMSC 029
> 121 N.M. 728 p.732
> 918 P.2d 7 p.11
Distinguished by:
Hartbarger v. Frank Paxton Co., 115 N.M. 665, 857 P.2d 776, 1993 N.M. LEXIS 187, 32 N.M. B. Bull. 635, 8 I.E.R. Cas. (BNA) 1114, 127 Lab. Cas. (CCH) P57664 (1993)
> **Distinguished by:**
> 115 N.M. 665 p.673
> 857 P.2d 776 p.784
> **Cited by:**
> 115 N.M. 665 p.669
> 857 P.2d 776 p.780
Cited by:
Chavez v. Manville Prods. Corp., 108 N.M. 643, 777 P.2d 371, 1989 N.M. LEXIS 241, 4 I.E.R. Cas. (BNA) 833, 122 Lab. Cas. (CCH) P56927 (N.M. 1989)
> **Cited by:**
> 108 N.M. 643 p.646
> 777 P.2d 371 p.374
Cited by:
Paca v. K-Mart Corp., 108 N.M. 479, 775 P.2d 245, 1989 N.M. LEXIS 189, 4 I.E.R. Cas. (BNA) 727 (N.M. 1989)
> **Cited by:**
> 108 N.M. 479 p.481
> 775 P.2d 245 p.247
Followed by:
Newberry v. Allied Stores, 108 N.M. 424, 773 P.2d 1231, 1989 N.M. LEXIS 139, 4 I.E.R. Cas. (BNA) 562 (N.M. 1989)
> **Followed by:**
> 108 N.M. 424 p.426
> 773 P.2d 1231 p.1233
Cited by:

ILLUSTRATION 11-1   *(continued)*

SHEPARD'S - 748 P.2d 507 - 19 Citing references

Kestenbaum v. Pennzoil Co., 108 N.M. 20, 766 P.2d 280, 1988 N.M. LEXIS 326, 4 I.E.R. Cas. (BNA) 67 (N.M. 1988)
    Cited by:
    108 N.M. 20 p.24
    766 P.2d 280 p.284

New Mexico Court of Appeals
Cited by:
Famiglietta v. Ivie-Miller Enters., Inc., 1998 NMCA 155, 126 N.M. 69, 966 P.2d 777, 1998 N.M. App. LEXIS 126, 37 N.M. B. Bull. 45, 37 N.M. B. Bull. No. 45 16 (1998)
    Cited by:
    1998 NMCA 155
    966 P.2d 777 p.782
    37 N.M. B. Bull. No. 45 16 p.18
Cited by:
Silva v. Town of Springer, 1996 NMCA 022, 1996 NMCA 22, 121 N.M. 428, 912 P.2d 304, 1996 N.M. App. LEXIS 4, 33 N.M. B. Bull. 11 (1996)
    Cited by:
    1996 NMCA 022
    121 N.M. 428 p.431
    912 P.2d 304 p.307
Cited by:
Delisle v. Avallone, 117 N.M. 602, 874 P.2d 1266, 1994 N.M. App. LEXIS 44, 33 N.M. B. Bull. 843 (1994)
    Cited by:
    117 N.M. 602 p.609
    874 P.2d 1266 p.1273

10th Circuit - Court of Appeals
Cited in Dissenting Opinion at:
Zaccardi v. Zale Corp., 856 F.2d 1473, 1988 U.S. App. LEXIS 12339, 3 I.E.R. Cas. (BNA) 1249, 110 Lab. Cas. (CCH) P55976 (10th Cir. Utah 1988)
    Cited in Dissenting Opinion at:
    856 F.2d 1473 p.1478
    Cited by:
    856 F.2d 1473 p.1476

10th Circuit - U.S. District Courts
Cited by:
Parker v. Hammons Hotel, 914 F. Supp. 467, 1994 U.S. Dist. LEXIS 20891, 135 Lab. Cas. (CCH) P58313 (D.N.M. 1994)
    Cited by:
    914 F. Supp. 467 p.470

California Courts of Appeal
Explained by:
Ladas v. California State Auto. Ass'n, 19 Cal. App. 4th 761, 1993 Cal. App. LEXIS 1058, 23 Cal. Rptr. 2d 810, 93 Cal. Daily Op. Service 7886, 93 D.A.R. 13441, 8 I.E.R. Cas. (BNA) 1628 (Cal. App. 1st Dist. 1993)
    Explained by:
    19 Cal. App. 4th 761 p.771
    23 Cal. Rptr. 2d 810 p.815

Washington Supreme Court
Cited by:
Swanson v. Liquid Air Corp., 118 Wash. 2d 512, 826 P.2d 664, 1992 Wash. LEXIS 71, 7 I.E.R. Cas. (BNA) 366, 125 Lab. Cas. (CCH) P57376, 126 Lab. Cas. (CCH) P57556 (1992)
    Cited by:
    118 Wash. 2d 512 p.524
    826 P.2d 664 p.671

ILLUSTRATION 11-1   *(continued)*

Page 3

SHEPARD'S - 748 P.2d 507 - 19 Citing references

Law Reviews and Periodicals (4 Citing References)
Cited by:
TRENDS IN NEW MEXICO LAW: 1995-96: CONTRACTS-Implied Employment Contracts Based on Written Policy Statements Are Not Subject to Governmental Immunity: Garcia v. Middle Rio Grande Conservancy District, 27 N.M. L. Rev. 649 (1997)
Cited by:
ARTICLE: RECONSIDERING THE LOUISIANA DOCTRINE OF EMPLOYMENT AT WILL: ON THE MISINTER-PRETATION OF ARTICLE 2747 AND THE CIVILIAN CASE FOR REQUIRING "GOOD FAITH" IN TERMINATION OF EMPLOYMENT, 69 Tul. L. Rev. 1513
Cited by:
SYMPOSIUM: BEYOND COLLECTIVE BARGAINING AND EMPLOYMENT AT WILL: THE FUTURE OF WRONGFUL DISMISSAL CLAIMS: WHERE DOES EMPLOYER SELF INTEREST LIE?, 58 U. Cin. L. Rev. 397
Cited by:
COMMENT: COMBATTING SEXUAL HARASSMENT IN THE WORKPLACE WITHOUT RISKING A WRONGFUL DISCHARGE LAWSUIT: AN EMPLOYER'S DILEMMA?*, 42 U. Kan. L. Rev. 437 (1994)

ALR Annotations (1 Citing Annotation)
Right to discharge allegedly "at-will" employee as affected by employer's promulgation of employment policies as to discharge, 33 A.L.R.4th 120, supp sec. 4

ILLUSTRATION 11-2   KeyCite Display, from Westlaw

```
KeyCite                                              Page 2
                               Date of Printing: DEC 30,1999


                          KEYCITE

CITATION: Lukoski v. Sandia Indian Management Co., 106 N.M. 664, 748 P.2d 507,
2 IER Cases 1650 (N.M., Jan 07, 1988) (NO. 16,462)
                        Citations
                   ****  Examined
    1 Zaccardi v. Zale Corp., 856 F.2d 1473, 1476+, 110 Lab.Cas.  P 55,976+,
         3 IER Cases 1249+ (10th Cir.(Utah) Sep 12, 1988) (NO. 86-1748)  ""
         HN: 1,2


                   ***  Discussed
    2 Hartbarger v. Frank Paxton Co., 857 P.2d 776, 780+, 115 N.M. 665, 669+,
         127 Lab.Cas.  P 57,664+, 8 IER Cases 1114+ (N.M. Jun 14, 1993)
         (NO. 19,913)  ""  HN: 2
    3 Newberry v. Allied Stores, Inc., 773 P.2d 1231, 1233+,
         108 N.M. 424, 426+, 4 IER Cases 562+ (N.M. May 01, 1989)
         (NO. 17,712)  ""  HN: 2
    4 Ladas v. California State Auto. Assn., 23 Cal.Rptr.2d 810, 816+,
         19 Cal.App.4th 761, 772+, 8 IER Cases 1628+
         (Cal.App. 1 Dist. Oct 22, 1993) (NO. A057353)  ""  HN: 2


                   **  Cited
    5 Garcia v. Middle Rio Grande Conservancy Dist., 918 P.2d 7, 11+,
         121 N.M. 728, 732+, 11 IER Cases 1328, 1328+ (N.M. May 21, 1996)
         (NO. 22,790)  ""  HN: 2
    6 Chavez v. Manville Products Corp., 777 P.2d 371, 374+,
         108 N.M. 643, 646+, 58 USLW 2084+, 122 Lab.Cas.  P 56,927+,
         4 IER Cases 833+ (N.M. Jul 05, 1989) (NO. 17,596)  HN: 2
    7 Paca v. K-Mart Corp., 775 P.2d 245, 247, 108 N.M. 479, 481,
         4 IER Cases 727 (N.M. May 31, 1989) (NO. 17,983)  HN: 2
    8 Kestenbaum v. Pennzoil Co., 766 P.2d 280, 284, 108 N.M. 20, 24,
         4 IER Cases 67 (N.M. Nov 30, 1988) (NO. 16,965)  HN: 2
    9 Famiglietta v. Ivie-Miller Enterprises, Inc., 966 P.2d 777, 782,
         126 N.M. 69, 1998-NMCA-155 (N.M.App. Aug 19, 1998) (NO. 17,922)
         HN: 1
   10 Silva v. Town of Springer, 912 P.2d 304, 307, 121 N.M. 428
         (N.M.App. Jan 29, 1996) (NO. 16,015)  HN: 2
   11 DeLisle v. Avallone, 874 P.2d 1266, 1273, 117 N.M. 602, 609
         (N.M.App. Jan 27, 1994) (NO. 13,652)  HN: 1
   12 Bayliss v. Contel Federal Systems, Inc., 930 F.2d 32+
         (10th Cir.(N.M.) Mar 21, 1991) (Table, text in WESTLAW,
         NO. 89-2310)  ""  HN: 2
   13 Parker v. John Q. Hammons Hotels, Inc., 914 F.Supp. 467, 470
         (D.N.M. Apr 26, 1994) (NO. CIV 93-0038MV/DJS)  HN: 2


                   © Copyright West Group 1999
```

ILLUSTRATION 11-2   *(continued)*

```
KeyCite                                                              Page 3
                              Citations
                           *   Mentioned
   14 Swanson v. Liquid Air Corp., 826 P.2d 664, 671, 118 Wash.2d 512, 524,
         125 Lab.Cas.  P 57,376, 126 Lab.Cas.  P 57,556, 7 IER Cases 366
         (Wash. Mar 05, 1992) (NO. 57358-1)  HN: 2


                           Secondary Sources
   15 Right to discharge allegedly "at-will" employee as affected by
         employer's promulgation of employment policies as to discharge,
         33 A.L.R.4th 120, §4a (1984)  HN: 2
   16  82 Am. Jur. 2d Wrongful Discharge s 91, PROMISSORY ESTOPPEL; RELIANCE
         HN: 2
   17  82 Am. Jur. 2d Wrongful Discharge s 93, MODIFICATION OF IMPLIED
         CONTRACTS  HN: 2
   18  82 Am. Jur. 2d Wrongful Discharge s 96, EFFECT OF HANDBOOKS AND POLICY
         MANUALS, GENERALLY  HN: 2
   19 CONTRACTS-IMPLIED EMPLOYMENT CONTRACTS BASED ON WRITTEN POLICY
         STATEMENTS ARE NOT SUBJECT TO GOVERNMENTAL IMMUNITY: GARCIA v.
         MIDDLE RIO GRANDE CONSERVANCY DISTRICT, 27 N.M. L. Rev. 649, 660+
         (1997)  HN: 2
   20 RECONSIDERING THE LOUISIANA DOCTRINE OF EMPLOYMENT AT WILL: ON THE
         MISINTERPRETATION OF ARTICLE 2747 AND THE CIVILIAN CASE FOR
         REQUIRING "GOOD FAITH" IN TERMINATION OF EMPLOYMENT,
         69 Tul. L. Rev. 1513, 1599 (1995)  HN: 2
   21 THE FUTURE OF WRONGFUL DISMISSAL CLAIMS: WHERE DOES EMPLOYER SELF
         INTEREST LIE?, 58 U. Cin. L. Rev. 397, 430 (1989)  HN: 2
   22 COMBATTING SEXUAL HARASSMENT IN THE WORKPLACE WITHOUT RISKING A
         WRONGFUL DISCHARGE LAWSUIT: AN EMPLOYER'S DILEMMA?,
         42 U. Kan. L. Rev. 437, 460 (1994)  HN: 2
   23 AT-WILL EMPLOYMENT: GOING, GOING . . ., 24 U. Rich. L. Rev. 187, 209+
         (1990)  HN: 2
   24 TRENDS IN WRONGFUL TERMINATION LAW AND COMMON LAW TORT CLAIMS,
         508 PLI/Lit 695, 735 (1994)  HN: 2
   25 WRONGFUL TERMINATION AND EMERGING TORTS, 416 PLI/Lit 703, 731+ (1991)
         HN: 2
   26 WRONGFUL TERMINATION AND EMERGING TORTS, 442 PLI/Lit 379, 449+ (1992)
         HN: 2
   27 RECENT DEVELOPMENTS IN THE LAW OF UNJUST DISMISSAL, 364 PLI/Lit 9, 78
         (1988)  HN: 2




                        © Copyright West Group 1999
```

ILLUSTRATION 11-3   Shepard's Citations in Paper, from *Shepard's Pacific Reporter Citations*

| PACIFIC REPORTER, 2d SERIES | | | | Vol. 748 |

—483—

Barnes v
Eighth Judicial
District Court
1987

(103Nev679)
801P2d¹1387
810P2d⁸1211

—488—

M & R
Investment
Company
Inc. v
Mandarino
1987

(103Nev711)
781P2d766
849P2d⁴315
853P2d106

—494—

Blanton
v North
Las Vegas
Municipal
Court
1987

(103Nev623)
a 489US538
a 103L𝔼550
a 109SC1289
a 57USLW4314
s 487US1203
s 488US810
s 488US938
s 101L𝔼880
s 102L𝔼23
s 102L𝔼351
s 108SC2843
s 109SC44
s 109SC360
f 752P2d²238
f 794P2d²706
844P2d804
   N J
553A2d360

—504—

C. Lambert
& Associates
Inc. v Horizon
Corp.
1988

(106NM661)

—507—

Lukoski v
Sandia Indian
Management
Co.
1988

(106NM664)
766P2d²284
773P2d²1233
775P2d²247
777P2d²374
   Cir. 10
856F2d²1476
856F2d1478
   Wash
826P2d671

—511—

Graff v
Glennen
1988

(106NM668)
853P2d723
   Cir. 10
857F2d731
935F2d1171

—512—

Morro v
Farmers
Insurance
Group
1988

(106NM669)
757P2d¹795
780P2d¹637
f 787P2d²839
787P2d³840
e 848P2d530
d 849P2d³369
   Cir. 10
923F2d1422

—516—

Allen v Board
of Education of
Albuquerque
1987

(106NM673)
d 845P2d137
   Ariz
775P2d²1164

—519—

Monroe v
Oklahoma
1987

—520—

Cunningham
v Oklahoma
1987

755P2d¹·94
762P2d¹·957
764P2d⁵904
781P2d⁵·330
813P2d531

—523—

Wood v
Oklahoma
1987

792P2d¹·80
813P2d¹·531

—526—

Thompson v
Oklahoma
1988

761P2d⁵·862
f 786P2d¹·1253
805P2d688
827P2d1342
   Wis
435NW303

—529—

Peterson
v Oklahoma
1988

—531—

King v
Oklahoma
1988

778P2d⁵·475

—535—

Simmons v
Oklahoma
1988

—536—

Ketcher v
Oklahoma
1988

767P2d²·436

—538—

Oklahoma v
Ebenhack
1985

787P2d⁴·478
q 853P2d795

—542—

In the Matter
of Ballot Title
of Robert
J. Wright's
Initiative
Petition
1988

(304Ore649)
752P2d⁶1218
767P2d¹71
774P2d¹1096
774P2d²1096
777P2d⁶409
781P2d²345
783P2d⁶1003
785P2d⁷1049
787P2d¹487
787P2d⁶487
788P2d¹⁰451
788P2d454
788P2d992
789P2d⁷260
789P2d652
789P2d¹652
789P2d¹657
799P2d⁶640
810P2d⁴838
813P2d¹39
815P2d¹699
822P2d⁶1166
j 849P2d522

—547—

Arena v
Gingrich
1988

(305Ore1)
s 733P2d75
768P2d²424
796P2d¹377
826P2d¹621
   La
531So2d453
553So2d402
   Ohio
596N𝔼525

—551—

Wicks v
O'Connell
1988

(89OrA236)

s 704P2d537
s 715P2d93
80A⅘937n

—555—

Oregon v
Larsen
1988

(89OrA260)

—558—

Utah v Egbert
1987

f 746P2d¹762
747P2d²1034
j 748P2d569
f 749P2d628
754P2d57
f 754P2d²58
j 754P2d60
754P2d667
f 758P2d²904
j 759P2d1157
f 760P2d²301
f 765P2d²1270
e 770P2d²996
j 770P2d997
f 779P2d²1137
f 784P2d145
790P2d86
791P2d²192

—568—

Utah v Bywater
1987

800P2d802

—569—

Rousay v Board
of Review of
Industrial
Commission
of Utah
1987

—572—

Peck v Eimco
Process
Equipment Co.
1987

785P2d¹1132
785P2d²1132
   Kan
832P2d⁸368

—579—

Stewart v
Coffman
1988

s 765P2d1277
763P2d²1213
767P2d¹139
771P2d684
790P2d589
793P2d394
f 852P2d¹1037

—582—

Wilburn
v Interstate
Electric
1988

s 765P2d1277
750P2d1229
751P2d257
751P2d261
755P2d²753
757P2d482
758P2d²929
763P2d816
765P2d9
768P2d977
768P2d¹978
771P2d²670
772P2d²469
784P2d1213
789P2d²56
790P2d582
793P2d931
800P2d819
814P2d1143
817P2d²347
817P2d835
818P2d1313
f 852P2d²1019
f 852P2d1023
852P2d1036

—588—

In the Matter
of K.O. v
Denison
1988

751P2d1156
752P2d905
755P2d²752
758P2d¹445
763P2d763
806P2d1208

—593—

Peterson v
Peterson
1988

761P2d³949
Continued

B.   WHY WOULD YOU RESEARCH WITH CASE CITATORS?

Case citators serve six primary functions relative to the case you have located and plan to rely upon (the cited cases):

(1) tracing its prior history,
(2) tracing its subsequent history,
(3) providing parallel citations to your cited case,
(4) helping you to determine the treatment of the cited case by leading you to other cases that have cited it,
(5) providing references to other sources that have cited the cited case, and
(6) updating your research to the present or nearly so.

Each of these functions is crucial to case law research.

Citators list the prior history and the subsequent history, if they exist, for the cited case. The history of the case (sometimes called the "direct history") is based on published decisions at all levels of the court system (recall that trial court decisions are not published as often as are appellate rulings). The prior history of the case consists of any previous decisions in the litigation; they provide the context in which the court issued the opinion you propose to rely on. The subsequent history of the case consists of decisions in the same litigation rendered after the opinion you propose to rely on; your decision may be on appeal or may have been affirmed, modified, reversed, superseded, or vacated. You should at least glance at all of the prior and subsequent history listings, and you should pay special attention to opinions modifying, reversing, superseding, or vacating the opinion you propose to rely upon.

Parallel citation listings indicate which other reporters have published a decision. Once you have a particular decision from a specific source in hand, you generally need not actually retrieve other versions. However, parallel citations are required for case citations in certain settings.

Citators also provide the treatment (also called "indirect history") of a cited case, by listing later cases, involving different parties, that cite the case and, as to some cases, by showing in what way a citing case referred to a cited case. The most negative treatment is a precedential court's overruling of the cited case's reasoning. (This is different from a reversal of the cited case on appeal, which would be within the history of the case, not the treatment.) Somewhat less negative treatment occurs in cases that criticize, disapprove of, disagree with, decline to follow, question, distinguish, or limit the cited case; these treatments indicate disfavor of the cited case or its reasoning. You should check all of these negative treatments of the cited case. If you want to locate cases reacting favorably to your case, you would look for cases paralleling or following the cited case or cases without any particular designation. Cases harmonizing or explaining the cited case might treat it negatively or positively.

Citators list other citing sources in addition to cases. Most of these are secondary sources such as encyclopedias, treatises, legal periodicals, and A.L.R. Annotations. If you consult a case citator early in your research, once you have a pertinent case citation, you can better focus the remainder of your research in secondary sources.

Incidentally, some citators indicate which topic a citing case or secondary source addresses, by appending a headnote number from the cited case to the citing source's reference.

Paper case citators are brought up to date (or nearly so) by supplements and other update services, while online case citators integrate the existing and updating information into a single collection. Thus, your research in case citators can furnish nearly up-to-date information on your case's prior and subsequent history, its parallel citation(s), its treatment in citing cases, and citations to other citing sources (especially secondary sources). This information allows you to judge your case's precedential value and importance and furthers your research in related subsequent sources.

C.   How Do You Research with Case Citators?

You should consider using case citators early in your research, because a citator may lead you to additional authority. In addition, you should citate cases as you conclude your research, to be sure they are good law at that time.

Case citators can be used online, in paper, and in CD-ROMs. Your choice among media will be based on availability, cost, editorial features, ease of use, and personal preference. Most prominent are the online and paper formats of this important research tool; the CD-ROM version is covered briefly in Part D.

Case citators in Westlaw or LEXIS:

▶ gain access to KeyCite (on Westlaw) or Shepard's online (on LEXIS)

▶ peruse the direct history and negative indirect history (treatment) of your cited case

▶ select the features and limitations needed to narrow your results

▶ peruse the chosen range of additional citing sources

▶ use the embedded links

Once you are signed onto Westlaw or LEXIS, you can gain access to the online citator directly from the case you wish to "citate." Or you can select the citator feature—KeyCite on Westlaw or Shepard's on LEXIS—and then type in the case citation. LEXIS gives you an initial choice between a KWIC view for "validation" (determining whether the case is still good law), versus a full view for "research"; the following discussion covers the full view. Exhibit 11.1 on page 155 presents the main features of the two systems, as of January 2000.

Both online citators use colorful graphic symbols to give you an at-a-glance indication of the precedential value of cited cases. For example, KeyCite uses a red status flag to warn that a case is no longer good law for at least one of the points it contains and a yellow flag to warn that a case has some negative history but has not been reversed or overruled. Shepard's uses a red stop sign to indicate a negative treatment such as reversal or overruling, a yellow caution sign to indicate a lesser negative treatment such as criticizing or limiting, and a green sign to indicate a positive treatment such as following or affirming.

The displayed information includes the full citation of the case, references to the direct history of the case (both prior and subsequent), and a list of cases and other sources that have cited the case. The citators separate the citing sources by type of source, with cases appearing first.

Within the listing of citing cases, the citators automatically separate direct from indirect case history, prior from subsequent direct history, and negative from positive treatments; or you can restrict the display in these ways. Shepard's allows you to separate citing cases by each type of treatment. KeyCite allows you to omit minor history and automatically ranks the citing cases by depth of discussion (that is, whether a citing case examines, discusses, cites, or merely mentions the cited case). In addition, the citators allow you to restrict the list of citing cases, for example, by jurisdiction, level of court.

Within noncase citing sources, both citators allow you to separate the citations by type of source. And all citing sources, cases and secondary sources, can be sorted by time period and by headnote number (West or other) of the cited case.

The editorial material contained in the online citators is within one or two days of being current, and certain material (for instance, overrulings and direct history) is current to within a few hours of receipt of the citing case by the citator's publisher.

Initially you should focus on the history of your cited case, with special attention to those rulings that occurred after your cited case. Your next priority should be to investigate any negative treatment of your cited case, especially cases within your jurisdiction that affect the precedential value of the case. You can link to the full text of each citing source.

Once you have assessed the precedential status of the cited case, you may use the list of citing cases as a means of finding additional pertinent cases, to fill out your research. If the overall list of citing cases is too cumbersome, you can restrict the display to cases from your jurisdiction, certain types of treatment or discussion, or a recent time period.

| EXHIBIT 11.1 | Main Features of KeyCite and Shepard's Online |

Features Common to Both Systems

- access is available from cited case or through separate operation
- colorful graphic symbol provides quick indication of status of cited case
- citator provides various parallel citations for cited case
- citator provides prior and subsequent history
- citator identifies negative treatment cases
- citator lists wide range of additional cases citing cited case
- citator lists some secondary sources that cite cited case
- citator shows headnote numbers for which cited case is cited
- citator permits restrictions, e.g., by type of citing source, date, type of treatment in citing source
- links connect to citing sources

KeyCite	*Shepard's*
• organizes case display by depth of discussion • provides more citing cases • provides more citing secondary sources • provides many links to West headnotes • indicates whether citing source quotes cited case	• organizes case display by court hierarchy • indicates type of treatment in citing case • covers headnotes from West and other publishers • offers Boolean search in citing cases

---

If you need sources on a particular topic, read the text of the headnotes to determine which are pertinent, then restrict the list of citing sources to the pertinent headnotes. (KeyCite refers only to the West headnotes, while Shepard's refers to the headnotes from various publishers.) Shepard's allows you to conduct a Boolean search within the text of the citing sources, to locate a particular fact situation or particular language of the court.

These display and restriction options are evolving on both online citators, so be sure to check the available options each time you use an online citator. Both systems have fairly clear directions for how to accomplish the steps listed above.

When researching the Canoga case, we used both of the online citators, for comparison's sake, to cite the *Lukoski* case discussed in Chapter 10. See Illustration 11-1 on pages 146–148 and 11-2 on pages 149–150. Both citators showed that the case had no direct history; the New Mexico Supreme Court disposition in 1988 was the final disposition, and there were no reported opinions before that opinion. Shepard's shows four parallel citations for that opinion, while KeyCite shows three.

Illustration 11-1 shows the full display from Shepard's on LEXIS. Thirteen citing cases are grouped by jurisdiction, starting with the New Mexico Supreme Court, then the New Mexico Court of Appeals, and then the federal and other state courts. The various entries note the type of reference (cited, followed, etc.) and the particular page of the reference. Shepard's provides a caution about possible negative treatment in *Hartbarger*, a New Mexico Supreme Court case that distinguishes *Lukoski*. The display also lists four law review articles and one A.L.R. Annotation.

Illustration 11-2 shows the citation list from KeyCite on Westlaw. The fourteen cases are grouped by depth of treatment (examined, discussed, cited, mentioned), and quote marks appear after each case that quotes *Lukoski*. The thirteen secondary sources are grouped by type but not so labeled; they include one A.L.R. Annotation, three Am. Jur. 2d encyclopedia sections, five law review articles, and four CLE materials. The pertinent West headnote numbers appear after each citing source. KeyCite listed more secondary sources than did Shepard's because it covers a wider range of secondary sources.

We did not further restrict the display of either online citator, because the listings were easy to comprehend and lacked the bulkiness that sometimes necessitates the use of restrictions.

Shepardizing in paper:

▶ determine which Shepard's citations and part(s) cover your cited case

▶ assemble all of the needed volumes and supplements

▶ locate the list(s) of citing sources for the cited case

▶ translate the abbreviations and codes

▶ review selected citing sources in priority order

Collect the appropriate volumes. First, you must pick the appropriate Shepard's title or titles. Shepard's publishes federal, state, and regional citators. If your research involves a United States Supreme Court case, use *Shepard's United States Citations, Case Edition*. Similarly, if you are researching a case reported in the *Federal Reporter* (court of appeals cases) or *Federal Supplement* (district court cases), use the appropriate part of *Shepard's Federal Citations* to Shepardize your case.

If your research involves a state court case, you may use a state citator. One part of a state citator allows you to Shepardize a case by its official reporter citation, if it has one, and another part allows you to Shepardize a citations by its regional reporter citation. Both parts of a state citator list parallel citations and citing cases from that state's courts and from federal courts. The official reporter part lists citations from additional sources; these citations appear in the regional reporter part of the state citator if there is no corresponding official reporter. See Exhibit 11.2 below for a chart of these differences. Because the official reporter part of the citator includes more citing sources but the regional reporter part contains citations from the more frequently published regional reporter, you generally should Shepardize your case in both parts of a state citator.

Shepard's also publishes a citator for each of the regional reporters. Regional citators include citing cases from the courts of every state, not just from federal courts and from the courts of the state in which the case arose. Review Exhibit 11.2.

A good strategy in paper citators is to start with the appropriate Shepard's state citator; check, if applicable, both the official reporter part and the regional reporter part to retrieve all mandatory case law authority from your state, as well as some commentary. Then expand your research to the appropriate Shepard's regional citator and search for persuasive authority. If your cited case is a persuasive precedent from a sister state, you would use a regional citator to learn whether that case has been cited by the courts of your state.

Make certain that you assemble all the main volumes and supplements needed for your research. To identify them, find the most recent paper supplement for the Shepard's title; it should generally be no more than a month old. Its cover should list what constitutes a complete set of Shepard's volumes for that title. Select from that set only those volumes and supplements

| **Exhibit 11.2** | Major Citing Sources in Various Shepard's Citations |

| | | New Mexico Citations | |
Citing Sources	*Pacific Reporter, Second Series, Citations*	*Regional Division*	*State/ Official Division*
United States Supreme Court reporters	√	√	√
Federal Reporter	√	√	√
Federal Supplement	√	√	√
Regional reporters	√	New Mexico cases from *Pacific Reporter*	
LEXIS	√	√	√
New Mexico Reports			√
ABA Journal	√		√
Selected law reviews			√
A.L.R. Annotations	√		√

that include citations to the reporter volume and series in which your case is printed.

Locate and peruse the entries for your case. Next, within each volume and supplement, turn to the appropriate part or parts; then locate the volume and page number that correspond to the cited case's citation. Read the entries for the cited case. Refer to Illustration 11-3 on page 151. The basic format of each listed citation is the case's volume number, its reporter title (in abbreviated format), and the page of the pertinent reference. A table of abbreviations of sources' titles appears in the front matter of each volume. Some citations are preceded by a letter; the code list for these letters appears in the front matter of Shepard's volumes. See Illustration 11-4 on pages 159–160.

Shepard's first lists (in parentheses) the parallel citations, if any, to your cited case in the official reporter, an unofficial reporter, or A.L.R. Annotations, as appropriate. Parallel citations are printed when they first become available and are not reprinted in subsequent volumes of Shepard's.

Shepard's next indicates the prior and subsequent history of a cited case. A history citation is preceded by one of Shepard's history abbreviations. Be especially alert for the "r," "m," and "v" abbreviations; "r" means the case has been reversed on appeal; "m" means it has been modified; and "v" means the decision has been vacated and no longer has precedential value.

Next, Shepard's lists citing cases. They are grouped in a predictable order; for example, in the regional citators, the first citations after the history citations are from the courts of the state that decided the cited case. Some of these cases are accompanied by treatment codes, so you can tell if a later case has explicitly overruled your case (noted by an "o"), criticizes your case ("c"), questions it ("q"), explains it ("e"), follows it ("f"), or distinguishes it ("d"). See Illustration 11-4 on pages 160–161. If a citing case does not have a treatment code, the case may be less significant. Some citations to citing cases include a superscript number to the left of a page number; it corresponds to the headnote number from the cited case that is discussed on that page of the citing case.

The last group of citations in a citation list are to secondary sources, such as A.L.R. Annotations. In state citators, these citations may be preceded by citations from state attorney general's opinions or other state sources.

Many Shepard's citation lists are very long and can appear overwhelming. To use Shepard's efficiently, check the history of your case to be sure it has not been reversed, vacated, or modified. Then check for cases from your jurisdiction that have significant treatment codes, address pertinent headnotes, and are recent.

Because there is a time lag between when a case is decided and when Shepard's lists the cases it cites, you should update your paper research. You may phone the Shepard's Daily Update at the number listed in the latest supplement. Or you may update your Shepard's research online on LEXIS or at the Shepard's web site.

Researching the Canoga case. We Shepardized *Lukoski,* which has both an official reporter citation (*New Mexico Reports*) and a regional reporter citation (*Pacific Reporter, Second Series*). Hence, we could Shepardize it in

Shepard's Pacific Reporter Citations, as well as in *Shepard's New Mexico Citations*, in both the official reporter part (*New Mexico Reports*) or the regional reporter part (*Pacific Reporter, Second Series*). The Shepard's entries for the *Lukoski* case in Illustration 11-3 on page 151 are from the 1994 main volume of *Shepard's Pacific Reporter Citations*.

In Illustration 11-3, immediately below the case name and date, the parallel citation to the case in *New Mexico Reports* appears. The *Lukoski* case has no reported prior or subsequent history. It has been followed by the New Mexico courts, cited in a dissenting opinion by the Tenth Circuit Court of Appeals, and cited in a Washington case, among other things. Many of the citing cases involve the issue that was reflected in headnote two of *Lukoski*, as printed in the *Pacific Reporter, Second Series*—the issue relevant to the Canoga case. We would focus on New Mexico cases dealing with headnote two, beginning with the case that clearly followed *Lukoski*; then we would check to see if the Tenth Circuit decisions involve New Mexico law and, if so, how the Tenth Circuit interprets state law. The Shepard's entry for the *Lukoski* case does not include citations from secondary sources.

To bring the paper Shepardizing of *Lukoski* up to date, we would, of course, consult supplements to the 1994 main volume and pursue the steps listed above to update paper Shepard's.

D. WHAT ELSE?

Citators Not Citable.   Because citators are a research tool, not a source, they should never be cited. Instead, you should cite to the sources found by means of citators.

Shepard's on CD-ROM.   The CD-ROM version of Shepard's Citations is a hybrid of the paper and online versions. It resembles the paper citators because it does not integrate the state and regional citators, or the official and regional parts of the state citator. You usually must bring your research up to date by using the Daily Update service, available by means of a CD-ROM connection to the Internet. In other respects, the CD-ROM Shepard's citator resembles Shepard's online, except for the following three additional features: Extract identifies all citations in a word-processed document and Shepardizes them for you; CiteFinder allows you to type in citations of several relevant authorities, then Shepardizes those authorities and provides a ranked list of authorities that are likely to be useful in your continuing research; and Underpinnings shows you whether any of the cases relied on in your cited case have potential problems with their precedential value.

Online Citing Sources.   At this juncture, KeyCite contains more secondary sources than does Shepard's. However, the list of citing sources covered by the online citators is expanding. As of late 1999, it could be checked in Westlaw by consulting the online publications list in KeyCite and in LEXIS

ILLUSTRATION 11-4	Shepard's Citations Abbreviations from *Shepard's Pacific Reporter* citation

ABBREVIATIONS—ANALYSIS
CASES

History of Case

a	(affirmed)	Same case affirmed on appeal to a higher level court.
cc	(connected case)	The case is related to your case in some way in that it involves either the same parties or arises out of the same subject matter. However, it is not the same action on the merits.
D	(dismissed)	An action which has been appealed from a lower court to a higher court has been discontinued without further hearing.
De	(denied)	Review or rehearing denied.
GP	(granted and citable)	Review granted and ordered published.
Gr	(granted)	Review or hearing granted.
m	(modified)	The lower court's decision is changed in some way, either during a rehearing or by action of a higher court. For example, if a court of appeals affirms a trial court decision in part and reverses it in part, that trial court decision is shown as modified by the court of appeals.
Np	(not published)	Reporter of Decisions directed not to publish this opinion.
Op	(original opinion)	Citation of original opinion.
r	(reversed)	The lower court is reversed on appeal to a higher court.
RE	(republished)	Reporter of Decisions directed to publish opinion previously ordered not published.
s	(same case)	The case is the identical action to your case, although at a different stage of the proceedings. "Same case" refers to many different situations, including motions and opinions that preceded your case. It is important to read these cases if you need to know exactly what occured.
S	(superseded)	A subsequent opinion has been substituted for your case.
v	(vacated)	The opinion has been rendered void and is no longer of precedential value.
#		Citing references may be of questionable precedential value as review was granted by California Supreme Court or case was ordered not published.
US	cert den	Certiorari has been denied by the U. S. Supreme Court.
US	cert dis	Certiorari has been dismissed by the U. S. Supreme Court.
US	reh den	Rehearing has been denied by the U. S. Supreme Court.
US	reh dis	Rehearing has been dismissed by the U. S. Supreme Court.
US	app pndg	Appeal pending before the U.S. Supreme Court

Treatment of Case

c	(criticized)	The court is disagreeing with the soundness of your decision, although the court may not have the jurisdiction or the authority to materially affect its precedential value.
d	(distinguished)	The case is different from your case in significant aspects. It involves either a dissimilar fact situation or a different application of the law.
e	(explained)	The court is interpreting your case in a significant way.

ILLUSTRATION 11-4		*(continued)*

f	(followed)	Your case is being relied upon as controlling or persuasive authority.
h	(harmonized)	The cases differ in some way; however, the court finds a way to reconcile the differences.
j	(dissenting opinion)	Your case is cited in the dissent of this opinion.
L	(limited)	The court restricts the application of your opinion. The court usually finds that the reasoning of your opinion applies only in very specific instances.
o	(overruled)	The court has determined that the reasoning in your case is no longer valid, either in part or in its entirety.
p	(parallel)	This letter is usually found in older cases where your case was described as "on all fours" or "parallel" to the citing case. Your case is being relied upon as controlling or persuasive authority.
q	(questioned)	The soundness of your case is at issue. For example, your decision may have been legislatively overruled, or its reasoning may have been overruled by an opposing line of authority.

ABBREVIATIONS—COURTS

Cir. DC–U.S. Court of Appeals, District of Columbia Circuit
Cir. (number)–U.S. Court of Appeals Circuit (number)
Cir. Fed.–U.S. Court of Appeals, Federal Circuit
CCPA–Court of Customs and Patent Appeals
CIT–United States Court of International Trade
ClCt–Claims Court (U.S.)
CtCl–Court of Claims (U.S.)
CuCt–Customs Court
ECA–Temporary Emergency Court of Appeals
ML–Judicial Panel on Multidistrict Litigation
RRR–Special Court Regional Rail Reorganization Act of 1973

xii

by consulting the Citation Abbreviations list within the online Product Guide for Shepard's Citations.

Citations Counter. To analyze the importance of the cited case, use Key-Cite's Citations counter feature. It determines how often and on what topics the cited case has been cited, as well as whether that number of citations is average, or above or below, for that year and jurisdiction.

KeyCite Alert. This Westlaw service automatically monitors the status of a specified case and sends you updates when its KeyCite information changes. When you select this option, you can specify how often the case should be checked and where the results should be delivered electronically.

Table of Authorities. Westlaw's Table of Authorities permits you to view the cases cited within your cited case, a "reverse citator" function. For each case, the table notes any red or yellow status flag and lists the page on which the case is discussed within your cited case and the depth of its treatment. This Westlaw feature is similar to Underpinnings in CD-ROM Shepard's.

Cite-Checking Software. Westcheck (connects to Westlaw) and Checkcite 2000 (connects to LEXIS) extract the citations from a word-processed document, check the accuracy of the citation information, run the citations through the online citator, check the accuracy of quotations, and allow you to link to the cited source. This software is a cost-efficient and thorough way to check some aspects of your research in a final document.

E. CONCLUDING POINTS

Case citators help you to ascertain the precedential status of a case, to locate related sources, and to update your case research. The online citators have many advantages over the paper citators, as well as several advantages over the CD-ROM citators. First, they search the equivalent of multiple paper citators at the same time, and they automatically search the correct parts of those citators. Second, they display older and newer information in a single integrated list. Third, they are easier to read. Fourth, you can ask the computer to show you only those citing documents that meet the criteria you specify and thereby create customized lists. Fifth, the online citators provide links between the citations of the citing documents and the full text of those documents, making it fast and easy for you to scan citing documents for relevance. Finally, the online citators are updated automatically.

Thus, even though online citators may be more expensive (depending on your contract with the online vendor), online citators, when used skillfully, make your research more cost-effective and comprehensive, because of the advantages listed above.

ENACTED LAW

PRELIMINARY POINTS

Thus far, you have learned how to use secondary sources to locate and understand primary authority, and you have learned how to research one form of primary authority—case law. In this chapter, you will learn to research an additional body of primary authority—enacted law, that is, statutes, constitutions, and related materials.

This unit has two chapters. Chapter 12 explains what statutes and constitutions are, how they relate to case law, and why they are so important in legal research. It then covers various ways of researching enacted laws and related case law. Chapter 13 covers methods of researching the legislative process; such research helps you discern what a legislature meant when it enacted a statute, as well as what a legislature is considering enacting for the future.

This unit continues to illustrate the re-search of the Canoga case stated on pages 3–4. One of the issues in that case, suggested by the research in secondary sources presented in Unit II, is whether the orchestra had the legal right to regulate employees' smoking outside of the workplace; this issue implicates the employee's interest in privacy. A second issue pertains to discrimination based on nicotine addiction, which might be considered a disability. This unit focuses on these two issues.

A note about terminology: This unit uses "bill" to refer to potential legislation under consideration by a legislature; "legislation" or "law" to refer to a bill that is passed, thereby becoming law; and "statute" to refer to the law on a particular topic that has been created by the legislature through one or more enacted laws and that is in effect on a specific date.

CODES AND SESSION LAWS

A. WHAT ARE CONSTITUTIONS AND STATUTES?

United States law is dominated by enacted law, created at the federal, state, and local levels. Federal and state constitutions and local charters create government structures, defining the powers of the government and the rights of the governed. Federal and state statutes and local ordinances govern a wide range of activities by public and private entities and individuals. Constitutions and statutes have somewhat different roles in the United States legal system, yet they resemble each other and are researched in much the same way.

1. What Is a Constitution?

a. How Is a Constitution Developed?

In the American Revolutionary War era, the colonial governments sent delegates to participate in a Continental Congress, which served as the first democratic government of the American colonies. The Second Continental Congress drew up the first Articles of Confederation; they were ratified by the colonies in 1781, thereby creating the United States of America. However, certain defects soon became apparent in the Articles of Confederation, and a constitutional convention was assembled in Philadelphia in 1787. The major political figures at that time submitted drafts that were debated and revised many times. With promises that a bill of rights spelling out specific protections afforded the governed would soon follow, the Constitution was finally ratified and became effective in 1789. The Bill of Rights, comprised of the first ten amendments to the Constitution, did soon follow.

One of the most important aspects of a constitution is its durable nature. Because it embodies the highest law, a constitution is not easily changed. To amend the United States Constitution, a proposed amendment first must pass two-thirds of both houses of Congress or the legislatures of two-thirds of the states; it then must be ratified by three-fourths of the states. In more than 200 years, only twenty-seven amendments (including the Bill of Rights) have been made to the United States Constitution.

Like the federal constitution, state constitutions generally are created by state constitutional conventions. Some states have had several constitutions. State constitutions are amended more frequently than the federal constitution. In the typical process, amendments are initiated by the state legislature or by public initiative and are then approved by public referendum.

b.   What Does a Constitution Do?

A constitution is the highest law in a constitutional democratic regime. A constitution describes the structure of the government, the inherent powers of the government, and the limits placed on the government's authority to govern with regard to certain matters.

The United States Constitution creates our three branches of government, describes the scope of power of each branch, and maintains the careful balance of powers so critical to our form of democratic governance. The Constitution creates the Congress, empowers it to enact legislation, and places limits on that power. For example, the First Amendment limits the power of Congress to pass statutes that infringe on the freedoms of speech, the press, and religion. The United States Constitution also creates the federal court system, detailing the process for selecting Supreme Court justices, defining the jurisdiction of the federal courts, and granting Congress the right to establish lower federal courts. Constitutional provisions pertaining to the executive branch detail how presidents are elected, impeached, and succeeded. The Constitution also provides for presidential powers such as the right to veto legislation (subject to congressional override), to negotiate international treaties, and to serve as commander-in-chief of the military.

Under our federalist system, each state also has its separate constitution which likewise details the structure of the state and local governments, grants them powers to act in certain areas, and protects the rights of persons within the state. Typically, the rights protected by a state constitution mirror the rights protected by the federal constitution; however, a state constitution may grant additional rights to its people, so long as those rights do not conflict with the federal constitution. Some state constitutions also govern the conduct of private citizens or entities.

A constitution states broad principles that are intended to stand the test of time. Most provisions have little detail or explanation. A constitution is organized by parts and subparts, such as articles and clauses. Generally, amendments are not integrated into the text of the original constitution, but rather appear as separate provisions in the order ratified.

Illustration 12-1 on page 170 is an excerpt from the New Mexico Constitution. It is a part of New Mexico's bill of rights.

2. What Is a Statute?

a. How Are Statutes Developed?

Statutes are created by a state legislature or the federal Congress in a highly collaborative process involving legislators, the executive branch, and members of the public, who act both as lobbyists and as interested individuals. Legislatures are both reactive and proactive institutions. Although interested individuals and groups bring concerns to the legislature, legislators also seek to anticipate or respond to trends and evolving issues they identify. The legislative process is open to all constituencies, so it inevitably is political in the sense that a government body listens to the diverse interests of its constituencies and decides how to honor those interests.

Nearly anyone may generate a bill—a new piece of proposed legislation. The bill itself must be introduced by a legislator. In a typical process, the bill then passes through committee hearings, committee deliberations, full-chamber floor debates, and eventual votes in both houses of the legislature before the bill is sent to the executive (governor or president) for approval or veto. Of course, the bill may be amended or may perish at any of these steps.

A law once passed is not written in stone. Should circumstances or public sentiment change, a legislature may return to the statute, to amend it or even repeal it, through the process described above. Some statutes are amended many times.

b. What Does a Statute Look Like?

Although the statutory law on a topic may consist of a single brief provision, many statutes consist of multiple related sections. An elaborate statute generally begins with a statement of the purpose of the statute, definitions, and a delineation of the scope, or coverage, of the statute. Next come the operative provisions: the general rule, any exceptions to the rule, consequences of violations of the rule, and enforcement provisions. The closing sections may include provisions on how the statute is to be severed if part of it is invalid and when the statute becomes effective. In an elaborate statute, the sections and subsections are separately numbered (sometimes with gaps in the numbering sequence to accommodate later additions and to set off separate topics).

Not all statutes fit this description. Compact statutes do not contain all of these components. In other statutes, the components may be unlabeled or presented in a different order.

When a statute is amended, the old text must of course give way to new text. Obsolete language is deleted, and new language is inserted. Generally this revision is accomplished within the organizational framework set by the original statute.

Regarding the Canoga case, Illustration 12-2 on pages 171–172 shows New Mexico's Employee Privacy Act, a six-section statute organized with definitions at the outset, the general rule in the third section, and the consequences of a violation in the remaining sections. Illustration 12-3 on pages 173–174 is a list of provisions in the federal Americans with Disabilities Act of 1990, a fifty-section statute broken into one preliminary unit and four topical subchapters (on employment, public services, public accommodations, and miscellaneous topics). Within each subchapter, definitions generally come first, operative provisions make up most of the sections, and enforcement provisions appear toward the end.

3.   How Does Enacted Law Relate to Case Law?

Although cases and statutes are both primary authority, they develop and are analyzed differently. As discussed in Chapter 10, case law develops case by case, each case focusing on the situation that prompted the litigation. Cases serve as binding or persuasive precedent for future disputes involving similar situations. In contrast, enacted laws are enacted by legislators who are seeking to describe and set rules for a broad class of situations that will arise in the future.

Constitutions are the supreme law in a jurisdiction, yet most provisions are framed in vague and general terms. Hence the courts play an active role in the development of constitutional law. It is up to the courts to discern what spare constitutional language means in myriad particular circumstances. As you research a constitutional issue, you most likely will find yourself grappling with a substantial body of case law.

Statutes bear various relationships to common law. Some statutes codify, clarify, or supplement pre-existing common law. Some statutes overturn the common law. Still other statutes create whole new areas of law not covered in the common law. Because the constitution grants the legislative branch broad powers, statutes usually take precedence over common law that conflicts with statutory provisions.

In turn, statutes become the subject of discussion in case law. Courts apply statutes to disputes that lead to litigation. Courts have two primary tasks in such cases, one common, the other rare. First, courts interpret the legislature's language and use it to resolve the parties' dispute. Second, less commonly, courts assess whether the statute is constitutional; if not, the statute is declared unconstitutional and has no further effect. The number of cases varies greatly from statute to statute, depending on the breadth of the statute's impact, the clarity of its language, and its age. Some statutes have no interpreting cases; some have thousands. Thus, as you research a statute, you should also research case law interpreting the statute; otherwise, your research will be incomplete.

4.   What Is a Uniform Act?

Uniform acts are statutory proposals drafted by public or private organizations that seek to standardize the statutory law of the fifty states. The drafters then recommend enactment of the proposal to the various state legislatures. Model acts address topics that may not be of critical concern to all jurisdictions or that likely will not be enacted by a substantial number of jurisdictions.

Uniform and model acts come from a variety of sources: The National Conference of Commissioners on Uniform State Laws (NCCUSL), formed in 1892, consists of attorneys, judges, legislators, and law professors appointed as commissioners from each state; the NCCUSL has approved more than 200 model and uniform acts. The American Law Institute (ALI) (which promulgates Restatements of the Law, discussed in Chapter 8) also drafts model acts. The ALI and NCCUSL occasionally work in tandem; the Uniform Commercial Code, a joint NCCUSL-ALI project, has nearly standardized commercial practice among the states, federal jurisdictions, and American territories. Section committees of the American Bar Association (ABA) and the Council of State Governments also promulgate model acts on occasion. Finally, private individuals, most notably law faculty, occasionally propose model legislation.

Achieving uniformity in state laws through these efforts generally benefits the public. Uniformity in state laws promotes and simplifies interstate activities. However, complete uniformity is rarely achieved because few acts are enacted by every jurisdiction and because few uniform or model acts are enacted verbatim. Even so, the act's effect, organization, and underlying policies generally remain unaltered, so that some degree of uniformity is achieved.

The organization of most uniform or model acts resembles the organization of other statutes: initial sections on purpose, scope, and definitions; operative provisions; consequences and enforcement provisions. Comments following the individual provisions clarify terms, concepts, or language and explain why the drafters adopted a certain approach or doctrine. In addition, notes accompanying the act may cover predecessor acts, the process and date of adoption by the drafting organization, the reasons for its adoption, and its key provisions.

| ILLUSTRATION 12-1 | New Mexico Constitution, from *New Mexico Statutes Annotated* |

Art. II, § 4   BILL OF RIGHTS   Art. II, § 4

Sec. 4. [Inherent rights.]

All persons are born equally free, and have certain natural, inherent and inalienable rights, among which are the rights of enjoying and defending life and liberty, of acquiring, possessing and protecting property, and of seeking and obtaining safety and happiness.

Rights described in this section are not absolute, but are subject to reasonable regulation. Otero v. Zouhar, 102 N.M. 493, 697 P.2d 493 (Ct. App. 1984), aff'd in part and rev'd in part on other grounds, 102 N.M. 482, 697 P.2d 482 (1985), overruled on other grounds, Grantland v. Lea Regional Hosp., Inc., 110 N.M. 378, 796 P.2d 599 (1990).

Unreasonable interference with others. — This section means that each person may seek his safety and happiness in any way he sees fit so long as he does not unreasonably interfere with the safety and happiness of another. 1966 Op. Att'y Gen. No. 66-15.

Graduated income tax provisions are in no way related to or in conflict with the inherent rights provision in this section. Such income tax provisions do not prevent or deny a person's natural inherent and inalienable rights. 1968 Op. Att'y Gen. No. 68-9.

Economic policy adopted by state. — A state is free to adopt an economic policy that may reasonably be deemed to promote the public welfare and may enforce that policy by appropriate legislation without violation of the due process clause so long as such legislation has a reasonable relation to a proper legislative purpose and is neither arbitrary nor discriminatory. Rocky Mt. Whsle. Co. v. Ponca Whsle. Mercantile Co., 68 N.M. 228, 360 P.2d 643, appeal dismissed, 368 U.S. 31, 82 S. Ct. 145, 7 L. Ed. 2d 90 (1961).

Laws 1937, ch. 44, § 2, Fair Trade Act (49-2-2, 1953 Comp., now repealed), was unconstitutional and void as an arbitrary and unreasonable exercise of the police power without any substantial relation to the public health, safety or general welfare insofar as it concerned persons who were not parties to contracts provided for in Laws 1937, ch. 44, § 1 (49-2-1, 1953 Comp., now repealed). Skaggs Drug Center v. General Elec. Co., 63 N.M. 215, 315 P.2d 967 (1957).

The right of association emanating from the first amendment is not absolute. Its exercise, as is the exercise of express first amendment rights, is subject to some regulation as to time and place. Futrell v. Ahrens, 88 N.M. 284, 540 P.2d 214 (1975).

The right of association has never been held to apply to the right of one individual to associate with another, and certainly it has never been construed as an absolute right of association between a man and woman at any and all places and times. Futrell v. Ahrens, 88 N.M. 284, 540 P.2d 214 (1975).

Constitutional rights of teachers and students. — Neither students nor teachers shed their constitutional rights to freedom of speech or expression at the schoolhouse gate; school officials do not possess absolute authority over their students, and among the activities to which schools are dedicated is personal communication among students, which is an important part of the educational process. Futrell v. Ahrens, 88 N.M. 284, 540 P.2d 214 (1975).

A regulation of the board of regents of the New Mexico state university which prohibited visitation by persons of the opposite sex in residence hall, or dormitory, bedrooms maintained by the regents on the university campus, except when moving into the residence halls and during annual homecoming celebrations, where the regents placed no restrictions on intervisitation between persons of the opposite sex in the lounges or lobbies of the residence halls, the

student union building, library or other buildings, or at any other place on or off the campus, and no student was required to live in a residence hall, did not interfere appreciably, if at all, with the intercommunication important to the students of the university, the regulation was reasonable, served legitimate educational purposes and promoted the welfare of the students at the university. Futrell v. Ahrens, 88 N.M. 284, 540 P.2d 214 (1975).

Although personal intercommunication among students at schools, including universities, is an important part of the educational process, it is not the only, or even the most important, part of that process. Futrell v. Ahrens, 88 N.M. 284, 540 P.2d 214 (1975).

Status of resident for divorce purposes. — The New Mexico legislature may constitutionally confer the status of resident for divorce purposes upon those continuously stationed within this state by reason of military assignment. Wilson v. Wilson, 58 N.M. 411, 272 P.2d 319 (1954).

Right to protect property. — The right to protect property being a specifically mentioned right, its presence in this section might provide the basis for additional protection against unreasonable searches and seizures. State v. Sutton, 112 N.M. 449, 816 P.2d 518 (Ct. App. 1991).

Reclamation district contract. — A provision of a reclamation contract allowing a reclamation district to enter into a lawful contract with the United States for the improvement of the district and the increase of its water supply does not violate this section or art. II, § 18. Middle Rio Grande Water Users Ass'n v. Middle Rio Grande Conservancy Dist., 57 N.M. 287, 258 P.2d 391 (1953).

Cause of action as property right. — Cause of action which Indian acquires when tort is committed against him is property which he may acquire or become invested with, particularly if tort is committed outside of reservation by a state citizen who is not an Indian; where Indian is killed as result of such tort, the cause of action survives. Trujillo v. Prince, 42 N.M. 337, 78 P.2d 145 (1938).

Recovery of damages as property right. — A tort victim's interest in full recovery of damages calls for a form of scrutiny somewhere between minimum rationality and strict scrutiny. Therefore, intermediate scrutiny should be applied to determine the constitutionality of the cap on damages in Subsection A(2) of 41-4-19 NMSA 1978 of the Tort Claims Act. Trujillo v. City of Albuquerque, 110 N.M. 621, 798 P.2d 571 (1990).

Ordinance denying right to canvass. — Green River ordinance was held valid despite contention that it deprived photographer who employed solicitors to canvass residential areas of right to acquire and enjoy property. Green v. Town of Gallup, 46 N.M. 71, 120 P.2d 619 (1941).

Comparable provisions. — Idaho Const., art. I, § 1.

Iowa Const., art. I, § 1.

Montana Const., art. II, § 3.

Utah Const., art. I, § 1.

Law reviews. — For survey, "The Statute of Limitations in Medical Malpractice Actions," see 6 N.M. L. Rev. 271 (1976).

Am. Jur. 2d, A.L.R. and C.J.S. references. —

3

ILLUSTRATION 12-2 New Mexico Statute Re Employee Privacy, from *Michie's Law on Disc* for New Mexico

1

ARTICLE 11
EMPLOYEE PRIVACY

Section
50-11-1. Short title.
50-11-2. Definitions.
50-11-3. Employers; unlawful practices.
50-11-4. Remedies.
50-11-5. Court fees and costs.
50-11-6. Mitigation of damages.

50-11-1. Short title.

This act [50-11-1 to 50-11-6 NMSA 1978] may be cited as the "Employee Privacy Act".

History: Laws 1991, ch. 244, § 1.

Am. Jur. 2d, A.L.R. and C.J.S. references. - What is "record" within meaning of Privacy Act of 1974 (5 USCS § 552a), 121 A.L.R. Fed. 465.

50-11-2. Definitions.

As used in the Employee Privacy Act [50-11-1 to 50-11-6 NMSA 1978]:
A. "employee" means a person that performs a service for wages or other remuneration under a contract of hire, written or oral, express or implied, and includes a person employed by the state or a political subdivision of the state;
B. "employer" means a person that has one or more employees and includes an agent of an employer and the state or a political subdivision of the state; and
C. "person" means an individual, sole proprietorship, partnership, corporation, association or any other legal entity.

History: Laws 1991, ch. 244, § 2.

50-11-3. Employers; unlawful practices.

A. It is unlawful for an employer to:
(1) refuse to hire or to discharge any individual, or otherwise disadvantage any individual, with respect to compensation, terms, conditions or privileges of employment because the individual is a smoker or nonsmoker, provided that the individual complies with applicable laws or policies regulating smoking on the premises of the employer during working hours; or
(2) require as a condition of employment that any employee or applicant for employment abstain from smoking or using tobacco products during nonworking hours, provided the individual complies with applicable laws or policies regulating smoking on the premises of the employer during working hours.

ILLUSTRATION 12-2   *(continued)*

2

B. The provisions of Subsection A of this section shall not be deemed to protect any activity that:

(1) materially threatens an employer's legitimate conflict of interest policy reasonably designed to protect the employer's trade secrets, proprietary information or other proprietary interests; or

(2) relates to a bona fide occupational requirement and is reasonably and rationally related to the employment activities and responsibilities of a particular employee or a particular group of employees, rather than to all employees of the employer.

History: Laws 1991, ch. 244, § 3.

50-11-4. Remedies.

Any employee claiming to be aggrieved by any unlawful action of an employer pursuant to Section 3 of the Employee Privacy Act [50-11-1 to 50-11-6 NMSA 1978] may bring a civil suit for damages in any district court of competent jurisdiction. The employee may be awarded all wages and benefits due up to and including the date of the judgment.

History: Laws 1991, ch. 244, § 4.

50-11-5. Court fees and costs.

In any civil suit arising from the Employee Privacy Act [50-11-1 to 50-11-6 NMSA 1978], the court shall award the prevailing party court costs and reasonable attorneys' fees.

History: Laws 1991, ch. 244, § 5.

50-11-6. Mitigation of damages.

Nothing in the Employee Privacy Act [50-11-1 to 50-11-6 NMSA 1978] shall be construed to relieve a person from the obligation to mitigate damages.

History: Laws 1991, ch. 244, § 6.

ARTICLE 12
EMPLOYER IMMUNITY FOR EMPLOYEE REFERENCES

Section
50-12-1. Employer immunity from liability for references on former employee.

50-12-1. Employer immunity from liability for references on former employee.

When requested to provide a reference on a former or current employee, an employer acting in good faith is immune from liability for comments about the former employee's job performance. The immunity shall not apply when the reference information supplied was knowingly false or deliberately misleading, was rendered with malicious purpose or violated any civil rights of the

ILLUSTRATION 12-3   Outline of Federal Statute Re Disability Discrimination, from *United States Code*

Page 643   TITLE 42—THE PUBLIC HEALTH AND WELFARE   § 12007

§ 12006. Reports

(a) Report by Secretary

One year after December 11, 1989, and annually thereafter, the Secretary shall report to Congress on the programs and projects supported under this chapter and the progress being made toward accomplishing the goals and purposes set forth in this chapter.

(b) National renewable energy and energy efficiency management plan

(1) The Secretary, in consultation with the Advisory Committee, shall prepare a three-year management plan to be administered and carried out by the Secretary in the conduct of activities under this chapter.

(2) After opportunity for public comment and consideration, as appropriate, of such comment, the Secretary shall publish the plan.

(3) In addition to describing the Secretary's intentions for administering this chapter, the plan shall include a comprehensive strategy for assisting the private sector—

(A) in commercializing the renewable energy and energy efficiency technologies developed under this chapter; and

(B) in meeting competition from foreign suppliers of products derived from renewable energy and energy efficiency technologies.

(4) The plan shall address the role of federally-assisted research, development, and demonstration in the achievement of applicable national policy goals of the National Energy Policy Plan required under section 7321 of this title and the plan developed under section 5905 of this title.

(5) In addition, the Plan [1] shall—

(A) contain a detailed assessment of program needs, objectives, and priorities for each of the programs authorized under section 12005 of this title;

(B) use a uniform prioritization methodology to facilitate cost-benefit analyses of proposals in various program areas;

(C) establish milestones for setting forth specific technology transfer activities under each program area;

(D) include annual and five-year cost estimates for individual programs under this chapter; and

(E) identify program areas for which funding levels have been changed from the previous year's Plan.[1]

(6) Within one year after October 24, 1992, the Secretary shall submit a revised management plan under this section to Congress. Thereafter, the Secretary shall submit a management plan every three years at the time of submittal of the President's annual budget submission to the Congress.

(c) Report on options

As part of the first report submitted under subsection (a) of this section, the Secretary shall submit to Congress a report analyzing options available to the Secretary under existing law to assist the private sector with the timely

---

[1] So in original. Probably should not be capitalized.

commercialization of wind, photovoltaic, solar thermal, biofuels, hydrogen, solar buildings, ocean, geothermal, low-head hydro, and energy storage renewable energy technologies and energy efficiency technologies through emphasis on development and demonstration assistance to specific technologies in the research, development, and demonstration programs of the Department of Energy that are near commercial application.

(Pub. L. 101-218, § 9, Dec. 11, 1989, 103 Stat. 1868; Pub. L. 102-486, title XII, § 1202(c), (d)(5), title XXIII, § 2303(b), Oct. 24, 1992, 106 Stat. 2959, 2960, 3093.)

AMENDMENTS

1992—Subsec. (a). Pub. L. 102-486, § 1202(d)(5), substituted "and projects" for ", projects, and joint ventures".

Subsec. (b)(1). Pub. L. 102-486, § 1202(c)(1), inserted "three-year" before "management plan".

Subsec. (b)(4). Pub. L. 102-486, § 2303(b), inserted before period at end "and the plan developed under section 5905 of this title".

Subsec. (b)(5), (6). Pub. L. 102-486, § 1202(c)(2), added pars. (5) and (6) and struck out former par. (5) which read as follows: "The plan shall accompany the President's annual budget submission to the Congress."

SECTION REFERRED TO IN OTHER SECTIONS

This section is referred to in section 12003 of this title.

§ 12007. No antitrust immunity or defenses

Nothing in this chapter shall be deemed to convey to any person, partnership, corporation, or other entity immunity from civil or criminal liability under any antitrust law or to create defenses to actions under any antitrust law. As used in this section, "antitrust laws" means those Acts set forth in section 12 of title 15.

(Pub. L. 101-218, § 10, Dec. 11, 1989, 103 Stat. 1869.)

CHAPTER 126—EQUAL OPPORTUNITY FOR INDIVIDUALS WITH DISABILITIES ◄

ILLUSTRATION 12-3   *(continued)*

B. WHY WOULD YOU RESEARCH WHICH CONSTITUTIONS AND STATUTES?

Succinctly stated, you research constitutions and statutes because they are the law. They are mandatory primary authority if validly enacted by the legislature in your jurisdiction. Courts in your jurisdiction then are compelled to follow the constitution and apply statutes to situations falling within their scopes.

Constitutions generally regulate only governmental action. They thus are primarily pertinent in two circumstances: (1) when a party seeks to assess the validity of a law or (2) when a party seeks to challenge some other action taken by a governmental actor, on constitutional grounds. On rare occasions, nongovernmental action may be regulated by constitutional law. Some non-governmental entities may be governed by constitutional law when their actions are quasi-governmental or tightly enmeshed in government functions. In addition, some state constitutional provisions are written broadly enough to apply to private actors as well.

Statutes have potentially broad application. Many apply to private actions, some to governmental actions, some to both. The statute itself typically indicates or implies how broadly it applies.

Often it may be unclear to you initially which law applies: federal, state, local, or a combination. Under our federal system, federal and state govern-ments each have separate as well as overlapping rights to enact law within constitutionally prescribed limits. For example, the federal government has authority to govern in areas that preserve its national sovereignty or that have been expressly granted to it by the United States Constitution. State governments have authority to govern matters that are state concerns, that have been delegated to them by Congress, or that are not expressly assigned to the federal government.

The federal system is hierarchical in that federal law sometimes preempts state law on the same topic. In areas of potential federal authority, Congress can dictate whether its laws preempt state laws or coexist with them. If Congress is silent, then the courts must decide whether the federal law impliedly preempts the state law. Courts consider the strength of the state interest and the potential for interference with the overall federal regulatory scheme.

If you are uncertain whose law governs a particular topic, begin with research in federal law, then turn to your state and then local law. Thereafter, you may seek guidance from another jurisdiction. This sequence obviously reflects the hierarchical system described above.

This sequence also reflects the role of persuasive precedent. A court asked to interpret a particular statute will, of course, first turn to mandatory precedent interpreting that statute. If the court finds no pertinent mandatory precedent, it may seek guidance in some other court's interpretation of a similarly, if not identically, worded statute from another jurisdiction. For example, if a state statute tracks the language of a federal statute and the federal courts have interpreted that language, the state court may well adopt the federal interpretation for its own statute.

Uniform and model acts operate in much the same way. When the language contained in a uniform or model act is enacted by a state legislature, that language becomes primary authority in that jurisdiction. If your jurisdiction's statute tracks or closely resembles a uniform or model act, you can use the comments of the drafters to explain the statute. In addition, case law interpreting parallel language in other jurisdictions may be persuasive to a court. Even if your jurisdiction has not adopted the uniform or model act, the act may provide persuasive authority about what the law should be. As you research uniform or model acts, keep in mind that sometimes a court or legislature may believe that important regional differences justify acting apart from other jurisdictions; then uniform or model acts would not be useful.

Timing is important in statutory research. To locate the correct law, you must discern which version of the law was in effect at the time of your client's fact situation. Legislation is presumed to be prospective, although a law can be retroactive if that effect is clearly stated. The effective date of a law is any date stated in the law's effective-date provision or, if none, a default date set by a separate statute governing all legislation. For federal legislation, the default effective date is the date of the president's approval. Once effective, a statute remains in effect unless it is repealed or replaced, is declared unconstitutional, or expires by operation of a provision in the statute so stating.

As for the Canoga case, the employer, as a private organization, is more likely to be governed by statutes than constitutions. Potentially pertinent provisions appear in a federal statute, the 1990 Americans with Disabilities Act (ADA), outlined in Illustration 12-3 on pages 173–174. A New Mexico statute on employee privacy, dating to 1991, reproduced in Illustration 12-2 on pages 171–172, is clearly pertinent.

C.   HOW DO YOU RESEARCH CONSTITUTIONS AND STATUTES?

Enacted laws appear in several forms over time. They also appear in multiple media.

A recently enacted law first appears in a slip law—that is, a copy of the individual act as enacted. The slip law carries the public law number (for federal laws) or chapter number (typically used for state laws). For some jurisdictions, these numbers reflect the session of the legislature in which the law was passed, as well as the order of passage during that session. Not long after the legislative session ends, the slip laws for the session are republished, in order of enactment, in one or more volumes. These volumes are called "session laws."

For example, the Americans with Disabilities Act, pertinent to the Canoga case, is Public Law Number (Pub. L. No.) 101-336, which means that it was the 336th statute enacted by the 101st Congress. At the state level, New Mexico's Employee Privacy Act, also pertinent to the Canoga case, was the 244th chapter of laws enacted by the 1991 New Mexico legislature.

Next the new law is codified; that is, it is inserted into the jurisdiction's code. A code is a set of statutes currently in force, organized topically. Thus if the new law amends an existing statute, the old language is displaced by the new language. If the new law covers new ground, it is inserted near other statutes on the same broad subject. A jurisdiction's code typically contains only public permanent laws, not private laws (which relate to a particular person or specific situation) or temporary laws (such as appropriations for government agencies). The numbering schemes for codes vary considerably. The federal code has fifty titles, which are subdivided into chapters and sections (although the chapter numbers are not necessary to derive the section numbers). Some state codes are similarly divided into titles or chapters and sections, while others use a single set of numbers, typically with decimals or other refinements.

For example, the federal Americans with Disabilities Act is a large statute, the core of which extends from § 12101 to § 12213 (although not every number is used in that range) within title 42, chapter 126. The first section is numbered 42 U.S.C. § 12101. New Mexico's six-section act on employee privacy comprises article 11 of title 50. Hence, the first section is numbered 50-11-1.

Many jurisdictions have multiple codes. One is the official code, published by the government; the other one (or two) is an unofficial code, published by a private publisher. Both use the same numbering scheme and should contain the same statutory language (subject to differences in updating). One significant difference is that most unofficial codes are annotated, while most official codes are not. An annotated code provides references to judicial cases interpreting the statute, related administrative materials, and secondary sources discussing the topic of the statute. Another significant difference is that unofficial codes are updated more frequently than official codes. Codes go by such names as "code," "statutes," "revised statutes," "consolidated laws," "general laws," or "compiled laws."

Although there rarely is conflict among session laws, official codes, and unofficial codes, there is a hierarchy among them. From time to time, Congress examines specific titles of the official federal statutory code, *United States Code,* and re-enacts those titles as so-called "positive law." Once re-enacted, those titles are the law. Titles that have not been re-enacted as positive law are only prima facie evidence of the law, and the session law governs in the event of a conflict. A similar process occurs at the state level.

Table T.1 of *The Bluebook* lists the statutory sources in paper media for United States jurisdictions, including session laws and codes.

With the development of computers and related information technology, researchers now have additional options. Statutory materials are available online from Westlaw and LEXIS, the two major online services for legal research; in CD-ROM products; and from private publishers, governments, and educational institutions through the Internet.

Quite often, you will find a reference to a pertinent statute through your research in secondary sources. Or you may become aware of a statute when you read a pertinent case that refers to it. However, you should not rely solely on such references; you also should research statutes directly.

This chapter discusses six statutory research practices; to a great extent, these practices operate identically for constitutions. The first two practices involve paper sources: annotated codes and session laws. Four are computer-based approaches: Westlaw/LEXIS, a CD-ROM product of the Michie Company supplemented by LEXIS, public web sites available through the Internet, and online citators. Exhibit 12.1 below provides an overview of the six statutory practices. This part concludes with a brief discussion of research materials used with uniform laws.

This chapter does not discuss several tools that have important but less central roles in statutory research. Chapter 13 discusses legislative process materials, which are used to establish the legislature's intent in passing a statute or to track pending bills.

EXHIBIT 12.1	Overview of Statutory Research Practices

Practice	Statutory Material Provided	Other Material Provided	Currency/Updating
Annotated code in paper	current statutory language and limited historical material	case descriptions and references to secondary sources	fairly current via pocket parts, pamphlets, advance legislative service
Session laws in paper	language passed in specific legislative session	——	limited to specific session
Westlaw and LEXIS	current statutory language and limited historical material in annotated code database; very recent language in session law database	case descriptions and references to secondary sources in annotated code database; authorities themselves through other databases	very current via various statutory updating features and case law research
Annotated code in CD-ROM	current statutory language and limited historical material	case descriptions and references to secondary sources	fairly current; supplemented by online search
Public web sites	current statutory language in code form; recent session laws	——	probably current
Online citators	statutory language through links; references to some session laws	descriptions or references to cases and references to secondary sources (with links to sources)	very current due to constant updating

---

Statutes in annotated codes in paper:

▶ select an appropriate annotated code
▶ use the index or statutory outlines or popular names table
▶ locate the statute's current language in the main volume and/ or updating materials—pocket parts, pamphlets, advance legislative service
▶ study the statutory language
▶ review the annotation: case descriptions, references to secondary sources, statutory cross-references, notes

---

Annotated codes exist at the federal and state levels. While each annotated code is unique, they share various general characteristics. This part focuses on federal statutory codes.

Select an appropriate code. Your first step is to select an annotated code for your jurisdiction. The federal code appears in three versions: *United States Code Annotated* (U.S.C.A.), published by West Group; *United States Code Service* (U.S.C.S.), once published by Lawyers Cooperative Publishing, now by LEXIS Law Publishing; and *United States Code* (U.S.C.), published by the United States government. These three versions contain the same statutory sections and use the same organizational scheme.

There are two important differences. The official code, U.S.C., is unannotated; it contains only the statutory text. By contrast, the two unofficial codes, U.S.C.A. and U.S.C.S., are annotated; accompanying the statute itself are descriptions of cases that interpret the statute, historical notes, and references to secondary sources that discuss the statute. See Illustration 12-4 on pages 184–186. (A note about vocabulary: the word "annotation" often is used to refer only to the case descriptions; for brevity, this discussion uses "annotation" to refer to the full range of case notes and references supplementing the statutory language.) Second, the unofficial codes are published and updated far more frequently than is the official code. These differences between official and unofficial codes occur at the state level as well. Thus, you generally will research in unofficial codes.

Use an index, outlines, or table. To locate a pertinent statute within a code, you generally will choose from three research approaches. The index approach is probably the most successful in most situations. U.S.C.A. and U.S.C.S. each have a multivolume General Index that is issued annually, so it is fairly current. In addition, each of the fifty titles in U.S.C.A. and U.S.C.S. has an individual title index, which usually is located in the last hardbound volume of the title. Because the title indexes are not updated, the General Index generally is more current than the individual title indexes.

A second method for finding a pertinent statute within a code is to use the statute's outlines. For many codes (including the federal codes), you will start with a list of titles, then move to a list of chapters within a title, and then to a list of sections within a chapter. Exhibit 12.2 on page 180 lists the

EXHIBIT 12.2	Titles of United States Code

1. General Provisions
2. The Congress
3. The President
4. Flag and Seal, Seat of Government, and the States
5. Government Organization and Employees; and Appendix
*6. [Surety Bonds]
7. Agriculture
8. Aliens and Nationality
9. Arbitration
10. Armed Forces; and Appendix
11. Bankruptcy; and Appendix
12. Banks and Banking
13. Census
14. Coast Guard
15. Commerce and Trade
16. Conservation
17. Copyrights
18. Crimes and Criminal Procedure; and Appendix
19. Customs Duties
20. Education
21. Food and Drugs
22. Foreign Relations and Intercourse
23. Highways
24. Hospitals and Asylums
25. Indians
26. Internal Revenue Code; and Appendix

27. Intoxicating Liquors
28. Judiciary and Judicial Procedure; and Appendix
29. Labor
30. Mineral Lands and Mining
31. Money and Finance
32. National Guard
33. Navigation and Navigable Waters
**34. [Navy]
35. Patents
36. Patriotic Societies and Observances
37. Pay and Allowances of the Uniformed Services
38. Veterans' Benefits; and Appendix
39. Postal Service
40. Public Buildings, Property, and Works; and Appendix
41. Public Contracts
42. The Public Health and Welfare
43. Public Lands
44. Public Printing and Documents
45. Railroads
46. Shipping; and Appendix
47. Telegraphs, Telephones, and Radiotelegraphs
48. Territories and Insular Possessions
49. Transportation
50. War and National Defense; and Appendix

*This title was enacted as law and has been repealed by the enactment of Title 31.
**This title has been eliminated by the enactment of Title 10.

current titles for the federal code. In U.S.C.A. and U.S.C.S., the list of chapters for each title appears at the front of each volume for the title or at the beginning of a new title in mid-volume; the list of sections within a chapter is found at the beginning of each chapter. The outline approach can be more difficult than the index approach if the title topics are very general, as is often true.

If you already know the name of the statute you are seeking, a third approach is to use a popular names table. Some, but not all, statutes have official or popular names for easy identification. The last volume of the softbound U.S.C.A. General Index contains a popular names table; the U.S.C.S. Tables volumes include a table of popular names, supplemented in a softbound cumulative supplement. Not all state codes include popular names tables.

Locate the current language. After you have identified a potentially pertinent statute, your next task is to locate its current language and study the statute. Much of the time, the current language will be in the main volume. Sometimes the language will be newer than the main volume and thus will appear in updating materials.

Most codes are updated in stages. The initial update generally is in the form of an annual pocket part or supplement pamphlet, filed in the back of or after the main hardbound volume to which it pertains; the initial update for a looseleaf code generally consists of supplement pages filed under a supplement tab in the same binder. See Illustration 12-5 on page 187. Even newer information appears in one or more supplements that update the entire code and accordingly are shelved at the end of the code; these pamphlets generally appear every few months and may or may not be cumulative. These various updating publications contain material that is similar in kind to that found in the main volume, and they typically are organized as the annotated code itself is, so it is easy to see whether there is any updating material for your statute. New statutory language is presented so that its relationship to the old language is clear. For example, there may be references to the main volume for sections or subsections that were not changed, while an amended section will be printed as amended. U.S.C.A. and U.S.C.S. both use these various supplements.

A different type of updating material is the advance legislative service. This service may be an adjunct to the annotated code or a separate publication. U.S.C.A. and U.S.C.S. both offer advance legislative services.

Advance legislative service pamphlets contain reprints of new acts; they do not contain annotation material. Because advance legislative service pamphlets typically are not organized so as to parallel the code, but rather by order of enacted laws, they typically have internal finding tools, such as tables of statutory sections affected by new legislation and subject indexes, which assist you in identifying pertinent material. The first is useful when you have located a pertinent statute in the code. See Illustration 12-6 on page 188. The second is most useful when there is no pertinent statute in the code; you should, however, check it even when there is a pertinent codified statute, to be sure the legislature has not added a statute without amending a preexisting statute.

The task of locating the current language and the task of studying the statute tend to overlap. You probably will skim the language you find first, typically in the main volume or perhaps in a pocket part, to ascertain whether it is indeed pertinent. Next you will want to check for newer language and discern how it fits with the older language. Then you will study the statute, as you have assembled it.

Study the statutory language. If you are working with a multisection statute, first read the title, any legislative findings, statement of purpose, or other introductory sections to obtain an overview of the intended effect of the statute. Then read any definitions so that you understand any particularized meanings of the statutory language. Also read any scope provision to determine the people, places, or situations regulated by the statute. Next read the operative sections of the statute; these sections include the general rule and also may include any exceptions and the consequences or enforcement provisions. They tell you what conduct the statute requires or prohibits, as well as the remedies and procedures for obtaining compliance with the statute.

As you work on understanding the statute, be sure to determine the version in force as of the date of your client's situation. First read the statutory history notes following pertinent sections to learn when the language you are reading was enacted. If you are not sure whether the language was effective when your client's situation occurred, discern the precise effective date of each of the laws enacting the pertinent language. You may need to consult the session laws (described below) for the year of the law in question; if the session law does not include an effective-date provision, check the code for your jurisdiction to determine the default effective date. If the version of the statute governing your client's situation is not the one in the current code, you will need to locate and read the applicable version in the session laws or a previous code.

Finally, pay close attention to every word in a statute. Unlike cases, statutes do not contain dicta. You should assume that each word has a purpose and is potentially significant. If you encounter vague, ambiguous, or conflicting language, you may wish to locate rules of statutory construction. Some jurisdictions have statutory provisions that set forth rules for analyzing statutory language; a general discussion of statutory construction can be found in Norman J. Singer, *Statutes and Statutory Construction* (5th ed. 1992; 6th ed. 2000).

Review the annotation. Once you have studied the statute itself, you should review the annotation, in both the main volume and updating volumes. Again, see Illustrations 12-4 on pages 184–186 and Illustration 12-5 on page 187. Of particular importance are the descriptions of cases interpreting the statute. There may be a few to literally hundreds of case descriptions, depending on how much litigation the statute has spawned. The editors may have created a topical framework for the case descriptions; if so, be sure to review that framework to discern where cases pertinent to your research problem should appear and focus on those portions of the annotation. As you read the case descriptions, look for cases that will be particularly useful to you, based on jurisdiction, legal issue, and factual similarity to your problem.

Next, review the other annotation material. You may find references to secondary sources on the topic governed by the statute, historical notes explaining older versions of the statute, drafter's notes, or cross-references to related statutes.

As to federal statutes, U.S.C.A. and U.S.C.S. both provide abundant annotation material. There are some differences. For example, U.S.C.A. typically provides more case descriptions than does U.S.C.S. Also, U.S.C.A. provides references to pertinent West key numbers. Because the two competing annotated codes are not identical, you may research in both at times, particularly when you have not located pertinent case law in one, or one does not present the case descriptions in a framework that fits your research needs.

Researching the Canoga case. We actually located the provision featured here via a reference in a treatise (Illustration 5-1 on page 60). The index in U.S.C.S. did not lead directly to the specific provision on smoking, but various index entries as well as a popular names table would lead to the Americans with Disabilities Act in general. We could then peruse the table of contents and skim statutory sections to locate specific provisions.

When we researched the Canoga case in the fall of 1999, the main volume of the pertinent title of U.S.C.S. was quite new—1997. It was updated by a 1999 pocket part issued in May 1999, an October 1999 pamphlet (called *U.S.C.S. Cumulative Later Case and Statutory Service*) covering multiple hardbound volumes and extending through Public Law No.106-40, and advance legislative service pamphlets (*U.S.C.S. Advance*) current through Public Law 106-55.

Illustration 12-4 on pages 184–186 is from U.S.C.S.'s 1997 main volume. It presents § 12201, a provision with some pertinence to the Canoga case; it was enacted in July 1990. There was no new language in the pocket part, Illustration 12-5 on page 187, or the October 1999 pamphlet. Illustration 12-6 on page 188 is the table of affected code sections from *U.S.C.S. Advance*; it has no entry for the Americans with Disabilities Act.

Section 12201 is only a small portion of the Americans with Disabilities Act (ADA). In general terms, that statute prohibits discrimination against employees based on disability and requires employers to provide reasonable accommodation of disabilities. The statute does not explicitly state whether nicotine addiction is a protected disability. Section 12201 does, however, address smoking, stating, on the topic of "relationship to other laws," that the ADA does not preclude prohibitions or restrictions on smoking in workplaces covered by the ADA. However, this provision does not squarely address the Canoga case, because the prohibition reached beyond the workplace and was imposed not by law but by the employer.

The annotation to § 12201 in U.S.C.S. is fairly short. The main volume annotation appears in Illustration 12-4 on pages 184–186; the pocket part annotation appears in Illustration 12-5 on page 187; there was no new material in the *Cumulative Later Case and Statutory Service*. The annotation includes references to several cases that appear to involve smoking restrictions or bans in fast-food restaurants, which may have been imposed to protect employees or patrons. Although the cases are not from the Tenth Circuit (which encompasses New Mexico), they would merit review because they may shed some light on what appears to be a rarely raised legal issue. The annotation to § 12201 also provides a cross-reference to another federal statute (29 U.S.C.S. §§ 791, 793, 794) as well as references to various secondary sources (including Am. Jur. 2d and law review articles, one on the topic of addiction as disability).

ILLUSTRATION 12-4   Provision of Americans with Disabilities Act and
Annotations, from *United States Code Service*

---

42 USCS § 12189   PUBLIC HEALTH AND WELFARE

minated her from her program of study because of   terminated from program. Goodwin v Keuka Col-
her disability, where student failed to show that   lege (1995, WD NY) 929 F Supp 90, 18 ADD 564.
college knew of her disability at time she was

MISCELLANEOUS PROVISIONS

§ 12201.   Construction

(a) **In general.** Except as otherwise provided in this Act, nothing in this Act
shall be construed to apply a lesser standard than the standards applied
under title V of the Rehabilitation Act of 1973 (29 U.S.C. 790 et seq.) or the
regulations issued by Federal agencies pursuant to such title.

(b) **Relationship to other laws.** Nothing in this Act shall be construed to
invalidate or limit the remedies, rights, and procedures of any Federal law
or law of any State or political subdivision of any State or jurisdiction that
provides greater or equal protection for the rights of individuals with disabilities than are afforded by this Act. Nothing in this Act shall be construed
to preclude the prohibition of, or the imposition of restrictions on, smoking
in places of employment covered by title I [42 USCS §§ 12111 et seq.], in
transportation covered by title II or III [42 USCS §§ 12131 et seq. or 12181
et seq.], or in places of public accommodation covered by title III [42 USCS
§§ 12181 et seq.].

(c) **Insurance.** Titles I through IV of this Act shall not be construed to prohibit or restrict—

(1) an insurer, hospital or medical service company, health maintenance
organization, or any agent, or entity that administers benefit plans, or similar organizations from underwriting risks, classifying risks, or administering such risks that are based on or not inconsistent with State law; or
(2) a person or organization covered by this Act from establishing,
sponsoring, observing or administering the terms of a bona fide benefit
plan that are based on underwriting risks, classifying risks, or administering such risks that are based on or not inconsistent with State law; or
(3) a person or organization covered by this Act from establishing,
sponsoring, observing or administering the terms of a bona fide benefit
plan that is not subject to State laws that regulate insurance.

Paragraphs (1), (2), and (3) shall not be used as a subterfuge to evade the
purposes of title I and III [42 USCS §§ 12111 et seq., 12181 et seq.].

(d) **Accommodations and services.** Nothing in this Act shall be construed to
require an individual with a disability to accept an accommodation, aid, service, opportunity, or benefit which such individual chooses not to accept.
 (July 26, 1990, P. L. 101-336, Title V, § 501, 104 Stat. 369.)

HISTORY; ANCILLARY LAWS AND DIRECTIVES

References in text:
"This Act", referred to in this section, is Act July 26, 1990, P. L. 101-
336, 104 Stat. 327, popularly referred to as the Americans with Disabili-

ILLUSTRATION 12-4   *(continued)*

INDIVIDUALS WITH DISABILITIES   **42 USCS § 12201**

ties Act of 1990, which appears generally as 42 USCS §§ 12101 et seq. For full classification, consult USCS Tables volumes.

"Title I through IV of this Act", referred to in this section, refers to Titles I-IV of Act July 26, 1990, P. L. 101-326, 104 Stat. 330, which appear generally as 42 USCS §§ 12111 et seq. For full classification of such Titles, consult USCS Tables volumes.

CROSS REFERENCES

 This section is referred to in 29 USCS §§ 791, 793, 794.

RESEARCH GUIDE

Am Jur:

45A Am Jur 2d, Job Discrimination (1993) §§ 19, 205, 208, 217, 453, 834.

Am Jur Proof of Facts:

33 Am Jur Proof of Facts 3d, Proof of "Disability" Under the Americans With Disabilities Act, p. 1.

Americans with Disabilities:

1 Am Disab, Programs, Services and Accommodations §§ 1:5, 109, 119; 2:1, 2, 18, 20, 22, 41, 43, 46, 47, 49; 3:1 4, 11–13, 52, 182, 302; 4:1–5, 15, 45, 52, 56, 67, 72.

4 Am Disab, Housing § 14:185.

CBC Coordinators:

3 Employment Discrim Coord, Employment Terms and Conditions ¶ ¶ 33,506; 35,009; 36,602.

3 Employment Discrim Coord, Selection and Hiring Practices ¶ 26,817.

3 Employment Discrim Coord, Types of Discrimination ¶ ¶ 20,701.5, 730.2, 730.6, 732.

5 Employment Discrim Coord, Summary of Law ¶ 82,006.5.

Law Review Articles:

Davidson. The Civil Rights Act of 1991. 1992 Army Law 3, March 1992.

Shaller. "Reasonable accommodation" under the Americans with Disabilities Act — what does it mean? 16 Empl Rel L J 431, Spring 1991.

Burgdorf. The Americans With Disabilities Act: analysis and implications of a second-generation civil rights statute. 26 Harv C R-C L L Rev 413, Summer 1991.

Ryan. Americans with disabilities: the legal revolution. 60 J Kan B A 13, Nov 1991.

Mahoney; Gibofsky. The Americans with Disabilities Act of 1990. 13 J Legal Med 51, March 1992.

Thornburgh. The Americans with Disabilities Act: what it means to all Americans. 41 Lab L J 803, December 1990.

Geslewitz. Understanding the 1991 Civil Rights Act. 38 Prac Law 57, March 1992.

Miller. How the Americans with Disabilities Act affects your clients. 8 Prac Real Est Law 13, March 1992.

Thornburgh. The Americans With Disabilities Act: what it means to all Americans. 64 Temp L Rev 375, Summer 1991.

ILLUSTRATION 12-4   *(continued)*

---

42 USCS § 12201   PUBLIC HEALTH AND WELFARE

Mikochik. The Constitution and the Americans with Disabilities Act: some first impressions. 64 Temp L Rev 619, Summer 1991.

Harkin. Our newest civil rights law: the Americans with Disabilities Act. 26 Trial 56, December 1990.

Addiction as disability: the protection of alcoholics and drug addicts under the Americans with Disabilities Act of 1990. 44 Vand L Rev 713, April 1991.

Buchanan. A dramatic expansion of rights and remedies: the Americans With Disabilities Act. 64 Wis Law 16, Nov 1991.

INTERPRETIVE NOTES AND DECISIONS

Congress did not intend to isolate effects of smoking from protections of ADA (42 USCS §§ 12101 et seq.) by leaving regulation of smoking to states and municipalities; rather, states and other political subdivisions remain free to offer greater protection for disabled individuals than ADA provides, but violations of ADA should not go unredressed merely because state has chosen to provide some degree of protection to those with disabilities; further, total ban on smoking is permissible if court finds it appropriate under ADA. Staron v McDonald's Corp. (1995, CA2 Conn) 51 F3d 353, 9 ADD 481, 4 AD Cas 353 (criticized in Neff v American Dairy Queen Corp. (1995, CA5 Tex) 58 F3d 1063, 11 ADD 92, 4 AD Cas 1170, 136 ALR Fed 671).

Where evidence shows that particular medical treatment is non-experimental, and insurance plan provides such treatment for other conditions directly comparable to one at issue, denial of that treatment arguably violates ADA (42 USCS §§ 12101 et seq.), and plaintiff is entitled to injunction requiring insurer to guarantee payment for treatment. Henderson v Bodine Aluminum (1995, CA8 Mo) 70 F3d 958, 12 ADD 77, 4 AD Cas 1505, 19 EBC 2047, mod, on reconsideration, reh gr, motion gr, application den (1995, CA8 Mo) 1995 US App LEXIS 31036.

Provision of employer's insurance plan which excluded coverage for treatment of infertility was not subterfuge to evade purposes of ADA § 501 (42 USCS § 12201) since exclusion did not adversely affect plaintiff's employment in any non-fringe benefit plan context, and plaintiff suffered no employment discrimination outside plan. Krauel v Iowa Methodist Medical Ctr. (1996, CA8 Iowa) 95 F3d 674, 18 ADD 112, 5 AD Cas 1503, 20 EBC 1809, 71 BNA FEP Cas 1326, 69 CCH EPD ¶ 44315 (criticized in Abbott v Bragdon (1997, CA1 Me) 107 F3d 934, 6 AD Cas 780).

Safe-harbor provision does not serve to insulate insurance industry completely from other requirements of ADA (42 USCS §§ 12101 et seq.) with regard to provision of insurance coverage; rather, insurance practices are protected by safe-harbor provision only to extent that they are consistent with "sound actuarial principles," "actual

reasonably-anticipated experience," and "bona fide risk classification." Parker v Metropolitan Life Ins. Co. (1996, CA6 Tenn) 99 F3d 181, 18 ADD 669, 5 AD Cas 1804, 20 EBC 2033, 1996 FED App 338P, vacated, reh, en banc, gr (1997, CA6) 107 F3d 359, 6 AD Cas 547.

When interpreting ADA (42 USCS §§ 12101 et seq.), 42 USCS § 12201(a) does not require court to incorporate into ADA more restrictive language of Rehabilitation Act (29 USCS §§ 701 et seq.), but rather directs court not to do so. McNely v Ocala Star-Banner Corp. (1996, CA11 Fla) 99 F3d 1068, 18 ADD 614, 10 FLW C542, 6 AD Cas 78, cert den (1997, US) 137 L Ed 2d 1028, 6 AD Cas 1314.

Given express provision of 42 USCS § 12201(b), ADA (42 USCS §§ 12101 et seq.) does not completely supplant state laws concerning discrimination against individuals with disabilities so that any action under such law would necessarily state federal claim; thus, action brought in state court, alleging violations of state's Civil Rights Act for Handicapped Persons, is not properly removed by defendant corporation to federal district court on theory that action necessarily states claim under ADA, and plaintiff's motion to remand case to state court will be granted. Beaumont v Exxon Corp. (1994, ED La) 4 ADD 684, 2 AD Cas 1865.

Plaintiff may properly pursue state law claim of fraud in conjunction with his claim under ADA (42 USCS §§ 12101 et seq.), since Act explicitly states that it is not intended to limit, preempt, or foreclose any state remedies which plaintiff might have which might potentially provide plaintiff with greater or different relief than he might be entitled to under ADA. Anderson v Martin Brower Co. (1994, DC Kan) 6 ADD 126, 3 AD Cas 829, 10 BNA IER Cas 1693.

ADA (42 USCS §§ 12101 et seq.) does not, by itself, mandate blanket ban on smoking in fast food restaurants; allergies to tobacco smoke must be considered on case-by-case basis. Staron v McDonald's Corp. (1994, DC Conn) 7 ADD 336.

In action alleging that nursing home violated ADA (42 USCS §§ 12101 et seq.) by denying plaintiff admission because of her size and medical condition, plaintiff is not required to exhaust her administrative remedies before bringing federal

ILLUSTRATION 12-5   Pocket Part, from *United States Code Service*

42 USCS § 12188   PUBLIC HEALTH AND WELFARE

§ 12188. Enforcement

INTERPRETIVE NOTES AND DECISIONS

8. Miscellaneous

1. Generally

Congressional intent not to provide private damages remedy for action allegedly based on violation of 42 USCS § 12182 was tantamount to congressional conclusion that presence of claimed violation of statute as element of state cause of action was insufficiently substantial to confer federal question jurisdiction. Jairath v Dyer (1998, CA11 Ga) 154 F3d 1280, 8 AD Cas 979, 12 FLW Fed C 88.

In action by disabled persons against organization which managed auditorium, alleging that disabled persons were not provided with minimum legally required access to auditorium, and that auditorium contained multiple architectural access barriers in violation of ADA (42 USCS §§ 12101 et seq.), class consisting of all physically disabled persons in state who have been denied right to full and equal access to auditorium is certified. Berlowitz ex rel. Berlowitz v Nob Hill Masonic Mgmt. (1996, ND Cal) 23 ADD 528.

2. Standing

Individual's request for injunctive and declaratory relief under ADA (42 USCS §§ 12181 et seq.) did not survive his death and could not be asserted by individual's wife who was substituted as plaintiff after his death. Plumley v Landmark Chevrolet (1997, CA5 Tex) 122 F3d 308, 23 ADD 583, 26 Media L R 1056.

Applicant who was denied life insurance coverage allegedly due to his partner's HIV-positive status had standing to bring action against insurance company under Title III of ADA (42 USCS §§ 12181 et seq.), even though he was not denied physical access to company's offices. Cloutier v Prudential Ins. Co. of Am. (1997, ND Cal) 964 F Supp 299, 23 ADD 359, 97 Daily Journal DAR 12841.

HIV-positive individual who was denied treatment by doctor did not have standing to pursue claim against doctor under ADA (42 USCS §§ 12181 et

seq.), since only injunctive relief was available under ADA, and injunction would not have offered any relief to individual because there was no chance of future harm, as treatment sought by individual had already been provided elsewhere. Jairath v Dyer (1997, ND Ga) 972 F Supp 1461, 25 ADD 476, 7 AD Cas 156.

By virtue of his relationship with his disabled son, father had standing to bring action under ADA (42 USCS §§ 12101 et seq.) alleging that proposed arena, once constructed, would violate ADA, since plaintiffs had reason to believe that they were about to be subjected to discrimination in violation of new construction provision of Title III. Johanson v Huizenga Holdings (19987, SD Fla) 963 F Supp 1175, 23 add 485.

5. Damages

Individual may not recover damages in action based on anti-discrimination provision of 42 USCS § 12182(a); rather, only injunctive relief is available. A.R. v Kogan (1997, ND Ill) 964 F Supp 269, 23 ADD 834.

8. Miscellaneous

Parents voluntarily waived their right to judicial forum when they signed enrollment agreement with school which provided that all disputes between parties would be subject to arbitration, and agreement to arbitrate was enforceable with regard to parents claims against school under ADA (42 USCS §§ 12181 et seq.). Bercovitch v Baldwin Sch. (1998, CA1 Puerto Rico) 133 F3d 141.

Plaintiff who brought action against restaurant alleging that he was denied service because of his physical disability substantially complied with requirement of notice to state, where plaintiff wrote to state's attorney general's office seeking that office's intervention against restaurant. Daigle v Friendly Ice Cream Corp. (1997, DC NH) 957 F Supp 8, 22 ADD 326, 6 AD Cas 554.

§ 12189. Examinations and courses

INTERPRETIVE NOTES AND DECISIONS

ADA (42 USCS §§ 12101 et seq.) does not completely preempt or displace state's procedures for administering bar examinations and licensing attorneys, but merely prohibits states from discriminating

on basis of disability. Ware v Wyoming Bd. of Law Examiners (1997, DC Wyo) 973 F Supp 1339, 24 ADD 854.

MISCELLANEOUS PROVISIONS

 § 12201. Construction

RESEARCH GUIDE

Forms:
12 Fed Procedural Forms L Ed, Job Discrimination (1998) §§ 45:296, 297, 320, 322.

INTERPRETIVE NOTES AND DECISIONS

Provision of Americans with Disabilities Act of 1990 (ADA) (42 USCS § 12201(a))—directing that except as otherwise provided, nothing in ADA shall be construed to apply lesser standard than standards applied under Title V of Rehabilitation Act of 1973 (29 USCS §§ 790 et seq.) or regulations issued by federal agencies pursuant to Title V—requires that

ADA be construed to grant at least as much protection as provided by regulations implementing Rehabilitation Act. Bragdon v Abbott (1998, US) 141 L Ed 2d 540, 118 S Ct 2196, 98 CDOS 5021, 98 Daily Journal DAR 6973, 8 AD Cas 239, 1998 Colo J C A R 3268, 11 FLW Fed S 726.

"Safe harbor" provision covering insurance indus-

76

ILLUSTRATION 12-6   Table of Code Sections Affected, from *U.S.C.S. Advance*

TABLE OF CODE SECTIONS ADDED, AMENDED, REPEALED, OR OTHERWISE AFFECTED
106TH CONGRESS FIRST SESSION
(106-1--106-55)

Section	Effect	Public Law No.	
TITLE 35			
3(d)	Amd.	106-44	Sec. 2(c)
TITLE 40			
270a(a)(2)	Amd.	106-49	Sec. 2(a)
270a nt.	New	106-49	Sec. 1
	New	106-49	Sec. 3
270b(a)	Amd.	106-49	Sec. 2(b)
270b(c)	Added	106-49	Sec. 2(c)
TITLE 42			
1305 nt.	New	106-4	Sec. 1
1396b(d)(3)	Amd.	106-31	Sec. 3031(a)
1396b(i)(18)	Amd.	106-31	Sec. 3031(b)(1)
1396b(i)(19)	Added	106-31	Sec. 3031(b)(2)
1396b nt.	New	106-31	Sec. 3031(c)
1396r(c)(2)	Amd.	106-4	Sec. 2(a)
1396r nt.	New	106-4	Sec. 2(b)
1962d-21	New	106-53	Sec. 455
2296b(b)	Amd.	106-36	Sec. 1002(g)(1)
2296b-6(c)	Amd.	106-36	Sec. 1002(g)(2)
3121 nt.	Amd.	106-31	Sec. 105(a)
6374(a)(3)	Amd.	106-36	Sec. 1002(h)
7401 nt.	New	106-40	Sec. 1
7412(r)(2)	Amd.	106-40	Sec. 2(5)
7412(r)(4)	Amd.	106-40	Sec. 2(1)-(4)
7412(r)(7)	Amd.	106-40	Sec. 3(a)
7412 nt.	New	106-40	Sec. 3(b)
	New	106-40	Sec. 3(c)
	New	106-40	Sec. 4
TITLE 43			
390h-6(a)	Amd.	106-53	Sec. 596(1)

> **Statutes in session laws in paper:**
>
> ▶ locate the pertinent act via public law number from a code or subject index
> ▶ study the language of the law

Because laws become effective on specific dates and can be amended over time, the law in effect on various dates can vary. The codes described above are designed to provide the law of the present, although they may provide some historical material as well. If your client's situation arose under law preceding that now stated or explained in the code, you will research in session laws (or an old code, if still available). As noted above, the new laws enacted during a legislative session eventually are published in a permanent hardbound form, the session laws.

Session law compilations are important research sources for several other reasons as well. They contain all the laws enacted during a particular legislative session, including private laws (which affect a particular person or specific situation) and temporary laws that are not codified. Session laws make it possible to track changes in a statute from year to year, which can assist you in discerning what a statute is intended to mean.

This discussion focuses on the federal session laws. Similar sources exist at the state level.

The official compilation of federal session laws is called *United States Statutes at Large (Statutes at Large)*. *Statutes at Large* is ordered by public law numbers (formerly by chapter numbers). Every *Statutes at Large* volume contains an index that pertains only to the acts contained in that volume. *Statutes at Large* is also available in a publication of West Group, *United States Code Congressional and Administrative News*. Illustration 12-7 on page 190 is an excerpt from *Statutes at Large*, showing a portion of the Americans with Disabilities Act as passed by Congress in 1990.

Your first task is to locate the pertinent act within the session law volume. Annotated codes generally provide references to the public law designations for statutes currently in force immediately following the text of the statute. Some also provide such references for obsolete language in historical notes. If you do not have a reference from a code or elsewhere, you may use the subject index to the session laws to locate laws on your topic.

Your second task is to study the law, as you would read a statute in a code. Be sure to examine any editorial enhancements, such as cross-references to related statutes and margin notes. Take particular note of the effective date provision, typically located at the end of the law.

When we researched the Canoga case, U.S.C.S. provided easy access to *Statutes at Large*. The text of § 12201 in U.S.C.S. is followed by references to the public law—P.L.101-336, Title V, § 501—and session laws—104 Stat. 369. Illustration 12-7 on page 190 shows § 12201 in session law form.

ILLUSTRATION 12-7   Portion of Public Law 101-336, from *Statutes at Large*

PUBLIC LAW 101–336—JULY 26, 1990   104 STAT. 369

"(i) within 180 days after the complaint is filed with such State; or

"(ii) within a shorter period as prescribed by the regulations of such State; or

"(B) the Commission determines that such State program is no longer qualified for certification under subsection (f).".

(b) CONFORMING AMENDMENTS.—The Communications Act of 1934 (47 U.S.C. 151 et seq.) is amended—

(1) in section 2(b) (47 U.S.C. 152(b)), by striking "section 224" and inserting "sections 224 and 225"; and

(2) in section 221(b) (47 U.S.C. 221(b)), by striking "section 301" and inserting "sections 225 and 301".

SEC. 402. CLOSED-CAPTIONING OF PUBLIC SERVICE ANNOUNCEMENTS.

Section 711 of the Communications Act of 1934 is amended to read   47 USC 611.
as follows:

"SEC. 711. CLOSED-CAPTIONING OF PUBLIC SERVICE ANNOUNCEMENTS.

"Any television public service announcement that is produced or funded in whole or in part by any agency or instrumentality of Federal Government shall include closed captioning of the verbal content of such announcement. A television broadcast station licensee—

"(1) shall not be required to supply closed captioning for any such announcement that fails to include it; and

"(2) shall not be liable for broadcasting any such announcement without transmitting a closed caption unless the licensee intentionally fails to transmit the closed caption that was included with the announcement.".

TITLE V—MISCELLANEOUS PROVISIONS

SEC. 501. CONSTRUCTION.   42 USC 12201.

(a) IN GENERAL.—Except as otherwise provided in this Act, nothing in this Act shall be construed to apply a lesser standard than the standards applied under title V of the Rehabilitation Act of 1973 (29 U.S.C. 790 et seq.) or the regulations issued by Federal agencies pursuant to such title.

(b) RELATIONSHIP TO OTHER LAWS.—Nothing in this Act shall be construed to invalidate or limit the remedies, rights, and procedures of any Federal law or law of any State or political subdivision of any State or jurisdiction that provides greater or equal protection for the rights of individuals with disabilities than are afforded by this Act. Nothing in this Act shall be construed to preclude the prohibition of, or the imposition of restrictions on, smoking in places of employment covered by title I, in transportation covered by title II or III, or in places of public accommodation covered by title III.

(c) INSURANCE.—Titles I through IV of this Act shall not be construed to prohibit or restrict—

(1) an insurer, hospital or medical service company, health maintenance organization, or any agent, or entity that administers benefit plans, or similar organizations from underwriting risks, classifying risks, or administering such risks that are based on or not inconsistent with State law; or

(2) a person or organization covered by this Act from establishing, sponsoring, observing or administering the terms

---

Statutes in Westlaw and LEXIS:

▶ select an appropriate database

▶ draft and run a Boolean or natural-language search in a statute database

▶ or search or peruse the index, table of contents, or popular names table

▶ sift the search results and browse adjacent sections

▶ update the statutory results

▶ study the statutory language

▶ review the annotation: case descriptions, references to secondary sources, statutory cross-references, notes

▶ update and expand the case law results in a cases database

Online statutory research has several advantages and disadvantages. You may use research terms, such as factual concepts, that an editorial staff would not use to create a statutory index, and you may create unique combinations of research terms. Information is very current and nearly totally cumulated online, so you need not use multiple volumes for the same type of information. On the other hand, some research topics lack the distinctive terms that make for an effective search online. And it is cumbersome to browse from statutory section to statutory section online.

Westlaw and LEXIS, the two major online subscription services for legal research, both provide access to federal and state statutory material and various options for gaining access to pertinent statutes. The following text focuses on the federal statute prohibiting disability discrimination.

Sometimes you will use an online service not to identify pertinent statutes, but to obtain a known statute. This research entails a find search, in which you enter the statutory citation to obtain the specified section and its annotation. If your research is not already this focused, you will follow several steps to locate pertinent provisions.

The first step is to select an appropriate database. The standard option is to search in an annotated code. Although an unannotated code is a smaller database and may seem desirable for that reason, it will lack the case descriptions in which your key words might appear. If you are researching federal statutory materials, which are voluminous, you may want to search in a subject-specific statutory database. As always, be sure you know the exact scope of your database, including its currency.

To identify pertinent statutory provisions within your database, you may choose to run a Boolean or natural-language search. The standard approach is to run the search in the statutory text and annotation material. If your search terms are common terms that are nearly certain to appear in the statutory language, you may want to confine your search to some smaller segment, such as the statutory text only or even the titles of the various chapters and sections.

Another option is to run your search in the statutory index database, which is much smaller than the statutes and annotations; your research terms may not be used in the statutes themselves but may have been recognized by the writer of the index. Furthermore, you may want to peruse the code's table of contents, if possible, or search a popular names table database.

Your next step is to sift your search results. An efficient means of doing so, given the generally informative nature of statutory section titles, is to skim a citation list. Other options include skimming the opening lines or the portion of the statute or annotation where your search terms appear. Note that you will, by researching in an annotated code, be retrieving not only statutory provisions, but also case descriptions and references to other sources.

Because your search may not retrieve all pertinent sections of a statute with multiple sections, you will want to browse beyond the retrieved section. You may order the computer to display sections preceding and following your retrieved section. Or you may browse a table of contents for the title or chapter in which your retrieved section appears.

Once you have found a pertinent statute, you should take care to update it. Although an annotated code database is very current and, unlike the paper code from which it derives, totally cumulated, there still may be very recent new legislation on your topic, which could amend or repeal your statute. A search by subject or code section, or both, in a current session law database, where new legislation is nearly instantly posted, will fill this gap. Furthermore, the provided online service may alert you to new legislation affecting a retrieved section or notice of bills that may affect a retrieved statute. Until the bills pass, of course, they are not law.

As you read a pertinent statute identified or retrieved online, you should look for the same information as is discussed above regarding statutes you locate in paper codes. Furthermore, you should peruse the annotation material carefully, looking for pertinent case descriptions, references to secondary sources, statutory cross-references, and notes.

Some very new cases will appear in case law databases, but not yet in annotated code databases. Furthermore, the case descriptions in statutory annotations do not encompass all cases; for example, unpublished cases are not included. Hence to bring your case law research up to date and expand your pool of cases, you should run a search in an appropriate case law database, with the statutory citation as your search term or part of your search.

Researching the Canoga case, we selected U.S.C.A., a Westlaw database containing the material in the print *United States Code Annotated*; in fall of 1999, it was current to mid-August 1999. We tried two different searches: [te(disabilit! & smok!)] and [disabilit! & nicotine]. The first confined the search to the statutory language; the second included the annotation material as well. The first search retrieved eleven documents, including § 12201, the provision featured above. See Illustration 12-8 on page 194. The second search retrieved § 12117, which relates to enforcement of the ADA in employment contexts. Similar searches in USCA-IDX, the index, retrieved nothing pertinent. Were we to browse around § 12117, we would have come across other provisions on employment discrimination.

No flag appeared for § 12201; however, a flag appeared for § 12117, indicating that there were then bills in Congress addressing litigation of discrimination cases. (A search of US-PL, which contains federal legislation (public laws) from the current session, revealed nothing new.)

The first statute retrieved, § 12201, is described above. The pertinent information retrieved by the second search appeared not in the statutory language, but in a case description of *Moore v. City of Overland Park*, 950 F. Supp. 1081 (D. Kan. 1996). There an employee complained to the federal agency about discrimination based on diabetes, then sued in court and expanded her claim to include nicotine addiction; the court dismissed the latter claim, without analysis of its merits, on the grounds that she had not properly pursued it with the agency.

To update our case law research, we ran a search for recent cases discussing our statutory section [42 /10 12201 da (aft 12/31/1998)] in both ALLFEDS, a broad federal case database, and NM-CS, which contains New Mexico state cases. No useful cases were retrieved.

Statutes in CD-ROM:

▶ select the statutes portion of the CD-ROM

▶ peruse outlines to locate the pertinent statute

▶ or draft and run a search, and sift results

▶ study the statute

▶ review the annotation: case descriptions, references to secondary sources, statutory cross-references, notes

▶ update your research online

CD-ROM research entails use of computer-based research methods in a fixed set of legal materials. Thus it is analogous to both the paper-based and computer-based practices described above. A wide range of statutes is available in CD-ROMs. Some CD-ROMs contain a range of materials including statutes. The following text focuses on the New Mexico state statute on employee privacy.

Your first step is to select an appropriate portion of the CD-ROM, the classic option being an annotated code. Be sure you know how current the material is, in particular which legislative session is the most recent one covered. Also be sure that you know how the CD-ROM is cumulated and updates information.

The second step is to identify pertinent statutes. You may be able to peruse outlines of the code and of individual titles or chapters. You may be able to run searches for particular key words.

As with other statutory research methods, you must carefully study the statute you have located. Attend carefully to its overall design, language, and effective dates. Finally, study the annotation to learn of cases interpreting

ILLUSTRATION 12-8	Westlaw Citations List, Run in USCADatabase

Citations List   Search Result Documents: 11
Database: USCA

1.   5 U.S.C.A. App. 1 REORG. PLAN 3 1967   UNITED STATES CODE ANNOTATED   TITLE 5.
            GOVERNMENT ORGANIZATION AND EMPLOYEES   APPENDIX 1. REORGANIZATION
            PLANS [FN1]   REORGANIZATION PLAN NO. 3 OF 1967

2.   5 U.S.C.A. App. 1 REORG. PLAN 3 1970   UNITED STATES CODE ANNOTATED   TITLE 5.
            GOVERNMENT ORGANIZATION AND EMPLOYEES   APPENDIX 1. REORGANIZATION
            PLANS [FN1]   REORGANIZATION PLAN NO. 3 OF 1970

3.   ▷   16 U.S.C.A. § 460l-6a   UNITED STATES CODE ANNOTATED   TITLE 16. CONSERVATION
            CHAPTER 1--NATIONAL PARKS, MILITARY PARKS, MONUMENTS, AND SEASHORES
            SUBCHAPTER LXIX--OUTDOOR RECREATION PROGRAMS   PART B--LAND AND WATER
            CONSERVATION FUND   § 460l-6a. Admission and special recreation use fees

4.   ▷   20 U.S.C.A. § 8283   UNITED STATES CODE ANNOTATED   TITLE 20. EDUCATION
            CHAPTER 70--STRENGTHENING AND IMPROVEMENT OF ELEMENTARY AND SECONDARY
            SCHOOLS   SUBCHAPTER X--PROGRAMS OF NATIONAL SIGNIFICANCE   PART J--URBAN
            AND RURAL EDUCATION ASSISTANCE   SUBPART 1--URBAN EDUCATION
            DEMONSTRATION GRANTS   § 8283. Urban school grants

5.   ▷   20 U.S.C.A. § 8294   UNITED STATES CODE ANNOTATED   TITLE 20. EDUCATION
            CHAPTER 70--STRENGTHENING AND IMPROVEMENT OF ELEMENTARY AND SECONDARY
            SCHOOLS   SUBCHAPTER X--PROGRAMS OF NATIONAL SIGNIFICANCE   PART J--URBAN
            AND RURAL EDUCATION ASSISTANCE   SUBPART 2--RURAL EDUCATION
            DEMONSTRATION GRANTS   § 8294. Uses of funds

6.   U.S.Ct. of App. D.C.Cir. Handbook, 28 U.S.C.A.   UNITED STATES CODE ANNOTATED
            UNITED STATES COURT OF APPEALS FOR THE DISTRICT OF COLUMBIA CIRCUIT
            HANDBOOK OF PRACTICE AND INTERNAL PROCEDURES   Handbook of Practice and Internal
            Procedures

7.   ▷   38 U.S.C.A. § 1117   UNITED STATES CODE ANNOTATED   TITLE 38. VETERANS' BENEFITS
            PART II--GENERAL BENEFITS   CHAPTER 11--COMPENSATION FOR SERVICE-CONNECTED
            DISABILITY OR DEATH   SUBCHAPTER II--WARTIME DISABILITY COMPENSATION   § 1117.
            Compensation for disabilities occurring in Persian Gulf War veterans

8.   ▷   42 U.S.C.A. § 242p   UNITED STATES CODE ANNOTATED   TITLE 42. THE PUBLIC HEALTH
            AND WELFARE   CHAPTER 6A--PUBLIC HEALTH SERVICE   SUBCHAPTER II--GENERAL
            POWERS AND DUTIES   PART A--RESEARCH AND INVESTIGATIONS   § 242p. National disease
            prevention data profile

9.   ▷   42 U.S.C.A. § 4321   UNITED STATES CODE ANNOTATED   TITLE 42. THE PUBLIC HEALTH
            AND WELFARE   CHAPTER 55--NATIONAL ENVIRONMENTAL POLICY   § 4321. Congressional
            declaration of purpose

10.   42 U.S.C.A. § 12201   UNITED STATES CODE ANNOTATED   TITLE 42. THE PUBLIC HEALTH
            AND WELFARE   CHAPTER 126--EQUAL OPPORTUNITY FOR INDIVIDUALS WITH
            DISABILITIES   SUBCHAPTER IV--MISCELLANEOUS PROVISIONS   § 12201. Construction

11.   USCA POPULAR NAME INDEX   UNITED STATES CODE ANNOTATED   POPULAR NAME
            TABLE FOR ACTS OF CONGRESS

the statute, statutory cross-references, secondary sources on the statute's topic, etc.

Because a CD-ROM is itself current only to its date of publication, you should update your research, typically via a supplemental online search, seeking both new legislation and additional annotation material.

Researching New Mexico statutes for the Canoga case, we used *Michie's Law on Disc* for New Mexico, a product of LEXIS Law Publishing. The New Mexico Statutes Annotated portion of the August 1999 CD-ROM was current through the first special session of the New Mexico Legislature in 1999; it cumulated old and new information that would be located in separate locations in the paper version.

We used both the outline and key-word approaches. On the list of seventy-seven chapters, we identified Chapter 50. Employment Law; within Chapter 50, we identified Article 11. Employee Privacy. The Boolean search [smok* and employ*] yielded thirty-one hits, scattered among the pertinent statute, other statutes (regarding clean indoor air, occupational safety and health, etc.), and the index. Some hits were in the statutory language itself; others were in the annotations. Illustration 12-2 on pages 171–172 is a print-out from the Michie CD-ROM.

As you can see from Illustration 12-2 on pages 171–172, New Mexico's Employee Privacy Act begins with the short title of the act, proceeds to a definitions section and the general rule, and ends with remedies and damages sections. Section 50-11-3 forbids employer regulation of smoker-employees' behavior when not at the workplace; it includes an exception for narrowly tailored constraints based on bona fide occupational requirements. The legislative history notes tell you that the statute was enacted in 1991 as chapter 244. According to the default effective date provision in the New Mexico Constitution, it became effective ninety days after passage, on June 14, 1991. The annotations to the New Mexico statute are very spare—only one secondary source. This statute is comparatively new (1991) and has not yet been interpreted in reported decisions.

To update our CD-ROM research on the Canoga case, we could shift to a LEXIS search.

Statutes via public Internet web sites:

▶ identify an appropriate web site
▶ ascertain how to search for pertinent statutes, e.g., by key-word searching or perusing table of contents, and do so
▶ or run a find search to obtain statute
▶ update your preliminary results as needed
▶ study the statute

There is an abundance of statutory material available through public web sites. Some sites are very current, an advantage when you are researching statutes, which can change regularly. The sophistication of search methods varies from site to site; if your problem is difficult to capture in distinctive search terms, Internet research may be difficult. Furthermore, web sites may not include annotation material, and you may find it difficult to browse across statutory sections. Finally because Internet web sites generally seek to provide the law as it now stands, they are not particularly useful should you need to discern the law as it used to be. This discussion covers both the federal and state statutory issues.

First, identify an appropriate web site and database for your jurisdiction's code, for example, by visiting a legal-information web site. Be sure to ascertain the precise scope of the database you have chosen, especially as to the most recent legislative session covered. Then figure out how you can search the database, whether by key-word searching, perusing a table of contents, or find searching (the latter being useful only if you already have a citation and are using the web site to obtain, but not locate, pertinent statutes). Then, update the preliminary results, most probably in a session law database. Once you have located a pertinent current statute, study it carefully.

Researching the state law privacy issue in the Canoga case in the fall of 1999, we used Findlaw to locate a collection of New Mexico legal materials, including New Mexico statutes, a joint effort of the state of New Mexico and a private publisher. The site was current through the 1999 special session of the New Mexico Legislature. We located the pertinent statute by perusing the list of chapters, then the list of articles. We also retrieved the pertinent statute via a simple Boolean search, [employee and smoking]. The statute as retrieved contained the same statutory language we could locate through other sources; there were no annotations.

Researching the federal discrimination issue in the Canoga case, we located the code portion of the United States House of Representatives web site (also entered via Findlaw). This site is, in a way, an official Internet code; it is provided by the Office of Law Revision Counsel, which also prepares the official *United States Code*. In the fall of 1999, the main statutory database was current to January of 1998 or 1999, depending on the title. The web site afforded an update signal (if you search for a specific statutory section, rather than conduct a key-word search) and a classification table in which you can look up your code section and find a list of new legislation affecting that section. (To obtain new legislation, you would use THOMAS, described in Chapter 13.) The ILL offers various search mechanisms, including Boolean searching, with segment restrictors if desired, and find searching. The search [disability and smoking] retrieved twelve statutory sections, including § 12201. See Illustration 12-9 on page 197 for a citation list. The information we retrieved paralleled the *United States Code*, that is, the statutory language with statutory cross-references but without case descriptions or references to secondary sources.

We also researched in the public laws available through the Government Printing Office at www.access.gpo.gov. In the fall of 1999, it covered three Congresses, including the 106th Congress, 1999–2000. The simple subject search [disability AND employ*] yielded six public laws, none on point. A search for ["Americans with disabilities"] yielded no public laws.

ILLUSTRATION 12-9	Facsimile Citation List, from United States House of Representatives Code Web site

12 documents found (12 returned) for Query:
(disability and smoking)

SIZE	SCORE	DOCUMENT		
31863	100	15 USC Sec. 2201	01/05/99	Sec. 2201 Congressional findings
33727	98	39 USC Sec. 1117	01/26/98	Sec. 1117 Compensation for disabilities occurring in Persian Gulf War...
117690	97	5 USC APPENDIX - REORGANIZATION PLAN NO. 3 OF 1967	01/05/99	REORGANIZATION PLAN NO. 3 OF 1967 {FOOTNOTE 1}
43524	96	5 USC APPENDIX - REORGANIZATION PLAN NO. 3 OF 1970	01/05/99	REORGANIZATION PLAN NO. 3 OF 1970
4250	96	42 USC Sec. 12201	01/26/98	Sec. 12201 Construction
3235	96	42 USC Sec. 242p	01/26/98	Sec. 242p. National disease prevention data profile
16194	95	20 USC CHAPTER 68 - NATIONAL EDUCATION REFORM	01/05/99	CHAPTER 68--NATIONAL EDUCATION REFORM
74691	95	42 USC Sec. 1395b-1	01/26/98	Sec. 13295b-1. Incentives for economy while maintaining or improving quality
35614	95	30 USC CHAPTER 22 - MINE SAFETY AND HEALTH	01/26/98	CHAPTER 22--MINE SAFETY AND HEALTH
9088	94	20 USC Sec. 8294	01/05/99	Sec. 8294 User of funds
10846	94	80 USC Sec. 8283	01/05/99	Sec. 8283 Urban school grants
175711	94	42 USC Sec. 4321	01/26/98	Sec. 4321 Congressional declaration of purpose

Online citators for statutes:

- ► Shepardize a statute on LEXIS; features include:
  - selection of section(s) or subdivision(s)
  - focus on negative or positive impact
  - restrictions on types of authority or time periods
  - focus on research terms
- ► or KeyCite statute on Westlaw; features include:
  - flags signifying legislative alteration
  - focus on specified topics
  - restrictions on types of authority or time periods
- ► attend to legislative activity, citing cases, useful secondary sources

Citators differ from the sources described above in that they do not provide ways to identify pertinent statutes. You use a citator once you have located and read a pertinent statute (your cited source) elsewhere. You then use a statutory citator to learn about later legislation affecting your statute, to learn about cases citing the statute, and to find references to secondary sources on the statute's topic (citing sources).

Other sources, such as annotated codes in paper and online, provide similar information, but there are some differences. For example, online citators provide a wider range of citing cases than one might find in an annotated code; however, for most cases, the information provided by a citator is not as extensive as the information in an annotated code. Online citators are very current, so they are good tools for updating research conducted in a paper annotated code. Online citators permit you to move quickly from a reference to a citing source to the source itself through the links.

For many years, the only statutory citators were the paper Shepard's Citations for various statutory codes. Fortunately, there now are two online statutory citators: an online version of Shepard's Citations, available through LEXIS, and KeyCite, available through Westlaw. Both cover federal and state statutes and build on the services' respective annotated codes. In both services, you simply enter a citation to the pertinent statute, or enter the citator program from a statutory database when you have located a pertinent section. Then the citator provides references to various citing sources. The two citators provide similar, but not identical, information and afford somewhat different means of tailoring your search to your particular needs. Both online citators afford links to the statutory language. The following discussion focuses on the federal statute regarding disability discrimination.

Shepard's provides a list of the session laws amending a statute. As for citing cases and secondary sources, Shepard's initially provides a means of focusing your research based on the range of the citing source's references to the statute. That is, it clumps together citing sources that cite a range of sections, a single section, or subdivisions of a section; this permits you to focus on citing sources that cite the precise statutory material of interest. See Illustration 12-10 on page 200. Within a citation list, Shepard's arrays the citing sources by type, for example, cases before secondary sources, federal cases before state court cases, federal cases from the same circuit together. For each citing case, Shepard's provides the case's citation and the location of the reference to the cited source. See Illustration 12-11 on page 201.

Shepard's offers several additional options. You can restrict your search to cases that Shepard's editors deem to have a negative or positive impact on the statute. An example of the former is a case declaring a statute unconstitutional; an example of the latter is a case upholding a statute as constitutional. You can restrict your search to sets of citing sources, for example, jurisdictions, law reviews, time periods. You can focus your search topically, by entering research terms that must appear in a citing source.

Researching the Canoga case, we Shepardized 42 U.S.C.S. § 12201 online. There were no entries for amendments. We selected the list of sources citing subdivision (b), because the language of interest is the second sentence in subdivision (b). (Review Illustration 12-4 on page 184.) Shepard's retrieved one case from the Tenth Circuit, but that case addressed the first sentence of subdivision (b). When we entered the research term [smoking] to focus our search, Shepard's retrieved three cases, the first being a federal appellate case, *Staron v. McDonald's Corp.* 51 F.3d 353 (2d Cir. 1995), which discusses the second sentence in the context of smoking restrictions in fast-food restaurants. See Illustration 12-11 on page 201.

When you KeyCite a statute, you can obtain several types of information. Some of the information permits you to track legislative activity involving the statute. In the credits, historical notes, and statutory notes, KeyCite provides a list of session laws and a description of the changes in your statute over time, as provided in West annotated codes. A flag may appear to indicate that the section has been amended or repealed (a red flag) or is the subject of pending bills (a yellow flag); KeyCite provides citations to the legislation or bills as appropriate.

The rest of the information provided by KeyCite permits you to track judicial and scholarly references to the statute in cases and secondary sources. In the annotations segment, KeyCite provides the same case descriptions you would find if you read the annotated code; these descriptions are fit into a topical framework that permits you to identify the most probably pertinent cases. In the citations segment, KeyCite provides a list of additional citations to cases that do not appear in the case descriptions in the annotated code; federal cases appear before state cases, higher court cases before lower court cases. See Illustration 12-12 on page 202. After the cases list, KeyCite lists references to various secondary sources, including A.L.R. Annotations, Am. Jur. 2d, and law reviews. Because the additional citations list can be long and is not divided topically, you may want to limit the citations, for example, by topic used in the annotated code (called "notes of decisions"), by type of authority, by court, or by date.

Researching the Canoga case, we KeyCited § 12201. There was no indication of amendments, repealers, or pending bills. An initial request for cases only (not secondary sources) yielded case descriptions of twenty-four cases and additional citations to over 150 additional cases. See Illustration 12-12 on page 202. (The *Staron* case was the thirty-sixth on the list.) When we limited that list to United States Supreme Court, Tenth Circuit, and New Mexico decisions on the most pertinent topic from the notes-of-decisions list, we obtained no such cases.

ILLUSTRATION 12-10   Shepard's Online Preliminary Screen, from LEXIS

Check a Citation - SHEPARD'S® - 42 uscs 12201   Page 1 of 1

Citation: **42 uscs 12201**

Shepard's® [   ] **Check**

SHEPARD'S has found 13 documents for the citation you entered. The number of
citing references indicated below are for those displayed in the FULL format. Select
one to start your research.

   1. <u>Exact match: 42 U.S.C. sec. 12201 , 26 Citing References</u>

   2. <u>42 U.S.C. sec. 12201 et seq. , 28 Citing References</u>

   3. <u>42 U.S.C. secs. 12201 to 12213 , 7 Citing References</u>

   4. <u>42 U.S.C. secs. 12201 to 12210 , 1 Citing References</u>

   5. <u>42 U.S.C. secs. 12201 to 12204 , 8 Citing References</u>

   6. <u>42 U.S.C. sec. 12201 (a) , 47 Citing References</u>

   7. <u>42 U.S.C. sec. 12201 (b) , 39 Citing References</u>

   8. <u>42 U.S.C. sec. 12201 (c) , 51 Citing References</u>

   9. <u>42 U.S.C. sec. 12201 (c) (1 to 3) , 1 Citing References</u>

  10. <u>42 U.S.C. sec. 12201 (c) (1) , 14 Citing References</u>

Citation: **42 uscs 12201**
    View: Cite
Date/Time: Thursday, November 11, 1999 - 3:28 PM EST

<u>About LEXIS-NEXIS</u> | <u>Terms and Conditions</u>

| ILLUSTRATION 12-11 | Shepard's Online List of Citing References, from LEXIS |

Check a Citation - SHEPARD'S® - 42 U.S.C. sec. 12201 (b)   Page 1 of 1

Citation: **42 uscs 12201** (Get this Document)
Focus: **smoking**

Shepard's® [   ] **Check**

42 U.S.C. sec. 12201 (b)

CITING REFERENCES (3 citing references)

2nd Circuit - Court of Appeals

Cited by:
Staron v. McDonald's Corp., 51 F.3d 353, 1995 U.S. App. LEXIS 7643, 1 Accom. Disabiliti Dec. (CCH) P1-255, 4 Am. Disabilities Cas. (BNA) 353, 9 Am. Disabilities Dec. 481 (2d Cir. Conn. 1995)

Cited by:
51 F.3d 353 p.357

7th Circuit - U.S. District Courts

Cited by:
Piquard v. City of E. Peoria, 887 F. Supp. 1106, 1995 U.S. Dist. LEXIS 11467, 4 Am. Disabilities Cas. (BNA) 1716, 11 Am. Disabilities Dec. 428 (C.D. Ill. 1995)

Cited by:
887 F. Supp. 1106 p.1118

West Virginia Supreme Ct. of Appeals

Cited by:
Paxton v. State Dep't of Tax & Revenue, 192 W. Va. 213, 451 S.E.2d 779, 1994 W. Va. LEXIS 199, 3 Am. Disabilities Cas. (BNA) 1689, 7 Am. Disabilities Dec. 894 (1994)

Cited by:
451 S.E.2d 779 p.782

Citation: **42 uscs 12201** (Get this Document)
Focus: **smoking**
View: Full
Date/Time: Thursday, November 11, 1999 - 3:42 PM EST

About LEXIS-NEXIS | Terms and Conditions

ILLUSTRATION 12-12   KeyCite Annotations and Additional Citations (Partial),
                          from Westlaw

KeyCite   Page 8

Citations: limited to Cases
Citations From U.S.C.A.

4. Subterfuge generally
    14 Krauel v. Iowa Methodist Medical Center, 95 F.3d 674, 676+, 65 USLW 2186+,
            71 Fair Empl.Prac.Cas. (BNA) 1326+, 69 Empl. Prac. Dec. P 44,315+,
            20 Employee Benefits Cas. 1809+, 5 A.D. Cases 1503+, 18 A.D.D. 112+,
            8 NDLR P 317+ (8th Cir.(Iowa) Sep 11, 1996) (NO. 95-3768)
    15 Piquard v. City of East Peoria, 887 F.Supp. 1106, 1118+, 4 A.D. Cases 1716+,
            11 A.D.D. 428+, 6 NDLR P 447+ (C.D.Ill. Apr 28, 1995) (NO. 94-1130)
    16 Krauel v. Iowa Methodist Medical Center, 915 F.Supp. 102, 105+, 64 USLW 2304+,
            69 Fair Empl.Prac.Cas. (BNA) 182+, 19 Employee Benefits Cas. 2145+,
            4 A.D. Cases 1734+, 13 A.D.D. 1128+, 7 NDLR P 363+ (S.D.Iowa Oct 02, 1995)
            (NO. 4-93-CV-10815)
    17 Doukas v. Metropolitan Life Ins. Co., 950 F.Supp. 422, 425+, 65 USLW 2429+,
            6 A.D. Cases 262+, 20 A.D.D. 245+, 9 NDLR P 121+ (D.N.H. Dec 19, 1996)
            (NO. CIV. 94-478-SD)
    18 Leonard F. v. Israel Discount Bank of New York, 967 F.Supp. 802, 805+, 7 A.D. Cases 1407+,
            23 A.D.D. 174+, 10 NDLR P 120+ (S.D.N.Y. Jun 26, 1997)
            (NO. 95 CIV. 6964 (CLB))

5. Regulations
    19 Caruso v. Blockbuster-Sony Music Entertainment Centre, 968 F.Supp. 210, 211,
            8 A.D. Cases 173, 23 A.D.D. 796, 10 NDLR P 196 (D.N.J. Jun 25, 1997)
            (NO. CIV.A. 95-3400 JEI)
    20 Anderson v. Gus Mayer Boston Store of Delaware, 924 F.Supp. 763, 779, 5 A.D. Cases 673,
            15 A.D.D. 955 (E.D.Tex. Mar 23, 1996) (NO. 1:94-CV-232)

6. Complete denial of insurance coverage
    21 Anderson v. Gus Mayer Boston Store of Delaware, 924 F.Supp. 763, 779, 5 A.D. Cases 673,
            15 A.D.D. 955 (E.D.Tex. Mar 23, 1996) (NO. 1:94-CV-232)

7. Preexisting conditions clauses
    22 Anderson v. Gus Mayer Boston Store of Delaware, 924 F.Supp. 763, 779, 5 A.D. Cases 673,
            15 A.D.D. 955 (E.D.Tex. Mar 23, 1996) (NO. 1:94-CV-232)

8. Actuarial data
    23 Chabner v. United of Omaha Life Ins. Co., 994 F.Supp. 1185, 1189+, 9 A.D. Cases 171+,
            12 NDLR P 43+ (N.D.Cal. Jan 16, 1998) (NO. C-95-0447-MHP)
    24 Doukas v. Metropolitan Life Ins. Co., 950 F.Supp. 422, 425+, 65 USLW 2429+,
            6 A.D. Cases 262+, 20 A.D.D. 245+, 9 NDLR P 121+ (D.N.H. Dec 19, 1996)
            (NO. CIV. 94-478-SD)

Additional Citations
    25 Theriault v. Flynn, 162 F.3d 46, 48, 8 A.D. Cases 1582, 14 NDLR P 65
            (1st Cir.(N.H.) Dec 08, 1998) (NO. 98-1420)
    26 Feliciano v. State of R.I., 160 F.3d 780, 788, 8 A.D. Cases 1520, 14 NDLR P 3
            (1st Cir.(R.I.) Nov 18, 1998) (NO. 98-1436)
    27 Dichner v. Liberty Travel, 141 F.3d 24, 32, 8 A.D. Cases 111, 12 NDLR P 164
            (1st Cir.(Mass.) Apr 13, 1998) (NO. 97-2046)
    28 Bercovitch v. Baldwin School, Inc., 133 F.3d 141, 154, 123 Ed. Law Rep. 1067,
            8 A.D. Cases 259, 11 NDLR P 273 (1st Cir.(Puerto Rico) Jan 12, 1998) (NO. 97-1739)
    29 Abbott v. Bragdon, 107 F.3d 934, 940, 65 USLW 2592, 6 A.D. Cases 780, 20 A.D.D. 616,
            9 NDLR P 215 (1st Cir.(Me.) Mar 05, 1997) (NO. 96-1643)

Sources for researching uniform laws:

- *Uniform Laws Annotated*
- specialized Shepard's Citators

You are most likely to research uniform and model acts when your jurisdiction has adopted one and you are seeking information about how it has been interpreted in other jurisdictions. Two sources are useful for this purpose.

First, *Uniform Laws Annotated*, published by West and available in paper and online, functions much like an annotated code. For each act, you can discern which states have adopted it and find NCCUSL commentary, West key numbers, references to cases from various jurisdictions, and references to selected secondary sources. *Uniform Laws Annotated* includes a directory of acts, index, and table of jurisdictions listing acts adopted by each.

Second, some uniform acts are the subject of specialized Shepard's, such as *Shepard's Uniform Commercial Code Citations*.

D. WHAT ELSE?

Conversion Tables. If you know a session law citation or public law number for a statute but not its codified citation, or if you have an outdated section number for a statute that has been renumbered, you can consult conversion tables. For example, the federal annotated codes' *Statutes at Large* tables list statutes in chronological order, by public law number, along with corresponding code sections. The federal annotated codes' tables of revised titles show where renumbered sections now appear.

Paper Shepard's Citations. Shepard's covering statutes also are available in paper. For example, *Shepard's Federal Statutes Citations* covers federal statutes.

KeyCite Alert. When you use this Westlaw service, you ask Westlaw to monitor the KeyCite record for a particular statute and notify you, for example, by fax or e-mail, when the record changes.

More on the Constitution. The United States Constitution is among the most analyzed legal texts in the world. *The Constitution of the United States of America: Analysis and Interpretation* is prepared by the Library of Congress and provides case summaries, historical information, and extensive commentary. Scholarly commentary includes treatises (such as those by Professors Tribe, Nowak, and Rotunda) and periodicals specializing in constitutional law. Some state annotated codes include the United States Constitution.

Treaties.   Treaties (compacts with other countries that are ratified by Congress) are not codified into the federal code. They appear in various publications, including *Treaties and Other International Act Series, United States Treaties and Other International Agreements*, and *Consolidated Treaties & International Agreements Current Document Service*. Other research options include Westlaw and LEXIS databases and web sites for particular treaties.

Interstate Compacts.   States may enter into agreements with each other, with the approval of Congress. These compacts appear in *Statutes at Large*, the session laws of the involved states, and *Interstate Compacts & Agencies* (a publication of the Council of State Governments).

Compilations of State Laws.   Should you seek information about the statutes of multiple states on a subject, you should check whether a compilation exists on that subject. The following compile state statutes on various major subjects: *Subject Compilations of State Laws; National Survey of State Laws;* and *Statutes Compared: A U.S., Canadian, Multinational Research Guide to Statutes by Subject.*

Local Government Laws.   Some local jurisdictions (municipalities and counties) publish their charters and ordinances; others do not. You are most likely to find such materials through a web site or through a clerk's office. *Ordinance Law Annotations* digests cases discussing local ordinances.

NCCUSL Handbook.   You can trace the ongoing work of the NCCUSL through its *Handbook of the National Conference of Commissioners on Uniform State Laws and Proceedings of the Annual Conference*. Among other things, the Handbook discusses the progress of acts currently under consideration.

Suggested State Legislation.   Similarly the Council of State Governments annually publishes its model acts in a publication entitled *Suggested State Legislation*.

E.   HOW DO YOU CITE CONSTITUTIONS AND STATUTES?

Constitutions are simply cited; here is an example (according to Rule 11 of *The Bluebook*):

N.M. Const. art. II, § 4.

Statutes have a somewhat more complicated citation form; various options are used in specific situations. The preferred source to cite is the official code; other options include the unofficial code, session laws, a computer database, and various other publications. The standard citation forms call for the following information: the source's abbreviated name; title, chapter, and volume numbers, as needed; section number; publisher (if not the government); and date of the volume where the information appears, including a "supp." designation if needed, or date of enactment if the citation is to the session laws. The statute's name is used when the statute is commonly cited by name and when the citation is to the session laws. Here are examples (according to Rule 12 of *The Bluebook*):

> state code: N.M. Stat. Ann. § 50-11-3 (Michie 1993)
> official federal code: 42 U.S.C. § 12201 (1994)
> unofficial federal code: 42 U.S.C.S. § 12201 (Law. Co-op. 1997)
> session law: Americans with Disabilities Act of 1990, Pub. L. No. 101-336, § 501, 104 Stat. 327, 369

F. CONCLUDING POINTS

Because constitutions and statutes are primary authority, your research will not be correct, comprehensive, or credible unless you competently research the enacted law on your problem. Early in your research, determine whether your problem is governed by a constitution or statute or both, at the federal or state or local levels, or some combination of these. Search not only for the statute itself but also for case law assessing and interpreting the statute.

Two types of paper-based sources are especially useful. Annotated codes are the major tool for statutory research. They present the law as it currently exists, organized topically; they also provide an abundance of useful material in the annotation, including descriptions of cases applying the statute and references to secondary sources. By contrast, session laws present the acts passed during a specific legislative session, organized chronologically and without annotation material. Session laws are useful in a narrower range of circumstances, for example, when your client's facts are governed by a statute that is no longer in effect or never was codified.

Westlaw and LEXIS both afford a wealth of statutory material online. Generally you will research in annotated code databases. The advantages of online research include the option to use key-word searching, the cumulated nature of the online database, and the currency of the database. CD-ROM research is similar in many respects to online research, although CD-ROMs are not themselves as current as online databases.

Various public web sites also offer a wealth of statutory material. This material should be very current, and the web site may be highly credible if a legislature is involved. However, a web site probably will not include annotation material, and the search options may be more limited than those afforded by the commercial online services.

Online statutory citators provide significant important information about legislative activity, cases interpreting the statute, and pertinent secondary sources along with ways of tailoring your research to your particular needs.

CHAPTER 13

LEGISLATIVE PROCESS MATERIALS

A. INTRODUCTION: THE LEGISLATIVE PROCESS

1. Introduction

This chapter covers the legislative process and its relationship to the statutory sources described in Chapter 12. Part A describes the legislative process. Part B identifies the legislative history materials generated during the process; then it explains how to locate those materials and evaluate their usefulness in discerning the legislative intent behind a vague or ambiguous law that has been enacted and now governs your client's situation. Part C covers how to track pending legislation to learn of its content or its progress; lawyers track pending legislation so as to counsel clients about laws that may affect their future operations and to assist clients who want to participate in the legislative process.

This chapter continues to illustrate the research of the Canoga case with a focus on Congress' enactment of the Americans with Disabilities Act (ADA), which is discussed in Chapter 12. If the Act governs Ms. Canoga's situation and she can prove that her smoking is caused by an addiction to nicotine, her employer may be prohibited from discriminating against her. Thus an issue is whether nicotine addiction is a "disability" under the ADA.

2. The Legislative Process

The process of enacting a law is similar at both the federal and state levels. The following discussion focuses on the United States Congress. See Exhibit 13.1 on page 208 for a graphic of how a bill becomes law. The illustration shows a common path; not all bills follow the exact same path.

The legislative process typically begins with the introduction of a bill into a session of Congress. While anyone can draft a bill, only a member of Congress can introduce a bill. Some bills have multiple sponsors, to reflect broad political support. When a bill is introduced, it is given a number that indicates both the body in which it is introduced and the order in which it is introduced. A Senate bill number begins with "S." for Senate, a House bill number with "H.R." for House of Representatives. Since bill numbering starts over again in each Congress, a complete bill number includes the number of the Congress in which a bill was introduced. The exact same bill may be introduced in both the House and Senate; the bill then has two bill numbers, and the two bills are called "companion bills." Different bills on the same subject also may be introduced in either or both chambers.

After a bill is introduced, it may be referred to one or more committees; or it may be held at the desk of the chamber; or it may be placed on a legislative calendar for floor action. (A bill that is held at the desk may be placed on a calendar at any time.)

If a bill is referred to a committee, the committee chair may refer the bill to one or more subcommittees, or the chair may handle the bill at the committee level. A subcommittee, the full committee, or (more rarely) both may hold a hearing on the bill. One or more of the bill's sponsors will appear. Witnesses may include representatives of the Administration and of groups affected by the proposed legislation, representatives of public interest groups, and experts on the topic. Other interested parties can submit written comments for the hearing record.

After the hearing, or at any time if there is no hearing, the subcommittee and the full committee may meet to consider and mark up the bill. If a subcommittee approves a bill (with or without amendment), it forwards the bill to the full committee. If the full committee approves the bill (with or without amendment), it reports the bill to its parent body and prepares a committee report, setting forth its analysis and recommendations on the bill and any amendments to it. Occasionally committee amendments to a bill are so extensive that the committee introduces a new bill with a new number.

Next, the bill goes to the floor of the House or the Senate for debate. Floor managers explain the bill and respond to questions about it. Other members may offer arguments for and against the bill, and amendments may be offered and either passed or defeated.

If the bill passes in one chamber, it becomes known as an "act," and it is reprinted and sent to the other chamber for its consideration. The second chamber may pass the bill without change, or it may amend the bill and return it to the first chamber. The first chamber may accept the amendment; or it may amend the amendment and return the bill to the other chamber;

| EXHIBIT 13.1 | How a Bill Becomes a Law (Congressional Quarterly's *Guide to Congress*) |

How a Bill Becomes a Law

This graphic shows the most typical way in which proposed legislation is enacted into law. There are more complicated, as well as simpler, routes, and most bills never become law. The process is illustrated with two hypothetical bills, House bill No. 1 (HR 1) and

Senate bill No. 2 (S 2). Bills must be passed by both houses in identical form before they can be sent to the president. The path of HR 1 is traced by a gray line, that of S 2 by a black line. In practice, most bills begin as similar proposals in both houses.

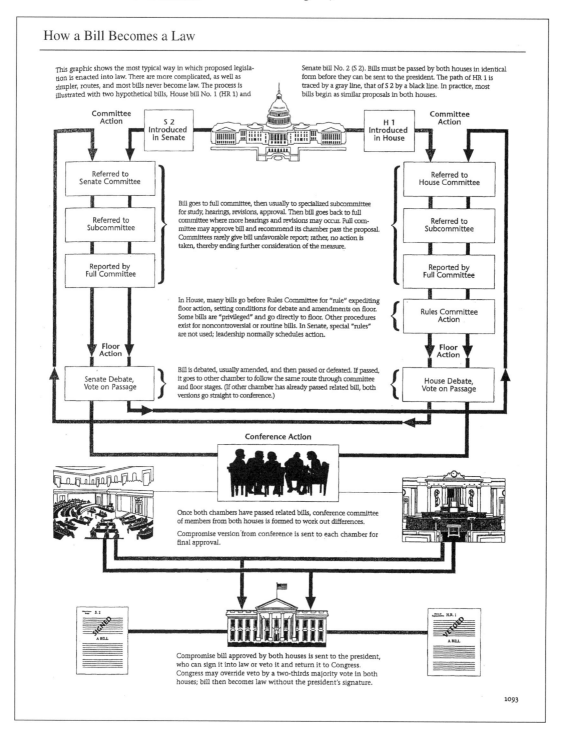

Committee Action

S 2 Introduced in Senate

H 1 Introduced in House

Committee Action

Referred to Senate Committee

Referred to House Committee

Referred to Subcommittee

Bill goes to full committee, then usually to specialized subcommittee for study, hearings, revisions, approval. Then bill goes back to full committee where more hearings and revisions may occur. Full committee may approve bill and recommend its chamber pass the proposal. Committees rarely give bill unfavorable report; rather, no action is taken, thereby ending further consideration of the measure.

Referred to Subcommittee

Reported by Full Committee

Reported by Full Committee

In House, many bills go before Rules Committee for "rule" expediting floor action, setting conditions for debate and amendments on floor. Some bills are "privileged" and go directly to floor. Other procedures exist for noncontroversial or routine bills. In Senate, special "rules" are not used; leadership normally schedules action.

Rules Committee Action

Floor Action

Floor Action

Senate Debate, Vote on Passage

Bill is debated, usually amended, and then passed or defeated. If passed, it goes to other chamber to follow the same route through committee and floor stages. (If other chamber has already passed related bill, both versions go straight to conference.)

House Debate, Vote on Passage

Conference Action

Once both chambers have passed related bills, conference committee of members from both houses is formed to work out differences.

Compromise version from conference is sent to each chamber for final approval.

S 2 / **H.R. 1**

Compromise bill approved by both houses is sent to the president, who can sign it into law or veto it and return it to Congress. Congress may override veto by a two-thirds majority vote in both houses; bill then becomes law without the president's signature.

1093

or it may insist on its version of the bill and request a conference committee to resolve the differences.

If the second chamber agrees to a conference committee, leaders of both chambers appoint conferees. If the conferees reach agreement, they prepare a conference committee report with the text of the compromise bill and an explanation. If both chambers vote to accept the compromise bill, it is sent to the President.

The President has ten days, excluding Sundays, in which to sign or veto a bill that has been presented by Congress. If the President signs a bill, the bill becomes effective upon signing, unless a different date is specified in the bill. If the President vetoes a bill, the bill and the President's objections are returned to Congress, where the bill dies unless two-thirds of each chamber vote to override the veto. If the President does not act on a bill within ten days and Congress is still in session, the bill becomes law without the President's signature. If Congress has adjourned, however, the bill dies; this is called a "pocket veto."

If a bill is not passed by the end of the Congress in which it was introduced (each Congress has two consecutive one-year sessions), the bill dies. It may be re-introduced with a new bill number in a subsequent Congress.

B.   LEGISLATIVE HISTORY

1.   What Are Legislative History Materials?

In the broadest sense, legislative history consists of all of the background and events giving rise to the enactment of a law. In a narrower sense, "legislative history" refers to the materials considered or created by the legislature at each stage of the legislative process. The legislative process just described generates seven categories of materials:

(1)   bill text and amendments,
(2)   hearing record,
(3)   committee prints,
(4)   House and Senate documents,
(5)   committee and conference committee reports,
(6)   floor debates and proceedings, and
(7)   presidential messages after passage of a bill.

Of course, not all of these materials are available for all legislation.

First, a bill is printed in various versions, including an introduced version; a reported version; an engrossed version—an official copy of a bill as it passed a particular chamber; an act version—the version as it passed one chamber and is printed for consideration in the other; and an enrolled version—the official version prepared for presentation to the President. Since each version reflects a different stage in the legislative process, it is important to understand which version you are reading. In addition, sometimes you may need to examine amendments that were proposed, but not adopted, and that therefore never appeared in any version of the bill. Illustration 13-1 on page 211 is an example of a bill as introduced.

Second, if a committee or subcommittee holds a hearing, it may publish a record of the hearing. The record may include the witnesses' oral and written statements, committee questions and answers, statements and exhibits submitted by interested parties, and supplemental material added to the hearing record by committee members and staff. See Illustration 13-2 on page 212 for an example of hearing testimony. Not all hearings are published.

Third, a committee may rely on research reports prepared by committee staff, consultants, the Library of Congress, or others. These reports, published as committee prints, may contain statistics, scientific and social studies, historical data, bibliographies, compilations of statutes, bill comparisons, and other analyses.

Fourth, if the President or an executive agency sends Congress a communication, such as a message proposing or vetoing a bill, the communication may appear as a House or Senate document. Reports of committee activities, the texts of committee-sponsored studies, background information reports, and some other miscellaneous materials also may be issued as House and Senate documents.

Fifth, committee reports are the publications by which congressional committees report to the full House or Senate on their deliberations and recommendations. Committee reports on bills typically include a description and analysis of the bill, a discussion of its background, the committee's findings and recommendations, the text of the recommended bill, any minority views, and an estimate of the costs or revenues produced by the bill. See Illustration 13-3 on pages 213–214. Of particular importance are conference committee reports, which contain the text of the compromise bill and an analysis of how the compromise was reached.

Sixth, floor debates and proceedings include statements made and actions taken in a chamber of Congress. The *Congressional Record* contains more or less verbatim transcripts of floor debates and reports of proceedings, including remarks by members of Congress, their votes, proposed amendments, conference committee reports, messages from the President, and on occasion the text of the bills under consideration. The *Congressional Record* report is not a completely accurate account of what transpired because members of Congress may revise their remarks, and they are allowed to add extended remarks, that is, comments never made on the floor. See Illustration 13-4 on page 215.

Seventh, presidential messages after passage of a bill by Congress include both signing statements and veto messages, as appropriate. See Illustration 13-5 on page 216.

Legislative history is a unique form of legal authority. The materials created during the legislative process are generated by a government body while creating primary authority—the legislation; but they are subordinate to the legislation itself. There is considerable disagreement about whether and to what extent any legislative process materials are themselves primary authority.

ILLUSTRATION 13-1   Senate Bill, from U.S. Government Printing Office

II

101ST CONGRESS
1ST SESSION
S. 933

To establish a clear and comprehensive prohibition of discrimination on the basis of disability.

IN THE SENATE OF THE UNITED STATES

MAY 9 (legislative day, JANUARY 3), 1989

Mr. HARKIN (for himself, Mr. KENNEDY, Mr. DURENBERGER, Mr. SIMON, Mr. JEFFORDS, Mr. CRANSTON, Mr. MCCAIN, Mr. MITCHELL, Mr. CHAFEE, Mr. LEAHY, Mr. STEVENS, Mr. INOUYE, Mr. COHEN, Mr. GORE, Mr. PACKWOOD, Mr. RIEGLE, Mr. GRAHAM, Mr. PELL, Mr. DODD, Mr. ADAMS, Ms. MIKULSKI, Mr. METZENBAUM, Mr. MATSUNAGA, Mr. WIRTH, Mr. BINGAMAN, Mr. CONRAD, Mr. BURDICK, Mr. LEVIN, Mr. LIEBERMAN, Mr. MOYNIHAN, Mr. KERRY, Mr. SARBANES, Mr. BOSCHWITZ, and Mr. HEINZ) introduced the following bill; which was read twice and referred to the Committee on Labor and Human Resources

---

A BILL

To establish a clear and comprehensive prohibition of discrimination on the basis of disability.

1   *Be it enacted by the Senate and House of Representa-*

2   *tives of the United States of America in Congress assembled,*

3   SECTION 1. SHORT TITLE; TABLE OF CONTENTS.

4   (a) SHORT TITLE.—This Act may be cited as the

5   "Americans with Disabilities Act of 1989".

6   (b) TABLE OF CONTENTS.—The table of contents is as

7   follows:

ILLUSTRATION 13-2   Hearing Testimony, from *CIS/Microfiche Library*

5

TESTIMONY OF

EVAN J. KEMP, JR., COMMISSIONER

U. S. EQUAL EMPLOYMENT OPPORTUNITY COMMISSION

BEFORE THE HOUSE SUBCOMMITTEES ON SELECT

EDUCATION AND EMPLOYMENT OPPORTUNITIES

SEPTEMBER 13, 1989 AT 10:00 A.M.

I am here today not as a Commissioner of the U.S. Equal Employment
Opportunity Commission, but as a person with a disability. I am
100% for the Americans With Disabilities Act. But there are those
who ask "Does it make economic sense to integrate disabled people
into society?" Other people inquire "How many disabled people are
there really?" While others ask "Does it really matter? Isn't
medical science going to cure most disabling conditions?" Both
disabled people and nondisabled and politician and nonpoliticians
have all asked these questions many times.

To answer these questions and others, I have found it necessary
and helpful to have a philosophical framework to work from. I
would like to share it with you.

The disability rights movement addresses the problems of all our
citizens who are different in some respect from what society
considers to be an acceptable American: the 28 year old, 5'10",

ILLUSTRATION 13-3   Committee Report, from *United States Code Congressional and Administrative News*

AMERICANS WITH DISABILITIES ACT OF 1990

P.L. 101–336, see page 104 Stat. 327

DATES OF CONSIDERATION AND PASSAGE

Senate: September 7, 1989; July 11, 13, 1990
House: May 22, July 12, 1990

Senate Report (Labor and Human Resources Committee)
No. 101–116, Aug. 30, 1989
[To accompany S. 933]

House Report (Public Works and Transportation Committee) No.
101–485(I), May 14, 1990
[To accompany H.R. 2273]

House Report (Education and Labor Committee) No. 101–485(II),
May 15, 1990
[To accompany H.R. 2273]

House Report (Judiciary Committee) No. 101–485(III), May 15,
1990
[To accompany H.R. 2273]

House Report (Energy and Commerce Committee) No. 101–
485(IV), May 15, 1990
[To accompany H.R. 2273]

House Conference Report No. 101–558, June 26, 1990
[To accompany S. 933]

House Conference Report No. 101–596, July 12, 1990
[To accompany S. 933]

Cong. Record Vol. 135 (1989)

Cong. Record Vol. 136 (1990)

The Senate bill was passed in lieu of the House bill after amending its language to contain much of the text of the House bill. The House Report (Parts I (this page), II (page 303), III (page 445), IV (page 512)) is set out below and the second House Conference Report (page 565) and the President's Signing Statement (page 601) follow.

HOUSE REPORT NO. 101–485(I)

[page 1]

The Committee on Public Works and Transportation, to whom was referred the bill (H.R. 2273) to establish a clear and comprehensive prohibition of discrimination on the basis of disability, having considered the same, report favorably thereon with an amendment and recommend that the bill as amended do pass.

*   *   *   *   *

267

ILLUSTRATION 13-3   *(continued)*

LEGISLATIVE HISTORY
HOUSE REPORT NO. 101–485(I)

[page 24]

*   *   *   *   *

INTRODUCTION

The Americans With Disabilities Act (ADA) will permit the United States to take a long-delayed but very necessary step to welcome individuals with disabilities fully into the mainstream of American society. The specific provisions of the bill which lie within the jurisdiction of the Committee on Public Works and Transportation are primarily within Titles II and III, dealing with publicly and privately provided transportation services.

With regard to publicly provided transportation services, the bill requires the purchase of new transit vehicles for use on fixed route systems which are readily accessible to, and usable by, individuals with disabilities, including individuals who use wheelchairs. The bill also requires the provision of paratransit services for those individuals whose disabilities preclude their use of the fixed route system.

Transit agencies across the United States have already made some progress in the provision of accessible transit services—35% of America's transit buses are currently accessible. As more and more transit authorities make the commitment to provide fully accessible bus service, the percentage of new bus purchases which are accessible has grown to more than 50% annually. By the mid-1990's many American cities will have completely accessible fixed route systems. Furthermore, many of the transit systems in America already provide some type of paratransit services to the disabled. So, the passage of the ADA will not break sharply with existing transit policy. It will simply extend past successes to even more cities, so that this country can continue to make progress in providing much needed transit services for individuals with disabilities.

With regard to privately provided transportation services, which do not receive the high levels of federal subsidies that publicly provided services do, the requirements of the bill vary according to the size and type of vehicle, as well as according to the type of system on which the vehicle operates.

Nonetheless, in all cases, the Americans with Disabilities Act provides strong guarantees that individuals with disabilities will be

[page 25]

treated with respect and dignity while using transporatation services. After all, the Americans With Disabilities Act is ultimately a civil rights bill. The history of the United States is rich with examples of diversity triumphing over discrimination, but not so rich that this country can ever afford to exclude, or segregate in any way, the significant number of its citizens who have disabilities.

SECTION 1. SHORT TITLE; TABLE OF CONTENTS

Subsection (a) of this section provides that the Act may be cited as the "Americans with Disabilities Act of 1990".

SECTION 2. FINDINGS AND PURPOSES

This section describes the findings and purposes of the Act.

ILLUSTRATION 13-4   Floor Debate, from *Congressional Record*

June 6, 1990   CONGRESSIONAL RECORD—SENATE   13063

Glenn	Kohl	Pell
Gore	Lautenberg	Riegle
Graham	Leahy	Robb
Harkin	Levin	Rockefeller
Hatfield	Lieberman	Sanford
Hollings	Metzenbaum	Sarbanes
Inouye	Mikulski	Simon
Jeffords	Mitchell	Wirth
Kennedy	Moynihan	
Kerrey	Packwood	

NAYS—53

Armstrong	Garn	Murkowski
Bentsen	Gorton	Nickles
Bond	Gramm	Nunn
Boren	Grassley	Pressler
Breaux	Hatch	Pryor
Bryan	Heflin	Reid
Bumpers	Heinz	Roth
Burns	Helms	Rudman
Byrd	Humphrey	Sasser
Coats	Johnston	Shelby
Cochran	Kassebaum	Simpson
Conrad	Kasten	Specter
D'Amato	Lott	Stevens
Dixon	Lugar	Symms
Dole	Mack	Thurmond
Exon	McCain	Wallop
Ford	McClure	Warner
Fowler	McConnell	

NOT VOTING—7

Baucus	DeConcini	Wilson
Boschwitz	Dodd	
Chafee	Kerry	

So the motion to lay on the table was rejected.

Mr. HELMS. Mr. President, I move to reconsider the vote by which the motion was rejected.

Mr. DOLE. I move to lay that motion on the table.

The motion to lay on the table was agreed to.

● Mr. KERRY. Mr. President, an important family commitment requires that I be in Boston during the time allotted this morning for debate and the subsequent vote on the motion offered by the Senator from North Carolina, to instruct the conferees on the Americans With Disabilities Act [ADA]. I want to make it clear for the record, however, that were I present for the upcoming vote, I would vote against the motion to instruct and in support of the motion to table offered by the majority leader.

The ADA, as passed by the Senate on a vote of 76-8, already excludes coverage of individuals with a contagious disease who pose a threat to the health or safety of others which cannot be eliminated by reasonable accommodation. Further, Mr. President, Dr. Roper, Director of the Center for Disease Control as well as Secretary Louis Sullivan of the Department of Health and Human Services, have stated that people with AIDS do not pose a threat to health or safety in food handling positions, because AIDS is not a foodborne illness.

We should not be in a position where we give rights and protections with one hand as we do with the ADA and then take them away with the other, which is exactly what we would accomplish by approving this motion. The ADA goes to the heart of opening the doors of opportunity and toward eliminating judgments based on fear,

prejudice and ignorance and we must protect the integrity of this legislation. As President Bush stated when he urged the Congress to pass the ADA, "I call on the Congress to get on the job of passing a law—embodied in the ADA that prohibits discrimination against those with HIV and AIDS. We won't tolerate discrimination.

Mr. President, we must move forward in helping to eliminate the discrimination faced by the Nation's 43 million disabled individuals. We have made a vitally important step in this regard with passage of the ADA. Let us continue to move forward in our fulfillment of this goal. I reiterate my strong opposition to the Helms motion and my strong support for the majority leader's motion to table.●

The PRESIDING OFFICER. All time having expired, the question is now on agreeing to the motion to instruct the conferees.

The Senator from North Carolina, [Mr. HELMS], is recognized.

Mr. HELMS. Mr. President, I think the Senate has made itself clear on this issue, and I see no point for a further rollcall vote.

I ask unanimous consent that the yeas and nays be vitiated.

The PRESIDING OFFICER. Without objection, the request of the Senator is agreed to.

The question now is on agreeing to the motion to instruct the conferees.

The motion was agreed to.

Mr. HELMS. Mr. President, I move to reconsider the vote by which the motion was agreed to.

Mr. HARKIN. I move to lay that motion on the table.

The motion to lay on the table was agreed to.

The PRESIDING OFFICER. Under the previous order, the Senator from Iowa [Mr. GRASSLEY] is now recognized.

MOTION TO INSTRUCT CONFEREES

Mr. GRASSLEY. Mr. President, I send a motion to the desk and ask for its immediate consideration.

The PRESIDING OFFICER. The clerk will report.

The assistant legislative clerk read as follows:

The Senator from Iowa, Mr. Grassley, moves that the Senate instruct the Senate conferees on S. 933, the Americans with Disabilities Act, to ensure that the rights, protections, and remedies made available under that Act with regards to employment shall extend to the employees, and prospective employees, of members of Congress or the instrumentalities thereof, and that such employees, or prospective employees, who are aggrieved by a violation of that Act shall have a private cause of action against the individual or entity that has engaged in the violation of such employees rights under the Act in the appropriate district court of the United States.

The PRESIDING OFFICER. The Senator from Iowa.

Mr. GRASSLEY. Under a previous unanimous-consent agreement, that motion is withdrawn.

The PRESIDING OFFICER. The Senator is correct; the motion is withdrawn.

Mr. GRASSLEY. Mr. President, I had planned to offer at this point a motion to instruct the conferees with respect to congressional coverage under S. 933. My motion would have instructed that the conferees provide to aggrieved congressional employees, or prospective employees, among other remedies, a private right of action against Congress, its members, or its instrumentalities.

This right is long overdue, and I am pleased that the Senate is about to turn over a new leaf, when it comes to meaningful congressional coverage of the laws that we apply to all other Americans.

Because of the assurances I have received from my colleagues, Senator HARKIN, on behalf of the conferees, I will not offer that motion. I truly appreciate the commitment of my colleague from Iowa on this point. I know he will be sensitive to the potentially significant constitutional issues involved, and balance them against the rights of victims of discrimination.

I also appreciate the interests of the leadership to move rapidly on this important bill. I agree and am prepared to move.

Mr. President, permitting a right to legal redress of grievances for more than 30,000 employees in and around Capitol Hill—and countless more prospective employees—would help put an end to the shameful practice around here where we say to the American people: "do as we say, not as we do."

Unfortunately Mr. President, the statesman who can best explain this principle can't be here in person. We do, however, have the benefit of his writings on precisely this point, more than 200 years ago.

James Madison, writing in "Federalist 57," explained why it was that Congress would be deterred from passing oppressive laws upon the people. His remedy—that Congress "could make no law which will not have its full operation on themselves and their friends, as well as on the great mass of society."

Madison continued:

This has always been deemed one of the strongest bonds by which human policy can connect the rulers and the people together. It creates between them a communion of interests and sympathy of sentiments * * * without which every government degenerates into tyranny.

Madison says:

If it be asked, what is to restrain the Congress from making legal discriminations in favor of themselves * * * the spirit which activates the people of America, a spirit which

| ILLUSTRATION 13-5 | Presidential Signing Statement, from *United States Code Congressional and Administrative News* |

SIGNING STATEMENT
P.L. 101–336

STATEMENT BY PRESIDENT OF THE UNITED STATES

STATEMENT BY PRESIDENT GEORGE BUSH UPON
SIGNING S. 933

26 Weekly Compilation of Presidential Documents 1165,
July 30, 1990

Today, I am signing S. 933, the "Americans with Disabilities Act of 1990." In this extraordinary year, we have seen our own Declaration of Independence inspire the march of freedom throughout Eastern Europe. It is altogether fitting that the American people have once again given clear expression to our most basic ideals of freedom and equality. The Americans with Disabilities Act represents the full flowering of our democratic principles, and it gives me great pleasure to sign it into law today.

In 1986, on behalf of President Reagan, I personally accepted a report from the National Council on Disability entitled "Toward Independence." In that report, the National Council recommended the enactment of comprehensive legislation to ban discrimination against persons with disabilities. The Americans with Disabilities Act (ADA) is such legislation. It promises to open up all aspects of American life to individuals with disabilities—employment opportunities, government services, public accommodations, transportation, and telecommunications.

This legislation is comprehensive because the barriers faced by individuals with disabilities are wide-ranging. Existing laws and regulations under the Rehabilitation Act of 1973 have been effective with respect to the Federal Government, its contractors, and the recipients of Federal funds. However, they have left broad areas of American life untouched or inadequately addressed. Many of our young people, who have benefited from the equal educational opportunity guaranteed under the Rehabilitation Act and the Education of the Handicapped Act, have found themselves on graduation day still shut out of the mainstream of American life. They have faced persistent discrimination in the workplace and barriers posed by inaccessible public transportation, public accommodations, and telecommunications.

Fears that the ADA is too vague or too costly and will lead to an explosion of litigation are misplaced. The Administration worked closely with the Congress to ensure that, wherever possible, existing language and standards from the Rehabilitation Act were incorporated into the ADA. The Rehabilitation Act standards are already familiar to large segments of the private sector that are either Federal contractors or recipients of Federal funds. Because the Rehabilitation Act was enacted 17 years ago, there is already an extensive body of law interpreting the requirements of that Act. Employers can turn to these interpretations for guidance on how to meet their obligations under the ADA.

The Administration and the Congress have carefully crafted the ADA to give the business community the flexibility to meet the requirements of the Act without incurring undue costs. Cost may be taken into account in determining how an employee is "reasonably accommodated," whether the removal of a barrier is "readily achievable," or whether the provision of a particular auxiliary aid would result in an "undue burden." The ADA's most rigorous access requirements are reserved for new construction where

601

2. Why Would You Research Which Legislative History Materials?

The meaning of a statute may be difficult to discern. Particular words of the statute may be vague or ambiguous, and statutory provisions may conflict. Rules of statutory construction emphasize the primacy of statutory language, of course. But if a close reading of a statute reveals an ambiguity, legislative history is one tool for resolving the ambiguity.

Legislative history analysis hinges on determining the legislature's intent as to two questions: First, did the legislature intend the law to cover the parties or the situation at hand? Second, if the law does apply, what effect did the legislature intend the law to have?

As you work with legislative history materials, keep several caveats in mind. First, the legislature may not have had any intent as to your situation. Your situation may not have been contemplated by those who drafted the legislation, or circumstances may have changed since the legislation's enactment. Second, legislative history materials often are themselves ambiguous or inconclusive; they may contain evidence both for and against a particular interpretation of a law. Third, some courts do not view arguments based on legislative history materials as credible. Legislative history research rests in part on the premise—or fiction—that some of the statements made by individual legislators and witnesses shed light on the intent of the whole legislature. It also rests on the premise (perhaps more believable) that one can tell something about legislative intent by reading committee reports or by studying the various drafts or amendments to the bill. In fact, none of the material making up a legislative history truly embodies the intent of the entire legislature—except the text of the law itself.

Various legislative history materials have differing weights of authority. The weightiness of legislative history materials generally depends on how well they represent the actual deliberative process of the legislature as a whole, rather than the personal view of an individual legislator or a witness. Furthermore, materials generated near the end of the legislative process may be more weighty than materials generated near the beginning, especially if a bill has been amended along the way.

The various versions of a bill as well as rejected and adopted amendments may be persuasive evidence of legislative intent. Furthermore, committee reports are usually considered key documents because they are formally adopted by a committee that has expertise on the topic and was charged with making a recommendation on the bill. Conference committee reports are especially important because they are adopted late in the legislative process and explain the resolution of differences between the House and Senate.

By comparison, hearing records typically carry less weight. While they may contain useful information, the testimony also may reflect the biased positions of those testifying. Floor debates are somewhat controversial as indications of legislative intent, because legislators sometimes seek to use them to establish a reading of the legislation that they were unable to incorporate into the legislation itself. Nevertheless, courts do rely on such statements, particularly when they are made by the bill's sponsors or managers.

Several categories of materials are less commonly used, but can provide some useful information. Committee prints may contain useful factual background and information from which you can infer the concerns or reasoning of the legislature. Reports of executive branch agencies can discuss the problems that a law was designed to remedy. Finally, the executive's action in approving or vetoing a bill is part of the legislative process and may be some evidence of legislative intent, particularly for legislation passed after a veto.

To use legislative history materials properly, you must acquaint yourself thoroughly with your law's full legislative history. Otherwise, you will be at risk of relying on unrepresentative fragments.

3. How Do You Research Legislative History?

As you no doubt have surmised, the federal legislative process and the materials it produces can be lengthy and complicated. Your research involves four tasks:

(1) identifying the public law enacting the pertinent statutory language;
(2) identifying the legislative steps leading to enactment of that law and the materials produced at each of those steps;
(3) identifying a source for each of those materials;
(4) locating, reading, and analyzing the materials.

If the legislature considered any related bills on the same subject prior to enacting the law you are researching, you also should know about these.

The following text discusses seven practices, each of which permits you to accomplish some of the four tasks to a greater or lesser extent. The first practice involves the transition from statutory research to legislative history research: the statutory code. The second practice works for major statutes only: use of a compiled legislative history, that is, a package of materials someone else has already prepared. Unfortunately, for most statutes, no compiled legislative history exists; furthermore, you may need to supplement a nonexhaustive compiled legislative history.

Thus, you often will need to compile your law's legislative history yourself. The remaining practices involve various sources that provide some range of federal legislative history documents and information. These sources vary in the range of documents provided for any congressional session, the number of sessions covered, and the sophistication of their editorial enhancements. Some sources are paper or microfiche sources; others are computer-based. The following discussion focuses on how to research the legislative history of relatively recent laws, because that is more probable than research into dated laws. Exhibit 13.2 on page 219–220 lists which documents are available in which sources. Exhibit 13.3 on pages 220–221 lists the major attributes of the research practices (other than the use of statutory codes and compiled legislative histories).

EXHIBIT 13.2	Legislative History Documents and Sources

Document	Explanation	Selected Sources
Bill text and amendments	proposed legislation and all versions of the bill, other proposed amendments	*CIS/Congressional Bills, Resolutions & Laws* *CIS Congressional Universe* *Congressional Record* (for floor amendments) GPO Access GPO bill collection on microfiche LEXIS THOMAS Westlaw
Hearing record	transcript of oral and written testimony presented to a committee, plus supplemental material entered on the record	*CIS Congressional Universe* *CIS/Microfiche Library* GPO (individual paper titles) GPO Access LEXIS Westlaw
Committee print	publication that provides information and analysis for a committee	*CIS Congressional Universe* *CIS/Microfiche Library* GPO (individual paper titles) GPO Access LEXIS
Committee report	committee publication of its findings and recommendations to the parent body on a proposed bill	*CIS Congressional Universe* *CIS/Microfiche Library* GPO (individual paper titles) GPO Access LEXIS THOMAS *United States Serial Set* U.S.C.C.A.N. Westlaw
Conference committee report	text of the compromise bill and analysis of how the compromise was reached	*CIS Congressional Universe* *CIS/Microfiche Library* *Congressional Record* GPO (individual paper titles) GPO Access LEXIS THOMAS *United States Serial Set* U.S.C.C.A.N. Westlaw
House or Senate document	presidential message proposing or vetoing legislation, executive agency's report to Congress, or committee publication not issued as a print	*CIS Congressional Universe* *CIS/Microfiche Library* GPO (individual paper titles) GPO Access LEXIS *United States Serial Set*

EXHIBIT 13.2	*(continued)*

Document	Explanation	Selected Sources
Floor debates and proceedings	daily transcript of congressional floor activity	*Congressional Record* (available from GPO in paper and on GPO Access; also available on *CIS Congressional Universe*, LEXIS, THOMAS, Westlaw)
Presidential signing statement	general comments concerning the purpose and value of legislation to the public	LEXIS *Public Papers of the Presidents* U.S.C.C.A.N. *Weekly Compilation of Presidential Documents* Westlaw
Presidential veto message	explanation for vetoing legislation	*CIS/Microfiche Library* *Congressional Record* LEXIS *Public Papers of the Presidents* U.S.C.C.A.N. *Weekly Compilation of Presidential Documents* Westlaw

EXHIBIT 13.3	Overview of Legislative History Research Practices

Practice	Legislative History Material	Strengths	Weaknesses
U.S.C.C.A.N.	*citations to: Congressional Record*, committee and conference committee reports *text:* reprints or excerpts of one or more committee or conference committee reports and perhaps a signing statement	it is the easiest paper source to use; it includes critical documents	content is limited
CIS	*citations to:* committee hearings, committee prints, House and Senate documents, committee and conference committee reports, *Congressional Record* debate, presidential signing statements, and the public law; additional citations for major laws *text: CIS/Microfiche Library* contains full text of all important documents except bills and	it offers comprehensive citations (especially for major laws), abstracts of documents, strong indexing including multiple access points; *CIS Congressional Universe* also offers links from some citations to the documents, full-text searching of documents, and currency of information	full-text coverage of documents on *CIS Congressional Universe* does not begin until 1985 and is somewhat limited until 1995

Exhibit 13.3   *(continued)*

Practice	Legislative History Material	Strengths	Weaknesses
	Congressional Record; *CIS Congressional Universe* adds the text of bills and *Congressional Record*		
THOMAS	*citations to:* bills, committee and conference committee reports, floor actions, public law *text:* bills, *Congressional Record*, committee reports, limited coverage of House hearings	it provides free access, currency, links to text of amendments and *Congressional Record*	citation coverage does not begin until 1973; full-text coverage does not begin until 1989 and is limited before 1995; coverage of hearings is limited; it does not contain committee prints or House or Senate documents
LEXIS; Westlaw	*citations to:* LEXIS contains *CIS/Legislative Histories*; Westlaw allows full-text searching of its full legislative history database *text:* bills, debates, hearings, committee and conference committee reports, signing statements, public laws; LEXIS also has House and Senate documents and committee prints	both offer full-text searching of documents; familiar standardized search processes; some compiled legislative histories, which provide for a single full-text search of a collection of documents	full-text coverage of most *Congressional Record* does not begin until 1985; coverage of most other documents begins later
GPO	*citations to:* no comprehensive list of legislative history documents for a bill or public law *text:* official text of all legislative history documents	*Congressional Record*'s History of Bills and Resolutions tracks a bill's progress by session of Congress; the *Monthly Catalog* provides indexing and description of documents	it provides no consolidated history of public laws; there is a time lag preceding publication of some documents

---

Preliminary legislative history research in statutory codes:

- identify the public law and its date of approval
- derive any additional information

To identify the appropriate public law to research, you would use the same source you use to find the statute you are researching: a statutory code. Look at the historical references that appear immediately after the statutory text. The *United States Code* (U.S.C.), *United States Code Annotated* (U.S.C.A.) and *United States Code Service* (U.S.C.S.) all provide references to the original and amending public laws, giving for each of those laws its public law number and section, the date the law was approved, and its citation in *Statutes at Large* (the federal session laws). See Illustration 13-6 on page 223.

If your statute has not been amended, you will have the one public law number you need. However, if your statute has been amended, you will need to discern which public law enacted the statutory language in question. The historical notes following the public law citations provide this information. You also may read the various public laws in *Statutes at Large.*

U.S.C.A. is the most helpful of the three codes because it provides an additional item of information—a citation to the legislative history of the statute as published in *United States Code Congressional and Administrative News* (U.S.C.C.A.N.), covered below.

Researching the Canoga case, we consulted U.S.C.A.'s version of § 12102 of the ADA, which defines "disability." Illustration 13-6 on page 223 shows that § 12102 of the ADA was enacted as § 3 of Pub. L. No. 101-336, which was approved on July 26, 1990 and published in *Statutes at Large* at 104 Stat. 329. U.S.C.A.'s Historical and Statutory Notes refer to a House report, a House conference report, and a signing statement by the President, printed at 1990 U.S. Code Cong. and Adm. News, p. 267.

Compiled legislative histories:

- ▶ consult a bibliography of compiled legislative histories
- ▶ procure and peruse the compilation
- ▶ or identify and search a LEXIS or Westlaw database for your statute

---

For efficiency, you should determine early on if there already exists a compiled legislative history for your law, that is, a collection of pertinent legislative materials or citations to those materials. As a general rule, compiled legislative histories exist for legislation of widespread importance.

To find out whether a compiled legislative history exists for a law, consult a source such as Nancy P. Johnson, *Sources of Compiled Legislative Histories: A*

| ILLUSTRATION 13-6 | Legislative History References in Statutory Code, from *United States Code Annotated* |

42 § 12101   OPPORTUNITY FOR THE DISABLED   Ch. 126
Note 7

7. Schools and universities

University's blanket policy prohibiting assignment of roommates to students with disabilities who require personal attendant care unnecessarily separated students with disabilities from those without disabilities and, thus, struck at essence of Americans with Disabilities Act (ADA) and specifically violated statute's stated purpose to provide clear and comprehensive national mandate for elimination of discrimination against individuals with disabilities. Coleman v. Zatechka, D.Neb. 1993, 824 F.Supp. 1360.

§ 12102. Definitions

As used in this chapter:

(1) Auxiliary aids and services

The term "auxiliary aids and services" includes—

(A) qualified interpreters or other effective methods of making aurally delivered materials available to individuals with hearing impairments;

(B) qualified readers, taped texts, or other effective methods of making visually delivered materials available to individuals with visual impairments;

(C) acquisition or modification of equipment or devices; and

(D) other similar services and actions.

(2) Disability

The term "disability" means, with respect to an individual—

(A) a physical or mental impairment that substantially limits one or more of the major life activities of such individual;

(B) a record of such an impairment; or

(C) being regarded as having such an impairment.

(3) State

The term "State" means each of the several States, the District of Columbia, the Commonwealth of Puerto Rico, Guam, American Samoa, the Virgin Islands, the Trust Territory of the Pacific Islands, and the Commonwealth of the Northern Mariana Islands.

 Pub.L. 101–336, § 3, July 26, 1990, 104 Stat. 329.)

HISTORICAL AND STATUTORY NOTES

Revision Notes and Legislative Reports
1990 Acts. House Report No. 101–485(Parts I–IV), House Conference Report No. 101–596, and Statement by President, see 1990 U.S. Code Cong. and Adm. News, p. 267.

CROSS REFERENCES

Auxiliary aids and services as defined in this section for purposes of national service trust fund program, see 42 USCA § 12581.

630

Bibliography of Government Documents, Periodical Articles, and Books (AALL Publication Series, No. 14, 1999) or Bernard D. Reams, *Federal Legislative Histories: An Annotated Bibliography and Index to Officially Published Sources* (1994). Illustration 13-7 on page 225 is a page from the Johnson bibliography. This publication is arranged by public law number and *Statutes at Large* citation, and it includes an index of statutory names. For each law, the table lists its compiled legislative histories, stating the standard bibliographic information (author, title, place of publication, publisher, and date) and some means by which to find a publication, such as its Library of Congress classification number. The table also notes which legislative history documents (if any) a compiled legislative history contains; whether those documents are available in full text or excerpts only; and whether a source discusses or cites the documents, without reprinting them.

Once you have learned that a compiled legislative history exists, your next task is, of course, to obtain it and peruse its contents. Some may be voluminous, others smaller and less complete. Some have an index, others only a table of contents.

Some compiled legislative histories appear online in LEXIS or Westlaw. The chief advantages of an online compilation are the availability of keyword and natural-language searching and the ability to search all documents simultaneously.

Researching the Canoga case, we learned from the Johnson bibliography that several publications about the ADA's legislative history exist. See Illustration 13-7 on page 225. They appear in a law review article, treatises, and other publications. The most extensive is the next-to-last entry, Reams' six-volume set, which contains a chronology of the ADA; a bibliography of ADA sources; and the full texts of bills, hearings, reports, debates, the presidential statement, and other materials.

Both LEXIS and Westlaw have separate databases for the Americans with Disabilities Act. We searched Westlaw's ADA database, which was compiled by the law firm of Arnold & Porter. The database included the public law, committee reports, the bill and amendments, the hearing record, excerpts of congressional debate, and other miscellaneous transcripts. We conducted a full-text search for [smok! cigarette nicotine] and retrieved twenty-one documents, none directly addressing the nicotine addiction issue in the Canoga case.

Legislative history in *United States Code Congressional and Administrative News* (U.S.C.C.A.N.):

▶ use a U.S.C.A. reference, public law number, *Statutes at Large* cite, or subject index to find pertinent materials

▶ read the opening material to obtain references to committee reports, conference committee reports, and the *Congressional Record*

▶ read the reprinted or excerpted documents

ILLUSTRATION 13-7	Bibliography of Compiled Legislative Histories, from *Sources of Compiled Legislative Histories*

PUBLIC LAW BILL NUMBER	STATUTE	ACT ENTRY	CONTENTS ACTUAL DOCS. REPORTS	HEARINGS	DEBATES	CITES TO DOCS. DISCUSSION	LISTS CITES
101-280 H.J.Res.553	104 Stat. 149	ETHICS REFORM ACT OF 1989: TECHNICAL AMENDMENTS					
		Tax Management Primary Sources, 101st Congress, Wash., D.C.: Bureau of National Affairs, 1989.	X				
101-311 H.R. 4612	104 Stat. 267	BANKRUPTCY: SWAP AGREEMENTS & FORWARD CONTRACTS					
		Collier on Bankruptcy, 15th ed., N.Y.: Matthew Bender, 1993, Legislative History: App. vols.				X	
101-336 S. 933	104 Stat. 327	AMERICANS WITH DISABILITIES ACT OF 1990					
		Americans with Disabilities Act of 1990: Law & Explanation, Chicago, IL: Commerce Clearing House, 1990. L.C.: KF480.A958 1990				X	X
		The Americans with Disabilities Act: A Practical and Legal Guide to Impact, Enforcement, and Compliance, Wash., D.C.: Bureau of National Affairs, 1990. L.C.: KF480.A957 1990				X	X
		Americans with Disabilities Act: A Survey of the Law, Regulations and Legislative History, New York, N.Y.: Practising Law Institute, 1992.				X	X
		BNA's Americans with Disabilities Act Manual, Wash., D.C.: Bureau of National Affairs, 1992. L.C.: KF480.A6B7	X				X
		The Disabled in the Workplace: Analysis of the Americans with Disabilities Act, N.Y.: Research Institute of America, 1990.				X	X
		Arlene Mayerson, The Americans with Disabilities Act— An Historic Overview, 7 Labor Lawyer 1 (1991).				X	X
		Henry H. Perritt, Jr., **Americans with Disabilities Act Handbook**, 2d ed., New York: Wiley, 1991. L.C.: KF3469.P47 1991				X	X
		Bernard D. Reams, Jr. et al., **Disability Law in the United States: A Legislative History of the Americans with Disabilities Act of 1990**, P.L. 101-336, 6 vols., Buffalo, N.Y.: Hein, 1992. L.C.: KF480.A32A15 1992	X	X	X		
		John G. Tysse & Edward E. Potter, **The Legislative History of the Americans with Disabilities Act**, Horsham, PA: LRP Publications, 1991. L.C.: KF480.A32A15	X	X			

U.S.C.C.A.N., or *United States Code Congressional and Administrative News*, published by West Group, is a convenient source for finding major legislative history references and reading major legislative materials. It does not, however, contain all or even most legislative history documents for a law.

Each year's bound volumes of U.S.C.C.A.N. cover a particular session of Congress and contain two sections: (1) a section of reprints of the *Statutes at Large* session laws and (2) a legislative history section. These sections generally appear in different volumes. Both sections are arranged by public law number. The legislative history section contains references to legislative history information, as well as reprints or excerpts of the legislative materials selected by the West editors as best reflecting the legislative history of the law. See Illustration 13-3 on pages 213–214.

There are four ways to find a pertinent legislative history in U.S.C.C.A.N. First, as stated previously, the U.S.C.A. annotations refer directly to the legislative history section of U.S.C.C.A.N. Second, if you know a statute's public law number, you can use the public law numbers on the spines of the U.S.C.C.A.N. volumes (since 1980) to select the correct volume of legislative history and to then find the appropriate legislative history material within that volume. Third, if you know the *Statutes at Large* citation for the law, you can locate the *Statutes at Large* reprint by relying on the spine labels (since 1975); the reprint refers you to the starting page of the law's legislative history materials. Fourth, the annual subject index in the final U.S.C.C.A.N. volume for the year gives page references to the legislative history sections.

Once you locate the pertinent material, note the information on the opening page. The legislative history section of U.S.C.C.A.N. typically provides the following information for a public law:

- its public law number and its *Statutes at Large* citation,
- the dates of consideration and passage of the legislation by both chambers,
- the numbers of the House and Senate bills,
- the committees to which the bills were assigned,
- the numbers and dates of committee reports,
- the numbers and dates of conference committee reports,
- the volumes and years of the *Congressional Record* in which the debates appear, and
- a list of the legislative history documents reproduced in U.S.C.C.A.N.

Then read the reprinted documents. U.S.C.C.A.N. typically includes one or more committee reports and perhaps a presidential signing statement. The committee reports are edited to remove duplicative or less helpful information; omissions are shown by asterisks, and the official page numbers are in brackets.

Researching the Canoga case, we found a fairly typical U.S.C.C.A.N.

legislative history for the ADA. The opening material, shown in Illustration 13-3 on page 213, reveals that the House and Senate considered separate bills for the law, the Senate bill was enacted, the legislation generated two committee reports (one of which was written by four House committees) and two conference committee reports, and debate on the law spanned two years of Congress. U.S.C.C.A.N. provides citations and dates for the materials listed.

U.S.C.C.A.N. has reprints of the House committee report, the second conference committee report, and President Bush's signing statement. Shown in part in Illustration 13-3 on pages 213–214, the House committee report includes each committee's recommendation on the bill; the text of the bill as recommended by each committee; section-by-section summaries of the bill; concurring and dissenting views of individual committee members; reports from the Congressional Budget Office, estimating the cost of the ADA as proposed by each committee; and analysis of changes that the bill as recommended would make in existing law. The House conference committee report catalogs the many differences between the House and Senate bills and notes which version prevailed on each differing provision. Shown in Illustration 13-5 on page 216, the presidential signing statement explains the origin of the bill, counters arguments against the ADA, and highlights the need for public education on the ADA. None of the documents address the issue of whether nicotine addiction is a disability under the ADA.

Legislative history in Congressional Information Service (CIS) sources:

▶ consult *CIS/Legislative Histories*, Legislative History Citations in *CIS/Abstracts*, or *CIS/Index* (paper tools) to compile a list of pertinent documents and read their abstracts

▶ or search *CIS Congressional Universe* (online) to compile a list of pertinent documents and read their abstracts

▶ retrieve potentially pertinent documents

▶ read the documents

The standard, most comprehensive tool for researching the legislative history of relatively recent federal statutes is a system developed by a private company, Congressional Information Service (CIS). CIS provides legislative history information for each significant public law enacted since 1970. The CIS system has two major components: tools that provide information about legislative events and references to legislative documents (finding tools) and the legislative documents themselves. Both components are available in multiple media. Generally, you will begin your research in a finding tool and proceed to the documents.

CIS finding tools are available in paper and online. The paper finding tools are *CIS/Annual Legislative Histories of U.S. Public Laws* (*CIS/Legislative Histories*), *CIS/Annual Index to Congressional Publications and Public Laws* (*CIS/Index*), and *CIS/Annual Abstracts of Congressional Publications* (*CIS/Abstracts*). The online product is *CIS Congressional Universe*.

Consult the paper finding tools and abstracts.   If you are researching the legislative history of a public law enacted in 1984 or later, a good place to begin is the *CIS/Legislative Histories* volume for the appropriate year. The *CIS/Legislative Histories* volumes are arranged by public law number. The legislative history information provided for a public law varies, depending on the significance of the law. For each public law, CIS provides at least an abstract of the law and its main committee reports, as well as citations to the relevant slip law, other committee reports (including, possibly, reports on predecessor bills), *Congressional Record* debate, committee hearings, committee prints, House and Senate documents, and presidential signing statements. This information constitutes a standard legislative history. For laws that CIS deems particularly important or likely to lead to litigation on issues of legislative intent, CIS also provides, in a special legislative history, citations for all relevant bills; abstracts for additional documents; *Congressional Record* citations for debate on predecessor legislation; and citations for related reports, hearings, prints, and House and Senate documents. See Illustration 13-8 on pages 231–233. Both types of legislative history provide CIS accession numbers for the various documents; these numbers assist you in locating the documents themselves within the CIS collection (described below).

CIS legislative histories are especially useful because they provide abstracts, or brief descriptions, of some documents' content. The abstracts assist you in assessing the value of a document to your research. You can supplement a standard legislative history, which does not abstract all documents, by locating additional abstracts in *CIS/Abstracts*. This publication contains abstracts of legislative materials, including committee hearings, committee prints, House and Senate documents, and committee reports, arranged by CIS accession numbers.

CIS/Legislative Histories volumes begin with 1984. If your research predates that year, use the public law tables in the Legislative History Citations section at the back of the *CIS/Abstracts* volumes. These tables provide information parallel to that in a standard legislative history. Check the *CIS/Abstracts* volume for both the year of your statute's enactment, plus the following year, since additional materials may have become available after the first listing for the public law.

You also may identify pertinent legislative history documents in the CIS books by looking under your subject in the *CIS/Index*. You would most likely do this if you had no citation information about a law (which is uncommon), you were researching all legislation concerning a specific subject (which is more plausible), or you were researching proposed legislation that did not pass. The *CIS/Index* is published monthly and cumulated quarterly, annually, and for four- or five-year periods. *CIS/Index* also has several specialized indexes covering bill numbers, report numbers, House and Senate document numbers, titles of publications, etc. Index entries provide the CIS accession numbers.

Or search *Congressional Universe.* *CIS Congressional Universe*, located at http://web.lexis-nexis.com/cis, provides another means of identifying legislative history documents in CIS. To obtain a legislative history, select CIS Index (legislative histories by number), and enter your public law number (or a *Statutes at Large* citation or enacted bill number). The information is presented in a slightly different order than in the paper version, and you must click on various citations to retrieve the abstracts for those citations. See Illustration 13-9 on pages 234–236.

CIS Congressional Universe, like its paper counterpart, offers many additional search options, including searches by subject, key word, title of a publication, committee, names or affiliations of witnesses, document number, and various bibliographic numbers, such as the CIS accession number.

Retrieve and read pertinent documents. Once you have a CIS accession number from one of the finding tools and you have read an abstract to determine that the document is likely to be pertinent, you can use that accession number to locate and read the legislative document in the CIS system.

CIS offers many legislative documents in microfiche. The *CIS/Microfiche Library* contains the full text of hearings, committee reports, committee prints, House and Senate documents, and some special publications, all arranged by CIS accession number. It does not contain the text of bills or floor debates. However, *CIS/Congressional Bills, Resolutions & Laws* provides the full text of various versions of House and Senate bills and resolutions, including amendments and revisions, beginning with 1933. For the full text of debates, CIS offers the permanent edition of the *Congressional Record* on microfiche as a separate set; coverage begins with the *Record*'s inception in 1873.

CIS Congressional Universe provides online the text of more types of documents than the *CIS/Microfiche Library*. The materials available on *CIS Congressional Universe* include bills, hearing transcripts, selected committee prints, House and Senate documents, committee reports, and the *Congressional Record*. However, its coverage does not extend as far back in time; when this text was written, hearing transcripts were available from 1988 forward, committee reports from 1990 forward, bills from 1989 forward, selected committee prints from 1995 forward, House and Senate documents from 1995 forward, and the *Congressional Record* from 1985 forward.

The online versions of the legislative history documents are unofficial versions, whereas the CIS fiche versions are official versions. The online versions omit charts, graphs, tables, page numbers, and supplementary materials from hearing records. Thus, you may want to look at the official version after checking an online version. On the other hand, *CIS Congressional Universe* offers full-text searching, and the information is current (for example, full-text testimony is available the day after it is given).

Researching the Canoga case. We first located the special legislative history excerpted in Illustration 13-8 on pages 231–233 in the *CIS/Legislative*

Histories volume. The legislative history for the ADA refers to forty-three documents, including the public law, committee reports, various bills, debates, hearings, and committee prints. We obtained the same information, albeit in a slightly different format, through *CIS Congressional Universe*. We perused the abstracts, but found no obvious reference to discussion of nicotine addiction as a disability. We thought that the testimony of Evan J. Kemp, Jr., commissioner of the Equal Employment Opportunity Commission, during hearings before the Subcommittee on Employment Opportunities, might be pertinent. So we noted the CIS accession number for the hearing record, 90:H341-4.

The committee reports, hearings, and committee prints we identified are all available in the *CIS/Microfiche Library*. We read Commissioner Kemp's testimony (a portion of which appears in Illustration 13-2 on page 212) in microfiche. He did not address the Canoga issue. *CIS Congressional Universe* provides links to the *Congressional Record* and contains (in the publications section) the text of one committee report and one conference committee report, but it does not include the text of the other reports, hearings, or prints. Because *CIS Congressional Universe* permits full-text searching for key words, we searched for [smok! or cigarette or nicotine] in the committee reports but did not locate any discussion of the issue of nicotine addiction as a disability.

Legislative history in THOMAS:

▶ select Public Laws by Law Number

▶ or search the Bill Summary section by word, phrase, subject, or other option

▶ or browse a list of laws in the Bill Summary section

▶ retrieve the pertinent Bill Summary & Status report

▶ skim the report, and compile a list of relevant documents

▶ retrieve and read the documents that are available on THOMAS

▶ retrieve the report for a related bill, if any

In 1995 the Library of Congress introduced THOMAS, a free federal legislative information system. You can find the THOMAS home page at http://thomas.loc.gov.

THOMAS tracks the history of bills, beginning with bills introduced in 1973. Its full-text coverage of legislative history documents begins later. When this text was written, THOMAS included the full text of bills from 1989 forward, the *Congressional Record* from 1989 forward (its index from 1994 forward), committee reports from 1995 forward, and House (but not Senate) hearing transcripts from 1997 forward. It did not include committee prints or House and Senate documents.

ILLUSTRATION 13-8   Special Legislative History, from *CIS/Legislative Histories*

Public Law 101-336   104 Stat. 327

Americans with Disabilities Act of 1990

July 26, 1990

Public Law

1.1   Public Law 101-336, approved July 26, 1990. (S. 933)

(CIS90:PL101-336   52 p.)

"To establish a clear and comprehensive prohibition of discrimination on the basis of disability."

Prohibits discrimination against disabled individuals in employment and public transportation, accommodations, and services.

Establishes a general definition of disability.

TITLE I, EMPLOYMENT.

Includes a provision to restrict use of pre-employment medical examinations and inquiries by employers, labor organizations, and employment agencies. Requires employers to make reasonable accommodations to the limitations of otherwise qualified job applicants or employees with disabilities.

Requires HHS to disseminate a list of infectious and communicable diseases transmissible by handling food.

Provides that the powers and civil and administrative remedies of the EEOC and Department of Justice under the Civil Rights Act of 1964 shall apply to employment discrimination against the disabled.

TITLE II, PUBLIC SERVICES.

Prohibits State and local governments and Amtrak from excluding from programs or services disabled individuals who meet specified eligibility requirements if reasonable modifications of policies or removal of barriers would enable them to participate.

Provides that enforcement for discrimination against the disabled by public entities shall be the remedies in the Rehabilitation Act of 1973.

Requires new vehicles purchased by public entities operating fixed route transportation systems to be readily accessible to and usable by the disabled.

Requires public entities operating fixed route transportation systems to provide paratransit services for individuals whose disabilities preclude the use of the fixed route system.

Requires Amtrak and all commuter rail systems to have at least one car per train readily accessible to and usable by disabled individuals within five years.

Requires Amtrak and key commuter stations to be made readily accessible to disabled individuals within specified time frames.

TITLE III, PUBLIC ACCOMMODATIONS AND SERVICES OPERATED BY PRIVATE ENTITIES.

Prohibits discrimination on the basis of disability by private businesses and other providers of goods, services, or accommodations. Requires businesses to remove barriers and make reasonable modifications of policies in order to provide equal benefits to the disabled, unless such changes are not readily achievable or would result in undue hardship.

Requires OTA to conduct a study to determine transportation access needs of the disabled, and the most cost-effective method of providing disabled individuals with access to buses and bus services.

Requires the Department of Justice to issue regulations regarding prohibition of discrimination in privately owned accommodations and services and DOT to issue regulations on land-based public transportation services.

TITLE IV, TELECOMMUNICATIONS.

Amends the Communications Act of 1934 to require that all telephone common carriers provide relay services for the hearing-impaired and speech-impaired so that they can communicate with persons who are not impaired. Extends FCC regulatory authority to intrastate common carriers for purposes of implementing the relay services requirement.

Requires closed-captioning of all TV public service announcements produced using Federal funds.

TITLE V, MISCELLANEOUS PROVISIONS.

Includes a provision to require the Architectural and Transportation Barriers Compliance Board to issue guidelines for removal of barriers that make goods and services inaccessible to the disabled.

Provides that nothing in the Wilderness Act shall be construed as prohibiting use of wheelchairs in wilderness areas.

Prohibits discrimination on the basis of disability by members of Congress and legislative branch employees.

Amends the Rehabilitation Act of 1973 to revise definitions and make conforming amendments.

P.L. 101-336 Reports

101st Congress

2.1   S. Rpt. 101-116 on S. 933, "Americans with Disabilities Act of 1989," Aug. 30, 1989.

(CIS89:S543-11   107 p.)
(Y1.1/5:101-116.)

Recommends passage, with an amendment in the nature of a substitute, of S. 933, the Americans with Disabilities Act (ADA) of 1989, to prohibit discrimination against disabled individuals in employment, housing, public accommodations, transportation, or telephone services. Includes provisions to:

a. Establish a comprehensive definition of disability.

b. Clarify ADA applicability to individuals with various diseases and disorders, including individuals infected with the human immunodeficiency virus (HIV).

c. Extend Rehabilitation Act of 1973 nondiscrimination requirements for Federal activities to State and local government entities.

d. Require various Federal departments and agencies to issue regulations and standards for ADA implementation and provide for Department of Justice enforcement procedures.

Includes additional views (p. 96-107).

S. 933 is related to 100th Congress S. 2345.

2.2   H. Rpt. 101-485, pt. 1 on H.R. 2273, "Americans with Disabilities Act of 1990," May 14, 1990.

(CIS90:H643-1   65 p.)
(Y1.1/8:101-485/pt.1.)

Recommends passage, with an amendment in the nature of a substitute, of H.R. 2273, the Americans with Disabilities Act of 1990, to amend the Communications Act of 1934 and the Rehabilitation Act of 1973 to prohibit discrimination against disabled individuals in employment; publicly

ILLUSTRATION 13-8   *(continued)*

Public Law 101-336   Item 3.5

101st Congress

ENACTED BILL

3.5   S. 933 as introduced May 9, 1989; as reported by the
       Senate Labor and Human Resources Committee Aug.
       30, 1989; as passed by the Senate Sept. 7, 1989; as
       passed by the House May 22, 1990.

COMPANION BILL

3.6   H.R. 2273 as introduced May 9, 1989; as reported by
       the House Public Works and Transportation Commit-
       tee, the House Education and Labor Committee, the
       House Judiciary Committee, and the House Energy
       and Commerce Committee May 15, 1990.

OTHER HOUSE BILLS

3.7   H.R. 3171 as introduced.

3.8   H.R. 4807 as introduced.

OTHER SENATE BILLS

3.9   S. 1452 as introduced.

P.L. 101-336 Debate

135 Congressional Record
101st Congress, 1st Session - 1989

4.1   Sept. 7, Senate consideration and passage of S. 933,
       p. S10701.

136 Congressional Record
101st Congress, 2nd Session - 1990

4.2   May 17, House consideration of H.R. 2273, p. H2410.

4.3   May 22, House consideration of H.R. 2273, consider-
       ation and passage of S. 933 with an amendment, and
       tabling of H.R. 2273, p. H2599.

4.4   May 24, House insistence on its amendments to S.
       933, request for a conference, and appointment of
       conferees, p. H3070.

4.5   June 6, Senate disagreement to the House amend-
       ments to S. 933, agreement to a conference, and ap-
       pointment of conferees, p. S7422.

4.6   June 26, Submission in the House of the conference
       report on S. 933, p. H4169.

4.7   July 11, Senate passage of motion to recommit the
       conference report on S. 933, p. S9527.

4.8   July 12, Submission in the House of the second con-
       ference report on S. 933, and House agreement to the
       conference report, p. H4582.

4.9   July 13, Senate agreement to the conference report on
       S. 933, p. S9684.

P.L. 101-336 Hearings

100th Congress

5.1   "Hearing on Discrimination Against Cancer Victims
       and the Handicapped," hearings before the Subcom-
       mittee on Employment Opportunities, House Educa-
       tion and Labor Committee, June 17, 1987.

(CIS88:H341-4   iii+115 p.)
(Y4.Ed8/1:100-31.)

Committee Serial No. 100-31. Hearing before the *Subcom on Employment
Opportunities* to consider the following bills:
   H.R. 192, to amend the Civil Rights Act of 1964 to prohibit employment
   discrimination against handicapped persons.
   H.R. 1546, the Cancer Patients' Employment Rights Act, to prohibit
   employment discrimination against cancer survivors.
Full Committee Member Mario Biaggi (D-NY) presents a statement *(see
H341-4.1)* and participates in questioning witnesses.
Includes correspondence (p. 113-115).

June 17, 1987. p. 2-37.
   Witnesses: **Moakley, Joe**, (Rep, D-Mass)
   Biaggi, Mario, (Rep, D-NY)
   Statements and Discussion: Need for H.R. 192; explanation of H.R.
   1546.
   Insertion:
   – Wolfe, M. Ann (CRS), "Survey of State Statutes Concerning Em-
     ployment Discrimination of Handicapped Persons" May 31, 1987
     (p. 16-27).

June 17, 1987. p. 38-86.
   Witnesses: **Hoffman, Barbara**, bd member, Natl Coalition for Cancer
   Survivorship (NCCS).
   Monaco, Grace P., atty, representing Candlelighters Childhood Cancer
   Foundation.
   Calonita, Timothy, cancer survivor.
   Statements and Discussion: Explanation of H.R. 1546; need for specific
   legislation to protect cancer patient employment rights; personal experi-
   ences with employment discrimination after cancer cure (related materi-
   als, p. 68-78).
   Insertion:
   – NCCS, newsletter, Mar. 1987 (p. 46-53).

June 17, 1987. p. 86-112.
   Witnesses: **Rodriguez, Alex**, chm, Mass Commission Against Discrimi-
   nation.
   Kiernan, William E., dir, Training and Research Inst for Adults with
   Disabilities, Boston Coll.
   Davila, Robert R., vp, precollege programs, Gallaudet Univ.

ILLUSTRATION 13-8   *(continued; pages omitted)*

Item 8.1   Public Law 101-336

Shishler, Janna, Law Clerk, p. 36-39.
Bowling, Nanette, Staff Liaison to the Mayor's Advisory Council for Handicapped Individuals, Kokomo, p. 40-62.
Turney, John D., Member, Mayor's Advisory Council for Handicapped Individuals, Kokomo; also representing Indiana Commission for the Handicapped, p. 46-62.
Williams, Michael L., Vice President for Ancillary Services, St. Josephs Hospital and Health Center, Kokomo, p. 56-62.
Edwards, Ric, p. 63-81.
Myers, Jeff, p. 68-81.
Hunt, Marchell, Chairperson, Common Concerns, p. 71-81.
Scott, David, representing Indianapolis Resource Center for Individual Living, p. 75-81.
May, Gary E., Commissioner, Indiana Department of Veterans' Affairs, p. 76-81.
Statements and Discussion: Perspectives on H.R. 2273.

5.13   "Americans with Disabilities Act," hearings before the House Small Business Committee, Feb. 22, 1990.

(CIS90:H721-24   iii+213 p.)
(Y4.Sm1:101-45.)

Committee Serial No. 101-45. Hearing to consider the potential effect on business of the Americans with Disabilities Act (ADA), to prohibit discrimination against the handicapped in various areas, including employment and public accomodations.
Supplementary material (p. 62-213) includes witnesses' written statements, and:
   GAO, "Persons with Disabilities: Reports on Costs of Accomodations" Jan. 1990, with tables (p. 186-213).

Feb. 22, 1990. p. 4-10.
Witness: Hoyer, Steny H., (Rep, D-Md)
Statement and Discussion: Endorsement of and need for the ADA.

Feb. 22, 1990. p. 10-56, 76-172.
Witnesses: Dragonette, Joseph J., President, Dragonette, Inc.; representing Chamber of Commerce of the U.S.
Lewis, Kenneth E., certified public accountant; representing National Federation of Independent Business.
Pinkus, David, Owner, North Haven Gardens; representing National Small Business United.
Frieden, Lex, Assistant Professor, Rehabilitation, Baylor College of Medicine; former Executive Director, National Council on the Handicapped.
Mayerson, Arlene B., Professor, Law School, University of California, Berkeley; representing Disability Rights Education and Defense Fund.
Statements and Discussion: Concerns about ADA provisions requiring modification of private buildings and structures for greater accessibility to the handicapped; potential excessive costs for small businesses of complying with ADA public accomodations and employment requirements; need to clarify ADA provisions regarding employment and public accomodations, with suggestions.
   Background and importance of the ADA, citing need to prohibit all forms of discrimination against the handicapped; adequacy of ADA provisions protecting small business from excessive costs for modifying facilities; nature and background of discriminatory treatment of the handicapped; assessment of discrimination against the handicapped in employment, with examples and results of various studies on employment discrimination.
   Merits of ADA provisions prohibiting employment discrimination; doubted negative impact on business of ADA employment provisions; overview of case law related to discrimination against the handicapped; extent of discrimination against the handicapped in public accomodations; views on discrimination issues and business concerns, with suggestions.

Feb. 22, 1990. p. 57-61, 173-185.
Witness: Turner, James P., Acting Assistant Attorney General, Civil Rights, Department of Justice.

101st Congress, 2nd Session

Statement and Discussion: Endorsement of the ADA; refutation of business concerns regarding ADA public accomodations provisions.

P.L. 101-336 Committee Prints

101st Congress

6.1   "Legislative History of Public Law 101-336, the Americans with Disabilities Act, Vol. 1," committee print issued by the House Education and Labor Committee, Dec. 1990. (Not available at time of publication.)

6.2   "Legislative History of Public Law 101-336, the Americans with Disabilities Act, Vol. 2," committee print issued by the House Education and Labor Committee, Dec. 1990. (Not available at time of publication.)

6.3   "Legislative History of Public Law 101-336, the Americans with Disabilities Act, Vol. 3," committee print issued by the House Education and Labor Committee, Dec. 1990. (Not available at time of publication.)

P.L. 101-336 Miscellaneous

8.1   Weekly Compilation of Presidential Documents, Vol. 26 (1990): July 26, Presidential remarks and statement.

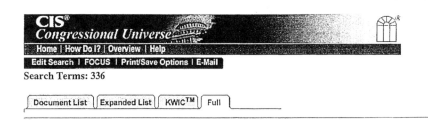

ILLUSTRATION 13-9   Legislative History, from *CIS Congressional Universe*

Search Terms: 336

Document List | Expanded List | KWIC™ | Full

Document 1 of 1.

CIS Legislative Histories
Copyright © 1990, Congressional Information Service, Inc.

90 CIS PL 101336; 101 CIS Legis. Hist. P.L. 336

LEGISLATIVE HISTORY OF: P.L. **101-336**

TITLE: Americans with Disabilities Act of 1990

CIS-NO: 90-PL101-336
CIS-DATE: December, 1990
DOC-TYPE: **Legislative History**
DATE: July 26, 1990
LENGTH: 52 p.
ENACTED-BILL: 101 S. 933 Retrieve Bill Tracking report
STAT: 104 Stat. 327
CONG-SESS: 101-2
ITEM-NO: 575

SUMMARY:
"To establish a clear and comprehensive prohibition of discrimination on the basis of disability."

Prohibits discrimination against disabled individuals in employment and public transportation, accommodations, and services.

Establishes a general definition of disability.

TITLE I, EMPLOYMENT.

Restricts use of pre-employment medical examinations and inquiries by employers, labor organizations, and employment agencies. Requires employers to make reasonable accommodations to the limitations of otherwise qualified job applicants or employees with disabilities.

Requires HHS to disseminate a list of infectious and communicable diseases transmissible by handling food.

Provides that the powers and civil and administrative remedies of the EEOC and Department of Justice

ILLUSTRATION 13-9   *(continued; pages omitted)*

Provides that nothing in the Wilderness Act shall be construed as prohibiting use of wheelchairs in wilderness areas.

Prohibits discrimination on the basis of disability by members of Congress and legislative branch employees.

Amends the Rehabilitation Act of 1973 to revise definitions and make conforming amendments.

CONTENT-NOTATION: Discrimination against the handicapped, prohibition

BILLS: 100 H.R. 192; 100 H.R. 1546; 100 H.R. 4498; 100 S. 2345; 101 H.R. 2273; 101 H.R. 3171; 101 H.R. 4807; 101 S. 1452 AMERICANS WITH DISABILITIES ACT; DISCRIMINATION AGAINST THE HANDICAPPED; DISCRIMINATION IN EMPLOYMENT; TRANSPORTATION OF THE HANDICAPPED; MEDICAL EXAMINATIONS AND TESTS; LABOR UNIONS; EMPLOYMENT SERVICES; DEPARTMENT OF HEALTH AND HUMAN SERVICES; GOVERNMENT INFORMATION AND INFORMATION SERVICES; COMMUNICABLE DISEASES; FOOD POISONING; EQUAL EMPLOYMENT OPPORTUNITY COMMISSION; DEPARTMENT OF JUSTICE; CIVIL RIGHTS ACT; ADMINISTRATIVE LAW AND PROCEDURE; CIVIL PROCEDURE; FEDERAL-STATE RELATIONS; FEDERAL-LOCAL RELATIONS; NATIONAL RAILROAD PASSENGER CORP.; ARCHITECTURAL BARRIERS; RAILROAD ROLLING STOCK; MOTOR BUS LINES; TRANSPORTATION REGULATION; GOVERNMENT AND BUSINESS; OFFICE OF TECHNOLOGY ASSESSMENT; DEPARTMENT OF TRANSPORTATION; TELECOMMUNICATION REGULATION; COMMUNICATIONS ACT; TELEPHONE AND TELEPHONE INDUSTRY; HEARING AND HEARING DISORDERS; SPEECH DISORDERS; TELEVISION; FEDERAL COMMUNICATIONS COMMISSION; REHABILITATION ACT; ARCHITECTURAL AND TRANSPORTATION BARRIERS COMPLIANCE BOARD; WILDERNESS ACT; WILDERNESS AREAS; CONGRESSIONAL EMPLOYEES

REFERENCES:

DEBATE:

135 Congressional Record, 101st Congress, 1st Session - 1989
  Sept. 7, Senate consideration and passage of S. 933, p. S10701.

136 Congressional Record, 101st Congress, 2nd Session - 1990
  May 17, House consideration of H.R. 2273, p. H2410.
  May 22, House consideration of H.R. 2273, consideration and passage of S. 933 with an amendment, and tabling of H.R. 2273, p. H2599.
  May 24, House insistence on its amendments to S. 933, request for a conference, and appointment of conferees, p. H3070.
  June 6, Senate disagreement to the House amendments to S. 933, agreement to a conference, and appointment of conferees, p. S7422.
  June 26, Submission in the House of the conference report on S. 933, p. H4169.
  July 11, Senate passage of motion to recommit the conference report on S. 933, p. S9527.
  July 12, Submission in the House of the second conference report on S. 933, and House agreement to the conference report, p. H4582.
  July 13, Senate agreement to the conference report on S. 933, p. S9684.

ILLUSTRATION 13-9   *(continued; pages omitted)*

"Americans with Disabilities Act of 1988," hearings before the Subcommittee on the Handicapped, Senate Labor and Human Resources Committee, and the Subcommittee on Select Education, House Education and Labor Committee, Sept. 27, 1988.
   CIS NO: 89-S541-17
   LENGTH: v+96 p.
   SUDOC: Y4.L11/4:S.hrg.100-926

"Oversight Hearing on H.R. 4498, Americans with Disabilities Act of 1988," hearings before the Subcommittee on Select Education, Committee on Education and Labor. House, Oct. 24, 1988.
   CIS NO: 89-H341-36
   LENGTH: v+235 p.
   SUDOC: Y4.Ed8/1:100-109

101st Congress

"Americans with Disabilities Act of 1989," hearings before the Subcommittee on the Handicapped, Committee on Labor and Human Resources. Senate, May 9, 10, 16, June 22, 1989.
   CIS NO: 89-S541-37
   LENGTH: v+849 p.
   SUDOC: Y4.L11/4:S.hrg.101-156

"Joint Hearing on H.R. 2273, the Americans with Disabilities Act of 1989," hearings before the Subcommittee on Select Education and the Subcommittee on Employment Opportunities, Committee on Education and Labor. House, July 18, 1989.
   CIS NO: 89-H341-81
   LENGTH: iii+146 p.
   SUDOC: Y4.Ed8/1:101-37

"Americans with Disabilities Act of 1989," hearings before the Subcommittee on Civil and Constitutional Rights, Committee on the Judiciary. House, Aug. 3, Oct. 11, 12, 1989.
   CIS NO: 90-H521-37
   LENGTH: iv+446 p. il.
   SUDOC: Y4.J89/1:101/58

"Field Hearing on Americans with Disabilities Act," hearings before the Subcommittee on Select Education, Committee on Education and Labor. House, Aug. 28, 1989.
   CIS NO: 90-H341-2
   LENGTH: iii+112 p.
   SUDOC: Y4.Ed8/1:101-56

"Hearing on H.R. 2273, the Americans with Disabilities Act of 1989," hearings before the Subcommittee on Employment Opportunities and the Subcommittee on Select Education, Committee on Education and Labor. House, Sept. 13, 1989.
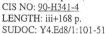
   CIS NO: 90-H341-4
   LENGTH: iii+168 p.
   SUDOC: Y4.Ed8/1:101-51

"Americans with Disabilities Act," hearings before the Subcommittee on Surface Transportation, Committee on Public Works and Transportation. House, Sept. 20, 26, 1989.

THOMAS is very current. For example, bills are generally available within a day or two of introduction, committee reports within several days, and the *Congressional Record* usually the day after the proceedings it reports.

THOMAS provides several ways to obtain information about a specific law. If you know your public law number, your best option is to search in Public Laws by Law Number. Alternatively, you may search THOMAS by word, phrase, subject, bill or amendment number, and some other methods in its Bill Summary section. Another approach is to browse various lists of laws in that section. Each search method leads to a Bill Summary & Status report for your bill.

A THOMAS Bill Summary & Status report identifies the bill, its sponsor, and its public law number or the last major action on the bill. Then it presents a table of contents from which you may select which additional information to view. Your choices include all bill summary and status information or selected parts of it, such as bill titles, bill status information (a listing of Senate, House, conference committee, and executive actions with page references to actions reported in the *Congressional Record*), committee information, amendments, cosponsors, and bill summary. A report does not identify all actions and documents for a companion bill, but it provides a link to related bills to help you obtain the information. Finally, THOMAS provides the text of the legislation. The information given in Bill Summary & Status reports and the order of the information varies over time. See Illustration 13-10 on pages 238–239.

Once you skim the report to compile a list of relevant documents, you should retrieve and read the documents that are available on THOMAS. Finally, to complete your research, retrieve the separate report for a related bill.

In addition to searching for bill summary and status information, THOMAS also allows you to do full-text searches of its documents, such as its bill text files, the *Congressional Record*, and committee reports.

Researching the Canoga case, we looked at the THOMAS Bill Summary & Status report for S. 933, the bill that became the ADA. It identified both House and Senate action on S. 933 and listed the actions and most of the documents you would expect to find listed in a legislative history of S. 933 (though it did not note the availability of some published 1989 Senate hearings). In addition, the report provided links to various information, including Bill Summary & Status reports for amendments. THOMAS did not contain the full text of committee reports for the 101st Congress, but it did contain the text of the *Congressional Record*, so we did a full-text search there for [nicotine]. We found no relevant information. As you might surmise, the report for S. 933 did not identify all House actions or documents for H.R. 2273, the companion bill, but it did provide a link to the Bill Summary & Status document for that bill, which we also researched.

| ILLUSTRATION 13-10 | Bill Summary & Status Report for Enacted Bill, from THOMAS |

Bill Summary & Status for the 101st Congress

NEW SEARCH | HOME | HELP

S.933
Public Law: 101-336 (07/26/90)
SPONSOR: Sen Harkin (introduced 05/09/89)
RELATED BILLS: H.R.2273

Jump to: Titles, Status, Abstracts, Committees, Amendments, Cosponsors, Summary

TITLE(S):

- SHORT TITLE(S) AS INTRODUCED:
  Americans with Disabilities Act of 1989

- SHORT TITLE(S) AS PASSED HOUSE:
  Americans with Disabilities Act of 1990

- SHORT TITLE(S) AS REPORTED TO SENATE:
  Americans with Disabilities Act of 1989

- SHORT TITLE(S) AS PASSED SENATE:
  Americans with Disabilities Act of 1989

- SHORT TITLE(S) AS ENACTED:
  Americans with Disabilities Act of 1990

- OFFICIAL TITLE AS INTRODUCED:
  A bill to establish a clear and comprehensive prohibition of discrimination on the basis of disability.

STATUS: Floor Actions
07/26/90 Public Law 101-336
07/17/90 Measure presented to President
07/17/90 Measure enrolled in Senate
07/17/90 Measure enrolled in House
07/13/90 Senate agreed to conference report, roll call #152 (91-6)
07/12/90 House agreed to conference report, roll call #228 (377-28)
07/12/90 Motion to recommit conference report with instructions rejected in House, roll call #227 (180-224)
07/12/90 Conference report filed in House, H. Rept. 101-596
07/11/90 Motion to recommit conference report with instructions passed Senate
07/11/90 Conference report considered in Senate
06/26/90 Conference report filed in House, H. Rept. 101-558
06/06/90 Motion to instruct Senate Conferees withdrawn in Senate
06/06/90 Motion to instruct Senate Conferees passed Senate
06/06/90 Conference scheduled in Senate
05/24/90 Motion to instruct House Conferees passed House

ILLUSTRATION 13-10   *(continued)*

05/24/90 Conference scheduled in House
05/22/90 Measure passed House, amended, in lieu of H.R. 2273
05/22/90 Measure considered in House
05/22/90 Measure called up by special rule in House
09/07/89 Measure passed Senate, amended, roll call #173 (76-8)
09/07/89 Measure considered in Senate
09/07/89 Measure called up by unanimous consent in Senate
08/30/89 Reported to Senate from the Committee on Labor and Human Resources with amendment, S. Rept. 101-116

STATUS: Detailed Legislative Status

Senate Actions

May 9, 89:
>   Read twice and referred to the Committee on Labor and Human Resources.
>   **May 9, 89:**
>> Committee on Labor and Human Resources. Hearings held.
>> **May 10, 89:**
>>> Subcommittee on Handicapped (Labor and Human Res.). Hearings held.
>   (May 16, 89).
>   **Jun 22, 89:**
>> Committee on Labor and Human Resources. Hearings held.
>   **Aug 2, 89:**
>> Committee on Labor and Human Resources. Ordered to be reported with an amendment in the nature of a substitute favorably.

Aug 30, 89:
>   Committee on Labor and Human Resources. Reported to Senate by Senator Kennedy under the authority of the order of Aug 2, 89 with an amendment in the nature of a substitute. With written report No. 101-116. Additional views filed.
>   Placed on Senate Legislative Calendar under General Orders. Calendar No. 216.

Sep 7, 89:
>   Measure laid before Senate by unanimous consent.
>   Amendment SP 708 proposed by Senator Hatch.
>   Amendment SP 708 agreed to in Senate by Voice Vote.
>   Amendment SP 711 proposed by Senator Harkin.
>   Amendment SP 712 proposed by Senator Harkin.
>   Amendment SP 711 agreed to in Senate by Voice Vote.
>   Amendment SP 712 agreed to in Senate by Voice Vote.
>   Amendment SP 709 proposed by Senator Hatch.
>   Point of order raised in Senate with respect to SP 709.
>   Motion to waive the Budget Act with respect to SP 709 rejected in Senate by Yea-Nay Vote. 48-44. Record Vote No: 170.
>   SP 709 ruled out of order by the chair.
>   Amendment SP 713 proposed by Senator Boschwitz.
>   Amendment SP 713 agreed to in Senate by Yea-Nay Vote. 90-0. Record Vote No: 171.
>   Amendment SP 714 proposed by Senator Hollings.
>   Amendment SP 714 agreed to in Senate by Voice Vote.
>   Amendment SP 715 proposed by Senator Helms.
>   Amendment SP 715 agreed to in Senate by Voice Vote.

Legislative history in LEXIS and Westlaw:

▶ select appropriate databases
▶ use a Boolean or natural-language search to identify pertinent documents
▶ retrieve and study the pertinent documents

As noted previously, LEXIS and Westlaw both contain some compiled legislative histories. Furthermore, LEXIS contains CIS legislative histories from 1970 forward.

In addition, you may use both systems, through a Boolean or natural-language search, to locate legislative history materials in the services' legislative history document databases. LEXIS and Westlaw both have several databases of legislative history materials, including bill text, committee hearings, committee reports, and the *Congressional Record*. LEXIS also contains databases of House and Senate documents and committee prints. Westlaw contains committee and conference committee reports from 1948 forward, coverage of the *Congressional Record* begins with 1985 on both systems, and coverage of other documents begins later.

Legislative history in United States Government Printing Office (GPO) sources:

● *Congressional Record* (paper and online through GPO Access)
● bills (paper, fiche, and online)
● other documents located via *Monthly Catalog of U.S. Government Publications* (paper) or *Catalog of U.S. Government Publications* (online)
● *Weekly Compilation of Presidential Documents* and *Public Papers of the President*

The United States Government Printing Office (GPO) publishes the official text of legislative history materials. Although you are likely to begin your research in some other source, you may use GPO publications to complete your research. For example, you may need to consult a *Congressional Record* volume that predates the coverage of THOMAS or *CIS Congressional Universe*. The following text summarizes the GPO sources.

The *Congressional Record* is the reporter of floor debates. See Illustration 13-4 on page 215. It is published daily in softbound pamphlets while Congress is in session. A permanent hardbound edition is published at the end of each session of Congress, though in recent years publication has been much delayed. In the daily edition, House and Senate proceedings are paginated separately, while the permanent edition uses a continuous numbering system. Each permanent volume includes an index that cumulates the information for a particular session of Congress. Each index has two parts: (1) a subject index and (2) a History of Bills and Resolutions. The History of Bills and Resolutions provides a synopsis of each bill's progress, as reported in the volume to which the index pertains; it is subdivided into one section on House bills and resolutions and one section on Senate bills and resolutions. See Illustration 13-11 on page 242.

The GPO makes the daily version of the *Congressional Record* available online, as well as in paper, through GPO Access, its online service. Online coverage for the text begins in 1994; the index is available from 1983 forward in two separate databases, the Congressional Record Index and the History of Bills.

In addition to the *Congressional Record*, the GPO makes available the text of all published versions of bills in paper, microfiche and, for bills introduced in 1993 or later, online through the GPO Access Congressional Bills database.

The GPO also publishes committee hearings, committee reports, and other legislative history documents. Its *Monthly Catalog of U.S. Government Publications* lists documents that are available to depository libraries. You can gain access to the paper, microfiche, or CD-ROM versions of the *Monthly Catalog* by using its author, title, subject, and series/report number indexes. See Illustration 13-12 on page 243. The index entry provides a number that refers you to *Monthly Catalog* text. The text, in turn, describes the document and provides a SuDoc number, which is a GPO classification number assigned by the Superintendent of Documents. See Illustration 13-13 on page 244. Because the GPO is slow to publish some documents, you may need to consult the issues of the *Monthly Catalog* for the year of enactment as well as a year or two thereafter. Government documents can be ordered from the GPO or may be found in federal depository libraries or other libraries.

A web version of the *Monthly Catalog* is available through GPO Access under the name *Catalog of U.S. Government Publications*. It includes bibliographic records generated since January 1994. The web version includes some enhancements over the paper and CD-ROM versions. For example, once you find a document of interest to you, you may identify a depository library that has it by doing an area code or state search.

Finally, GPO publishes the *Weekly Compilation of Presidential Documents*, which contains the text of most presidential communications, including presidential communications to Congress. The title is available from the GPO in paper and on GPO Access. The annual *Public Papers of the President* is an edited version of the *Weekly Compilation*; since 1977 it includes virtually all of it.

Researching the Canoga case, we looked in the title keyword indexes for the *Monthly Catalog* from 1989 through 1992 under "Americans with Disabilities Act" and found a reference to document 91-15677. See Illustration 13-12 on page 243. That document is a legislative history of the ADA, prepared for the House Committee on Education and Labor. See Illustration 13-13 on page 244.

ILLUSTRATION 13-11   History of Bills and Resolutions, from *Congressional Record*

SENATE BILLS

27254—Examined and signed in the House, 28006—Examined and signed in the Senate, 28077—Presented to the President, 28135—Approved [Public Law 101-441], 33293

S. 840—A bill to amend the Internal Revenue Code of 1986 to allow a deduction for education loan interest incurred by doctors, nurses, and allied health professionals while serving in medically underserved areas; to the Committee on Finance.—Cosponsors added, 3999

S. 845—A bill to amend the Federal Food, Drug, and Cosmetic Act to revitalize the Food and Drug Administration, and for other purposes; to the Committee on Labor and Human Resources.—Reported with amendments (S. Rept. 101-242), 1063—Amendments, 33545, 33566—Debated, 33564, 35152—Amended and passed Senate. 33567—Referred to Committee on Energy and Commerce, 34451—Rules suspended. Passed House, 36848

S. 849—A bill to repeal section 2036(c) of the Internal Revenue Code of 1986, relating to valuation freezes; to the Committee on Finance.—Cosponsors added, 5669, 15614, 22874

S. 865—A bill to amend the Sherman Act regarding retail competition; to the Committee on the Judiciary.—Reported with amendments (S. Rept. 101-251), 3967—Cosponsors added, 11785, 13113, 16051, 17425

S. 874—A bill to establish national voter registration procedures for Presidential and Congressional elections, and for other purposes; to the Committee on Rules and Administration.—Cosponsors added, 2595, 3999, 4189, 5190, 5669, 7621, 8093, 12719, 14463, 15207—Debated, 25114—Amendments, 25418—Cloture failed of passage, 25906

S. 878—A bill to grant a Federal charter to the Michael Jackson International Research Institute; to the Committee on the Judiciary.—Cosponsors added, 205

S. 891—A bill to provide for the modernization of testing of consumer products which contain hazardous or toxic substances; to the Committee on Commerce, Science, and Transportation.—Cosponsors added, 17425, 21863, 23574

S. 892—A bill to exclude Agent Orange settlement payments from countable income and resources under Federal means-tested programs; to the Committee on Finance.—Approved [Public Law 101-201], 134

S. 915—A bill to authorize appropriations to the National Aeronautics and Space Administration for research and development, space flight, control and data communications, construction of facilities. and research and program management, and for other purposes; to the Committee on Commerce, Science, and Transportation.—Amended and passed House (in lieu of H.R. 5649), 26582—Title amended, 26589—House insisted on its amendments and asked for a conference., 26589—Conferees appointed, 27033

S. 933—A bill to amend the Occupational Safety and Health Act of 1970 to establish an Office of Construction, Safety, Health and Education within OSHA, to improve inspections investigations, reporting, and recordkeeping in the construction industry, to require certain construction contractors to establish construction safety and health programs and onsite plans and appoint construction safety specialists, and for other purposes; to the Committee on Labor and Human Resources.—Cosponsors added, 13894, 15614, 16051, 16490, 19441—Reported with amendment (S. Rept. 101-558), 36580

S. 931—A bill to protect a segment of the Genesee River in New York; to the Committee on Energy and Natural Resources.—Approved [Public Law 101-175], 134

S. 933—A bill to establish a clear and comprehensive prohibition of discrimination on the basis of disability; to the Committee on Labor and Human Resources.—Debated, 11476—Amended and passed House (in lieu of H.R. 2273), 11491—House insisted on its amendments and asked for a conference. Conferees appointed, 12226—Senate disagreed to House amendments and agreed to a conference., 13035—Conferees appointed, 13064—Conference report (H. Rept. 101-558); submitted in House, 15669—Explanatory statement, 15684, 17267—Conference report considered in Senate, 17028—Amendments, 17033, 17044, 17097—Conference report (H. Rept. 101-596) submitted in House, 17251—Conference report submitted in the House and agreed to, 17280—Conference report submitted in the Senate and agreed to, 17364—Examined and signed in the Senate, 17703—Presented to the President, 17703—Examined and signed in the House, 17839—Approved [Public Law 101-136], 33292

S. 963—A bill to authorize a study on methods to commemorate the nationally significant highway known as Route 66, and for other purposes; to the Committee on Energy and Natural Resources.—Passed House, 20753—Senate concurs in House amendment, 24474—Examined and signed in the Senate, 24849—Examined and signed in the House, 25015—Presented to the President, 25070—Approved [Public Law 101-400], 33292

S. 970—A bill to promote low-input agricultural production systems, to maintain farm profitability to encourage land, resource, and wildlife stewardship in connection with Federal farm programs and for other purposes; to the Committee on Agriculture, Nutrition, and Forestry.—Cosponsors added, 1428

S. 971—A bill to authorize and encourage Federal agencies to use mediation, conciliation, arbitration, and other techniques for the prompt and informal resolution of disputes and for other purposes; to the Committee on Governmental Affairs.—Reported with amendment (S. Rept. 101-543), 31339—Rereferred to Committee on the Judiciary, 31423—Ordered placed on calendar, 31871—Amendments, 33546, 33569, 33574, 33575, 33576—Debated, 33569—Indefinitely postponed, 33577

S. 972—A bill to transfer to the Secretary of Health and Human Services the authority of the Secretary of Energy to conduct epidemiological studies of the effects of radiation and for other purposes; to the Committee on Energy and Natural Resources.—Cosponsors added, 612

S. 974—A bill to designate certain lands in the State of Nevada as wilderness, and for other purposes; to the Committee on Energy and Natural Resources.—Approved [Public Law 101-195], 134

S. 977—A bill entitled the "White House Conference on Small Business Authorization Act"; to the Committee on Small Business.—Cosponsors added, 25399

S. 978—A bill to authorize the establishment within the Smithsonian Institution of the National Museum of the American Indian, to establish a memorial to the American Indian, and for other purposes; to the Committee on Rules and Administration—Approved [Public Law 101-185], 134

S. 980—A bill to amend the Internal Revenue Code of 1986 to improve the effectiveness of the low-income housing credit; to the Committee on Finance.—Cosponsors added, 3216, 7621, 11671, 13410

S. 982—A bill to repeal a provision of Federal tort claim law relating to the civil liability of Government contractors for certain injuries, losses of property and deaths and for other purposes; to the Committee on the Judiciary.—Cosponsors added, 11786, 15207, 22874—Reported (no written report), 29609

S. 985—A bill to amend the Internal Revenue Code of 1986 to allow the Secretary of the Treasury to release information to participants of a qualified pension plan; to the Committee on Finance.—Cosponsors added, 15207

S. 993—A bill to implement the Convention on the Prohibition of the Development, Production, and Stockpiling of Bacteriological (Biological) and Toxin Weapons and Their Destruction, by prohibiting certain conduct relating to biological weapons, and for other purposes; to the Committee on the Judiciary.—Passed Senate, 9663—Examined and signed in House, 9902—Examined and signed in Senate, 10056—Presented to the President, 10056—Approved [Public Law 101-298], 16761

S. 994—A bill to amend the Clayton Act regarding interlocking directorates and officers; to the Committee on the Judiciary.—Cosponsors added, 10185, 21150—Reported with amendments (S. Rept. 101-286), 10267—Indefinitely postponed, 36295

S. 995—A bill to amend the Clayton and Sherman Acts regarding antitrust procedures; to the Committee on the Judiciary.—Cosponsors added, 10185—Reported with amendments (S. Rept. 101-287), 10267

S. 996—A bill to amend the Clayton Act regarding damages for the United States; to the Committee on the Judiciary.—Cosponsors added, 10185—Reported (S. Rept. 101-288), 10267

S. 1000—A bill to amend the Agricultural Act of 1949 to require the Secretary of Agriculture to exclude the malting barley price from the national weighted market price for barley in determining the payment rate used to calculate deficiency payments for the 1989 and 1990 crops of barley, and for other purposes; to the Committee on Agriculture, Nutrition, and Forestry.—Cosponsors added, 205, 834, 2824

S. 1006—A bill to encourage innovation and productivity, stimulate trade, and promote the competitiveness and technological leadership of the United States; to the Committee on the Judiciary.—Cosponsors added, 966, 4189, 5669, 5926, 6541, 7621

S. 1007—A bill to amend title 23, United States Code, regarding the reduction in apportionment of Federal-aid highway funds to certain States, and for other purposes; to the Committee on Environment and Public Works.—Cosponsors added, 22874

S. 1016—A bill to change the name of "Marion Lake," located northwest of Marion, KS, to "Marion Reservoir"; to the Committee on Environment and Public Works.—Rules suspended. Passed House, 2666—Examined and signed in the House, 3100—Examined and signed in the Senate. 3186—Presented to the President, 3399—Approved (Public Law 101-253), 10055

2523

ILLUSTRATION 13-12 Title Keyword Index, from *Monthly Catalog of U.S. Government Publications*

American Air Filter   Title Keyword Index

" submarines, 1914-1940 /, Building	91-19659
" workers /, Employee benefits for	91-12397
" workers /, Federal policies affecting	91-24600
" youth, Trends in the well-being of	91-16371
" , Operator, organizational, direct support	91-17892
American Air Filter models), CH-420-1, 400 hertz,	91-6571
American Air Filter Co., model CH609-3) [sic] NSN	91-4527
American Air Filter Co., Inc. ... Engineered Air S. ....,	
Operation and maintenance instructions wit	91-23025
American Athletes Participating in the 1992 Olympi	91-15843
American Bosch APE-6BB (4910-01-005-2850), America	91-17892
American Canal at El Paso, Texas., An Act to Provi	91-15854
American Citizens Stationed or Held Hostage in the	91-12755
American Education Research Association annual mee	91-4665
American Falls Reservoir area, Idaho, 1988-89 /, R	91-16733
American Families Act : report together with minor	91-19040
American Federation of Government Employees, Natio	91-2876
American Heritage Trust Act of 1989 :	91-4120
American Indian enrichment activities /	91-14467
" music for the classroom : an India	91-14519
American Indian/Alaska Native women business owner	91-22065
American Indians and Alaska natives., 1990 census	91-1668
" , and other minorities., 1987 econ	91-22784
American Kleaner Mfg. Co., Inc., Operator's, organ	91-17895
American Kleaner Mfg. Co. Inc., model 6000-OM), Op	91-17894
American Legion so as to redefine eligibility for	91-12580
" , National Convention of the	91-17492
" ., Proceedings of ... National Conv	91-17492
American Legion So As to Redefine Eligibility for	91-15859
American Mathematics, Science, and Engineering Edu	91-10703
American Military Forces and American Citizens Sta	91-12755
American People to the Importance of Adult Educati	91-22764
American Propulsion Technology /, Engines and inno	91-22154
American Psychological Association /, Psychology i	91-5985
American Public; Stimulate the Professional Develo	91-10703
American Revolution.	91-2252
American River National Recreation Area feasibilit	91-5270
American Samoa, and for Other Purposes., An Act to	91-12768
" , and the Commonwealth of the Northe	91-24328
" : summary report /, Report to Congre	91-20377
" ., 1987 census of agriculture. Volum	91-14251
American Shoal /, United States—east coast, Florid	91-4427
American States in the 1990's ; The role of the O	91-8561
American Statistical Association., Selected papers	91-19374
American Technology Preeminence Act :	91-21070
" of 1991 : repo	91-22348
" of 1991 : repo	91-24433
American Textile Industry Bicentennial Week.", Jo	91-8715
American University and the General Board of Highe	91-8720
American University", Approved February 24, 1893,	91-8720
American University Incorporation Amendments Act o	91-3959
Americans /, Significant incidents of political vi	91-22193
" , Significant incidents of political vi	91-5969
" :, A Consumer guide to prescription drug	91-24532
" :, Housing for older	91-15630
" :, In poor health, the federal commitmen	91-12408
" :, Rising out-of-pocket health care cost	91-17513
" : the report of the National Trails Agen	91-24008
" against overpayment of income taxes :, P	91-13952
" are not eating enough fruit and vegetabl	91-14924
" assess their health : United States, 198	91-23762
" exercise freedoms guaranteed by the Cons	91-22362
" in agriculture : portraits of diversity.	91-6309
" with Disabilities Act., Facts about the	91-19101
" with Disabilities Act :, Legislative his	91-15677
" with Disabilities Act., The	91-20410
" with Disabilities Act, The	91-2871
" with Disabilities Act : questions and an	91-20409
" with Disabilities Act : questions and an	91-24474

" ., Nutrition and your health : dietary gu	91-6314
" ., Tax information for older	91-20694
Americas :, Enterprise for the	91-10395
" initiative., Enterprise for the	91-5971
Americas Board : report (to accompany H.R. 1294 ..	91-20826
Americas Initiative :, The Enterprise for the	91-15701
" , and for other purposes., Ente	91-3882
" , and for, Proposed legislation	91-15600
" , S. 3064 :, Enterprise for the	91-15709
Americas Initiative Act of 1990 : message from the	91-3882
" of 1990 : report (to accom	91-12360
" of 1991 : message from the	91-15600
Americus, Georgia, Sumter County., Flood insurance	91-16393
Amertech Corporation model no. APP-1), NSN 6115-00	91-10870
" model no. APP-1), NSN 6115-00	91-6584
Ames 40- by 80- foot and the 80- by 120-foot wind	91-9741
Ames-Dryden water tunnel, Vortex breakdown and con	91-24167
Ames-Dryden Flight Research Facility, The PC/AT co	91-11896
Ames Research Center since its inception, Some inn	91-9806
" (1987 Forum on Federal Techno	91-5550
" , A static data flow simulatio	91-9829
" , November 1983, Phase 4 stati	91-8028
Amesville, Ohio, Athens County., Flood insurance s	91-11067
Amherst, Wisconsin, Portage County., Flood insuran	91-16516
amines, and nitroso compounds., Cancergram. Series	91-841
" , and nitroso compounds, Azo dyes, aryl	91-841
" , and nitroso compounds, Chemical carcinogen	91-841
" , and related compounds, Cancergram. Series	91-828
" , and related compounds, Azo dyes, aryl	91-828
" , and related compounds, Chemical carcinogen	91-828
amino acids., Cancergram. Series CB27, Molecular b	91-812
" acids, Molecular biology. Proteins, polypept	91-812
" acids, Proteins, polypeptides,	91-812
Amistad National Recreation Area /	91-18658
Ammo operations in the desert.	91-19648
Ammonia boiling in long tubes heat transfer and ch	91-13833
" cracking resistance, The Manufacturing met	91-12205
" formation caused by the presence of water	91-24123
" mixtures, Low power dc arcjet operation wi	91-9855
" , Interaction of vinylidene fluoride - tetr	91-13825
Ammonites and some characteristic bivalves from th	91-11144
ammonium perchlorate crystal shape on Missions 51-	91-9727
Ammophila Arenaria, Carpobrotus Edulis, Cortaderia	91-11957
ammunition : acquisition of the M762 electronic ti	91-9304
" : the Mississippi plant will be closed	91-9288
" and explosives : improved controls are	91-11255
" container contract : briefing report to	91-11250
" for training, target practice, and comb	91-1940
" peculiar equipment., Army equipment dat	91-10942
" support and review programs : logistics	91-16033
" , tracked : M992 (NSN 2350-01-110-4660).	91-10897
ammunition budget : report to Congressional request	91-11259
amnesty program :, The feasibility and revenue imp	91-17582
AMO gallium arsenide grating solar cell, A 25.5 pe	91-9764
amorphous carbon films grown from methane plasma,	91-2959
" hydrogenated carbon (a-C:H) films, Rapid	91-7898
amortization., 1990 instructions for Form 4562 : d	91-10296
AMOS plan, environmental analysis final report., L	91-3469
amount of petroleum products that may be withdrawn	91-12328
amounts due and unpaid 90 days or more on foreign	91-1303
" from the contingent fund of the House for	91-15615
" over land /, Global distribution of total	91-2108
" under sections 179 and 280F)., 1990 instru	91-10298
" , burial allowances, special benefits., Adj	91-12307
amp AC straight polarity, 10 to 00 amp DC reverse	91-23015
" AC, 5 to 350 amp DC (Miller model 330A/B/SP)	
" F	91-23017
" DC arc, wheel MTD ...., Direct and general sup	91-23016

ILLUSTRATION 13-13	Document Description, in *Monthly Catalog of U.S. Government Publications*

Government Publications — July 1991

1990"—Pt. 38. Includes bibliographical references. ●Item 1000-B, 1000-C (MF)
 1. Labor supply — United States. 2. Unemployment — United States. I. Title. II. Title: Employment unemployment. III. Series: United States. Congress. Senate. S. hrg. ; 101-151. OCLC 08895693

91-15674
Y 4.Ec 7:So 8/21
United States. Congress. Joint Economic Committee.
 The Soviet economic crisis : hearing before the Joint Economic Committee, Congress of the United States, One Hundred First Congress, second session, April 25, 1990. — Washington : U.S. G.P.O. : For sale by the Supt. of Docs., Congressional Sales Office, U.S. G.P.O. 1990
 iii, 42 p. : 24 cm. — (S. hrg. 101-1204) Distributed to some depository libraries in microfiche. Shipping list no.: 91-271-P. ●Item 1000-B, 1000-C (MF)
 1. Soviet Union — Economic conditions — 1985- 2. Soviet Union — Politics and government — 1985- 3. Soviet Union — Foreign economic relations — United States. 4. United States — Foreign economic relations — Soviet Union. I. Title. II. Series: United States. Congress. Senate. S. hrg. ; 101-1204. OCLC 23379440

91-15675
Y 4.Ec 7:W 19/3
United States. Congress. Joint Economic Committee.
 Economic adjustment after the Cold War : hearings before the Joint Economic Committee, Congress of the United States, One Hundred First Congress, first and second sessions, December 12 and 19, 1989, and March 20, 1990. — Washington : U.S. G.P.O. : For sale by the Supt. of Docs., Congressional Sales Office, U.S. G.P.O., 1990 [i.e. 1991]
 iv, 310 p. : ill. ; 24 cm. — (S. hrg. ; 101-1215) Distributed to some depository libraries in microfiche. Shipping list no.: 91-322-P. Includes bibliographical references. ●Item 1000-B, 1000-C (MF)
 1. United States — Economic conditions — 1981- 2. United States — Appropriations and expenditures. 3. United States. Dept. of Defense — Appropriations and expenditures. 4. Cold War. I. Title. II. Series: United States. Congress. Senate. S. hrg. ; 101-1215. OCLC 23609743

EDUCATION AND LABOR, Committee on, House
Washington, DC 20515

91-15676
Y 4.Ed 8/1:101-132
United States. Congress. House. Committee on Education and Labor.
 Hearing on the Department of Education, Office of [i.e. for] Civil Rights policy on student financial assistance : hearing before the Committee on Education and Labor, House of Representatives, One Hundred First Congress, second session, hearing held in Washington, DC, December 19, 1990. — Washington : U.S. G.P.O. : For sale by the Supt. of Docs., Congressional Sales Office, U.S. G.P.O., 1991.
 v, 428 p. : ill. ; 24 cm. Distributed to some depository libraries in microfiche. Shipping list no.: 91-272-P. Includes bibliographical references. "Serial no. 101-132." ●Item 1015-A, 10@RB@5-B (MF)
 1. United States. Dept. of Education. Office for Civil Rights. 2. Minority students — Scholarships, fellowships, etc. — United States. 3. Scholarships — Government policy — United States. 4. Student financial aid administration — United States. I. Title. OCLC 23458329

91-15677
Y 4.Ed 8/1:102-A
Y 4.Ed 8/1:102-B
Y 4.Ed 8/1:102-C
Legislative history of Public Law 101-336, the Americans with Disabilities Act : prepared for the Committee on Education and Labor, U.S. House of Representatives, One Hundred First Congress, second session. — Washington : U.S. G.P.O. : For sale by the Supt. of Docs., Congressional Sales Office, U.S. G.P.O., [1990]
 3 v. : ill. ; 24 cm. At head of title: Committee print. Distributed to some depository libraries in microfiche. Shipping list no.: 91-247-P (v. 1), 91-256-P (v. 2), 91-267-P (v. 3). "December 1990." "Serial no. 102-A"—Vol. 1. "Serial no. 102-B"—Vol. 2. "Serial no. 102-C"—Vol. 3. Includes bibliographical references. ●Item 1015-A, 1015-B (MF)
 1. United States. Americans with Disabilities Act of 1990. 2. Handicapped — Legal status, laws, etc. — United States. I. United States. Congress. House. Committee on Education and Labor. OCLC 23368329

ENERGY AND NATURAL RESOURCES, Committee on, Senate
Washington, DC 20510

91-15678
Y 4.En 2:S.hrg.101-1137
United States. Congress. Senate. Committee on Energy and Natural Resources. Subcommittee on Energy Regulation and Conservation.
 Vehicular Natural Gas Jurisdiction Act of 1990 : hearing before the Subcommittee on Energy Regulation and Conservation of the Committee on Energy and Natural Resources, United States Senate, Once Hundred First Congress, second session on S. 3085 ... September 25, 1990. — Washington : U.S. G.P.O. : For sale by the Supt. of Docs., Congressional Sales Office, U.S. G.P.O., 1991.
 24 p. ; 24 cm. — (S. hrg. ; 101-1137) Distributed to some depository libraries in microfiche. Shipping list no.: 91-145-P. Includes bibliographical references. ●Item 1040-A, 1040-B (MF)
 1. Gas, Natural — United States. 2. Motor vehicles — United States. I. Title. II. Series: United States. Congress. Senate. S. hrg. ; 101-1137. OCLC 23163428

91-15679
Y 4.En 2:S.hrg.101-1178
United States. Congress. Senate. Committee on Energy and Natural Resources. Subcommittee on Energy Research and Development.
 Renewable and other alternative energy sources : hearing before the Subcommittees on Energy Research and Development and Mineral Resources Development and Production of the Committee on Energy and Natural Resources, United States Senate, One Hundred First Congress, second session ... Albuquerque, NM, November 1, 1990. — Washington : U.S. G.P.O. : For sale by the Supt. of Docs., Congressional Sales Office, U.S. G.P.O., 1991.
 iii, 127 p. : ill. ; 24 cm. — (S. hrg. ; 101-1178) Distributed to some depository libraries in microfiche. Shipping list no.: 91-226-P. Includes bibliographical references. ●Item 1040-A, 1040-B (MF)
 1. Energy policy — United States. 2. Renewable energy sources — United States. 3. Power resources — United States. I. United States. Congress. Senate. Committee on Energy and Natural Resources. Subcommittee on Mineral Resources Devel-

Page 195

4. What Else?

Legislative Histories of Older Statutes. For legislative materials prior to 1970, CIS has published the following indexes, which may be researched separately in paper or with one search in CIS's *Congressional Masterfile 1* (currently on CD-ROM):

- *CIS US Serial Set Index* (1789-1969)
- *CIS US Congressional Committee Hearings Index* (1833-1969)
- *CIS Index to Unpublished US Senate Committee Hearings* (1823-1972)
- *CIS Index to Unpublished US House of Representatives Committee Hearings* (1833-1958)
- *CIS US Congressional Committee Prints Index* (1830-1969)
- *CIS Index to US Senate Executive Documents and Reports* (1817-1969)

For all of these indexes, CIS microfiche sets contain the related documents.

United States Serial Set. This source contains House and Senate committee reports, House and Senate documents (including presidential messages on legislation), and many other materials. It is published by the GPO and is compiled roughly in chronological order, in the order in which the reports and documents are produced. As you can imagine, the *Serial Set* is a massive source, so access to it is difficult. The best way to gain access to the *Serial Set* between 1789 and 1969 is through the *CIS US Serial Set Index,* which is designed for use with the *CIS US Serial Set on Microfiche.*

Congressional Masterfile 2. CIS's *Congressional Masterfile 2* on CD-ROM includes the *CIS/Index* and legislative histories for 1970 to 1998. Its current service was discontinued in 1998.

Additional Documents Available Through GPO Access. GPO Access contains a limited number of committee prints, documents, hearing transcripts, and reports, starting with the 104th Congress.

Predecessors to *Congressional Record.* To find debates concerning older legislation, you would consult the *Annals of Congress* (1789-1824), the *Register of Debates* (1824-1837), and the *Congressional Globe* (1833-1873).

State Legislative History. In many states, it is difficult to research state legislative history. Some materials may not be published. Some may be available only on audiotape, without any comprehensive list or index. Many materials may be available only in a single location, generally a state capitol. You should seek the advice of your state's legislative reference librarian or consult one of the texts that provide an overview of state legislative history, such as Lynn Hellebust, *State Legislative Sourcebook: A Resource Guide to Legislative Information in the Fifty States* (1999).

5.   How Do You Cite Legislative Materials?

Each type of legislative history document has its own citation requirements. For committee reports the form includes the name of the chamber, the numbers of the Congress and of the report, page number (if you are citing a particular page), and year. If the report is published in U.S.C.C.A.N., a U.S.C.C.A.N. citation should be added. Here are examples (according to Rule 13.4 of *The Bluebook*):

S. Rep. No. 101-116 (1989)
H.R. Rep. No. 101-485 (1990), *reprinted in* 1990 U.S.C.C.A.N. 267.

The form for a hearing transcript includes the subject matter title, the bill number, the names of the subcommittee (if any) and the committee, the number of the Congress, the page number, the year, and identifying information about the witness. Here is an example (according to Rule 13.3):

Americans with Disabilities Act of 1989: Hearing on H.R. 2273 Before the Subcomm. on Employment Opportunities and the Subcomm. on Select Education of the House Comm. on Education and Labor, 101st Cong. 5 (1989) (statement of Evan J. Kemp, Commissioner, EEOC).

As for bills, enacted bills are cited as statutes unless they are used to document legislative history, in which case they are cited as unenacted bills. Unenacted bills are cited with the chamber's abbreviation, the bill number, the number of the Congress, the section number (if any), and the year. The name of the bill may be included; if the unenacted bill can be found in published hearings, that information may be added. Here is an example (according to Rule 13.2):

S. 933, 101st Cong. § 1 (1989).

Congressional debates are cited to the *Congressional Record*; the permanent version must be cited if available. Here is an example (according to Rule 13.5):

136 Cong. Rec. 13,063 (1990).

C.   PENDING LEGISLATION

Legislative process materials also can be used to track pending legislation. Although legislation generally does not operate retroactively, some clients are concerned enough about future statutes to want to affect legislation or to adjust their affairs by planning ahead. This part briefly describes four research options for tracking pending legislation, one in paper, three online.

Exhibit 13.4 below presents an overview of the four options. The bill number is the key to tracking pending legislation.

The following discussion shifts from the enacted ADA to a bill that was pending at the time this book was written. S.121 in the 106th Congress would amend the ADA to preclude compelled arbitration of employment discrimination claims, including claims based on disability discrimination.

Pending legislation in *Congressional Index*:

▶ use the subject, author, or headline legislation indexes to find potentially relevant bill numbers

▶ use the Senate Bills or House Bills section to obtain a summary of a potentially relevant bill

▶ use the Status table to determine actions taken on the bill

---

The standard paper source for tracking the progress of pending legislation is *Congressional Index*, a two-volume looseleaf service published by Commerce Clearing House (a commercial publisher). *Congressional Index* is updated weekly while Congress is in session and at least six weeks after adjournment. This service does not provide the full text of bills or other legislative materials; it simply describes actions on a bill. (In addition to

EXHIBIT 13.4	Overview of Research Practices for Pending Legislation

Practice	Strengths	Weaknesses
Congressional Index	multiple indexes, including Headline Legislation; use of subject headings in bill descriptions to facilitate finding related legislation; concise Status report	lack of currency compared to online sources; updates not integrated into prior text; no full-text documents
CIS Congressional Universe	multiple search methods, including Hot Bills; detailed tracking report; citations to *Congressional Record*; links to bill text and *Congressional Record*; links to related news stories; use of subject headings for a bill to facilitate finding related legislation; very current	not very compact
THOMAS	multiple indexes, including Major Legislation; full text of bills; easy to track amendments; very current; free	variations in format over time, which may be confusing
LEXIS/Westlaw	both are very current; both offer Billcast; LEXIS offers the same report provided by *CIS Congressional Universe*	Westlaw's US-BILLTRK lacks citations or links to *Congressional Record*

information on bills and resolutions, *Congressional Index* also provides information on members, committees and subcommittees, presidential nominations, and treaties.)

If you do not know the number of your bill, you can use the subject, author (sponsor), or Headline Legislation indexes to obtain the bill number. Once you have the bill number, you can turn to the Senate Bills or House Bills section to obtain a description of the bill. This description includes the main subject heading under which the bill is indexed (which is useful for tracking related bills), the bill's sponsors, a brief summary of the bill, and either the committee to which the bill was referred or the first action taken on the bill in lieu of referral to a committee.

Then you may look up the bill in the Status of Senate Bills or Status of House Bills section. These sections show progress on a bill from its introduction through presidential action. See Illustration 13-14 on page 249. However, a bill is not listed in this section until it receives action beyond its initial referral or first action.

Researching for bills that would amend the ADA or enact new laws governing employee smoking, we searched *Congressional Index*'s subject index and its update and found several possibilities, including S. 121, under the heading "Labor and employment." Turning to the Senate Bills section for a description of the bill, we learned that S. 121 would amend certain (unnamed) civil rights statutes to prevent the involuntary arbitration of claims that arise from unlawful employment discrimination based on certain characteristics, including disability. We noted that S. 121 had been referred to the Health, Education, Labor, and Pensions Committee. Turning next to the Status of Senate Bills section and its updates, we found no entry for S. 121, so we concluded the bill was still in committee. See Illustration 13-14 on page 249.

Pending legislation in *CIS Congressional Universe:*

▶ select the bills database

▶ select key-word, sponsor, bill number, or Hot Bills search

▶ enter a search

▶ retrieve and read the bill tracking report

▶ link to the full text of the bill, *Congressional Record*, related news search stories

---

CIS Congressional Universe also has a bill tracking service, dating back to 1989. It offers not only information about legislative activity, but also the text of bills and related news stories.

Your first step is to select the bills database and a search method. You may search this database several ways: by bill number, key word, sponsor, or so-called "Hot Bills." The Hot Bills option provides links to bill tracking

ILLUSTRATION **13-14**   Status of Senate Bills, from *Congressional Index*

21,002   **Status of Senate Bills**   51 12-23-99
                    See also Status at pages 20,101 and 20,501.
                 For digest, see "Bills" and "Resolutions" Divisions.

93

Introduced 1/19/99
Ref to S Budget; Govt Affairs Coms 1/19/99
Hrgs by Budget Com 1/27/99
Hrgs by Govt Affairs Com 1/27/99

96

Introduced ...;.................... 1/19/99
Ref to S Commerce Com.............. 1/19/99
Hrgs by Commerce Com.............. 2/9/99
Ordered reptd w/amdts by Commerce Com
.... 3/3/99
Reptd w/amdts, S Rept 106-10, by Commerce
Com............................ 3/10/99
S began consideration 4/22/99
S continued consideration............. 4/26/99
S invoked cloture (94 to 0; S Leg 91) 4/26/99
S continued consideration............. 4/27/99
S continued consideration............. 4/28/99
Amdts rejected (44 to 55; S Leg 94)..... 4/28/99
S continued consideration............. 4/29/99
S failed to invoke cloture by 3/5 vote (52 to 47; S
Leg 95) 4/29/99
S continued consideration............. 5/14/99
S continued consideration............. 5/17/99
S continued consideration............. 5/18/99
S failed to invoke cloture by 3/5 vote (53 to 45; S
Leg 120) 5/18/99
S continued consideration.............. 6/9/99
Amdts adopted (Voice)............... 6/9/99
Amdts rejected (41 to 57; S Leg 159)..... 6/9/99
Amdts rejected (32 to 65; S Leg 160)..... 6/9/99
S continued consideration............. 6/10/99
Amdts adopted (Voice)............... 6/10/99
Amdts rejected (41 to 57; S Leg 161).... 6/10/99
Amdts rejected (36 to 62; S Leg 162).... 6/10/99
Amdts rejected (32 to 66; S Leg 163).... 6/10/99
Amdts adopted (Voice)............... 6/15/99
Amdts adopted (71 to 28; S Leg 164) ... 6/15/99
Placed on S calendar................. 6/15/99
See H 775, text incorporated therein 6/15/99

97

Introduced 1/19/99
Ref to S Commerce Com.............. 1/19/99
Hrgs by Commerce Com............... 3/4/99
Hrgs by Commerce Com.............. 5/20/99
Ordered reptd w/amdts by Commerce Com
.... 6/23/99
Reptd w/amdts, S Rept 106-141, by Commerce
Com............................. 8/5/99

101

Introduced 1/19/99
Ref to S Finance Com................ 1/19/99
Hrgs by Agriculture Com 1/26/99

109

Introduced 1/19/99
Ref to S Energy Com 1/19/99
Hrgs by National Parks Subcom 4/15/99
Ordered reptd w/amdts by Energy Com. 5/19/99
Reptd w/amdts, S Rept 106-62, by Energy Com
.... 6/7/99

S 93

140

Introduced 1/19/99
Ref to S Energy Com 1/19/99
Hrgs by National Parks Subcom 5/25/99
Ordered reptd w/amdts by Energy Com. 6/16/99
Reptd w/amdts, S Rept 106-89, by Energy Com
.... 6/24/99

148

Introduced 1/19/99
Ref to S Environment Com 1/19/99
Ordered reptd w/o amdts by Environment Com
.... 3/17/99
Reptd w/o amdts, S Rept 106-36, by
Environment Com 3/26/99
Passed by S (Voice).................. 4/13/99

161

Introduced 1/19/99
Ref to S Energy Com 1/19/99
Hrgs by Energy Com 6/29/99
Hrgs by Energy Com 7/15/99

167

Introduced 1/19/99
Ref to S Energy Com 1/19/99
Hrgs by National Parks Subcom 10/13/99

185

Introduced 1/19/99
Ref to S Finance Com................ 1/19/99
Finance Com discharged 11/3/99
Passed by S (Voice)................... 11/3/99
Ref to H Ways & Means Com 11/4/99

187

Introduced 1/19/99
Ref to S Banking Com 1/19/99
Hrgs by Banking Com 6/9/99

188

Introduced 1/9/99
Ref to S Environment Com 1/9/99
Introduced 1/19/99
Ref to S Environment Com 1/19/99
Hrgs by Environment Com 10/13/99

211

Introduced 1/19/99
Ref to S Finance Com................ 1/19/99
Hrgs by Finance Com................ 3/3/99

225

Introduced 1/19/99
Ref to S Indian Affairs Com.......... 1/19/99
Ordered reptd w/o amdts by Indian Affairs Com
.... 6/30/99
Reptd w/amdts, S Rept 106-192, by Indian
Affairs Com..................... 10/14/99
Amdts adopted (Voice).............. 11/4/99
Passed by S (Voice).................. 11/4/99
Ref to H Banking Com 11/5/99

reports for proposed or recently enacted legislation that has received national attention.

A *Congressional Universe* bill tracking report includes the date of introduction of the bill, date of last action, status (in committee, etc.), sponsor, a synopsis, actions on the bill, and a legislative chronology of activity on the bill as noted in the *Congressional Record*, along with citations to the *Congressional Record*. This information is followed by a digest of the bill and additional information. See Illustration 13-15 on pages 251–252.

The bill tracking report also provides links to several sets of materials: the bill's text, the *Congressional Record*, and news stories. A related news search retrieves a citation list of news stories related to the legislation, gathered from news wires, legal newspapers, and general interest newspapers. You can go directly from the citation list to the stories.

Researching potential amendments to the ADA in the 106th Congress, we searched *CIS Congressional Universe* using the phrase ["Americans with disabilities"]. We found four bills, including S. 121. The bill tracking report appears as Illustration 13-15 on pages 251–252. Although a link to the *Congressional Record* established that Senator Feingold mentioned S. 121 on the floor in May 1999, the report confirmed that the bill was still in committee.

Pending legislation in THOMAS:

▶ search by bill or amendment number, word, phrase, subject, or other method in Bill Summary & Status for the current Congress

▶ or browse a list of legislation in the Bill Summary & Status section

▶ or search in Major Legislation for the current Congress

▶ retrieve the pertinent Bill Summary & Status report

▶ skim the report, and compile a list of relevant documents

▶ retrieve and read the documents that are available on THOMAS

▶ retrieve the report for a related bill, if any

You search for pending legislation on THOMAS much as you would search for legislative history information. You generally will begin your search in the Bill Summary & Status section, because that section permits searches by bill and amendment number, as well as by word, phrase, subject, and some other methods. Another approach is to browse a list of legislation in that section. Alternatively, you may begin your search in the Major Legislation section, which provides a shortcut by topics to selected bills that have been the subject of hearings, debate, or floor action, or that have received media attention. The result of your search will be the Bill Summary & Status report, with which you are familiar from Part B. See Illustration 13-16 on page 253. THOMAS includes the full text of proposed bills.

ILLUSTRATION 13-15   Bill Tracking Report, from *CIS Congressional Universe*

Search Terms: S., 121

| Document List | Expanded List | KWIC™ | Full |

Document 1 of 1.

More Like This

Copyright 1999 Congressional Information Service, Inc

Bill Tracking Report

106th Congress
1st Session

U. S. Senate

S 121

1999 Bill Tracking **S. 121**; 106 Bill Tracking **S. 121**

CIVIL RIGHTS PROCEDURES PROTECTION ACT OF 1999

Related news search
Retrieve full text version

DATE-INTRO: January 19, 1999

LAST-ACTION-DATE: May 12, 1999

STATUS: In committee

SPONSOR: Senator Russell Feingold D-WI

TOTAL-COSPONSORS: 3 Cosponsors: 3 Democrats / 0 Republicans

SYNOPSIS: A bill to amend certain Federal civil rights statutes to prevent the involuntary application of arbitration to claims that arise from unlawful employment discrimination based on race, color, religion,

ILLUSTRATION 13-15   *(continued)*

sex, age, or disability, and for other purposes.

ACTIONS:
Committee Referrals:
01/19/1999 Senate Committee on Health, Education, Labor, and Pensions Committee

Legislative Chronology:

1st Session Activity:

01/19/1999 145 Cong Rec S 341
                        Referred to the Senate Committee on Health,
                        Education, Labor, and Pensions Committee
01/19/1999 145 Cong Rec S 550
                        Remarks by Sen. FEINGOLD, RUSSELL D (D-WI)
05/12/1999 145 Cong Rec S 5158
                        Remarks by Sen. FEINGOLD, RUSSELL D (D-WI)

BILL-DIGEST:
(from the CONGRESSIONAL RESEARCH SERVICE)

Digest :

Rights Procedures Protection Act of 1999 Civil Rights Procedures

Protection Act of 1999 - Amends specified Federal civil rights
statutes (including title VII of the Civil Rights Act of 1964,
the Age Discrimination in Employment Act of 1967, the Rehabilitation
Act of 1973, the Americans With Disabilities Act of 1990, the
equal pay requirement under the Fair Labor Standards Act of 1938,
and the Family and Medical Leave Act of 1993) to prevent
the involuntary application of arbitration to claims that arise
from unlawful employment discrimination based on race, color,
religion, sex, national origin, age, or disability.

CRS Index Terms:

Civil rights
Age discrimination in employment
Aged
Alternative dispute resolution
Civil liberties
Civil rights enforcement
Contracts
Disabled
Discrimination against the disabled

| ILLUSTRATION 13-16 | Bill Summary & Status Report for Pending Bill, from THOMAS |

Bill Summary & Status for the 106th Congress

Item 1 of 1

PREVIOUS:ALL | NEXT:ALL
NEW SEARCH | HOME | HELP

S.121
Sponsor: Sen Feingold, Russell D. (introduced 1/19/1999)
Latest Major Action: 1/19/1999 Referred to Senate committee
Title: A bill to amend certain Federal civil rights statutes to prevent the involuntary application of arbitration to claims that arise from unlawful employment discrimination based on race, color, religion, sex, age, or disability, and for other purposes.

Jump to: Titles, Status, Committees, Related Bill Details, Amendments, Cosponsors, Summary

TITLE(S): *(italics indicate a title for a portion of a bill)*

- SHORT TITLE(S) AS INTRODUCED:
  Civil Rights Procedures Protection Act of 1999

- OFFICIAL TITLE AS INTRODUCED:
  A bill to amend certain Federal civil rights statutes to prevent the involuntary application of arbitration to claims that arise from unlawful employment discrimination based on race, color, religion, sex, age, or disability, and for other purposes.

STATUS: *(italics indicate Senate actions)* (Floor Actions/Congressional Record Page References)

1/19/1999:
  Read twice and referred to the Committee on HELP.

COMMITTEE(S):

Committee/Subcommittee:	Activity:
Senate Health, Education, Labor, and Pensions	Referral

RELATED BILL DETAILS:

NONE

AMENDMENT(S):

NONE

> **Pending legislation in LEXIS and Westlaw:**
>
> ▶ select an appropriate database
> ▶ do a Boolean or natural-language search to retrieve the bill tracking report
> ▶ read the report
> ▶ check the likelihood of the bill's passage in Billcast

Both LEXIS and Westlaw provide databases for tracking pending federal legislation. The LEXIS database, BLTRCK, contains the same bill tracking report provided by *CIS Congressional Universe*. You may retrieve a bill tracking report from BLTRCK by using the format [cite (S. 121)].

Westlaw's database, US-BILLTRK, which is supplied by Information for Public Affairs, Inc., provides a simpler report that consists of the sponsor; main topic, subtopic, and title of the legislation (as assigned by the publisher); a short summary of the bill; a list of legislative actions on the bill (by date); and a list of the topics under which the publisher indexes the bill. See Illustration 13-17 on page 255. Unlike BLTRCK, US-BILLTRK does not provide citations or links to legislative actions as reported in the *Congressional Record*. To search for a bill by number on US-BILLTRK use the format ["S.B. 121"] or ["H.R. 121"].

After you have identified pending legislation of interest to you and tracked its current status, you may want to learn about its likelihood of passage. LEXIS and Westlaw both offer Billcast, a service of Information for Public Affairs, Inc., which provides the odds for passage of a public bill in committee and on the floors of the House and Senate. According to data provided on LEXIS, Billcast had a ninety-four percent accuracy rate from 1977 to 1999. Researching Billcast for the likelihood of passage of S. 121, we learned that it had less than a five percent chance of passage in committee or on the floor.

LEXIS and Westlaw have additional databases for tracking federal legislation. You may identify those databases in their print or online directories.

What Else?

Other Sources.   Other popular online updating and legislative tracking systems include LEGI-SLATE, a service of the Washington Post Company, and *CQ Washington Alert*, published by *Congressional Quarterly* and available in some Westlaw systems.

Unnumbered Federal "Bills."   Occasionally a bill is written in a committee or subcommittee, then introduced and given a number when it is reported.

ILLUSTRATION 13-17   STATE NET's US-BILLTRK, from Westlaw

```
                                                                    Page

Citation                  Search Result     Rank 1 of 1      Database
1999 US S.B. 121 (SN)                                        US-BILLTR
 1999 United States Senate Bill No. 121 1st Session of the 106th Congress
(SUMMARY - STATE NET)

                    UNITED STATES BILL TRACKING

AUTHOR:    Feingold
TOPIC:     LAW AND JUSTICE
SUBTOPIC:  CIVIL LAW- OTHER
TITLE:     Civil Rights Statutes

SUMMARY:   Amends certain Federal civil rights statutes to prevent the
involuntary application of arbitration to claims that arise from unlawful
employment discrimination based on race, color, religion, sex, age, or
disability.

STATUS:
01/19/1999  INTRODUCED.
01/19/1999  To SENATE Committee on HEALTH, EDUCATION, LABOR, AND PENSIONS.

TOPIC LIST:
LABOR AND EMPLOYMENT
FAIR EMPLOYMENT PRACTICES [PRIVATE SECTOR]
Employment Discrim & Harassment [Private Sector]
PUBLIC EMPLOYEES
Public Employee Wages and Hours
LAW AND JUSTICE
CIVIL LAW- OTHER
Civil Rights, Discrimination, Harassment- Other
1999 US S.B. 121 (SN)
END OF DOCUMENT
```

If you are unable to track one of these bills by number, try searching secondary sources, such as newspapers, for further information.

State Bill Tracking.   LEXIS and Westlaw both offer state bill text and bill tracking databases. You may use a source such as Lynn Hellebust, *State Legislative Sourcebook: A Resource Guide to Legislation Information in the Fifty States* (1999), or a comprehensive web site, such as WashLaw Web, to identify state bill tracking sources in addition to those provided by LEXIS and Westlaw.

D.   CONCLUDING POINTS

Legislative process materials can be used (1) to locate legislative history materials, so as to discern the legislative intent behind an ambiguous law that has been enacted, or (2) to track pending legislation for an interested client.

The legislative materials pertinent to legislative intent have varying weights, depending on how well they represent the views of the legislature. The first step in legislative history research is to identify the public law that enacted the ambiguous statutory language, typically by using a statutory code. Your next step is to attempt to find a compiled legislative history. If none is available, the next sensible step is to consult U.S.C.C.A.N. There you can find a list of the major legislative documents and events and the actual text of at least one of the documents.

Should you need to extend your research, you have several options, depending on the date of your law. One set of sources is published by CIS. You may use various CIS paper sources or *CIS Congressional Universe* online to trace the history of legislation. Alternatively, you may use the Library of Congress' THOMAS database to trace the history of recent legislation.

The next step is to read the documents. The debates and remarks are contained in the CIS and GPO versions of the *Congressional Record*. Other materials (committee prints, hearings, reports, House and Senate documents, and other special publications) are usually available in a CIS publication or a government publication or database. Some of those materials also are available on LEXIS and Westlaw.

In addition to legislative history research, legislative process materials also can be used to track pending legislation. This research may involve use of the *Congressional Index* or various online bill-tracking systems, including those provided by *CIS Congressional Universe*, THOMAS, LEXIS, and Westlaw.

ADMINISTRATIVE MATERIALS

UNIT

V

In the United States, law is made not only by the judiciary and the legislature, but also by administrative agencies. Administrative agencies are involved in almost every aspect of American life. They operate at the federal, state, and local levels. For some matters, a single agency may operate alone; in other fields, there may be an overlap.

Many agencies regulate an industry (such as nuclear energy); others regulate certain practices (such as employment relations) of various industries. An agency may have the power to promulgate regulations, adjudicate cases, prosecute violations of the law, inspect operations, issue licenses, or conduct studies. Some gather data (such as the Census Bureau), and some provide scientific or other expertise in a specialized field.

Agencies have two lawmaking functions: rulemaking and case adjudication. Rulemaking resembles legislative activity, and case adjudication resembles judicial activity. As to both, the agency acts in concert with and under the supervision of the legislature, executive, and courts.

The legislature creates the agency through an enabling statute. This statute establishes the scope of the agency's authority; it identifies the goals the agency is to pursue and the lawmaking functions it may engage in. When the agency departs from what the legislature wants it to do, the agency may experience legislative oversight, loss of funding, or an amendment of its enabling statute.

The links between an agency and the executive branch vary. Typically agency commissioners are appointed by the executive, and the agency may be highly influenced by the executive on matters of policy and budget.

Additionally, the courts review agency actions. If a court finds the agency's action to be unconstitutional, unauthorized by the enabling statute, inadequately supported by the factual record, or insufficiently explained, it will invalidate or void the action.

Agencies generally are bound to follow not only their particular enabling statutes, but also a jurisdiction's administrative procedure act. These statutes, which exist at the federal and state levels, specify, for example, how regulations may be promulgated and cases adjudicated.

This unit has three chapters. Chapter 14 discusses regulations, the product of agency rulemaking. Chapter 15 discusses agency decisions, the product of case adjudication. Chapter 16 discusses what we call "mini-libraries," sources that present multiple authorities in one package. Because they are especially useful in areas governed by agencies, due to the multiplicity of legal authorities, mini-libraries are discussed in this unit.

This unit explores a new issue in the Canoga case. Recall that Ms. Canoga's concern over the no-smoking policy was shared to some extent by her co-workers. See the Canoga case on pages 3–4. Hence, she might claim that the orchestra violated her right to act in concert with her co-workers. A federal statute, the National Labor Relations Act (NLRA), safeguards this right and enables the operations of a major federal agency, the National Labor Relations Board (Board). The Board's better-known task is to protect the rights of employees to form unions and bargain with employers, but it also protects employees who engage in concerted activity, even though there is no union on the scene. The Board has the authority to promulgate rules (which it has chosen to do only rarely) and prosecute and decide cases involving violations of the NLRA, called "unfair labor practices."

This unit focuses throughout on federal law. There are analogous authorities, sources, and research methods at the state level.

Two notes about terminology: To clearly distinguish various types of legal authority, this unit uses "regulation" to refer to the product of agency rulemaking; "rule" is a synonym of "regulation." And this unit uses "decision" to refer to the product of case adjudication by an agency; "case" is a synonym of "decision."

REGULATIONS

A.   WHAT IS A REGULATION?

1.   How Is a Regulation Created?

Federal and state agencies promulgate various types of regulations. Legislative, or substantive, regulations are based on a specific statutory delegation of power from the legislature. The statute typically sets forth, in general terms, what conduct is to be regulated and what penalties may be assessed; the legislature delegates authority to the agency to provide the specific regulatory scheme, consistent with the statute. Nonlegislative regulations include interpretative and procedural regulations, as well as policy statements. Interpretative regulations have substantially less force than legislative regulations; they are an agency's statement of its interpretation of its enabling statute. Procedural regulations address how the agency operates.

In general, when an agency promulgates a legislative regulation, it functions as a quasi-legislative body. The agency may act because its enabling statute compels it to act, because the public pressures or petitions it to do so, or because its own studies have identified an area of concern. To create the regulation, the agency may follow one of several processes, as specified in the administrative procedure act or enabling statute. The dominant model is notice-and-comment rulemaking, which begins when the agency gives notice to the public of the topic it is about to consider. The public may provide pertinent information to the agency through written submissions or, at the agency's discretion, through written or oral testimony at agency hearings. The agency considers these comments as it develops the final regulation and then issues the regulation with a statement of its basis and purpose. A less common second possibility is formal rulemaking, which entails a trial-type hearing, in which participants may cross-examine witnesses and provide evidence. Furthermore, the agency must issue findings and conclusions to support its regulation. A third possibility is that some agencies engage in hybrid rulemaking processes for particular rules.

By contrast, when an agency promulgates interpretative or procedural regulations or policy statements, it need not engage in such formal processes. The agency may simply issue a final regulation based on its own internal deliberations, although it may provide for public participation, in its discretion.

2.   What Does a Regulation Look Like?

In form, an agency regulation resembles a statute. See Illustration 14-1 on page 261. A regulation consists of general rules applicable to a range of persons engaging in certain conduct. Regulations use fairly specific terms because they are intended to give precision to vague statutory language and are to be applied to specific situations. Many employ numerical tests or use technical concepts.

Illustration 14-1 is one of the few regulations promulgated by the National Labor Relations Board. It pertains to the Board's exercise of jurisdiction over orchestras.

B.   WHY WOULD YOU RESEARCH WHICH REGULATIONS?

All regulations provide insight into what the law is. Indeed, a legislative regulation constitutes the law so long as the regulation meets constitutional requirements, conforms to all applicable statutes, was properly promulgated, and is not arbitrary or capricious. Somewhat in contrast, an interpretative regulation is a significant statement of the agency's interpretation of the pertinent statute, but it may be disregarded by a court that interprets the statute differently. Generally courts do defer to agencies, in recognition of their expertise. Regulations pertaining to agency procedures are important for obvious reasons: they set out the steps, time lines, and details of how to handle a case involving the agency. As you analyze a client's situation, you either must or should take the regulation into account.

As noted above, agencies exist at various levels of government. Which level of agency governs a particular subject is fixed by statute. Typically, if a

| ILLUSTRATION 14-1 | National Labor Relations Board Regulation, from *Code of Federal Regulations* |

National Labor Relations Board   **§ 103.30**

Las Vegas .... 8:30 a.m.–5 p.m.
29—Brooklyn .... 9 a.m.–5:30 p.m.
30—Milwaukee .... 8 a.m.–4:30 p.m.
31—Los Angeles .... 8:30 a.m.–5 p.m.
32—Oakland .... 8:30 a.m.–5 p.m.
33—Peoria .... 8:30 a.m.–5 p.m.
34—Hartford .... 8:30 a.m.–5 p.m.

[57 FR 4158, Feb. 4, 1992]

PART 103—OTHER RULES

Subpart A—Jurisdictional Standards

Sec.
103.1   Colleges and universities.
103.2   Symphony orchestras.
103.3   Horseracing and dogracing industries.

Subpart B—Election Procedures

103.20   Posting of election notices.

Subpart C—Appropriate Bargaining Units

103.30   Appropriate bargaining units in the health care industry.

Subpart E [Reserved]

Subpart F—Remedial Orders

103.100   Offers of reinstatement to employees in Armed Forces.

AUTHORITY: 29 U.S.C. 156, in accordance with the procedure set forth in 5 U.S.C. 553.

Subpart A—Jurisdictional Standards

§ 103.1   Colleges and universities.

The Board will assert its jurisdiction in any proceeding arising under sections 8, 9, and 10 of the Act involving any private nonprofit college or university which has a gross annual revenue from all sources (excluding only contributions which, because of limitation by the grantor, are not available for use for operating expenses) of not less than $1 million.

[35 FR 18370, Dec. 3, 1970]

§ 103.2   Symphony orchestras.

The Board will assert its jurisdiction in any proceeding arising under sections 8, 9, and 10 of the Act involving any symphony orchestra which has a gross annual revenue from all sources (excluding only contributions which are because of limitation by the grant-

or not available for use for operating expenses) of not less than $1 million.

[38 FR 6177, Mar. 7, 1973]

§ 103.3   Horseracing and dogracing industries.

The Board will not assert its jurisdiction in any proceeding under sections 8, 9, and 10 of the Act involving the horseracing and dogracing industries.

[38 FR 9507, Apr. 17, 1973]

Subpart B—Election Procedures

§ 103.20   Posting of election notices.

(a) Employers shall post copies of the Board's official Notice of Election in conspicuous places at least 3 full working days prior to 12:01 a.m. of the day of the election. In elections involving mail ballots, the election shall be deemed to have commenced the day the ballots are deposited by the Regional Office in the mail. In all cases, the notices shall remain posted until the end of the election.

(b) The term *working day* shall mean an entire 24-hour period excluding Saturdays, Sundays, and holidays.

(c) A party shall be estopped from objecting to nonposting of notices if it is responsible for the nonposting. An employer shall be conclusively deemed to have received copies of the election notice for posting unless it notifies the Regional Office at least 5 working days prior to the commencement of the election that it has not received copies of the election notice.

(d) Failure to post the election notices as required herein shall be grounds for setting aside the election whenever proper and timely objections are filed under the provisions of § 102.69(a).

[52 FR 25215, July 6, 1987]

Subpart C—Appropriate Bargaining Units

§ 103.30   Appropriate bargaining units in the health care industry.

(a) This portion of the rule shall be applicable to acute care hospitals, as defined in paragraph (f) of this section: Except in extraordinary circumstances and in circumstances in which there

111

federal statute governs, a federal agency will be created, and federal regulations will govern too. Similarly, if a state statute governs, you will be concerned with a state agency and its regulations. If more than one statute governs (e.g., federal and state statutes overlap), then more than one regulation may apply.

To locate the correct law, you must identify the regulation in effect as of the time of your client's fact situation. A regulation is presumed to be prospective, applying to events arising after its promulgation, until it is amended or removed. Hence, as you research regulations, you must attend to their currency.

As for the Canoga case, the statute on concerted activity is a federal statute, so the regulations of interest are federal regulations. Section 103.2 in Illustration 14-1 on page 261 was promulgated in 1973 and is still in force. (Incidentally, some states have so-called "baby NLRA" statutes paralleling the federal statute. New Mexico does not have a private-sector labor statute; it does have a public-sector labor statute.)

C.   HOW DO YOU RESEARCH REGULATIONS?

Regulations appear in two different forms over time. They also appear in multiple media.

A recently promulgated regulation first appears in a daily publication containing the written record of many activities of various agencies. There are various names for this type of publication; a common name, and the name used for the federal version, is "register." Registers are analogous to legislative session laws, in that they are organized chronologically, not topically, and contain recently promulgated regulations, rather than all regulations currently in effect. Registers also differ from session laws, in that they contain proposed regulations and other materials.

Sometime after promulgation, regulations are codified, that is, inserted into the jurisdiction's code of regulations. A regulatory code is a topically organized set of regulations currently in force. If a new regulation alters an existing regulation, the new one displaces the old one in the code. If the new regulation covers new ground, it is inserted near other regulations on the same broad subject. Regulatory codes are analogous to statutory codes, in that they are organized topically and contain all regulations currently in effect.

Indeed, the organization of some regulatory codes parallels, to a greater or lesser extent, the organization of the jurisdiction's statutory code. This is natural, because agencies derive their authority to create regulations from their enabling statutes. The organization of most regulatory codes is reflected in a scheme of numbered titles, chapters, parts, and sections.

Most jurisdictions have one regulatory code, which is published by the government. Regulatory codes typically do not contain significant annotation material; rather their purpose is to present the regulations themselves.

Table T.1 of *The Bluebook* lists the paper sources of regulations for United States jurisdictions, including registers and codes.

With the development of computers and related information technology, researchers now have additional options. Some regulations are available through the Internet, directly from the government and in other public web sites. Westlaw and LEXIS offer a wide range of federal regulations and some state regulatory materials. Finally, regulations also appear in CD-ROM products, which typically package together various primary authorities from a particular jurisdiction or for a particular major practice area.

Often you will begin your research with a reference to a pertinent regulation from some other source: a secondary source perhaps, or a pertinent case, or most likely an annotated version of the statute enabling the agency to promulgate the regulation. Generally you should not only locate and read the cited regulation, but also conduct additional research into regulations to verify that you have located all pertinent material. Furthermore, your regulations research is not complete unless you fully understand the enabling statute and the courts' response (if any) to the regulation.

Hence the following discussion opens and closes with brief discussions of statutory research and case law research, respectively, in the context of agency regulations. In between, it discusses four ways to research regulations themselves. The first two involve paper sources: codes and registers. The last two are computer-based: the Internet and LEXIS or Westlaw. Exhibit 14.1 below provides an overview of regulations research practices.

This chapter does not discuss CD-ROM research. Rather, CD-ROMs are covered in Chapter 16, which discusses various types of "mini-libraries."

EXHIBIT 14.1   Overview of Regulations Research

Preliminary step: statutory research in annotated codes		
Regulations research: regulatory code → administrative register		
paper sources	public Internet sources	LEXIS or Westlaw
Concluding step: case law research • reporters and digests • online and CD-ROM alternatives to reporters and digests • case citators • annotated codes in various media • Shepard's or KeyCite for regulations		

Preliminary regulations research in annotated codes:

● read the enabling statute for the legal standard and the agency's authority to promulgate regulations
● seek references to the regulatory code

Because an agency is created by statute and its actions must conform to that statute, an important step in regulations research is locating and reading the enabling statute. Chapter 12 covers statutory research.

More specifically, as you read the statute, look for the legal standard that the legislature has set for the conduct you are concerned with, as well as indications of the agency's power to promulgate regulations. Furthermore, you should look in the annotation for references to relevant regulations. See Illustration 14-2 on pages 265–267.

Researching the Canoga case, we learned that the enabling statute states that the Board's jurisdiction extends to "employers" whose businesses "affect commerce." These terms are defined broadly, and no exclusions apply on these facts. *See* 29 U.S.C. § 152(2), (6), (7) (1994). Congress gave the Board the authority to decline to assert jurisdiction over categories of employers where the impact on commerce is not sufficient to warrant federal involvement, *id.* § 164(c)(1), as well as the general authority to issue regulations, *id.* § 156. The annotation in *United States Code Service* for § 164, shown in Illustration 14-2 on pages 266–267, includes general references to 29 C.F.R. parts 101 and 102 as well as a specific reference to § 103.2 of title 29; the references are to the *Code of Federal Regulations*, described below. (The parallel annotation in *United States Code Annotated* gives a general reference to parts 101 and 102 of title 29 of C.F.R.)

Regulations in paper regulatory code *(Code of Federal Regulations):*

▶ identify the regulation via the index, outline of the code, or parallel table of statutes and regulations
▶ read the regulation
▶ note information about the promulgation of the regulation

The federal government, most states, and some larger cities and counties publish codes containing their agency regulations. The *Code of Federal Regulations* (C.F.R.) is a codification of the permanent rules adopted by federal administrative agencies. C.F.R. is published by the United States Government Printing Office and is the official compilation of current federal regulations. Indeed, it is the only such compilation in paper, so it is a major research tool.

ILLUSTRATION 14-2 Statute re National Labor Relations Board Jurisdiction and Annotation, from *United States Code Service*

---

29 USCS § 163, n 16   LABOR

which protects against interferring with, impeding or diminishing in any way right to strike. Quaker State Oil Refining Corp. v NLRB (1959, CA3) 270 F2d 40, 44 BNA LRRM 2297, 37 CCH LC ¶ 65535, cert den (1959) 361 US 917, 4 L Ed 2d 185, 80 S Ct 261, 45 BNA LRRM 2249.

17. Miscellaneous

Strike, in which employees distribute handbills defaming quality of employer's product as concerted activity, is not protected by 29 USCS § 163. NLRB v International Brotherhood of Electrical Workers (1953) 346 US 464, 98 L Ed 195, 74 S Ct 172, 33 BNA LRRM 2183, 24 CCH LC ¶ 68000.

Union is clearly outside its legitimate function when it demands employer discharge foreman for reason that he or she is "crabby" or too-strict disciplinarian, so that strike called following employer's refusal to discharge foreman is illegal. NLRB v Aladdin Industries, Inc. (1942, CA7) 125

F2d 377, 9 BNA LRRM 548, 5 CCH LC ¶ 60879, cert den (1942) 316 US 706, 86 L Ed 1773, 62 S Ct 1310, 10 BNA LRRM 939.

Wildcat strike in which discharged employees were engaged and for which they were discharged is not such concerted action as falls within protection of 29 USCS § 157. NLRB v Draper Corp. (1944, CA4) 145 F2d 199, 15 BNA LRRM 580, 8 CCH LC ¶ 62368, 156 ALR 989.

Where employer is given notice by two unions that each of them represents his employees, and one union calls strike without offering proof of its majority representation or giving employer opportunity to request such proof or to talk to union's officials, strike is illegal; thus, company is within its rights in discharging strikers, and they are not entitled to reinstatement. Ohio Ferro-Alloys Corp. v NLRB (1954, CA6) 213 F2d 646, 34 BNA LRRM 2327, 26 CCH LC ¶ 68496.

§ 164. Supervisory employees' rights to organize—Membership as condition of employment—Local law applicable—Declination of jurisdiction by board

(a) Supervisors as union members. Nothing herein shall prohibit any individual employed as a supervisor from becoming or remaining a member of a labor organization, but no employer subject to this Act [29 USCS §§ 151–158, 159–169] shall be compelled to deem individuals defined herein as supervisors as employees for the purpose of any law, either national or local, relating to collective bargaining.

(b) Agreements requiring union membership in violation of State law. Nothing in this Act [29 USCS §§ 151–158, 159–169] shall be construed as authorizing the execution or application of agreements requiring membership in a labor organization as a condition of employment in any State or Territory in which such execution or application is prohibited by State or Territorial law.

(c) Power of Board to decline jurisdiction of labor disputes; assertion of jurisdiction by State and Territorial courts. (1) The Board, in its discretion, may, by rule of decision or by published rules adopted pursuant to the Administrative Procedure Act, decline to assert jurisdiction over any labor dispute involving any class or category of employers, where, in the opinion of the Board, the effect of such labor dispute on commerce is not sufficiently substantial to warrant the exercise of its jurisdiction: Provided, That the Board shall not decline to assert jurisdiction over any labor dispute over which it would assert jurisdiction under the standards prevailing upon August 1, 1959.

(2) Nothing in this Act [29 USCS §§ 151–158, 159–169] shall be deemed to prevent or bar any agency or the courts of any State or Territory (including the Commonwealth of Puerto Rico, Guam, and the Virgin Islands), from assuming and asserting jurisdiction over labor disputes over

30

ILLUSTRATION 14-2   *(continued)*

LABOR-MANAGEMENT RELATIONS   **29 USCS § 164**

which the Board declines, pursuant to paragraph (1) of this subsection, to assert jurisdiction.

(July 5, 1935, ch 372, § 14, 49 Stat. 457; June 23, 1947, ch 120, Title I, § 101 in part, 61 Stat. 151; Sept. 14, 1959, P. L. 86-257, Title VII, § 701(a), 73 Stat. 541.)

HISTORY; ANCILLARY LAWS AND DIRECTIVES

References in text:

"The Administrative Procedure Act," referred to in subsec. (c)(1), is Act June 11, 1946, ch 324, 60 Stat. 237, which was repealed by Act Sept. 6, 1966, P. L. 89-554, § 8, 80 Stat. 653, which re-enacted similar provisions as 5 USCS §§ 551–559, 701–706, 1305, 3105, 3344, 5362, and 7521.

Amendments:

1947. Act June 23, 1947 (effective 60 days after enactment, as provided by § 104 of such Act, which appears as 29 USCS § 151 note), amended this section generally. The section formerly related to resolution of conflicts of this Act with other laws; see 29 USCS § 165.

1959. Act Sept. 14, 1959, added subsec. (c).

CODE OF FEDERAL REGULATIONS

National Labor Relations Board–Statements of procedures, 29 CFR Part 101.
National Labor Relations Board–Rules and regulations, Series 8, 29 CFR Part 102.

CROSS REFERENCES

This section is referred to in 18 USCS § 1951.

RESEARCH GUIDE

Federal Procedure L Ed:

22 Fed Proc L Ed, Labor and Labor Relations §§ 52:878, 903, 904, 911, 934, 938.

Am Jur:

48 Am Jur 2d, Labor and Labor Relations §§ 13, 15, 16, 20, 164, 183, 271, 359, 432, 546, 628, 629, 631, 639, 649, 685, 970, 1190.

48A Am Jur 2d, Labor and Labor Relations §§ 1729, 1730, 1797, 2004, 2014.

Am Jur Proof of Facts:

Union's Breach of Duty of Fair Representation, 15 POF2d 65.

Forms:

12 Fed Procedural Forms L Ed, Labor and Labor Relations § 46:677.

WGL Coordinators:

10 Employment Coord, Coverage ¶¶ LR-10,702; 11,901.1; 11,904; 11,907.

11 Employment Coord, Prohibited Labor Practices ¶¶ LR-21,402; 22,505; 26,055; 26,677.

12 Employment Coord, Prohibited Labor Practices ¶ LR-35,005.

31

ILLUSTRATION 14-2   *(continued; pages omitted)*

29 USCS § 164, n 94   LABOR

outside state and also purchased materials in excess of that amount, despite employer's denial of substantially identical commerce allegations in complaint without asserted reason, where, having stipulated to jurisdiction, employer is estopped from denying it in absence of valid ground. Capitan Drilling Co. (1967) 167 NLRB 144, 66 BNA LRRM 1015, 1967 CCH NLRB ¶ 21706, enforced (1969, CA5) 408 F2d 676, 70 BNA LRRM 3258, 59 CCH LC ¶ 13360.

95. Orchestras

NLRB's retail jurisdictional standard applies to orchestras performing "club dates," defined as single engagements, such as at wedding, commencement, bar mitzvah, debutante party, fashion show, or other social event; however, bands selling music to commercial enterprises are governed by the prevailing nonretail standard. Levitt (1968) 171 NLRB 739, 68 BNA LRRM 1161, 1968-1 CCH NLRB ¶ 22512.

NLRB will assert jurisdiction over symphony orchestras having gross annual revenue from all sources of not less than $1 million, excluding only contributions unavailable for use for operating expenses because of limitation by grantor. 29 CFR § 103. 2.

96. Pharmacies

Pharmacy is retail enterprise governed by monetary requirements of NLRB's retail standard. Booker Family Medical Care Center (1975) 219 NLRB 220, 89 BNA LRRM 1702, 1974-75 CCH NLRB ¶ 16041.

97. Private clubs

NLRB has jurisdiction over nonprofit corporation operating private athletic club of 2,300 members, which, in addition to health and recreation facilities, also operates restaurant and furnishes hotel-type accommodations, where during prior fiscal year club derived over $500,000 from sale of food and beverages and made direct and indirect purchases of goods in interstate commerce exceeding $50,000. Denver Athletic Club (1967) 164 NLRB 677, 65 BNA LRRM 1136, 1967 CCH NLRB ¶ 21356.

NLRB will not assert jurisdiction over employer-membership corporation, operating nonprofit singing and eating club, where employer is basically retail enterprise with annual gross income of business, not including membership dues, of less than NLRB's discretionary standard of $500,000 for assertion of jurisdiction over retail enterprise. Syracuse Liederkranz, Inc. (1967) 166 NLRB 782, 65 BNA LRRM 1645, 1967 CCH NLRB ¶ 21651.

In determining NLRB's discretionary standard for retail businesses, membership dues will not be included in calculating volume of business of membership corporation, operating nonprofit singing and eating club. Syracuse Liederkranz, Inc. (1967) 166 NLRB 782, 65 BNA LRRM 1645, 1967 CCH NLRB ¶ 21651.

98. Public transportation systems

Where interstate commerce is unquestionably involved to extent not inconsequential, question of whether NLRB will require showing by bus company of dollar-amount of interstate traffic as predicate to jurisdiction is matter of Board's policy with which court will not interfere in absence of abuse of Board's discretion. NLRB v Parran (1956, CA4) 237 F2d 373, 38 BNA LRRM 2774, 31 CCH LC ¶ 70266.

Jurisdiction will be asserted over bus company, licensed by state and federal authorities, which supplies exclusive chartered and scheduled passenger transportation to nearby United States Air Force base and serves as interstate link with large bus company and numerous commercial airlines to and from such base, where bus company is not only required to maintain adequate transportation service but also to maintain employment conditions in accordance with Air Force regulations, and where labor dispute disrupting bus service would have serious and adverse impact on national defense, in that base served by bus company is vital link in air service between North American continent and Far East, and bus service is only public mass transportation available. Simmons (1968) 171 NLRB 1469, 69 BNA LRRM 1064, 1968-1 CCH NLRB ¶ 22588, supp op (1969) 179 NLRB 641, 72 BNA LRRM 1425, 1969 CCH NLRB ¶ 21362.

NLRB would assert jurisdiction over surface transportation company having tour business and operating buses in Honolulu, where company met standard for public utility or transit system, and for nonretail enterprises. Transportation Associates of Hawaii, Ltd. (1975) 216 NLRB 357, 88 BNA LRRM 1216, 1974-75 CCH NLRB ¶ 15452.

Privately-owned toll bridge connecting mainland to island met Board's discretionary standards for jurisdiction as transit system. Margate Bridge Co. (1980) 247 NLRB 1437, 103 BNA LRRM 1335, 1980 CCH NLRB ¶ 16787.

Privately-owned toll bridge connecting mainland to island met Board's discretionary standards for jurisdiction as transit system. Margate Bridge Co. (1980) 247 NLRB 1437, 103 BNA LRRM 1335, 1980 cch NLRB ¶ 16787.

99. Public utilities

NLRB does not abuse its discretion in asserting jurisdiction over public utility by retroactively applying $250,000 "volume of business" jurisdictional standard, where, at time alleged unfair labor practice occurred, jurisdictional standard was $3,000,000 annual gross volume of business, which

C.F.R. is a large, multivolume set, published in paper pamphlets. It is organized topically, and the organization roughly parallels the organization of the federal statutory code, *United States Code*. For example, labor statutes are covered in title 29 of U.S.C., and labor regulations in title 29 of C.F.R. C.F.R. is divided into titles and from there into subtitles, chapters, subchapters, parts, and sections.

Unlike U.S.C., an entire updated set of C.F.R. is published annually: titles 1-16 by January 1, titles 17-27 by April 1, titles 28-41 by July 1, and titles 42-50 by October 1. Because there is a new color each year, you can readily see the updating pattern. C.F.R. does not itself have updating pocket parts or pamphlets.

If you do not already have a reference, you most likely will use *CFR Index and Finding Aids,* a separate volume accompanying C.F.R., to locate a pertinent regulation within C.F.R. Your goal is to find the most specific part or section possible. *CFR Index* affords three options.

First, you may look up your research terms in the subject index. Often the name of your agency is a useful research term.

Second, you may skim the List of CFR Titles, Chapters, Subchapters, and Parts, which outlines C.F.R. See Illustration 14-3 on page 270. If you have a statutory cite, you may take advantage of the strong parallel between the organization of the federal statutory code and C.F.R.

Third, you may use the Parallel Table of Authorities and Rules. There you can look up the title and section of the enabling statute, pursuant to which the agency acted in promulgating the regulations. You will find a reference to the corresponding regulations. See Illustration 14-4 on page 271.

Depending on the particular research project, one of these methods may be more effective than the others, so you should be flexible in your approach. In general, you will be able to discern a pertinent C.F.R. title and part, but probably not a specific section, through these methods.

Once you have identified a potentially pertinent part, you should, of course, examine that material carefully. Examine the table of contents encompassing your part. Because a regulation, like a statute, may consist of several or many interlocking sections, you should examine all sections within the pertinent part or chapter you have located. Be sure to look for definition provisions, which may apply to a whole chapter. Once you have discerned the full range of specific sections pertinent to your client's situation and read them, you should take note of the administrative history material in small print at the end of the outline for a part or the specific section. The small print includes the regulation's date of final promulgation and the *Federal Register* citation, which can be used to research the administrative history of your regulation. The small print also includes the statutory authority for the regulation. See Illustration 14-1 on page 261.

Finally, ascertain how current your research is. The first pages of each C.F.R. volume indicate the dates of coverage for the regulations contained within it. You will need to update your research from that date forward in sources described below.

Researching the Canoga case, we knew from our research in secondary sources and the federal annotated statutory codes that the pertinent regulation was § 103.2 of title 29. Had we not had such a specific reference, we would have looked under title 29 in the List of CFR Titles and found Subtitle B—Regulations Relating to Labor, Chapter 1—National Labor Relations Board, Part 103—Other Rules. See Illustration 14-3 on page 270. Or we could have checked the Parallel Table of Authorities and Rules, as shown in Illustration 14-4 on page 271. Section 103.2 is presented in Illustration 14-1 on page 261.

According to that regulation, the orchestra must have gross annual revenues (excluding certain grants) of at least $1 million for the Board to address Ms. Canoga's case. As indicated at the end of § 103.2, it was promulgated on March 7, 1973, and it appears in final form in volume 38 of the *Federal Register* at page 6177. The C.F.R. volume we used in the fall of 1999 was current through July 1, 1999.

Regulations in paper administrative registers (*Federal Register*):

▶ look up the regulation in *List of CFR Sections Affected*

▶ look up the regulation in *Federal Register* Reader Aids

▶ or consult a *Federal Register* subject index for new regulations

▶ read the regulation

▶ read the explanatory material

The *Federal Register* is a virtually daily publication covering the activities of federal agencies. It focuses on proposed and adopted regulations. The *Federal Register* serves three purposes. First, as noted above, C.F.R. is generally within a few months to about a year of being current. New regulations are proposed and promulgated daily, so you must update your research beyond C.F.R.; this is done in the *Federal Register*. The new material may amend an earlier regulation or address a previously unregulated area. Second, a regulation that has been removed will no longer appear in C.F.R.; you can find it in the *Federal Register* issued on its date of promulgation. Third, if your regulation is not clear as you apply it to your facts, you may want to learn about the agency's thinking behind the regulation. This information appears in the *Federal Register*. See Illustration 14-5 on page 273.

The *Federal Register* is voluminous; a daily issue in paper may contain more than one hundred pages. Although the material within each issue of the *Federal Register* is arranged alphabetically by agency and there are indexes and tables, it would be very burdensome to look through all of the daily issues published since the C.F.R. volume you are using was published. Two finding tools assist you in finding any recent changes to your federal rule: (1) *List of CFR Sections Affected* (L.S.A.), which is a separate set of softcover pamphlets typically shelved at the end of the C.F.R. set, and (2) the Reader Aids material printed within the *Federal Register*.

ILLUSTRATION 14-3   List of CFR Titles, Chapters, Subchapters, and Parts, from *CFR Index*

List of CFR Titles, Chapters, Subchapters, and Parts

TITLE 29—LABOR—Continued

70	Production or disclosure of information or materials.
71	Protection of individual privacy and access to records under the Privacy Act of 1974.
75	Department of Labor review and certification procedures for rural industrialization loan and grant programs under the Consolidated Farm and Rural Development Act of 1972.
90	Certification of eligibility to apply for worker adjustment assistance.
93	New restrictions on lobbying.
95	Grants and agreements with institutions of higher education, hospitals, and other non-profit organizations, and with commercial organizations, foreign governments, organizations under the jurisdiction of foreign governments, and international organizations.
96	Audit requirements for grants, contracts and other agreements.
97	Uniform administrative requirements for grants and cooperative agreements to State and local governments.
98	Governmentwide debarment and suspension (nonprocurement) and governmentwide requirements for drug-free workplace (grants).

Subtitle B—Regulations Relating to Labor

Chapter I—National Labor Relations Board (Parts 100—199)

100	Administrative regulations.
101	Statements of procedures.
102	Rules and regulations, Series 8.
103	Other rules.

Chapter II—Office of Labor-Management Standards, Department of Labor (Parts 200—299)

215	Guidelines, section 5333(b), Federal Transit Law.
220	Airline employee protection program.

Chapter III—National Railroad Adjustment Board (Parts 300—399)

301	Rules of procedure.

Chapter IV—Office of Labor-Management Standards, Department of Labor (Parts 400—499)

SUBCHAPTER A—LABOR-MANAGEMENT STANDARDS

401	Meaning of terms used in this subchapter.
402	Labor organization information reports.
403	Labor organization annual financial reports.
404	Labor organization officer and employee report.
405	Employer reports.
406	Reporting by labor relations consultants and other persons, certain agreements with employers.
408	Labor organization trusteeship reports.
409	Reports by surety companies.
417	Procedure for removal of local labor organization officers.
451	Labor organizations as defined in the Labor-Management Reporting and Disclosure Act of 1959.
452	General statement concerning the election provisions of the Labor-Management Reporting and Disclosure Act of 1959.
453	General statement concerning the bonding requirements of the Labor-Management Reporting and Disclosure Act of 1959.

SUBCHAPTER B—STANDARDS OF CONDUCT

457	General.
458	Standards of conduct.
459	Miscellaneous.

SUBCHAPTER C—EXECUTIVE ORDER 12800, NOTIFICATION OF EMPLOYEE RIGHTS CONCERNING PAYMENT OF UNION DUES OR FEES

Chapter V—Wage and Hour Division, Department of Labor (Parts 500—899)

SUBCHAPTER A—REGULATIONS

500	Migrant and seasonal agricultural worker protection.

903

ILLUSTRATION 14-4 CFR Parallel Table of Authorities and Rules, from *CFR Index*

Authorities

28 U.S.C.—Continued	CFR
	28 Part 543
	32 Part 536
	38 Part 14
	39 Part 912
	43 Part 22
2671—2672	32 Part 842
2672	5 Part 177
	10 Parts 14, 1014
	13 Part 114
	14 Part 15
	15 Part 2
	20 Part 429
	22 Parts 304, 604
	24 Part 17
	28 Part 14
	29 Parts 15, 100
	31 Part 3
	32 Part 1280
	33 Part 25
	34 Part 35
	45 Part 35
	46 Part 204
	49 Part 1
2674—2680	32 Part 842
2675	14 Part 15
2679	10 Part 14
	28 Part 15

29 U.S.C.

	CFR
9a	29 Part 580
37	45 Parts 95, 204
41a—41b	29 Part 1924
49 et seq	20 Parts 621, 651, 652—656, 658
	29 Parts 42, 507, 508
49k	20 Parts 601, 652, 654
	29 Part 31
49l–2	29 Part 44
50	29 Parts 29, 30
141	5 Part 7101
	29 Part 100
151	29 Parts 101—103
156	5 Part 7101
	29 Parts 100—103
158	29 Part 1420
171	29 Part 1420
172—173	29 Parts 1402—1403
172	29 Part 1401, 1404
173—174	29 Part 1420
173 et seq	29 Part 1404
175a	29 Parts 1470, 1471
183	29 Part 1420
201 et seq	29 Parts 42, 510, 516, 536, 548, 775, 782, 790, 1620, 1621
201—219	29 Parts 525, 553, 570, 776, 778—780, 783—786, 788, 789, 791, 793, 794
203	29 Parts 531, 579, 580
204	5 Part 551
204f	5 Part 551
205—206	29 Parts 511, 616, 617, 619, 697, 699, 700, 701, 720, 721, 723—730
206	29 Parts 552, 1614
207	29 Parts 536, 547—550
208	29 Parts 511,

29 U.S.C.—Continued	CFR
	616, 617, 619, 697, 699, 700, 701, 720, 721, 723—730
211—212	29 Parts 575, 579, 580
211	29 Parts 515, 516, 519, 525, 530, 1627
213	29 Parts 536, 541, 551, 552
214	29 Parts 519, 520, 528
216	29 Parts 578—580
218	29 Part 575
251 et seq	29 Part 775
259	29 Parts 1, 5
402	29 Parts 401, 451
431	29 Parts 402, 403, 408
432	29 Part 404
433	29 Parts 405, 406
437—438	29 Part 406
437	29 Parts 402—405, 408, 409
438	29 Parts 401—405, 408, 409, 451
441	29 Part 409
461	29 Parts 401, 403, 408
481—482	29 Parts 401, 417, 452
481	29 Part 451
502	29 Part 453
504	28 Part 4
526	28 Part 4
551	29 Part 98
557a	30 Parts 56, 57
577a	30 Parts 1, 40—44, 50, 70, 77, 100
	42 Part 84
621	29 Part 1625
626	29 Part 1627
628	29 Part 1626
631	29 Parts 1625, 1627
633a	29 Part 1614
651 et seq	29 Part 42
	42 Part 84
651—653	29 Part 1975
651	34 Part 75
653	29 Parts 1910—1912, 1915, 1917—1919, 1926, 1928, 1975, 1990
655—657	29 Part 1912
655	29 Parts 1905, 1910, 1911, 1915, 1917—1920, 1926, 1928, 1990
	40 Part 311
655 note	29 Part 1910
656—657	29 Part 1912a
656	29 Part 1908
657—658	29 Part 1903
657	29 Parts 1902, 1904—1905, 1909—1913, 1915, 1917—1919, 1926, 1928, 1975, 1977, 1978, 1990
	30 Part 11
	42 Parts 84—87
660	29 Parts 1977, 1978
661	29 Parts 2200—2203
665	29 Part 1905
667	29 Parts 1902, 1952—1956
668	29 Part 1960
670	29 Parts 1908, 1949
	42 Part 86
673	29 Parts 1904, 1960

L.S.A. lists regulations that have been affected by recent regulatory activity reported in the *Federal Register*. The nature of the "affect" varies; a regulation may have been added, amended, corrected, or removed. See Illustration 14-6 on page 275. L.S.A. is published monthly, with later issues cumulating the material from earlier issues. Recall that C.F.R. is republished on a rolling basis; hence the time periods covered in an L.S.A. issue vary by C.F.R. title. The titles and dates covered are listed on the first page of each paper pamphlet.

The entries in L.S.A. are arranged by title and section number. If your regulation has an entry, it will include the action taken and a reference to page number(s) in the *Federal Register*. You may use the Table of Federal Register Issue Pages and Dates within L.S.A. to learn which daily issues of the *Federal Register* contain the pages you need.

You must further update your research using the Reader Aids material within the *Federal Register* itself. One table is organized by C.F.R. titles and parts, and it lists page numbers where corresponding material appears in the *Federal Register*. See Illustration 14-7 on page 276. The Reader Aids material appears near the end of each issue of the daily *Federal Register*, and it is cumulative, but only for material printed during that month. Hence, you may need to examine several issues of the *Federal Register* to bring your research current to date.

If you are not updating a regulation in C.F.R., but rather looking for new regulations on your topic, you still may want to use the tables described above. Rather than looking for entries related to a specific known regulation, you would look for activity listed under the title or part pertaining to your agency. Another option is to consult the subject index to the *Federal Register*, which is organized by agency and then by topic.

The final step, of course, is to read the material you have identified in the *Federal Register*. There you will find whatever changes have been made, along with explanations of them. The explanatory material typically provides a summary; states the regulation's effective date and people to contact within the agency about the regulation; and discusses the legal background of the regulation, including its enabling statute, the material received during the rulemaking process, and any evolution in the language of the regulation. This information can be invaluable in helping you to understand the regulation.

Researching the Canoga case in the fall of 1999, we found that the most recent C.F.R. volume for § 103.2 of title 29 was current through July 1, 1999. Illustration 14-6 on page 275, from a later issue of L.S.A., indicates that various regulations in title 29 underwent change, in 1999; however, there was no activity involving § 103.2. We then checked the Reader Aids material in the *Federal Register*. As you can see from Illustration 14-7 on page 276, it has no entries for part 103 of title 29.

Should we wish to know more about § 103.2, we would read about it in the 1973 *Federal Register*. See Illustration 14-5 on pages 273–274. The first page is the background and explanatory material; the regulation itself appears on the second page. (Both pages have been reproduced from microfilm.)

ILLUSTRATION 14-5   Final Rule, from *Federal Register*

6176

RULES AND REGULATIONS

written statements of exceptions and allegations as to applicable fact and law. Upon request of any party made within such 20-day period, a reasonable extension of time for filing such briefs or statements may be granted and upon a showing of good cause such period may be extended, as appropriate.

(b) *By a court.* Where a case has been remanded by a court, the Board may proceed in accordance with the court's mandate to issue a decision or it may in turn remand the case to a deputy commissioner or judge with instructions to take such action as is ordered by the court and any additional necessary action and upon completion thereof to return the case with a recommended decision to the Board for its action.

§ 802.406   Finality of Board decisions.

A decision rendered by the Board pursuant to this subpart shall become final 60 days after the issuance of such decision unless an appeal pursuant to section 21(c) of the LHWCA is filed prior to the expiration of the 60-day period herein described, or unless a timely request for reconsideration by the Board has been filed as provided in § 802.407.

RECONSIDERATION

§ 802.407   Reconsideration of Board decisions—generally.

(a) Any party in interest may, within no more than 10 days from the filing of a decision pursuant to § 802.403(b) request a reconsideration of such decision.

(b) Failure to file a request for reconsideration shall not be deemed a failure to exhaust administrative remedies.

§ 802.408   Notice of request for reconsideration.

(a) In the event that a party in interest requests reconsideration of a final decision and order, he shall do so in writing, stating the supporting rationale for the request and include any material pertinent to the request.

(b) The request shall be sent or delivered in person to the Clerk of the Board, and copies shall be served upon the parties.

§ 802.409   Grant or denial of request.

All requests for reconsideration shall be reviewed by the Board and shall be granted or denied in the discretion of the Board.

JUDICIAL REVIEW

§ 802.410   Judicial review of Board decisions.

Within 60 days after a decision by the Board has been filed pursuant to § 802.403(b), any party adversely affected or aggrieved by such decision may take an appeal to the U.S. Court of Appeals pursuant to section 21(c) of the LHWCA.

§ 802.411   Certification of record for judicial review.

The record of a case including the record of proceedings before the Board shall be transmitted to the appropriate

court pursuant to the rules of such court.

Signed at Washington, D.C., this 1st day of March 1973.

PETER J. BRENNAN,
Secretary of Labor.

[FR Doc.73-4262 Filed 3-6-73;8:45 am]

Title 29—Labor

CHAPTER I—NATIONAL LABOR RELATIONS BOARD

PART 103—OTHER RULES

Jurisdictional Standards Applicable to Symphony Orchestras

By virtue of the authority vested in it by the National Labor Relations Act, approved July 5, 1935,[1] the National Labor Relations Board hereby issues the following rule which it finds necessary to carry out the provisions of said Act.

This rule is issued following proceedings conforming to the requirements of 5 U.S.C. 553 in which notice was given that any rule adopted would be immediately applicable. On August 19, 1972, the Board published notice of proposed rule making requesting responses from interested parties with respect to the assertion of jurisdiction over symphony orchestras and the establishment of jurisdictional standards therefor. The Board having considered the responses and its discretion under sections 9 and 10 of the Act has decided to adopt a rule asserting jurisdiction over any symphony orchestra having a gross annual revenue of not less than $1 million. The National Labor Relations Board finds for good cause that this rule shall be effective on March 7, 1973, and shall apply to all proceedings affected thereby which are pending at the time of such publication or which may arise thereafter.

Dated at Washington, D.C., March 2, 1973.

By direction of the Board.

[SEAL]   JOHN C. TRUESDALE,
Executive Secretary.

On August 19, 1972, the Board published in the FEDERAL REGISTER, a notice of proposed rule making which invited interested parties to submit to it (1) data relevant to defining the extent to which symphony orchestras are in commerce, as defined in section 2(6) of the National Labor Relations Act, and to assessing the effect upon commerce of a labor dispute in those enterprises, (2) statements of views or arguments as to the desirability of the Board exercising jurisdiction, and (3) data and views concerning the appropriate jurisdictional standards which should be established in the event the Board decides to promulgate a rule exercising jurisdiction over those enterprises. The Board received 26 responses to the notice. After careful

---

[1] 49 Stat. 449; 29 U.S.C. 151–166, as amended by act of June 23, 1947 (61 Stat. 136; 29 U.S.C. Supp. 151–167), act of Oct. 22, 1951 (65 Stat. 601; 29 U.S.C. 158, 159, 168), and act of Sept. 14, 1959 (73 Stat. 519; 29 U.S.C. 141–168).

consideration of all the responses, the Board has concluded that it will best effectuate the purposes of the Act to assert jurisdiction over symphony orchestras and apply a $1 million annual gross revenue standard, in addition to statutory jurisdiction. A rule establishing that standard has been issued concurrently with the publication of this notice.

It is well settled that the National Labor Relations Act gives to the Board a jurisdictional authority coextensive with the full reach of the commerce clause.[1] It is equally well settled that the Board in its discretion may set boundaries on the exercise of that authority.[2] In exercising that discretion, the Board has consistently taken the position that it would better effectuate the purposes of the Act, and promote the prompt handling of major cases, not to exercise its jurisdiction to the fullest extent possible under the authority delegated to it by Congress, but to limit that exercise to enterprises whose operations have, or at which labor disputes would have, a pronounced impact upon the flow of interstate commerce.[3] The standard announced above, in our opinion, accommodates this position.

The Board, in arriving at a $1 million gross figure,[4] has considered, inter alia, the impact of symphony orchestras on commerce and the aspects of orchestra operations as criteria for the exercise of jurisdiction. Symphony orchestras in the United States are classified in four categories: college, community, metropolitan, and major.[5] Community orchestras constitute the largest group with over 1,000 in number and, for the most part, are composed of amateur players. The metropolitan orchestras are almost exclusively professional and it is estimated that there are between 75 and 80 orchestras classified as metropolitan. The annual budget for this category ranges approximately from $250,000 to $1 million. The major orchestras are the largest and usually the oldest established musical organizations. All of them are completely professional, and a substantial number

---

[1] See N.L.R.B. v. Fainblatt, 306 U.S. 601.

[2] Office Employees International Union, Local No. 11 [Oregon Teamsters] v. N.L.R.B., 353 U.S. 313; sec. 14(c)(1) of the Act.

[3] Siemons Mailing Service, 122 NLRB 81; Hollow Tree Lumber Company, 91 NLRB 635, 635. See also, e.g., Floridan Hotel of Tampa, Inc., 124 NLRB 261, 264; Butte Medical Properties, d.b.a. Medical Center Hospital, 168 NLRB 266, 268.

[4] As reflected in the rule, this figure includes revenues from all sources, excepting only contributions which, because of limitations placed thereon by the grantor, are not available for operating expenses. These contributions encompassing, for example, contributions to an endowment fund or building fund, are excluded because of their generally nonrecurring nature. (Cf. Magic Mountain, Inc., 123 NLRB 1170.) Income derived from investment of such funds will, however, be counted in determining whether the standard has been satisfied.

[5] The latter three categories are defined by the American Symphony Orchestra League principally on the basis of their annual budgets.

ILLUSTRATION 14-5　　　　*(continued)*

---

operates on a year-round basis. For this category the minimum annual budget is approximately $1 million. Presently, there are approximately 28 major symphony orchestras in the United States. Thus, statistical projections based on data submitted by responding parties, as well as data compiled by the Board, disclose that adoption of such a standard would bring approximately 2 percent of all symphony orchestras, except college, or approximately 28 percent of the professional metropolitan and major orchestras, within reach of the Act. The Board is satisfied that symphony orchestras with gross revenues of $1 million have a substantial impact on commerce and that the figure selected will not result in an unmanageable increase on the Board's workload. The adoption of a $1 million standard, however, does not foreclose the Board from reevaluating and revising that standard should future circumstances deem it appropriate.

In view of the foregoing, the Board is satisfied that the $1 million annual gross revenue standard announced today will result in attaining uniform and effective regulation of labor disputes involving employees in the symphony orchestra industry whose operations have a substantial impact on interstate commerce.

§ 103.2　Symphony Orchestras.

The Board will assert its jurisdiction in any proceeding arising under sections 8, 9, and 10 of the Act involving any symphony orchestra which has a gross annual revenue from all sources (excluding only contributions which are because of limitation by the grantor not available for use for operating expenses) of not less than $1 million.

[FR Doc.73-4374 Filed 3-6-73;8:45 am]

CHAPTER XVII—OCCUPATIONAL SAFETY AND HEALTH ADMINISTRATION, DEPARTMENT OF LABOR

PART 1952—APPROVED STATE PLANS FOR ENFORCEMENT OF STATE STANDARDS

New Jersey Plan; Plan Description; Amendment

In a document issued by this office on January 22, 1973, and published in the FEDERAL REGISTER on January 26, 1973 (37 FR 2426), the New Jersey developmental plan to assume responsibility for the development and enforcement of State occupational safety and health standards in accordance with Part 1902 of Title 29 of the Code of Federal Regulations and section 18 of the Occupational Safety and Health Act of 1970 (29 U.S.C. 667) was approved.

Provisions of that plan require that owners of any structures to be erected and used as places of employment submit plans for approval and comply with specific provisions of special State building codes. However, the decision did not indicate that the pertinent safety and health codes (N.J.A.C. 12:115—Building Code and N.J.A.C. 12:110—Plan Filing) have as their stated and clear purpose

the protection of employees even though the codes may afford some incidental protection to others. Codes that more directly concern other matters such as the protection of the environment and the public at large are properly not incorporated in the plan, and are dealt with elsewhere by the State of New Jersey and its political subdivisions.

The description of the plan in § 1952.140(b) is accordingly amended to indicate these features of the codes involved by adding a new subparagraph (3) to read as follows:

§ 1952.140　Description of the plan.

＊　　＊　　＊　　＊　　＊

(b) ＊ ＊ ＊

(3) Safety and health codes which are established by the State of New Jersey to protect employees and which incidentally protect others are considered occupational safety and health standards for the purposes of this subpart.

＊　　＊　　＊　　＊　　＊

(Sec. 18, Pub. L. 91-596, 84 Stat. 1608 (29 U.S.C. 667))

Signed at Washington, D.C., this 1st day of March 1973.

CHAIN ROBBINS,
Acting Assistant Secretary of Labor.
[FR Doc.73-4355 Filed 3-6-73;8:45 am]

Title 32—National Defense

CHAPTER XVII—OFFICE OF EMERGENCY PREPAREDNESS

PART 1709—REIMBURSEMENT OF OTHER FEDERAL AGENCIES UNDER PUBLIC LAW 91-606.

Eligibility of Certain Expenditures for Reimbursement

1. Section 1709.2 is amended by deleting paragraphs (d), (e), and (f).

Effective date. This amendment shall be effective as of March 1, 1973.

Dated: March 1, 1973.

DARRELL M. TRENT,
Acting Director,
Office of Emergency Preparedness.
[FR Doc.73-4380 Filed 3-6-73;8:45 am]

Title 41—Public Contracts and Property Management

CHAPTER 3—DEPARTMENT OF HEALTH, EDUCATION, AND WELFARE

PART 3-16—PROCUREMENT FORMS

Subpart 3-16.8—Miscellaneous Forms

Chapter 3, Title 41, Code of Federal Regulations is amended as set forth below. The purpose of this amendment is to inform the public of HEW's use of miscellaneous procurement forms.

It is the general policy of the Department of Health, Education, and Welfare to allow time for interested parties to take part in the rule making process. However, since the amendment herein involves minor technical matters, the public rule making process is deemed unnecessary in this instance.

1. The table of contents of Part 3-16 is amended to add Subpart 3-16.8 as follows:

Subpart 3-16.8—Miscellaneous Forms

3-16.804	Report on procurement.
3-16.804-2	Agencies required to report.
3-16.804-3	Standard Form 37, Report on Procurement by Civilian Executive Agencies.
3-16.852	Equal Opportunity Clause (HEW 386).
3-16.853	Request for Equal Opportunity Clearance of Contract Award (HEW 511).
3-16.854	Notice to Prospective Bidders (HEW 512).
3-16.855	Transmittal Letter (HEW-513).
3-16.856	Procurement Activity Report.

AUTHORITY:　S.C. 301; 40 U.S.C. 486(c).

Subpart 3-16.8—Miscellaneous Forms

2. Subpart 3-16.8 is added to read as follows:

§ 3-16.804　Report on procurement.

§ 3-16.804-2　Agencies required to report.

Each operating agency, the Office of Regional and Community Development, and the Office of Administrative Services, OS-OASAM, shall report its procurement to the Office of Procurement and Materiel Management, OS-OASAM, for the organization as a whole.

§ 3-16.804-3　Standard Form 37, Report on Procurement by Civilian Agencies.

(a)–(e) [Reserved]
(f) *Frequency and due date for submission of Standard Form 37.* Each report shall be submitted in the original and three copies to arrive at OPMM not later than 30 calendar days after the close of each reporting period.

§ 3-16.852　Equal Opportunity Clause (HEW-386).

Use Form HEW-386, Equal Opportunity Clause, if it is prescribed.

§ 3-16.853　Request for Equal Opportunity Clearance of Contract Award.

Form HEW-511, Request for Equal Opportunity Clearance of Contract Award, is prescribed for use in communicating and transmitting information between the contracting officer and the Office of Civil Rights.

§ 3-16.854　Notice to Prospective Bidders (HEW-512).

Form HEW-512, Notice to Prospective Bidders, is prescribed for use with invitation for bids when bids are estimated to exceed $10,000.

§ 3-16.855　Transmittal Letter (HEW-513).

Form HEW-513, Transmittal Letter, is prescribed for transmitting awards which are subject to the Equal Opportunity clause.

§ 3-16.856　Procurement Activity Report.

(a) *General.* The Procurement Activity Report is designed to provide the Department with essential procurement records and statistics necessary for procurement management purposes and to

ILLUSTRATION 14-6   List of Recent Agency Activity, from *List of CFR Sections Affected*

JULY 1999   65

CHANGES JULY 1, 1999 THROUGH JULY 30, 1999

TITLE 28—JUDICIAL ADMINISTRATION

Chapter I—Department of Justice (Parts 0—199)

0.14 Removed	37042
0.137 Removed	46846
0.138 Revised	46846
0.157 (b), (c) and (d) revised; (e) removed	46846
20 Authority citation revised	47102
20.25 Amended	47102
22 Authority citation revised	47102
22.29 Revised	47102
36 Authority citation revised	47103
36.504 (a)(3)(i) and (ii) revised	47103
71 Authority citation revised	47103
71.3 Amended; (a) introductory text and (f) introductory text revised; (a) concluding text and (f) concluding text	47103
76 Authority citation revised	47103
76.3 (a) revised	47103
85 Added	47103
90 Authority citation revised	39783
90.100—90.106 (Subpart E) Added	39783

Chapter V—Bureau of Prisons, Department of Justice (Parts 500—599)

505 Revised	43881
553 Authority citation revised	36753
553.10 Amended	36753
553.11 Revised	36753
553.12 Revised	36754
553.13 (b)(2)(iii) amended	36754
553.14 Revised	36754

Chapter VI—Offices of Independent Counsel, Department of Justice (Parts 600—699)

600 Revised	37042

Proposed Rules:

5	37065
540	40718

TITLE 29—LABOR

Subtitle A—Office of the Secretary of Labor (Parts 0—99)

18.9 (e)(2) revised	47089

Chapter II—Office of Labor-Management Programs, Department of Labor (Parts 200—299)

215 Guidelines	40990

Chapter X—National Mediation Board (Parts 1200—1299)

1203.1 Amended	40287
1203.2 Amended	40287
1203.3 (a) amended	40287
1205.4 Amended	40287
1209 Authority citation revised	40287
1209.7 (f) amended	40287
1209.8 (d) amended	40287

Chapter XIV—Equal Employment Opportunity Commission (Parts 1600—1699)

1610.4 Regulation at 63 FR 1341 confirmed	45164
1610.5 Regulation at 63 FR 1341 confirmed	45164
1610.8 Regulation at 63 FR 1341 confirmed	45164
1610.9 Regulation at 63 FR 1341 confirmed	45164
1610.10 Regulation at 63 FR 1342 confirmed	45164
1610.11 Regulation at 63 FR 1342 confirmed	45164
1610.14 Regulation at 63 FR 1342 confirmed	45164
1610.15 Regulation at 63 FR 1342 confirmed	45164
1610.18 Regulation at 63 FR 1342 confirmed	45164
1610.21 Regulation at 63 FR 1342 confirmed	45164
1610.34 Regulation at 63 FR 1342 confirmed	45164
1614.102 (b)(2) through (6) redesignated as (b)(3) through (7); (b)(2) added; (c)(5) revised	37655
1614.103 (b)(3) amended; (b)(4) revised; (5), (6), and (7) added	37655

ILLUSTRATION 14-7   Reader Aids Table of Parts Affected, from *Federal Register*

ii   Federal Register / Vol. 64, No. 189 / Thursday, September 30, 1999 / Reader Aids

400	52678	205	49699	**17 CFR**		570	50140
780	52678	213	49713	30	50248	572	50140
928	48115	226	49722	240	52428	573	50140
1126	51083	230	49740	**Proposed Rules:**		574	50140
1137	50777	327	48719	146	52695	576	50140
1735	50476	340	51084	270	52476	582	50140
		380	48968			583	50140
9 CFR		701	52694	**18 CFR**		585	50140
93	48258			153	51209	761	49900, 50140
130	51421	**13 CFR**		157	51209	881	50140
381	49640	107	52641	375	51209	882	50140
Proposed Rules:		121	48275	385	51222	883	50140
3	48568	123	48275	**Proposed Rules:**		886	50140
94	50014			35	51933	888	51860
101	52247	**14 CFR**				891	50140
130	51477, 52680	21	52646	**19 CFR**		901	50140
		23	49365, 49367	12	48091	903	51045
10 CFR		25	47649, 51423, 51424	113	48528	906	50140
1	48942	39	47651, 47653, 47656,	151	48528	941	50140
2	48942		47658, 47660, 47661, 48277,	178	48528	965	50140
7	48942		48280, 48282, 48284, 48286,	351	48706, 50553, 51236	968	50140
9	48942		49080, 49961, 49964, 49966,	**Proposed Rules:**		970	50140
50	48942, 51370		49969, 49971, 49974, 49977,	141	49423	982	49656, 50140
51	48496, 48507, 48942		49979, 50439, 50440, 50442,			983	50140
52	48942		50749, 51189, 51190, 51192,	**20 CFR**		1000	50140
60	48942		51193, 51195, 51196, 51198,	404	51892	1003	50140
62	48942		51199, 51200, 51202, 51205,	416	51892	1005	50140
72	48259, 48942, 50872,		51681, 51683, 51684, 51686,			**Proposed Rules:**	
	51187		52219, 52221, 52423, 52424,	**21 CFR**		203	49958
75	48942		52649	5	47669, 49383	905	49924
76	48942	71	47663, 47664, 47665,	74	48288	906	49932
100	48942		48085, 48086, 48088, 48089,	101	50445	943	49942
110	48942		48527, 48703, 48897, 49646,	173	49981	990	48572
Proposed Rules:			49647, 49648, 49981, 50246,	175	48290		
20	50015		50247, 50331, 50443, 50445,	178	47669, 48291, 48292	**25 CFR**	
31	48333		51208, 51430, 52121, 52426,	210	52696	**Proposed Rules:**	
51	48117		52427	211	52696	151	49756
61	50778	73	47665, 48090, 49373,	343	49652		
72	51270, 51271		49374, 49376	510	48293, 51241	**26 CFR**	
73	49410	91	51430	520	48295, 48543	1	48545, 52650
430	52248	97	49377, 49378, 49649,	522	48293, 48544	301	48547, 51241
			51432, 51433	524	48707, 49082	602	51241
11 CFR		121	49981	556	48295, 48544	**Proposed Rules:**	
9003	49355	**Proposed Rules:**		558	48295, 49082, 49383,	1	48572, 49276, 50026,
9004	49355	23	49413		49655		50783
9008	49355	39	47715, 48120, 48333,	820	52696		
9032	49355		48721, 48723, 490105,	876	51442	**27 CFR**	
9033	49355		49110, 49112, 49113, 49115,	1271	52696	1	49984
9034	49355, 51422		49413, 49420, 49752, 50016,	1308	49982	4	49385, 50252, 51896
9035	49355		50018, 50020, 50022, 50023,	**Proposed Rules:**		24	50252, 51896
9036	49355		50781, 51479, 51481, 51483,	2	47719	200	49083
			51484, 51486, 52259, 52260,	111	48336	**Proposed Rules:**	
12 CFR			52263	212	51274	4	50265, 51933
Ch. IX	52148	71	47718, 48123, 48459,	1401	51275	9	52483
26	51673		49754, 49755, 51273, 51587,			24	50265, 51933
30	52638		52475	**22 CFR**			
201	48274	1260	50334	40	50751	**28 CFR**	
212	51673	1274	50334	514	51894	0	52223
230	49846					16	52223
331	50429	**15 CFR**		**23 CFR**		20	52223
348	51673	742	47666, 49380, 50247	658	48957	32	49954
563f	51673	745	49380	**Proposed Rules:**		50	52223
615	49959	746	49382	Ch. I	47741, 47744, 47746,	68	49659
795	49079	774	47666, 48956		47749	**Proposed Rules:**	
917	52163	902	52427			16	49117
925	52163	**Proposed Rules:**		**24 CFR**		302	48336
930	52163	806	48568	35	50140		
940	52163			91	50140	**29 CFR**	
954	52163	**16 CFR**		92	50140	697	48525
955	52163	1051	48703	200	50140	2700	48707
958	52163	1615	48704	203	50140	4044	49986, 51587
965	52163	1616	48704	206	50140	**Proposed Rules:**	
966	52163	**Proposed Rules:**		280	50140	1926	51722
980	52163	432	51087	291	50140	2510	51277
1730	50246	460	48024	511	50140		
Proposed Rules:						**30 CFR**	
202	49688					46	53080

> **Regulations through GPO Access on the Internet:**
>
> ▶ select an appropriate web site
> ▶ locate the regulation in a C.F.R. database via a find search, Boolean search, or search-or-browse
> ▶ read the retrieved regulation, and browse adjacent material
> ▶ search the *List of CFR Sections Affected* for updates
> ▶ read any new material in the *Federal Register*

The United States Government Printing Office (GPO) has developed a free web site that contains the *Code of Federal Regulations*, the *List of CFR Sections Affected*, and the *Federal Register*, located at www.access.gpo.gov. Some states also have developed web sites covering their state administrative materials.

Especially if you already know the pertinent regulation's citation or at least the agency name, Internet research can offer an efficient and low-cost alternative to paper-based sources. If you use a government web site, the information should be highly reliable and fairly current. Search options vary depending on the site.

After selecting an appropriate web site, your first step in Internet research is to locate the pertinent regulation. There are three ways to find a federal administrative regulation using the GPO's web site.

First, if you know the regulation's citation, you can retrieve it by designating the C.F.R. edition year and the title/part/section or title/part/subpart. Second, you may perform a key-word search in the entire C.F.R. database, using basic Boolean commands (AND, ADJ (adjacent), OR, NOT), truncation (* expands the root word), and phrases (such as the agency name). Third, you may use the search-or-browse function, which is actually a combination of the first two methods. In this mode, you limit your key-word search to one or several titles or parts of titles. See Illustration 14-8 on page 279.

You also have a set of options as to reviewing your retrieved documents. You may be able to review sections, subparts, or parts. See Illustration 14-8 on page 279. The latter choices facilitate browsing, which is important in a codified source. As with paper-based research in regulatory codes, read the regulation you locate carefully. Explore all sections pertaining to your problem. Note when the regulation was promulgated.

Because the GPO database is based on the paper publication, the C.F.R. database is no more current than the paper volumes. Hence, the next step is to update your research using the online *List of CFR Sections Affected*, containing the monthly issues of the L.S.A. and Current List of CFR Sections Affected, which covers changes since the last monthly L.S.A. issue was published. One option is to browse the most recent L.S.A. issue and Current List of CFR Sections Affected. Another option is to perform a key-word search using your C.F.R. citation as the search term. If there are any changes to your regulation, L.S.A. will report the change. Unfortunately, there is no link from the L.S.A. to the *Federal Register,* so you should print out any pertinent L.S.A. lists you retrieve.

Your next step is to read the material identified by the L.S.A. in the *Federal Register* database. You can locate pertinent information there by a search for year and page number, as revealed in L.S.A., or by a search for the citation of your regulation.

As with paper-based research, when you find pertinent material in the *Federal Register,* be sure to read the regulation itself carefully, so you understand how it relates to any previous regulation. Also read the explanatory material for background information that may help you understand it.

Researching the Canoga case, we searched the C.F.R. database using the search-or-browse method. In this mode, we selected title 29 from a list of C.F.R. titles and used [orchestra] as a key word. The search retrieved § 103.2, part 103, and subpart A. See Illustration 14-8 on page 279. We reviewed part 103, because doing so permitted us to browse related sections.

Our next step was to search for any changes to § 103.2, using the L.S.A. database. We entered a search based on the C.F.R. citation we had previously found: ["title 29" AND 103 ADJ 2]. (It is necessary to use the ADJ connector because the decimal point is not searchable.) And we updated by searching Current List of CFR Sections Affected. We retrieved no documents; no changes had been made to § 103.2 since it was published in the C.F.R. If we had retrieved any documents in L.S.A., we would have turned to the *Federal Register* database.

Regulations in LEXIS and Westlaw:

▶ select an appropriate regulatory code database
▶ draft and run a Boolean or natural-language search in the regulatory code database
▶ or search a table of contents database
▶ sift the search results, and browse adjacent sections
▶ read the regulation
▶ run updating searches in a register database

LEXIS and Westlaw both provide a database with the full text of C.F.R.; several subject-specific administrative law databases, for example, CFR-Labor Titles for LEXIS; and a *Federal Register* database. They also provide a fair amount of state administrative materials for some states. For example, in the fall of 1999, LEXIS offered the administrative code and state register for New Mexico; Westlaw offered materials from selected New Mexico agencies and a regulation tracking database.

Online research through LEXIS and Westlaw has several advantages and disadvantages. You may create a search using terms that the index does not

ILLUSTRATION 14-8   CFR Search Results, from GPO Access

CFR Search Results

Search Database:

Title 29 All Volumes (1999)

For: "ORCHESTRA"

Total Hits: 5

[1]
((LIST OF AVAILABLE CFRs ONLINE))
 Size: 63947 , Score: 1000

[2]
[1999] 29CFR103.2-- Sec. 103.2 Symphony orchestras.
 Size: 805 , Score: 1000

[3]
[1999] 29CFR103-- Subpart A--Jurisdictional Standards
 Size: 1463 , Score: 883

[4]
[1999] 29CFR103-- PART 103--OTHER RULES
 Size: 8291 , Score: 658

[5]
Query Report for this Search
 Size: 650 , Score: 1

This document is sponsored by the Office of the Federal Register, National Archives and Records Administration on the United States Government Printing Office web site.

use. The code database may be nearly up to date, requiring less updating. However, you may find it difficult to draft an effective search, and indexes may not be available online. Browsing from section to section or part to part can be cumbersome online. The following text focuses on LEXIS; Westlaw offers similar options.

If you already know your regulation's citation, you would conduct a find search to retrieve the regulation. If not, you would follow several steps to locate the pertinent regulation.

The first step is to select an appropriate database. Because the C.F.R. database is so large, it often is better to use a subject-specific C.F.R. database, if possible. Be sure to check the currency of the database you choose.

LEXIS permits Boolean and natural-language searches for regulations. Searching the full text, rather than a segment, generally is sensible, especially if you are working in a subject-specific database. See Illustration 14-9 on page 281. LEXIS affords an alternative approach: to search or browse the C.F.R. table of contents in its CFRTOC database.

Your next step is to sift your search results. One option is to skim the captions of retrieved documents, which generally are quite descriptive. You should read the pertinent regulation carefully and browse adjacent sections in the same part.

C.F.R. online is more up to date than C.F.R. in paper; new information is integrated regularly, so that the online version is generally only two to four weeks old. Nonetheless, you must update your C.F.R. database research.

Updating information appears in the *Federal Register* database, FEDREG in LEXIS. When you have found a regulation in C.F.R., a good strategy is to use its citation as a search term along with a date restrictor aimed at confining your search to issues of the *Federal Register* postdating the endpoint of the C.F.R. database. If your research in C.F.R. yields no pertinent regulation, you would conduct a Boolean search for your subject in the FEDREG database, often including the name of the agency and another key word or two along with a date restrictor.

Researching the Canoga case, we first used the CFR-Labor Titles database in LEXIS. The simple Boolean search ["title 29" and orchestra] retrieved three documents, including § 103.2 of title 29, the only pertinent section. See Illustration 14-9 on page 281. We then updated our research in the FEDREG database; we used the regulation citation as a search term [29 cfr pre/3 103!] and restricted the dates of our search to the past month. We retrieved no documents; no changes affecting our regulation had occurred.

ILLUSTRATION 14-9   LEXIS Citations List, Run in CFR-Labor Titles Database

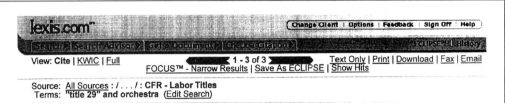

lexis.com™ | Change Client | Options | Feedback | Sign Off | Help

Search | Search Advisor | Get a Document | Check a Citation | ECLIPSE™ | History

View: Cite | KWIC | Full   ◄ 1 - 3 of 3 ►   Text Only | Print | Download | Fax | Email
FOCUS™ - Narrow Results | Save As ECLIPSE | Show Hits

Source: All Sources : / . . . / : **CFR - Labor Titles**
Terms: **"title 29" and orchestra** (Edit Search)

1. 29 CFR 103.2, TITLE 29 -- LABOR, SUBTITLE B -- REGULATIONS RELATING TO LABOR, CHAPTER I -- NATIONAL LABOR RELATIONS BOARD, PART 103 -- OTHER RULES, SUBPART A -- JURISDICTIONAL STANDARDS, § 103.2 Symphony orchestras., 58 words, CODE OF FEDERAL REGULATIONS

2. 29 CFR PART 510 APPENDIX B, TITLE 29 -- LABOR, SUBTITLE B -- REGULATIONS RELATING TO LABOR, CHAPTER V -- WAGE AND HOUR DIVISION, DEPARTMENT OF LABOR, SUBCHAPTER A -- REGULATIONS, PART 510 -- IMPLEMENTATION OF THE MINIMUM WAGE PROVISIONS OF THE 1989 AMENDMENTS TO THE FAIR LABOR STANDARDS ACT IN PUERTO RICO, SUBPART C -- CLASSIFICATION OF INDUSTRIES, APPENDIX B TO PART 510 -- NONMANUFACTURING INDUSTRIES ELIGIBLE FOR MINIMUM WAGE PHASE-IN, 5745 words, CODE OF FEDERAL REGULATIONS

3. 29 CFR 776.12, TITLE 29 -- LABOR, SUBTITLE B -- REGULATIONS RELATING TO LABOR, CHAPTER V -- WAGE AND HOUR DIVISION, DEPARTMENT OF LABOR, SUBCHAPTER B -- STATEMENTS OF GENERAL POLICY OR INTERPRETATION NOT DIRECTLY RELATED TO REGULATIONS, PART 776 -- INTERPRETATIVE BULLETIN ON THE GENERAL COVERAGE OF THE WAGE AND HOURS PROVISIONS OF THE FAIR LABOR STANDARDS ACT OF 1938, SUBPART A -- GENERAL, ENGAGING "IN COMMERCE", § 776.12 Employees traveling across State lines., 319 words, CODE OF FEDERAL REGULATIONS

View: Cite | KWIC | Full   ◄ 1 - 3 of 3 ►   Text Only | Print | Download | Fax | Email
FOCUS™ - Narrow Results | Save As ECLIPSE | Show Hits

Source: All Sources : / . . . / : **CFR - Labor Titles**
Terms: **"title 29" and orchestra** (Edit Search)
View: Cite
Date/Time: Monday, November 22, 1999 - 1:34 PM EST

Search | Search Advisor | Get a Document | Check a Citation
ECLIPSE(TM) | History | Change Client | Options | Feedback | Sign Off | Help
About LEXIS-NEXIS | Terms and Conditions

> **Concluding case law research regarding regulations:**
>
> - case reporters and digests, their electronic alternatives, case citators
> - annotated codes in paper and computer-based media
> - regulations citators: *Shepard's Code of Federal Regulations Citations*, Shepard's online, KeyCite

Your research in federal or state regulations is not complete unless you have read the case law involving your regulation. When a court is asked to apply a regulation to a specific set of facts, the court interprets the regulation. Furthermore, a court also may address the regulation's validity in light of the enabling statute, constitutional principles, or both.

To find case law interpreting a regulation, you would use sources covered in detail elsewhere in this book. Secondary sources discussed in Unit II may lead you to cases discussing your regulation. Case reporters and digests, online and CD-ROM alternatives to reporters and digests, and case citators are discussed in Unit III. Because cases interpreting regulations involve statutes as well, annotated codes (available in paper, in CD-ROMs, and online) are useful; they are discussed in Unit IV. If, as will generally be true, you are looking for case law regarding a known regulation, you can use the regulation's citation as a search term in case law databases in various computer-based sources.

Another option is a citator for regulations. *Shepard's Code of Federal Regulations Citations* is a paper citator. Electronic Shepard's, available on LEXIS, and KeyCite, available on Westlaw, both cover federal regulations. They provide information similar to that provided for statutes, including citing cases. Furthermore, both afford various means of tailoring your research, such as date and jurisdiction restrictions. See Illustration 14-10 on page 283.

Researching the Canoga case, we first searched the Tenth Circuit database on LEXIS and used the regulation's citation as our search; we obtained no cases. We then expanded our search to cover all federal courts. We retrieved thirty-nine cases that discuss regulations within part 103 of title 29, including *NLRB v. Rochester Musicians Ass'n Local 66*, 514 F.2d 988 (2d Cir. 1975), a Second Circuit case addressing § 103.2. There the court upheld the Board's assertion of jurisdiction brought under the 1973 regulation, but the court did not discuss the regulation in detail.

We also KeyCited the regulation. The results appear in Illustration 14-10 on page 283. The cited sources include the *Rochester Musicians* case, two agency decisions, and secondary sources.

In addition, some agencies decide cases and issue decisions involving agency regulations. See Chapter 15 for a discussion of research in agency decisions.

ILLUSTRATION 14-10   KeyCite Display, from Westlaw

KeyCite   **Page 1**

Date of Printing: NOV 20,1999

KEYCITE

CITATION: **29 CFR s 103.2**
Citations
1 N.L.R.B. v. Rochester Musicians Ass'n Local 66, 514 F.2d 988, 990+,
        89 L.R.R.M. (BNA) 2193+, 76 Lab.Cas. P 10,850+ (2nd Cir. Apr 28, 1975) (NO. 471,
        74-1940)

Administrative Materials
2 Spring Library and Museums Ass'n, 221 NLRB 1209, 1210, 221 NLRB No. 194,
        1975 WL 6564, *3, 91 L.R.R.M. (BNA) 1043 (N.L.R.B. Dec 18, 1975) (NO. AO-173)
3 Rochester Musicians Assn. Local 66, 207 NLRB 647, 648, 207 NLRB No. 110,
        1973 WL 4660, *4, 85 L.R.R.M. (BNA) 1345 (N.L.R.B. Nov 29, 1973)
        (NO. 3-CB-1939)

Secondary Sources
4 48 Am. Jur. 2d Labor and Labor Relations s 826, NONPROFIT INSTITUTIONS
5 THE BIRTH OF A RULE: THE NATIONAL LABOR RELATIONS BOARD'S USE OF
        INFORMAL RULEMAKING TO PROMULGATE A RULE FOR HEALTH CARE
        BARGAINING UNIT DETERMINATIONS, 1989 Det. C.L. Rev. 1105, 1132+ (1989)
6 NLRB RULEMAKING ON HEALTH CARE COLLECTIVE BARGAINING UNITS:
        PREDICTABILITY, BUT AT WHAT COST, 9 Hofstra Lab. L.J. 483, 513 (1992)
7 RULEMAKING: THE NATIONAL LABOR RELATIONS BOARD'S PRESCRIPTION FOR THE
        RECURRING PAINS OF THE HEALTH CARE INDUSTRY,
        9 J. Contemp. Health L. & Pol'y 377, 418 (1993)
8 QUESTIONING THE PREEMPTION DOCTRINE: OPPORTUNITIES FOR STATE-LEVEL
        LABOR LAW INITIATIVES, 5 Widener J. Pub. L. 35, 86 (1995)

D.   WHAT ELSE?

Administrative History.   As noted above, if you are seeking the history of a federal regulation to help you understand its purpose or background or to determine whether it has been promulgated properly, you should consult its publication in the *Federal Register*. For thorough research into the background of a regulation, you would consult not only the *Federal Register* materials published at the time of final promulgation, but also those appearing when the regulation was proposed.

Proposed Regulations.   If you are monitoring a federal agency's activities for a client concerned about the impact of possible future regulations, you could locate proposed regulations in the *Federal Register*. A proposed regulation typically is accompanied by an explanation of the agency's plans, background on the rule, and the name of a person to contact about it. You can locate information about proposed rules through the L.S.A. and Reader Aids listings of proposed rules, appearing at the end of each title's entries.

Removed Regulations.   If your client's facts occurred some time ago and the regulation in force then no longer is in force, you have two options. First, you may locate the regulation in the *Federal Register*. Second, you may research in an old version of C.F.R., possibly in LEXIS or Westlaw's historic C.F.R. databases, or in microforms for even older regulations.

Further Information about the *Federal Register*.   If you wish to learn more about the *Federal Register*, which has uses beyond those described here, consult the pamphlet entitled *The Federal Register: What It Is and How to Use It*.

United States Code Service.   This annotated statutory code also provides procedural regulations of major federal agencies, along with annotations that include notes of judicial and agency decisions and references to secondary sources.

CIS Products.   If you find the finding tools within C.F.R. difficult to use, you may want to consult *CIS* (Congressional Information Service) *Index to the Code of Federal Regulations,* which features frequent updating and detailed indexing. CIS also provides the text of federal regulations and the *Federal Register* in its *Congressional Universe* service. CIS is a commercial publisher.

Guides to Federal and State Agencies.   To learn what federal agencies do, how to contact them, and what resources they provide, consult a source such as *The United States Government Manual* (available on the Internet via www.access.gpo) and the *Federal Regulatory Directory*. Many states have similar manuals. BNA's *Directory of State Administrative Codes and Registers* provides background on the publications of administrative material at the state level.

Presidential Documents.   Two major types of presidential documents are executive orders (typically directed to government officials) and proclamations (general announcements and policy statements). These appear in various publications, including the *Federal Register*, Title 3 of C.F.R., and *U.S. Code Congressional and Administrative News*; some also appear in the federal statutory codes. LEXIS and Westlaw provide online access to some presidential documents. The *Weekly Compilation of Presidential Documents* and the annual *Public Papers of the President* compile not only executive orders and proclamations, but also other documents, such as announcements and nominations.

E.   How Do You Cite Regulations?

Regulations generally are cited to the regulatory code. You need to provide the regulation's name, if it is commonly known by a name; the code's abbreviation; the numbers needed to identify the regulation; and the date of the code. Regulations not appearing in a regulatory code are cited to the register. You must provide the regulation's commonly used name, the register's name, the volume and the page number on which the discussion of the regulation or the regulation itself begins, the page number where the portion you are citing appears, the year, and the regulation's eventual codification. Here are examples (according to Rule 14 of *The Bluebook*):

> 29 C.F.R. § 103.2 (1999)
> 38 Fed. Reg. 6176, 6177 (1973) (to be codified at 29 C.F.R. § 103.2).

F.   Concluding Points

When a legislature creates an agency, it may authorize the agency to promulgate regulations. Some regulations have the force of law, so long as they do not affront the Constitution and accord with the enabling statute. Other regulations are less authoritative, but nonetheless significant.

Regulations research always involves a statute, for agencies come into being and derive their authority by statute.

Two types of sources are key to regulations research. A regulatory code (such as the *Code of Federal Regulations*) contains regulations currently in force, topically organized. A register (such as the *Federal Register*) contains the daily or periodic output of agencies, including new regulations. Codes are the main source used in regulations research; registers are used to update codes, as well as to provide background and regulations no longer in force. Regulatory codes and registers may be researched in paper and online, through the Internet, LEXIS, and Westlaw.

Case law rounds out regulations research because courts interpret and assess the validity of regulations. Shepard's and KeyCite are among the many sources you can use to locate cases interpreting regulations.

AGENCY DECISIONS

A. WHAT IS AN AGENCY DECISION?

1. How Is an Agency Case Decided?

Federal and state agencies make many decisions. Agency officials decide how to conduct an investigation, which issues to study, whether to prosecute an alleged offender, etc. This chapter focuses on decisions that are the output of case adjudication.

Agency decisions are the end product of some type of litigation before the agency, just as judicial opinions are the end product of litigation in the courts. Agency litigation varies considerably.

In formal adjudication, the parties typically are the government, acting as a quasi-prosecutor or claims administrator, and the private party. The case begins with some form of notice, typically in pleadings, which may be construed fairly broadly. There may be discovery (or development of the facts by the lawyers) before the hearing, and preliminary issues may be handled by motion (that is, by written and oral argument rather than presentation of evidence). The typical hearing resembles a trial with counsel, direct testimony and cross-examination, and exhibits. Some evidence may be submitted in writing, and evidentiary rules typically are relaxed, so evidence that may not be admissible in court during a jury trial may be admitted during the hearing. The parties then submit proposed findings to the judge, known as an "administrative law judge" (ALJ) or "hearing officer," who then renders a decision.

The case generally proceeds to higher levels within the agency, ultimately to the commissioners or members of the agency, who may adopt the ALJ's decision or develop their own decision in response to the arguments of counsel. In some sense, the commissioners act as an appeals court, because they do not hear the evidence themselves; however, unlike the judicial process, the ALJ decision is only a recommendation to the commissioners. The agency decision is not the terminus of the litigation; agency decisions are subject to judicial review.

In contrast, informal agency decisions typically are not the product of an adversarial process. An agency staff member may render an informal opinion based on information provided by the party seeking advice, an independent investigation undertaken by the agency itself, or perhaps a written response provided by an adverse party. If the informal decision constitutes final agency action, it has some precedential impact, in that the agency would have to explain a later change of course.

If litigation were pursued in the Canoga case under the federal labor statute, it would begin with Ms. Canoga filing a charge against the employer. The National Labor Relations Board's staff would investigate the facts. If the investigation indicated that the labor statute had been violated, a Board lawyer would file a complaint against the employer and proceed to litigate the case on Ms. Canoga's behalf before an ALJ. The Board would review the ALJ's recommendation and determine whether to adopt the recommendation or write its own decision. The Board's decision would be subject to review in turn by the Courts of Appeals for the Tenth Circuit (which encompasses New Mexico) or the District of Columbia (where the Board's offices are) and thereafter by the United States Supreme Court.

2. What Does an Agency Decision Look Like?

A state or federal formal agency decision more or less resembles a case decided by a court. It includes a statement of the facts as found by the agency, the agency's decision based on those facts, and the reasoning behind the decision. That reasoning typically includes discussion of the statute, any pertinent regulations, and previous decisions of the agency. See Illustration 15-1 on pages 288–291. As with case law, an agency decision not only resolves the dispute for the litigants, but also operates as precedent for similar situations involving other parties.

Illustration 15-1 on pages 288–291 is an excerpt from a Board decision in a case with some parallel to the Canoga case. It involves the federal issue raised in Ms. Canoga's case: protection of nonunion activities that involve concerted action by employees.

ILLUSTRATION 15-1   *Morton International* Decision, from *Decisions and Orders*
                           of the National Labor Relations Board

Morton International, Inc. *and* Martin D. Howell.
Case 9–CA–30898

November 10, 1994

DECISION AND ORDER

BY MEMBERS DEVANEY, BROWNING, AND COHEN

On July 20, 1994, Administrative Law Judge Claude R. Wolfe issued the attached decision. The Respondent filed exceptions and a supporting brief.

The National Labor Relations Board has delegated its authority in this proceeding to a three-member panel.

The Board has considered the record in light of the exceptions and brief and has decided to affirm the judge's rulings, findings,[1] and conclusions and to adopt the recommended Order.

ORDER

The National Labor Relations Board adopts the recommended Order of the administrative law judge and orders that the Respondent, Morton International, Inc., West Alexandria, Ohio, its officers, agents, successors, and assigns, shall take the action set forth in the Order.

---

[1] The Respondent has excepted to some of the judge's credibility findings. The Board's established policy is not to overrule an administrative law judge's credibility resolutions unless the clear preponderance of all the relevant evidence convinces us that they are incorrect. *Standard Dry Wall Products*, 91 NLRB 544 (1950), enfd. 188 F.2d 362 (3d Cir. 1951). We have carefully examined the record and find no basis for reversing the findings.

Joseph C. Devine, Esq., for the General Counsel.
David J. Millstone and *William A. Nolan, Esqs.*, for the Respondent.

DECISION

STATEMENT OF THE CASE

CLAUDE R. WOLFE, Administrative Law Judge. This proceeding was litigated before me at Dayton, Ohio, on May 17, 1994, pursuant to charges filed on July 15, 1993, and amended on August 24 and October 22, 1993,[1] and complaint issued October 25 alleging Martin D. Howell and Robert Boerner were unlawfully suspended and discharged for engaging in protected concerted activity. Morton International, Inc. (the Respondent) contends the suspensions and discharges were for cause and did not violate Section 8(a)(1) of the National Labor Relations Act (the Act) as alleged.

Upon the entire record, and after considering the demeanor of the witnesses and the posttrial briefs of the parties, I make the following

---

[1] All dates are 1993 unless otherwise stated.

FINDINGS AND CONCLUSIONS

I. THE RESPONDENT'S BUSINESS

The Respondent is a corporation engaged in the manufacture and nonretail sale of adhesives at West Alexandria, Ohio, and during the 12 months preceding the issuance of the complaint, sold and shipped its products valued in excess of $50,000 from its West Alexandria facility to points located outside the State of Ohio. The Respondent is an employer engaged in commerce within the meaning of Section 2(2), (6), and (7) of the Act.

II. SUPERVISORS AND AGENT

At all times material to this proceeding, the individuals named below held the positions set forth opposite their names and have been supervisors and agents of the Respondent within the meaning of Section 2(11) and (13) of the Act.

Randall Bittner—Plant Manager
Jane Paxton—Manager for Human Resources
Leigh Walling—Polyester Supervisor
Bob Napier—Maintenance Supervisor

III. THE ALLEGED UNFAIR LABOR PRACTICES

A. *Chronology*

The facts are not in dispute with respect to the conduct of Boerner and Howell which led to their discharge, and all these facts were known to the Respondent at the time the two were discharged.

On the morning of June 14, at about 2 or 2:30 a.m., Boerner was lunching with a custodian named Snider "Butch" Neusock, and another employee. All were smokers. Snider had placed a memo on the table.[2] The memo was addressed to the Respondent's safety committee and signed, "Morton employee." The memo, in substance complained that the Respondent was not rigidly enforcing its no-smoking policy. The last sentence in the lengthy memo reading, "Also, what about the employees who do not use tobacco products—when will we be able to have a 'non-smoke' break of ten minutes or more every hour?" was composed by Brenda Holfinger, an assistant to the health and safety administrator. Holfinger is a regular hourly paid employee.

Indignant at the content of this memo, Boerner wrote comments on it in bold letters reading in one instance, "Chicken Shit" after the anonymous "Morton employee" appearing as the originator of the memo, and at another point made the observation, without an aquerbian mark "could this be racist" in reference to a sentence reading, "I hate to see them [the Respondent] back down because of pressure from a minority of the employee [i.e., smokers]" warning to his task, Boerner enlarged his commentary by noting at the bottom of the purloined memo. Again in very large letters, "I think the non-smokers should quit their damm [sic] crying and put their thoughts to a more useful purpose for the company!" In the course of his composition of this broadside, Boerner sought assistance in the spelling of a word from Neusock

---

[2] The custodian was later discharged on the ground he had removed the document from company records in a locked office.

ILLUSTRATION 15-1   *(continued)*

MORTON INTERNATIONAL, INC.   565

who obliged. What word he assisted with is not specified, but I seriously doubt it was, "Damm."

Apart from the minuscule assistance included by Neusock, who made no other contribution to Boerner's effort, none of the three men lunching with Boerner, whom he states shared his views, were in any way party to the writing on or posting of the memo by Boerner, nor is there any evidence they designated him as their representative for any purpose. Boerner left the area after posting the memo with his comments on it.

Enter Howell. At about 4 a.m. he entered the empty lunchroom. Noticing the posted memo with Boerner's amendations, he took it to a table and read it. A smoker himself, Howell was then inspired to add further commentary on the memo. At the very top of the memo he wrote, "Gee, Brenda this isn't you is it? Get a real job you glorified secretary." In response to a statement in the memo referring to "the old days" he penned, "What do you know about the "old days." Directing his attention to the memo claim the company was retreating from a policy, he noted, "what policy? be specific Brenda." Concerning a statement in the memo to the effect that forcing smokers to do so outside in all weather would deter smoking, Howell wrote, "then more of us would miss work for being sick." To this point none of the memo was composed by Brenda Holfinger who typed the memo. Now, however, her sentence quoted above closed the memo and moved Howell to expound, "has production suffered, no, so shut up and stay the hell out of the trailer."[3] Finally, at the bottom of the page, Howell commented on Boerner's adjuration to nonsmokers that they should put their thoughts to a more useful purpose, stating this would be quite difficult for this nonsmoker cause *she* has no "useful thoughts!" Finished with his commentary, Howell made copies and posted them in the breakroom, the smoke trailer, and on a bulletin board by the health and safety office.

Discovering the altered and posted memo, Respondent launched an investigation. As a result the custodian who admitted taking the document from company files as a joke was fired. Boerner and Howell each candidly advised the Respondent of their conduct with reference to the memo. They were suspended pending the results of the Respondent's investigation. Each received a letter from Jane Paxton dated June 15 and reading as follows:

Subject: Suspension Notification Without Pay

As we discussed, the Company is investigating concerns that you may have violated our policies. In particular, we are reviewing policies including but not limited to:

a. Harassment or intimidating language or conduct, . . .

b. Conduct that reflects unfavorably upon the Corporation.

c. Making malicious, false or derogatory statements that may damage the integrity or reputation of the Corporation, its products and performance, or its employees.

d. Destruction, damage, improper disposition, or unauthorized possession or removal from Company

premises of property that does not belong to the employee.

e. Posting, distributing, or circulating any written materials in work areas deemed inappropriate or disruptive.

Pending the outcome of this investigation, you have been suspended. I will be the person investigating these concerns.

What you can expect was discussed as the investigation is conducted. I will review the information and documentation you provided. As appropriate, I will consult with other employees and managers to assist in addressing and resolving the issues, and I will strive to keep you informed of the progress of this investigation.

I want to emphasize some of our expectations of you during this investigation. If you have any questions or concerns about any of these expectations, or about any part of this investigation, please contact me immediately. The expectations for you include the following:

You are expected to cooperate fully throughout the investigation, and be completely honest in answering questions and providing information to the Company.

You are expected to provide us with all of the information and documentation that you believe may help us in conducting this investigation. If you have any information or documentation that may be relevant to this matter and which you have not already provided, please provide immediately.

While this investigation is being conducted, you will be suspended without pay. During this time you must devote your full efforts to help bring this matter to closure. You must remain available during normal working hours to meet and/or provide information to Company representatives.

This is a confidential investigation. You must not discuss this investigation with any person who does not have a legitimate business need to know this information. If you have any questions or concerns about this requirement at any time, please feel free to discuss it further with me.

If you have any questions or concerns about any of these expectations, or about any part of this investigation, you will contact me immediately. I will contact you within the next three days to let you know of the progress of the investigation.

Please let me know if you have any questions, additional information, or want to discuss any of this. As you know, you can reach me at 839–4612.

Completing its investigation, the Respondent gave Boerner and Howell identical dismissal letters dated June 18 and reading as follows:

Subject: Investigation—Termination

We have completed the investigation of the alleged violation of policy listed in your suspension letter of June 15, 1993.

Our conclusions, based on interview with employees and your statement are:

---

[3] Respondent has a trailer to which employees may repair to smoke on their breaks.

ILLUSTRATION 15-1   *(continued)*

566   DECISIONS OF THE NATIONAL LABOR RELATIONS BOARD

While working third shift on Sunday night, June 13th, an employee removed a confidential memo from the locked office of Health & Safety, made a copy and gave it to the Polyester third shift employees. You and one other Polyester employee co-authored derogatory, inflammatory and false comments on the memo, made additional copies and distributed it.

WAL cannot tolerate such actions and multiple violations of company policy. Therefore, your termination is effective immediately due to misconduct. Your final paycheck will include 32 hours of vacation payoff.

B. *Discussion and Conclusions*

The facts are clear and undisputed, but do they show the discharges were unlawful or legitimate? As I have previously stated in *Gatliff Coal*,[4] the answer to such questions depend on whether concerted action is present, whether that action is protected if it is in fact concerted, whether the General Counsel has set forth a prima facie case, the terminations were precipitated by protected concerted activity, and, if General Counsel has such a prima facie case, would Respondent have taken the same action in the absence of the protected activity? The first step in the process of determining these issues is measuring the facts found against the guide set forth in *Meyers Industries*, 268 NLRB 493, 497 (1984) (*Meyers I*), in the following terms:

In general, to find an employee's activity to be "concerted," we shall require that it be engaged in with or on the authority of other employees, and not solely by and on behalf of the employee himself. Once the activity is found to be concerted, an 8(a)(1) violation will be found if, in addition, the employer knew of the concerted nature of the employee's activity, the concerted activity was protected by the Act, and the adverse employment action at issue (e.g., discharge) was motivated by the he employee's protected concerted activity. [Footnotes deleted.]

and as recited in *Meyers Industries*, 281 NLRB 882, 887 (1986) (*Meyers II*):

We reiterate, our definition of concerted activity in *Meyers I* encompasses those circumstances where individual employees seek to initiate or to induce or to prepare for group action, as well as individual employees bringing truly group complaints tot he attention of management.

General Counsel, relying on *Meyers I*; *Amelio's*, 301 NLRB 182 fn. 4 (1991); and *Dayton Typographical Service*, 273 NLRB 1205 (1984), contends Boerner's conduct was concerted because other employees were opposed to the suggestions in the memo, Neusock assisted Boerner in the drafting of his comments on the memo, and Boerner's posting of the memo was a solicitation of employee actions and a logical outgrowth of the employees' joint complaint about the memo's stance on smoking.

I do not believe Boerner's conduct was concerted merely because others were opposed to the memo's suggestions inasmuch as there is no persuasive evidence the other three

memo readers, or any one else, authorized him to act on their behalf, or, with respect to the reference to the footnote in *Amelio's*, that Boerner's writings on the memo were necessarily a logical outgrowth of the concerns expressed by the group at the lunchroom table. Moreover, I do not agree that mere assistance in the spelling of a word threw Neusock into concert with Boerner. I do, however, conclude in accord with *Meyers II*, supra, that Boerner was engaged in concerted activity because his uncontroverted and credible testimony that he posted the memo, with his comments thereon. "To let the other people in the plant know—the other smokers know that this had been written and to see if—maybe if they had any comments or any hard feelings, maybe they would express their feelings" warrants a fair conclusion that he was seeking "to initiate or to induce or to prepare for group action" by fellow smokers in opposition to the sentiments expressed in the memo which were contrary to the interest of employees who smoked and in support of his writings on the memo.[5]

When Howell added his words to the memo, he endorsed and joined Boerner's effort in protest of the memo's attack on the existing smoking policy. That he did not then know Howell was the one who added the commentary to the memo is of no consequence. Here two employees reacted adversely to the memo and took complementary action to oppose it because they were smokers concerned in a common goal of preserving the status quo as it related to the policy on smoking. Howell's conduct in copying the notice, with his comments added thereon and posting it in several additional areas was an enlistment in and enlargement of Boerner's effort to inform other smokers of the threat the memo posed to existing smoking policy which was acceptable to employees who smoked.

The Respondent's smoking policy is a term or condition of employment, *Allied Signal*, 307 NLRB 752, 754 (1992), and the concerted activity of Boerner and Howell directed at protesting any change in policy thus concerns a term or condition of employment and is protected. The dismissal letters given to Howell and Boerner flatly stated the reason for their discharge to be "You and one other Polyester employee co-authored derogatory, inflammatory and false comments on the memo, made additional copies and distributed it." This evidences that the Respondent believed they were acting concertedly in writing and posting the altered memo, and terminated them for engaging in such activity. It is well settled that discharges based on suspected concerted activities violate Section 8(a)(1) of the Act even if the suspected concert did not exist. See, e.g., *American Poly Therm Co.*, 298 NLRB 1057, 1065 (1990); *Gulf-Wandes Corp.*, 233 NLRB 772, 778 (1977).

I conclude the evidence warrants an inference the known or suspected participation of Boerner and Howell in protected concerted activities was a motivating factor in the Respondent's decision to discharge them. The burden rests on the Respondent to show the discharges would have taken place in the absence of protected concerted activity. *Wright Line*, 251 NLRB 1083 (1980); *NLRB v. Transportation Management Corp.*, 462 U.S. 393 (1983).

---

[4] *Gatliff Coal Co.*, 301 NLRB 793 (1991).

[5] The testimony of Jane Paxton that her investigation received a report that the comments at issue were designed to start up trouble evidences that the Respondent recognized the comments were of interest to other employees and would tend to inspire debate.

ILLUSTRATION 15-1   *(continued; pages omitted)*

therefore not shown the rule was violated,[6] and I find it was not because no postings were made in work areas. The use of the rule by Respondent as a defense therefore can not prevail. Here again, I conclude Respondent has consciously manufactured a reason that does not exist in order to disguise its true motivation.

The evidence shows Howell and Boerner were engaged in protected concerted activity when they placed their comments on and posted the memo, those activities were a motivating factor in Respondent's decision to discharge them, and General Counsel has made out a prima facie case the Act has been violated. The burden on the Respondent to prove the discharges would have taken place in the absence of any protected activity has not been met. Accordingly, I find General Counsel has proved by a preponderance of the credible evidence that Howell and Boerner were discharged in violation of Section 8(a)(1) of the Act.

To the extent the complaint alleges their suspension during investigation violated the Act, I do not so find. It was not unreasonable for the Respondent to suspend the employees involved in the handling of a document wrongfully extracted from its files while it conducted an appropriate investigation. It is its conduct after it ascertained the facts which runs afoul of the Act.

CONCLUSIONS OF LAW

1. Respondent is an employer within the meaning of Section 2(2), (6), and (7) of the Act.

2. Respondent violated Section 8(a)(1) of the Act by discharging Martin Howell and Robert Boerner on June 18, 1993, because they engaged in protected concerted activity.

3. The unfair labor practices found affect commerce within the meaning of Section 2(6) and (7) of the Act.

THE REMEDY

In addition to the usual notice posting and cease-and-desist requirements, my recommended Order will require Respondent to offer Howell and Boerner immediate and full reinstatement to their former jobs or, if those jobs no longer exist, to substantially equivalent positions without prejudice to their seniority, or other rights and privileges previously enjoyed, and make them whole for any loss of earnings suffered as a result of the discrimination against them. Backpay shall be calculated and interest thereon computed in the manner prescribed in *F. W. Woolworth Co.*, 90 NLRB 289 (1950), and *New Horizons for the Retarded*, 283 NLRB 1173 (1987). I shall further recommend that Respondent be required to remove from its files any reference to their discharges and notify them in writing that this has been done and that the discharges will not be used against them in any way.

On these findings of fact and conclusions of law and on the entire record, I issue the following recommended[7]

---

[6] Whether the posting rule is valid or not is not before me.

[7] If no exceptions are filed as provided by Sec. 102.46 of the Board's Rules and Regulations, the findings, conclusions, and recommended Order shall, as provided in Sec. 102.48 of the Rules, be adopted by the Board and all objections to them shall be deemed waived for all purposes.

ORDER

The Respondent, Morton International, Inc., West Alexandria, Ohio, its officers, agents, successors, and assigns, shall

1. Cease and desist from

(a) Discharging or otherwise discriminating against employees because they engage in protected concerted activity.

(b) In any like or related manner interfering with, restraining, or coercing employees in the exercise of the rights guaranteed them by Section 7 of the Act.

2. Take the following affirmative action necessary to effectuate the policies of the Act.

(a) Offer Martin D. Howell and Robert Boerner immediate and full reinstatement to their former jobs or, if those jobs no longer exist, to substantially equivalent positions, without prejudice to their seniority or any other rights or privileges previously enjoyed, and make them whole for any loss of earnings or benefits suffered as a result of the discrimination against them, in the manner set forth in the remedy section of this decision.

(b) Remove from its files any reference to the discharges of Howell and Boerner on June 18, 1993, and notify them in writing that this has been done and that the discharges will not be used against them in any way.

(c) Preserve and, on request, make available to the Board or its agents for examination and copying, all payroll records, social security payment records, timecards, personnel records and reports, and all other records necessary to analyze the amount of backpay due under the terms of this Order.

(d) Post at its place of business in West Alexandria, Ohio, copies of the attached notice marked "Appendix."[8] Copies of the notice, on forms provided by the Regional Director for Region 9, after being signed by the Respondent's authorized representative, shall be posted by the Respondent immediately upon receipt and maintained for 60 consecutive days in conspicuous places including all places where notices to employees are customarily posted. Reasonable steps shall be taken by the Respondent to ensure that the notices are not altered, defaced, or covered by any other material.

(e) Notify the Regional Director in writing within 20 days from the date of this Order what steps the Respondent has taken to comply.

---

[8] If this Order is enforced by a judgment of a United States court of appeals, the words in the notice reading "Posted by Order of the National Labor Relations Board" shall read "Posted Pursuant to a Judgment of the United States Court of Appeals Enforcing an Order of the National Labor Relations Board."

APPENDIX

NOTICE TO EMPLOYEES
POSTED BY ORDER OF THE
NATIONAL LABOR RELATIONS BOARD
An Agency of the United States Government

The National Labor Relations Board has found that we violated the National Labor Relations Act and has ordered us to post and abide by this notice.

Section 7 of the Act gives employees these rights.

To organize
To form, join, or assist any union

B.   WHY WOULD YOU RESEARCH WHICH AGENCY DECISIONS?

As with agency regulations, the reason for researching formal agency decisions is that they constitute the law. An agency decision must conform, of course, to statutory and constitutional requirements, as determined by the courts. Furthermore, the agency's process must be fair, and there must be substantial evidence to support the decision. The agency properly may be seen as subordinate to the legislature and courts. Even so, the decision is law and functions as precedent for other similar situations coming within the agency's jurisdiction. Although stare decisis does not operate as forcefully with agencies as with courts, an agency must explain any deviations from earlier decisions.

Once you have located the pertinent statute enabling an agency to act, you will know which agency's decisions to research. Federal statutes give rise to federal agency decisions, and state statutes creating state agencies give rise to state agency decisions.

C.   HOW DO YOU RESEARCH AGENCY DECISIONS?

As with judicial cases, an agency decision first appears in slip form, that is, a single decision, without editorial enhancement. Decisions are compiled periodically into reporters. Each such reporter contains the decisions of a specific agency, and each volume contains that agency's decisions for a specific time period. These agency reporters typically are government publications, and their utility as research sources varies widely.

Agency decisions now may be found online via Westlaw and LEXIS and via government web sites on the Internet. Furthermore, for major practice areas, they appear as well in the mini-libraries discussed in Chapter 16. These alternatives to the official paper-based reporters often are good choices, especially if your agency's official reporter is cumbersome to use or updated slowly.

Comprehensive research into agency decisions, like research in agency regulations, involves statutes and case law from the courts. You should consult annotated codes early in your research, and judicial case law may conclude your research.

The following text opens and closes with brief discussions of statutory and judicial case law research, respectively. The text describes how to use four groups of research sources: official agency reporters and digests, Westlaw and LEXIS, government web sites, and citators for agency decisions. Exhibit 15.1 on page 293 shows the relationships among the various research practices.

The discussion focuses on federal agency decisions, in particular those from the National Labor Relations Board. The research sources for agency decisions under the federal labor statute are among the most extensive and

EXHIBIT 15.1	Overview of Agency Decisions Research

Preliminary step: statutory research in annotated codes

Major step: research agency decisions		
official reporter and digest	Westlaw or LEXIS	public Internet sources
citators		

Concluding step: case law research
• reporters and digests, their computer-based alternatives, citators
• annotated codes in various media

sophisticated. For less prominent federal agencies as well as for state agencies, you may find fewer sources and options. A good practice is to contact the agency or a reference librarian in an academic law library for assistance.

Preliminary research for agency decisions in annotated codes:

● study enabling statute
● obtain references to agency decisions and judicial cases

When an agency that has the authority to decide cases does so, it implements the language of its enabling statute. Hence you should begin your research with the enabling statute. Chapter 12 covers statutory research.

As you research in the annotated code, you should first examine the statutory language guiding your agency's actions. You then should examine the annotation for descriptions of pertinent cases. While most cases noted in the annotation likely will be judicial cases, you may find some references to agency decisions as well. See Illustration 15-2 on page 294.

Researching the Canoga case, we saw that the labor statute indicates that it protects not only activities involving unions but also other "concerted activities for the purpose of . . . mutual aid or protection." *See* 29 U.S.C. § 157 (1994). We found references to various Board and court decisions in the annotation in *United States Code Service* (U.S.C.S.) under the topic of "activities as concerted activities—generally." See Illustration 15-2 on page 294.

ILLUSTRATION 15-2   Case Descriptions in Annotated Code, from *United States Code Service*

---

29 USCS § 157, n 45   LABOR

A conversation may constitute a concerted activity although it involves only a speaker and listener, but to qualify as such it must appear at the very least that it was engaged in with the object of initiating or introducing or preparing for group action or that it had some relation to group action in the interest of the employees. Mushroom Transp. Co. v NLRB (1964, CA3) 330 F2d 683, 56 BNA LRRM 2034, 49 CCH LC ¶ 18921.

In order to protect concerted activities in full bloom, protection must be extended to "intended, contemplated or even referred to" group action lest employer retaliation destroy incipient employee initiative aimed at bettering terms of employment and working conditions. Hugh H. Wilson Corp. v NLRB (1969, CA3) 414 F2d 1345, 71 BNA LRRM 2827, 60 CCH LC ¶ 10205, cert den (1970) 397 US 935, 25 L Ed 2d 115, 90 S Ct 943, 73 BNA LRRM 2600, 62 CCH LC ¶ 10724.

Activities of employees engaged in, with, or on behalf of, other employees, and not solely by or on behalf of particular employees themselves, are concerted activities for purpose of mutual aid or protection within meaning of 29 USCS § 157. Top of Waikiki, Inc. v NLRB (1970, CA9) 429 F2d 419, 74 BNA LRRM 2678, 63 CCH LC ¶ 10999.

"Concerted activity" means the employee must be acting with or on behalf of other employees, and not solely by and on behalf of the discharged employee himself. NLRB v C &I Air Conditioning, Inc. (1973, CA9) 486 F2d 977, 84 BNA LRRM 2625, 72 CCH LC ¶ 14048.

For individual claim or complaint to amount to concerted action, it must not be made solely on behalf of individual employee, but must be made on behalf of other employees or at least be made with object of inducing or preparing for group action and have some arguable basis in collective bargaining agreement. ARO, Inc. v NLRB (1979, CA6) 596 F2d 713, 101 BNA LRRM 2153, 86 CCH LC ¶ 11250, 56 ALR Fed 728.

Concerted activity includes activity of individual employee when that employee is acting on behalf of only one other employee. Wilson Trophy Co. v NLRB (1993, CA8) 989 F2d 1502, 143 BNA LRRM 2008, 124 CCH LC ¶ 10622, reh, en banc, den (1993, CA8) 125 CCH LC ¶ 10740.

Two employees as well as a dozen or a thousand can act in concert for their mutual aid and protection. Tex-Togs, Inc. (1955) 112 NLRB 968, 36 BNA LRRM 1129, enforced (1956, CA5) 231 F2d 310, 37 BNA LRRM 2768, 30 CCH LC ¶ 69849.

It is not necessary for employees to band together and overtly manifest by physical action discontent before NLRB will find that concerted activity, for even individual protests which resound to groups' benefit are protected concerted activity. Aro, Inc. (1976) 227 NLRB 243, 94 BNA LRRM 1010, 1976-77 CCH NLRB ¶ 17662, enforcement

den (1979, CA6) 596 F2d 713, 101 BNA LRRM 2153, 86 CCH LC ¶ 11250, 56 ALR Fed 728.

Contrary to prior decision in Alleluia Cushion Co. (1975) 221 NLRB 999, Board will not find protected concerted activity unless employee engages in or with or own authority of other employees, and not solely on behalf of employee himself. Meyers Industries, Inc. (1984) 268 NLRB 493, 115 BNA LRRM 1025, 1983-84 CCH NLRB ¶ 16019, remanded (1985) 244 US App DC 42, 755 F2d 941, 118 BNA LRRM 2649, 102 CCH LC ¶ 11346, cert den (1985) 474 US 948, 88 L Ed 2d 294, 106 S Ct 313, 120 BNA LRRM 3392 and cert den (1985) 474 US 971, 88 L Ed 2d 320, 106 S Ct 352, 120 BNA LRRM 3392, 103 CCH LC ¶ 11585, on remand (1986) 281 NLRB 882, 123 BNA LRRM 1137, 1986-87 CCH NLRB ¶ 18184, affd (1987) 266 US App DC 385, 835 F2d 1481, 127 BNA LRRM 2415, 107 CCH LC ¶ 10226, cert den (1988) 487 US 1205, 101 L Ed 2d 884, 108 S Ct 2847, 128 BNA LRRM 2664, 129 BNA LRRM 3016, 109 CCH LC ¶ 10534.

46. Activity of single employee, generally

Employee who was discharged after acting alone in complaining to employer about violation would have been protected from discharge under 29 USCS § 157 by simply getting together with co-workers to complain. Prill v NLRB (1987) 266 US App DC 385, 835 F2d 1481, 127 BNA LRRM 2415, 107 CCH LC ¶ 10226, cert den (1988) 487 US 1205, 101 L Ed 2d 884, 108 S Ct 2847, 128 BNA LRRM 2664, 129 BNA LRRM 3016, 109 CCH LC ¶ 10534.

Activity of single employee in enlisting support of fellow employees for their mutual aid and protection is as much concerted activity as is ordinary group activity. Owens-Corning Fiberglas Corp. v NLRB (1969, CA4) 407 F2d 1357, 70 BNA LRRM 3065, 59 CCH LC ¶ 13356.

Truckdriver engaged in concerted activity by refusing to drive truck which he felt unsafe where he obtained instructions to do so from union official, sought to involve other union members and have them present during dispute with employer, and employer was aware of union involvement. McLean Trucking Co. v NLRB (1982, CA6) 689 F2d 605, 111 BNA LRRM 3185, 97 CCH LC ¶ 10166.

Single employee's filing of worker's compensation claim is not protected concerted activity, notwithstanding employee is member of collective bargaining group. Flick v General Host Corp. (1983, ND Ill) 573 F Supp 1086, 114 BNA LRRM 3576.

Employee who, in good faith, refuses to drive tractor-trailor truck on ground that condition of truck constitutes abnormally dangerous working condition is engaged in concerted activity under 29

> **Agency decisions in official reporters:**
>
> ► identify the agency's reporter
> ► use the index or digest to locate potentially pertinent cases
> ► consult the updating mechanism
> ► read the decisions

There is no reporter system for agency decisions that is equivalent to West Group's National Reporter System. However, the federal government does publish some agency decisions in official reporters. The federal segment of Table T.1 of *The Bluebook* lists these official reporters. These publications vary considerably, especially as to editorial enhancements and updating.

Reporters of agency decisions publish decisions in rough chronological order. Hence, your first step in finding an agency decision pertinent to your problem is to use a topically organized digest or index. The digest or index may come in several volumes, each covering a certain time period. Furthermore, you should examine whatever source, if any, that the agency uses to inform researchers of very recent decisions. Of course, you should read with care the decisions you have located. As with judicial cases, you should learn the outcome of the case, discern the rule used by the agency to decide the case, understand the facts of the case and the court's reasoning about those facts, identify the leading authorities cited in the reasoning, and examine any dissenting and concurring opinions. Be sure you fully understand how the decision is structured. Many agency commissioners incorporate the recommended findings and conclusions of the ALJ.

Researching the Canoga case, we examined the list in Table T.1 in *The Bluebook* and determined that the National Labor Relations Board issues *Decisions and Orders of the National Labor Relations Board* (N.L.R.B.). To locate pertinent Board decisions within this reporter, we used two closely related government publications.

The first, *Classification Outline with Topical Index for Decisions of the National Labor Relations Board and Related Court Decisions* (*Classification Outline*), contains an outline of Board decisions (and related court decisions). The Board has developed a detailed numerical classification scheme, with topics and subtopics. You can look up your research terms in the Topical Index to identify a pertinent part of the outline, or you can skim the Table of Contents and then the Classification Outline itself. See Illustration 15-3 on page 297. We thus arrived at topic 506, subtopic 2001-5000 (employee rights protected by section 7—nature of activities protected—generally—concerted activity defined).

The second publication is the *Classified Index of National Labor Relations Board Decisions and Related Court Decisions* (*Classified Index*). Although it is called an index, it is really a digest of cases, with the case descriptions arranged according to the topics found in the *Classification Outline*. See

Illustration 15-4 on page 298. Unfortunately, the *Classified Index* is not cumulative; each volume covers several years of decisions. Thus, you need to examine multiple volumes to find all of the relevant digest entries. In a recent volume of the *Classified Index*, under topic 506, subtopic 2001-5000, we found several agency decisions, including one for *Morton International, Inc.*, cited as "315 NLRB No. 71."

New decisions are summarized in a pamphlet, *Weekly Summary of NLRB Cases*. There is no index or other finding aid, and the only method to find a pertinent decision is to skim the summaries. If you identify a potentially pertinent decision in the *Weekly Summary*, you could visit the Board's web site or contact the Board to obtain a slip opinion.

We looked for *Morton International* in volume 315 of the *Decisions and Orders of the National Labor Relations Board*. See again Illustration 15-1 on pages 288–291. The decision number is not the page designation; the cross-reference table of decisions in the front of volume 315 indicates that No. 71 begins on page 564. From *Morton International*, we learned that when two employees handwrote comments on a memo posted by the employer addressing the company's no-smoking policy, they engaged in protected concerted activity, as they acted together to protest a change in the terms and conditions of employment.

Agency decisions in Westlaw and LEXIS:

► select an appropriate database

► draft and run a Boolean or natural-language search

► sift the search results

► read the decisions

LEXIS and Westlaw both contain extensive databases of federal agency decisions. New decisions are added as they become available, and the databases extend backward in time as well. The two online services also make some state agency decisions available.

Online research through Westlaw and LEXIS for agency decisions has several advantages and disadvantages. The databases are more current than paper reporters, and you can circumvent a difficult or cumbersome index or digest by running a search online. On the other hand, you do not obtain the advantages of a well written and well maintained index or digest. Compared to a government web site, LEXIS and Westlaw are more expansive and offer more search options. However, the cost is, of course, higher.

If you already have a citation or name for an agency decision, you would conduct a find or title search to obtain the decision. If not, your first step is to select an appropriate database. The obvious choice is the database containing the decisions of the agency you have identified. You may use Boolean and natural-language searches, most probably in the full text of the decisions.

ILLUSTRATION 15-3   Classification Outline, from *Classification Outline with Topical Index for Decisions of the National Labor Relations Board and Related Court Decisions*

506 EMPLOYEE RIGHTS PROTECTED BY SECTION 7

0100	**GENERALLY**
0114	RIGHT OF SELF-ORGANIZATION
0128	RIGHT TO FORM, JOIN, OR ASSIST LABOR ORGANIZATIONS
0142	RIGHT TO BARGAIN COLLECTIVELY THROUGH REPRESENTATIVE OF OWN CHOOSING
0156	RIGHT TO ENGAGE IN OTHER CONCERTED ACTIVITIES FOR PURPOSE OF COLLECTIVE BARGAINING
0170	RIGHT TO ENGAGE IN OTHER CONCERTED ACTIVITIES FOR MUTUAL AID OR PROTECTION
0180	ATTITUDE TOWARD MANAGEMENT REFLECTING DISSATISFACTION WITH WORKING CONDITIONS AND/OR LACK OF SUCCESS OF UNION CAMPAIGN, ETC.
0184	RIGHT TO REFRAIN FROM EXERCISE OF SECTION 7 RIGHTS
0184-0100	Generally
0184-5000	Subject to membership requirement of valid agreement
0188	RIGHT TO BE FREE FROM UNFAIR, IRRELEVANT, OR INVIDIOUS TREATMENT BY REPRESENTATIVE
0188-5000	Differentiation on basis of sex
0192	RIGHTS DERIVED FROM OTHER FEDERAL LABOR STATUTES
2000	**NATURE OF ACTIVITIES PROTECTED**
2001	GENERALLY
2001-5000	Concerted activity defined
2017	NOT ALL CONCERTED ACTIVITIES PROTECTED
2017-0800	Activity of such character as to render employee unfit for further service
2017-1700	Activities tending to disrupt employer's or union's operations
2017-2500	Activities relating to intra-union affairs
2017-3300	Cessation of work for personal reasons
2017-4000	No impact upon terms and conditions of employment
2017-5000	Resort to prohibited means

82

2017-6700	Activities prohibited by statute
2017-8300	Conduct violating valid provisions of contract
2017-9100	Conduct in derogation of bargaining representation
2033	BOARD HAS FUNCTION OF BALANCING CONFLICTING EMPLOYEE AND EMPLOYER INTERESTS
2033-5000	Exercise of economic pressure not unlawful per se
2050	EMPLOYER'S MISTAKEN BELIEF AS TO ACTIVITY'S PROTECTED STATUS IMMATERIAL
2060	EMPLOYEES' MISTAKEN BELIEF AS TO VALIDITY OF GRIEVANCE IMMATERIAL
2067	UNION MEMBERSHIP IMMATERIAL
2083	UNION ACTIVITY NEED NOT BE INVOLVED OR COLLECTIVE BARGAINING CONTEMPLATED
3000	**REFUSAL TO CROSS PICKET LINE**
3001	GENERALLY
3001-5000	Employer may replace non-striking employee refusing to cross line if business reasons so require
3033	AT PREMISES OF ANOTHER EMPLOYER
3033-0100	Generally
3033-2500	Right protected by 8(b)(4) proviso
3033-5000	Primary picket line
3033-7500	Secondary picket line
3033-8700	Picket line at state subdivision
3067	AT OWN EMPLOYER'S PREMISES
3067-0100	Generally
3067-1700	Primary line of another union at employee's place of work
3067-3300	Primary line of union representing unit of which employee is not member
3067-5000	As result of sympathy strike
3067-6700	Secondary picket line which is primary line of another union
4000	**OBJECTIVE AS DETERMINANT OF PROTECTED STATUS OF ACTIVITY**
4001	GENERALLY
4001-5000	Racial discrimination
4033	OBJECTIVES WARRANTING PROTECTION OF ACTIVITY
4033-0100	Generally

ILLUSTRATION 15-4   Case Descriptions, from *Classified Index of National Labor Relations Board Decisions and Related Court Decisions*

506-EMPLOYEE RIGHTS PROTECTED BY SECTION 7
0180—Cont.

expressing a group concern to management and when Ee told coworkers what he had done, one of them indicated that if he had known, he would have accompanied the complaining Ee in approaching management; in instant case, Ee's refusal to follow up on problems by arranging group meeting weakens his argument that he was acting on behalf of other drivers]

Manimark Corporation v. N.L.R.B.   7 F.3d 547 (6th Cir.,
                                                  October 21, 1993);
                                                  144 LRRM 2521

[E's discharge of Ee for his disruptive behavior and negative attitude, lawful, since Ee's discussion with an assistant to E's controller about policy of unused sick pay and his expressed intention to speak to management about policy was not concerted activity; Ee action of speaking up in front of group of Ees does not rise to level of a *protest;* instant case distinguishable from *NLRB v. Evans Packing Co.,* 463 F.2d 193 (6th Cir. 1972) as in *Evans* there was clear evidence that complaining Ee was speaking on behalf of others who were equally concerned and in this case, there was little, if any, evidence that others also wanted to complain about policy rather than merely seeking a clarification of the policy]

**0184   RIGHT TO REFRAIN FROM EXERCISE OF
             SECTION 7 RIGHTS**

0184-0100   Generally

Sheet Metal Workers International   SDR 312 NLRB No. 049
  Association Local 550

[under *Scofield* (394 U.S. 423), U is free to enforce properly adopted rule which reflects legitimate U interest, impairs no congressional policy contained in labor laws, and is reasonably enforced against U members who are free to leave U and escape rule; accordingly, U's mere maintenance of rule requiring presence of U representative during investigatory interviews was not unlawful, absent argument by GC that rule was not properly adopted or communicated to U's members]

Sheet Metal Workers International   SDR 312 NLRB No. 049
  Association Local 550

[U's mere maintenance of rule requiring presence of U representative during investigatory interviews held not unlawful, since rule did not interfere with Ee's right to refrain from engaging in U activities; members who choose to decline U representation at investigatory interviews were free to resign their membership and thereby avoid application of rule; and here U did not seek to apply or enforce its rule against nonmembers, there were no unlawful restrictions on members' right to resign, and rule was not somehow binding on nonmembers]

Sheet Metal Workers International   SDR 312 NLRB No. 049
  Association Local 550

[U unlawfully attempted to enforce its rule requiring presence of U representative during investigatory interviews of Ee/members, since rule interfered with E's right to secure Ee testimony in preparation for grievance arbitration hearings, and was not applied to protect Ee/members from discipline; while Ees have right to assistance of U in disciplinary matters, such right is personal to them and does not reside in U; Ees also have statutory right to decline U assistance or participation, and rule interfered with their right to refrain from U activities]

**0188   RIGHT TO BE FREE FROM UNFAIR,
             IRRELEVANT, OR INVIDIOUS TREATMENT
             BY REPRESENTATIVE**

International Brotherhood of   SDO 308 NLRB No. 026
  Teamsters, Local 101, AFL-CIO
  (Allied Signal Corporation)

[breach of duty of representation requires credible proof that demonstrates, with reasonable preciseness, that bargaining agent has crossed line of rationality and acted to detriment of member or members for reasons that are arbitrary, discriminatory, or in bad faith; negotiating process which leads to decision which does not meet everyone's perception of fairness is not itself offensive to this standard; and mere negligence would not state a claim for breach of duty]

0188-5000   Differentiation on basis of sex

Dispatch Printing Company   SDR 306 NLRB No. 003

[alleged discriminatory failure to assign priority rights, i.e. seniority concept involving continuous service within a job classification and within unit designated by newspaper publisher as a *chapel*, to three female Ees, held not the cause of layoff, but rather cause attributed

to contract's facially nondiscriminatory guarantee of lifetime or term-of-contract jobs for named Ees, thus layoff was legal]

Dispatch Printing Company   SDR 306 NLRB No. 003

[failure to assign seniority rights to female Ees was not sexual discrimination despite earlier case which found the U displayed hostility to female Ees, where prior 2 year old case did not concern itself with seniority rights, and there was no record evidence of animus toward females by either the U or the E; Further, U steward, who supposedly was chief protagonist against these female Ees, supported a change in the seniority system which, although defeated, would have benefitted these female Ees, and past practice was consistent in that the only similarly situated male Ee was treated the same way]

2000   NATURE OF ACTIVITIES PROTECTED

2001   GENERALLY

Brother Industries (U.S.A.), Inc.   GBC 314 NLRB No. 198

[notwithstanding giving false statements to Bd agent was serious violation of law and not condoned, fired Ee and other Ees who falsely said in Bd affidavits that ptn complaining about a supervisor and working conditions was circulated and signed only during breaktimes, were protected by the Act and fired Ee was fit for further employment, where Ees gave corrected affidavits and fully and credibly testified before ALJ, since Ees acted out of fear because of E's attempt to disparately enforce no-solicitation no-distribution rule against Ees]

Blue Circle Cement Company, Inc.   SDO 311 NLRB No. 065
  and International Brotherhood
  of Boilermakers, AFL-CIO

[Bd's decision in *Mike Yurosek & Son, Inc.,* 306 NLRB No. 210, which concerned whether action of individual Ees, in protesting working conditions, was concerted, while instant case purportedly presented *fundamentally different question* of whether Ee's activity was protected held pertinent since instant case plainly concerned whether Ee's activity was concerted *and* protected]

2001-5000   Concerted activity defined

Neff-Perkins Co.   GSC 315 NLRB No. 157

[Ees engaged in protected concerted activities when during a group meeting called by the E in which a representative from its major customer was present, Ees questioned management about the placement of a control panel on a press which was causing back problems for the operators, whether the major customer was involved in setting wages of the Ees, and criticized management over maintenance of equipment and training, since such comments and questions concerned working conditions]

Avery Leasing, Inc.   GBC 315 NLRB No. 73

[Discharged Ee engaged in protected concerted activity; where an Ee, in the presence of other Ees, complains to management concerning wages, hours, or other terms and conditions of employment, such complaints constitute protected concerted activity, even though the Ee purports to speak on behalf of himself or herself; protected concerted activity established where an Ee complained to a supervisor because discharged Ee sought to invoke a seniority system, regardless of whether discharged Ee would have personally benefited; further, supervisor's designation of discharged Ee as an instigator indicates that the company believed Ee was inciting the Ees to assert their grievances]

Morton International, Inc.   DBC 315 NLRB No. 71

[E's suspension and discharge of 2 Ees for writing on and posting memo dealing with enforcement of E's no-smoking policy, unlawful, since Ees were engaged in protected concerted activity; Ees' action of altering memo was taken to initiate or induce other fellow smokers in opposition to sentiments of memo; Ees took action to oppose memo in attempt to preserve status quo as it related to smoking policy; E's smoking policy is term and condition of employment and Ees' concerted action directed at protesting change in policy thus concerns a term and condition of employment and is protected activity; E's dismissal letters, stating *You and one other ... Ee,* indicates E believed Ees were acting concertedly in writing on and posting memo]

Morton International, Inc.   DBC 315 NLRB No. 71

[E's use of word *chicken shit* to describe Ee who wrote memo and other Ee's attack of person he believed to be author by stating that she had no *useful thoughts* does not make Ees'conduct unprotected; Ees were engaged in protected concerted activity of altering memo dealing with E's smoking policy in effort to induce other smokers to oppose sentiments in memo requesting that E change the smoking policy; use of *chicken shit* as a descriptive term of disapproval is

248

Next you would sift results, for example, by skimming the portions of the retrieved decisions where your search terms appear. Then you would read the cases, as described above.

Researching the Canoga case, we used Westlaw's FLB-NLRB database, containing the Board's decisions from 1935 (its establishment) to date. We ran the search ["concerted activit!" /p smok!] and obtained sixty documents. See Illustration 15-5 on page 300. The *Morton International* case was the sixth on the list.

Agency decisions via public Internet web sites:

► select an appropriate web site and database
► run a find search
► or draft and run a Boolean search
► sift the results
► read the decisions

Many major federal agency decisions and an increasing share of state agency decisions may be found online through the Internet. The federal Government Printing Office (GPO) web site offers some agency decisions published by the GPO; other online material may be found through Findlaw.

There are several advantages to this approach. A government database is inexpensive, very credible, and probably very current. With basic Boolean search capabilities, you should be able to locate pertinent decisions, given the specialized language used in most areas of administrative law. However, the database is unlikely to contain cases decided before the 1990s.

As in other Internet research, your first step is to locate an appropriate web site and database; then determine its scope, especially as to older decisions. Then draft and run a search, sift your results, and read pertinent cases as you would read a case in a paper reporter.

More specifically, National Labor Relations Board decisions can be found in the GPO database at www.nlrb.gov. This database contains all Board decisions published since August 1991 (volume 304). As soon as a new decision is released for publication, it is made available online. Hence, the database is current, but limited to fairly recent decisions. If you know the title and citation of a specific decision, you can use the table of decisions within the volume to find the text of the case. Or you can perform a Boolean search (using AND, ADJ, OR, NOT; root words; and phrases) for all volumes in the database or for individual volumes.

Researching the Canoga case, we performed a simple Boolean search ["concerted activity" AND smok*] in the GPO NLRB database. We obtained forty decisions (the default number), including the *Morton International* decision, the second on the list. See Illustration 15-6 on page 301. Note that the citation list is not particularly revealing, compared to the information generated by Westlaw or LEXIS.

ILLUSTRATION 15-5   Westlaw Partial Citations List, Run in FLB-NLRB
                           Database

Citations List   Search Result Documents: 60
Database: FLB-NLRB

1.   Regional Home Care, Inc., d/b/a North Atlantic Medical Services and Truck Drivers Union Local No.
       170, a/w International Brotherhood of Teamsters, AFL-CIO, 329 NLRB No. 6, 1999 WL 713975
       (N.L.R.B., Sep 09, 1999) (NO. CASES 1-CA-32995 (1-)

2.   Tracer Protection Services, Inc. and Shane Crump Ormet Primary Aluminum Corporation and Shane
       Crump, 328 NLRB No. 94, 1999 WL 416183, 162 L.R.R.M. (BNA) 1079 (N.L.R.B., Jun 16, 1999)
       (NO. CASES 15-CA-12970 AN)

3.   In re Honda, 321 NLRB 482, 321 NLRB No. 69, 1996 WL 338371, 154 L.R.R.M. (BNA) 1050,
       1995-96 NLRB Dec. P 16,044 (N.L.R.B., Jun 17, 1996) (NO. 14-CA-23169, 4-CA-23575,
       14-CA-23318, 14-CA-23501)

4.   Hospital Linen Service, 316 NLRB 1151, 316 NLRB No. 177, 1995 WL 214641,
       149 L.R.R.M. (BNA) 1167, 1995-96 NLRB Dec. P 15,735 (N.L.R.B., Apr 10, 1995) (NO.
       6-CA-26123, 6-CA-26152)

5.   Zurn Nepco, 316 NLRB 811, 316 NLRB No. 133, 1995 WL 128054, 149 L.R.R.M. (BNA) 1193,
       1995-96 NLRB Dec. P 15,697 (N.L.R.B., Mar 23, 1995) (NO. 4-CA-19725, 4-CA-19725-3,
       4-CA-19725-4, 4-CA-20187)

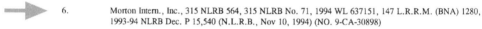

6.   Morton Intern., Inc., 315 NLRB 564, 315 NLRB No. 71, 1994 WL 637151, 147 L.R.R.M. (BNA) 1280,
       1993-94 NLRB Dec. P 15,540 (N.L.R.B., Nov 10, 1994) (NO. 9-CA-30898)

7.   Farmer Bros. Co., 303 NLRB 638, 303 NLRB No. 92, 1991 WL 262405, 138 L.R.R.M. (BNA) 1390,
       1991-92 NLRB Dec. P 16,736 (N.L.R.B., Jun 27, 1991) (NO. 31-CA-17677)

8.   Yokohama Tire Corp., 303 NLRB 337, 303 NLRB No. 50, 1991 WL 123552,
       138 L.R.R.M. (BNA) 1155, 1991-92 NLRB Dec. P 16,699 (N.L.R.B., Jun 11, 1991) (NO.
       22-CA-16571)

9.   Adam's Rib Restaurant, 299 NLRB 717, 299 NLRB No. 108, 1990 WL 141911,
       136 L.R.R.M. (BNA) 1064, 1989-90 NLRB Dec. P 16,219 (N.L.R.B., Sep 14, 1990) (NO.
       34-CA-4403)

10. ▷ Aspen, 298 NLRB 401, 298 NLRB No. 49, 1990 WL 122379, 134 L.R.R.M. (BNA) 1135,
       1989-90 NLRB Dec. P 16,044 (N.L.R.B., Apr 30, 1990) (NO. 22-CA-15851, 22-CA-16148,
       22-CA-16060)

11.   Hussmann Corp., 290 NLRB 1108, 290 NLRB No. 145, 1988 WL 214167, 131 L.R.R.M. (BNA) 1171,
       1988-89 NLRB Dec. P 15,109 (N.L.R.B., Sep 15, 1988) (NO. 15-CA-10270-2)

12.   St. John's Hosp., 281 NLRB 1163, 281 NLRB No. 157, 1986 WL 54417, 124 L.R.R.M. (BNA) 1311,
       1986-87 NLRB Dec. P 18,296 (N.L.R.B., Sep 30, 1986) (NO. 6-CA-14603, 6-CA-15496)

13.   Rockwell Corp., 278 NLRB 55, 278 NLRB No. 13, 1986 WL 54057, 122 L.R.R.M. (BNA) 1285,
       1986-87 NLRB Dec. P 18,157 (N.L.R.B., Jan 16, 1986) (NO. 10-CA-20815)

14.   Bechtel Power Co., 277 NLRB 882, 277 NLRB No. 88, 1985 WL 46102, 120 L.R.R.M. (BNA) 1291,
       1985-86 NLRB Dec. P 17,547 (N.L.R.B., Nov 27, 1985) (NO. 4-CA-14361)

15.   J.T. Cullen Co., 271 NLRB 114, 271 NLRB No. 19, 1984 WL 36577, 116 L.R.R.M. (BNA) 1339,

ILLUSTRATION 15-6   NLRB Files Partial Search Results, from GPO Access

Search Results (v2)   Page 1 of 6

Search Results

Search Database:

NLRB Files

For: "SMOK AND "concerted activity""*

Total Hits: 40

[1]
No Title Found
     Size: 685112 , **Score:** 1000 , TEXT , PDF

[2]
No Title Found
     Size: 40733 , **Score:** 523 , TEXT , PDF

[3]
[325 NLRB No. 161] Roma One Enterprises, d/b/a Tony Roma's Restaurant and Mauro S. Ruiz. Case 21-CA-31485
     Size: 56368 , **Score:** 290 , TEXT , PDF

[4]
[319 NLRB No. 135] Brown & Root USA, Inc. and International Brotherhood of Boilermakers, Iron Shipbuilders, Blacksmiths, Forgers and Helpers, AFL-CIO and West Virginia Building & Construction Trades Council, AFL-CIO. Cases 9-CA- 27460 and 9-CA-27674
     Size: 913849 , **Score:** 247 , TEXT , PDF

[5]
No Title Found
     Size: 164736 , **Score:** 196 , TEXT , PDF

[6]
[326 NLRB No. 29] Beverly California Corporation f/k/a Beverly Enterprises, its Operating Divisions, Regions, Wholly-Owned Subsidiaries and Individual Facilities and each of them and Service Employees' International Union, Local 606, AFL-CIO and United Food and Commercial Workers International Union Local 917, AFL-CIO and Peggy M. Urban and District 199P, National Union of Hospital and Health Care Employees, SEIU, AFL-CIO and New England Health Care Employees Union, District 1199/S.E.I.U. AFL-CIO and Gladys Hahn and Hospital and Health Care Workers Local 250, SEIU, AFL-CIO-CLC and United Food and Commercial Workers International Union, Local 1161, AFL-CIO and District 1199W/United Professional for Quality Health Care and Service Employees International Union, Local 150, AFL-CIO and United Steelworkers of America, AFL-CIO-CLC. Cases 6-CA- 20188-46 (formerly 16- CA-13556), 6-CA-20188-48 (formerly 25-CA-19478), 6-CA-20188-49

http://frwebgate.access.gpo.gov/cgi-bin/multidb.cgi   11/23/99

Citators for agency decisions:

- various Shepard's Citations in paper
- Shepard's online on LEXIS
- KeyCite on Westlaw

Just as you must learn the subsequent history and treatment of a case decided by a court, so must you be sure an agency decision has not lost its precedential force through adverse subsequent history, adverse treatment in later cases, or statutory developments. The later cases may be other agency decisions or judicial cases.

Some agency decisions may be updated through the paper publication *Shepard's United States Administrative Citations.* This Shepard's covers a fairly wide range of federal agencies. Some agency decisions are covered in specialized Shepard's. For example, labor law cases are covered by *Shepard's Labor Law Citations*; the cited sources include Board decisions and federal court cases involving labor law issues. Citing sources in these administrative Shepard's include federal cases from the United States Supreme Court to the federal district courts, state court cases, agency decisions, and secondary sources.

The alternatives to paper Shepard's are the electronic citators, Shepard's via LEXIS and Westlaw's KeyCite. These citators provide information similar to that provided for judicial cases, including the decision's history, later citing cases, and secondary sources that cite your decision. Furthermore, the electronic citators afford various means of tailoring your research, such as date and jurisdiction restrictions. See Illustration 15-7 on page 303.

Researching the Canoga case, we Shepardized the *Morton International* decision online. Illustration 15-7 on page 303 shows both the prior history of the decision, that is, where the ALJ decisions can be found, and a set of Board decisions citing *Morton International*. The "interim decision" references are to decisions in which the ALJ, rather than the Board itself, referred to *Morton International*. There is no indication that *Morton International* was reviewed by an appellate court.

Concluding judicial case law research regarding agency decisions:

- case reporters and digests, their computer-based alternatives, citators
- annotated codes in paper and computer-based media

Agency decisions operate in tandem with judicial case law. You must, of course, be aware of any judicial opinions reviewing the agency decisions you have located and intend to rely upon. More broadly, you should be aware

| ILLUSTRATION 15-7 | Shepard's Online Display (Partial), from LEXIS |

Check a Citation - SHEPARD'S® - 315 N.L.R.B. 564   Page 1 of 2

Citation: **315 nlrb 564** (Get this Document)   *Shepard's*® [   ] **Check**

Morton Int'l, 315 N.L.R.B. 564, 1994 N.L.R.B. LEXIS 910, 147 L.R.R.M. (BNA) 1280, 93-94 NLRB Dec. (CCH) P15540, 1993-94 NLRB Dec. (CCH) P15540, 315 N.L.R.B. No. 71 (1994)

PRIOR HISTORY (1 citing reference) ◆ **Hide Prior History**

    ▦ Morton Int'l, 1994 N.L.R.B. LEXIS 534 (N.L.R.B. July 20, 1994)

⊁   **Affirmed by, Adopted by (CITATION YOU ENTERED):**
      ▦ Morton Int'l, 315 N.L.R.B. 564, 1994 N.L.R.B. LEXIS 910, 147 L.R.R.M. (BNA) 1280, 9 94 NLRB Dec. (CCH) P15540, 1993-94 NLRB Dec. (CCH) P15540, 315 N.L.R.B. No. 71 (1994)

CITING REFERENCES (6 citing references)

National Labor Relations Board

   Cited by:
   ▦ BTNH, Inc., 1998 N.L.R.B. LEXIS 514 (N.L.R.B. July 29, 1998)

   Cited by:
   ▦ Vets Int'l Armored Car, 1998 N.L.R.B. LEXIS 38 (N.L.R.B. Jan. 29, 1998)

   Interim decision at:
   ▦ Timekeeping Sys., 323 N.L.R.B. 244, 1997 N.L.R.B. LEXIS 177, 154 L.R.R.M. (BNA) 1233, 323 N.L.R.B. No. 30 (1997)

      Interim decision at:
      323 N.L.R.B. 244 p.248

   Cited by:
   ▦ Timekeeping Sys., 1996 N.L.R.B. LEXIS 740 (N.L.R.B. Nov. 12, 1996)

   Interim decision at:
   ▦ World Fashion, 320 N.L.R.B. 922, 1996 N.L.R.B. LEXIS 125, 153 L.R.R.M. (BNA) 1120, 32 N.L.R.B. No. 90 (1996)

      Interim decision at:
      320 N.L.R.B. 922 p.925

   Cited by:
   ▦ Securitites Indus. Automation Corp., 1996 N.L.R.B. LEXIS 28 (N.L.R.B. Jan. 30, 1996)

Annotated Statutes (1 Citing Statute)

of the judicial case law on your topic. That case law may develop somewhat independently of the agency decisions you have researched.

This phenomenon is best illustrated with an example. On the concerted activity issue in the Canoga case, your research in agency decisions would yield, among others, the *Morton International* decision, which appears to be good law. *Morton International* provides guidance on how the Board would analyze the issue. Should Ms. Canoga's situation lead to an unfair labor practice proceeding before the Board, the case could be reviewed by the Tenth Circuit or the D.C. Circuit. Accordingly, you would want to know how these courts, as well as the Board, approach the issue of concerted activity.

Research into judicial case law is covered in other chapters. Your options include secondary sources (discussed in Unit II); case reporters and digests, their computer-based alternatives, and case citators (Unit III); and annotated codes in various media (Unit IV).

Researching the Canoga case, we discerned that one of the leading judicial cases in the area of concerted activity is *Prill v. NLRB*, 835 F.2d 1481 (D.C. Cir. 1987), *cert. denied*, 487 U.S. 1205 (1988). The Board's rulings in that case go by the name *Meyers Industries*. *Prill* and *Meyers Industries* are both described in the U.S.C.S. annotation. See Illustration 15-2 on page 294.

D.   WHAT ELSE?

Informal Decisions.   Some agencies issue opinion letters about specific situations on which advice is sought, so as to avoid litigation. An example is the private letter ruling of the Internal Revenue Service. To learn how to research such informal decisions, contact the agency, check its web site, or check a library catalog.

E.   HOW DO YOU CITE AGENCY DECISIONS?

To properly cite an agency decision, you would provide the case's name, official reporter citation (where available), date, and subsequent history. If the decision is not published in an official reporter, typically because it is a very new decision, it should be cited to the slip decision along with a citation to an unofficial source, such as a looseleaf service (covered in Chapter 16). Here is an example of an official reporter citation (following Rule 14 and related rules of *The Bluebook*):

Morton International, Inc., 315 N.L.R.B. 564 (1994).

F. CONCLUDING POINTS

When a legislature creates an agency, it may authorize the agency to adjudicate cases. The resulting decisions have the force of law, so long as they conform to constitutional and statutory requirements, including requirements of procedural fairness.

Research in agency decisions involves a statute because the statute enables the agency's decisionmaking. The main sources used to research agency decisions themselves loosely resemble sources used to research judicial case law: paper reporters and digests, Westlaw or LEXIS databases, public Internet web sites, and citators. Furthermore, one must also research judicial case law, through the standard case law sources, to learn of the courts' response to the agency's decisionmaking.

MINI-LIBRARIES

A. WHAT ARE MINI-LIBRARIES?

For some areas of the law, commercial publishers compile what we are calling "mini-libraries," comprehensive and current collections of primary and secondary authorities. The traditional term for this type of source is "looseleaf service." Mini-libraries do indeed appear in multivolume paper looseleaf volumes; they also appear in online subscription services and in CD-ROM disks. We are discussing these sources in this unit because they are particularly useful for locating administrative materials. Although they vary considerably, mini-libraries share three important characteristics.

First, they bring together, into one source, a wide range of primary and secondary authority. Comprehensive mini-libraries include judicial case law, statutes, administrative regulations, and agency decisions, at the federal and state levels. Many mini-libraries also contain commentary, and the most comprehensive include practice materials (such as forms), reports of pending cases or bills, and summaries of interesting conferences or studies.

Second, mini-libraries are updated frequently and thereby provide fairly current material. They are published in formats that facilitate updating.

Third, the best mini-libraries provide significant assistance to the researcher through refined finding tools, such as indexes, topic outlines, and case digests. Because a mini-library covers only one area of law, these tools can be very detailed, and one set of tools covers various types of legal authority.

B.   WHY WOULD YOU RESEARCH IN MINI-LIBRARIES?

Mini-libraries are useful for several main reasons, all suggested by the preceding description. First, because a mini-library provides comprehensive coverage of an area of law, you can efficiently cover a range of authorities within a single source; this promotes efficiency. Second, because it covers only one area of law, a mini-library benefits from a sharp editorial focus on that area; this permits focused research. Furthermore, it affords a wide range of finding tools. Third, a mini-library contains material not easily available elsewhere; this promotes comprehensive research. Fourth, the information in a mini-library is relatively current, and the current information may be integrated into the older material.

C.   HOW DO YOU RESEARCH IN MINI-LIBRARIES?

Because each mini-library is unique, research in such sources varies considerably. The following discussion covers several classic steps you might take in many looseleafs and in online mini-libraries, with research into the federal concerted activity issue featured in this unit serving as the example. This discussion also touches briefly on CD-ROM products that combine various types of authority.

Administrative materials in looseleaf services:

► locate an appropriate looseleaf service
► examine it and its instructional material
► consult the general index
► read the commentary for background and references
► locate and read the statutes and administrative regulations
► use the case digest to locate pertinent cases
► read judicial case law and agency decisions
► update the primary authority

A looseleaf service uses binders that can be easily opened for insertion and deletion of pages; as new material arrives, it is slipped into the binder, adding to or replacing older material. The set of materials usually includes several binders, each with one or more sections set off by tabs. Extensive

looseleaf services also include separate volumes for older material of permanent value, such as cases or agency decisions.

Because some treatises are published in binders, the dividing line between
looseleaf services and looseleaf treatises can be blurry. You should think of a
looseleaf service as a source that contains significant primary authority; in
contrast, a treatise usually has more analytical commentary.

Locate and examine the looseleaf.   To determine whether an appropriate looseleaf service exists, consult the library catalog, examine *Legal Looseleafs in Print,* by Arlene L. Eis, or check Table 15 in *The Bluebook*
(abbreviations for services).

Once you have identified a pertinent looseleaf, it is best to look over
the entire set. Examine the many binders, and gain some understanding of
the materials each contains. Look for a section describing how to use the
looseleaf, typically located in the first binder, and read it. Also locate the
general index and any updates, as well as tables of authorities, such as statutes
or regulations. Figure out where the commentary material, statutes, regulations, and cases appear. Locate the most recent information, typically in a
separate binder or section of a binder; also locate any hardbound or other
volumes containing more dated information, such as cases or agency decisions.

Consult the index.   Next, turn to the general index. Many looseleafs
are divided into multiple, discrete parts, by topic, by types of authority (for
example, commentary, statutes), or by jurisdiction (federal, individual states).
Thus there may be more than one index: a general index for the entire
looseleaf and subsidiary indexes for discrete parts. Furthermore, some of
these indexes may have one or more updates, so you should be sure to note
the currency of each index. The date a page was printed generally may be
found in small print on the bottom of the page. In general, it is wise to
consult the general index first and then any pertinent subsidiary indexes; be
sure to pursue various research terms. See Illustration 16-1 on page 311.

As you move from the index to the text, take special care to discern the
looseleaf's numbering scheme. Your looseleaf may be numbered by chapter,
section, paragraph, or page, or, most likely, a combination of these. You must
follow the numbering scheme precisely or risk not locating the material you
are seeking.

Read the commentary.   Ordinarily you will move from the index references to the commentary portion of your looseleaf. The commentary is likely
to be fairly current, present a detailed discussion, and contain references to
primary authority. To discern how current the discussion is, you can look at
the date of the most recent new material added to the set; the pages you are
reading may not have been changed recently if the law has not changed
recently. See Illustration 16-2 on page 312.

Research statutes and regulations.   If you are using a looseleaf service
to research an area of law governed by an administrative agency, you will
want to read the pertinent statute and any regulations the agency has promulgated on your subject. Most looseleafs afford several means of locating statutes
and regulations: through the overall index, through references in the commentary section, through a subsidiary index to the section containing the

statutes and regulations, through a table of contents at the beginning of a set of statutes or regulations, and through tables of statutes or regulations. Federal and state materials typically appear in separate sections or binders. See Illustration 16-3 on page 314. Some looseleafs include citators that can be used to update your research or to determine the status of your statute or regulation.

Research cases and decisions.   A looseleaf service covering an area of law governed by an administrative agency may also contain agency decisions and judicial case law. Indeed, a looseleaf service may well encompass judicial cases not reported in general case reporters, informal agency decisions that are difficult to locate in government sources, and very new decisions.

Looseleafs containing cases also typically contain detailed, topically arranged digests of the cases. The digest may appear in multiple volumes, for example, the newest digest material in the looseleaf binders, older materials in softcover or hardbound books. Thus you typically must work through recent material and then back in time. You may well have a helpful citation to a digest topic from the overall index or commentary. You also may find it useful to skim an outline of the digest topics to identify additional topics. See Illustration 16-4 on page 315. You then would examine the digest material under those topics and subtopics to identify potentially pertinent cases or agency decisions. See Illustration 16-5 on page 316.

Once you have identified potentially pertinent cases, you would, of course, read them in the looseleaf service. They may appear in hardbound or softcover volumes or looseleaf volumes. The looseleaf may or may not give the official citation to material published in official reporters.

The final step in researching case law and agency decisions is to update and expand your research, using the looseleaf's citator, if one exists. If there is none, you would use a paper or online citator, such as Shepard's or KeyCite.

Researching the Canoga case.   We used a comprehensive looseleaf service covering employment law, *Labor Relations Reporter* (L.R.R.), published by the Bureau of National Affairs (BNA). The general index and other finding aids appear in the *Master Index* binders. The *Labor Relations Expediter* binders contain commentary, statutes, and regulations, while *State Laws* binders contain state statutes and regulations. L.R.R. presents case material in a digest and reporter, with the most recent material appearing in binders and the dated material in the bound volumes. There is no citator.

In the General Index, we looked up "termination of employment" and focused on the subheading "protected activities, discrimination, LMRA." ("LMRA" is the abbreviation for the Labor Management Relations Act, a name used to refer to the private sector labor statute.) See Illustration 16-1 on page 311. The two references are to the Labor Relations Outline (LR) and to the Labor Relations Expediter (LRX). Material at the bottom of the pages of the General Index explains its abbreviations and tells you how current this index is (September 1999 when this research was conducted in the fall of 1999).

We pursued the reference to LRX 510.207 and located a portion of the

Labor Relations Expediter that discusses concerted activities. See Illustration 16-2 on pages 312–313. The commentary mentions several agency decisions, including the landmark case, *Meyers Industries*. (If you did not have a cite to LRX from the General Index, you could skim the list of chapters at the outset of LRX for possibilities.)

We could locate both the federal statute and the Board's regulations in the Text of Laws and Regulations section in the *Labor Relations Expediter* binder. As to the latter, the publisher has provided references to the enabling statute and the citation to the *Federal Register* where the regulation was promulgated in final form.

To determine whether a comparable statute exists at the state level, we looked in the *State Laws* binder covering New Mexico. Illustration 16-3 on page 314 is the beginning of the pertinent material. As you can see, although New Mexico does not have a labor statute for the private sector, it does have a labor statute governing public employment. The looseleaf contains that statute, its regulations, and case descriptions.

To research case law backwards from the present in L.R.R. entails reviewing the very recent materials filed under the Cumulative Digest and Index (CDI) tab in the *Master Index* binder, then older softcover volumes, and then even older hardbound volumes. When we researched the Canoga case in the fall of 1999, three issues of the CDI in the *Master Index* binder covered 1999; three softcover pamphlets covered 1996, 1997, and 1998; and hardbound volumes extended back farther in time. The most recent cases appear in the *Labor Management Relations: Decisions of Boards and Courts* binder, while older ones appear in hardbound volumes called the *Labor Relations Reference Manual* (L.R.R.M.).

We turned to our case law research with a good lead: both the General Index and the discussion of concerted activity at LRX 510:207 pointed to LR 52.2532 et seq. See Illustrations 16-1 on page 311 and 16-2 on page 312. "LR" refers to the Labor Relations Outline of Classifications, which is a very refined topical outline that covers exclusively labor relations topics and appears in the *Master Index* binder. Topic 52 is Employer Discrimination in Regard to Employment, and subtopic .2532 is one of the series of subtopics of concerted activities. See Illustration 16-4 on page 315.

We then read the case descriptions under the various pertinent subtopics. Illustration 16-5 on page 316 is the material from the hardbound CDI covering 1991-1995; it includes the Board decision, *Morton International*. That case appears in volume 147 of the L.R.R.M. reporter. The L.R.R. digest covers court cases as well as Board decisions.

The featured looseleaf does not itself include a citator. It is possible, however, to Shepardize L.R.R.M. cases in *Shepard's Labor Law Citations*.

ILLUSTRATION 16-1 Looseleaf Service General Index, from *BNA's Labor Relations Reporter*

TERMINATION OF EMPLOYMENT—Contd.
Just cause—Contd.
—Rule of reason, LRX 510:221
"Justice and dignity clause," LA ▸ 118.301
Labor Relations Cases, LR ▸ 118.01 et seq.
Layoffs distinguished
  LR ▸ 117.105
  LRX 510:202
—Discrimination, LMRA, LR ▸ 52.242
Leniency of unions enforcing union-security clauses, LRX 730:314
Liability of employer, ULPs, LR ▸ 56.4212
Lie detectors
—Employee Polygraph Protection Act, IERM 595:1201
—Refusal to take test
  LA ▸ 118.644
  IERM 509:312, 313
—Results, LA ▸ 118.644
LMRA limits on, LRX 510:201 et seq.
Loafing
  LR ▸ 118.654
  LA ▸ 118.654
  LRX 510:236
—Discrimination, LMRA, LR ▸ 52.2716
—Public employees, LA ▸ 100.552555
Maintenance of membership
  LR ▸ 8.633
  LA ▸ 8.633
Managerial employees, discrimination, LMRA
  LR ▸ 52.05
  LRX 510:207
Mental health and disability
  LR ▸ 118.655
  LA ▸ 118.655
  LRX 510:236 et seq.
—Discrimination, LMRA, LR ▸ 52.2726
—Public employees, LA ▸ 100.552565
—Troubled employees, LRX 510:238
Mixed motive cases. *See* MIXED MOTIVE DISCHARGES
Model Uniform Employment Termination Act, IERM 540:21 et seq.
Modifications or reductions of penalties, LA ▸ 118.03, ▸ 118.806
—Public employees, LA ▸ 100.559565
Moonlighting
  LA ▸ 118.6482
  LRX 510:229
—Public employees, LA ▸ 100.552560
Motive of union in seeking discharges, union-security contracts, LRX 730:314
Name calling
  LR ▸ 118.640
  LA ▸ 118.640
  LRX 510:227
National origin discrimination, FEP ▸ 108.1215
—Federal employees, FEP ▸ 110.6515
Negligence
  LR ▸ 118.651
  LA ▸ 118.651
  LRX 510:233

—Public employees, LA ▸ 100.552535
No reason given, evidence of discrimination, LMRA, LR ▸ 52.2780
Notice, LA ▸ 118.305
—Public employees, LA ▸ 100.5520
Obscenity
  LR ▸ 118.640
  LA ▸ 118.640
  LRX 510:227
—Discrimination, LMRA, LR ▸ 52.2728
—Management, employee use toward, LA ▸ 118.6523
—Public employees, LA ▸ 100.552510
Off-duty or off-premises misconduct, LA ▸ 118.634
—Public employees, LA ▸ 100.552505
Overtime, refusal to work
  LR ▸ 118.658
  LA ▸ 118.658
  LRX 510:235
—Discrimination, LMRA, LR ▸ 52.2731
—Public employees, LA ▸ 100.552570
Past practice, LA ▸ 24.355
Performance. *See* Incompetence and inefficiency, *this heading*
Personal appearance, LA ▸ 118.639
—Public employees, LA ▸ 100.552529
Personnel files, remedies for discrimination
  FEP ▸ 228.251
  AD ▸ 228.251
Physical disabilities. *See* Disabled employees, *this heading*
Physical tests, failure to submit, LA ▸ 118.655
—Public employees, LA ▸ 100.552565
Picketing
  LR ▸ 118.660
  LA ▸ 118.6601
—Discrimination, LMRA, LR ▸ 52.341
—Employees' failure to repudiate illegal strike or violent picketing, LMRA, LRX 670:310
Polygraph tests. *See* Lie detectors, *this heading*
Poor performance, LRX 510:233
Post leaving, LA ▸ 118.654
—Public employees, LA ▸ 100.552555
Pregnancy, FEPM 421:509
—Federal employees, FEP ▸ 110.4018
Procedure
  LR ▸ 118.301 et seq.
  LA ▸ 118.301 et seq.
  LRX 510:224
—Public employees, LA ▸ 100.5523
Productivity. *See* Incompetence and inefficiency, *this heading;* Loafing, *this heading*
Promotion before, LRX 650:107
Protected activities, discrimination, LMRA
  LR ▸ 52.2532 et seq.
  LRX 510:207
Protest against, picketing objects, LR ▸ 81.257
Psychological evaluations, LA ▸ 118.655
—Public employees, LA ▸ 100.552565
Public employees
  LR ▸ 100.641, ▸ 100.647
  LA ▸ 100.5501 et seq.

Consult individual Manual indexes for more recent information.
LA▸ = Labor Arbitration Outline; LR▸ = Labor Relations Outline;
*LRX = Labor Relations Expediter; *SLL = State Labor Laws;
WH▸ = Wages and Hours Outline; *WHM = Wages and Hours Manual

  9-99   Copyright © 1999 by The Bureau of National Affairs, Inc., Washington, D.C.   855
ISSN 1043-5506

ILLUSTRATION 16-2   Looseleaf Service Commentary, from *BNA's Labor Relations Reporter*

No. 660   DISCHARGE   LRX 510:207

42 LRRM 2620 (CA 2 1958); *NLRB v. Coal Creek Co.*, 204 F2d 579, 32 LRRM 2089 (CA 10 1953); *NLRB v. Mallick & Schwalm Co.*, 198 F2d 477, 30 LRRM 2529 (CA 3 1952).

However, the NLRB's view is that the facts in each case determine whether employees are protected by the act when they take concerted action to protest the selection or termination of a supervisor. Where the identity and capability of a supervisor has a direct impact on employees' own job interests, the board has found that they are legitimately concerned with his identity and have a protected right to protest his termination. *Puerto Rico Foods Products Corp.*, 242 NLRB 899, 101 LRRM 1307 (1979).

Strikes to protest the discharge of supervisors have been found unprotected because the means of protest were not reasonably related to the ends sought. *Dobbs Houses v. NLRB*, 325 F2d 531, 54 LRRM 2726 (CA 5 1963); *Abilities & Goodwill v. NLRB*, 612 F2d 6, 103 LRRM 2029 (CA 1 1979). The NLRB has disagreed, saying that reasonableness is not a test for determining whether a strike is protected. The test, the board says, is whether the discharge of the supervisor had an impact on the strikers in the performance of their jobs. *Plastilite Corp.*, 153 NLRB 180, 59 LRRM 1401 (1965). "The application of Section 7 does not depend on the manner or method by which employees choose to press their dispute, but rather on the matter they are protesting," the court said. *Puerto Rico Food Products*, 242 NLRB 899, 101 LRRM 1307 at 1309 (1979).

The NLRB's order in *Puerto Rico Food Products* was denied enforcement. It was not shown that the work stoppage in fact was a protest over the actual conditions of the strikers' own employment, the court said, adding that the means of protest must also be "reasonable." *Puerto Rico Food Products v. NLRB*, 619 F2d 153, 104 LRRM 2304 (CA 1 1980).

The same court held that an employer lawfully fired 11 supervisors and employees for sending its president a letter requesting the discharge of the general manager at one of the employer's hotels. Reversing the NLRB, the court said the case involved "simply a dispute among managerial employees into which several non-supervisory employees were drawn." *NLRB v. Sheraton Puerto Rico Corp.*, 651 F2d 49, 107 LRRM 2735 (CA 1 1981).

One court has held that a strike seeking the reinstatement of supervisors may be protected if the individuals involved are not employer representatives for the purpose of adjusting grievances or collective bargaining. *NLRB v. Puerto Rico Rayon Mills*, 293 F2d 941, 48 LRRM 2947 (CA 1 1961).

Discharge of 'managerial' employee (LR ▶ 52.041, 52.05) — Reversing the NLRB, the Eighth Circuit upheld the discharge of a managerial employee for failing to remain neutral during an organizing campaign. The purpose of the act, the court said, is to protect "workers," not individuals who are not members of any bargaining unit and who are more closely aligned with management than with the bargaining unit. *NLRB v. North Arkansas Electric Co-op*, 446 F2d 602, 77 LRRM 3114 (CA 8 1971)

§ 7. **Concerted employee activities under LMRA.** (LR ▶ 52.2532 et seq.) LMRA Sec. 7. declares the employees' right "to engage in other concerted activities for the purpose of collective bargaining or other mutual aid or protection." The obvious forms of concerted activities are joining a union, soliciting other employees to join, attending union meetings, going on strike, etc. But the area of "concerted activities" protected by the LMRA is broader.

To be "concerted," an employee's activity must be engaged in with or on the authority of others, not solely by and on behalf of the employee himself. To establish the illegality of discipline based on such activity, the NLRB's general counsel must show not only that the activity was "concerted," but that the employer knew of its concerted nature, that it was

ILLUSTRATION 16-2 *(continued)*

LRX 510:208   DISCHARGE   No. 660

"protected" by the LMRA, and that the discipline in fact was motivated by this protected concerted activity. *Meyers Industries*, 268 NLRB 493, 115 LRRM 1025 (1984), overruling *Alleluia Cushion Co.*, 221 NLRB 999, 91 LRRM 1131 (1975); see also *Walls Mfg. Co.*, 128 NLRB 487, 46 LRRM 1329 (1960) and *Myers Products Corp.*, 84 NLRB 32, 24 LRRM 1216 (1949).

The District of Columbia Circuit ordered the board to reconsider its *Meyers* ruling. *Prill v. NLRB* (Meyers Industries), 755 F2d 941, 118 LRRM 2649 (1985).

On reconsideration, the board adhered to its definition of concerted activities. It also stressed that its *Meyers I* definition encompasses those circumstances where individual employees seek to initiate, induce, or prepare for group action, as well as individual employees bringing truly group complaints to the attention of management. *Meyers Industries*, 281 NLRB No. 118, 123 LRRM 1137 (1986).

The District of Columbia Circuit affirmed. The board's definition under which an employee's conduct is not "concerted" unless it is engaged in with or on the authority of other employees, is a reasonable interpretation of Section 7 of the act, the court said. *Prill v. NLRB* (Meyers Industries), 835 F2d 1481, 127 LRRM 2415 (1987).

An individual employee who reasonably and honestly invokes a right set forth in his collective-bargaining contract is engaged in concerted activity, the U.S. Supreme Court held, approving the NLRB's *Interboro* doctrine. An employee's refusal to drive a truck he claimed had bad brakes was concerted even though he did not refer explicitly to the contract's safety provision, the court concluded. *NLRB v. City Disposal Systems*, 465 US 822, 115 LRRM 3193 (1984); *Interboro Contractors*, 157 NLRB 1295, 61 LRRM 1537 (1965), enforced, 388 F2d 495, 67 LRRM 2083 (CA 2 1967).

In *Prill II*, the District of Columbia Circuit ruled that the board's *Meyers I* definition of concerted activities was not inconsistent with the *Interboro* doctrine.

Concerted activity may take place where only "one person is seeking to induce action from a group." *Salt River Valley Assn. v. NLRB*, 206 F2d 325, 32 LRRM 2598 (CA 9 1953). Thus, it is illegal to discharge one employee for seeking overtime for company workers. *NLRB v. Lion Brand Mfg. Co.*, 146 F2d 773, 15 LRRM 870 (CA 5 1945). Where "one employee discusses with another the need for union organization, their action is 'concerted' . . . for it involves more than one employee, even though one be in the role of speaker and the other of listener." *Root-Carlin*, 92 NLRB 1313, 27 LRRM 1235 (1951). Two employees' informal protest against the elimination of overtime work was held protected although the employees had no authorization from other employees. *Ohio Oil Co.*, 92 NLRB 1597, 27 LRRM 1288 (1951).

Employees have the right to engage in concerted activities "even though no union activity be involved," and even though no collective bargaining is "contemplated" by the employees involved. *NLRB v. Phoenix Mutual Life Insurance Co.*, 167 F2d 983, 22 LRRM 2089 (CA 7 1948), cert. denied, 335 US 845, 22 LRRM 2590 (1948). A meeting of dissident union members to seek a change in the union's bargaining policy is protected. *NLRB v. NuCar Carriers*, 189 F2d 756, 28 LRRM 2160 (CA 3 1951), cert. denied, 342 US 919, 29 LRRM 2384 (1952).

Employees who quit work about five minutes early to hold a grievance meeting in a nonunion plant were engaged in protected activity, NLRB has held. *Quaker Alloy Casting Co.*, 135 NLRB 805, 49 LRRM 1578 (1962), enforced, 320 F2d 260, 53 LRRM 2532 (CA 3 2963).

Processing a grievance is concerted activity. *NLRB v. City Disposal Systems*, supra; *Farmers Union Coop. Marketing Assn.*, 145 NLRB 1, 54 LRRM 1298 (1963).

Refusing to remove pro-boycott signs from a car in an employer's parking lot is concerted activity. *Firestone Tire &*

ILLUSTRATION 16-3   Looseleaf Service State Statute Reprint, from *BNA's Labor Relations Reporter*

No. 984   SLL 41:221

Labor Relations Acts—

New Mexico has no labor relations act comparable to the federal Labor Management Relations Act or similar laws enacted in some of the states. However, Sec. 50–1–5 of the act establishing the state labor and industrial commission, above, makes it unlawful for the commission's director or agents to advocate organization or disorganization of a labor union.

Public Employees: Bargaining Rights

Full text of Ch. 10, Article 7D, Secs. 10-7D-1 to 10-7D-26 of the New Mexico Statutes Annotated, comprising the state collective bargaining statute providing rights, responsibilities, and procedures in the employment relationship between public employees and public employers, as enacted by Ch. 9, L. 1992, and as last amended by Ch. 212, L. 1997, effective June 20, 1997.

Sec. 10-7D-1. Short title.—Secs. 10-7D-1 through 10-7D-26 of this Act may be cited as the "Public Employee Bargaining Act."

Sec. 10-7D-2. Purpose of Act.—The purpose of the Public Employee Bargaining Act is to guarantee public employees the right to organize and bargain collectively with their employers, to promote harmonious and cooperative relationships between public employers and public employees, and to protect the public interest by assuring, at all times, the orderly operation and functioning of the state and its political subdivisions.

Sec. 10-7D-3. Conflicts.—In the event of conflict with other laws, the provisions of the Public Employee Bargaining Act shall supersede other previously enacted legislation; provided, that the Public Employee Bargaining Act shall not supersede the provisions of the Bateman Act, the State Personnel Act, Secs. 10-7-1 through 10-7-19 NMSA 1978, the Group Benefits Act, the Per Diem and Mileage Act, the Retiree Health Care Act, public employee retirement laws, or the Tort Claims Act.

Sec. 10-7D-4. Definitions.—As used in the Public Employee Bargaining Act:

A. "Appropriate bargaining unit" means a group of public employees designated by the board or local board for the purpose of collective bargaining;

B. "Appropriate governing body" means the policymaking body or individual representing a public employer as defined in Sec. 10-7D-7 NMSA 1978;

C. "Board" means the public employee labor relations board;

D. "Certification" means the designation by the board or local board of a labor organization as the exclusive representative for all public employees in an appropriate bargaining unit;

E. "Collective bargaining" means the act of negotiating between a public employer and an exclusive representative for the purpose of entering into a written agreement regarding wages, hours, and other terms and conditions of employment;

F. "Confidential employee" means a person who assists and acts in a confidential capacity with respect to a person who formulates, determines, and effectuates management policies;

G. "Exclusive representative" means a labor organization that, as a result of certification, has the right to represent all public employees in an appropriate bargaining unit for the purposes of collective bargaining;

H. "Factfinding" means the procedure following mediation whereby the parties involved in an impasse submit their differences to a third party for an advisory recommendation;

I. "Impasse" means failure of a public employer and an exclusive representative, after good–faith bargaining, to reach agreement in the course of negotiating a collective bargaining agreement;

| ILLUSTRATION 16-4 | Looseleaf Service Outline of Case Digest, from *BNA's Labor Relations Reporter* |

C-I 112   MASTER INDEX BINDER

► 52.—Contd.

.243 —Layoffs in general; permanent or temporary layoffs; disciplinary layoff
.247 —Successive layoffs or discharges; discharge following reinstatement
.251 —Contracts with unions, violation of; termination of contract
—Concerted activities; protected activities
.2532 ——In general
.2533 ——Abstention from concerted activity
.2534 ——Activities in advance of or apart from organization; individual activities
.2535 ——Boycotts; "disloyalty" to employer
.2536 ——Grievances generally; bypassing contract procedure; union officers and agents, protection in performance of union duties
.2537 ——Meetings, conferences, and hearings
.2538 ——Wage demands
.2539 ——Strikes, picketing, and slowdowns as protected
.2541 ——Minority demands; dissident groups; intraunion disputes
.2542 ——False or abusive statements or threats
.2543 ——Racial, national origin, or sex discrimination, protest against
.2544 ——Work jurisdiction disputes
.257 —Quit or discharge; constructive discharge; retraction of resignation
.259 —Discharge following transfer or refusal to accept transfer; attempt to discredit employee; entrapment
—Reasons for discharge, discipline, layoff or refusal to reinstate
.2672 ——In general
.2678 ——Demand by union or fellow employees; intraunion disputes and rival unions
.2682 ——Absence or tardiness; leave of absence; overstaying leave: leaving plant or work place
.2683 ——Accident record, driving rules, law violations, criminal record
.2684 ——Altercations with others; fighting; violence
.2690 ——Communist activities; refusal to testify
.2692 ——Damage to or loss of machines, materials, etc.
.2695 ——Discourtesy toward or complaints by customers

► 52.—Contd.

.2696 ———Dishonesty, false statements, theft, or disloyalty to employer; lie-detector tests
.2697 ———Dissatisfaction, or criticism of management
.2698 ———Garnishment of wages
.2700 ———Horseplay
.2704 ———Insubordination
.2708 ———Intoxication; use or possession of liquor, drugs
.2716 ———Loafing, sleeping, or talking
.2718 ———Low production or impeding production
.2722 ———Negligence, inefficiency, or incompetence
.2724 ———Offensive personal characteristics; quarrelsomeness; "troublemakers"; bad attitude
.2725 ———Outside work; competing business; "moonlighting"
.2726 ———Physical or mental disability; failure to submit to physical examination or give doctor's certificate; age of employee; contagious diseases
.2728 ———Profanity, name calling, obscene language or conduct
.2729 ———Plant rules generally; successive violations
.2730 ———Reduction or redistribution of work; elimination of jobs; availability of work after discharge or layoff; automation
.2731 ———Refusal to work overtime or accept job assignment
.2738 ———Solicitation or other union activity on company time or property
.2740 ———Threats by employees
.2744 ———Wearing union buttons or other display of insignia
—Background circumstances indicating or rebutting discrimination in discharge, discipline, layoff, or refusal to reinstate
.2751 ——In general
.2752 ——Anti-union background of employer, proof of; union animus
.2756 ——Comparative treatment
.2758 ——Timing of dismissal; extent of union activity
.2764 ——Grievances or bargaining demands, presentation of; suits against employers
.2767 ——Knowledge of employee's union activities, proof of; surveillance or questioning
.2769 ——Majority status affected by termination

ILLUSTRATION 16-5   Looseleaf Service Case Digest, from *BNA's Labor Relations Reporter*

▶ 52.2536 (Contd.)

that her selection for termination was "aggravated" by "maternity thing."—*Id.*

Employer lawfully discharged *EEO* officer, where employer made business decision to discharge relatively highly paid, skilled employee, and to redistribute her duties among remaining, less skilled but lower paid employees, in order to reduce its significant operating losses.—*Id.*

Employee's conduct in opposing, together with co-workers, property management company's selection of leasing agent as its property manager constitutes protected concerted activity within meaning of LMRA, despite claim that employee's opposition was based on personal antipathy which existed between him and agent. —*Atlantic-Pacific Construction Co. d/b/a Atlantic-Pacific Management* (312 NLRB 242, 9/20/93) 145 LRRM 1176

Employer that manages apartment complex unlawfully terminated employee, since termination was motivated by employee's protected concerted activity of opposing, together with co-workers, employer's selection of leasing agent as property manager.—*Id.*

Employer unlawfully discharged employee who it believed was acting with co-workers in complaining about work assignments and other working conditions; it failed to demonstrate that discharge would have occurred even in absence of employee's protected concerted activity. —*U.S. Service Industries Inc.* (314 NLRB 30, 6/13/94) 146 LRRM 1203

Employer unlawfully discharged employee who discussed recently announced "advanced training class" with co-workers, since employee's conduct constitutes protected concerted activity; class was mandatory condition of employment, where workers who failed to attend it were subject to disciplinary action. —*Goemon America Inc.* (314 NLRB 504, 7/22/94) 146 LRRM 1282

Employer unlawfully appraised adversely employee's performance and then reprimanded him, since these actions were motivated by his protected concerted activity of participating in discussion and presentation of complaints concerning pay and other working conditions. —*FPC Holdings Inc. d/b/a Fiber Products* (314 NLRB 1169, 9/16/94) 147 LRRM 1127

Employer unlawfully designated two employees for layoff at future date; designation occurred after employer unlawfully had reprimanded employees because of their protected concerted activity of participating in discussion and presentation of complaints concerning pay and other working conditions.—*Id.*

Employer unlawfully issued written reprimands to three employees and discharged six others, since these actions were motivated by employees' protected concerted activity of walking off their jobs after painting contractor left their work area in chaotic condition. —*Vemco Inc.* (314 NLRB 1235, 9/21/94) 147 LRRM 1139

Employer unlawfully suspended and then discharged employee who, after conferring with co-workers, drafted and then solicited signatures on letter which was presented to employer's president and which complained about working conditions, particularly personnel director's alleged "favoritism" and "unfairness." —*Brother Industries (U.S.A.) Inc.* (314 NLRB 1218, 9/20/94) 147 LRRM 1230

Two employees were engaged in protected concerted activity when, after seeing co-worker's memorandum claiming that safety committee has failed to rigidly enforce no-smoking policy, they wrote on memo their opposition to its message and posted copies; one employee testified that posting was intended to elicit comments or opinions of fellow smokers. —*Morton International Inc.* (315 NLRB 564, 11/10/94) 147 LRRM 1280

Employer unlawfully discharged two employees who, after seeing co-worker's memorandum criticizing safety committee for allegedly failing to rigidly enforce no-smoking policy, wrote on memo their opposition to its message and then posted copies of memo.—*Id.*

Employer unlawfully declared lawfully laid-off employee ineligible for rehire, since reason was employee's protected concerted activity of being "loudest complainer" in group of workers who protested allegedly low wages and lack of benefits; employee never was intoxicated on the job and his drinking never interfered with production or caused safety problem. —*Cardinal Industries Inc. International Grooving & Grinding Div.* (315 NLRB 1303, 1/13/95) 148 LRRM 1187

Employer whose bargaining agreement provides for payment for certain amount of time spent by stewards in handling of grievances unlawfully refused union steward's re-

> **Options for administrative material research in online mini-libraries:**
>
> - search the table of contents or indexes
> - run a Boolean search in one or more directories
> - peruse the case digest
> - use the embedded links
> - employ the citator

Increasingly, commercial publishers are offering the contents of looseleaf services online, accessible by paid subscription. The online mini-library may have a wide range of content: primary authority, including federal and state law; commentary; finding aids; citators; forms; and information about conferences and studies. Furthermore, material is frequently updated.

In some ways, online mini-libraries resemble looseleaf services. The online materials generally are organized into directories by topic or jurisdiction, just as looseleaf binders and tabs separate materials. Typically, you can search a detailed table of contents, the general index, or subsidiary indexes.

There are differences between the paper and online mini-libraries as well. You can elect to search one or several of the directories simultaneously. You can perform a Boolean search, typically by use of truncated words, phrases, and proximity connectors. You may be able to move quickly from one portion to another through embedded links. Also, the online materials are completely cumulated so you need not look in several places for current materials. However, the retrospective coverage of the online service may vary from the paper service, so it is important to determine its beginning date of coverage.

Researching the Canoga case, we used BNA's Labor and Employment Law Library online at http://laborandemploymentlaw.bna.com. We began by reading the help section, to learn the scope of the database (older case reporters are not accessible online), the organization of the materials, display options, and permitted search strategies. We chose to focus on case law and selected the LRRM—Decisions of Court and the LRRM—Decisions of NLRB directories. We entered the Boolean search [smoking and "concerted activity"]. The search retrieved nine NLRB documents, including the *Morton International* decision, but no court decisions. See Illustration 16-6 on page 318. We could display just the headnotes or the full text. In the headnotes for *Morton International*, there were two embedded links. See Illustration 16-7 on page 319. These links led us to the outline of digest topics, including topic 52.2536, a subtopic of Employer Discrimination in Regard to Employment. See Illustration 16-8 on page 320. In turn, we could move from a topic to digests of judicial cases or NLRB decisions. Finally, we consulted the citator function, called "cites," to look for cases or agency decisions citing *Morton International*. We entered *Morton International*'s unofficial reporter citation, 147 LRRM 1280, but found no such cases or decisions.

ILLUSTRATION 16-6   BNA Labor and Employment Law Library Citations List,
                           Run in LRRM–Decisions of Court and LRRM–Decisions
                           of NLRB Directories

Labor and Employment Law Library   Page 1 of 1

9 ▭ All Other Cases
    1 ▭ MANNO ELECTRIC INC., 152 LRRM 1107 (NLRB 1996)
        1 ▭ Headnotes
            1 ▩
    1 ▭ MORTON INTERNATIONAL INC. and MARTIN D. HOWELL 147 LRRM 1280 (NLRB 1994)
        1 ▭ Headnotes
            1 ▩
    1 ▭ MULLICAN LUMBER CO., 143 LRRM 1019 (NLRB 1993)
        1 ▭ Headnotes
            1 ▩
    1 ▭ GOLD COAST RESTAURANT, 139 LRRM 1256 (NLRB 1991)
        1 ▭ Headnotes
            1 ▩
    1 ▭ ADAM'S RIB RESTAURANT, 136 LRRM 1064 (NLRB 1990)
        1 ▭ Headnotes
            1 ▩
    1 ▭ ADVERTISER'S MFG. CO., 124 LRRM 1017 (NLRB 1986)
        1 ▭ Headnotes
            1 ▩
    1 ▩ CHEMTRONICS, INC., 98 LRRM 1559 (NLRB 1978)
    1 ▩ WESTERN CLINICAL LABORATORY, INC., 93 LRRM 1292 (NLRB 1976)
    1 ▩ GENERAL ELECTRIC CO., 104 LRRM 1498 (NLRB GenCoun AdMem 1980)

| ILLUSTRATION 16-7 | *Morton International* Case Headnotes, from BNA Online Labor and Employment Law Library |

Labor and Employment Law Library   Page 1 of 1

All Other Cases
MORTON INTERNATIONAL INC. and MARTIN D. HOWELL 147 LRRM 1280 (NLRB 1994)

MORTON INTERNATIONAL INC. and MARTIN D. HOWELL 147 LRRM 1280 (NLRB 1994)

MORTON INTERNATIONAL INC. and MARTIN D. HOWELL

National Labor Relations Board
147 LRRM 1280
November 10, 1994
Case 9-CA-30898
315 NLRB No. 71

Administrative Law Judge
Administrative Law Judge Claude R. Wolfe

Judges
Before Devaney, Browning, and Cohen, Members.

Headnotes

Interference (▧ 52.2536)
Two employees were engaged in protected ▶concerted activity◀ when, after seeing co-worker's memorandum claiming that safety committee had failed to rigidly enforce no-▶smoking◀ policy, employees wrote on memo their opposition to its message and then posted copies of memo, where one employee testified that his posting of memo was intended to elicit comments or opinions of fellow smokers; other employee's comments endorsed first employee's protest of memo's attack on enforcement of existing ▶smoking◀ policy.

Interference (▧ 52.2536)
Employer violated Section 8(a)(1) of LMRA by discharging two employees who, after seeing co-worker's memorandum criticizing safety committee for allegedly failing to rigidly enforce no-▶smoking◀ policy, wrote on memo their opposition to its message and then posted copies of memo. (1) Employees' conduct constitutes protected ▶concerted activity◀; (2) it is contended that employee who wrote "chicken shit" on memo was engaged in angry personal attack on author of memo, but it was content of memo to which he was reacting, and word "shit" is common expression in employer's facility; (3) it is contended that second employee's comments directed to author of memo will have "negative effect" on author, but there is no showing that author ever had favorable status in eyes of workers who smoke, and fact that she was "vilified" by other employee is not likely to lower her status in eyes of non-smokers; (4) it was not established that any worker has ever been disciplined for breaching company rule against "harassment or intimidating language or conduct"; (5) there is no evidence that the two employees were aware they were dealing with "purloined" document, memo does not on its face show its possession by employees was unauthorized, nor is there evidence that they should have known that was the case; (6) employer had rule against posting of written materials in "work areas," but discharged employees posted copies of memo in breakroom, timeclock area, ▶smoking◀ trailer, and on bulletin board of health and safety office.

ILLUSTRATION 16-8	Outline of Digest Topics, from BNA Online Labor and Employment Law Library

---

Labor and Employment Law Library   Page 1 of 1

Division V Labor Relations Acts: Unfair Labor Practices
  52. Employer Discrimination in Regard to Employment

52.2536 **CT** **NLRB**   ----Grievances generally; bypassing contract procedure; union officers and
agents, protection in performance of union duties

> [For wage demands, see 52.2538.
> For strike over grievances, see 52.2539 and 52.346.
> For minority or dissident group grievances, see 52.2541.
> For discharge for union activity on company time or property, see 52.2738.]
> [See also 52.2764 and 54.17.]

52.2537 **CT** **NLRB**   ----Meetings, conferences, and hearings

> [For work stoppages, see 52.2539 and 52.341 et seq.]
> [See also 52.2738.]

52.2538 **CT** **NLRB**   ----Wage demands

52.2539 **CT** **NLRB**   ----Strikes, picketing, and slowdowns as protected

> [Limited to protected concerted activities.]
> [See also 52.2738.]

52.2541 **CT** **NLRB**   ----Minority demands; dissident groups; intraunion disputes

> [For strikes, see 52.2539 and 52.341 et seq.]
> [See also 52.2678 and 59.233.]

52.2542 **CT** **NLRB**   ----False or abusive statements or threats

Administrative materials in CD-ROM mini-libraries

Various commercially published CD-ROM disks also contain mini-libraries of important federal and state materials. These CD-ROM mini-libraries offer the same principal advantages offered by looseleafs and online subscription services: comprehensive, frequently updated compilations of primary and secondary authorities usually found in diffuse sources.

Some CD-ROM mini-libraries contain the same materials as a parallel looseleaf service; an example is BNA's Labor and Employment Law Library. Some companies include only primary authorities; for instance, a less comprehensive labor law CD-ROM library might contain selected titles of the *United States Code* and *Code of Federal Regulations* that pertain to labor law, along with related federal case law and agency decisions.

Some CD-ROM mini-libraries have a different focus: the entire primary authority of a specific jurisdiction. For instance, the New Mexico state law CD-ROM library published by LEXIS Law Publishing contains the current statutes, case law, court rules, and some administrative materials for that state. (Its use has been illustrated in Chapters 10 and 12.)

CD-ROM disks are updated periodically, typically monthly or quarterly, when new disks are issued. Hence, there may be a gap between the time the CD-ROM you are using was issued and the present, and you must update your research using other updating sources.

Research techniques vary from CD-ROM to CD-ROM. Hence, just as with looseleafs and online subscription services, the best approach is to read the introductory or help section first. Typically, the disks can be searched by browsing the table of contents or index, if any, or by using Boolean search strategies, including truncated words, phrases, and proximity connectors.

D.   WHAT ELSE?

Current Awareness Publications.   Comprehensive looseleafs have current awareness publications, which are frequently published pamphlets that permit a regular reader to keep abreast of recent developments. The pamphlet may contain synopses of recent legal authorities, analyze significant new laws, recount the results of recent studies, report on important conferences, and list upcoming events. In addition, some legal authorities, especially new statutes and regulations, often are first available in paper media in pamphlets issued by looseleaf publishers. Current awareness publications may be filed in their own binder and covered by a periodic index.

Westlaw and LEXIS.   Westlaw and LEXIS offer databases containing some looseleaf materials. The offering may be selective, that is, only portions of a paper looseleaf service.

E. HOW DO YOU CITE TO MINI-LIBRARIES?

Most authorities located in a mini-library appear elsewhere in preferred sources, such as a code of regulations or official reporter of agency decisions. Nonetheless, you may cite to a looseleaf on occasion. The most common instance is when you are citing to a very recent agency decision not yet available in the agency's official reporter. When citing to a looseleaf, you must provide identifying information about the authority as well as its location in the looseleaf. Here is an example (following Rule 18 of *The Bluebook*):

> *Morton International, Inc.,* 315 N.L.R.B. No. 71, 147 L.R.R.M. (BNA) 1280 (Nov. 10, 1994).

(This example assumes that the decision is so new that it does not yet appear in the official reporter.)

F. CONCLUDING POINTS

To conduct comprehensive research into an area governed by an administrative agency, you must research not only the law created by the agency, but also the statute creating the agency and judicial cases reviewing the agency's actions. The law created by the agency may consist of regulations or decisions or both. This complex body of law may be researched in the various sources described in Chapters 14 and 15. These research processes can be very time-consuming, although they should yield correct results if performed carefully.

A mini-library, whether a looseleaf, online subscription, or CD-ROM source, may provide a convenient alternative. These sources typically contain commentary, statutes, regulations, cases from the courts, and agency decisions. The mini-library materials are comprehensive and updated frequently. And your research will benefit from the editorial and technological enhancements available through such sources.

RULES OF PROCEDURE AND LEGAL ETHICS

UNIT

VI

This unit explores the methods and materials used to research rules that govern litigation and the practice of law. These rules are primary authority because they are created by various government bodies acting in their official capacities. This unit has two chapters.

Chapter 17 discusses rules governing the procedural aspects of litigation in the courts. Each jurisdiction has its own rules of procedure, and most have several sets for different phases and types of litigation. These overarching rules for a jurisdiction may be supplemented by rules developed by a single court or district. (There also are more or less formal rules governing other legal proceedings, such as international disputes and commercial arbitration. Although these specialized rules may bear some similarity to the rules of procedure discussed here, they are beyond the scope of this book.)

Chapter 18 discusses the law governing the ethical conduct of lawyers, known as rules of professional responsibility. This discussion focuses on the state rules of professional responsibility and the model rules and codes prepared by the American Bar Association.

For examples, this unit turns again to the Canoga case, stated on pages 3–4. Assume that, as Ms. Canoga's lawyer, you have identified viable claims and unsuccessfully sought a settlement from the orchestra. Ms. Canoga has decided to pursue litigation. The two specific issues to be researched are stated within the two chapters.

RULES OF PROCEDURE

A. WHAT ARE RULES OF PROCEDURE?

Although the distinction is not always clear, most lawyers distinguish "substantive law" from "procedural law." Substantive law governs the rights, duties, and powers of people and entities as they carry out their personal and business affairs. By contrast, procedural law regulates how a case is brought before a particular court and how the case proceeds from its inception until a final outcome is reached. It provides guidelines that the lawyers and parties must observe in carrying out the litigation and that assist the court and lawyers in administering justice fairly and efficiently.

Most jurisdictions have several sets of rules of procedure, each addressing certain phases and types of litigation. Exhibit 17.1 on page 326 diagrams the typical arrangement. Furthermore, a particular court (such as family or small claims court) or district may have additional so-called "local rules" outlining the details of its practice.

In most jurisdictions, some procedural law appears not in the rules of procedure, as this chapter uses that term, but in the statutes of the jurisdiction. For example, statutes typically govern how quickly you must bring a claim (statutes of limitation) and which court has the power to adjudicate a claim (jurisdiction).

	Civil Cases	*Criminal Cases*
Pre-trial pleadings discovery motions	Civil procedure	Criminal procedure
Trial	Evidence, civil procedure	Evidence, criminal procedure
Post-trial	Civil procedure	Criminal procedure
Appeals	Appellate procedure	Appellate or criminal appellate procedure

EXHIBIT 17.1 — Types of Rules of Procedure

1.   How Are Rules of Procedure Developed?

Procedural rules are created either by the legislature, by the court, or by interaction of both branches of government.

At the federal level, it is not clear in the United States Constitution whether Congress or the federal courts have primary authority for procedural rules. Most commentators believe that Congress has the right to prescribe rules of procedure for the federal courts, while the individual federal courts are free to issue local rules on matters not covered by Congress' rules. As a practical matter, Congress has delegated a great deal of authority to the United States Supreme Court.

The enactment of the Federal Rules of Civil Procedure (FRCP) is an example of this delegation. Under the Rules Enabling Act of 1934, ch. 651, 48 Stat. 1064 (1934), Congress gave the Supreme Court the power to prescribe rules of procedure for the federal district courts and the District of Columbia, as well as the obligation to report to Congress. In 1935, the Supreme Court appointed an Advisory Committee on Civil Rules to prepare a draft. After making some changes, the Supreme Court adopted the rules in 1937 and submitted them to Congress via the Attorney General. Although these rules were never formally adopted by both houses of Congress, the rules became effective in 1938. The FRCP have been amended by the Supreme Court from time to time since then.

Most states have delegated authority to make procedural rules to the highest state court or a special governmental body; some state legislatures then review and adopt the rules. In other states, the legislature or other advisory body drafts a bill containing the needed procedural rules, and the legislature enacts the bill according to its usual process of statutory enactment. In many states, the procedural rules are modeled after the FRCP, an indication of the success of the federal rules.

The development of the law of evidence—which governs the presentation of testimony and other evidence during trial—is similar, yet also different. The Federal Rules of Evidence (FRE) were drafted by a committee appointed by the Supreme Court and then adopted jointly by Congress and the Court in 1975. Many states have evidence rules based on the FRE. Some have adopted rules based on the model codes developed by law reform organizations. Of course, courts interpret the rules in specific situations. Should there be no evidentiary rule on a topic, the common law governs.

2.   What Do Rules of Procedure Look Like?

Each set of rules is organized topically, generally chronologically. The FRCP, for example, are arranged roughly in the sequence in which litigation usually proceeds in the trial court, from initiation of the lawsuit until judgment. The introductory rules indicate that the FRCP pertain to civil matters brought before the federal district courts. The next few rules address commencement of a lawsuit, covering such matters as service of process, filing of pleadings, the form of pleadings and motions, and designation of parties to the suit. The next two parts of the rules regulate discovery, such as depositions and interrogatories, and the trial itself. Rules concerning judgments and remedies follow. The last several rules cover specialized and miscellaneous matters.

Each rule describes in general terms the litigation practice it covers, stating what is or is not permissible. Each rule is separately numbered, generally with subdivisions. Notes or comments prepared by the advisory committee that worked on the rules generally accompany the rules. These notes typically discuss the purpose of the rule, previous rules that have been superseded or amended, and perhaps proposed amendments that were rejected. Although the notes of the advisory committee do not carry mandatory authority, they are highly persuasive. See Illustration 17-1 on pages 328–330.

Illustration 17-1 on pages 328–330 is Rule 11 of the Federal Rules of Civil Procedure, a rule that is at once mundane and profound. Subdivision (a) states the requirement that a lawyer sign pleadings. Subdivisions (b) and (c) provide that such a signature conveys the lawyer's belief about the propriety of the pleading and specify sanctions for improper pleadings. Illustration 17-1 also presents a portion of the Advisory Committee Notes to Rule 11.

B.   WHY WOULD YOU RESEARCH WHICH RULES OF PROCEDURE?

If your client's case is being or likely will be litigated, you would research procedural rules to learn the proper steps for carrying out litigation. Procedural rules are binding on the litigants and their lawyers. Failure to follow the applicable procedural rules impedes the efficient resolution of the case and may be grounds for dismissal of the suit or for sanctions against the party or the lawyer.

| ILLUSTRATION 17-1 | Federal Rule of Civil Procedure 11 and Advisory Committee Notes, from *Federal Civil Judicial Procedure and Rules* |

PLEADINGS AND MOTIONS   Rule 11

make it unnecessary to consider the admiralty claim and have the same effect on the case and parties as disposition of the admiralty claim. Or the admiralty and nonadmiralty claims may be interdependent. An illustration is provided by Roco Carriers, Ltd. v. M/V Nurnberg Express, 899 F.2d 1292 (2d Cir.1990). Claims for losses of ocean shipments were made against two defendants, one subject to admiralty jurisdiction and the other not. Summary judgment was granted in favor of the admiralty defendant and against the nonadmiralty defendant. The nonadmiralty defendant's appeal was accepted, with the explanation that the determination of its liability was "integrally linked with the determination of nonliability" of the admiralty defendant, and that "section 1292(a)(3) is not limited to admiralty claims; instead, it refers to admiralty cases." 899 F.2d at 1297. The advantages of permitting appeal by the nonadmiralty defendant would be particularly clear if the plaintiff had appealed the summary judgment in favor of the admiralty defendant.

It must be emphasized that this amendment does not rest on any particular assumptions as to the meaning of the § 1292(a)(3) provision that limits interlocutory appeal to orders that determine the rights and liabilities of the parties. It simply reflects the conclusion that so long as the case involves an admiralty claim and an order otherwise meets statutory requirements, the opportunity to appeal should not turn on the circumstance that the order does—or does not—dispose of an admiralty claim. No attempt is made to invoke the authority conferred by 28 U.S.C. § 1292(e) to provide by rule for appeal of an interlocutory decision that is not otherwise provided for by other subsections of § 1292.

GAP Report on Rule 9(h). No changes have been made in the published proposal.

Rule 10.   Form of Pleadings

(a) **Caption; Names of Parties.** Every pleading shall contain a caption setting forth the name of the court, the title of the action, the file number, and a designation as in Rule 7(a). In the complaint the title of the action shall include the names of all the parties, but in other pleadings it is sufficient to state the name of the first party on each side with an appropriate indication of other parties.

(b) **Paragraphs; Separate Statements.** All averments of claim or defense shall be made in numbered paragraphs, the contents of each of which shall be limited as far as practicable to a statement of a single set of circumstances; and a paragraph may be referred to by number in all succeeding pleadings. Each claim founded upon a separate transaction or occurrence and each defense other than denials shall be stated in a separate count or defense whenever a separation facilitates the clear presentation of the matters set forth.

(c) **Adoption by Reference; Exhibits.** Statements in a pleading may be adopted by reference in a different part of the same pleading or in another pleading or in any motion. A copy of any written instrument which is an exhibit to a pleading is a part thereof for all purposes.

ADVISORY COMMITTEE NOTES
1937 Adoption

The first sentence is derived in part from the opening statement of former Equity Rule 25 (Bill of Complaint—Contents). The remainder of the rule is an expansion in conformity with usual state provisions. For numbered paragraphs and separate statements, see Conn.Gen.Stat., 1930, § 5513; Smith-Hurd Ill.Stats. ch. 110, § 157(2); N.Y.R.C.P., (1937) Rule 90. For incorporation by reference, see N.Y.R.C.P., (1937) Rule 90. For written instruments as exhibits, see Smith-Hurd Ill.Stats. ch. 110, § 160.

Rule 11.   Signing of Pleadings, Motions, and Other Papers; Representations to Court; Sanctions

(a) **Signature.** Every pleading, written motion, and other paper shall be signed by at least one attorney of record in the attorney's individual name, or, if the party is not represented by an attorney, shall be signed by the party. Each paper shall state the signer's address and telephone number, if any. Except when otherwise specifically provided by rule or statute, pleadings need not be verified or accompanied by affidavit. An unsigned paper shall be stricken unless omission of the signature is corrected promptly after being called to the attention of the attorney or party.

(b) **Representations to Court.** By presenting to the court (whether by signing, filing, submitting, or later advocating) a pleading, written motion, or other paper, an attorney or unrepresented party is certifying that to the best of the person's knowledge, information, and belief, formed after an inquiry reasonable under the circumstances,—

(1) it is not being presented for any improper purpose, such as to harass or to cause unnecessary delay or needless increase in the cost of litigation;

(2) the claims, defenses, and other legal contentions therein are warranted by existing law or by a nonfrivolous argument for the extension, modification, or reversal of existing law or the establishment of new law;

(3) the allegations and other factual contentions have evidentiary support or, if specifically so identified, are likely to have evidentiary support after a reasonable opportunity for further investigation or discovery; and

(4) the denials of factual contentions are warranted on the evidence or, if specifically so identified, are reasonably based on a lack of information or belief.

(c) **Sanctions.** If, after notice and a reasonable opportunity to respond, the court determines that subdivision (b) has been violated, the court may, subject to the conditions stated below, impose an appropriate sanction upon the attorneys, law firms, or

---

Complete Annotation Materials, see Title 28 U.S.C.A.
85

ILLUSTRATION 17-1   *(continued)*

Rule 11   RULES OF CIVIL PROCEDURE

parties that have violated subdivision (b) or are responsible for the violation.

(1) **How Initiated.**

(A) **By Motion.** A motion for sanctions under this rule shall be made separately from other motions or requests and shall describe the specific conduct alleged to violate subdivision (b). It shall be served as provided in Rule 5, but shall not be filed with or presented to the court unless, within 21 days after service of the motion (or such other period as the court may prescribe), the challenged paper, claim, defense, contention, allegation, or denial is not withdrawn or appropriately corrected. If warranted, the court may award to the party prevailing on the motion the reasonable expenses and attorney's fees incurred in presenting or opposing the motion. Absent exceptional circumstances, a law firm shall be held jointly responsible for violations committed by its partners, associates, and employees.

(B) **On Court's Initiative.** On its own initiative, the court may enter an order describing the specific conduct that appears to violate subdivision (b) and directing an attorney, law firm, or party to show cause why it has not violated subdivision (b) with respect thereto.

(2) **Nature of Sanction; Limitations.** A sanction imposed for violation of this rule shall be limited to what is sufficient to deter repetition of such conduct or comparable conduct by others similarly situated. Subject to the limitations in subparagraphs (A) and (B), the sanction may consist of, or include, directives of a nonmonetary nature, an order to pay a penalty into court, or, if imposed on motion and warranted for effective deterrence, an order directing payment to the movant of some or all of the reasonable attorneys' fees and other expenses incurred as a direct result of the violation.

(A) Monetary sanctions may not be awarded against a represented party for a violation of subdivision (b)(2).

(B) Monetary sanctions may not be awarded on the court's initiative unless the court issues its order to show cause before a voluntary dismissal or settlement of the claims made by or against the party which is, or whose attorneys are, to be sanctioned.

(3) **Order.** When imposing sanctions, the court shall describe the conduct determined to constitute a violation of this rule and explain the basis for the sanction imposed.

(d) **Inapplicability to Discovery.** Subdivisions (a) through (c) of this rule do not apply to disclosures and discovery requests, responses, objections, and motions

that are subject to the provisions of Rules 26 through 37.

(As amended Apr. 28, 1983, eff. Aug. 1, 1983; Mar. 2, 1987, eff. Aug. 1, 1987; Apr. 22, 1993, eff. Dec. 1, 1993.)

ADVISORY COMMITTEE NOTES
1937 Adoption

This is substantially the content of [former] Equity Rules 24 (Signature of Counsel) and 21 (Scandal and Impertinence) consolidated and unified. Compare former Equity Rule 36 (Officers Before Whom Pleadings Verified). Compare to similar purposes, *English Rules Under the Judicature Act* (The Annual Practice, 1937) O. 19, r. 4, and *Great Australian Gold Mining Co. v. Martin*, L.R. 5 Ch.Div. 1, 10 (1877). Subscription of pleadings is required in many codes. 2 Minn.Stat. (Mason, 1927) § 9265; N.Y.R.C.P. (1937) Rule 91; 2 N.D.Comp.Laws Ann. (1913) § 7455.

This rule expressly continues any statute which requires a pleading to be verified or accompanied by an affidavit, such as: U.S.C., Title 28:

§ 381 [former] (Preliminary injunctions and temporary restraining orders)

§ 762 [now 1402] (Suit against the United States)

U.S.C., Title 28, § 829 [now 1927] (Costs; attorney liable for, when) is unaffected by this rule.

For complaints which must be verified under these rules, see Rules 23(b) (Secondary Action by Shareholders) and 65 (Injunctions).

For abolition of former rule in equity that the averments of an answer under oath must be overcome by the testimony of two witnesses or of one witness sustained by corroborating circumstances, see 12 P.S.Pa. § 1222; for the rule in equity itself, see *Greenfield v. Blumenthal*, C.C.A.3, 1934, 69 F.2d 294.

1983 Amendment

Since its original promulgation, Rule 11 has provided for the striking of pleadings and the imposition of disciplinary sanctions to check abuses in the signing of pleadings. Its provisions have always applied to motions and other papers by virtue of incorporation by reference in Rule 7(b)(2). The amendment and the addition of Rule 7(b)(3) expressly confirms this applicability.

Experience shows that in practice Rule 11 has not been effective in deterring abuses. See 6 Wright & Miller, *Federal Practice and Procedure: Civil* § 1334 (1971). There has been considerable confusion as to (1) the circumstances that should trigger striking a pleading or motion or taking disciplinary action, (2) the standard of conduct expected of attorneys who sign pleadings and motions, and (3) the range of available and appropriate sanctions. See Rodes, Ripple & Mooney, *Sanctions Imposable for Violations of the Federal Rules of Civil Procedure* 64–65, Federal Judicial Center (1981). The new language is intended to reduce the reluctance of courts to impose sanctions, see Moore, **Federal Practice** ¶ 7.05, at 1547, by emphasizing the responsibilities of the attorney and reenforcing those obligations by the imposition of sanctions.

The amended rule attempts to deal with the problem by building upon and expanding the equitable doctrine permitting the court to award expenses, including attorney's fees, to

ILLUSTRATION 17-1   *(continued; page 87 omitted)*

Rule 11   RULES OF CIVIL PROCEDURE

A party seeking sanctions should give notice to the court and the offending party promptly upon discovering a basis for doing so. The time when sanctions are to be imposed rests in the discretion of the trial judge. However, it is anticipated that in the case of pleadings the sanctions issue under Rule 11 normally will be determined at the end of the litigation, and in the case of motions at the time when the motion is decided or shortly thereafter. The procedure obviously must comport with due process requirements. The particular format to be followed should depend on the circumstances of the situation and the severity of the sanction under consideration. In many situations the judge's participation in the proceedings provides him with full knowledge of the relevant facts and little further inquiry will be necessary.

To assure that the efficiencies achieved through more effective operation of the pleading regimen will not be offset by the cost of satellite litigation over the imposition of sanctions, the court must to the extent possible limit the scope of sanction proceedings to the record. Thus, discovery should be conducted only by leave of the court, and then only in extraordinary circumstances.

Although the encompassing reference to "other papers" in new Rule 11 literally includes discovery papers, the certification requirement in that context is governed by proposed new Rule 26(g). Discovery motions, however, fall within the ambit of Rule 11.

1987 Amendment

The amendments are technical. No substantive change is intended.

1993 Amendments

Purpose of revision. This revision is intended to remedy problems that have arisen in the interpretation and application of the 1983 revision of the rule. For empirical examination of experience under the 1983 rule, see, *e.g.*, New York State Bar Committee on Federal Courts, *Sanctions and Attorneys' Fees* (1987); T. Willging, *The Rule 11 Sanctioning Process* (1989); American Judicature Society, *Report of the Third Circuit Task Force on Federal Rule of Civil Procedure 11* (S. Burbank ed., 1989); E. Wiggins, T. Willging, and D. Stienstra, *Report on Rule 11* (Federal Judicial Center 1991). For book-length analyses of the case law, see G. Joseph, *Sanctions: The Federal Law of Litigation Abuse* (1989); J. Solovy, *The Federal Law of Sanctions* (1991); G. Vairo, *Rule 11 Sanctions: Case Law Perspectives and Preventive Measures* (1991).

The rule retains the principle that attorneys and pro se litigants have an obligation to the court to refrain from conduct that frustrates the aims of Rule 1. The revision broadens the scope of this obligation, but places greater constraints on the imposition of sanctions and should reduce the number of motions for sanctions presented to the court. New subdivision (d) removes from the ambit of this rule all discovery requests, responses, objections, and motions subject to the provisions of Rule 26 through 37.

Subdivision (a). Retained in this subdivision are the provisions requiring signatures on pleadings, written motions, and other papers. Unsigned papers are to be received by the Clerk, but then are to be stricken if the omission of the signature is not corrected promptly after being called to

the attention of the attorney or pro se litigant. Correction can be made by signing the paper on file or by submitting a duplicate that contains the signature. A court may require by local rule that papers contain additional identifying information regarding the parties or attorneys, such as telephone numbers to facilitate facsimile transmissions, though, as for omission of a signature, the paper should not be rejected for failure to provide such information.

The sentence in the former rule relating to the effect of answers under oath is no longer needed and has been eliminated. The provision in the former rule that signing a paper constitutes a certificate that it has been read by the signer also has been eliminated as unnecessary. The obligations imposed under subdivision (b) obviously require that a pleading, written motion, or other paper be read before it is filed or submitted to the court.

Subdivisions (b) and (c). These subdivisions restate the provisions requiring attorneys and pro se litigants to conduct a reasonable inquiry into the law and facts before signing pleadings, written motions, and other documents, and prescribing sanctions for violation of these obligations. The revision in part expands the responsibilities of litigants to the court, while providing greater constraints and flexibility in dealing with infractions of the rule. The rule continues to require litigants to "stop-and-think" before initially making legal or factual contentions. It also, however, emphasizes the duty of candor by subjecting litigants to potential sanctions for insisting upon a position after it is no longer tenable and by generally providing protection against sanctions if they withdraw or correct contentions after a potential violation is called to their attention.

The rule applies only to assertions contained in papers filed with or submitted to the court. It does not cover matters arising for the first time during oral presentations to the court, when counsel may make statements that would not have been made if there had been more time for study and reflection. However, a litigant's obligations with respect to the contents of these papers are not measured solely as of the time they are filed with or submitted to the court, but include reaffirming to the court and advocating positions contained in those pleadings and motions after learning that they cease to have any merit. For example, an attorney who during a pretrial conference insists on a claim or defense should be viewed as "presenting to the court" that contention and would be subject to the obligations of subdivision (b) measured as of that time. Similarly, if after a notice of removal is filed, a party urges in federal court the allegations of a pleading filed in state court (whether as claims, defenses, or in disputes regarding removal or remand), it would be viewed as "presenting"—and hence certifying to the district court under Rule 11—those allegations.

The certification with respect to allegations and other factual contentions is revised in recognition that sometimes a litigant may have good reason to believe that a fact is true or false but may need discovery, formal or informal, from opposing parties or third persons to gather and confirm the evidentiary basis for the allegation. Tolerance of factual contentions in initial pleadings by plaintiffs or defendants when specifically identified as made on information and belief does not relieve litigants from the obligation to conduct an appropriate investigation into the facts that is reasonable under the circumstances; it is not a license to join parties, make claims, or present defenses without any factual basis or

As already noted, reflecting our federalist system, rules of procedure exist at both the federal and state levels. To ascertain which set of rules applies, determine whether your claim will be pursued in federal or state court. The federal courts apply federal rules, and each state court applies its state's rules. Federal procedural rules apply even when a federal court is adjudicating a claim based on the substantive law of a state, as occurs in diversity jurisdiction cases. Furthermore, you should figure out which specific state or federal court is involved and research that court's local rules.

Even when you are in state court and your issue is governed by a state rule, you may research federal law, because many state rules parallel federal rules. See Illustration 17-2 on pages 332–333, the New Mexico state court rule paralleling federal Rule 11. There are far more published cases regarding federal rules than state rules, in part because some federal trial court opinions are published. Hence, when researching state rules, lawyers often look to federal cases as persuasive precedent. Of course, if a state rule differs in significant part from a federal rule, federal case law would not be persuasive.

C. HOW DO YOU RESEARCH RULES OF PROCEDURE?

The focus of research in procedural rules is, of course, the text of the rule, but the rule is not often the endpoint of your research. You generally will look to case law for additional authority. The courts assess the constitutionality of and apply procedural rules in specific cases, just as they do with statutes. If the language of the rule is less than clear in its application to your client's situation, you also may use commentary to help you understand the rule.

To obtain this combination of authorities, you will use sources used in other forms of research; you also will use sources unique to research in procedural rules. The following discussion leads off with deskbooks, a source most litigators turn to first. It then touches on various sources covered in detail elsewhere and notes what is distinctive about their use for procedural research. The discussion closes with a description of one specialized procedural law source and a survey of sources containing local rules. Federal procedure in particular is one of the most thoroughly covered areas of law. Accordingly the following discussion is not exhaustive.

This part addresses the following issue: Assume, as Ms. Canoga's lawyer, that you decided to file suit on her behalf. The complaint concludes with a signature block: a blank for your signature, your name typed below the blank, and information about your firm typed below that. Somehow the complaint was filed with the clerk of court without your signature. Instead, it carries the signature of Ms. Canoga, who came into your office the day the complaint was filed to review it and sign some other papers. So, you need to learn whether the complaint is valid as filed and, if not, how to correct it, if possible.

The following discussion focuses on the federal rules. Comparable sources and methods exist at the state level.

ILLUSTRATION 17-2   New Mexico Rule of Civil Procedure 1-011 and
                          Annotation, from *New Mexico Rules Annotated*

1-011. Signing of pleadings, motions and other papers; sanctions.

Every pleading, motion and other paper of a party represented by an attorney, shall be signed by at least one attorney of record in the attorney's individual name, whose address and telephone number shall be stated. A party who is not represented by an attorney shall sign the party's pleading, motion or other paper and state the party's address and telephone number. Except when otherwise specifically provided by rule or statute, pleadings need not be verified or accompanied by affidavit. The rule in equity that the averments of an answer under oath must be overcome by the testimony of two witnesses or of one witness sustained by corroborating circumstances is abolished. The signature of an attorney or party constitutes a certificate by the signer that the signer has read the pleading, motion or other paper; that to the best of the signer's knowledge, information and belief there is good ground to support it; and that it is not interposed for delay. If a pleading, motion or other paper is signed with intent to defeat the purpose of this rule, it may be stricken as sham and false and the action may proceed as though the pleading or other paper had not been served. If a pleading, motion or other paper is not signed, it shall be stricken unless it is signed promptly after the omission is called to the attention of the pleader or movant. For a willful violation of this rule an attorney or party may be subjected to appropriate disciplinary or other action. Similar action may be taken if scandalous or indecent matter is inserted. A "signature" means an original signature, a copy of an original signature, a computer generated signature or any other signature otherwise authorized by law.
[As amended, effective January 1, 1987; August 1, 1989; January 1, 1997.]

Committee commentary. — New Mexico has enacted an Electronic Authentication Documentation Act which provides for the Secretary of State to register electronic signatures using the public key technology. See Section 14-15-4 NMSA 1978.

Cross references. — As to verification of petition in divorce actions, see 40-4-6 NMSA 1978. As to verification of pleadings in action for seizure of illegal oil, see 70-2-32 NMSA 1978.

The 1997 amendment, effective January 1, 1997, added the last sentence defining "signature".

Compiler's notes. — This rule, in conjunction with Rule 1-005, is deemed to have superseded 105-510 and 105-705, C.S. 1929. It is further deemed to partially supersede 105-415, C.S. 1929, and to supersede 105-424, 105-425, 105-821, C.S. 1929.

Purpose. — The primary goal of this rule is to deter baseless filings in district court by testing the conduct of counsel. Rivera v. Brazos Lodge Corp., 111 N.M. 670, 808 P.2d 955 (1991).

The objectives sought by this rule and the wording of the rule primarily place a moral obligation upon the lawyer to satisfy himself that there are good grounds for the action or defense. This requires honesty and good faith in pleading. Rivera v. Brazos Lodge Corp., 111 N.M. 670, 808 P.2d 955 (1991).

The "good ground" provision in this rule is to be measured by subjective standards at the time of the signing of the pleading. Any violation depends on what the attorney or litigant knew and believed at the relevant time and involves the question of whether the litigant or attorney was aware that a particular pleading should not have been brought. Rivera v. Brazos Lodge Corp., 111 N.M. 670, 808 P.2d 955 (1991).

The "good ground" provision of this rule is measured by a subjective standard: Any violation depends on what the attorney or litigant knew and believed at the relevant time (the signing of the pleading) and involves the question of whether the litigant or attorney was aware that a particular pleading should not have been brought. Lowe v. Bloom, 112 N.M. 203, 813 P.2d 480 (1991).

Husband signing pleading as attorney-in-fact equivalent to wife signing. — Where defendant did not personally sign the answer in the prior suit, in which appeared the admission of the debt later sued upon, but in her answer in the later suit she admitted her deceased husband signed the answer in the prior suit as attorney for her and himself, and no question had been raised as to his authority to sign the answer as her attorney or to make the admission on her behalf, then his signature on her behalf to the answer in the prior suit had the same effect as if she had personally signed. Smith v. Walcott, 85 N.M. 351, 512 P.2d 679 (1973).

Where an appellant is obviously present before the court and vigorously pursuing his case — although his name is missing from the caption of the case and he has erroneously designated someone else as the appellant — the court and all those concerned may yet have sufficient knowledge of the parties and their positions to hear the merits of the case. Mitchell v. Dona Ana Sav. & Loan Ass'n, 111 N.M. 257, 804 P.2d 1076 (1991).

Pleading stricken when required verification omitted. — Where a verification is required and is omitted, the pleading may be stricken out or judgment may be had on the pleadings. Hyde v. Bryan, 24 N.M. 457, 174 P. 419 (1918) (decided under former law).

Where the attorney objected to the judgment which included sanction, and the court also gave him notice through the order to show cause, this afforded the attorney not only the essential facts but also the notice and an opportunity to be heard; the attorney was afforded all the process he was due. Dona Ana Sav. & Loan Ass'n v. Mitchell, 113 N.M. 576, 829 P.2d 655 (Ct. App. 1991).

Sworn statement not required. — Service of a sworn statement before imposing sanctions is not required. Dona Ana Sav. & Loan Ass'n v. Mitchell, 113 N.M. 576, 829 P.2d 655 (Ct. App. 1991).

Motion to vacate a judgment need not be verified. Sheppard v. Sandfer, 44 N.M. 357, 102 P.2d 668 (1940) (decided under former law).

ILLUSTRATION 17-2   *(continued)*

45   RULES OF CIVIL PROCEDURE FOR THE DISTRICT COURTS   1-012

District court improperly imposed sanctions against an attorney for willfully failing to disclose the pendency of an action in another state involving the same issue, where the sanction awarded was based on what the attorney failed to disclose to the court, as opposed to a defect in his pleading. Cherryhomes v. Vogel, 111 N.M. 229, 804 P.2d 420 (Ct. App. 1990).

Sanctions should be entered against an attorney rather than a party for violation of the "good ground" requirement of this rule only when a pleading or other paper is unsupported by existing law rather than unsupported by facts. Rivera v. Brazos Lodge Corp., 111 N.M. 670, 808 P.2d 955 (1991).

Procedural due process. — Rule 11 sanctions should be imposed rarely, they should be levied only if the mandates of procedural due process are obeyed. Rivera v. Brazos Lodge Corp., 111 N.M. 670, 808 P.2d 955 (1991).

Determining whether process is due in a Rule 11 case requires an application of familiar principles of due process. The timing and content of the notice and the nature of the hearing will depend upon an evaluation of all the circumstances and an appropriate accommodation of the competing interests involved. Rivera v. Brazos Lodge Corp., 111 N.M. 670, 808 P.2d 955 (1991).

Appellate review of Rule 11 determination. — An appellate court should apply an abuse-of-discretion standard in reviewing all aspects of a trial court's Rule 11 determination. An abuse of discretion will be found when the trial court's decision is clearly untenable or contrary to logic and reason. Rivera v. Brazos Lodge Corp., 111 N.M. 670, 808 P.2d 955 (1991).

Case was remanded to the district court for the entry of findings and conclusions on the imposition of Rule 11 sanctions, where the supreme court was unable to review whether an abuse of discretion occurred in the imposition of sanctions for the filing of plaintiff's complaint without speculation about the subjective knowledge of the relevant facts and applicable law held by plaintiff and his attorney at the time of filing. Rivera v. Brazos Lodge Corp., 111 N.M. 670, 808 P.2d 955 (1991).

Evidence of willful violation lacking. — An earlier action for attorney fees was disposed of through a voluntary dismissal without prejudice and with no answer having been filed. The later filing of a malpractice claim against the plaintiffs in the earlier action was not a violation of this rule. Whether the claim for malpractice was a compulsory counterclaim in the earlier action was a question on which reasonable lawyers and judges could have differed. Lowe v. Bloom, 112 N.M. 203, 813 P.2d 480 (1991).

Am. Jur. 2d, A.L.R. and C.J.S. references. — 61A Am. Jur. 2d Pleading §§ 339 to 349.

Sufficiency of verification of pleading by person other than party to action, 7 A.L.R. 4.

Perjury in verifying pleadings, 7 A.L.R. 1283.

Civil liability of attorney for abuse of process, 97 A.L.R.3d 688.

Comment Note—General principles regarding imposition of sanctions under Rule 11, Federal Rules of Civil Procedure, 95 A.L.R. Fed. 107.

Imposition of sanctions under Rule 11, Federal Rules of Civil Procedure, pertaining to signing and verification of pleadings, in actions for defamation, 95 A.L.R. Fed. 181.

Imposition of sanctions under Rule 11, Federal Rules of Civil Procedure, pertaining to signing and verification of pleadings, in action for wrongful discharge from employment, 96 A.L.R. Fed. 13.

Imposition of sanctions under Rule 11, Federal Rules of Civil Procedure, pertaining to signing and verification of pleadings, in actions for securities fraud, 97 A.L.R. Fed. 107.

Imposition of sanctions under Rule 11, Federal Rules of Civil Procedure, pertaining to signing and verification of pleadings, in actions for infliction of emotional distress, 98 A.L.R. Fed. 442.

Imposition of sanctions under Rule 11, Federal Rules of Civil Procedure, pertaining to signing and verification of pleadings, in antitrust actions, 99 A.L.R. Fed. 573.

Procedural requirements for imposition of sanctions under Rule 11, Federal Rules of Civil Procedure, 100 A.L.R. Fed. 556.

71 C.J.S. Pleading §§ 339 to 366.

1-012. Defenses and objections; when and how presented; by pleading or motion; motion for judgment on the pleadings.

A. **When presented.** A defendant shall serve his answer within thirty (30) days after the service of the summons and complaint upon him. A party served with a pleading stating a cross-claim against him shall serve an answer thereto within thirty (30) days after the service upon him. The plaintiff shall serve his reply to a counterclaim in the answer within thirty (30) days after service of the answer, or, if a reply is ordered by the court, within thirty (30) days after service of the order, unless the order otherwise directs. The service of a motion permitted under this rule alters these periods of time as follows, unless a different time is fixed by order of the court:

(1) if the court denies the motion or postpones its disposition until the trial on the merits, the responsive pleading shall be served within ten (10) days after the court's action;

(2) if the court grants a motion for a more definite statement, the responsive pleading shall be served within ten (10) days after the service of the more definite statement.

B. **How presented.** Every defense, in law or fact, to a claim for relief in any pleading, whether a claim, counterclaim, cross-claim or third-party claim, shall be asserted in the responsive pleading thereto if one is required, except that the following defenses may at the option of the pleader be made by motion:

(1) lack of jurisdiction over the subject matter;

(2) lack of jurisdiction over the person;

> **Procedural rules in deskbooks:**
>
> ▶ choose an appropriate deskbook
> ▶ consult the index or table of contents
> ▶ read the main rule and related rules
> ▶ read the advisory committee notes
> ▶ look for pertinent forms

Procedural rules are published in their most compact form in deskbooks. A deskbook is a one- or two-volume set that usually contains the text of a jurisdiction's various sets of rules of procedure, notes or comments of the advisory committees on those rules, and some model forms. See Illustration 17-3 on page 335, the table of contents for a representative federal rules deskbook. However, deskbooks do not contain case descriptions or extensive commentary. Most deskbooks are published annually and are not updated until the next edition is published. Thus deskbooks are fairly current, but not necessarily completely up to date.

There are several means of locating a pertinent rule within a deskbook. If you are not sure which set of rules covers your topic, you may use a general index for the deskbook. If you know which set of rules is pertinent, you may prefer to use the index to that set of rules. Some deskbooks have a general index or specific indexes, but not both. Or you can skim the table of contents at the beginning of a set of rules.

Once you have located the pertinent rule, you should read it much as you would read a statute. You should read the entire rule, not just a section that seems to be on point. Indeed, it often is wise to skim nearby and related rules as well. You should read any other rules to which your rule refers. In addition, you should read advisory committee notes to learn about the drafters' intent and any amendments to the rule (so that your research in case law will be focused on cases arising under the current language).

Furthermore, you should check for forms that accompany your rule. Such forms are intended only to illustrate an appropriate format of pleadings. These forms generally are printed in an appendix to the set of rules. See Illustration 17-4 on page 336, a federal form for various types of jurisdictional allegations.

Researching the signature issue in the Canoga case, we selected West Group's *Federal Civil Judicial Procedure and Rules.* In the table of contents for the FRCP, we quickly found Rule 11 in part III. Pleadings and Motions. Rule 11's title refers to signing of pleadings. Subdivision (a) requires a pleading to be signed by the attorney (or the party, but only where the party is not represented by an attorney); an unsigned pleading is stricken unless promptly corrected after being called to the attorney's attention. See Illustration 17-1 on page 328. The Advisory Committee Notes to the 1993 amendments explain how to correct the omission: by signing the filed pleading or submitting a signed duplicate.

ILLUSTRATION 17-3	Deskbook's Table of Contents, from *Federal Civil Judicial Procedure and Rules*

TABLE OF CONTENTS

*

VII

ILLUSTRATION 17-4   Sample Form, from *Federal Civil Judicial Procedure and Rules*

Form 1B   RULES OF CIVIL PROCEDURE

pursuant to section 2074 of this title, which was to take effect Dec. 1, 1991, was nullified by Congress, see section 11 of Pub.L. 102–198, set out as a note under section 2074 of this title.

Form 2.   Allegation of Jurisdiction

(a) Jurisdiction founded on diversity of citizenship and amount.

Plaintiff is a [citizen of the State of Connecticut] [1] [corporation incorporated under the laws of the State of Connecticut having its principal place of business in the State of Connecticut] and defendant is a corporation incorporated under the laws of the State of New York having its principal place of business in a State other than the State of Connecticut. The matter in controversy exceeds, exclusive of interest and costs, the sum of fifty thousand dollars.

(b) Jurisdiction founded on the existence of a Federal question.

The action arises under [the Constitution of the United States, Article ___, Section ___]; [the ___ Amendment to the Constitution of the United States, Section ___]; [the Act of ___, ___ Stat. ___; U.S.C., Title ___, § ___]; [the Treaty of the United States (here describe the treaty)] [2] as hereinafter more fully appears.

(c) Jurisdiction founded on the existence of a question arising under particular statutes.

The action arises under the Act of ___, ___ Stat. ___; U.S.C., Title ___, § ___, as hereinafter more fully appears.

(d) Jurisdiction founded on the admiralty or maritime character of the claim.

This is a case of admiralty and maritime jurisdiction, as hereinafter more fully appears. [If the pleader wishes to invoke the distinctively maritime procedures referred to in Rule 9(h), add the following or its substantial equivalent: This is an admiralty or maritime claim within the meaning of Rule 9(h).]

[1] Form for natural person.

[2] Use the appropriate phrase or phrases. The general allegation of the existence of a Federal question is ineffective unless the matters constituting the claim for relief as set forth in the complaint raise a Federal question.

NOTES

1. **Diversity of citizenship.** U.S.C., Title 28, § 1332 (Diversity of citizenship; amount in controversy; costs), as amended by PL 85–554, 72 Stat. 415, July 25, 1958, states in subsection (c) that "For the purposes of this section and section 1441 of this title [removable actions], a corporation shall be deemed a citizen of any State by which it has been incorporated and of the State where it has its principal place of business." Thus if the defendant corporation in Form 2(a) had its principal place of business in Connecticut, diversity of citizenship would not exist. An allegation regarding the principal place of business of each corporate party must be made in addition to an allegation regarding its place of incorporation.

2. **Jurisdictional amount.** U.S.C., Title 28, § 1331 (Federal question; amount in controversy; costs) and § 1332 (Diversity of citizenship; amount in controversy; costs), as amended by PL 85–554, 72 Stat. 415, July 25, 1958, require that the amount in controversy, exclusive of interest and costs, be in excess of $10,000. The allegation as to the amount in controversy may be omitted in any case where by law no jurisdictional amount is required. See, for example, U.S.C., Title 28, § 1338 (Patents, copyrights, trade-marks, and unfair competition), § 1343 (Civil rights and elective franchise).

3. **Pleading venue.** Since improper venue is a matter of defense, it is not necessary for plaintiff to include allegations showing the venue to be proper. See 1 *Moore's Federal Practice*, par. 0.140[1–4] (2d ed. 1959).

(As amended Apr. 17, 1961, eff. July 19, 1961; Feb. 28, 1966, eff. July 1, 1966; Apr. 22, 1993, eff. Dec. 1, 1993.)

ADVISORY COMMITTEE NOTES

1966 Amendment

Since the Civil Rules have not heretofore been applicable to proceedings in Admiralty (Rule 81(a)(1)), Form 2 naturally has not contained a provision for invoking the admiralty jurisdiction. The form has never purported to be comprehensive, as making provision for all possible grounds of jurisdiction; but a provision for invoking the admiralty jurisdiction is particularly appropriate as an incident of unification.

Certain distinctive features of the admiralty practice must be preserved in unification, just as certain distinctive characteristics of equity were preserved in the merger of law and equity in 1938. Rule 9(h) provides the device whereby, after unification, with its abolition of the distinction between civil actions and suits in admiralty, the pleader may indicate his choice of the distinctively maritime procedures, and designates those features that are preserved. This form illustrates an appropriate way in which the pleader may invoke those procedures. Use of this device is not necessary if the claim is cognizable only by virtue of the admiralty and maritime jurisdiction, nor if the claim is within the exclusive admiralty jurisdiction of the district court.

Omission of a statement such as this from the pleading indicates the pleader's choice that the action proceed as a conventional civil action, if this is jurisdictionally possible, without the distinctive maritime remedies and procedures. It should be remembered, however, that Rule 9(h) provides that a pleading may be amended to add or withdraw such an identifying statement subject to the principles stated in Rule 15.

1993 Amendments

This form is revised to reflect amendments to 28 U.S.C. §§ 1331 and 1332 providing jurisdiction for federal questions without regard to the amount in controversy and raising the amount required to be in controversy in diversity cases to fifty thousand dollars.

Complete Annotation Materials, see Title 28 U.S.C.A.

> **Procedural rules in general-purpose sources:**
>
> - secondary sources
> - case reporters and related sources, for example, digests, online databases, citators
> - annotated codes and rules citators

Rules of procedure are included in many of the sources described in the earlier chapters of this book. Rather than reiterate what is stated there, the following discussion simply points out how those sources, whether in paper or computer-based media, can be used in procedural rules research.

Most secondary sources (see Unit II) cover procedural rules. The exception is the Restatements, which focus on restating the substantive common law, not procedural rules. You will find procedural topics discussed in sources that also cover substantive law and in sources focused only on procedural law, for example, encyclopedias dedicated to federal procedure. The most credible and extensive discussions of procedural rules appear in treatises. Exhibit 17.2 on page 338 lists the better known treatises regarding federal procedure and the law of evidence. Many states have one or more well recognized procedural treatises.

Case reporters contain procedural cases, of course. (See Chapter 10.) Many procedural cases are interspersed among the general federal and regional reporters in the West National Reporter System. For example, recent Tenth Circuit cases interpreting the federal rules would appear in F.3d; New Mexico state court cases interpreting the New Mexico state rules appear in the *Pacific Reporter*. In addition, West publishes *Federal Rules Decisions* (F.R.D.), which contains federal district court cases discussing the Federal Rules of Civil Procedure and the Federal Rules of Criminal Procedure. (F.R.D. also provides such useful information as proposals for rule changes and articles on procedural topics by judges, lawyers, and professors.)

As you research procedural cases, you also may employ the full array of case law sources that complement or substitute for case reporters. These sources include case digests, Westlaw and LEXIS databases, CD-ROM collections of case law, public web sites offering cases, and paper and online case citators. (See Unit III.) For example, F.R.D. cases are digested in the *Federal Practice Digests*.

Even though rules of procedure typically are not enacted in the same way as statutes, they generally appear in or along with a jurisdiction's statutory code. (See Chapter 12.) They may appear in one or more separate volumes, or they may be integrated into the statutory codification. For example, *United States Code Annotated* presents the FRCP after Title 28, which is about the judiciary; *United States Code Service* presents procedural rules in rules volumes at the end of the set. (A few states publish procedural rules not with the statutory code, but with the administrative code.)

The rules volumes typically have their own index, whereas court rules

| EXHIBIT 17.2 | Federal Procedure and Evidence Treatises |

Fleming James, Jr., et al., *Civil Procedure* (4th ed. 1992) (single-volume treatise).

James W. Moore et al., *Moore's Federal Practice* (3d ed. 1997-present) (multivolume looseleaf treatise covers civil, criminal, appellate, and admiralty rules).

Charles A. Wright, *The Law of Federal Courts* (5th ed. 1994) (single-volume treatise).

Charles A. Wright et al., *Federal Practice and Procedure* (1969-present) (multivolume treatise covers civil, criminal, appellate, and evidentiary rules; various volumes have various authors).

Jack B. Weinstein & Margaret A. Berger, *Weinstein's Federal Evidence: Commentary on Rules of Evidence for the United States Courts* (Joseph M. McLaughlin ed., 2d ed. 1997-present) (multivolume treatise).

John H. Wigmore, *Evidence in Trials at Common Law* (rev. ed. Peter Tillers, 1983-present) (multivolume treatise).

McCormick on Evidence (John W. Strong ed., 5th ed. 1999) (single-and two volume treatise).

---

incorporated into the statutory codification are indexed in the general index. Some general indexes cover court rules under the title of the rules, such as "Rules of Civil Procedure." Others disperse the court rules topics throughout the general index, in which case you may need to use research terms such as "signature" or "pleadings."

Two main advantages of researching in the annotated code, whether in paper or in computer-based media, are the descriptions of pertinent cases and the references to other sources in the annotation. See Illustration 17-2 on pages 332–333, which is drawn from the *New Mexico Rules Annotated*, a companion set to the *New Mexico Statutes Annotated*.

Furthermore, online databases contain procedural rules. Westlaw, for example, provides US-RULES, which includes the four main sets of federal procedural rules, and comparable databases for the states.

As with statutes, procedural rules can be cited, in paper Shepard's Citations, specifically the statutes editions, and online through Shepard's on LEXIS and KeyCite on Westlaw. You would cite a rule for the same reasons you would cite a statutory section: to learn of amendments, cases declaring the rule void or unconstitutional, cases interpreting the rule, and secondary sources discussing the rule. The results you get may vary from citator to citator, depending on how extensive the LEXIS or West publications are for the jurisdiction. (See Chapter 12.)

> **Procedural rules in *Federal Rules Service* (specialized reporter):**
>
> ▸ discern the Findex number
> ▸ locate pertinent cases under that Findex number in the *Federal Rules Digest*
> ▸ read the cases in reporters
> ▸ peruse recent releases

Federal Rules Service, published by West Group, contains cases construing the Federal Rules of Civil Procedure and the Federal Rules of Appellate Procedure. *Federal Rules of Evidence Service* is a similar publication for evidence issues. Cases often appear in these sources sooner than in other publications, and some cases are not published elsewhere. The following discussion focuses on use of *Federal Rules Service*.

Using the *Federal Rules Service* involves several steps. The first step is to find an applicable Findex number. The Findex is a detailed topical index with a numerical scheme roughly paralleling the numbering of the rules. The Findex uses whole numbers, letters, and decimal numbers to divide the rules and their subdivisions into subtopics. See Illustration 17-5 on page 340. Each rule's Findex is preceded by the rule itself. If you do not know the rule's number, you can use the Word Index to find a pertinent Findex number. The Findex and the Word Index are located in the Finding Aids volume.

The second step is to locate descriptions of pertinent cases. The *Federal Rules Digest* contains descriptions of the cases reported in the *Federal Rules Service* and is organized by Findex number. See Illustration 17-6 on page 341. The *Federal Rules Digest* groups the case descriptions by court levels and provides citations to the *Federal Rules Service* reporters and to other reporters, such as West reporters, if the cases are published in them.

The third step is to read any pertinent cases. The full texts of the cases digested in the *Federal Rules Digest* are printed in the *Federal Rules Service* reporters, and some are printed in other reporters.

To update your research in the *Federal Rules Service*, you can use the paper advance sheets, called "releases," which are published monthly. Each release contains the full text of recent cases and a Findex case table containing a cumulative listing of cases ordered by Findex numbers.

Researching the omitted signature issue in the Canoga case, we focused on Findex number 11.21, which pertains to the attorney of record as the signatory; 11.21 is a subtopic of 11.2, who may sign. See Illustration 17-5 on page 340. The *Federal Rules Digest* describes *White v. American Airlines, Inc.*, 915 F.2d 1414 (10th Cir. 1990). There, a plaintiff signed a motion, and the attorney's name was typed but not signed. The court deemed the motion unsigned by the attorney for purposes of Rule 11 sanctions for filing an unfounded motion. See Illustration 17-6 on page 341.

ILLUSTRATION 17-5   Findex, from *Federal Rules Service*

FEDERAL RULES SERVICE—F̶i̶n̶d̶e̶x̶™   **RULE 11**

➤   .21   Attorney of record
              .211   Member of firm
       .22   Party
   .3   Verification or affidavit
       .31   In general (see also F̶i̶n̶d̶e̶x̶™ 1.342)
       .32   When required by other Rules
              .321   Secondary action by shareholders: see F̶i̶n̶d̶e̶x̶™ 23–1.2
              .322   Perpetuation of testimony: see F̶i̶n̶d̶e̶x̶™ 27a.45
              .323   Injunction: see F̶i̶n̶d̶e̶x̶™ 65b.13
       .33   When required by statute
       .34   When required by local rule
   .4   Effect of signature; good faith
       .41   In general
       .42   Allegations upon information and belief (see also F̶i̶n̶d̶e̶x̶™
              8e.2)
       .43   "Reasonable inquiry"
              .431   General statements
              .432   Objective standards
              .433   Inquiry into law
                     .4331   In general
                     .4332   Existing law
                     .4333   Argument for extension, modification, or
                             reversal of law
                     .4334   Jurisdiction (see also F̶i̶n̶d̶e̶x̶™ 11.4344)
                     .4335   Res judicata (see also F̶i̶n̶d̶e̶x̶™ 11.4345)
              .434   Inquiry into facts
                     .4341   In general
                     .4342   Misrepresentation of facts
                     .4343   Conclusory statements
                     .4344   Citizenship of party (see also F̶i̶n̶d̶e̶x̶™
                             11.4334)
                     .4345   Prior history of case (see also F̶i̶n̶d̶e̶x̶™
                             11.4335)
                     .4346   Filing in order to obtain discovery
                     .4347   Attorney's reliance on information from
                             client
              .435   Investigation after filing
              .436   Represented and unrepresented parties; duty to
                     inquire
              .437   Factors in determining reasonableness; time
                     constraints
       .44   General denial
       .45   Denials upon or for lack of information and belief: see
              F̶i̶n̶d̶e̶x̶™ 8b.15
   .5   Sanctions for violation of Rule
       .50   In general
              .501   Jurisdiction of court; general statements
                     .5011   Inherent powers of court

[For digests of cases in point, see applicable F̶i̶n̶d̶e̶x̶™ number in Federal Rules Digest.]

Rule 11—Page 3

Release 14—Copyright © 1996, Lawyers Cooperative Publishing   Pub 4/96

ILLUSTRATION 17-6   Case Descriptions, from *Federal Rules Digest, Federal Rules Service*

SIGNING OF PLEADINGS   **11.21**

The fact that defendant municipality's counsel did not personally sign the notice of appeal in an action challenging the constitutionality of certain police procedures did not deprive the court of appellate jurisdiction where someone else in counsel's office had signed counsel's name and placed his own initials next to the signature. The city's municipal code made its counsel legally accountable for all matters filed on the city's behalf; moreover, anything signed by an authorized agent of his was to be treated under Rule 11 as if he himself had signed it. Thus, the notice satisfied both the letter and purpose of that Rule. Moreover, an unsigned notice of appeal meets the jurisdictional requirements for appeal under Appellate Rule 3(c), even if it does not meet the demands of Rule 11. Robinson v. City of Chicago, 13 Fed Rules Serv 3d 377, 848 F2d 959 (CA7 1989).

The district court did not abuse its discretion in a wrongful discharge action by refusing to impose sanctions against an attorney for filing an unfounded motion for a protective order where plaintiff signed the motion and the attorney's name appeared only in typewritten form. Rule 11 focuses on the individual who signs the document in question. Thus, a typewritten name is not sufficient to satisfy the Rule. White v. American Airlines, Inc., 17 Fed Rules Serv 3d 1199, 915 F2d 1414 (CA10 1990).

In a doctor's antitrust suit against a hospital, the district court did not abuse its discretion in refusing to grant the doctor's motion for Rule 11 sanctions against defendant insurance company based on the fact that one of the company's attorneys had not been admitted to practice in the district. The district court construed the local rule not to require admission to practice in order merely to take a deposition. Although counsel also participated in a conference call and signed the motion to dismiss, the motion was argued by other attorneys who were admitted to practice. Negligent failure to secure local admission has been held not to justify sanctions for violation of a rule generally regarded as a technicality absent a showing of bad faith, recklessness or willfulness. That showing was not made. Further, the doctor's efforts were seen as a retaliatory measure. Castillo v. St. Paul Fire & Marine Ins. Co., 20 Fed Rules Serv 3d 295, 938 F2d 776 (CA7 1991).

The district court did not abuse its discretion in refusing to hold substitute counsel susceptible to Rule 11 sanctions on the basis of a complaint signed by a predecessor. When substitute counsel takes up a claim, some new pleading should be necessary to serve as the basis for the imposition of sanctions against the successor counsel. Although Rule 11 imposes upon substitute counsel a duty to investigate the legal and factual sufficiency of the claims taken up, until substitute counsel files some paper indicating an intention to continue prosecution of the suit, such a decision will not be presumed by looking to the complaint itself. Since substitute counsel's actions in the case were limited to discovery requests and were made with movant's acquiescence or nonobjection, the disallowance of sanctions was not an abuse of discretion. Bakker v. Grutman, 20 Fed Rules Serv 3d 779, 942 F2d 236 (CA4 1991).

DISTRICT COURTS

A complaint alleging defendants' conspiracy to defraud the court will not be stricken where the attesting attorney testified that before the commencement of the action he and his associates intensively investigated the facts upon which the complaint was based and that he knew of "good ground" to support the complaint

35

> **Sources containing local rules of procedure:**
>
> - deskbooks
> - statutory codes
> - *Federal Local Court Rules*
> - clerk of court's office or web site
> - online and CD-ROM sources

As noted above, local rules are rules that are created by and apply to proceedings before specific courts within a court system. Local rules typically deal with matters of detail not addressed by the general rules for the jurisdiction, such as size of pages, page ranges, and time limits. Although they may not seem as weighty as the general rules, you must know and follow all pertinent local rules. See Illustration 17-7 on page 343, an excerpt from the rules of the United States District Court for the District of New Mexico.

Federal local court rules appear in various sources. The rules of the courts of appeals appear, with annotations, in the federal statutory codes. *Federal Local Court Rules*, a set of looseleaf binders supplementing *Federal Rules Service*, contains the local rules for the federal appellate and district courts. The deskbook for a state may include the rules of the local federal courts. Of course, a clerk of court can provide a copy as well. To identify cases interpreting local federal rules, consult *Shepard's Federal Statutes Citations*. Local court rules also are available in computer-based media. Some courts make their rules available through their web sites. Federal local court rules also are available from LEXIS and Westlaw and in CD-ROM products.

At the state level, the state's deskbook or annotated code may contain the local rules for the various courts. Other options are to contact the clerk of the particular court, whether in person or through the court's web site. Again, these local rules may be found in LEXIS, Westlaw, and CD-ROM products.

Researching the issue of the omitted signature in the Canoga case, we located Rule 10.3(b) of the New Mexico federal district court in *Federal Local Court Rules*. Note that the local rule provides detail lacking in Rule 11: the correction must be made within fourteen calendar days, or the pleading will be stricken. See Illustration 17-7 on page 343.

| ILLUSTRATION 17-7 | Local Civil Rule 10 of the United States District Court for the District of New Mexico, from *Federal Local Court Rules* |

Rule 10   NEW MEXICO

RULE 10. FORM OF PAPERS

10.1 F'orm. A paper presented for filing must be on size 8½″ by 11″ white, opaque, unglazed paper of good quality and be typewritten or printed on one side without interlineations. Except for footnotes and quotations, the text of all papers must be double spaced. The first page of each paper must have the case file number and initials of the assigned Judges.

10.2 Titles of Papers.

(a) *Identification of Substance.* The title of a paper must clearly identify its substance.

(b) *Responses or Replies.* The title of a response or a reply must identify by title and approximate date of filing the paper to which it responds.

(c) *Affidavit.* The title of an affidavit must identify by title and approximate date of filing of the paper it supports.

10.3 Filing of Non-conforming Papers.

(a) *Acceptance of Papers.* The Clerk will not refuse to file any paper because it is not in proper form.

(b) *Signature.* Any paper filed without signature will be stricken unless it is signed within fourteen (14) calendar days after the omission is called to the party's attention.

(c) *Non-conforming Papers.* The Clerk will give to the submitting party written notice of a deficiency and deadline for correcting the deficiency. The Clerk will also provide any applicable forms and instruction sheets. Failure to remedy a deficiency or to show good cause for non-compliance within forty-five (45) calendar days from the date of notice may result in dismissal of the action without prejudice in accordance with D.N.M.LR–Civ. 41.2.

10.4 Attachments to Pleadings. Exhibits are not attached to a pleading unless the documents attached form the basis for the action or defense.

10.5 Page Limit for Exhibits. Exhibits to a motion, response or reply, including excerpts from a deposition, must not exceed fifty (50) pages unless all parties agree otherwise. If agreement cannot be reached, then the party seeking to exceed the page limit must file a motion in accordance with D.N.M.LR–Civ. 7. A party may file only those pages of an exhibit which are to be brought to the Court's attention.

10.6 Highlighting of Exhibits. The portions of the exhibit the party wishes to bring to the Court's attention must be highlighted in the original, the copy for the Court and copies to all parties.

10.7 Non-duplication of Exhibits. An exhibit should be submitted only once and may later be referred to by document title and filing date. An exhibit may be submitted more than once, however, if the submitting party wishes to bring to the Court's attention portions of the exhibit different from those previously highlighted under D.N.M.LR–Civ. 10.6.

[Effective January 1, 1996.]

RULE 11. SIGNING OF DOCUMENTS

11.1 Duplicate Signature. The Court will treat a duplicate signature as an original signature.

[Effective January 1, 1996.]

12

D.   WHAT ELSE?

Advance Notice of Rules Amendments.   In recognition of the importance of rules of procedure, various publications provide prompt notice of rules amendments. For example, advance sheets of West's federal reporters do so for federal rules. State legal newspapers and bar publications typically do so for state rules. Some states have advance rules services similar to advance legislative services. Many lawyers, especially litigators, monitor such developments regularly.

Form Books.   Many practitioners rely on form books, which contain sample forms and pleadings. These sample forms can be useful, but they must be used with care. Major difficulties can result from selecting the wrong form, an outdated form, or a standard form that does not precisely fit the needs of a particular case. Sources of forms for use in federal courts include *Bender's Federal Practice Forms; West's Federal Forms; Federal Local Court Forms;* and *Federal Procedural Forms, Lawyers' Edition*. State forms may be available in local practice publications, such as state practice treatises and continuing legal education materials.

Specialized Courts.   For some specialized courts, such as the Bankruptcy Court, the court rules, along with other primary authority, commentary, and forms, can be found in comprehensive mini-libraries. Likewise, rules for some specialized courts can be Shepardized in specialized citators.

E.   HOW DO YOU CITE RULES OF PROCEDURE?

If a procedural rule is not codified as a statute but rather is part of a rules set, a proper citation includes the appropriate abbreviation for the title of the rules and the number of the rule being cited. Here are examples, both citing to a rules set (following Rule 12.8 of *The Bluebook*):

> Fed. R. Civ. P. 11(a)
> N.M. R. Civ. P. 1-011.

If a rule of procedure is part of the statutory codification, it is cited as a statute.

If a case in *Federal Rules Service* also has been published in an official or a West regional or federal reporter, use that citation, to the exclusion of the *Federal Rules Service* citation. For cases reported only in *Federal Rules Service*, provide the case name, the volume number, abbreviated names of the service and publisher, the page number where the case begins, and the name of the court and the year. Here is an example (following Rule 18 of *The Bluebook*):

> *White v. American Airlines, Inc.*, 17 Fed. R. Serv. 3d (West Group) 1199 (9th Cir. 1990).

F. CONCLUDING POINTS

Rules of procedure govern the conduct of various types of litigation. Most jurisdictions have several sets, governing civil, criminal, and appellate procedure, as well as evidence issues. Many states' rules parallel the federal rules to some or a great extent. Furthermore, many courts supplement the main rules with local rules; these add detail and fill in gaps.

Some sources used in procedural research are used to research other topics as well; these include treatises, case reporters, digests, annotated codes, citators, and various computer-based alternatives to these sources. Some sources used for procedural research are unique to that area. Deskbooks provide a jurisdiction's rules in one compact source and are a litigator's basic tool. Another specialized source is *Federal Rules Service*, a specialized digest and case reporter.

<table>
<tr><td></td><td align="right">CHAPTER</td></tr>
</table>

RULES OF LEGAL ETHICS

CHAPTER

18

A. What Are Rules of Professional Responsibility?

B. Why Would You Research a Rule of Professional Responsibility?

C. How Do You Research Rules of Professional Responsibility?

D. What Else?

E. How Do You Cite Rules of Professional Responsibility?

F. Concluding Points

A. WHAT ARE RULES OF PROFESSIONAL RESPONSIBILITY?

Lawyers have a unique role in our society. Lawyers affect the decisions of their clients and the outcomes of matters that often are confidential and difficult. Because of their expertise and training, lawyers often serve in decisionmaking positions as judges, legislators, executive officers, or administrators. Lawyers also are major participants in law reform efforts. Thus, lawyers often are in positions to exert enormous power over the affairs of their clients and over the public at large.

With power comes the obligation to assure that lawyers act responsibly and are held accountable for irresponsible actions. Early on, the profession policed itself. Over time, that tradition has given way to modified self-regulation. In each state the legal profession now is governed by rules of professional responsibility, also called codes of conduct, canons of ethics, or similar nomenclature.

1. How Are Rules of Professional Responsibility Developed?

Regulation of the legal profession is a matter primarily of state law. Either the state supreme court or the state legislature promulgates rules of professional responsibility. Typically, an advisory committee recommends and drafts new rules and changes to existing rules, which are then published for review and comment by the legal community and the public before adoption.

The American Bar Association (ABA) has had a major role in the development of rules of professional responsibility. The ABA adopted its first rules in the 1908 Canons of Professional Ethics. These canons were not mandatory, but bar associations and courts did look to them for guidance in establishing standards of conduct and in disciplining lawyers.

The ABA later adopted a more comprehensive set of rules, the 1969 Model Code of Professional Responsibility (Model Code). This code subsequently was widely adopted. It had a three-part structure: the Canons serving as broad principles; Ethical Considerations (ECs) providing aspirational and explanatory provisions; and Disciplinary Rules (DRs) setting minimum, mandatory standards. Some states continue to use rules patterned after the 1969 Model Code.

In response to criticism of the 1969 Model Code, the ABA appointed a Special Commission on Evaluation of Professional Standards (the Kutak Commission) to study and revise the Model Code. After wide debate, the ABA adopted the Model Rules of Professional Conduct (Model Rules) in 1983. The Model Rules, which have a simpler structure, have been adopted by many states, often with some modifications. The Model Rules have been revised from time to time. They are complemented by the Model Rules for Lawyer Disciplinary Enforcement, which address procedural systems to implement attorney discipline.

2. What Do Rules of Professional Responsibility Look Like?

The overall structure of a set of professional responsibility rules is, of course, topical. The 1983 Model Rules of Professional Conduct for example, begin with a preamble on a lawyer's responsibilities, a scope note, and a terminology section. Parts 1 through 4 address a lawyer's role in the practice of law (such as attorney-client relationships and the attorney as counselor and advocate), and parts 5 through 8 address related matters (such as the structure and responsibilities of law firms and the provision of pro bono legal service).

The format of an individual rule varies from state to state, depending on whether the state follows the three-part structure of the Model Code, the unitary rule structure of the Model Rules, or a variation on these models. Most publications of state rules include some type of commentary, whether the ABA commentary or commentary from the state's drafting committee.

Illustration 18-1 on pages 348–350 is the ABA's Model Rule governing conflicts of interest, with a portion of the drafting committee's commentary. Illustration 18-2 on pages 351–353 is the New Mexico rule on the same topic, along with some explanatory material.

ILLUSTRATION 18-1   ABA Model Rules of Professional Conduct 1.7 and
                               Comment, from *ABA Compendium of Professional
                               Responsibility Rules and Standards*

ABA MODEL RULES OF PROFESSIONAL CONDUCT   Rule 1.7

Model Code Comparison

   Rule 1.6 eliminates the two-pronged duty under the Model Code in favor of a
single standard protecting all information about a client "relating to representation."
Under DR 4-101, the requirement applied to information protected by the attorney-client privilege and to information "gained in" the professional relationship that
"the client has requested be held inviolate or the disclosure of which would be
embarrassing or would be likely to be detrimental to the client." EC 4-4 added that
the duty differed from the evidentiary privilege in that it existed "without regard to
the nature or source of information or the fact that others share the knowledge." Rule
1.6 imposes confidentiality on information relating to the representation even if it is
acquired before or after the relationship existed. It does not require the client to indicate information that is to be confidential, or permit the lawyer to speculate whether
particular information might be embarrassing or detrimental.
   Paragraph (a) permits a lawyer to disclose information where impliedly authorized to do so in order to carry out the representation. Under DR 4-101(B) and (C),
a lawyer was not permitted to reveal "confidences" unless the client first consented
after disclosure.
   Paragraph (b) redefines the exceptions to the requirement of confidentiality.
Regarding paragraph (b)(1), DR 4-101(C)(3) provided that a lawyer "may reveal [t]he
intention of his client to commit a crime and the information necessary to prevent the
crime." This option existed regardless of the seriousness of the proposed crime.
   With regard to paragraph (b)(2), DR 4-101(C)(4) provided that a lawyer may
reveal "[c]onfidences or secrets necessary to establish or collect his fee or to defend
himself or his employers or associates against an accusation of wrongful conduct."
Paragraph (b)(2) enlarges the exception to include disclosure of information relating to claims by the lawyer other than for the lawyer's fee; for example, recovery of
property from the client.

RULE 1.7[1]   CONFLICT OF INTEREST:
GENERAL RULE

   (a) A lawyer shall not represent a client if the representation of that client will
be directly adverse to another client, unless:
      (1) the lawyer reasonably believes the representation will not adversely
   affect the relationship with the other client; and
      (2) each client consents after consultation.

---

1. Amended February 17, 1987, American Bar Association House of Delegates, New Orleans,
Louisiana, per Report No. 121.

ILLUSTRATION 18-1   *(continued)*

COMPENDIUM OF PROFESSIONAL REPSONSIBILITY RULES AND STANDARDS

(b) A lawyer shall not represent a client if the representation of that client may be materially limited by the lawyer's responsibilities to another client or to a third person, or by the lawyer's own interests, unless:

(1) the lawyer reasonably believes the representation will not be adversely affected; and

(2) the client consents after consultation. When representation of multiple clients in a single matter is undertaken, the consultation shall include explanation of the implications of the common representation and the advantages and risks involved.

Comment

Loyalty to a Client

[1]   Loyalty is an essential element in the lawyer's relationship to a client. An impermissible conflict of interest may exist before representation is undertaken, in which event the representation should be declined. The lawyer should adopt reasonable procedures, appropriate for the size and type of firm and practice, to determine in both litigation and non-litigation matters the parties and issues involved and to determine whether there are actual or potential conflicts of interest.

[2]   If such a conflict arises after representation has been undertaken, the lawyer should withdraw from the representation. See Rule 1.16. Where more than one client is involved and the lawyer withdraws because a conflict arises after representation, whether the lawyer may continue to represent any of the clients is determined by Rule 1.9. See also Rule 2.2(c). As to whether a client-lawyer relationship exists or, having once been established, is continuing, see Comment to Rule 1.3 and Scope.

[3]   As a general proposition, loyalty to a client prohibits undertaking representation directly adverse to that client without that client's consent. Paragraph (a) expresses that general rule. Thus, a lawyer ordinarily may not act as advocate against a person the lawyer represents in some other matter, even if it is wholly unrelated. On the other hand, simultaneous representation in unrelated matters of clients whose interests are only generally adverse, such as competing economic enterprises, does not require consent of the respective clients. Paragraph (a) applies only when the representation of one client would be directly adverse to the other.

[4]   Loyalty to a client is also impaired when a lawyer cannot consider, recommend or carry out an appropriate course of action for the client because of the lawyer's other responsibilities or interests. The conflict in effect forecloses alternatives that would otherwise be available to the client. Paragraph (b) addresses such situations. A possible conflict does not itself preclude the representation. The critical questions are the likelihood that a conflict will eventuate and, if it does, whether it will materially interfere with the lawyer's independent professional judgment in considering alternatives or foreclose courses of action that reasonably should be pursued on behalf of the client. Consideration should be given to whether the client wishes to accommodate the other interest involved.

32

ILLUSTRATION 18-1 *(continued)*

ABA MODEL RULES OF PROFESSIONAL CONDUCT   Rule 1.7

Consultation and Consent

[5] A client may consent to representation notwithstanding a conflict. However, as indicated in paragraph (a)(1) with respect to representation directly adverse to a client, and paragraph (b)(1) with respect to material limitations on representation of a client, when a disinterested lawyer would conclude that the client should not agree to the representation under the circumstances, the lawyer involved cannot properly ask for such agreement or provide representation on the basis of the client's consent. When more than one client is involved, the question of conflict must be resolved as to each client. Moreover, there may be circumstances where it is impossible to make the disclosure necessary to obtain consent. For example, when the lawyer represents different clients in related matters and one of the clients refuses to consent to the disclosure necessary to permit the other client to make an informed decision, the lawyer cannot properly ask the latter to consent.

Lawyer's Interests

[6] The lawyer's own interests should not be permitted to have an adverse effect on representation of a client. For example, a lawyer's need for income should not lead the lawyer to undertake matters that cannot be handled competently and at a reasonable fee. See Rules 1.1 and 1.5. If the probity of a lawyer's own conduct in a transaction is in serious question, it may be difficult or impossible for the lawyer to give a client detached advice. A lawyer may not allow related business interests to affect representation, for example, by referring clients to an enterprise in which the lawyer has an undisclosed interest.

Conflicts in Litigation

[7] Paragraph (a) prohibits representation of opposing parties in litigation. Simultaneous representation of parties whose interests in litigation may conflict, such as coplaintiffs or codefendants, is governed by paragraph (b). An impermissible conflict may exist by reason of substantial discrepancy in the parties' testimony, incompatibility in positions in relation to an opposing party or the fact that there are substantially different possibilities of settlement of the claims or liabilities in question. Such conflicts can arise in criminal cases as well as civil. The potential for conflict of interest in representing multiple defendants in a criminal case is so grave that ordinarily a lawyer should decline to represent more than one codefendant. On the other hand, common representation of persons having similar interests is proper if the risk of adverse effect is minimal and the requirements of paragraph (b) are met. Compare Rule 2.2 involving intermediation between clients.

[8] Ordinarily, a lawyer may not act as advocate against a client the lawyer represents in some other matter, even if the other matter is wholly unrelated. However, there are circumstances in which a lawyer may act as advocate against a client. For example, a lawyer representing an enterprise with diverse operations may accept employment as an advocate against the enterprise in an unrelated matter if doing so will not adversely affect the lawyer's relationship with the enterprise or conduct of the suit and if both clients consent upon consultation. By the same

ILLUSTRATION 18-2	New Mexico Rule of Professional Conduct 16-107 and Annotation, from *New Mexico Rules Annotated*

16-107   RULES OF PROFESSIONAL CONDUCT   476

the client, the lawyer may respond to the extent the lawyer reasonably believes necessary to establish a defense. The same is true with respect to a claim involving the conduct or representation of a former client. The lawyer's right to respond arises when an assertion of such complicity has been made. Paragraph (b)(2) [D] does not require the lawyer to await the commencement of an action or proceeding that charges such complicity, so that the defense may be established by responding directly to a third party who has made such an assertion. The right to defend, of course, applies where a proceeding has been commenced. Where practicable and not prejudicial to the lawyer's ability to establish the defense, the lawyer should advise the client of the third party's assertion and request that the client respond appropriately. In any event, disclosure should be no greater than the lawyer reasonably believes is necessary to vindicate innocence, the disclosure should be made in a manner which limits access to the information to the tribunal or other persons having a need to know it, and appropriate protective orders or other arrangements should be sought by the lawyer to the fullest extent practicable.

If the lawyer is charged with wrongdoing in which the client's conduct is implicated, the rule of confidentiality should not prevent the lawyer from defending against the charge. Such a charge can arise in a civil, criminal or professional disciplinary proceeding, and can be based on a wrong allegedly committed by the lawyer against the client, or on a wrong alleged by a third person; for example, a person claiming to have been defrauded by the lawyer and client acting together. A lawyer entitled to a fee is permitted by paragraph (b)(2)

[D] to prove the services rendered in an action to collect it. This aspect of the rule expresses the principle that the beneficiary of a fiduciary relationship may not exploit it to the detriment of the fiduciary. As stated above, the lawyer must make every effort practicable to avoid unnecessary disclosure of information relating to a representation, to limit disclosure to those having the need to know it, and to obtain protective orders or make other arrangements minimizing the risk of disclosure.

Disclosures Otherwise Required or Authorized
The attorney-client privilege is differently defined in various jurisdictions. If a lawyer is called as a witness to give testimony concerning a client, absent waiver by the client, Rule 1.6(a) [16-106A] requires the lawyer to invoke the privilege when it is applicable. The lawyer must comply with the final orders of a court or other tribunal of competent jurisdiction requiring the lawyer to give information about the client.

The Rules of Professional Conduct in various circumstances permit or require a lawyer to disclose information relating to the representation. See Rules 2.2, 2.3, 3.3 and 4.1 [16-202, 16-203, 16-303 and 16-401]. In addition to these provisions, a lawyer may be obligated or permitted by other provisions of law to give information about a client. Whether another provision of law supersedes Rule 1.6 [16-106] is a matter of interpretation beyond the scope of these Rules, but a presumption should exist against such a supersession.

Former Client
The duty of confidentiality continues after the client-lawyer relationship has terminated.

COMPILER'S ANNOTATIONS

Cross references. — For privileged communication between attorney and client, see 38-6-6 NMSA 1978.

When duty of confidentiality attaches. — The duty of confidentiality under this rule may attach when the lawyer agrees to consider whether a client-lawyer relationship shall be established. In re Lichtenberg, 117 N.M. 325, 871 P.2d 981 (1994).

"Substantial relationship" test, as applied to one's former attorney in prior litigation serving as counsel for one's opponent in present litigation, requires a three-tiered analysis: (1) A factual reconstruction of the scope of the prior legal representation; (2) a determination of whether it is reasonable to presume that the lawyer would have received confidential information of the type alleged by his former client; and (3) a determination of whether the alleged confidential information is relevant to the issues raised in the litigation pending against the former client. Leon, Ltd. v. Carver, 104 N.M. 29, 715 P.2d 1080 (1986) (decided under former rules).

Substantial relationship standard requires disqualification if an attorney represents a party in a matter in which the adverse party is that attorney's former client, and the subject matter of the two representations are substantially related. United Nuclear Corp. v. General Atomic Co., 96 N.M. 155, 629 P.2d 231 (1980), appeal dismissed, 451 U.S. 901, 101 S. Ct. 1966, 68 L. Ed. 2d 289 (1981) (decided under former rules).

Law reviews. — For article, "Attorney as Interpreter: A Return to Babble," 20 N.M.L. Rev. 1 (1990).

Am. Jur. 2d, A.L.R. and C.J.S. references. — 7 Am. Jur. 2d Attorneys at Law §§ 119, 120.

Propriety of attorney who has represented corporation acting for corporation in controversy with officer, director, or stockholder, 1 A.L.R.4th 1124.

Applicability of attorney-client privilege to evidence or testimony in subsequent action between parties originally represented contemporaneously by same attorney, with reference to communication to or from one party, 4 A.L.R.4th 765.

Applicability of attorney-client privilege to communications made in presence of or solely to or by third person, 14 A.L.R.4th 594.

Attorney-client privilege as extending to communications relating to contemplated civil fraud, 31 A.L.R.4th 458.

Attorney's work product privilege, under Rule 26(b)(3) of the Federal Rules of Civil Procedure, as applicable to documents prepared in anticipation of terminated litigation, 41 A.L.R. Fed. 123.

Propriety of law firm's representation of client in federal court where lawyer affiliated with firm is disqualified from representing client, 51 A.L.R. Fed. 678.

7A C.J.S. Attorney and Client §§ 234, 237.

16-107. Conflict of interest; general rule.

A. **Representation adverse to other client considered.** A lawyer shall not represent a client if the representation of that client will be directly or substantially adverse to another client, unless:

ILLUSTRATION 18-2   *(continued)*

---

477   RULES OF PROFESSIONAL CONDUCT   16-107

(1) the lawyer reasonably believes the representation will not adversely affect the relationship with the other client; and

(2) each client consents after consultation. The consultation shall include explanation of the implications of the common representation and the advantages and risks involved.

B. **Lawyer's other responsibilities considered.** Unless otherwise required by these rules, a lawyer shall not represent a client if the representation of that client may be materially limited by the lawyer's responsibilities to another client or to a third person, or by the lawyer's own interests, unless:

(1) the lawyer reasonably believes the representation will not be adversely affected; and

(2) the client consents after consultation. When representation of multiple clients in a single matter is undertaken, the consultation shall include explanation of the implications of the common representation and the advantages and risks involved.

COMMENT TO MODEL RULES

Compiler's notes. — The New Mexico rule differs from the ABA model rule in that the New Mexico version inserts "or substantially" in the first sentence, adds the second sentence in Paragraph A(2), and inserts "Unless otherwise required by these rules," at the beginning of Paragraph B.

ABA COMMENT:

Loyalty to a Client

Loyalty is an essential element in the lawyer's relationship to a client. An impermissible conflict of interest may exist before representation is undertaken, in which event the representation should be declined. If such a conflict arises after representation has been undertaken, the lawyer should withdraw from the representation. See Rule 1.16 [16-116]. Where more than one client is involved and the lawyer withdraws because a conflict arises after representation, whether the lawyer may continue to represent any of the clients is determined by Rule 1.9 [16-109]. See also Rule 2.2(c) [16-202C]. As to whether a client-lawyer relationship exists or, having once been established, is continuing, see Comment to Rule 1.3 [16-103] and Scope.

As a general proposition, loyalty to a client prohibits undertaking representation directly adverse to that client without that client's consent. Paragraph (a) [A] expresses that general rule. Thus, a lawyer ordinarily may not act as advocate against a person the lawyer represents in some other matter, even if it is wholly unrelated. On the other hand, simultaneous representation in unrelated matters of clients whose interests are only generally adverse, such as competing economic enterprises, does not require consent of the respective clients. Paragraph (a) [A] applies only when the representation of one client would be directly adverse to the other.

Loyalty to a client is also impaired when a lawyer cannot consider, recommend or carry out an appropriate course of action for the client because of the lawyer's other responsibilities or interests. The conflict in effect forecloses alternatives that would otherwise be available to the client. Paragraph (b) [B] addresses such situations. A possible conflict does not itself preclude the representation. The critical questions are the likelihood that a conflict will eventuate and, if it does, whether it will materially interfere with the lawyer's independent professional judgment in considering alternatives or foreclose courses of action that reasonably

should be pursued on behalf of the client. Consideration should be given to whether the client wishes to accommodate the other interest involved.

Consultation and Consent

A client may consent to representation notwithstanding a conflict. However, as indicated in paragraph (a)(1) [A(1)] with respect to representation directly adverse to a client, and paragraph (b)(1) [B(1)] with respect to material limitations on representation of a client, when a disinterested lawyer would conclude that the client should not agree to the representation under the circumstances, the lawyer involved cannot properly ask for such agreement or provide representation on the basis of the client's consent. When more than one client is involved, the question of conflict must be resolved as to each client. Moreover, there may be circumstances where it is impossible to make the disclosure necessary to obtain consent. For example, when the lawyer represents different clients in related matters and one of the clients refuses to consent to the disclosure necessary to permit the other client to make an informed decision, the lawyer cannot properly ask the latter to consent.

Lawyer's Interests

The lawyer's own interests should not be permitted to have adverse effect on representation of a client. For example, a lawyer's need for income should not lead the lawyer to undertake matters that cannot be handled competently and at a reasonable fee. See Rules 1.1 [16-101] and 1.5 [16-105]. If the probity of a lawyer's own conduct in a transaction is in serious question, it may be difficult or impossible for the lawyer to give a client detached advice. A lawyer may not allow related business interests to affect representation, for example, by referring clients to an enterprise in which the lawyer has an undisclosed interest.

Conflicts in Litigation

Paragraph (a) [A] prohibits representation of opposing parties in litigation. Simultaneous representation of parties whose interests in litigation may conflict, such as co-plaintiffs or co-defendants, is governed by paragraph (b) [B]. An impermissible conflict may exist by reason of substantial discrepancy in the parties' testimony, incompatibility in positions in relation to an opposing party or the fact that there are substantially different possibilities of settlement of the claims or liabilities in question. Such conflicts can arise in criminal cases as well as civil. The potential for conflict of

ILLUSTRATION 18-2   *(continued)*

16-107   RULES OF PROFESSIONAL CONDUCT   478

interest in representing multiple defendants in a criminal case is so grave that ordinarily a lawyer should decline to represent more than one codefendant. On the other hand, common representation of persons having similar interests is proper if the risk of adverse effect is minimal and the requirements of paragraph (b) [B] are met. Compare Rule 2.2 [16-202] involving intermediation between clients.

Ordinarily, a lawyer may not act as advocate against a client the lawyer represents in some other matter, even if the other matter is wholly unrelated. However, there are circumstances in which a lawyer may act as advocate against a client. For example, a lawyer representing an enterprise with diverse operations may accept employment as an advocate against the enterprise in an unrelated matter if doing so will not adversely affect the lawyer's relationship with the enterprise or conduct of the suit and if both clients consent upon consultation. By the same token, government lawyers in some circumstances may represent government employees in proceedings in which a government agency is the opposing party. The propriety of concurrent representation can depend on the nature of the litigation. For example, a suit charging fraud entails conflict to a degree not involved in a suit for a declaratory judgment concerning statutory interpretation.

A lawyer may represent parties having antagonistic positions on a legal question that has arisen in different cases, unless representation of either client would be adversely affected. Thus, it is ordinarily not improper to assert such positions in cases pending in different trial courts, but it may be improper to do so in cases pending at the same time in an appellate court.

Interest of Person Paying for a Lawyer's Service

A lawyer may be paid from a source other than the client, if the client is informed of that fact and consents and the arrangement does not compromise the lawyer's duty of loyalty to the client. See Rule 1.8(f) [16-108F]. For example, when an insurer and its insured have conflicting interests in a matter arising from a liability insurance contract, and the insurer is required to provide special counsel for the insured, the arrangement should assure the special counsel's professional independence. So also, when a corporation and its directors or employees are involved in a controversy in which they have conflicting interests, the corporation may provide funds for separate legal representation of the directors or employees, if the clients consent after consultation and the arrangement ensures the lawyer's professional independence.

Other Conflict Situations

Conflicts of interest in contexts other than litigation

sometimes may be difficult to assess. Relevant factors in determining whether there is potential for adverse effect include the duration and intimacy of the lawyer's relationship with the client or clients involved, the functions being performed by the lawyer, the likelihood that actual conflict will arise and the likely prejudice to the client from the conflict if it does arise. The question is often one of proximity and degree.

For example, a lawyer may not represent multiple parties to a negotiation whose interests are fundamentally antagonistic to each other, but common representation is permissible where the clients are generally aligned in interest even though there is some difference of interest among them.

Conflict questions may also arise in estate planning and estate administration. A lawyer may be called upon to prepare wills for several family members, such as husband and wife, and, depending upon the circumstances, a conflict of interest may arise. In estate administration the identity of the client may be unclear under the law of a particular jurisdiction. Under one view, the client is the fiduciary; under another view the client is the estate or trust, including its beneficiaries. The lawyer should make clear the relationship to the parties involved.

A lawyer for a corporation or other organization who is also a member of its board of directors should determine whether the responsibilities of the two roles may conflict. The lawyer may be called on to advise the corporation in matters involving actions of the directors. Consideration should be given to the frequency with which such situations may arise, the potential intensity of the conflict, the effect of the lawyer's resignation from the board and the possibility of the corporation's obtaining legal advice from another lawyer in such situations. If there is material risk that the dual role will compromise the lawyer's independence of professional judgment, the lawyer should not serve as a director.

Conflict Charged by an Opposing Party

Resolving questions of conflict of interest is primarily the responsibility of the lawyer undertaking the representation. In litigation, a court may raise the question when there is reason to infer that the lawyer has neglected the responsibility. In a criminal case, inquiry by the court is generally required when a lawyer represents multiple defendants. Where the conflict is such as clearly to call in question the fair or efficient administration of justice, opposing counsel may properly raise the question. Such an objection should be viewed with caution, however, for it can be misused as a technique of harassment. See Scope.

COMPILER'S ANNOTATIONS

Attorney cannot represent two clients with possible conflicting interests. State v. Aguilar, 87 N.M. 503, 536 P.2d 263 (Ct. App. 1975).

Representation of two defendants by lawyers who became partners. — While two defendants were, in effect, represented by the same attorney since their lawyers became partners, nothing prohibited this dual representation as long as there was no actual conflict of interest adversely affecting the lawyers' performance. State v. Martinez, 102 N.M. 94, 691 P.2d 887 (1984).

Office-sharing agreement with former partner of former prosecutor not conflict. — A defendant is not entitled to the disqualification of his appointed counsel on the grounds of appearance of impropriety or

potential conflict of interest where the counsel has an office-sharing arrangement with a former partner of a former prosecutor who had prosecuted defendant on a prior conviction. State v. Martinez, 100 N.M. 532, 673 P.2d 509 (Ct. App. 1983).

Attorney general's prosecution of officer he formerly represented. — The appointment of the New Mexico attorney general, and a deputy attorney general, to act as special assistant United States attorneys for prosecution of criminal charges against the state investment officer and an assistant state treasurer alleging a conspiracy to extort a political contribution, involved no inherent or actual conflict of interest under former Canons 4 or 9 (now see this rule) or 8-5-2 NMSA

B. WHY WOULD YOU RESEARCH A RULE OF PROFESSIONAL RESPONSIBILITY?

Because the ABA is a voluntary association to which only a portion of all lawyers belong, the standards set by the ABA are not themselves binding on any attorney. However, the rules adopted by a state lawmaking body do bind lawyers licensed in that state. Some rules set mandatory standards of conduct (for example, a lawyer shall not commingle client funds). Others set aspirational guidelines (for example, a lawyer should aspire to provide fifty hours of pro bono service annually).

Professional responsibility rules are enforced through various mechanisms. In a typical model, a state disciplinary committee hears complaints regarding allegations of professional misconduct, issues decisions, and disciplines noncomplying lawyers. Professional sanctions include public or private censure, suspension of one's license to practice law, and disbarment. In addition to the state regulatory entity, local bar associations may have ethics committees that hear complaints about attorney misconduct and make findings and recommendations to the state authorities.

A violation of an ethical standard also may expose an attorney to liability to the client for malpractice. In assessing the seriousness of a lawyer's misconduct, courts in legal malpractice often look to the rules of professional responsibility. In some circumstances, professional misconduct also can result in criminal penalties. In short, failure to meet ethical standards not only harms the client and the profession, but also can carry grave personal consequences for the attorney.

C. HOW DO YOU RESEARCH RULES OF PROFESSIONAL RESPONSIBILITY?

Research in legal ethics involves, of course, the state's rules of professional responsibility. You are likely to research judicial cases interpreting the rule as well because, as noted above, courts interpret and apply rules of professional responsibility in a variety of contexts. As always, you may use commentary to help you understand the rule.

Furthermore, you also may research disciplinary and ethics opinions. Some state regulatory entities issue disciplinary opinions, in which they explain their discipline (or nondiscipline) of attorneys whose conduct has prompted disciplinary proceedings. Furthermore, an ABA committee and most state regulatory entities occasionally issue advisory ethics opinions. Written either as a general statement of what the rules require or in response to a specific inquiry, these advisory opinions shed light on the rules, even if they are not mandatory authority. More specifically, the ABA's formal opinions are statements that are intended to clarify a rule or to address subjects of general interest to the practicing bar; informal opinions are responses to specific questions that are narrow in scope and arise infrequently.

To obtain this combination of authorities, you will use sources used in other forms of research, especially procedural research. The following discussion first describes the major sources you may use to learn about your own state's rule, accompanying judicial case law, disciplinary opinions, and ethics opinions. It then describes some major sources regarding the ABA model standards, including ethics opinions and commentary. For an overview, see Exhibit 18.1 below.

This part addresses the following issue arising out of the Canoga case: Assume that you have learned, a few weeks into the litigation, that one of your other clients is a member of the board of the orchestra that Ms. Canoga has sued. The individual is Sharon Anderson. You wrote her estate plan several years ago and update it on an annual basis. Ms. Anderson changed her name upon her divorce about eight months ago, which you did not know until last week. Hence you did not recognize her name on the recent list of the orchestra's board members that you reviewed before agreeing to represent Ms. Canoga. Ms. Anderson could be a witness in Ms. Canoga's case, because she may have information about the board's handling of Ms. Canoga's termination. Does your representation of Ms. Anderson involve a conflict of interest so as to preclude your representing Ms. Canoga?

| **EXHIBIT 18.1** | Legal Ethics Authorities |

In Your Own State	*Material from ABA and Other States*
• rule and comments • judicial cases • disciplinary opinions • ethics opinions	• ABA model standard and comments • cases from other states • ethics opinions from other states • ABA ethics opinions

---

Sources of state professional responsibility rules, cases, and opinions:

- state deskbooks
- codes in various media
- bar journals and legal newspapers
- rules citators
- reporters and digests
- CD-ROM and online alternatives to reporters
- case citators
- looseleaf services
- ethics databases in LEXIS and Westlaw

For most states, the text of professional responsibility rules is published in the same deskbook that contains various procedural rules. (See Chapter 17.) A state deskbook also typically contains some explanatory material as well, such as the comments of the advisory committee or adopting authority, but not cases or references to other sources. Deskbooks are issued annually; thus, very recent amendments and new rules will not be included.

In addition, the state code typically includes the rules. (See Chapter 12.) You can consult the general index for the entire code, the separate index for the rules (if any), and the table of contents for the rules. In an annotated code, the rules are annotated in a manner similar to statutory provisions, including any comments of the state advisory committee, historical notes regarding previous rules, case descriptions, and references to secondary sources. See Illustration 18-2 on pages 351–353. The rules are updated using the same updating materials that update annotated statutes.

Proposed amendments and recently adopted rules of professional responsibility generally are published in state bar journals or legal newspapers. (See Chapter 6.) These publications also may contain comments explaining the new rules.

Furthermore, state rules of professional responsibility are available in computer-based sources. You may find them on CD-ROMs that contain the state's primary authority as well as in various Westlaw and LEXIS databases (the most obvious choices being the state's rules or code databases).

To research judicial cases interpreting a state's rules, you can use standard case law sources: West regional reporters and digests; online alternatives available through Westlaw, LEXIS, and public web sites on the Internet; CD-ROM case collections; and case citators. (See Chapters 10 and 11.) Furthermore, the annotation to a rule in an annotated statutory code refers to pertinent judicial cases. Another means of identifying cases citing a state rule of professional responsibility is via that state's Shepard's Citations in paper or online. (See Chapter 12.)

Similarly, you have various options for researching the disciplinary and ethics opinions of a state regulatory entity. One option is a looseleaf service, such as *ABA/BNA Lawyer's Manual on Professional Conduct* or *National Reporter on Legal Ethics and Professional Responsibility.* See Illustration 18-3 on page 358. (See Chapter 16.) A state bar association journal and local legal newspaper may publish the state entity's ethics opinions. Westlaw offers ethics opinion databases for many states, a combined database METH-EO, and the *ABA/BNA Lawyers' Manual.* LEXIS offers ethics opinions in ETHOP (based on the *National Reporter*).

Researching the conflict-of-interest issue in the Canoga case, we began in the *New Mexico Rules Annotated* (an adjunct to the annotated code). There we found the rule, ABA comments (but not comments by a New Mexico drafting committee), descriptions of cases interpreting the rule and its predecessor, and references to secondary sources. See Illustration 18-2 on pages 351–353. Rule 16-107 proscribes representation of one client that is directly or substantially adverse to another client, as well as representation of one client that is materially limited by responsibilities to another client, except in specified circumstances, including consent of each client after consultation.

The annotation to Rule 16-107 lists various cases interpreting the rule. As an example, the first case reverses a criminal conviction on conflict-of-interest grounds because the defendant's lawyer represented the crime victim in her civil suit against third parties. *State v. Aguilar*, 536 P.2d 263 (N.M. Ct. App. 1975), *recognized as overruled in part in Churchman v. Dorsey*, 919 P.2d 1076 (N.M. 1996). We did not find New Mexico ethics opinions directly on point. See Illustration 18-3 on page 358.

Sources regarding ABA model standards of professional responsiblity:

- deskbooks
- annotated rules publications
- treatises
- case law sources
- looseleaf services
- ethics databases in LEXIS, Westlaw, CD-ROMs, and public web sites on the Internet
- citators

ABA model standards (and related materials) have little persuasive authority unless they have been adopted by your state. Therefore, you first need to know whether your state rule is based on an ABA model, and if so, which version—the 1969 Model Code or the 1983 Model Rules. You also need to know whether the specific standard was adopted verbatim by your state or differs in pertinent part. This information typically may be found in the state compiler's notes for the state rule.

Once you decide to expand your research to include ABA model standards, you should seek several types of materials: the applicable ABA standards and comments; cases from other states interpreting that language, in the form of rules adopted in those states; disciplinary and ethics opinions from other states as well as the ABA's Standing Committee on Ethics and Professional Responsibility; and commentary. The materials are listed from most to least authoritative.

Various deskbooks, published by the ABA and other publishers, contain the ABA model standards. Some contain the 1983 Model Rules only, others various sets of standards. One example is the *ABA Compendium of Professional Responsibility Rules and Standards*, which includes both the Model Rules and the Model Code, along with related materials such as the ABA Model Code of Judicial Conduct and federal civil procedure rules that address lawyer conduct in litigation. Deskbooks typically provide the rules and the drafters' comments, and perhaps a comparison of the two model standards, but no other explanatory material. See Illustration 18-1 on pages 348–350.

To learn about materials beyond the rules and comments, you will need to research in a more expansive source. For example, the ABA publication,

| ILLUSTRATION 18-3 | Synopses of New Mexico Ethics Opinions, from *ABA/ BNA Lawyers' Manual on Professional Conduct* |

No. 165   **1001:6001**

ETHICS OPINIONS

New Mexico

STATE BAR OF NEW MEXICO

Opinions are issued by the Advisory Opinions Committee of the State Bar of New Mexico. The bar may be contacted at Springer Square, 121 Tijeras N.E., Garden Level, P.O. Box 25883, Albuquerque, NM 87125, (505) 842-6132, fax (505) 843-8765.

Opinion 1992-1 (11/14/92) **Conflicts of interest; Real estate transactions; Referrals.** A lawyer may not participate in an arrangement in which real estate brokers direct title companies to require that closing documents in certain transactions be prepared by the lawyer, with the lawyer's providing free legal advice to the brokers in return.

Opinion 1992-2 (12/7/92) **Attorney-client privilege; Confidentiality; Deceased client.** A lawyer whose deceased client was the subject of a criminal investigation must continue to assert the client's privilege during the police investigation into the client's death until either an appointed personal representative makes an informed waiver upon consultation or a court orders the lawyer to reveal information.

Opinion 1993-1 (3/29/93) **Referrals.** A lawyer may not participate in a for-profit lawyer referral service in which the lawyer pays a fee to be referred to the service's panel of lawyer members on a rotating basis. A lawyer may not associate with a network of independent non-lawyer professionals who refer business to each other.

Opinion 1995-1 (8/12/95) **Lawyer-client relationship; Decision-making authority of client; Independent professional judgment; Withdrawal.** A lawyer whose client insists on appearing in court without the lawyer and drafting documents on his own must seek leave of court to withdraw if the client renders the representation unreasonably difficult, or if the representation will result in a violation of the ethics rules or other law. Rules 1-011, 1-089, 16-101, 16-102(A)(C)(E), 16-107(B), 16-201,16-116, 16-301, 16-302.

Opinion 1995-2 (9/9/95) **Fees; Fee agreements; Contingent fees; Discharge of lawyer.** A lawyer may use a contingent fee agreement that gives the lawyer a claim to a quantum meruit fee upon the occurrence of the contingency, if the client fires the lawyer without cause or if some behavior of the client gives the lawyer cause to withdraw. The agreement must give the client some guidance as to what constitutes "cause" for this purpose, and the fee must not exceed what the lawyer would have received had the contract been fully performed. Rules 16-105(A), 16-107(B), 16-116(B).

Annotated Model Rules of Professional Conduct, provides topically organized references to cases and ethics opinions interpreting the Model Rules. See Illustration 18-4 on page 360. Another source of references, as well as well respected commentary, is *The Law of Lawyering: A Handbook on the Model Rules of Professional Conduct*, a looseleaf treatise by Geoffrey C. Hazard, Jr. and W. William Hodes. This text also includes the authors' analysis of specific scenarios. See Illustration 18-5 on page 361.

You can research judicial cases from other states in the standard sources of case law, such as West reporters and digests. To locate digests or the full text of ethics opinions of other states or ABA ethics opinions in paper, consult *ABA/BNA Lawyers' Manual on Professional Conduct* or *National Reporter on Legal Ethics and Professional Responsibility*. Review Illustration 18-3 on page 358. The ABA publication *Recent Ethics Opinions* contains both formal and informal opinions, published in looseleaf bound volumes, and includes a citator.

Computer-based research in specialized databases also is a good option for research into legal ethics law nationwide. LEXIS offers a variety of databases in its ETHICS library, including cases regarding ethics from all states and ABA formal and informal opinions. Westlaw similarly offers state case law databases and databases of ABA and state ethics opinions. See Illustration 18-6 on page 362. Alternatively, the American Legal Ethics Library is an example of a "library" of state and ABA materials on legal ethics available in CD-ROM and on the Internet.

Shepard's Professional and Judicial Conduct Citations lists cases or opinions citing professional responsibility rules. The cited sources include the ABA Model Rules, the ABA Model Code, and formal and informal opinions. Citing sources include cases, state ethics opinions, and selected secondary sources. This Shepard's is available online.

Researching the Canoga case, we learned from the compiler's note to the New Mexico rule that it substantially parallels, but is not identical to, the ABA model rule. Hence, we turned to ABA and other states' materials for persuasive authority. We found pertinent information in several sources. The *ABA Annotated Model Rules* provides a synopsis of a 1993 West Virginia case with analogous facts, *Committee on Legal Ethics v. Frame*, 433 S.E.2d 579 (W. Va. 1993). See Illustration 18-4 on page 360. The Hazard and Hodes treatise discusses the issue of inadvertence. See Illustration 18-5 on page 361. A Westlaw search yielded ABA Formal Opinion 92-367, which addresses an issue that is quite similar to the Canoga issue. See Illustration 18-6 on page 362; Shepard's indicated that Opinion 92-367 has been cited several times, in the West Virginia case and later formal opinions.

D. WHAT ELSE?

Specialized Rules of Professional Conduct. From time to time, starting in the early 1970s, the ABA has adopted standards relating to the practice of criminal law, which regulate the role and conduct of prosecuting and

ILLUSTRATION 18-4   Commentary, from *Annotated Model Rules of Professional Conduct*

513 So. 2d 1052 (Fla. 1987) (lawyer improperly represented holder of note in suit against debtor for whom lawyer drafted note); *Florida Bar v. Milin*, 502 So. 2d 900 (Fla. 1986) (lawyer represented employee in suit against employer for unemployment compensation; improper to later represent employer in employee's defamation suit against employer); *In re Horine*, 661 N.E.2d 1206 (Ind. 1996) (lawyer violated Rule 1.7(a) by negotiating sale of one client's automobile to another client without obtaining consent of purchasing client to adverse representation); *Molitoris v. Woods*, 618 A.2d 985 (Pa. Super. Ct. 1992) (no conflict of interest when law firm represented plaintiff in personal injury suit and employee benefit plan in its subrogation claim arising from payment of medical benefits to plaintiff; subrogation interest of plan identical to interest of plaintiff in recovery against defendants).

REPRESENTING A PARTY IN AN UNRELATED SUIT
AGAINST AN EXISTING CLIENT

Rule 1.7 may also apply when the lawyer is asked to represent a party in unrelated litigation against an existing client. The Comment notes, however, that an impermissible conflict is not created when the simultaneous representation concerns an unrelated matter involving clients whose interests, such as competing economic interests, are only generally adverse. *See* American Bar Association, *The Legislative History of the Model Rules of Professional Conduct* 56 (1987) ("[Rule 1.7(a)] was intended to allow a lawyer to represent a client in one matter and be engaged in representation adverse to that client in a different matter, if both clients consent"); *see also Harrison v. Fisons Corp.*, 819 F. Supp. 1039 (M.D. Fla. 1993) (law firm disqualified from representing defendant in civil action brought by bank serving as minor plaintiff's guardian, because of firm's concurrent representation of bank in unrelated matter); *Committee on Legal Ethics v. Frame*, 433 S.E.2d 579 (W. Va. 1993) (firm representing plaintiff suing corporation for personal injuries should not have represented corporation's manager and controlling shareholder in divorce action; even though personal injury suit did not name manager/shareholder individually, she was cross-examined in it); *In re Walsh*, 515 N.W.2d 263 (Wis. 1994) (lawyer publicly reprimanded for representing county in deputy sheriff's disability appeal, even though firm already defending deputy in civil rights action); ABA Comm. on Ethics and Professional Responsibility, Formal Op. 95-390 (1995) (lawyer who represents corporate client may not take on representation of corporate affiliate that is also client and has interests directly adverse to corporate client, unless lawyer reasonably believes no adverse effect on relationship with corporate client and both corporate client and affiliate consent after consultation); ABA Comm. on Ethics and Professional Responsibility, Formal Op. 91-361 (1991) (simultaneous representations of partnerships and individual partners, even on basically unrelated matters, may result in lawyer possessing confidences of one client that may not be revealed to another, leading to requirement that lawyer withdraw from one or both representations); Ill. State Bar Ass'n Comm. on Professional Ethics, Op. 95-15 (1996) (no per se prohibition against parent corporation's lawyer representing plaintiff suing subsidiary on matter unrelated to representation of parent); Ill. State Bar Ass'n Comm. on Professional Ethics, Op. 94-21 (1995) (not per se improper for lawyer to represent city as defendant in personal injury suit and to sue same city in zoning case, if both clients consent after full disclosure); Mass. Bar Ass'n Ethics Comm., Op. 92-3 (1992)

ILLUSTRATION 18-5   Illustrative Case and Commentary, from *The Law of Lawyering*

§1.7:108   THE LAW OF LAWYERING

Subsection (a) of Rule 1.7 governs conflict of interest situations involving concurrent and *direct* adversity, whereas subsection (b) governs the myriad of situations in which the conflict is muted or indirect. Not surprisingly, Rule 1.7(a) imposes something akin to a *per se* ban on continued representation. Rule 1.7(b), by contrast, requires a subtle calculus to determine the likelihood that the quality of the lawyer's representation will be affected.

§1.7:108   ILLUSTRATIVE CASE: INADVERTENT REPRESENTATION OF ADVERSE PARTIES

> A female employee filed gender discrimination charges against her employer with the Equal Employment Opportunity Commission. The EEOC entered into negotiations with the employer, which was represented throughout by lawyer L. During the negotiations, the identity of the complaining party was never revealed.
>
> The negotiations broke down, and the EEOC prepared to file suit. Meanwhile, strictly by chance, the employee hired L to obtain the annulment of her marriage, unaware of his role in the other matter. (By the same token, he was unaware that she was the unnamed party in the EEOC matter.) Shortly after the annulment became final, the EEOC did file suit against the employer, and, when L's interim relationship with the employee became known, sought his disqualification from further representation of the defendant company.

This odd coincidence actually took place in *EEOC v. Orson N. Gygi Co.*, 749 F.2d 620 (10th Cir. 1984). The court disqualified L even though his concurrent representation of adverse parties was both temporary and inadvertent. Although the court mitigated the burden on the employer somewhat by permitting L to turn his work product over to successor counsel, the result seems wrong, and is a good demonstration of the need for

1998 SUPPLEMENT   232.10

ILLUSTRATION 18-6   ABA Formal Ethics Opinion, from Westlaw

FOR EDUCATIONAL USE ONLY   Page 1
ABA Formal Op. 92-367
ABA Comm. on Ethics and Professional Responsibility, Formal Op. 92-367

American Bar Association

LAWYER EXAMINING A CLIENT AS AN ADVERSE WITNESS, OR CONDUCTING THIRD
PARTY DISCOVERY OF THE CLIENT

October 16, 1992

Copyright (c) 1992 by the American Bar Association

A lawyer who in the course of representing a client examines another client as an adverse witness in a matter unrelated to the lawyer's representation of the other client, or conducts third party discovery of the client in such a matter, will likely face a conflict that is disqualifying in the absence of appropriate client consent. Any such disqualification will also be imputed to other lawyers in the lawyer's firm.

The Committee has been asked whether a lawyer who has a doctor as a general client may cross-examine the doctor when the doctor testifies as an adverse expert witness in a medical malpractice case. The central issue posed by the inquiry--whether a potentially disqualifying conflict of interests arises when the lawyer while representing one client in litigation must deal with another client as a third-party witness--has resonance in an array of familiar situations that go well beyond the particular circumstances prompting the present inquiry. The potential for conflict does not depend on the client being an expert, rather than a fact, witness, nor on the setting being trial rather than pretrial discovery. Nor, indeed, does it depend on testimonial evidence being involved: documentary third-party discovery of a client, on behalf of another client, may well present the same core issue. [FN1]

The Committee concludes that a lawyer's examining the lawyer's client as an adverse witness, or conducting third party discovery of a client, will ordinarily present a conflict of interest that is disqualifying absent consent of one or both of the clients involved (depending, as will be explained, on the nature and degree of the conflict), and that the individual lawyer's disqualification will, again in the absence of consent, be imputed to all other lawyers in the lawyer's firm as well.

The principal applicable provisions of the Model Rules of Professional Conduct (1983, amended 1992) are to be found in Rule 1.7, dealing with conflicts of interest generally: paragraph (a) of that Rule prohibits representations "directly adverse" to another client, unless the lawyer reasonably believes that the lawyer's relationship with that client will not be adversely affected, and both clients consent; and paragraph (b) prohibits a representation that "may be materially limited by the lawyer's responsibilities to another client," unless the lawyer reasonably believes that that representation will not be adversely affected, and the client involved in the representation (but not both clients) consents. [FN2] Also pertinent are Rule 1.10, governing imputation of a lawyer's disqualification; [FN3] Rule 1.6, governing the obligation of confidentiality; [FN4] Rule 1.8(b), which prohibits using information relating to a client's representation to the client's detriment; [FN5] and the obligations of competence and diligence set forth, respectively, in Rules 1.1 and 1.3. [FN6]

The applicable provisions of the predecessor Model Code of Professional Responsibility include DR 5-105, which addresses a lawyer's refusing to accept or continue employment if the interests of another client may impair the lawyer's independent professional judgment; Canon 5 and EC 5-1, which call upon a lawyer to exercise independent professional judgment on a client's behalf; EC 7-1 and DR 7-101, regarding zealous representation of a client; EC 5-14, 5-15, and 5-16, which deal with a lawyer's responsibilities with respect to the interests of multiple clients; and EC 4-5 and Canon 4, which require preservation of client confidences.

The Committee believes that as a general matter examining one's own client as an adverse witness on behalf of another client, or conducting third party discovery of one client on behalf of another client, is likely (1) to pit the duty of loyalty to each client against the duty of loyalty to the other; (2) to risk breaching the duty of confidentiality to the client-witness; and (3) to present a tension between the lawyer's own pecuniary interest in continued employment by the client-witness and the lawyer's ability to effectively represent the litigation client. The first two of these hazards

defense attorneys. In 1972, the ABA first adopted the Model Code of Judicial Conduct, which regulates the conduct of judges; it has been amended since then.

Additional Shepard's Citations. *Shepard's Federal Statutes Citations* also covers the Model Rules, the Model Code, and the Code of Judicial Conduct. Federal court decisions construing these professional rules are listed.

Proposed Rules. Drafts of new rules and the reports of studies that the ABA undertakes concerning new rules often are published as separate publications to permit the ABA membership to make comments. Furthermore, proposed amendments as well as recently adopted rules and comments are published in the *ABA Journal.*

Drafting History. The ABA has published the *Legislative History of the Model Rules of Professional Conduct: Their Development in the ABA House of Delegates,* which provides additional insight into the meaning of the rules.

Restatement of the Law Governing Lawyers. This new Restatement, pending as this text was written, covers a wide range of topics including disciplinary matters, legal malpractice, and disqualification issues.

E. HOW DO YOU CITE RULES OF PROFESSIONAL RESPONSIBILITY?

To cite a state's professional responsibility rule, you would provide at least the title of the set of rules and the rule number. You may also find it useful to provide a date, whether the date of the publication or the date of promulgation; *The Bluebook* is not clear. Here is a sample (without a date, cited as procedural rules are cited):

> N.M. Rules of Professional Conduct Rule 16-107.

To cite a model rule, first give the designation or type of rule, rule number, and the year that the code was adopted or last amended. Here is an example (following Rule 12.8.6 of *The Bluebook*):

> Model Rules of Professional Conduct Rule 1.7 (1998).

Citations to ethics opinions include the name of the issuing body, the opinion number, and the year. Here is an example (following Rule 12.8.6 of *The Bluebook*):

> ABA Comm. on Ethics and Professional Responsibility, Formal Op. 367 (1992).

F.   CONCLUDING POINTS

Issues concerning the professional obligations of an attorney are governed by state rules of professional responsibility, many of which are based on model standards of the American Bar Association. These rules typically are published as part of state codes and also may be published in state law deskbooks. To understand these rules fully, you often will also research case law, advisory committee comments, and state ethics opinions. Because state rules of professional responsibility often are based on the ABA model rules or code, persuasive authority may exist in the comments of the ABA advisory committee, ABA ethics opinions, and case law from other jurisdictions that have adopted language based on the same ABA model. These materials can be found in various paper sources. State rules of professional responsibility and the ABA materials also can be found online using Westlaw or LEXIS.

CONCLUSION

UNIT

VII

Developing an Integrated Research Strategy

A.   INTRODUCTION: THE AP*ART*MENT PROBLEM

Now that you have worked with a range of legal research sources, you should realize that there is no one "right" or "best" way to research any particular situation. You have options as to which commentary to explore, which media to use for case law research, which publication of court rules to employ, etc. At the same time, you must somehow accomplish the necessary task—locating the law that governs your situation.

To help you see how varied legal research can be, we asked four law students to research the following situation, which we invented for this purpose:

A nonprofit organization, ap*ART*ment, is negotiating for a loan from a large commercial bank in Baltimore, Maryland. The loan would fund ap*ART*ment's renovation of an abandoned building near downtown Baltimore. The site is now known as the Rainbow Building, and apARTment believes it would convert easily to mixed-use space. The lower level would consist of shops, galleries, and other small businesses clustered around an open gathering space. The upper levels would consist of studio spaces and residential apartments for artists with limited financial resources. The hope is that the project would help to rejuvenate an area that once was a thriving light-industrial area, but now is largely abandoned.

One concern is the potential for crime committed against tenants. Property crimes are common in the vicinity of the Rainbow Building (indeed, the Rainbow Building has been heavily vandalized), and the incidence of assault in the area is well above the city's average. City officials hope that projects such as the one under discussion will lead to improvements in safety in the area as the number of abandoned buildings drops. Nonetheless, the area now is, and probably will continue to be, a somewhat risky location. In light of this, ap*ART*ment proposes to use various safety measures, such as lighting, security systems, and surveillance cameras.

During the last meeting between the bank's lending officer and ap*ART*ment's executive director, the twin issues of safety and liability arose. The bank expressed concern that ap*ART*ment could be exposed to a significant liability should a serious crime against a tenant occur. (Given ap*ART*ment's thin capitalization, a large recovery against the organization could threaten the financial viability of the project.) Furthermore, should a lawsuit be brought and not resolved promptly, the adverse publicity could scare away tenants and undermine the financial stability of the project.

In response, the executive director of ap*ART*ment expressed doubt that ap*ART*ment would be liable for crimes committed by other people against its tenants, suggested that perhaps the tenants could agree in the lease not to seek recovery against ap*ART*ment should such a situation occur, and noted that the court probably would promptly dismiss any lawsuit brought against ap*ART*ment in such a situation.

Both representatives agreed that their concerns merit assessment by a lawyer.

We assigned two students—Jennifer Henderson and Richard Soderberg—to research the situation for the bank. Two students—Steve Brunn and Vickie Loher—researched the situation for ap*ART*ment. Their journals and their conclusions follow. Following the journals are our observations.

B. THE RESEARCH JOURNALS

As you read the following journals, keep these points in mind: The journals chronicle research processes; they are not complete analyses of the legal issues and facts. We have presented the main steps each researcher took and have omitted detail for purposes of brevity. Full citations appear only for the major authorities and then only for the first reference to an authority. The research was conducted for purposes of providing the "lay of the land" to the respective clients; had we presented the four researchers with a specific case in litigation, they probably would have researched further.

Between each journal and the researcher's conclusion is a simplified statement of the research process. Regular typeface connotes paper research; italics connotes online research.

1. Researching for the Bank

a. Jennifer Henderson

I had a vague recollection of discussion in torts class of a building owner's liability for crimes of third parties, as well as discussion in contracts class of clauses similar to that proposed here. Because torts and contracts generally are state law issues, I decided I would be researching Maryland law.

I generated a list of key words. The list included: landlord, tenant, contracts, leases, apartment.

Because I did not have a state encyclopedia for Maryland, I consulted *Corpus Juris Secundum* and *American Jurisprudence 2d*. I found general information in C.J.S. about a landlord's liability to tenants for injuries from dangerous and defective conditions and a discussion of exculpatory contracts in Am. Jur. 2d. In particular, the Am. Jur. 2d discussion provided the term "exculpatory clause" that I had not remembered before. I also read the Am. Jur. 2d discussion of assault and battery, which provided a cross-reference to A.L.R. Annotations.

Taking that clue, I moved to A.L.R. In the A.L.R. Index, I found references to two pertinent annotations: "Validity of Exculpatory Clause in Lease Exempting Lessor from Liability," 49 A.L.R.3d 321, and "Landlord's Obligation to Protect Tenant against Criminal Activities of Third Persons," 43 A.L.R.3d 331.

I moved to Westlaw and did a find search for the first annotation. I found three Maryland cases listed in the jurisdictional table, including *Eastern Avenue Corp. v. Hughes*, 180 A.2d 486 (Md. Ct. App. 1962), a case which was also mentioned in C.J.S. for the proposition that a landlord may absolve itself from liability for a tenant's injury, absent a statutory prohibition.

I jumped into the *Eastern Avenue* case, my first primary authority. I saw a red flag, indicating that the case is no longer good law. So I jumped into KeyCite and learned that *Hughes* has been superseded by a Maryland statute, Md. Code Ann., Real Property § 8-105 (1996 & Supp. 1998). That statute provides that exculpatory clauses encompassing a landlord's negligence "on or about the leased premises" in areas "not within the exclusive control of the tenant" are void as against public policy.

To obtain cases interpreting the statute, I examined the annotation to § 8-105 and reviewed the list of cases from the A.L.R. Annotation; I also KeyCited the first cases I found and followed up on the list of citing cases. I found several cases interpreting the statute, from both the Maryland state courts and the federal courts sitting in diversity, including *White v. Walker-Turner Division*, 841 F. Supp. 704 (D. Md. 1993), and *Prince Phillip Partnership v. Cutlip*, 582 A.2d 992 (Md. Ct. App. 1990). KeyCiting the *Prince Phillip* case, I discovered a 1998 law review article on exculpatory clauses in Maryland, published in volume 27 of the *University of Baltimore Law Review*. According to KeyCite, the cases interpreting the statute are good law.

Shifting to the liability issue, I did a find search on Westlaw for the A.L.R. Annotation at 43 A.L.R.3d 331. A red flag appeared, signaling that there is a new annotation on the topic, at 43 A.L.R.5th 207, "Landlord's

Liability for Failure to Protect Tenant from Criminal Acts of Third Person." The opening material of that annotation states that the previous rule favoring landlords is giving way to a rule favoring tenants.

Through the newer annotation, I found two important state court cases, *E.G. Rock v. Danly*, 633 A.2d 485 (Md. Ct. App. 1993), and *Scott v. Watson*, 359 A.2d 548 (Md. Ct. App. 1976); the latter appears to be the leading case. *Scott* holds that a landlord may be liable in certain instances for crimes committed against tenants by third parties in the premises' common areas; key factors include the landlord's actual or constructive knowledge of earlier criminal activity on the premises, the landlord's voluntary assumption of a duty to protect the tenant, and the reasonableness of the protective measures at issue. When I KeyCited my cases, I found they are good law. I also found additional cases, including unpublished federal appellate cases, a published federal district court case, and some state court cases involving attacks by dogs. KeyCite again directed me to a potentially pertinent periodical article, this time regarding the liability issue, published in the summer 1998 issue of *Real Estate Law Journal*.

I then wondered whether ap*ART*ment might be protected from suit on the grounds that it is a nonprofit organization. I ran a search or two in Maryland state case law databases, but found nothing to support this premise.

My client also is concerned about obtaining a speedy resolution of any litigation. I paged through the Maryland Rules books that are part of Michie's *Annotated Code of Maryland*. I looked for the two rules that are familiar to me from the federal rules (Rule 12 on motions to dismiss and Rule 56 on summary judgment). This did not work, so I consulted the index. There I found references to Circuit Court Rules 2-322 (motions to dismiss) and 2-501 (summary judgment). I reviewed these rules in the Maryland Rules book, perused the case descriptions in the annotations, and KeyCited the rules and the main cases.

I learned from the rules and cases that ap*ART*ment could move for dismissal even before answering, by asserting that the complaint on its face is deficient. On such a motion, the court must accept the facts as pleaded. The court may grant the motion, deny it, grant the tenant the opportunity to correct the deficiencies by filing an amended complaint, or defer ruling on the motion until trial. A second alternative is a motion for summary judgment later in the proceedings. To prevail, ap*ART*ment would have to show there is no genuine issue of material fact and that it is entitled to judgment as a matter of law. Again the court favors the nonmovant, and the court may grant the nonmovant additional time to develop the case through discovery.

Jennifer Henderson

---

exculpatory clause	encyclopedias → A.L.R. Index → *A.L.R.* → *cases* → *statute* → *cases* → *KeyCite* → *periodical article*
liability	A.L.R. Index → *A.L.R.* → *cases* → *KeyCite* → *periodical article*
dismissal	rules book → cases → *KeyCite*

Conclusion.   I would advise the bank that it should proceed with caution on the loan. If ap*ART*ment gets sued for a crime against a tenant, it may very well be held liable, depending on the circumstances. Moreover, a clause extinguishing liability would probably be unenforceable, and there is no guarantee that the suit could be disposed of quickly. Nevertheless, the bank may want to proceed. The benefits to the community from the project and the bank's image as a good citizen contributing to those benefits may outweigh the risks involved.

b.   Richard Soderberg

I started by brainstorming terms for the following categories:

- who: tenant, landlord, artist, professional;
- what: living quarters, apartment, lease, rental space, business space, professional building, crime, liability, waiver, release;
- where: Baltimore, Maryland, apartment building, residential area;
- why: recover damages, avoid liability, attract tenants, promote artistic development, improve the area;
- legal: landlord liability, premises liability, waiver, release;
- relief: damages.

I began by looking, in paper sources, for secondary authority. I found a Landlord and Tenant volume of Am. Jur. 2d and reviewed the table of contents until I identified section 551. That section indicates that there is no liability for landlords with regard to crimes against tenants. It provided a reference to 43 A.L.R.3d 331. (I neglected, however, to check the encyclopedia's pocket part.)

I moved to that A.L.R. Annotation. The scope note warned that the annotation does not cover statutes. The general rule stated in the annotation was consistent with that stated above, although the annotation also mentioned a provision in the Restatement (Second) of Torts that imposes liability for failure to protect another from crime when the plaintiff and defendant stand in a special relationship. There were no Maryland cases covered in the annotation. Then I learned from the pocket part that there is a newer, superseding annotation at 43 A.L.R.5th 207. (Had I checked the Am. Jur. 2d pocket part, I would have been directed to the newer annotation.)

The annotation at 43 A.L.R.5th 207 was more detailed than the older annotation and included descriptions of three Maryland cases, including *E.G. Rock* and *Scott*. [See the first journal for a brief description of the *Scott* rule.] I looked in the annotation for key words related to the other issue, such as release, waiver, disclaimer, and exculpation, but found nothing. The pocket part did not discuss Maryland cases.

I then decided to research Maryland statutory law. In the *Annotated Code of Maryland*, I looked for my key terms under the subject heading "landlord and tenant" in the index. I learned of a statute regarding exculpatory clauses in the landlord-tenant setting, § 8-105 of the Real Property article. [See the first journal for a brief statement of that statutory rule.] I also found some less pertinent statutes, one (§ 2-120) providing that the occurrence of crimes does not constitute a latent defect in the premises.

I wanted to strengthen my case law research, so I looked in the *Maryland Digest 2d* in the Landlord and Tenant materials, in particular under key numbers 162 and following, regarding injuries from dangerous conditions. I looked in the pocket part and the pamphlet supplementing the pocket part. I found the *E.G. Rock* and *Scott* cases, as well as some others.

I decided to verify that my leading cases were still good law. I used Westlaw's KeyCite program. *E.G. Rock* had no negative history; *Scott* had been distinguished by a Massachusetts case, which would not affect its status in Maryland.

I also wanted to find case law interpreting the exculpatory clause statute, § 8-105, so I proceeded to the MD-ST-ANN database on Westlaw and entered the search [exculpat! /s landlord]. I learned of seven cases and six secondary sources citing the statute. The list included *White*, *Prince Phillip*, and *Shell Oil Co. v. Ryckman*, 403 A.2d 379 (Md. Ct. App. 1979). The latter explains that the statute does not apply if the premises are exclusively within the control of the tenant.

I looked in the cases I had already located for indications of the likelihood of a prompt dismissal of any lawsuit that might arise. In *White*, the defendant obtained summary judgment on the basis of a valid exculpatory clause. On the other hand, the *Prince Phillip* court held the clause invalid, and the case went on to fairly prolonged litigation.

Richard Soderberg

liability	encyclopedia → A.L.R. → (Restatement) → cases
exculpatory clause	annotated code → statute
liability	digest → cases → *KeyCite*
exculpatory clause	*statutory database → cases*
dismissal	cases → procedural rule

Conclusion.   I would counsel the bank to consider giving apARTment the loan. There is reliable authority that apARTment would not be held liable to its tenants if it takes reasonable precautionary measures. Should crimes occur on the premises, apARTment must act reasonably to prevent future crimes, and it appears prepared to do so, since it is already willing to take precautionary measures. A landlord also must act properly in carrying out any safety measures it takes on, and I see no reason to fear that apARTment would act improperly. We should, however, forget the idea of apARTment seeking to exculpate itself. Any attempt to do so will not be upheld by the courts if the clause violates the statutory prohibition.

2.   Researching for ap*ART*ment

a.   Steve Brunn

I started with a short list of research terms: landlord, tenant, crime, third person, lease, liability, vicarious liability, negligence, and exculpatory clause.

As for the issue of liability, I read the Am. Jur. 2d discussion of "landlord's liability for disturbances." The most useful reference I found there was to an A.L.R. Annotation regarding crimes by third persons, found at 43 A.L.R.3d 331. I looked over that annotation and read the accompanying case, *Kline v. 1500 Massachusetts Avenue Apartment Corp.*, 439 F.2d 477 (D.C. Cir. 1970). That case holds that a landlord does owe a duty to take reasonable steps to protect a tenant from foreseeable criminal acts by intruders. Although it is a leading case, it is not mandatory precedent in Maryland.

To locate primary mandatory authority on this issue, I turned first to the *Annotated Code of Maryland*. I explored various subheadings of "landlord and tenant" in the index, but found nothing on the liability issue. Nor did I find anything pertinent in the session law service.

I then turned to the *Maryland Digest 2d* and skimmed the table of contents for the Landlord and Tenant topic. I identified *Doe v. Montgomery Mall Ltd. Partnership*, 962 F. Supp. 58 (D. Md. 1997) as a pertinent case. I read it in the reporter and found that Maryland law does recognize landlord liability for criminal acts by third persons under some circumstances. *Doe* led me to several Maryland state court cases and identified one, *Scott*, as the seminal case. [See the first journal for a brief description of the *Scott* rule.]

As for the issue of exculpatory clauses, I learned from Am. Jur. 2d that the law on such clauses differs from state to state. I did not find any useful citations to Maryland cases in the encyclopedia. So I read a discussion in the Williston treatise on contracts, which was not easy to locate, and another in the Friedman treatise on leases, which was much easier to locate. I learned from my treatise research that courts do not look favorably on exculpatory clauses for public policy reasons and strictly construe such clauses in leases. Furthermore, the Williston treatise provided a reference to a Maryland case, *Adloo v. H.T. Brown Real Estate, Inc.*, 686 A.2d 298 (Md. Ct. App. 1996). That case sets out general principles limiting the enforceability of exculpatory clauses and identifies the fairness of the transaction and the public interest as pertinent factors.

Seeking additional mandatory primary authority, I searched the index of the *Annotated Code of Maryland*. Nothing stood out among the many subheadings under "landlord and tenant."

I turned to the *Maryland Digest 2d* and looked under various headings, such as contracts, leases, limitations on liability, and bailments. The most useful find was a description of *White*, a 1993 federal court case, digested in the pocket part. The *White* court relied on a state statute, § 8-105. I turned to that statute (which I had not found earlier for some reason). I read it in the annotated code and noted additional cases from the annotation. [See the first journal for a brief statement of that statutory rule.] I checked for updates in the session law service, but found nothing.

Before I shifted to computer-based sources, I researched in the Maryland Rules volumes. Their index directed me to Rule 2-501 regarding summary judgment. I read that rule and the annotation material and checked a few of the listed cases. I learned that the Maryland rule resembles the federal summary judgment rule. [See the first journal for a brief discussion of summary judgment.]

At this point, I turned to online research, which, for cost reasons, I use primarily to doublecheck and update my paper research. I KeyCited *Doe*, which had only two citing sources, one a 1999 law review article in volume 33 of the *University of San Francisco Law Review*. I looked at that article and learned about a California case in which a key factor was whether a neighborhood is inherently dangerous. I KeyCited *Scott*, which has been cited by nearly seventy cases, none undermining its status as good law; I looked at the "examined" cases, but found nothing new. I KeyCited *Adloo*, which led me to a federal case, *Cornell v. Council of Unit Owners Hawaiian Village Condominiums, Inc.*, 983 F. Supp. 640 (D. Md. 1997), which in turn referred to an older (1962) Maryland case, *Eastern Avenue Corp.*, in which the court favored exculpatory clauses on the grounds of freedom of contract. I KeyCited *White* and § 8-105 along with the other cases listed in the annotated code as interpreting that statute; these sources all checked out, and I came across no new authorities.

As one last step, I ran Westlaw searches in the Maryland state court cases (MD-CS) database. The first two natural-language searches addressed the two main issues I had been researching; I found nothing new. The third search [rejuvenation or revitalization] was aimed at deriving discussion by the courts of a policy concern in ap*ART*ment's project—the public's interest in revitalizing the city. I found one useful case in the dozen I retrieved, *Donnelly Advertising Corp. v. City of Baltimore*, 370 A.2d 1127 (Md. 1977), in which the court discussed this policy, although the legal issue was not the same as in our case.

	Steve Brunn
liability	encyclopedia → A.L.R. → annotated code → digest → cases
exculpatory clause	encyclopedia → treatises → cases → annotated code → digest → cases → statute → cases
dismissal	rules book → rule → cases
liability	*KeyCite → periodical article → persuasive precedent*
exculpatory clause	*KeyCite case and statute*
liability	*natural-language search*
exculpatory clause	*natural-language search*
policy issue	*Boolean search → case*

Conclusion.   I believe there is some risk of liability for crimes committed against tenants. The dangerousness of the neighborhood contributes to the foreseeability of harm. As for breach of duty, ap*ART*ment's current plans may meet the standard of reasonableness, but it may need to increase its protective measures if criminal activity does occur. As for an exculpatory clause, Maryland law has shifted, from favoring them to restricting their use. Ap*ART*ment should include a clear clause in its leases, but not expect it to be enforced in court unless it conforms to the statute, there was no unfairness in the parties' transaction, and the public policy favoring revitalization of the city benefits ap*ART*ment. The exculpatory clause issue could well be decided on summary judgment, but the liability issue may or may not be amenable to summary judgment.

b.   Vickie Loher

I discerned three issues: (1) whether ap*ART*ment could be liable for crimes committed against tenants by third parties, (2) whether ap*ART*ment could limit that liability by a term in its lease, and (3) what standards the court would follow in dismissing a lawsuit by a tenant on summary judgment. Because I was fairly confident of my background understanding of the issues, I proceeded directly to primary authority.

I started in the *Annotated Code of Maryland,* more specifically the index. I read the entries under the subject heading "landlord and tenant." I identified nine potentially pertinent sections, including such topics as homicide, implied covenant of quiet enjoyment, and disclosures about property. The sections all appeared in the Real Property volume. I reviewed each section in the main volume and the pocket part. The only actually pertinent section is § 8-105. [See the first journal for a brief statement of that statutory rule.]

I then perused the annotation to that section. I identified three cases as fitting the research problem the best: *Prince Phillip, White,* and *Cornell.*

I turned to the *Maryland Digest 2d* to look for cases on the first issue in particular. I reviewed the outline of the Landlord and Tenant topic and decided to focus on cases under the heading "premises and enjoyment and use thereof" and subheading "injuries from dangerous or defective condition," that is, key numbers 162-170. I reviewed the case descriptions to identify the most useful cases. I selected fourteen cases, including *Scott, E.G. Rock, Adloo,* and *Doe.* [See the first journal for a brief description of the *Scott* rule.]

I updated my cases through KeyCite. The cases are still good law. I did discover additional cases through KeyCite, including a recent federal appellate decision.

To locate the information I needed about the procedural issue, I searched in Westlaw's MD-RULES database; my search was ["summary judgment"]. This search retrieved Maryland's summary judgment rule. The rule itself states the two-part standard (absence of a genuine issue of material fact, entitlement to judgment as a matter of law). The cases appearing in the annotation further develop the rule's standard. Furthermore, I reviewed a case I had encountered earlier, *Pittman v. Atlantic Realty Co.*, 732 A.2d 912 (Md. Ct. App. 1999), which does not address my substantive issues, but does discuss summary judgment; I KeyCited it as well. As persuasive precedent, in a federal case, the appeals court upheld summary judgment on the grounds the landlord had no duty to protect against armed robbery when there had been only a single robbery, not involving a gun or actual harm to the victim. *Nails v. Community Realty*, 166 F.3d 333 (4th Cir. 1998) (per curiam).

Vickie Loher

---

exculpatory clause	annotated code → statute → cases
liability	digest → cases
liability/ exculpatory clause	*KeyCite → additional cases*
dismissal	*rules database → cases → KeyCite*

Conclusion.   Should ap*ART*ment take over the building, it would have a duty to exercise reasonable diligence to keep the common areas safe. It is already aware of break-ins and must take reasonable measures to eliminate conditions contributing to break-ins. If it becomes aware of assaults, it must similarly act to prevent assaults. If ap*ART*ment voluntarily undertakes to provide security for tenants, it must be sure it does so properly. By statute, ap*ART*ment cannot enforce a lease provision regarding liability for losses that occur in areas not within the exclusive control of the tenant. However, the statute would not void a provision covering injuries in an area within the exclusive control of the tenant. Hence, it would be advisable for ap*ART*ment to place a clause of the latter sort within the leases. As for the likelihood of a prompt resolution of any lawsuit, ap*ART*ment might prevail if it can argue that its duty had not yet arisen, due to low crime levels within the building; otherwise a lawsuit is likely to raise fact issues for a jury's determination.

C.   OUR OBSERVATIONS

Ultimately, all four researchers came to focus on the same few leading authorities: the *Scott* case, § 8-105, Rule 2-501, and related cases. There are, of course, both similarities and differences among the four research processes described above. The differences tend to be matters of detail, while the similarities reveal matters of importance.

All four researchers began with an analysis of the facts, so as to generate research terms or issues. For all of them, as to the two main issues, two concepts proved to be key: landlord-tenant and exculpatory clause. The former was apparent at the outset; for some, the latter term took some research to identify. All four also zeroed in quickly on Maryland state law as the law to research.

Most of the four researchers began in secondary sources. They used encyclopedias, treatises, and A.L.R.s for background and references to primary authority.

Most of the researchers used a state digest to identify pertinent cases. All used the state's annotated code and drew from that source not only the statutory language but also descriptions of pertinent cases. Most took a similar approach to the procedural issue.

All of the researchers took care to update their research and verify the status of their leading authorities as good law, through such tools as pocket parts, supplementary pamphlets, session law services, KeyCite, and computer searches.

All researchers mixed paper-based research and computer-based research. All four used KeyCite. Beyond that, they differed as to how much they used Westlaw. Two notes: Due perhaps to William Mitchell's proximity to the headquarters of the West Group, Westlaw tends to be more popular than LEXIS in our region. It did not surprise us that no one used Internet or CD-ROM sources, because we have not emphasized them as much in our research course as Westlaw.

Each of the four journals shows the truth of the saying, "one thing led to another." For example, one researcher found pertinent law review articles while KeyCiting leading cases. As another example, one researcher found the statute through a leading federal court case. Even so, there is a clear sense of direction in each research journal; each researcher pursued each of the three issues as distinct, but related, tasks.

The four journals also show the truth of the saying, "nobody's perfect." For example, one researcher did not initially realize that there was a new annotation because he did not check an encyclopedia pocket part. Another did not initially identify the statute in the index to the annotated code. Nonetheless, they both corrected their missteps; their research processes were thorough enough to provide safeguards against missteps.

When we designed the problem, we wondered whether the lawyers for the bank would approach the task any differently than the lawyers for apARTment. As you can see, all four researchers came to the same set of authorities. This is as it should be, for the role of a lawyer in a counseling setting is to find and apply the pertinent law to the client's situation, as a neutral looking at the problem would, and build a legal strategy for the client on that objective assessment.

We hope that the four research journals, and indeed the rest of this book, have shown you how to accomplish legal research. We also hope that you will use your research skills to benefit your clients and those affected by their actions.

RESEARCH SITUATIONS AND PROBLEM SETS

The following materials constitute research exercises, each consisting of two parts. First, we have provided realistic research situations to be researched. Most of the time, you will have a choice of situation or state in which to research. Second, we have provided sets of questions—the problem sets; each set of questions guides you through a research process (such as development of research terms and issues, encyclopedia research, computer-based research in cases). Some problem sets have their own research situations; other problem sets share research situations, so you can see how various sources work together. There are problem sets for all chapters but Chapters 1, 2, 9, and 19; some chapters have one problem set, others more than one.

All pages in this part of the book are perforated. Thus you can tear out the problem sets for submission to your professor. Do not tear out the research situations that are used for multiple problem sets.

LEGAL LANGUAGE AND RESEARCH TERMS

SECONDARY SOURCES

You will be selecting one of the research situations stated below for the following problem sets for Units I and II:

Chapter 3.   Legal Language and Research Terms
Chapter 4.   Encyclopedias
Chapter 5.   Treatises
Chapter 6.   Legal Periodicals
Chapter 7.   A.L.R. Annotations
Chapter 8.   Restatements

Unless otherwise instructed by your professor, you should select one research situation to work for all of these problem sets. We suggest that you leave pages 381–384 in your book (or at least do not turn them in to your professor), so you will have ready access to the texts of the research situations as you work through each problem set.

Research Situation A:

Clarence Murphy, your client, is a month-to-month tenant at Parkside Manor Apartments in Appleton, Wisconsin. Recently, Mr. Murphy's bathroom pipes began to leak. Mr. Murphy reported the problem to the landlord's manager of the apartment complex. After one month passed without management fixing the leak, Mr. Murphy, suspecting that the leaking pipes might be a housing code violation, contacted the local city housing inspector. The inspector found multiple housing code violations while she was at the complex inspecting the leaky pipes. The inspector ordered the landlord to fix the code violations and also fined the landlord. One week after the order from the housing inspector, Mr. Murphy received a letter from the landlord of Parkside Apartments, stating that he had "10 days to find a new residence and vacate the premises." Mr. Murphy was shocked by the letter; he has never been late paying his rent and believes that the landlord is retaliating against him for calling the housing inspector. Can Mr. Murphy raise any defenses to an unlawful detainer action, based on his belief that the landlord is retaliating against him for calling the housing inspector?

Research Situation B:

In anticipation of their upcoming marriage, Marline Ciatti presented her fiancé, Ben Brown, your client, with an expensive braided-gold engagement ring. Two months before the wedding was scheduled to take place, Mr. Brown discovered that Ms. Ciatti had been unfaithful to him. He canceled the wedding plans but refused to give back the engagement ring. Ms. Ciatti is furious at Mr. Brown's refusal to give back the ring, especially since he is the one who called off the wedding. These events took place in Akron, Ohio. Who is entitled to the ring?

Research Situation C:

Over lunch break, Li Chang, your client, entered a local clothing store in Joplin, Missouri, looking for a new tie. Mr. Chang spent about twenty-five minutes looking at the ties, picking some of them up and closely examining them. Mr. Chang was undecided about which tie to buy, so he decided to leave the store. Just as Mr. Chang was about to exit the store, a security guard grabbed him and told Mr. Chang to come to the manager's office. Once inside the manager's office, Mr. Chang was accused of shoplifting. Mr. Chang attempted to leave the office, but the security guard blocked the door. After a half hour of questioning, the manager was finally convinced of Mr. Chang's innocence. The manager apologized for the "inconvenience," but Mr. Chang is upset about being detained. Does he have a cause of action for being falsely imprisoned?

Research Situation D:

Alexander Schwartz, the son of Anna and Mikel Schwartz, your clients, recently returned home after a six-month stay at the Safe Haven Group Home. Safe Haven is a residential facility located in Albany, New York, for teenagers who need to live away from home temporarily, for any number of reasons. Upon returning home, Alexander alleged that Sam Oke, the director of Safe Haven, sexually abused him. Mr. and Mrs. Schwartz investigated Mr. Oke's background and found that he was arrested ten years ago for fifth-degree assault, an incident in which Mr. Oke hit his wife in the face. Could Safe Haven itself be liable as an employer for negligence in hiring Mr. Oke as an employee, without first checking his criminal record? (This is not a question of agency status or respondeat superior.)

Research Situation E:

Billy's New Car & Truck Mega-Store, your client, located in Bloomington, Minnesota, printed the following ad in the local paper:

> We sell the most cars and trucks in the metro area. If you buy a new truck from us this weekend, valued at over $21,000, we will include leather interior for free (valued at over $3,000!).

The only other information in the ad was the company's logo, address, and phone number. Roger Nelsova saw the ad and decided to purchase a truck from Billy's on the specified weekend. After paying the purchase price, $22,550, Mr. Nelsova inquired about the leather interior. Billy's owner said that the manufacturer of the truck that Mr. Nelsova chose does not make leather interiors. Mr. Nelsova told the owner that the ad promised a free leather interior and that he expects Billy's to provide it even if it has to be custom made. The owner refused, saying that the ad was not a binding offer, but merely a general advertisement for customers to visit his Mega-Store. Did the ad constitute a binding offer?

Research Situation F:

Your client is Macey Seymour, whose beloved dog, a beagle, was hit and killed by a woman who was negligently speeding through Ms. Seymour's neighborhood in Miami Beach, Florida. Ms. Seymour is very distraught over the death of her dog, which could have easily been avoided. The woman who killed the dog has offered Ms. Seymour an amount of money equal to the value of a new beagle at the local pet store. Ms. Seymour feels that the woman also should be required to pay damages for Ms. Seymour's emotional distress for losing the dog. Can Ms. Seymour recover these damages?

Research Situation G:

You represent the family of Wayne Roy. Mr. Roy was injured in an auto accident while driving home from work one evening in Austin, Texas. Mr. Roy suffered serious injuries during the accident, including brain injuries. He sued the driver of the other vehicle, alleging that the driver was negligent in driving through a red light. Mr. Roy recovered a fair judgment as a result of his personal injury accident. One year later, he died as a result of complications stemming from his brain injury. His family would like to pursue a wrongful death action against the driver of the car that caused Mr. Roy's injuries. What effect will Mr. Roy's previous lawsuit and judgment have on his family's possible wrongful death claim?

Research Situation H:

Jack Habera, your client, lived with Mary Nosko, unmarried, in Nome, Alaska, for fifteen years. During that time, Ms. Nosko was the sole source of income. She worked as an engineer, while Mr. Habera stayed at home, rendering domestic services: meal preparation, shopping, cleaning, and childcare. They never memorialized their domestic arrangement. They have recently decided to end their fifteen-year relationship. Now that the relationship is ending, Mr. Habera is without income or support. Is he legally entitled to restitution for the domestic services he rendered to Ms. Nosko during the course of their relationship?

Research Situation I:

Ben Guare, your client, is a musician who plays in a jazz band, in a woodwind quartet, and as a soloist in Providence, Rhode Island. He entered into an agreement to play at the wedding reception of Joan Chu and Ron Venn, six months in advance of the date. Three months before the wedding, Mr. Guare's jazz band released a CD recording that was an instant and huge success. Because of this success, Mr. Guare was able to increase his hourly rate for future musical bookings by 30%. When Ms. Chu and Mr. Venn heard of the CD's success, they called Mr. Guare to make sure that he still intended to play at their reception. Mr. Guare assured them that he would and that he was not increasing his rates for those jobs that were already under contract. Nonetheless, Ms. Chu and Mr. Venn offered to pay him 30% more than the agreement specified, and, after some hesitation, Mr. Guare gratefully accepted their offer. He did indeed play at their wedding reception. However, Ms. Chu and Mr. Venn then paid Mr. Guare at the rate of the original agreement, not the additional 30%. Is the modification of their agreement invalid because it lacked new consideration? (Ignore other issues, such as the statute of frauds.)

Research Situation J:

Andrea Yod, a resident of Salt Lake City, Utah, promised her roommate, Danielle Ryan, that she would buy several lottery tickets during her vacation in San Francisco, California, and that the two of them would share any winnings equally. Ms. Yod purchased the lottery tickets as promised, and returned to Utah. One of the tickets, still in Ms. Yod's possession, turned out to be worth $1.5 million; she has refused to share any of the winnings with her roommate. From your preliminary research, you have already established that the ticket was a state-sponsored California lottery ticket and that the agreement would be enforceable in California. However, Utah prohibits any type of gambling or games of chance. Ms. Ryan, your client, needs to know whether the Utah court will enforce the contract; in other words, if she brings suit in Utah, will the Utah court apply California or Utah law in resolving the conflict of laws.

PROBLEM SET FOR CHAPTER 3. LEGAL LANGUAGE AND RESEARCH TERMS

Your Name   Professor

_____   _____

Circle the letter of the research situation you selected (see pages 381–384):

A   B   C   D   E   F   G   H   I   J

1. Read through the research situation carefully. List the main concepts for each of the eight categories below. If you are not able to identify concepts for a category, leave it blank.

factual "who"

_____

_____

factual "what"

_____

_____

factual "when"

_____

_____

factual "where"

_____

_____

factual "why"

_____

_____

legal theory

_____

_____

relief

_____

_____

procedure

_____

_____

2. Select three factual or legal concepts you have listed. For each, think of related terms, such as synonyms, antonyms, broader terms, and narrower terms. Present them here, whether in ladder, wheel, or list form, or a combination of these.

3. Look up one of your legal terms in a legal thesaurus. List your initial term and up to five related terms that could be pertinent to your research situation.

_____

_____

_____

4. Look up one of your legal terms in a legal dictionary.

(a) Write out or paraphrase the definition; you need not include references to other sources.

_____

_____

_____

_____

_____

(b) Provide the proper citation for the above definition.

_____

_____

5. Based on your work in Questions 1 through 4, formulate at least one potential research issue for your research situation. The issue should link pertinent factual concepts with related legal concepts.

_____

_____

_____

_____

6. Draft a search you might run in a computer-based source. Follow the LEXIS or Westlaw Boolean protocols described in Chapter 3.

(a) Write out your draft search.

_____

_____

_____

(b) Check which set of protocols you followed:

_____ LEXIS   _____ Westlaw

(c) What does this search ask the computer to do?

_____

_____

PROBLEM SET FOR CHAPTER 4. ENCYCLOPEDIAS

Your Name   Professor

_____   _____

Circle the letter of the research situation you selected (see pages 381–384):

A   B   C   D   E   F   G   H   I   J

Note: If you have not yet developed research terms for the research situation you selected, do so before you begin this problem set. See the problem set for Chapter 3 for assistance.

1. Circle the encyclopedia you will be using:

Am. Jur. 2d   C.J.S.   state encyclopedia identified by your professor

2. Locate pertinent sections in your chosen encyclopedia. Describe your research process. Example: I looked up the following terms in the index: . . . .

_____

_____

_____

3. From the pertinent sections, note here the law that pertains to your research situation.

_____

_____

_____

_____

_____

_____

_____

_____

_____

_____

4. Examine the footnotes to those sections for references to primary authority. List two or three references that could be pertinent to your research situation. If possible, find primary authority from the jurisdiction in your research situation. (You need not use proper citation form.)

_____

_____

_____

_____

_____

5. If you are researching in paper, to update and expand your research, consult updating material, such as a pocket part or pamphlet supplement. Did you find any additional information that is pertinent to your research situation? If so, record it here. If not, write "none."

_____

_____

_____

_____

6. Provide the proper citation to the material you read in the encyclopedia, including the updating material as appropriate.

_____

_____

7. Has your research in the encyclopedia brought forth any legal or factual concepts that you had not yet identified? If so, state them here.

_____

_____

_____

_____

PROBLEM SET FOR CHAPTER 5. TREATISES

Your Name   Professor

_____   _____

Circle the letter of the research situation you selected (see pages 381–384):

A   B   C   D   E   F   G   H   I   J

Note: If you have not yet developed research terms for the research situation you selected, do so before you begin this problem set. See the problem set for Chapter 3 for assistance.

Your research situation involves the following area(s) of law:

Research Situation A:	property, real property, landlord, and tenant
Research Situation B:	property, personal property
Research Situation C:	torts
Research Situation D:	employment, torts
Research Situation E:	contracts
Research Situation F:	torts
Research Situation G:	judgments, civil procedure
Research Situation H:	remedies, restitution
Research Situation I:	contracts
Research Situation J:	conflict of laws, civil procedure

1. Use the library catalog and the research terms that you have developed to locate a treatise covering the subject of your research situation.

(a) Which subject heading(s) and subheading(s), if any, did you use in the catalog?

_____

_____

(b) List the title and call number of a treatise on your subject.

_____

_____

2. By browsing the shelves containing treatises with that call number, locate another treatise on your subject. State its title.

_____

_____

3. Select one of the treatises you have located. By use of its index or table of contents, locate the pertinent part(s) of the treatise.

(a) Note here the law that pertains to your research situation, as explained in the treatise.

_____

_____

_____

_____

_____

_____

_____

_____

_____

_____

(b) If the treatise critiques the law, summarize that critique. If not, write "none."

_____

_____

_____

_____

4. Examine the footnotes to the material you read for references to primary authority. List two or three references that could be pertinent to your research situation. If possible, find primary authority from the jurisdiction in your research situation. (You need not use proper citation form.)

_____

_____

_____

_____

5. To update and expand your research, consult a pocket part or other supplement, if any. Did you find any additional information that is pertinent to your research situation? If so, record it here. If not, write "none."

_____

_____

_____

6. By reference to the factors discussed in Chapter 5, evaluate the treatise's usefulness.

_____

_____

_____

_____

_____

_____

7. Provide the proper citation to the material you read in the treatise, including the updating material as appropriate.

_____

_____

_____

8. Has your research in treatises brought forth any legal or factual concepts that you had not yet identified? If so, state them here.

_____

_____

_____

_____

PROBLEM SET FOR CHAPTER 6. LEGAL PERIODICALS

Your Name   Professor

_____   _____

Circle the letter of the research situation you selected (see pages 381–384):

A   B   C   D   E   F   G   H   I   J

Note: If you have not yet developed research terms for the research situation you selected, do so before you begin this problem set. See the problem set for Chapter 3 for assistance.

1. Select a legal periodical index, and search for one or two articles pertinent to your research situation.

(a) Which index did you select?

_____

(b) Describe your research process. Example: I ran a search for . . . in the subject index.

_____

_____

_____

(c) List the titles of up to three potentially pertinent articles. (You need not use proper citation form.)

_____

_____

_____

_____

_____

2. Select one of the two articles listed below for your research situation. Locate the article in paper or online. Remember that some student-written articles show the author's

name only at the end of the article, not on the title page or in the table of contents. Circle your choice of article:

A	Vermont Law Review, Sullivan, 1997	Part III B 1 c
	Utah Law Review, Owens, 1997	Part VI C
B	Washburn Law Journal, Kruckenberg, 1998	Part IV
	Yale Law Journal, Tushnet, 1998	Part II
C	St. Mary's Law Journal, Gibson, 1987	Part IV A-C
	Mercer Law Review, Hicks, 1997	Part I B-C
D	South Dakota Law Review, Swedlund, 1996	Part IV
	Whittier Law Review, Camacho, 1993	Part III
E	Stanford Law Review, Craswell, 1996	Part IV intro, A
	California Law Review, Eisenberg, 1994	Part III C 1
F	New York University Law Review, Squires-Lee, 1995	Part II
	New York Law School Law Review, Barton & Hill, 1989	Part IV A-C
G	University of Puget Sound Law Review, Clark, 1993	Parts III, IV
	Arkansas Law Review, Olsen, 1986	Part III
H	University of Puget Sound Law Review, Lewis, 1991	Parts II B, VI
	William & Mary Law Review, Estin, 1995	Part II B
I	Loyola (L.A.) Law Review, Wessman, 1996	Part III A, D
	Alabama Law Review, Teeven, 1996	Parts III B 2, VI
J	American Journal of Trial Advocacy, Thompson, 1994	all
	Nova Law Review, Southerland, 1997	Part III

What type of article does it appear to be—a student comment or note, a lead article, an essay, or something else?

_____

    3. Skim the introduction and conclusion of your article, if any, to get a sense of the article. Then read the segment of the article listed above.

    (a) Note here the law that pertains to your research situation, as explained in the article.

_____

_____

_____

_____

_____

_____

_____

(b) Does the article critique current law or propose changes in the law? If so, summarize the author's position. (If you do not find a critique in the segment we assigned, check other segments.)

_____

_____

_____

_____

_____

4. Examine the footnotes for the segment listed above for references to primary authority. List up to three references that could be pertinent to your research situation. If possible, find primary authority from the jurisdiction in your research situation. (You need not use proper citation form.)

_____

_____

_____

_____

_____

5. By reference to the factors discussed in Chapter 6, assess the article's quality.

_____

_____

_____

_____

_____

_____

6. Provide the proper citation to the article you have reviewed.

_____

_____

_____

7. Has your research in legal periodicals brought forth any legal or factual concepts that you had not yet identified? If so, state them here.

_____

_____

_____

_____

8. **Optional Question:** Use *Shepard's Law Review Citations* in paper to follow up on your research.

(a) Is your journal covered by Shepard's?

_____

(b) If so, the article you read is the cited source. Locate its entry, if any, and record the first two citing sources listed there. (Use the table of abbreviations at the front of the volume to decipher the entries.) If there is no entry, write "none."

_____

_____

(c)   How current was your Shepardizing? How do you know?

_____

_____

PROBLEM SET FOR CHAPTER 7. A.L.R. ANNOTATIONS

Your Name   Professor

_____   _____

Circle the letter of the research situation you selected (see pages 381–384):

A   B   C   D   E   F   G   H   I   J

Note: If you have not yet developed research terms for the research situation you selected, do so before you begin this problem set. See the problem set for Chapter 3 for assistance.

1. Locate one or more annotations pertinent to your research situation.

(a) Describe your research process. Example: I ran the following search in Westlaw/ LEXIS: . . . ; I looked up the following terms in the index: . . . .

_____

_____

_____

(b) State the title(s) of up to three pertinent annotations.

_____

_____

_____

_____

_____

2. Locate one of the annotations you listed in your answer to Question 1. Examine the editorial aids at the outset of the annotation, to locate pertinent sections of the annotation. Which sections appears to be most pertinent? How did you identify that material?

_____

_____

_____

_____

_____

3. Read the pertinent sections of the same annotation. Note here the law that pertains to your research situation, as well as any guidance the annotation provides as to patterns in the case law.

_____

_____

_____

_____

_____

_____

_____

_____

_____

4. List the names of up to three cases from your jurisdiction. If there are none, list the names of up to three cases from other jurisdictions, and note their jurisdictions. Be sure to check the supplement, if you are researching in paper. (You need not use proper citation form.)

_____

_____

_____

_____

_____

5. List up to three secondary sources, listed in the opening pages, that you would consider pursuing. (You need not use proper citation form.)

_____

_____

_____

_____

6. Provide the proper citation to your annotation, including any additional material in the supplement.

_____

_____

_____

_____

7. Has your research in A.L.R.s brought forth any legal or factual concepts that you had not yet identified? If so, state them here.

PROBLEM SET FOR CHAPTER 8. RESTATEMENTS

Your Name _____   Professor _____

Circle the letter of the research situation you selected (see pages 381–384):

A   B   C   D   E   F   G   H   I   J

Note: If you have not yet developed research terms for the research situation you selected, do so before you begin this problem set. See the problem set for Chapter 3 for assistance.

Although you sometimes would do a comprehensive search of more than one Restatement topic and series, for this assignment, use the following Restatement topic and series for your research situation:

Research Situation A:	Property 2d (Landlord and Tenant)
Research Situation B:	Property 2d (Donative Transfers)
Research Situation C:	Torts 2d
Research Situation D:	Agency 2d
Research Situation E:	Contracts 2d
Research Situation F:	Torts 2d
Research Situation G:	Judgments 2d
Research Situation H:	Restitution 1st
Research Situation I:	Contracts 2d
Research Situation J:	Conflict of Laws 2d

1. Locate one or more Restatement sections pertinent to your research situation.

(a) Describe your research process. Example: I looked up the following terms in the index: . . . .

_____

_____

_____

(b) List the section numbers and their topics.

_____

_____

_____

2. Read the rules in the sections you listed above, and determine which rule is most pertinent to your research situation. Write out that rule, or paraphrase it if it is lengthy.

_____

_____

_____

_____

_____

_____

_____

3. Read the material following that rule (comments, illustrations, and reporter's note). Also skim any cross-referenced sections and the sections in the vicinity of your section. Note here additional legal concepts or refinements of the rule that pertain to your research situation.

_____

_____

_____

_____

_____

_____

_____

4. Provide the proper citation to the Restatement rule as well as specific comments and illustrations, if applicable.

_____

_____

5. Locate and review the case summaries for the Restatement section you cited above. List the names of up to three cases from your jurisdiction. If there are none, list the names of up to three cases from other jurisdictions, and note their jurisdictions. (You need not use proper citation form.)

_____

_____

_____

_____

6. Has your research in Restatements brought forth any legal or factual concepts that you had not yet identified? If so, state them here.

_____

_____

_____

_____

RESEARCH
SITUATION
AND
BACKGROUND
READING FOR
UNIT III AND
UNIT IV

CASE LAW

ENACTED LAW

(STATE STATUTES)

You will be researching the research situation stated below for the following problem sets for Units III and IV:

Chapter 10 First Problem Set.	Paper Reporters and Digests
Chapter 10 Second Problem Set.	Computer-Based Research in Case Law
Chapter 11 Problem Set.	Case Citators
Chapter 12 First Problem Set.	State Paper Codes and Session Laws
Chapter 12 Second Problem Set.	Computer-Based Research in State Statutes

You will have a choice of states for some of these problem sets. Unless otherwise instructed by your professor, you should select the same state for all such problem sets. For other problem sets, you will be assigned a state.

We suggest that you leave pages 407–413 in your book (or at least do not turn them in to your professor), so you will have ready access to the research situation and background material as you work through each problem set.

Your Research Situation:

Your client, Per Johanson, has developed a new line of high-quality vitamins. For various reasons, Mr. Johanson has decided that instead of selling the vitamins through retail stores, he would rather sell his vitamins through a multi-level marketing distribution plan.

The distribution plan would use salespersons called vita-managers. Vita-managers would pay $250 to Mr. Johanson for the privilege of becoming a salesperson; in return Mr. Johanson would provide the individual with a badge, a sales record ledger, and fifty brochures describing the vitamins. Each vita-manager would be required to buy the product from Mr. Johanson at wholesale prices, which are 80% of retail prices. Mr. Johanson would not buy back unsold product, but vita-managers would not be required to buy product before entering into a contract with a customer at the retail level.

Mr. Johanson is hopeful that vita-managers will recruit additional vita-managers. If vita-manager A persuades B to become a vita-manager, A would then receive a 5% discount on the wholesale price of A's next vitamin purchase from Mr. Johanson. Vita-manager A could earn more than one 5% discount per wholesale purchase. Vita-manager A would not receive any portion of the $250 fee that B pays to Mr. Johanson or any monetary reward for product bought by B. All product at the wholesale level would be purchased from Mr. Johanson, not from other vita-managers.

Based on detailed market analysis, Mr. Johanson has selected the following states in which to begin his marketing plan: Alabama, Arizona, Illinois, Indiana, Minnesota, Missouri, New York, Ohio, Pennsylvania, and Texas. Mr. Johanson is aware that some marketing plans are deemed to be fraudulent or to violate state statutes that regulate or restrict pyramid schemes, multi-level marketing plans, and chain referrals. Mr. Johanson has tried—successfully, he hopes—not to structure his plan along the lines of a prohibited typical pyramid scheme. He would like you to examine the case and statutory law of your assigned state. Ignore federal law, such as Federal Trade Commission (FTC) or Securities Exchange Commission (SEC) regulation.

Assume that your research in secondary sources has yielded the following pertinent commentary, which we suggest you review before beginning each problem set.

Erwin S. Barbre, Annotation, *Validity of Pyramid Distribution Plan*, 54 A.L.R.3d 217, 220 (1974).

While bearing some similarity to the traditional referral selling plan,[3] the pyramid program differs from a referral selling plan in that under the latter the party who supplies the names of potential buyers is normally purchasing a product for his own consumption, while under the pyramid program, the party who brings another into the program is normally purchasing products for resale rather than his own consumption. Also, in a pyramid distribution program, the participants constitute the entire distribution system for the manufacturer of the product, while in a referral plan, the participant is merely a consumer who receives goods after they have gone through traditional distribution outlets.

---

[3]Described in the annotation at 14 ALR3d 1420, which deals with the enforceability of transactions entered into pursuant to referral sales arrangements, the traditional referral sales program is used in connection with house-to-house sales of high-cost consumer items, such as encyclopedias and color televisions. Under such a program, a purchaser is offered the opportunity to receive a commission to be applied against the purchase price of the article purchased if he submits a certain number of names of persons who might make a purchase and if those persons actually do make a purchase. In some instances, the plan may allow the consumer to earn commissions above the sales price of the article purchased.

Utah Legislative Survey–1983, 1984 Utah L. Rev. 115, 209-212

No. 1]   UTAH LEGISLATIVE SURVEY   209

A pyramid scheme is a fraudulent version of a multilevel marketing organization, which victimizes members of the organization. Multilevel marketing plans differ from conventional distribution in that each level in the multilevel marketing network is comprised of independent contractors, rather than employees.[640] Multilevel marketing also is different in that it is organized to expand in a pyramid fashion. Each distributor is encouraged to recruit additional distributors to work under him, thus allowing for multiple levels with an expanding number of distributors at lower levels.[641] Each distributor buys the product from the distributor above him in the distribution network and retails it to consumers or wholesales it to those below him in the distribution network, usually distributors whom he has recruited.[642] Distributors profit from sales made by their recruited distributors as well as from their own retail sales.[643]

Two factors distinguish pyramid schemes from legitimate multilevel marketing organizations. First, on joining the organization, new members of pyramid schemes must pay for the right to sell the product and for the right to recruit other distributors.[644] Typi-

---

accompanying text.

638. UTAH CODE ANN. § 76-6a-2(4) (Supp. 1983).

639. *See infra* notes 669 & 687-88 and accompanying text. Additionally, certain defenses to the charge of operating a pyramid scheme are eliminated. UTAH CODE ANN. § 76-6a-5 (Supp. 1983).

640. Comment, *Multi-Level or Pyramid Sales Systems: Fraud or Free Enterprise*, 18 S.D.L. REV. 358, 359-61 (1983). For a detailed description of one multilevel marketing organization, see Amway Corp., 93 F.T.C. 618, 634-78 (1979).

641. Comment, *supra* note 640, at 359-61.

642. *Id.*

643. *Id.*

644. Koscot Interplanetary, Inc., 86 F.T.C. 1106 (1975), *aff'd sub nom.* Turner v. FTC, 580 F.2d 701 (D.C. Cir. 1978). In 1975, the Federal Trade Commission defined an illegal pyramid scheme as one

> characterized by the payment by participants of money to the company in return for which they receive (1) the right to sell a product *and* (2) the right to receive in return for recruiting other participants into the program rewards which are unrelated to the sale of the product to ultimate users . . . . As is apparent, the presence of this second element, recruitment with rewards unrelated to product sales, is nothing more than an elaborate chain letter device in which individuals who pay a valuable consideration with the expectation of recouping it to some degree via recruitment are bound to be disappointed.

Id. at 1180. A pyramid scheme constitutes an unfair and deceptive act and practice and an unfair method of competition in violation of section 5 of the Federal Trade Commission Act. *Id.* (holding pyramid schemes to be in violation of 15 U.S.C. § 45 (1973)).

Although the emphasis on recruitment and the promise of future profits are key characteristics of pyramid schemes, pyramids are not always easily distinguishable from legitimate

cally a new member purchases those rights by buying an amount of nonreturnable inventory[645] and a portion of the money paid is retained by the person who recruited the new member.[646] Second, in pyramid schemes recruiting new distributors is not a means to selling more of the product but is, itself, a source of profit.[647] The product is relatively unimportant, except as a vehicle for recruitment.[648]

When these two factors become present in a multilevel marketing organization, the basis for creating wealth becomes unsound, thus often leading to the use of deception to recruit new members and eventually resulting in financial loss to at least some

---

multilevel marketing plans. Because multilevel marketing typically involves door-to-door selling, and door-to-door selling is a difficult occupation, multilevel marketing plans typically suffer from a high rate of attrition among their distributors. Three out of four Amway distributors, for example, quit after the first year, a turnover rate said to be lower than that of most direct selling companies. Amway Corp. 93 F.T.C. 618, 679 (1979). Of necessity, multilevel marketing plans emphasize and offer incentives for recruitment of new distributors. Hence, the distinction between a legitimate multilevel marketing plan and a pyramid scheme is a subtle one—it turns on whether the rewards offered for recruitment are derived primarily from the recruitment process itself or whether the rewards are derived from the enterprise of selling to consumers, the success of which, at least in part, is dependent on recruitment. Comment, *supra* note 640, at 361-65.

Furthermore, even legitimate multilevel marketing plans are subject to pyramid scheme abuses. In light of the difficulties of door-to-door sales, the stress on recruitment for the purpose of increased consumer sales easily can shift to an emphasis on recruitment per se, accompanied by misleading claims of easy profits, "inventory loading" (requiring or encouraging new distributors to purchase an excessive amount of inventory) or other related deceptive practices. *Id.* Amway Corp., for example, is a multilevel sales organization that appears to have come quite close to crossing over the line into illegal pyramid scheme activity. The Federal Trade Commission found that although Amway was not a pyramid scheme, it was guilty of deceptive recruitment practices similar to those typically used by pyramid schemes. Amway Corp., 93 F.T.C. at 659-70, 715-17, 729-32.

645. *See, e.g.,* Koscot Interplanetary, Inc., 86 F.T.C. 1106, 1179 (1975), *aff'd mem. sub nom.* Turner v. FTC, 580 F.2d 701 (D.C. Cir. 1978); Ger-Ro-Mar, Inc., 84 F.T.C. 95, 108-10 (1974).

646. Koscot Interplanetary, Inc., 86 F.T.C. 1106, 1179 (1975), *aff'd sub nom.* Turner v. FTC, 580 F.2d 701 (D.C. Cir. 1978). New members in the Koscot marketing plan paid an initial amount up to $5000 for inventory and for the right to recruit others; $2650 of the $5000 was received by the recruiting member. *Id.*

647. *Id.* at 1180.

648. Holiday Magic, Inc., 84 F.T.C. 748, 1035 (1974). In a suit against Koscot Interplanetary, Inc. for alleged pyramid scheme violations, a Kansas court found "[t]hat the sale of Koscot Cosmetics was an incidental part of the business conducted by the defendants; that the sale of cosmetics was used as a vehicle through which to conduct a spurious wholesale business with nothing much to wholesale except the sale of so-called 'positions' within the company." State *ex rel.* Sanborn v. Koscot Interplanetary, Inc., No. C 22475 (Dist. Ct. Sedgwick County, Kan. 1972), *quoted in* Comment, *supra* note 640, at 365. For a description of the recruiting techniques and promises employed in one major pyramid scheme, see Note, *Dare To Be Great, Inc.: A Case Study of Pyramid Sales Plan Regulation,* 33 Ohio St. L.J. 676, 676-86 (1972).

members of the organization. New members are recruited into pyramid schemes by promises of high profits to be made by recruiting additional distributors who will, in turn, recruit others.[649] Those promises rarely are fulfilled for the very reason that they appear so alluring to the uninitiated—the geometric increase in the number of new distributors as one level recruits another.[650] The fatal flaw in the scheme is that the number of new recruits needed to sustain the growing pyramid soon exceeds the available supply of potential recruits.[651] For example, a pyramid scheme in which each recruit would recruit five others would exceed the population of the United States at the thirteenth level.[652] When the point of market saturation is reached, which may occur quickly and unexpectedly, the pyramid collapses and a great many distributors are left with the worthless "right to recruit," accumulated debts from the costs of recruiting or nonreturnable inventory.[653] Because there is no sound basis for creating wealth, but money merely is channeled from the pockets of many to the pockets of a few, pyramid schemes typically engage in numerous deceptive practices such as promising unrealistically high earnings or claiming that recruiting and selling are easy.[654] The fundamental deception, however, lies in the fact that pyramid schemes are not true sales organizations[655] and market saturation precludes most members from ever recovering their investments.[656] Some courts have viewed pyramid schemes as disguised chain letter schemes, not organized to sell goods to consumers, but rather aimed at extracting money from their own members.[657]

649. Note, *Pyramid Schemes: Dare To Be Regulated*, 61 GEO. L.J. 1257, 1259 (1973).

650. Oregon Attorney General's Office, Multilevel Sales Plans in Oregon 2 (undated) (copy on file with UTAH L. REV.).

651. *Id.*

652. Comment, *supra* note 640, at 361 n.8. In addition to exhausting the supply of potential recruits, the geometric growth in the number of distributors also undercuts the possibility of success in making consumer sales. Annot., 54 A.L.R.3d 217, 220 (1973).

653. Note, *supra* note 648, at 686-87; Oregon Attorney General's Office, *supra* note 650, at 2.

654. Comment, *supra* note 640, at 363-69.

655. *See supra* note 648 and accompanying text.

656. Oregon Attorney General's Office, *supra* note 650, at 2.

657. *See, e.g.,* Koscot Interplanetary, Inc., 86 F.T.C. 1106, 1180 (1975), *aff'd sub nom.* Turner v. FTC, 580 F.2d 701 (D.C. Cir. 1978); Holiday Magic, Inc., 84 F.T.C. 748, 1035 (1974); People v. Koscot Interplanetary, Inc., 37 Mich. App. 447, 195 N.W.2d 43, 53 (1972). A chain letter is "[a] letter sent to a number of recipients requesting each to write similar letters to an equal number of recipients and often employed as a money-making scheme by the inclusion with each letter of a list of persons to whom money is to be sent." WEBSTER'S NEW INTERNATIONAL DICTIONARY 369 (3d ed. unabridged 1961). Like a pyramid scheme, a

212   UTAH LAW REVIEW   [1984: 115

chain letter is a recruiting scheme that grows downward from its origin, expanding at its base like a pyramid. Each new member recruits additional members who, in turn, recruit more members. An individual joins a chain letter by paying money to members higher in the chain in the hope that he will receive a greater amount of money from the growing number of members who join after him. One who is fortunate enough to join a chain letter early in its growth may profit by receiving money from others joining later. However, because a chain letter is only a scheme for channeling money from the pockets of many persons into the hands of a few, and because the scheme cannot expand indefinitely, it will collapse with most members losing money.

Restatement (Second) of Torts §§ 525, 526, 531, 537, 538 (1966).

§ 525. Liability for Fraudulent Misrepresentation

One who fraudulently makes a misrepresentation of fact, opinion, intention or law for the purpose of inducing another to act or to refrain from action in reliance upon it, is subject to liability to the other in deceit for pecuniary loss caused to him by his justifiable reliance upon the misrepresentation.

§ 526. Conditions Under Which Misrepresentation Is Fraudulent (Scienter)

A misrepresentation is fraudulent if the maker
(a) knows or believes that the matter is not as he represents it to be,
(b) does not have the confidence in the accuracy of his representation that he states or implies, or
(c) knows that he does not have the basis for his representation that he states or implies.

§ 531. General Rule (Expectation of Influencing Conduct)

One who makes a fraudulent misrepresentation is subject to liability to the persons or class of persons whom he intends or has reason to expect to act or to refrain from action in reliance upon the misrepresentation, for pecuniary loss suffered by them through their justifiable reliance in the type of transaction in which he intends or has reason to expect their conduct to be influenced.

§ 537. General Rule (Justifiable Reliance)

The recipient of a fraudulent misrepresentation can recover against its maker for pecuniary loss resulting from it if, but only if,
(a) he relies on the misrepresentation in acting or refraining from action, and
(b) his reliance is justifiable.

§ 538. Materiality of Misrepresentation

(1) Reliance upon a fraudulent misrepresentation is not justifiable unless the matter misrepresented is material.
(2) The matter is material if
    (a) a reasonable man would attach importance to its existence or nonexistence in determining his choice of action in the transaction in question; or
    (b) the maker of the representation knows or has reason to know that its recipient regards or is likely to regard the matter as important in determining his choice of action, although a reasonable man would not so regard it.

FIRST PROBLEM SET FOR CHAPTER 10. PAPER REPORTERS AND DIGESTS

Your Name   Professor

_____   _____

Your research situation is stated on pages 407–408, followed by some useful excerpts from secondary sources. Your secondary-source research has suggested the following issue to pursue in case law:

What are the elements of common law fraud? Do these facts meet the elements of common law fraud?

Look for a case that thoroughly lays out the elements of fraud for your jurisdiction. You need NOT find a case involving a marketing plan similar to Mr. Johanson's idea. Do not address statutory law, which will be covered in later problem sets.

Circle the state in which you will perform your research:

Alabama	Missouri
Arizona	New York
Illinois	Ohio
Indiana	Pennsylvania
Minnesota	Texas

1. List at least five research terms suggested by the research situation and the secondary sources we have provided.

_____

_____

2. Name the appellate courts in your selected state and the reporters in which their recent (1990s and later) decisions appear. (Remember that Table T.1 in *The Bluebook* provides this information.)

_____

_____

_____

3. Which West digests cover cases decided by the appellate court(s) in the state you selected?

_____

_____

4. Select one of those digests. Identify several potentially useful topics and key numbers. List them, and explain how you found them. Example: I looked up the following terms in the Descriptive Word Index: . . . .

_____

_____

_____

5. Assemble the main volumes and supplements (including pocket parts and supplement pamphlets) needed to research one of the topics you have identified, back to 1970. Identify the digest and series, types of volumes you gathered, and their dates. Example: state digest, second series, main volume 1984, pocket part 1999.

_____

_____

6. Skim the digest paragraphs under promising key topics and numbers until you locate the case listed below. (We are directing you to a single case to facilitate your professor's evaluation of your work on the following questions.)

Alabama:	*Voyager Guaranty Insurance Company* (1993)
Arizona:	*Peery* (1978)
Illinois:	*Jeffrey M. Goldberg & Associates* (1994)
Indiana:	*Soft Water Utilities* (1974)
Minnesota:	*Gorham* (1995)
Missouri:	*Next Day Motor Freight* (1997)
New York:	*Graubard Mollen Dannett & Horowitz* (1995)
Ohio:	*Walter* (1987)
Pennsylvania:	*Shoemaker* (1997)
Texas:	*Brush* (1998)

Locate a digest paragraph describing that case in the digest.

(a) Record the full reference to that case, as it appears in the digest.

_____

_____

(b) Under which topic and key number did you find the digest paragraph?

_____

7. Locate that case in a West reporter, read it, and provide the following information about the case:

(a) the elements of fraud

_____

_____

_____

_____

_____

_____

_____

_____

_____

(b) the number(s) of the headnote(s) corresponding to the definition of fraud

_____

(c) whether there is a concurrence or dissent and, if so, its main point

_____

_____

_____

8. Provide two proper citations for your case:

(a) if you were writing to the court that decided the case

_____

(b) if you were writing to a court in a different state

_____

Notes: In some situations your answers to (a) and (b) will be the same. If you do or may need information beyond that provided in the West reporter to properly cite your case, state here what is or may be missing.

9. What would your next research step be, as to the case you read and cited?

_____

10. Locate a recent advance sheet for the West reporter you have been using.

(a) Record the reporter volume(s) and page numbers contained in that advance sheet.

_____

(b) Locate the digest material in that advance sheet. Does it contain any digest paragraphs under the topic and key numbers you have been researching? If so, note the name(s) of the case(s). If not, write "none."

_____

_____

11. Based on your reading for this problem set, should Mr. Johanson be concerned about fraud? Why, or why not?

_____

_____

_____

_____

_____

_____

_____

_____

SECOND PROBLEM SET FOR CHAPTER 10. COMPUTER-BASED RESEARCH IN CASE LAW

Your Name   Professor

_____   _____

Your research situation is stated on pages 407–408, followed by some useful excerpts from secondary sources. Your secondary-source research has suggested the following issue to pursue in case law:

Do these facts meet the elements of common law fraud?

Do not address statutory law, which will be covered in later problem sets.

For this problem set, research the case law of **Connecticut.**

1. Select a computer-based (online or CD-ROM) source for Connecticut state and federal cases that permits at least Boolean and natural-language searching. Indicate your choice:

        LEXIS _____   Westlaw _____   Other _____

2. Select the database (or portion of a CD-ROM) containing decisions of the Connecticut state courts. State the name of the database. Which courts' decisions are included, and, as to each court, what are the years of coverage?

_____

_____

_____

3. First run one or more Boolean searches until you obtain a reasonable number of cases, including at least one pertinent case.

(a) Write out your successful search.

_____

_____

_____

(b) By running that search, what did you ask the computer to do?

_____

_____

_____

_____

_____

4. Print the list of citations from that search, as well as the first pages of up to three pertinent cases. Attach your print-outs to this problem set, and mark them Q4.

5. Now run one or more natural-language searches until you obtain at least one pertinent case. Write out your successful search, including any revisions you made with the computer program's assistance.

_____

_____

_____

_____

6. Print the list of citations from that search, as well as the first pages of up to three pertinent cases. Attach your print-outs to this problem set, and mark them Q6. If the cases for this question are the same as for Question 4, you need not make additional first-page print-outs, rather mark the same print-out Q6 as well as Q4.

7. Does your source permit any other types of searches for pertinent case law by subject matter? If so, try the additional method(s). Describe your research process and results. Example: On Westlaw, I searched for the following key numbers: . . . ; I obtained . . . cases, the following being most useful: . . . .

_____

_____

_____

_____

_____

_____

_____

_____

8. Select the most useful case you have found through your online research. Read that case (you may want to read the case in a reporter or download or print it, rather than read it online). State the name of the case. Based on that case, should Mr. Johanson be concerned about fraud? Why, or why not?

_____

_____

_____

_____

_____

_____

_____

_____

9. Select a database (or portion of a CD-ROM) containing decisions of the federal district court for Connecticut. State the name of the database. What are the years of coverage for that court?

_____

_____

10. Assume that a colleague has alerted you to a potentially pertinent decision from the federal district court for Connecticut, decided by Judge Eginton in 1993 or 1994. An employee sued his employer, Textron or Omnitron, for fraud or misrepresentation. Run one or more searches to locate the case.

(a) Write out your successful search.

_____

_____

(b) By running that search, what did you ask the computer to do?

_____

_____

_____

_____

11. Print out the first page of that case, attach your print-out to this problem set, and mark it Q10.

PROBLEM SET FOR CHAPTER 11. CASE CITATORS

Your Name _____   Professor _____

Your research situation is stated on pages 407–408. Assume that you are researching that situation in **New Jersey**. You have located the fairly lengthy case of *Kugler v. Koscot Interplanetary, Inc.*, decided by the Superior Court of New Jersey, Chancery Division in 1972. Among other points, the court discussed whether Koscot's business amounted to "fraud" under a broadly worded New Jersey consumer fraud statute. Here are excerpts from the opening pages of its report at 293 A.2d 682, with pertinent headnotes bracketed:

George F. KUGLER, Jr., Attorney General of New Jersey, Plaintiff,

v.

KOSCOT INTERPLANETARY, INC., a Florida corporation, and Glenn W. Turner, Defendants.

Superior Court of New Jersey, Chancery Division.

July 26, 1972.

Action against manufacturer and its principal stockholder for alleged violations of Consumer Fraud Act, Antitrust Act, and Corporation Act. The Superior Court, Chancery Division, Mehler, J. S. C., held that manufacturer's multilevel distribution system based on pyramid sales violated Consumer Fraud Act and Antitrust Act and that manufacturer was subject to fine for doing business in State without qualifying.

Judgment accordingly.

1. Fraud ⊜1

Statements made to prospective purchasers which are aimed to induce purchase by them may not be characterized as mere puffery.

2. Trade Regulation ⊜861

Consumer Fraud Act may be violated even though one has not in fact been misled or deceived by an unlawful act or practice. N.J.S.A. 56:8–1 et seq., 2, 8.

3. Trade Regulation ⊜861

Where manufacturer which operated multilevel distribution system based on pyramid sales provided training manual used by distributors to induce others to enter into distributorship contracts with manufacturer and most meetings for prospective distributors were organized and conducted by manufacturer's employee, manufacturer could not escape liability for misrepresentations on ground that distributors who made misrepresentations were independent contractors. N.J.S.A. 56:8–1 et seq., 2, 8.

4. Contracts ⊜143

Courts of equity will go behind form of contract or relationship to its substance.

5. Trade Regulation ⊜861

Manufacturer's referral or pyramid sales practice was prohibited by Consumer Fraud Act. N.J.S.A. 56:8–1 et seq., 2, 8.

6. Trade Regulation ⊜861

Where manufacturer operated multilevel distribution system based on pyramid sales and prospective distributors were unaware of pitfalls of market saturation, State had vital interest in protection of its

---

KUGLER v. KOSCOT INTERPLANETARY, INC.   N. J.   **683**
Cite as 293 A.2d 682

citizens from fraud and from consequences of their own ignorance or folly. N.J.S.A. 56:8-1 et seq., 2, 8.

7. Trade Regulation ⊜861

Fact that manufacturer's multilevel distribution system based on pyramid sales had quota for number of distributors in State did not save program from constituting violation of Consumer Fraud Act. N.J.S.A. 56:8-1 et seq., 2, 8.

8. Trade Regulation ⊜864

Evidence established that representations made to prospective distributors to enter into distributorship with manufacturer which operated multilevel distribution system based on pyramid sales violated Consumer Fraud Act. N.J.S.A. 56:8-2.

9. Trade Regulation ⊜864

Purchasers of distributorships in multilevel distribution plan based on pyramid sales were ascertainable class with sufficient community of interest to justify action by Attorney General against manufacturer which operated multilevel distribution system for violation of Consumer Fraud Act. N.J.S.A. 56:8-1 et seq., 2, 8.

10. Trade Regulation ⊜864

Attorney General is not required to give notice of class action when he commences class action for violation of Consumer Fraud Act. N.J.S.A. 56:8-1 et seq.; R. 4:32-2; R. 4:32-2(b).

11. Courts ⊜97(6)

Federal decisions interpreting sections 1 and 2 of the Sherman Act provide court with guidelines for interpreting similar sections of state Antitrust Act. N.J.S.A. 56:9-3, 4, subd. a, 10, subds. a, c, 18; Sherman Anti-Trust Act, §§ 1, 2, 15 U.S.C.A. §§ 1, 2.

12. Contracts ⊜105

Contract, legal at time it was entered into, violates law proscribing its terms and effect if it continues in force after passage of law.

13. Monopolies ⊜17(1)

Where distributors participating in manufacturer's multilevel distributorship system agreed by terms of their contract that they were independent contractors, and contract required each distributor to indicate his status as independent contractor at all times and risk of loss of merchandise was transferred to distributor, distributors were independent contractors for purposes of application of state Antitrust Act. N.J.S.A. 56:9-1 et seq.

14. Monopolies ⊜17(1.3)

Where manufacturer which operated multilevel distribution system had regulations limiting persons from whom and to whom distributors could purchase and sell manufacturer's products, manner and method by which distributors sell or advertise product, and right of distributors to associate and cooperate with other distributors in retail sales effort, manufacturer was guilty of unlawful restraint of trade and commerce in violation of state Antitrust Act. N.J.S.A. 56:9-3.

15. Monopolies ⊜30

Evidence failed to establish that price differentials and overrides established by manufacturer which operated multilevel distribution system tended to create monopoly in violation of state Antitrust Act. N.J.S.A. 56:9-4, subd. a.

16. Monopolies ⊜30

Antitrust Act provision that violator of Act shall be liable to penalty of not more than greater of $100,000 or $500 per day for each and every day of said violation did not mean that $100,000 was minimum penalty to be imposed on manufacturer which violated Act in its operation of multilevel distribution system, and court had discretion to impose lesser penalty. N.J.S.A. 56:9-10, subd. a.

17. Monopolies ⊜30

Penalty of $25,000 would be assessed against manufacturer which violated state

684   N. J.   293 ATLANTIC REPORTER, 2d SERIES

Antitrust Act in operating multilevel distribution system. N.J.S.A. 56:9–10, subd. a.

18. Corporations ⟨key⟩652

Penalty of $1,000 would be imposed on manufacturer which was foreign corporation and which did business in State without procuring certificate of authority. N. J.S.A. 14A:13–3.

19. Corporations ⟨key⟩1.4(1)

There are exceptions to rule that corporation is entity wholly separate and distinct from individuals who compose it and that entity may not be disregarded.

20. Corporations ⟨key⟩1.4(2)

Equity will go behind corporate form where necessary to do justice.

21. Corporations ⟨key⟩1.6(13)

Where party who held 95% of stock of corporation, with wife holding other 5%, authorized corporation to issue scripts containing false statements which formed basis for fraudulent representations made to prospective distributors of corporation's products, completely identified himself with corporation and was active in corporation's activities, corporation was his alter ego and stockholder would be held personally liable for corporation's violation of Consumer Fraud Act and violation of state Antitrust Act. N.J.S.A. 56:8–1 et seq., 56:9–1 et seq.

22. Process ⟨key⟩166

Failure of nonresident to object to service of process by answer or timely motion waived defect in allowance and service of process. R. 4:4–4(e); R. 4:6–2; R. 4:6–3; R. 4:6–7.

23. Monopolies ⟨key⟩24(7)

Trade Regulation ⟨key⟩864

Where manufacturer was guilty of violating Consumer Fraud Act and state Antitrust Act, injunction against further vio-

lations would be issued. N.J.S.A. 56:8–8, 56:9–10, subd. a.

24. Trade Regulation ⟨key⟩864

Where manufacturer and principal stockholder had been found guilty of violating Consumer Fraud Act by operation of multilevel distribution system, manufacturer and stockholder would be ordered to refund to all distributors in State who asked for refund all monies paid by such distributors. N.J.S.A. 56:8–1 et seq.

———◆———

Richard W. Grieves, Deputy Atty. Gen., and Elias Abelson, Asst. Atty. Gen., for plaintiff.

Gross, Demetrakis & Donohue, Hackensack (Richard J. Donohue, Hackensack), for defendants.

MEHLER, J. S. C.

This is an action brought by the Attorney General under the Consumer Fraud Act, N.J.S.A. 56:8–1 et seq., the New Jersey Antitrust Act, N.J.S.A. 56:9–1 et seq., and the Corporation Act, N.J.S.A. 14A:13–11.

The defendants are Koscot Interplanetary, Inc. (Koscot), a Florida corporation, which is engaged in the sale and distribution of cosmetics through non-exclusive distributorships throughout the United States, and Glenn W. Turner, who founded Koscot, and at all times relevant to this action was chairman of its Board of Directors and its principal, if not sole stockholder.

The Attorney General charges that defendants have employed fraudulent and deceptive practices in connection with the sale of Koscot distributorships to residents of New Jersey and that its multilevel distribution program is predicated upon a referral sales and pyramiding concept which is inherently fraudulent and deceptive within the meaning of N.J.S.A. 56:8–2. At the commencement of this action that sec-

1. Peruse the following excerpt from the 1994 bound volume of *Shepard's Atlantic Reporter Citations.*

ATLANTIC REPORTER, 2d SERIES   **Vol. 293**

9A3203s
25A4947n

—671—

Bialkowski
v Ridgefield
1972
(120NJS194)
s 287A2d479
s 299A2d76
342A2d587
343A2d[3]161
353A2d156
353A2d[2]157
362A2d1228
372A2d683
f 457A2d[1]1211

—672—

New Jersey
v Morales
1972
(120NJS197)
s 299A2d75
301A2d[4]735
301A2d[5]735
319A2d260
319A2d[7]261
330A2d[4]621
371A2d[7]770
406A2d[2]212
446A2d[4]1216
601A2d[1]204
Calif
108CaR96
Mich
234NW470
257NW750
S C
211SE658
Va
283SE200
36LE1089n

—676—

New Jersey
v Horn
1972
(120NJS203)
s 283A2d561
329A2d[1]101
397A2d[3]1107
410A2d[1]65
512A2d[1]547
Ind
395NE815
75A3376s

—678—

New Jersey
v Sidoti
1972
(120NJS208)
s 280A2d864
s 341A2d670
300A2d[8]349
308A2d[6]83
d 349A2d[6]137
f 350A2d[4]486
380A2d[1]708
403A2d[1]4
427A2d[7]546
427A2d[6]547
450A2d[1]968
484A2d1267
534A2d[1]35
f 540A2d[6]236
j 561A2d582
Minn
337NW656
N Y
353NYS2d990

—682—

Kugler v
Koscot
Interplanetary
Inc.
1972
(120NJS216)
295A2d[10]387
325A2d[14]515
326A2d101
365A2d[24]964
370A2d[2]24
382A2d[23]47
383A2d[11]1184
385A2d[10]291
405A2d[19]873
405A2d[20]873
429A2d[24]430
445A2d[19]1156
445A2d[20]1156
481A2d[4]832
497A2d544
506A2d[16]384
510A2d1201
510A2d[5]1202
515A2d249
527A2d[16]1375
565A2d[3]1136
618A2d[5]375
624A2d[20]617
Cir. 2
545FS[24]73
Cir. 3
843F2d[21]151
567FS549
784FS[20]1165
70BRW[21]851
95BRW335
95BRW[21]338

Conn
351A2d[5]884
Pa
321A2d[3]693
Ala
283So2d177
Calif
141CaR26
569P2d131
Ill
321NE392
461NE82
471NE242
Kan
512P2d421
Ky
600SW462
La
354So2d775
Mass
316NE756
Mo
600SW176
Nev
530P2d110
N M
741P2d439
N Y
360NYS2d494
N C
284SE337
54A21187s
54A3222n
54A3234n
89A3496n

—706—

Kugler v
Haitian
Tours Inc.
1972
(120NJS260)
315A2d[2]685
391A2d[2]538
Cir. 1
835F2d[2]942
Cir. 2
77BRW381
Del
542A2d1203
Fla
297So2d306
N Y
496NYS2d660
13A31419s
59A31237n
89A3413n
89A3508n

—711—

B & L Motor
Freight Inc. v
Heymann
1972
(120NJS270)
a 311A2d184
380A2d1191
510A2d303
f 510A2d[4]305
510A2d[6]305
510A2d[7]305
510A2d[8]305
f 510A2d[3]307
534A2d[4]15
q 534A2d[4]16
j 544A2d36
Me
503A2d218
Okla
806P2d602
17A2421s

—720—

Inganamort v
Fort Lee
1972
(120NJS286)
a 303A2d298
s 299A2d721
cc 371A2d34
cc 362FS581
294A2d436
295A2d13
301A2d486
f 301A2d[15]492
330A2d[2]645
342A2d[4]890
e 344A2d343
350A2d[4]31
350A2d[1]832
350A2d[1]733
356A2d741
357A2d[10]317
f 359A2d[1]868
365A2d[10]13
365A2d[7]241
380A2d[12]1192
399A2d[4]1032
404A2d1193
412A2d820
e 416A2d[19]359
436A2d[12]941
476A2d[17]276
493A2d590
624A2d[12]1375
628A2d[4]826
Cir. 3
605FS[9]1166
Md
306A2d[2]521
306A2d[1]543
Fla
305So2d766

339So2d236

—744—

Riley v Savary
1972
(120NJS331)
307A2d[5]573
324A2d[5]587
380A2d[5]1150
Cir. 3
395FS[5]93
40A4153n
40A4158n

—747—

New Jersey v
Palendrano
1972
(120NJS336)
303A2d891

—752—

New Jersey
v Anderson
1972
(120NJS345)
a 333A2d291
342A2d[2]553
Colo
626P2d736
Iowa
286NW159

—755—

Barry v Bank
of New
Hampshire
1972
(112NH226)
s 304A2d879
s 348A2d364
315A2d[3]186
Cir. 2
58BRW891
17A31010s
30A39s
100A376n
100A31015n
100A31077n
4A4941n

—757—

Whitten
Oil Inc. v
Fireman's Fund
Insurance Co.
1972
(112NH257)
328A2d781

365A2d[2]745
Mo
550SW194
58A348n
58A3111n

—760—

Corbeil v
Rouslin
1972
(112NH295)
304A2d[2]371
319A2d[1]299
498A2d[1]723
32A481n

—762—

Stephenson
v Starks
1972
(112NH291)
339A2d[1]31
f 343A2d646
359A2d[3]197

—764—

Fisk v Atlantic
National
Insurance Co.
1972
(112NH255)
s 236A2d688
Ind
448NE1228

—766—

New
Hampshire
v Martineau
1972
(112NH278)
cc 175A2d814
cc 196A2d52
cc 342A2d634
cc 369US879
cc 369US881
cc 8LE282
cc 8LE283
cc 82SC1153
cc 82SC1155
cc 495FS287
367A2d[2]1337
498A2d[1]328
Cir. 1
655F2d[2]2
Cir. 9
367FS[2]86
410FS[2]966
Md
297A2d[2]701

1583

Answer the following questions with the information provided by the excerpt on page 426:

(a) Where, in addition to 293 A.2d 682, is *Kugler* published?

_____

(b) Did a higher court review the superior court decision? Explain.

_____

(c) Has *Kugler* been cited in subsequent decisions of New Jersey state courts? If so, in how many cases?

_____

(d) Has *Kugler* been cited in subsequent federal court cases? If so, in how many cases?

_____

(e) Has *Kugler* been cited in subsequent decisions in state court cases outside New Jersey? If so, how many states?

_____

(f) Has any New Jersey court cited *Kugler* for the propositions of concern to you? (Note the headnote numbers in the excerpt on pages 423–425.) If so, provide the listings for those cases.

_____

(g) On page 426, highlight or circle the listings for the three to five cases you would read first.

(h) What else do you need to do before you are done Shepardizing *Kugler* in paper?

_____

2. Select an electronic citator, and indicate your choice below:

KeyCite on Westlaw _____ Shepard's online on LEXIS _____

Enter the *Kugler* citation, and examine the results. Then answer the following questions, and make the requested print-outs:

(a) Where, aside from 293 A.2d 682, is *Kugler* published?

_____

(b) Is *Kugler* good law? Explain.

_____

_____

_____

_____

(c) To focus on mandatory precedents, restrict your display to New Jersey state court cases. Print out that display, attach it to this problem set, and mark it Q2(c). On the print-out, highlight or circle the three to five cases you would read first, and jot a brief note of explanation of your choices on the print-out.

(d) Now focus on cases from any jurisdiction that appear to discuss the propositions of concern to you. You may use a headnote restriction in KeyCite or Shepard's; you also may use a focus search in Shepard's. (Note: West has reclassified some of the headnotes, from Trade Regulation to Consumer Protection, since *Kugler* was published in paper. The numbers of the pertinent headnotes have not changed.) Explain how you restricted your search.

_____

_____

_____

_____

Print out that display, attach it to this problem set, and mark it Q2(d). On the print-out, highlight or circle the three to five cases that you would read first, and jot a brief note of explanation of your choices on the print-out.

(e) Peruse the list of citing secondary sources. List here up to three potentially useful secondary sources (by volume, abbreviation of the source, and page number).

_____

_____

_____

First Problem Set for Chapter 12. State Paper Codes and Session Laws

Your Name   Professor

_____   _____

    Your research situation is stated on pages 407–408, followed by some useful excerpts from secondary sources. Your secondary-source research has suggested the following issue to pursue in statutory law:

> *Does Mr. Johanson's business plan fall within the scope of any state statutes concerning pyramid schemes, multi-level marketing plans, chain referrals, or the like? Could the state prohibit the business from operating?*

Assume that this topic is governed by a state statute specifically addressing pyramid schemes, multi-level marketing plans, or chain referrals.

    Circle the state in which you will perform your research:

Alabama	Missouri
Arizona	New York
Illinois	Ohio
Indiana	Pennsylvania
Minnesota	Texas

    1. List at least five research terms suggested by the research situation and the secondary sources we have provided.

_____

_____

    2. Name the statutory code(s) for your jurisdiction. (Remember that Table T.1 in *The Bluebook* lists codes for the various states.)

_____

_____

    3. Identify the pertinent statute in the annotated code, in paper, for your state. Describe your research process. Example: I looked up the following terms in the index: . . . .

_____

_____

_____

4. Assemble the volumes you need to locate the current language of the pertinent statute: generally a bound volume, a pocket part or supplement pamphlet for the bound volume, and soft-cover updates covering the entire code (typically shelved at the end of the code). Give the types of volumes, including their dates of coverage, you must use to be sure your statutory research is current.

_____

_____

5. Review the pertinent statute carefully. Read especially carefully the provisions needed to answer the two following questions:

(a) How does the statute define pyramid schemes that are prohibited by the statute? Note the section(s) you used for your answer.

_____

_____

_____

_____

_____

_____

_____

_____

_____

(b) Does the statute grant a state official, such as an attorney general or county attorney, the power to seek a court order restraining or enjoining a prohibited pyramid scheme? Note the section(s) you used for your answer.

_____

_____

_____

6. Provide the proper citation for the section(s) you used to answer Question 5(a).

_____

7. Examine the statutory history notes following the section (or the first section if you used more than one) you used to answer Question 5(a).

(a) State the year that statutory section was originally enacted, and give the session law reference for the original act. (You need not use proper citation form.)

_____

(b) If the code section has been amended since it was first enacted, note the reference to the most recent amendment by its session law citation. (You need not use proper citation form.)

_____

(c) If you were researching a situation that occurred on April 1, 1995, would the language of the current statute have been in effect then? Explain your answer.

_____

_____

_____

_____

(d) If a different, earlier version of the statute was in effect on April 1, 1995, what source would you examine to find the statutory language that was in effect then?

_____

8. Examine the annotation for the section(s) you used to answer Question 5(a).

(a) List the names of up to three cases, if any, that could be pertinent to your research situation. **Note:** If you were doing actual research, you would, of course, read the cases, but you need not do so for this problem set. (You need not use proper citation form.)

_____

_____

_____

_____

(b) List the references to one or two secondary sources, if any, that could be pertinent to your research situation.

_____

_____

_____

_____

9. Based on your reading for this problem set, should Mr. Johanson be concerned about the statute? Why, or why not?

_____

_____

_____

_____

_____

_____

_____

_____

_____

SECOND PROBLEM SET FOR CHAPTER 12. COMPUTER-BASED RESEARCH IN STATE STATUTES

Your Name   Professor

_____   _____

Your research situation is stated on pages 407–408, followed by some useful excerpts from secondary sources. Your secondary-source research has suggested the following issue of statutory law:

Does Mr. Johanson's business plan fall within the scope of any state statutes concerning pyramid schemes, multi-level marketing plans, chain referrals, or the like? Could the state prohibit the business from operating?

Assume that this topic is governed by a state statute specifically addressing pyramid schemes, multi-level marketing plans, or chain referrals.

For this problem set, research the law of **Virginia.**

1. Select a computer-based (online or CD-ROM) source for Virginia statutes, including annotation materials, that permits Boolean searching and at least one other search method (such as natural-language searching or browsing of a table of contents). Indicate your choice:

    LEXIS _____   Westlaw _____   Other _____

2. Select the pertinent database (or portion of a CD-ROM). State its name. How recent is the information in that database?

_____

_____

3. First run one or more Boolean searches, in the full text of the statutes and annotations, until you obtain a reasonable number of statutory sections, including pertinent sections.

(a) Write out your successful search.

_____

_____

_____

(b) By running that search, what did you ask the computer to do?

_____

_____

_____

_____

4. Print the list of citations from that search, as well as the section of the statute that defines the statute's term for illegal pyramid schemes and its annotation. Attach your print-outs to this problem set, and mark them Q4. Peruse the annotation to that section. On the print-out, highlight or circle the references to up to three cases you would read to further your understanding of the statute.

5. Browse through the three sections preceding the definitional section and the three sections following the definitional section.

(a) List the section numbers and titles of whichever of those six sections addresses pyramid schemes.

_____

_____

_____

_____

_____

_____

(b) Do any of those sections indicate whether a state official can seek an injunction against an illegal pyramid scheme? Explain.

_____

_____

_____

6. Return to the definitional section. Does the service you are using provide any indication that that section has recently been or may soon be amended? If so, explain what you have learned.

_____

_____

_____

7. Now search for the definitional section in the same database, but by a different method. Describe your research process. Example: I ran the following natural-language search: . . . .

_____

_____

_____

_____

8. Shift to a session law database for Virginia.

(a) What is the name of the database?

_____

(b) What search would you enter in that database to locate new legislation on your situation?

_____

_____

(c) Run that search. What did you learn?

_____

_____

9. Now select a computer-based source for Virginia state cases that permits Boolean searching.

(a) Indicate the source and database (or portion of a CD-ROM) that you have chosen.

_____

(b) What search would you enter to locate cases, within the past year, that cite the definitional section of the statute?

_____

(c) Run that search. What did you learn?

_____

_____

_____

10. Finally, select an online statutory citator (KeyCite on Westlaw or Shepard's online on LEXIS), and enter the citation of the definitional section of the statute. Print out the display, and attach the print-out, marked Q10, to this problem set. Compare the information in the display to the information in the annotation you printed out for Q4 and the results of your search for Question 9; write a check beside any new information that appears on your Q10 display. On the Q10 print-out, highlight or circle the references to two to three sources you would read first, and jot a brief note of explanation of your choices on the print-out.

11. Based on your reading for this problem set, should Mr. Johnason be concerned about the state statute? Why, or why not?

_____

_____

_____

_____

_____

_____

_____

_____

_____

ENACTED LAW
(FEDERAL STATUTES)

You will be selecting one of the research situations below for the following problem sets for Unit IV:

Chapter 12 Third Problem Set.   Federal Codes and Session Laws
Chapter 13 Problem Set.   Legislative Process Materials

Unless otherwise instructed by your professor, you should select one research situation to work for both problem sets.

We suggest that you leave pages 437–440 in your book (or at least do not turn them in to your professor), so you will have ready access to the research situations as you work your way through both problem sets.

Research Situation A:

Your client, Amy Frazier, applied for food stamps when she lost her job. When she filed her application, she owned a car with a fair market value of $7,500, but she owed $8,000 on the loan that she had taken to finance the purchase of the car. Her application for food stamps was denied because the fair market value of her car exceeded the amount permitted by statute in the eligibility formula for food stamps. Your research in secondary sources has suggested the following issue: *Is a car an "inaccessible resource," so that it should be excluded from calculation of a household's resources for purposes of determining eligibility for food stamps, if the lien incumbrance on the car exceeds its fair market value?*

Research Situation B:

Your client, Alice Crocker, was employed by a nonprofit corporation. At the end of her probationary period, she received a satisfactory evaluation, but her supervisor noted concerns about her ability to meet deadlines. During Ms. Crocker's maternity leave, her supervisor allegedly discovered that she had failed to acknowledge eighty-five donor gifts, and he notified her that she would be demoted when she returned to work. Alice was told that her new job paid half of what her other position paid. She declined to accept the job because of the pay. The person who took it received almost twice as much as she was offered. Alice believes that her demotion may have been based on her status as a new mother, since her supervisor told her that she was being given a position "for a new mom to handle." Your research in secondary sources has suggested the following issue: *Is discrimination based on one's status as a new mother prohibited by the federal statute that prohibits discrimination based on pregnancy, childbirth, or related medical conditions?*

Research Situation C:

Your client, Susan Jackson, is suing a debt collection agency. She claims that on three separate occasions an attorney working for the agency failed to identify that he was employed by the agency when speaking to her by phone, in violation of a federal statute that regulates fair debt collection practices for consumer debts. Your research in secondary sources has suggested the following issue: *In a consumer action against a debt collection agency for unfair fair debt collection practices, is a plaintiff entitled to an award of statutory damages for each violation proved, or is a plaintiff limited to a single award of statutory damages per lawsuit?*

Research Situation D:

Your client, Maria Gonzales, wants to challenge her state's voter purge law. That law provides for cancellation of a voter's registration if the voter fails to vote within the last two years, although a voter whose registration is cancelled may re-register at any time. Ms. Gonzales has evidence that African-American and Latino voters are purged from the voter registration rolls at a higher rate than white voters, and she believes that the law adversely affects the civil rights of minorities. Your research in secondary sources has suggested the following issue to research in federal statutes: *Does a state voter purge law constitute a per se violation of federal voting rights statutes? If not, what criteria apply to determine if the voter purge law violates federal law?*

Research Situation E:

Your client, Roger Kurkowski, is a gunmaker and gun collector. He recently filed with the Bureau of Alcohol, Tobacco and Firearms an application to make and register a machine gun for his personal collection. His application was denied. Your research in secondary sources has suggested the following issue: *Does a federal statute prohibit a private citizen from possessing a machine gun that he or she did not possess when the statute was enacted?*

Research Situation F:

Your client, the Campus Coalition for Students with Disabilities, wants to challenge the failure of your state's state universities and colleges to provide voter registration services on campus. Your research in secondary sources has suggested the following issue: *Do national voter registration laws require state institutions of higher education to serve as voter registration agencies for persons with disabilities?*

Research Situation G:

Your client, a company whose CEO is Phong Nguyen, manufactures medical devices used in back surgery. Ms. Nguyen is unhappy with a set of guidelines on acute lower back pain that the federal government distributes to doctors. These guidelines suggest that doctors should rarely use the medical devices her company manufactures to treat back problems. A group of experts and consumers convened by the federal Agency for Health Care Policy created the guidelines. Ms. Nguyen argues that the group is an "advisory committee" and, since it failed to follow "advisory committee" regulations, distribution of its guidelines should be discontinued. Your research in secondary sources has suggested the following issue: *Do federal statutes governing advisory committees apply to a panel whose stated purpose is to advise private health care practitioners, if Congress also intends that the panel address a medical condition of importance to the Medicare program and the federal government subsequently uses some of the panel's work?*

Research Situation H:

Your client, Amanda Lynn, was fired from her job as a mill worker at a local paper factory. Shortly before her termination, Ms. Lynn injured her back. She saw her doctor, who manipulated her back and recommended that she take three days off work for the injury. He did not prescribe any medication or recommend any treatment. She had one follow-up appointment with the doctor, who excused her from work for another week. Ms. Lynn missed ten days of work beyond those excused by her doctor, and after she returned to work her attendance was erratic. She was soon terminated. Her termination notice stated that she was discharged for poor performance, and her employment record shows that she had been placed on a performance improvement plan for eight reasons, including absentee-ism. She claims that she was wrongfully terminated because of absences caused by her back injury. Your research in secondary sources has suggested the following issue: *Was Ms. Lynn's back injury a serious health condition that entitled her to leave under federal statutes ensuring family and medical leave?*

Research Situation I:

Your client, Creative Investments, Inc., is a defendant in a private securities fraud action that has been brought as a class action. The company seeks a writ directing the district court in which the action is pending to stay the initial disclosure requirements of Federal Rule of Civil Procedure 26(a)(1), pending disposition of its motion to dismiss the action. Rule 26(a)(1) requires that parties to an action must, without waiting for discovery requests, provide certain specified information to the other parties. Your research in secondary sources has suggested the following issue to research in federal statutes: *Do the initial disclosure requirements of Federal Rule of Civil Procedure 26(a)(1) constitute "discovery" or "other proceedings" for purposes of the stay provision governing private securities fraud actions?*

Research Situation J:

Your client, Fay Bishop, was fired from the Postal Service for drinking alcohol on the job. She appealed her dismissal to the Merit Systems Protection Board, an administrative law court which hears appeals from federal government employees on employment issues. The Board determined that Ms. Bishop was properly removed from her job. She is appealing the Board's final decision. Your research in secondary sources has suggested the following issue: *In an employee's appeal of a decision of the Merit Systems Protection Board upholding a dismissal for cause, is the proper respondent the agency that terminated the employee or the Merit Systems Protection Board that upheld the agency's decision?*

THIRD PROBLEM SET FOR CHAPTER 12. FEDERAL CODES AND SESSION LAWS

Your Name   Professor

_____   _____

Circle the letter of the research situation you selected (see pages 437–440):

A   B   C   D   E   F   G   H   I   J

1. List at least three research terms suggested by your research situation and the issue we stated.

_____

_____

2. Select one of the two annotated federal codes, *United States Code Annotated* or *United States Code Service*; you may research in paper or computer-based media. Identify the pertinent statute. Describe your research process. Example: I looked up the following terms in the index: . . . ; I ran the following search in LEXIS: . . . .

_____

_____

_____

3. Obtain the current language of the pertinent statute. Indicate how you assured that your research is current. Example: I checked the following volumes of U.S.C.S.: . . . ; the online database was current to . . . .

_____

_____

_____

4. Review the pertinent statute carefully. State the statutory language that governs your research situation.

_____

_____

_____

_____

_____

_____

_____

_____

_____

5. Provide the proper citation for the section(s) you used to answer Question 4.

_____

6. Examine the statutory history notes following the section containing the language that most directly addresses your research situation.

(a) Identify the section you selected.

_____

(b) State the year that code section was originally enacted, and give the session law reference for the original act. (You need not use proper citation form.)

_____

(c) If the code section has been amended since it was first enacted, note the reference to the most recent amendment by its session law citation. (You need not use proper citation form.)

_____

7. Examine the annotation for the section you used to answer Question 6(a).

(a) Identify a case that appears pertinent to your research situation. For purposes of this exercise, identify the case described below. If you were doing actual research, you would, of course, examine all pertinent annotations.

Research Situation A:	a 1995 Fourth Circuit case
Research Situation B:	a 1997 Eighth Circuit case
Research Situation C:	a 1991 District of Delaware case
Research Situation D:	a 1993 Eastern District of Pennsylvania case
	or a 1994 Third Circuit case
Research Situation E:	a 1990 Eleventh Circuit case
Research Situation F:	a 1998 Fourth Circuit case
Research Situation G:	a 1995 District of Columbia Circuit case
Research Situation H:	a 1997 Southern District of Iowa case
Research Situation I:	a 1996 Ninth Circuit case
Research Situation J:	a 1991 Federal Circuit case

Provide the name of the case as given in the annotation.

_____

_____

    (b) What, according to the annotation, does that case say that is pertinent to your research situation? **Note:** If you were doing actual research, you would, of course, read the case itself.

_____

_____

_____

_____

_____

_____

_____

    (c) List the references to one or two secondary sources, if any, that could be pertinent to your research situation.

_____

_____

_____

_____

_____

    8. Update and expand your research by citing the section you noted for Question 6(a).

    (a) Select an electronic citator, and indicate your choice below:

        KeyCite on Westlaw _____   Shepard's on LEXIS _____

    (b) Determine whether your code section or its pertinent language has been adjudicated unconstitutional. Record the name and citation of one such case, if any.

_____

9. Based on the materials you have read, what is the probable answer to your research issue?

_____

_____

_____

_____

_____

_____

_____

_____

PROBLEM SET FOR CHAPTER 13. LEGISLATIVE PROCESS MATERIALS

Your Name   Professor

_____   _____

Circle the letter of the research situation you selected (see pages 437–440):

A   B   C   D   E   F   G   H   I   J

Legislative History

1. If you have not already done so, locate and read in *United States Code Annotated* or *United States Code Service* the statute that pertains to your research situation. Note the title and section number of the statutory section containing the language that most directly addresses your research situation.

_____

2. Locate the statutory history notes for the statutory section you identified for Question 1. That material typically is located immediately following the statute. Record the following legislative history information for the public law enacted in the year stated below. Your answers need not be in proper citation form.

Research Situation A:	1990
Research Situation B:	1978
Research Situation C:	1977
Research Situation D:	1982
Research Situation E:	1986 (first law)
Research Situation F:	1993
Research Situation G:	1972
Research Situation H:	1993
Research Situation I:	1995
Research Situation J:	1989

(a) public law number

_____

(b) date of bill's approval by the President

_____

(c) *Statutes at Large* citation

_____

3. Check at least one source to see if a compiled legislative history exists for your law. Good sources for this task include *Sources of Compiled Legislative Histories, Federal Legislative Histories*, LEXIS, and Westlaw.

(a) Note here the source you checked.

_____

(b) Provide the reference to one compiled legislative history, if you found any.

_____

_____

4. Using the sources of your choice, identify the following information, if any, for your public law. Good sources for this task include *United States Code Congressional and Administrative News, CIS/Legislative Histories* or *CIS/Abstracts, CIS Congressional Universe, Congressional Record,* and THOMAS' Bill Summary & Status reports.

Source(s) used: _____

(a) the bill number of the enacted law

_____

(b) the bill number of any companion bill

_____

(c) a pertinent hearing from the Congress that enacted the bill

_____

_____

_____

_____

(d) a pertinent committee print from the Congress that enacted the bill

_____

_____

_____

(e) a House report number for the bill from the Congress that enacted the bill

_____

(f) a Senate report number for the bill from the Congress that enacted the bill

(g) the conference committee report number

(h) three to five citations to the *Congressional Record* for a discussion of the bill that was enacted (volume and date, or volume and page, and a description of the action taken)

(i) one important legislative history document for the law from a Congress prior to the Congress that enacted the law

5. Obtain the legislative history document(s) listed below. Recall that many committee reports are available in *United States Code Congressional and Administrative News*; the CIS library (in fiche and online) also contains reports. Scan the pertinent portions, and note any pertinent guidance.

Research Situation A:	H.R. Rep. No. 101-916, at 1089 (1990)
Research Situation B:	H.R. Rep. No. 95-948, at 4-5 (1978)
Research Situation C:	S. Rep. No. 95-382, at 8 (1977)
Research Situation D:	S. Rep. No. 97-417, at 27-30 (1982)
Research Situation E:	132 Cong. Rec. 9602 (1986) (statement of Sen. Metzenbaum); 132 Cong. Rec. 9605 (1986) (statement of Sen. Lautenberg); 132 Cong. Rec. 9600-01 (1986) (exchange between Sen. Dole and Sen. Hatch)
Research Situation F:	H.R. Rep. No. 103-9, at 12 (1993)
Research Situation G:	H.R. Rep. No. 92-1017, at 4 (1972)
Research Situation H:	S. Rep. No. 103-3, at 29 (1993)
Research Situation I:	141 Cong. Rec. H13,699, H13,700 (daily ed. Nov. 28, 1995); 141 Cong. Rec. S19,146, S19,151 (daily ed. Dec. 22, 1995)
Research Situation J:	S. Rep. No. 100-413, at 21-22, 36 (1988)

_____

_____

_____

_____

_____

_____

_____

_____

6. In the *CIS/Legislative Histories* or *CIS/Annual Abstracts* volumes or through *Congressional Universe* online, locate and scan the CIS abstract for the committee hearing that you identified for Question 4(c). If you did not find one, choose a pertinent committee hearing from the prior Congress.

(a) Which document did you pick?

_____

(b) What does the abstract indicate about the likely relevance of the document for your research situation?

_____

_____

_____

_____

(c) What is the CIS accession number for the document?

_____

7. Locate the document you identified for Question 6(a) in CIS (the microfiche library or *Congressional Universe* online), from the GPO (via GPO Access), or through LEXIS or Westlaw. Skim its first ten pages. What guidance, if any, does it provide on your research situation? Also, if you find some guidance, print out any pages on which you base your answer. If you find none, briefly summarize your reading.

_____

_____

_____

_____

_____

_____

_____

8. Locate and read one of the *Congressional Record* excerpts you identified for Question 4(h). What guidance, if any, does it provide on your research situation? Also if you find some guidance, print out any pages on which you base your answer. (Omit this question if you are researching research situation E or I.)

_____

_____

_____

_____

_____

_____

_____

_____

9. Provide the proper citation for two of the documents that you used to answer Questions 5, 7, and 8.

_____

_____

_____

_____

_____

_____

_____

_____

10. If all of the documents you read provided some guidance on your research situation, which would you rely on as the most authoritative? Why?

_____

_____

_____

_____

_____

Pending Legislation

11. Select a source to assist you in locating pending legislation that could be pertinent to your research situation. Good options include *Congressional Index, CIS Congressional Universe,* THOMAS', and a bill tracking database on LEXIS or Westlaw.

(a) Name here the source you selected.

_____

(b) Describe your search method in that source.

_____

_____

_____

_____

(c) Note here the bill name and number for a pending bill pertinent to your research situation, if any.

_____

_____

(d) Note the most recent action taken on that bill, if any.

_____

_____

ADMINISTRATIVE MATERIALS

Your Name   Professor

_____   _____

Select one of the research situations stated below for the problem set for Unit V, Administrative Materials:

Research Situation A:

Xiong Phia was an engineer who worked for a manufacturing company which was under contract with the United States Department of Energy to make various components used in nuclear power cooling systems. Mr. Xiong found that some tests required by the contract to be run on the components were not being done. He so advised his supervisor, but no action was taken, so Mr. Xiong then contacted the vice-president of his division. A few days later, Mr. Xiong was fired by his supervisor. The reason given for his dismissal was frequent tardiness, yet Mr. Xiong had been late only once, following a bad ice storm. Mr. Xiong believes he was dismissed in retribution because he was a "whistleblower," so he filed a complaint with the Department of Energy. *Who has the burden of proof in the administrative hearing on the issue of the motive behind the discharge?*

Research Situation B:

Tulasha Fjorel, a non-resident alien, originally entered the United States on a temporary visa, but now seeks asylum as a permanent resident. She has petitioned the *Immigration and Naturalization Service* for asylum, on the grounds that she fears persecution and physical harm if she were forced to return to her home country. Ms. Fjorel was an outspoken advocate for lesbian and gay rights in her home country and, prior to the time she fled, was threatened with arrest and physical injury if she did not cease to advocate the rights of lesbians and gays. *What must she show to establish her eligibility for asylum?*

Research Situation C:

An employer who hired seasonal migrant farm laborers found it convenient to require the workers to stay in furnished lodgings on the farm. The employer deducted housing costs from the workers' wages, which brought their wages below the federal minimum wage. The housing is grossly substandard. The workers believe that the housing costs exceed reasonable fair market value, and that the wages received thus violate federal labor laws. *Under the circumstances, may the employer withhold the cost of housing from the wages paid to farm laborers, if the housing costs then reduce the wage to less than minimum wage?*

Research Situation D:

Sally LeJong had lived with Terry LeJong for more than thirty years, raised their three children, and in every respects acted as Terry's wife. However, Terry had never legally divorced his first wife, Gina. Terry recently died from pneumoconiosis, or black lung disease, which was a consequence of working for more than twenty years in the coal mines. Sally and Gina both filed for Social Security benefits, and the local administrator denied Sally's request for survivor's benefits because she was not legally married to Terry. Sally seeks to appeal that decision. *Is a common law wife a "deemed spouse" eligible for survivor's Social Security benefits, although she was not legally married to a coal miner who died from black lung disease?*

Research Situation E:

Several current and former employees of Warehouse Terminal, Inc. have had respiratory illnesses. One of the employees alerted the *Occupational Safety and Health Administration* about the problem, and OSHA commenced an investigation. The OSHA investigator asked Warehouse, Inc. to provide any medical records it had for its employees, especially records related to possible exposure to asbestos. Warehouse has refused, citing privacy concerns for its employees. *Does OSHA have the right to gain access to employee medical records?*

Research Situation F:

First National Banking and Loan is a member of the *Federal Deposit Insurance Corporation* (FDIC). Recently, it discovered a series of transactions involving the transfer of money to Antigua and Barbuda that it believes may involve money laundering. The amount of money involved in each transaction is never over $7,500. *Is the bank obligated to report the suspicious activity to the FDIC?*

Research Situation G:

Modern Homes Design, Inc. remodels kitchens and baths. As part of its services, Modern Homes also sells appliances, including dishwashers, ovens, microwaves, washers, and dryers. The display areas in the Modern Homes store contain many of the appliances that are for sale. The designers think that the energy consumption labels on the appliances are ugly and have instructed the manager to remove all of the labels. These labels contain information about the amount of energy and water the appliances consume. *Does removal of the labels violate federal trade regulations?*

Research Situation H:

Crocus Hills Condominiums, Inc. is a residential homeowners' association whose membership includes only the owners of the condominiums in that development. Recently, one of the condominium units was offered for sale, and it was suggested that the association buy the unit, rent it, and apply the income received to pay for the external maintenance of the buildings in the development. About 80% of the association's income would then be derived from membership dues; 20% would come from the rental income. The president of the homeowners' association has heard that normally homeowners' associations are tax-exempt organizations not required to pay income tax on membership dues. *Is the rental income received by a homeowners' association exempt from federal income taxation?*

Research Situation I:

Malcolm's Gas Station dispenses leaded and unleaded gasoline at the station's retail fuel pumps. A first-time customer, Grant Therrien, accidentally pumped leaded gasoline into his car, which was rated for unleaded gasoline only. The error led to smoky emissions and damage to the car's engine. When the matter was fully investigated, it was discovered that the fuel pumps at Malcolm's all had nozzles with the same circumference, making it possible to pump leaded gas into cars rated for unleaded only. Furthermore, the fuel had excessive leaded additives, which cause air pollution. *Do the size of the pump nozzles and the fuel additives violate federal environmental standards?*

Research Situation J:

Surja Devgun applied to drive a bus for the local school and passed the various safety and driving tests. However, Ms. Devgun was denied employment because she refused to remove the scarf used to cover her head. Ms. Devgun explained that she was compelled by her religious beliefs and practices to wear the scarf at all times that she was in public. Although Ms. Devgun had worn the scarf when taking the driving test, the school officials believed that the scarf might slip sometime in the future while she was driving the bus and cause a safety risk. Ms. Devgun asked the school board to make an accommodation for her religious practices, but it refused. She believes she was denied employment because of her sincerely held religious beliefs, in violation of equal employment standards. *May an employer lawfully refuse an applicant employment due to safety concerns related to clothing worn for religious purposes?*

Circle the letter of the research situation you selected:

A   B   C   D   E   F   G   H   I   J

1. Locate the pertinent federal regulation in the *Code of Federal Regulations.* Good sources for this task include the annotated statutory codes (for references), paper C.F.R., looseleaf services or other "mini-libraries," Internet web sites, and LEXIS or Westlaw databases. You may need to use more than one source.

(a) Identify the source(s) you selected.

_____

(b) Explain how you located the regulation. Example: I first used the following terms in the index: . . . ; I selected the following databases and ran the following searches: . . . .

_____

_____

_____

(c) State the language of the rule that governs your research situation.

_____

_____

_____

_____

_____

_____

_____

_____

_____

_____

(d) Which administrative agency is responsible for enforcing the regulation?

_____

(e) Provide a reference to the enabling legislation for the regulation.

_____

(f) When was the regulation first adopted, and where in the *Federal Register* was the regulation published upon adoption?

_____

_____

(g) Provide a proper citation to the regulation.

_____

(h) How current is the source you selected?

_____

2. Update the regulation you found; look both for recent changes and proposed changes. Good sources for this task include the *Federal Register* and related tools in various media.

(a) Identify the source you used.

_____

(b) Describe your research process. Example: I looked in L.S.A. for . . . ; I used the following key-word search in L.S.A. online: . . . .

_____

_____

_____

(c) Have there been any recent changes, or are there any proposed changes? If so, state how the language of the regulation has changed or would change.

_____

_____

_____

_____

_____

3. Identify a source you would use to find judicial case law applying or interpreting the regulation. (You need not actually find judicial case law unless directed to do so by your professor.)

_____

_____

4. Locate at least one administrative decision pertinent to your research situation. You may use a formal decision or informal opinion, such as an advisory letter or administrative ruling. Good sources for this task include official agency decision reporters, looseleaf services or other "mini-libraries," Internet web sites, and LEXIS or Westlaw databases. You may need to use more than one source.

(a) Identify the source(s) you selected.

_____

(b) Explain how you located the decision. Example: I used the following terms in the index: . . . ; I selected the . . . database and ran the following search: . . . .

_____

_____

_____

(c) Briefly state the facts and pertinent holding of the decision.

_____

_____

_____

_____

_____

_____

_____

_____

(d) Attach to this problem set a copy or print-out of the first page of that decision and the page(s) containing the pertinent discussion, and mark the copy or print-out Q4.

(e) What must you do before you rely upon that decision?

_____

(f) Provide a proper citation to the decision.

_____

_____

5. Based on the materials you have read, what is the probable answer to your research issue? Explain.

_____

_____

_____

_____

_____

_____

_____

RESEARCH
SITUATIONS
AND
PROBLEM SET
FOR UNIT VI,
CHAPTER 17

RULES OF PROCEDURE

Your Name   Professor

_____   _____

Select one of the research situations stated below for the problem set for Unit VI, Chapter 17, Rules of Procedure:

Research Situation A:

Dr. Manop Suthera sued DeJong Sporting Goods, Inc. for breach of contract. In his complaint, Dr. Suthera included alternative claims for relief: rescission of the contract and specific performance. In a pre-trial motion, DeJong objected to the inconsistency of the pleadings. *Is the complaint defective for this reason? Can a plaintiff recover on inconsistent claims?* Research your situation in Idaho.

Research Situation B:

After she was evicted for non-payment of rent, Gracie Simons filed several lawsuits against her former landlord, Frances Latham. Ms. Latham successfully defended each of the numerous lawsuits, but she was forced to incur attorney's fees. Ms. Latham's attorney has now petitioned the court to assess sanctions against Ms. Simons for what the attorney claims were baseless or frivolous legal actions. Ms. Simons had signed each of the pleadings herself as a pro se litigant and was not represented by an attorney. *If the court believes that the plaintiff's suits were without merit and were filed primarily to harass the defendant, may the court assess sanctions against a pro se plaintiff?* Research your situation in Hawaii.

Research Situation C:

Some time ago, Timothy George filed suit for wrongful discharge from his employment with Therrien Ag Corporation, but he voluntarily dismissed it a few months later. Mr. George then filed a second such suit, but failed to appear for trial on the date scheduled. So Therrien moved to dismiss the case for failure to prosecute the case and argued that

Mr. George had been fully advised of the date of the trial and had adequate time to prepare the case. *May a court dismiss a case with prejudice for failure to prosecute (especially where the plaintiff has voluntarily dismissed a similar suit)?* Research your situation in Ohio.

Research Situation D:

Roberta Josephson, a well known songwriter, claims that Andre Daniels made defamatory comments concerning the originality of her musical compositions. At a pre-trial conference, the court required the parties to exchange lists of witnesses to be called at trial. Later, during the trial, the court permitted Ms. Josephson to call a witness whose name had not been included on the witness list. That witness, an expert in musicology, has been recuperating from a serious car accident; Ms. Josephson's lawyer learned only recently that the witness could testify. *Did the court have the discretion to permit the unlisted witness to testify at the trial?* Research your situation in Louisiana.

Research Situation E:

Miller Corporation was recently served with several sets of interrogatories. Many of the questions can be answered by reading the corporation's business records, but it will be a time-consuming job as there are many records, covering several years, that must be read. *May one answer interrogatories by sending several boxes of copies of a corporation's records to the opposing party?* Research your situation in Pennsylvania.

Research Situation F:

Prof. Jeffers brought suit against Loretan College for breach of his employment contract. Prof. Jeffers' attorney wants to depose a faculty member of another school, who is on sabbatical out of state. The deponent has just informed Prof. Jeffers' attorney that he is available a week from today. Prof. Jeffers' attorney would like to hold the deposition next week. *What must the attorney do in order to give adequate notice of the depositions? Is one week notice sufficient?* Research your situation in Vermont.

Research Situation G:

Nearly two years ago, Michelle Cantarutti filed suit against a turkey-processing plant near her home, alleging that the plant emitted contaminants into the air and water, adversely affecting her property. Information about the case was published widely in local newspapers. One week after the jury verdict and entry of judgment for Ms. Cantarutti, Jay Chock, a neighbor of Ms. Cantarutti, applied to the court for permission to intervene as a co-plaintiff. Mr. Chock moved into his home three months ago and only gradually became aware of the contaminants. *Does the court have the right to deny the application to intervene as too late?* Research your situation in Arkansas.

Research Situation H:

Diane Dental Enterprises sued Manbeck Limited for negligence in manufacturing of Manbeck products purchased by Diane Dental; Diane Dental requested a jury trial. At a pretrial conference held before Judge Spencer in her chambers, the attorneys for both parties thought that the technical aspects of the case would be difficult for a jury to understand, so they both orally stipulated that a trial by the court, without a jury, would be acceptable. Judge Spencer then docketed the trial accordingly. A few days before trial, the attorney for Diane Dental filed a written demand for a jury trial. Defendant Manbeck has objected. *Is an oral stipulation for a judge trial effective?* Research your situation in Indiana.

Research Situation I:

Sharon Ternes, an up-and-coming sculptor, has sued the owner of the building where she rents a studio. She claims that the landlord's negligence in providing security permitted an intruder to break into her studio, which led to an assault during which her hands were badly injured. The landlord's attorney seeks to try the liability issue separately from damages, on the grounds that trial of the latter will be lengthy and complex, involve evidence unrelated to liability, and unfairly evoke sympathy toward Ms. Ternes. *Should the court try the liability and damages issues separately?* Research your situation in Georgia.

Research Situation J:

Assume that the applicable paternity statute provides for initial determinations in district court (an inferior trial court) and appeal, within sixty days, to circuit court (the main trial court). Attorney Steve Sanders' client received an adverse adjudication in a paternity case in district court and wants to appeal. The sixtieth day falls on a Saturday. It is the preceding Friday afternoon, and Mr. Sanders' quadruplets are ill. He would like to head home to care for them, but he is concerned that the notice of appeal is due tomorrow and believes that the clerk of court's office is open on Saturday mornings. *How do the timing rules account for due dates that fall on a weekend?* (Assume that the civil procedure rule on timing applies.) Research your situation in Kentucky.

Circle the letter of the research situation you selected:

A   B   C   D   E   F   G   H   I   J

1. Locate the pertinent state rule and accompanying comments, if any. Good sources for this task include a deskbook, the state's annotated code or rules volume, and LEXIS or Westlaw databases.

(a) Identify the source you selected.

_____

(b) Explain how you located the pertinent rule. Example: I scanned the table of contents; I used the following terms in the index: . . . ; I ran the following search: . . . .

_____

_____

_____

(c) State the language of the rule that governs your situation.

_____

_____

_____

_____

_____

_____

_____

_____

(d) Provide a proper citation to the rule.

_____

(e) Read the comments or explanatory notes following the rule, if any. If they provide any insight into the rule that is pertinent to the situation, note it here.

_____

_____

_____

_____

_____

2. Locate a state court case interpreting the rule. Good sources for this task include reporters and digests, the state's annotated code or rules volume, and LEXIS or Westlaw databases.

(a) Identify the source(s) you selected.

_____

_____

(b) Explain how you located the case. Examples: I scanned the case descriptions under the topic . . . in the annotation to the rule; I ran the following search: . . . .

_____

_____

_____

(c) Briefly state the facts and pertinent holding of the case.

_____

_____

_____

_____

_____

_____

_____

_____

_____

(d) What must you do before you rely upon that case?

_____

(e) With the information you have from your research to this point, provide the proper citation to that case. Assume that you are citing it in a memorandum to the state court.

_____

_____

3. Assume that you deem it useful to examine federal law on the same issue. Select one or more sources that provide the federal rules of civil procedure, their advisory committee notes, and federal cases. (For lists of good types of sources, see Questions 1 and 2 above.)

(a) Locate the pertinent federal rule and the advisory committee notes. Describe your research process; state the source(s) you used and the means of access you used.

_____

_____

_____

_____

_____

(b) How closely does the federal rule's language parallel the language of the state rule you have examined? Explain.

_____

_____

_____

_____

_____

(c) If the advisory committee notes provide any insight into the rule that is pertinent to the situation, note it here.

_____

_____

_____

_____

_____

(d) Provide a proper citation for the federal rule.

_____

(e) Locate a case addressing your issue, decided by any federal district court or federal circuit court of appeals. Describe your research process; state the source(s) you used and the means of access you used.

_____

_____

_____

_____

_____

(f) Attach a copy or print-out of the first page of the pertinent case and the page(s) containing the pertinent discussion to this problem set, and mark it Q3.

4. Based on the materials you have read, what is the probable answer to your research issue? Explain.

_____

_____

_____

_____

_____

_____

_____

_____

RESEARCH
SITUATION
AND
PROBLEM SET
FOR UNIT VI,
CHAPTER 18

RULES OF LEGAL ETHICS

Your Name

Professor

You will be researching the research situation stated below for the problem set for Unit VI, Chapter 18, Rules of Legal Ethics:

Your Research Situation:

Frances Latham and Min Sean both joined the law firm of Grant, Luke & Therrien after they graduated from law school, about ten years ago. Ms. Latham and Mr. Sean are now partners in the law firm and have developed a special expertise in representing clients with disabilities. They now wish to leave Grant, Luke & Therrien to form their own boutique law firm specializing in that area of law. When they announced their plans to leave Grant, Luke & Therrien, the managing partner reminded them that, pursuant to the agreement they signed when they first joined the law firm, they were not permitted to compete against the law firm; specifically they could not represent, in the future, any clients they had represented while they had been at Grant, Luke & Therrien. The employment agreement also stipulates that, if they violate the non-compete clause, they must return 50% of the equity they have earned while at the law firm. *Does the restrictive covenant impose impermissible restrictions on the practice of law, violating the state rules of professional conduct?*

Circle the state in which you will perform your research:

Illinois	Minnesota
Indiana	New Jersey
Iowa	Oregon
Louisiana	Tennessee
Massachusetts	Texas

1. Locate the pertinent rule of professional responsibility and accompanying comments, if any. Good sources for this task include a deskbook, the state's annotated code or rules volume, and LEXIS or Westlaw databases.

(a) Identify the source you selected.

_____

(b) Explain how you located the pertinent rule. Examples: I scanned the table of contents; I used the following terms in the index: . . . ; I ran the following search: . . . .

_____

_____

_____

(c) State the language of the rule that governs your situation.

_____

_____

_____

_____

_____

_____

_____

_____

_____

(d) Provide a proper citation to that rule.

_____

(e) Read the comments or explanatory notes following the rule, if any. If they provide any insight into the rule that is pertinent to the situation, note it here.

_____

_____

_____

_____

2. Locate a state court case interpreting the rule (or its predecessor). The case need not be a disciplinary case; indeed this issue typically arises in a breach-of-contract case. If there are several pertinent cases, select the most recent. Good sources for this task include reporters and digests, the state's annotated code or rules volume, and LEXIS or Westlaw databases.

(a) Identify the source(s) you selected.

_____

_____

(b) Explain how you located the case. Examples: I scanned the case descriptions under topic . . . in the annotation to the rule; I ran the following search: . . . .

_____

_____

_____

(c) Briefly state the facts and pertinent holding of the case.

_____

_____

_____

_____

_____

_____

_____

_____

_____

(d) What must you do before you rely upon that case?

_____

(e) With the information you have from your research to this point, provide the proper citation to that case. Assume that you are citing it in a memorandum to the state court.

_____

_____

3. Assume that you deem it useful to examine the ABA Model Rules on your topic. Select one or more sources that provide the Model Rules along with the ABA comments and a comparison to the ABA Model Code. Good sources for this task include deskbooks, ABA publications (such as _Annotated Model Rules of Professional Conduct_), and treatises.

(a) Identify the source you selected.

_____

_____

(b) Locate the language of the pertinent model rule. How closely does the ABA Model Rule's language parallel the language of the state rule you have researched? Explain.

_____

_____

_____

_____

_____

(c) What does your source indicate about the Model Code's provision on this topic?

_____

_____

(d) If the ABA comments, or any additional explanatory material provided by your source, provide any insight into the rule that is pertinent to the situation, note it here.

_____

_____

_____

_____

_____

4. Select one or more sources that provide ethics or disciplinary opinions from the ABA or the appropriate state entity. Good sources for this task include *ABA/BNA Lawyers' Manual on Professional Conduct, National Reporter on Legal Ethics and Professional Responsibility*, and LEXIS and Westlaw databases.

(a) Identify the source you selected.

_____

_____

(b) Locate an opinion addressing the topic of restrictions on practice by departing lawyers. First search for an opinion from the state entity for the state you selected; if you do not find one, look for an ABA opinion. Explain how you located the opinion. Example: I ran the following search: . . . .

_____

_____

_____

(c) State the legal point made in the opinion.

_____

_____

_____

_____

_____

(d) Provide the proper citation to that opinion.

_____

5. Based on the materials you have read, what is the probable answer to your research issue? Explain.

_____

_____

_____

_____

_____

_____

_____

_____

INDEX

This index is alphabetized word-by-word. Page numbers appearing in italic type refer to pages that contain illustrations.